THE CIVIL WAR

THE CIVIL WAR

IRONWEED AMERICAN NEWSPAPERS
AND PERIODICALS PROJECT

Edited by Brayton Harris

IRONWEED PRESS · NEW YORK

Ironweed Press, Inc.
P.O. Box 754208
Parkside Station
Forest Hills, NY 11375

Manufactured in the United States of America.
Printed on acid-free paper.

Cover photo of the paperback edition:
City Point, Virginia, 1864.
Courtesy of the Library of Congress.

Library of Congress Cataloging-in-Publication Data

The Civil War / edited by Brayton Harris
p. cm. — (Ironweed American newspapers and periodicals project)
Includes index.
ISBN 1-931336-00-8 (hard: alk. paper)
ISBN 1-931336-01-6 (paper: alk. paper)
1. United States—History—Civil War, 1861–1865—Sources. I. Harris, Brayton, 1932– II. Series.
E464.C437 2002
973.7—dc21 2002068519

CONTENTS

ACKNOWLEDGMENTS

Special gratitude is owed to the following individuals and institutions for the courtesies extended: Philip Lampi, Dennis Laurie, and Russell Martin, Newspapers and Periodicals Department, American Antiquarian Society; Martin King and Francis Pollard, Virginia Historical Society; Errol Somay, Virginia Newspaper Project, Library of Virginia; Gayle Cooper, Albert and Shirley Small Special Collections Library, University of Virginia; Nancy Keating, United States Military Academy Library; Cathy Martin, Legislative Library, General Assembly of North Carolina; Virginia Camerman, New York State Library; Charleston Library Society; New-York Historical Society; South Carolina Historical Society; Charleston County Library; New York Public Library; Boston Public Library; and Library of Congress.

INTRODUCTION

This book marks a departure in the presentation of Civil War journalism. For the most part, newspaper studies of the Civil War have been written for academic audiences, with a narrow, topical orientation, or have focused on the exploits of individual reporters. Even among scholars, newspapers have yet to be fully appreciated as primary sources. From the surviving issues of the Civil War press, little has been reprinted and made widely available for a critical examination. This neglect is measurably redressed in *The Civil War*.

The text is wholly drawn from the pages of four leading period dailies—the *Richmond Daily Dispatch,* the *Charleston Daily Courier,* the *Boston Evening Transcript,* and the *New York Tribune*. Since the overabundance of material precludes an exhaustive presentation, items are drawn in each of the newspapers from the third Saturday issue of every month for the duration of the war, a total of some fifty-five dates. Thus, the war unfolds as a series of time-lapse snapshots. While the emphasis falls perforce on the military and political aspects, the narrative is much broader and succeeds in conveying the human dimension of the conflict.

In style and content, the selected articles will not seem markedly dissimilar from those in present-day newspapers. Between the 1830s and the eve of the Civil War, American journalism underwent a major transformation; many of the organizational changes and editorial innovations introduced in this period remain standard today. But newspapers from the early nineteenth century were quite different from their modern counterparts and, in fact, did not contain much "news." They were journals of opinions and political cheerleading and often served as vehicles for cultural discourse and, just as likely, cultural pretension. Little effort was made to gather information in the field, and much of what was published about the world at large came in the mail: letters from subscribers; copies of speeches, which may or may not have been actually delivered; and, in an informal system of exchange, other newspapers, from which interesting items were liberally appropriated. Reporters were deemed unnecessary, and "war correspondence" was no more than the home letters of men in military service. As in Ben Franklin's day, printing at the smaller weeklies was done on flatbed handpresses, which might produce 250 impressions an hour, as long as the pressman could endure the pace. From the 1820s, larger papers employed rotary presses, which raised the output to around 1,000 impressions an hour. Regardless of the type of press used, the maximum length of a newspaper was four pages, the two leaves of a large single folded sheet. Given the high cost of production, newspapers, at six cents a copy, were prohibitively expensive and were read regularly only by the upper classes.

Then, propelled by technological advances and journalistic enterprise, the newspaper came of age. Enterprise, however, preceded technology. In 1835, James Bennett, sensing a market for an inexpensive, more lively newspaper, founded the *New York Herald*. He covered crime and scandal and introduced the Wall Street report and the personal interview, the first of which was with the proprietor of a brothel in which one of the residents had been murdered. It may be said that Bennett invented the modern newspaper and then sold it for a penny a copy. His immediate success inspired a gaggle of imitators.

After the onset of the industrial revolution, the newspaper trade soon emerged as a fully commercial endeavor. By the 1850s, steam-powered printing presses permitted the more highly capitalized newspapers to churn out as many as twenty thousand impressions an hour and to issue eight- and even twelve-page editions. The telegraph, invented in 1844, had a network spanning some fifty thousand miles by 1860; it allowed reports of an afternoon event in New Orleans to be off the press in New York by midnight and, thanks to rail service, arrive on the president's desk in the morning. Three New York papers even offered same-day home delivery in Washington, D.C.

In the year Bennett founded the *Herald,* there were perhaps 900 newspapers in the nation. By 1860, there were more than 2,500; of these, at least 373 were published daily, 80 of them in the less-populous South. New York City alone supported seventeen daily newspapers, Washington, D.C., three, and Richmond four. The larger papers in New York City, Boston, and Chicago began issuing Sunday editions; several of the New York papers published both morning and evening editions. The growth of the newspaper trade gave rise to a permanent corps of professional reporters, some working full-time, some under contract for piecework.

But, as earlier, newspapers remained unabashedly partisan. At the beginning of the Civil War, newspapers in the North belonged to one of four general political categories: Radical Republican, moderate Republican, Independent, and Democratic. Radical Republicans, moderate Republicans, and Independents all supported the government, but differed principally on the question of slavery. For Radical Republican papers like the *New York Tribune,* the *Chicago Tribune,* and the *Philadelphia Inquirer,* the overriding aim of the war was the abolition of slavery, whereas moderate Republican papers, such as the *New York Times,* the *Boston Journal,* and the *Boston Evening Transcript,* though ideologically abolitionist, viewed the war mainly as a struggle to preserve the Union. Independents, on the other hand, either opposed abolition or stayed neutral on the issue. The most prominent of the Independent papers was the *New York Herald,* although most Republican editors regarded it as a Democratic organ.

Intractably hostile to the Lincoln administration, Northern Democrats identified politically with Democrats of the South and, on the whole, supported the claims of slaveholders. To Democrats on both sides of the Mason-Dixon Line, the war represented a "Black Republican" plot to overthrow civil liberties and the rule of law and to force full racial equality on an unwilling nation. Democratic papers, notably the *Chicago Times,* the *Cincinnati Enquirer,* and the *New York World,* called for sectional differences to be resolved through rational discourse rather than by force of arms. The Democratic position aroused deep suspicion among the Radicals, who charged that Democrats serving in the army, particularly Major General George McClellan, were not committed to victory; McClellan's apparent reluctance to engage the enemy served to reinforce this belief. A subset called the Peace Democrats were militant and openly pro-Southern and were pejoratively dubbed "Copperheads" by the Radicals, after the venomous snake of the same name.

Most Southern papers were Democratic, although a few were aligned with the moribund Whigs, the philosophical predecessors of the Republicans. Regardless of political persuasion, Southern papers quickly fell in line behind the cause, or were put out of business. A number of papers, in both the North and the South, were forcibly shuttered, either by government edict or mob action.

Arguably the most important Southern paper was the *Richmond Daily Dispatch,* whose daily circulation exceeded that of any other paper in the South and, indeed, that of all other Richmond papers combined. This four-page, tabloid-size paper was founded in 1850, to offer New York–style journalism to the South. The editorials of its Civil War issues were written by Hugh Pleasants, Oliver Baldwin, and the publisher, James Cowardin. Baldwin, who worked part-time as a clerk for the Confederate War Department, gave the *Dispatch* an insider's edge. Unlike its chief rivals in Richmond, the *Enquirer* and the *Examiner,* the *Dispatch* stayed above politics as a matter of long-standing editorial policy. Of the four papers presented in this volume, the *Charleston Daily Courier,* founded in 1803, is the oldest. The *Courier* steadfastly opposed secession until Lincoln's election in 1860. Aaron Willington served as senior editor until his death in 1862, when Richard Yeadon and Thomas Simons assumed editorial duties. In contrast to the *Dispatch,* the *Courier* strongly favored the Davis administration; its main competitor, the *Charleston Mercury,* was prowar but antiadministration.

The *Boston Evening Transcript* began as a Whig penny sheet in 1830 and evolved into a moderate Republican paper. During the war years, much of the copy was written by its editors Daniel Haskell and Thomas Fox. For direct war coverage the *Transcript,* then one of seven papers in Boston, relied on exchanges, official dispatches, and letters from men serving in the field, as was the common journalistic practice at the time. In this volume the reader will find frequent references to "our exchanges," in which more than fifty newspapers are cited or quoted, often at great length. In one instance the *Courier* reproduces an item from the *Richmond Examiner* that was originally copied from the *New York Herald*.

The *New York Tribune* was founded in 1841 by Horace Greeley, with the announced intention "to advance the interests of the people and to promote their moral, political, and social well-being." Greeley promised his readers that "the immoral and degrading police reports, advertisements, and other matters which have been allowed to disgrace the columns of our leading penny papers"—meaning the *New York Herald*—"will be carefully excluded from this, and no exertion will be spared to render it worthy of the virtuous and refined, and a welcome visitant at the family fireside." The *Tribune* was by far the largest of the four newspapers in this volume. At the start of the war the paper had 212 employees, 28 of whom were editors. Some sixty men provided war coverage from the field, and two women reported from Washington. Although Greeley set the policy, most of the editorials were written by the managing editor Charles Dana for the first two years of the war and then by Sydney Gay.

The *Tribune* was the quintessential Radical paper and was unquestionably the most influential paper of the day. As one of the leading voices against slavery, it earned the undying enmity of the South. To the *Tribune* may go the credit for goading the Lincoln administration into sending a woefully unprepared army to a crushing defeat at the First Battle of Bull Run. Every day, between June 26 and July 4, 1861, the *Tribune* proclaimed, "Forward to Richmond! Forward to Richmond! The Rebel Congress must not be allowed to meet there on the 20th of July! *By that date the place must be held by the national army!*"

The majority of the contributors in this collection cannot be positively identified. By general policy, few wartime reporters were allowed to write under their full names. Some were permitted the use of initials, but most articles were published unsigned or under fanciful pseudonyms. William Shepardson was known to the readers of the *Richmond Daily Dispatch* as "Bohemian" and Felix Gregory de Fontaine to those of the *Charleston Daily Courier* as "Personne." An executive of the *New York Tribune* wrote, "The anonymous greatly favors freedom and boldness in newspaper correspondence. I will not allow *any* letter writer to attach his initials to his communications, unless he is a widely known and influential man like Greeley. . . . Besides the responsibility it fastens on a correspondent, the signature inevitably detracts from the powerful impersonality of a journal." In 1863, the Union general Joseph Hooker, frustrated over security leaks and personal attacks by "injudicious correspondents of an anonymous character," issued General Order No. 48, requiring that all news items thenceforth be signed. Only some reporters complied, however.

As Union forces marched inexorably across the South, many Confederate newspapers were seized by the Federal authorities and abruptly became "loyal Union" sheets, as the *Courier* did in February 1865, or shut down for a time, as the *Dispatch* did, following the disastrous fire in Richmond in April of that year. By the end of the war, only some twenty daily newspapers were still being published in the South, fewer than in Virginia alone before the war. Given the circumstances, it was no small miracle that newspapers were being published at all in the Confederate states. News coming from Northern papers had to be smuggled through military lines; shoe polish was sometimes substituted for ink, when there was enough paper on which to print even a truncated edition. By contrast, newspapers of the North flourished. James Bennett, who had borrowed $500 to start the *Herald,* turned down a purchase offer of $2 million.

But the story ends on a note of irony. The *Charleston Daily Courier,* the oldest Southern daily, is now, after two mergers, the *Post and Courier*. The *Richmond Daily Dispatch,* after three mergers, is now the *Times-Dispatch*. The *Boston Evening Transcript,* eleven years after its centennial celebration, ceased publication in 1941. The *New York Tribune* bought its archrival *Herald* in 1924, becoming the *Herald Tribune*. It went out of business in 1963; only the name survives in the *International Herald Tribune,* published in Paris, France. Of the four newspapers featured here, only two remain in business. Both are in the South.

Brayton Harris
Mission Hills, Kansas

A NOTE ON THE TEXT

The articles presented in the volume are drawn directly from the original newspapers. Obvious errors have been emended. In a small number of instances, words have been silently inserted or changed for clarity. Where appropriate, modern standards in spelling and punctuation have been imposed to enhance readability.

Headlines and datelines have been modified to render them uniform. The beginning of an article is signaled by the absence of indention in the opening sentence of the lead paragraph. If an article is part of, or related to, the preceding article(s), as, for example, is the "Van Dorn Reinforced and Coming Forward Again" item on page 330, the opening sentence is accordingly indented.

Only the bracketed comments pertaining to the publication history of the two Southern newspapers are those of the editor; the rest are part of the original articles. As an aid to the reader, a timeline of the major events is provided at the beginning of each section, and throughout the text, terms and references are explained in the footnotes.

The racial and social attitudes expressed in some of the selections are objectionable in the extreme. As distasteful and offensive as these passages are, their exclusion would have produced an incomplete and misleading account of the Civil War. The editor sincerely apologizes for any offense caused by the material.

PROLOGUE

TIMELINE

January 1808: The importation of slaves into the United States is outlawed. But the traffic in slavery continues, stirring abolitionist sentiment in the North.

March 1820: In an attempt to maintain a political balance between the free and the slave states, Kentucky Senator Henry Clay brokers the Missouri Compromise. Under the terms of the compromise, Missouri is to be admitted as a slave state to offset the admission of Maine as a free state, and the Louisiana Purchase is to be divided along latitude 36°30′, slavery being banned north of the line but permitted to the south.

September 1850: Legislative compromises avert threatened disunion. As an accommodation to the Southern states, Congress passes the Fugitive Slave Act, mandating that runaway slaves, wherever apprehended, be returned to their owners. Honored more in the breach than in the observance, the law becomes a rallying point for both the North and the South.

June 1851–April 1852: Harriet Beecher Stowe's novel *Uncle Tom's Cabin* appears as a serial in the abolitionist journal *National Era*. The novel is published as a book in March 1852 and sells 300,000 copies by the year's end.

May 19–22, 1856: Massachusetts Senator Charles Sumner denounces the Kansas-Nebraska Act (1854), which opened the western territories to slavery, and lambastes its authors, Senators Andrew Butler and Stephen A. Douglas. Two days later, Senator Sumner is beaten nearly unconscious on the Senate floor by Senator Butler's nephew, South Carolina Representative Preston Brooks.

August–October 1858: Abraham Lincoln, the Republican candidate for senator of Illinois, declares, "I believe this government cannot endure half slave and half free." In a series of debates with the incumbent, Stephen A. Douglas, Lincoln argues against the extension of slavery beyond its present boundaries; Douglas, reiterating his support for the doctrine of "popular sovereignty," maintains that each state or territory should decide the issue for itself. Although Douglas is elected to the Senate by the Democratic-controlled Illinois legislature, Lincoln achieves national prominence.

October 1859: The abolitionist John Brown leads an abortive raid on the Federal arsenal at Harpers Ferry, Virginia, and is captured by a company of marines under the command of Robert E. Lee. Convicted of treason, Brown is hanged in December.

May 1860: Lincoln is nominated as the Republican candidate for president. In an effort to appeal to Southern voters, Republicans promote a platform which would permit slavery to continue in the states where it has been already established but prohibit it in the territories. In June, Northern Democrats nominate Stephen A. Douglas for president and affirm the right to own slaves. Southern Democrats nominate John Breckinridge; the Whigs nominate John Bell. Southern politicians predict that if Lincoln is elected, Southern states will withdraw from the Union. Lincoln's name does not even appear on the ballot in ten Southern states.

November 1860: Lincoln is elected by a majority of electoral votes, but wins only a plurality in the popular vote.

December 1860: South Carolina votes to secede from the Union on December 20. Though sympathetic to the South, President James Buchanan, a Democrat, refuses to accede to the demand that all Federal troops be removed from Charleston, South Carolina. Major Robert Anderson, commanding the garrison at two Federal forts in Charleston Harbor, moves his forces to the larger of the two, Fort Sumter. A few days later, state forces occupy the smaller Fort Moultrie. Buchanan announces that Fort Sumter will be defended. Fort Sumter is not under blockade, and mail and messages pass freely.

January–February 1861: Seizing Federal military and government facilities, other Southern states withdraw from the Union: Mississippi,

January 9; Florida, January 10; Alabama, January 11; Georgia, January 19; Louisiana, January 26; Texas, February 1.

February 4, 1861: Former president John Tyler convenes the "Peace Convention" in Washington, D.C., on the same day the Provisional Congress of the Confederate States of America meets in Montgomery, Alabama. Unable to effect a compromise, the Peace Convention disbands on February 27.

February 9: The Confederates select Jefferson Davis as provisional president. He is inaugurated on February 18; the appointment becomes permanent a year later. In Tennessee a secession convention is rejected by a margin of ten thousand votes; the state will join the Confederacy without a vote.

February 27: Davis sends a three-man "peace delegation" to Washington. Its legitimacy is not recognized by the Federal government, for to do so would be tantamount to recognizing the seceded states as an independent political entity.

March 4, 1861: Lincoln is inaugurated as sixteenth president of the United States. Southern threats to prevent the ceremony do not materialize.

March 16: The Confederates adopt a constitution. The Territory of Arizona votes to join the Confederacy. Over time, more states secede: Virginia, April 17; Arkansas and Tennessee, May 6; North Carolina, May 20. Kentucky claims neutrality, and Missouri is unable to reach a decision. For a time both states have parallel Union and Confederate governments.

JANUARY 19, 1861

SOUTH

RICHMOND DAILY DISPATCH
January 19, 1861

FROM WASHINGTON

Special Correspondence of the *Dispatch*

Washington, January 17, 1861

So Virginia is to act as mediator between the parties belligerent. But does not this estop action? Kentucky members tell me that the very fact of Virginia's disposition to remain inert until Lincoln comes in has impaired the Southern movement in their state. If, when it comes to a settlement, Virginia will put up with not one whit less than her entire equality and the power—guaranteed by constitutional amendments—to enforce that equality, well and good. Settlements are doubtful things. Time and time again we have been told that this or that compromise was the "finality of the finality." In vain! There is but one settlement with a moment's consideration, and that is a restoration of fraternal feeling between the two sections and a common understanding as to the nature of our government. This is the one, sole, true, lasting foundation for the Union; without it all else is but a cheat and a snare.

So fixed is the Northern mind in the belief that the Federal government is paramount to the states that I am told by Mr. Vallandigham that there is not now in all the populous state of Ohio a single states'-rights paper.[1] One will shortly be established. He says, moreover, that he has lately heard Democratic congressmen of Illinois declare that they owed no allegiance to their state whatever, but to the Federal government directly, solely, entirely. While we of the South hold doctrines precisely the reverse of those entertained by the North on this all-important point (for out of it the whole theory of coercion has grown), how is it possible for us to get along in a common government? The only conceivable plan is that advocated yesterday by Mr. Garnett in the House—to wit, distinct governments for the two sections and a league of customs, with an alliance offensive and defensive.

Mr. Crittenden, aided by Mr. William C. Rives, who is now here, does not yet despair of his compromise, so utterly defeated yesterday by the abolitionists in the Senate.[2] Seward and company are scared somewhat and will give back a little—just enough to "placate" (that's the *Tribune*'s slang phrase for "please" or "soothe") the border states.[3] It seems a pity that Northern and Middle men cannot be brought to realize the fact that the Southern Confederacy is a fixed thing, and act accordingly. All the friends of the South at the North are eager for Southern unity, as the best position in any event, whether of final separation or reconstruction—best for themselves and best for us.

Patrick Henry, in 1788, foresaw and predicted the trouble which would arise from giving the Federal power absolute authority over the forts and arsenals within the states' limits. Among other things to be settled, this is one of the very first moment. Before long I will send you a quotation from Henry's speech on this subject.

1. In 1863, the Ohio Democratic politician Clement Vallandigham was imprisoned by General Ambrose Burnside for his pro-Southern speeches and was tried and convicted of treason and banished to the Confederacy, where the authorities expelled him for his criticism of President Davis's management of the war.

2. Refers to the Crittenden Compromise. In December 1860, in an attempt to halt the march toward secession and war, Kentucky Senator John Crittenden proposed six constitutional amendments, defining where slavery was to be prohibited, where it was to be permitted, and where it might be open to public referendum; affirming regulations for the interstate transportation of slaves; and providing compensation to slave owners for "rescued" slaves. The legislation stood a good chance of passage, but was opposed by President Lincoln and was killed in committee. However, the senator called upon the full Senate to approve a public referendum on the compromise; he was defeated, 23 to 25. Senator Crittenden had two sons: Fittingly, Thomas became a major general in the Union army and George a major general in the Confederate army.

3. Border states: Delaware, Maryland, Kentucky, and Missouri. Slavery existed in all four, but the allegiances of their citizens were divided. Delaware remained loyal to the North; Maryland largely supported the Union war effort, under the watchful eye of Federal troops; dual governments were established in Kentucky and Missouri.

Gurley, of Ohio, once a Universalist preacher, and notorious for his pusillanimity, made the bitterest coercion speech of the season in the House yesterday. One of his colleagues complimented him, at the close of his tirade, for so far departing from his religious convictions as to give his Southern brethren a plentiful supply of that subterranean fire in the existence of which he did not for a moment believe.

Holt is foaming at the idea of Washington's being invaded by Virginians at the time of Lincoln's inauguration. The very thought of such a thing is said to make him tremble with rage.

What the Scott–Buchanan dynasty intends to do at Charleston is not known certainly.[4] Some say they will back Anderson with his whole power. Others say they won't send another man. I hear that Anderson himself is utterly opposed to the coercion system and would gladly resign if he could do so with honor. If he had known of the understanding between the South Carolina authorities and the president in regard to the maintenance of the status, he would never have put himself and his men to the trouble of fortifying Fort Moultrie; still less would he have gone to Sumter.[5] This I get from first-rate authority. Two of Anderson's wife's brothers are in the South Carolina army, and as I have perhaps already told you, he is himself a large slaveholder.

Zed

CHARLESTON DAILY COURIER
January 19, 1861

CORRESPONDENCE OF THE COURIER

Washington, January 16, 1861

Although the excitement here is subsiding, the secession movements among us are nonetheless formidable. They do not, however, seem to have any effect upon the Republicans, who maintain the same inactive position and steadily vote against all concessions and compromises. In the Senate there are some Democrats, too, who prefer the consideration of their own peculiar measures in preference to anything which would tend to settle existing difficulties. The California senators take every occasion to crowd in the Pacific Railroad Bill, and this measure is generally considered in the Senate two or three days during the week, in the

4. Winfield Scott, general in chief (1841–61); James Buchanan, moderate Democrat, president (1857–61).

5. Fort Moultrie and Fort Sumter guarded Charleston Harbor, South Carolina.

presence of empty seats and thin galleries. There is some probability of its passage. It is advocated in private circles on the ground that it will create an immense national debt, which will bind the diversified portions of the republic together again, while the progress of the work will call into active life all of the material elements of the country. But with the credit of the government ruined and the Treasury empty, the corporators will not find so much Union strength in their bill as they are led to imagine.

The House has fairly inaugurated bunkum, and in the Committee of the Whole we sometimes have four or five speeches a day. It is very rarely that they are listened to, while in some instances they are printed in the *Globe* without ever having been delivered in the House. They, of course, go out to the astonished constituents of the member with an immense flourish of trumpets, flattering them that listening senates sat in mute admiration at the "eloquence," and no doubt lulling them into a false security of the dangers which hourly threaten the country. Nothing but the abolition of the franking privilege will ever put an end to these manufactured speeches for "home consumption."[6] But *vive la humbug* while the republic lasts!

The owners of brick and mortar in this city are beginning to despair of any relief. The same state of things continues to exist. Indeed, I may add that they are growing worse. Property is in such a condition that it will not bring a dollar under the hammer, nor will it be taken for security. Some of our wealthiest citizens have entirely suspended payment, while others have been driven to such desperation that if rumor be true, they will soon *suspend* themselves. I see it published that one of them has been released from this voluntary act and conveyed to the insane asylum. This is one of many incidents.

The lobby, the great lobby, which has flourished like a green bay tree during former sessions, has been completely prostrated at this one. The halls of the Capitol are often deserted in the busiest part of the day, and not even the ghost of a lobbyite is seen listlessly leaning against their marble columns watching for his claimant. Committees are no longer troubled with idle claims, and their prosecutors but pass quietly through their duties. The cause of all this is the crisis.

The president had a reception last night. It was very thinly attended. A few of the belles and beaux who loiter still were present, but they voted it "stale, flat, and unprofitable," for the most welcome piece of

6. franking: sending mail without charge.

music was that of "Yankee Doodle," the usual signal for everybody to leave. The president kept up the usual handshaking process, Miss Lane graciously "received," the Marine band drummed out its usual operatic airs, but there was no heart to the reception.[7] As early as ten, the lights were turned out, the band packed off to the barracks, and the spectators left to wander home amid the driving snow and the bitter cold. Thus ended the first reception.

Several of our daily journals are retrenching their limits. The *Intelligencer* has reduced its size, and the *States* ditto. The latter journal is advertised for sale, but nobody will buy it. It has undergone at least a dozen ownerships since it was first started, and has therefore dwindled down to almost nothing. Under the management of Messrs. Pryor and Heiss, it paid handsomely.

The *Constitution* will be continued, notwithstanding the petty spite of the president in withdrawing patronage from it.

We have had shocking weather—so the ladies say. It snows and then rains, and the streets of Washington are filled with the "slush." Balmorals and Wellingtons are consequently quite numerous.

Kritick

FICTIONS OF THE PRESS

It is encouraging to note that some of our Northern exchanges, mindful of truth, are directing attention to the mischievous effects of the falsehoods manufactured for the unscrupulous abolition journals. When the Northern mass of intelligent and honest readers learn that certain journals, which have been accepted as influential organs for years, are now wholly given up to misstatements, one grand step will be taken toward a permanent adjustment, whether in or out of the late Union. Thousands of the most fanatical and furious of Northern citizens have acted and voted consistently and logically according to their premises, but unfortunately they have acted on premises that had no basis in truth.

Were it not an unpleasant task, we could take up from any package of Northern exchanges a paper, and go through its columns of intelligence and supposed correspondence from the South, and prove the falsehood of almost every statement. Such a task, however, would scarcely repay the time and space occupied, for the papers that have habitually and perseveringly employed falsehood as a necessary means of inciting the Northern mind have generally no Southern circulation.

7. James Buchanan's niece Harriet Lane assumed the duties of first lady during his presidency. Buchanan was the only bachelor to ever serve as president.

With the exception of the *New York Herald,* we now recall no one that has or had a Southern circulation to be compared to its Northern circulation. The *Herald* has had the singularly satanic privilege of stirring up discord, by exciting either section against the other, but its gratuitous use of falsehood has, in some degree, neutralized its power for evil by destroying its credit.

Other papers that circulate largely and almost exclusively North are believed by Northern readers for want of better evidence, and when a Southern journal contradicts them flatly and absolutely, as Southern editors are often compelled to do, the denial does not reach the original circle of readers who are deceived, or is attributed merely to partisanship.

Let the Northern journals whose conductors still recognize truth as of paramount obligation over all utterances correct plainly and pointedly the misstatements, or, in plain English, the falsehoods of their unscrupulous neighbors, and something may even yet be done to bring the North and South face-to-face understandingly.

These hints are suggested by a letter from Charleston to the *Hartford* (Connecticut) *Times,* from "Amos," who thus writes:

FALSEHOODS ABOUT SOUTH CAROLINA

Charleston, South Carolina, January 9, 1861

To Editors of the *Hartford Times*

It is wonderful to note the immense number of absolute falsehoods about the South that are published in some of the Northern papers. It really does seem as though men were busy manufacturing these stories in order to deceive their neighbors and exasperate the men of the South. I have had the curiosity to notice their stories in one number of the *Hartford Courant* which a friend sent me, and have cut them out and now enclose them to you with brief comments. It is not important to republish them, and I enclose them only to show you how little importance is to be attached to these kinds of stories. Some of these are original in the *Courant,* and some are credited to other papers.

Here follow, in order, eleven distinct assertions, all false, and of such a character that the falsehood must have been known to, or could easily have been ascertained by, the author or authors. . . .

NORTH

BOSTON EVENING TRANSCRIPT
January 19, 1861

MOVEMENTS OF THE ALABAMA AND GEORGIA DELEGATIONS—NATIONAL FEELING AT THE SOUTH—CHANGE OF POLICY TOWARD MAJOR ANDERSON BY SOUTH CAROLINA—MOVEMENTS OF FOREIGN MINISTERS—UNION SENTIMENT INCREASING IN THE SLAVE STATES—THE BORDER STATES PATRIOTIC—THE SKIES BRIGHTENING

Special Dispatch to the *Transcript*
Washington, January 19, 1861

The Alabama delegation in Congress will leave their seats next Monday, regardless of the telegrams from their state directing them to remain.

They are much mortified at the refusal of the Union delegates to sign the secession ordinance, and fear it may check the revolution in their state. These Unionists refuse to sign unless they are specially instructed to do so by their respective constituents, and a spirited correspondence is going on with them. The result is watched with great interest by all parties here.

I am reliably informed this morning that there is a good prospect of a satisfactory arrangement between Mr. Hayne, the South Carolina messenger, and the president. Mr. Hayne informs me that the reports of his mission here, published in the *New York Herald,* are baseless fabrications.

An official dispatch was received here from South Carolina last evening, saying that according to the advice of Senators Davis and Hunter, Major Anderson now has the free use of the market of Charleston. A return of the former social relations between the officers of the United States and the local authorities of South Carolina is expected at an early day.

It is reported here that Major Anderson approves of the leading object of Mr. Hayne's mission and that his dispatches sent from Fort Sumter by Lieutenant Hall were of a pacific nature.

Several of the foreign ministers deny that they have asked the opinion of the secretary of state on points of international law concerning clearances from Southern seaports. Their governments, they assume, will act, regardless of the special wishes or intentions of the Cabinet at Washington, should vessels leaving Southern ports without proper clearances be interrupted.

The correspondence between Judge Black and Mr. Lyons, the British minister, with reference to clearances from Charleston, will be sent to the Senate next week.

The Union feeling is strengthening here every hour. The border-slave-state leaders admit that the pacific policy of the administration and the radical course of the disunionists will strangle the secession rebellion against the Federal government.

Very favorable telegrams have been received from Richmond today, by prominent officials, and Virginia does not seem in any haste to copy the insane policy of South Carolina.

The Honorable William C. Rives, one of the leaders of the National party of the Old Dominion, is confident that all will yet be well with the Union.

NEW YORK TRIBUNE
January 19, 1861

A FEW DAYS' MORE PATIENCE

Recent advices indicate that the secession tide in the "border states" is beginning to ebb. It has been unnaturally stimulated by ambitious and wily leaders, mainly for the purpose of frightening the free states and extorting humiliating concessions and compromises from their senators and representatives in Congress. When they find that this game of bluff proves ineffectual and that talking secession and treason is far easier and safer than committing the overt act, reason will resume its sway, and the storm will wholly blow over or expend its force in fitful gusts. If the North, in and out of Congress, will keep cool and stand firm twenty or thirty days longer, the border states will leave the cotton states to "play it alone."[8] It is evident that Virginia is disposed to look before she leaps into the dark chasm of disunion. North Carolina holds back from the brink of the precipice, while Maryland, Kentucky, Tennessee, and Missouri can hardly be said to have taken any decisive steps toward it.

8. The Southern states were also called the "cotton states," after their chief cash crop. On the eve of the war, Southern cotton constituted some 60 percent of the nation's net export and no less than 75 percent of England's annual import. The Southerners imposed a voluntary embargo on cotton exports, believing that the loss of supply would motivate Europeans to intervene, diplomatically or militarily, on the side of the Confederacy; however, wanting to avoid the appearance of blackmail, the Confederate government withheld formal approval. The embargo proved to be a gross miscalculation. The bumper crops in 1859 and 1860 had created a glut on the market, and later, when the surplus was depleted, planters in India, Egypt, and Brazil increased production to meet the shortfall.

Let the senators and representatives of the free states maintain a "masterly inactivity," and all will yet be well.

BLACK AND WHITE

For every slave that has run away from the South during the last twenty-five years, there has been at least one white Northern free man who has been maltreated in the Southern states and deprived of his rights, on suspicion that he did not love their "peculiar institution."[9] For every slave that has been enticed away, there have been more than two white men from the free states who have been forcibly ejected from the South without cause, or lynched on the spot, in violation of law and right. For every Negro that has been rescued from officers while executing the Fugitive Slave Law, and for every case of successful resistance to the enforcement of that law, there have been at least five Northern white men, guilty of no crime, who have been put to death in the South because they were suspected of being opposed to slavery.[10] With these palpable facts before them, we do not perceive that those Republicans who are overhauling the Constitution at Washington propose to do anything to give effect to that provision which declares that "the citizens of each state shall be entitled to all privileges and immunities of citizens in the several states." When *will* our legislators "stop agitating the Negro question and attend to the interests of white men"? Why will not some white Republican introduce a bill into Congress, or propose an amendment to the Constitution, to secure the rights of men guilty of a skin colored like his own?

THE CONSPIRACY TO SEIZE WASHINGTON

The plot to seize upon Washington and proclaim a revolutionary government from the steps of the Capitol was well matured and complete in every part. It rested upon the confident expectation of the secession of both Virginia and Maryland before the 1st of March and the continuance in office of the traitors who have been ejected from the Cabinet. Floyd was the undoubted center of the conspiracy and expected to re-

9. peculiar institution: a Southern euphemism for slavery, possibly coined by John C. Calhoun (circa 1828), meaning it was an institution peculiar to the South.

10. To protect Southern "property" rights, Congress passed two Fugitive Slave acts (1793, 1850), requiring that escaped slaves, wherever found, be returned to their owners. The first act was in large part nullified by legislation in the Northern states; the second, bearing penalties that included six months' imprisonment and a thousand-dollar fine, was enacted as a concession to the South, in response to the growing antislavery sentiment in the North. The law was openly and flagrantly violated. Few escaped slaves were ever sent back South, and it remained a source of bitter contention.

main in office and superintend its consummation.[11] The plan has long been the subject of general conversation in Washington, and we are able to lay its details before our readers.

Immediately after the secession of Virginia and Maryland, a concerted movement was to be made just previous to Lincoln's inauguration, by which a hostile force was to be suddenly thrown into Washington to seize upon and garrison all the public buildings, expel Congress, and hold the town. A declaration to the effect that the regular government had been superseded was next to be issued and a provisional president and vice president to be proclaimed on the 4th of March. The departments, containing all the archives of the government, were at once to be occupied by provisional heads, and orders promptly issued therefrom to the army and navy, claiming from the officers everywhere obedience to the authorities in possession of the capital—to the government de facto. At the same time, the foreign ministers were to be called upon to recognize the new authorities and to announce the success of a peaceable revolution in the United States to their several governments.

It was expected that this program, which, but for its premature exposure, might have been easily carried out, would divide the allegiance of the army and navy everywhere, confounding the officers by its audacity, so that all whose sympathies or proclivities were with the South would have a reasonable excuse to go over to the revolutionary government without being amenable to the charge of deliberate treason. In this way the Southern slaveholding Confederacy expected to get its start before the world and be ready to maintain its claim to the flag and to be considered the actual possessor of the government of the United States. It would have the great advantage of being in control of the national capital and national archives and whatever portion of army and navy it might be able to seduce. Whatever contests, successful or otherwise, might have grown out of this attempt, a great object would have been gained. The military and naval force of the country would have been divided, and foreign nations made to doubt and hesitate and delay, before being able to decide whether the de jure or the de facto government of the United States was actually in power.

If, as we have said, the plot had not been unexpectedly exploded by the discovery of the robberies in the Department of the Interior, where Floyd was implicated, and by Major Anderson's occupation of Fort Sumter, it might have been executed with just as much ease and sud-

11. John Floyd, governor of Virginia (1849–52), secretary of war (1857–60), and Confederate general (1861–63).

denness as the seizure of the Florida, Georgia, Alabama, and Louisiana forts has been executed by the Rebels in those states. It is here to be remarked that the revelation of the conspiracy by Floyd was accidental and unpremeditated. Through fear that his confederates would distrust his good faith in the common treachery, he demanded Anderson's return to Fort Moultrie. To escape suspicion, and as a means of extorting that concession from the president, he resigned, supposing, from previous experience, that Mr. Buchanan would give way. But it so happened that he did not. Floyd immediately saw his mistake and offered to remain, as is stated by the president in his letter accepting Floyd's resignation. But it was now too late. It was said at the time, and has been said ever since, that the conspirators were thunderstruck at this faux pas of Floyd; at any rate, they were loud in its condemnation. They supposed it would prove fatal to their cherished plans, and the event has shown that there was reason in the opinion.

But the conspiracy is by no means destroyed. Its total defeat, even now, depends upon two grave contingencies yet undecided. One is whether Maryland will be held back from seceding, and the other is whether the military preparations in Washington are adequate to the emergency. The Rebels are desperate, as they have been from the start. Of course, they now labor under the great disadvantage of seeing their plans exposed and of being ousted from their influential positions in the government. Still, what they can do they will do; and if they can yet succeed in taking Maryland out along with the other seceding states, they will unquestionably undertake to carry Washington with them also. Then it can only be preserved by force of arms. And how are troops to be conveyed to Washington from the North, with Maryland engaged in the rebellion, Baltimore in the hands of an armed mob, and railroad communication cut off? It is even possible that the defense of Washington may have to be begun on the soil of Maryland.

Such is the outline of the atrocious conspiracy to overthrow the government and take possession of the capital, as it circulates in the highest political circles of Washington. We know that no doubt is there expressed of its being substantially correct by those who have the best opportunities of knowing the truth. And we repeat that there is no certainty that some such scheme will not even yet be carried out. The most determined efforts are still afoot to force Maryland to secede, and the movement is extremely threatening and formidable. If it succeeds, nothing is certain in the future but a fight with the Rebels for the possession of the Federal capital.

Yet, in the midst of these foul conspiracies, we have men and presses everywhere begging and praying that a compromise be made with the traitors engaged in this diabolical business! Is it not amazing that every man of every party who desires to preserve the republic does not hold with the grave and conservative senator from Rhode Island, who declares that he is afraid to compromise in the face of such perils for fear of demoralizing the government and bringing on general confusion and anarchy?

FEBRUARY 16, 1861

SOUTH

RICHMOND DAILY DISPATCH
February 16, 1861

ENGLISH INTEGRITY

We heard it lately remarked that notwithstanding the intense abolitionism of England, there can be no doubt that if, like the Northern states, she had ever promised to restore fugitive slaves, she would fulfill that promise, no matter how galling it might be to her own prejudices and passions. This remark was made in a large circle of gentlemen, almost every one of whom, by the way, had lost a slave. Nor can there be any doubt of its truth. Abolitionism would probably prevent England from ever entering into any such engagements, but her engagements, once made, whether political or commercial, are faithfully regarded. This is a great compliment to England, but it is well deserved. Everyone knows how much more faithfully every kind of work is done by English manufacturers than by those of New England, from the massive engine of a steamship down to a penknife. The English article is always what it professes to be, the New England hardly ever. In their social intercourse the English people are generally more reserved and less demonstrative than those of our own country, but what they say, as a general thing, can be relied on. The woeful absence of truthfulness is one of the most striking and ominous characteristics of the Puritan race. But for this radical defect of character, it would be utterly impossible for whole communities to sanction deliberately such violations of the constitutional compact as those which have occurred in New England communities, and which they have never dreamed of redressing till their money nerve was touched and the path to their conscience was found through their pockets. If justice can be done now in those states which are now promising to perform their constitutional obligations, why was it not done long ago? And how long will it continue to be done after their interests are no longer in danger? We must do the mother country the justice to say that while she is woefully bedeviled by antislavery fanaticism, she adheres to her contracts with a true English stamina of principle that we should like to see adopted in this boastful republic, which claims to be the best and purest of all nations.

CHARLESTON DAILY COURIER
February 16, 1861

CORRESPONDENCE OF THE COURIER

New York, February 12, 1861

In these trying times we are getting patriotic. Our city authorities have not made any provision to celebrate the 22nd—Washington's birthday—but they are accepting invitations to unite with others in so doing. The Order of United Americans will observe the day, and the Honorable Morrison Harris, M.C., of Maryland, will deliver an oration.

Divorce cases are as plentiful as blackberries in summertime. The crop this season is unusually large, and, strangely enough, most of the parties let off from the matrimonial bonds are husbands. There was a divorce case a day or two ago in which the persons figuring were about three quarters of a century old. New York furnishes peculiar advantages for violations of married rights, and the courts seem to be equally accommodating in putting asunder those whom the clergymen supposed they were uniting for better or for worse, and forever.

Tomorrow Lent commences, and it will afford many poor proud people an opportunity of feigning that they are Roman Catholics or High Churchmen, and thus almost starve themselves on principle. It will not, for forty days at least, be a badge of poverty to have it known that there is scarcely anything in the house to eat.

As usual, the opera has taken a fresh start just as Lent intervenes, and one half of its cultivated patrons will be compelled, from religious scruples, to keep away from its performances.

Our Central Park is going to be a very pretty, but a rather expensive toy. During the year 1860, there were employed on it about 3,579

aided by designing politicians. My advice to them is to keep cool. If the great American people will only keep their temper on both sides of the line, the trouble will come to an end and the question be settled just as surely as all other difficulties of a like character which have originated in this government have been adjusted.

Let the people on both sides keep their self-possession, and just as other clouds have cleared away in due time, so will this great nation continue to prosper as heretofore. But I have spoken longer on this subject than I intended.

As this is the first opportunity that I have had to address a Pennsylvania assembly, it seems fitting to indulge in a few remarks on the important question of the tariff, a subject of great magnitude and attended with many difficulties, owing to the variety of interests involved. So long as direct taxation is not resorted to, a tariff is necessary. A tariff to government is what meat is to a family.

This admitted, it still is necessary to modify and change its operations according to new interests and circumstances. So far there is little difference in opinion among politicians, but the question as to how far imports may be adjusted for protection to home industry gives rise to numerous objections. I don't understand the subject in all its multiform bearings, but I promise to give it my closest attention and fully to comprehend it. And here I may remark that the Chicago platform contains a plank on the subject which I think should be regarded as law for the incoming administration.[13] [*Immense applause.*] In fact, this question as well as other subjects embodied in that platform should not be varied from. [*At the request of Mr. Lincoln, his secretary here read the tariff (twelfth) section of the Chicago platform.*]

Mr. Lincoln continued:

I must confess there are shades of difference in construing even this platform; but I am not discussing these differences, but merely give you a general idea of the subject. I have long thought

13. The 1860 Republican convention, held in Chicago, nominated Abraham Lincoln for president. The party reaffirmed the antislavery position of its 1856 platform, but allowed that the militant abolitionist John Brown had committed the "gravest of crimes" in his raid on the Federal arsenal at Harpers Ferry, then part of Virginia, on October 16, 1859. The platform pointedly warned against "contemplated treason, which it is the imperative duty of an indignant people sternly to rebuke and forever silence."

that if there be any article of necessity which can be produced at home with as little or nearly the same labor as abroad, it would be better to protect that article. Labor is the true standard of value. If a bar of iron be got out of the mines in England and a bar of iron taken from the mines of Pennsylvania at the same cost, it follows that if the English bar is shipped from Manchester to Pittsburgh and the American bar from Pittsburgh to Manchester, the cost of carriage is appreciably lost. [*Laughter.*]

If we had no iron here, then we should encourage shipments from foreign countries, but not when we can make it as cheaply in our own country. The Treasury is in such a low condition as to demand the attention of Congress, and will demand the immediate attention of the new administration. The tariff bill now before Congress may not pass the present session. I confess I do not understand the precise provisions of this bill. It may or may not become the law of the land, but if it does, that will be an end of the matter until modifications can be effected. If it does not pass—and the latest advices I have are to this effect—it is still pending, and the next Congress will have to give it their earliest attention.

According to my political education, I am inclined to believe the people should have their own views carried out through their representatives in Congress. No subject should engage the attention of your representatives more than the tariff. If I have any recommendation to make, it will be that every man who is called upon to serve the people in a representative capacity should study the whole subject thoroughly, as I intend to do myself, looking to all the varied interests of the country, so that when the time for action arrives, adequate protection shall be extended to the coal and iron of Pennsylvania, the corn of Illinois, and the reapers of Chicago. Permit me to express the hope that this important subject may receive such consideration at the hands of your representatives that the interests of no part of the country may be overlooked, but that all sections may share in the common benefits of a just and equitable tariff.

Thanking them for their kindly attention, Mr. Lincoln bade the assemblage adieu amid immense applause. He was then escorted by a procession to the depot, where he took a special train for Cleveland. The utmost enthusiasm prevailed. Every street was filled with people.

Cleveland, 15th—The special train conveying Mr. Lincoln and suite arrived at half past four this afternoon. He was received with great enthusiasm. A procession composed of the military and fire companies escorted him to his hotel.

Mr. Lincoln, after reaching the Weddell House, was welcomed by Acting Mayor Masters. Mr. Lincoln, briefly replying, said:

> The large numbers here testify that you are in earnest about something. You have assembled to testify your respect to the Union, Constitution, and the laws; and here let me say that it is with you, the people, to advance the great cause of the Union and the Constitution, and not with any one man. It rests with you alone. This fact is strongly impressed on my mind in a community like this whose appearance testifies to its intelligence. I am convinced the Union can never be in danger. Frequent allusion is made to the excitement at present existing in our national politics. I think there is no occasion for any excitement. The crisis, as it is called, is altogether an artificial crisis.
>
> In all parts of the nation, there are differences of opinion in politics, as there are different opinions even here. You did not all vote for the person who now addresses you. What is happening now will not hurt those who are farther away from here.
>
> Have they not all their rights now as they ever have had? Do they not have their fugitive slaves returned now as they ever have? Have they not the same Constitution that they have lived under for the last seventy-odd years? Have they not a position as citizens of this common country, and have we any power to change that position? What, then, is the matter with them? Why all this excitement—why all these complaints?
>
> As I said before, this crisis is all artificial. It has no foundation in fact; it was not argued up, as the saying is, and cannot therefore be argued down. Let it alone, and it will go down of itself. [*Laughter*.]

He thanked them for their reception, but pleaded fatigue, and thanked them for the votes they gave him last fall, and quite as much for the efficient aid they had given the cause he represented—a cause which he would say was a good one.

He had one word more to say. He understood this reception was irrespective of party. This was as it should be. "If Judge Douglas had been elected and was on his way to Washington, the Republicans should have joined in welcoming him, as his friends have joined with mine tonight.[14] If all do not join now to save the good old ship of the Union this voyage, nobody will have a chance to pilot her on another voyage."

Several bouquets were presented to Mr. Lincoln, and the crowd separated, cheering for Lincoln and the Union. Thousands attended the levee this evening. He leaves at nine in the morning for Buffalo.

Mr. Lincoln has requested a suspension of all contemplated party or Wide Awake demonstrations.[15]

A FORCE BILL TO BE PASSED BY CONGRESS—KELLOGG'S ATTACK UPON THE CHICAGO EDITOR—PROSPECTS OF A COMPROMISE LESS FAVORABLE

Washington, February 16, 1861

A force bill for collecting the revenue in the seceded states has been agreed on by the Republican caucus and will pass both houses of Congress.

The leading Republicans in this city are much incensed at the attack upon the editor of the *Chicago Tribune* by Mr. Kellogg at the National Hotel last night.

The secretary of the Treasury, Mr. Dix, positively refuses to discount 1 percent on the deposits made by the bidders for the $10 million loan.

Present indications are less promising than formerly of an adjustment of the slavery question by a compromise. The Honorable James Guthrie is reported to have remarked at the president's dinner table yesterday that there was no hope of a settlement.

NEW YORK TRIBUNE
February 16, 1861

SOUTHERN UNIONISM

If we were to give full credit to the bulletins transmitted from the slave states, the people of those states are divided into two parties: (1) those who hold that the North is inveterately Republican, and therefore are intent on disunion; and (2) those who still hope that the North can be bullied out of Republicanism, and therefore incline to give us another chance to humble ourselves before breaking away from us. We must

14. Stephen A. Douglas, Northern Democratic presidential candidate in 1860.
15. Wide Awake: a secret pro-Union militia.

confess that these two positions seem not at all diverse in principle, while the latter is by far the less flattering to the North.

But, in truth, neither of these positions does justice to the better instincts of the South. What calls itself the Union party of the South does injustice to itself because it has been led to do injustice to us. Having indolently adopted the current Southern assumption that Republicanism menaces the rights and the safety of the South, it has piled thereon the further assumption that part of us are blind fanatics and the rest simply unprincipled knaves who have conspired to humor the fanatics in order thus to ride into office and fill their own pockets. They thereupon conclude that if they seriously threaten disunion, the Republican knaves will desert the fanatics and concede whatever may be tenaciously required.

We beg leave to assure the South that these impressions do injustice to the North, as their attitude based thereon does injustice to themselves. Let us understand each other.

It is the clear conviction of the great mass of the Northern people today—that is, of those who have any moral convictions by which they abide—that slavery is essentially wrong; hence that they cannot conscientiously permit themselves to be implicated in its extension. Such has been, such is, their conviction. The whole subject has been studied, considered, contested, debated, until there is no longer any rational ground for hope that this conviction will be changed.

He who asks us, therefore, to acquiesce in the Crittenden or some kindred arrangement may not mean to insult us, but he *does*. He says, in effect, "Your consciences are in the market, and you are ready to defy your sense of duty, provided you can make gain thereby. If we only promise or threaten you sufficiently, you will consent to do what you have long insisted and still feel is wrong."

We beg the true friends of the Union at the South to reconsider this matter. We ask them to do nothing, say nothing, inconsistent with their own sense of duty. If they think slavery ought to be extended, we do not blame them for seeking its extension, but we insist that they shall not seek to constrain us to do what our consciences imperatively forbid. If they want slavery extended, let them rely on the votes of those who approve or are indifferent to "the institution"; and there are quite as many of these, even at the North, as there ought to be. But to ask Republicans to make any bargain, compact, arrangement, compromise, whereby they shall be pledged to acquiescence in, or nonresistance to, slavery extension is to ask them to disgrace and stultify themselves. If they respect their own moral convictions, let them prove it by respecting those of their neighbors.

If the Union is to be saved, it must be by upholding the Constitution and obeying the laws and constituted authorities. Whoever uses others' threats of secession to compass a partisan or sectional triumph is but one remove from treason. The true compromise is a universal agreement to respect all rightful authority and obey the laws.

MARCH 16, 1861

SOUTH

RICHMOND DAILY DISPATCH
March 16, 1861

FROM CHARLESTON

Special Correspondence of the *Dispatch*
Charleston, South Carolina, March 13, 1861

If a man who has the reputation of tolerable veracity tells me anything, I am disposed to believe him, but when a Washington official assures me, I feel inclined to doubt him, no matter how he may pledge himself. We have been so duped and swindled with Buchanan that we do not feel inclined to believe anything from Washington; for it has always been infected with deep corruption, and we can hardly respect anything else now, under Black Republican keeping.

I told you yesterday that news had been received here that Fort Sumter was to be vacated but that I did not believe it; that on the bulletin boards is a further confirmation of it; and that a special messenger starts today at four o'clock to carry the dispatch to Major Anderson. I do not yet believe it, and shall not until I see Anderson and his men on the cars with their faces northward. By the way, Anderson, and his friends for him, have assured the public that he was a true Southern man and that his feelings and sympathies were all with the South. He will have a fine opportunity now to show to the world whether he and his friends have been sincere.

It is understood in Washington—so says the correspondent of the *Courier*—that Anderson and his command are to strengthen Fortress Monroe.[16] Yes, strengthen your forts. Virginia is not quite to be relied on yet by the Black masters. She has shown lately some little sign of life

16. Located at Old Point Comfort, on the Peninsula of Virginia, Fortress (or Fort) Monroe guarded the entry to the James River from the Chesapeake Bay.

and pluck; hence, she is not exactly as *tame* as she ought to be. Some few signs of the return of the Virginia-blooded stock—perhaps Daniel of the *Examiner*—coming home just now may have affected the nerves of the "rightful masters," and some plucky speeches in your convention, all put together, may have alarmed your masters, and they now consider "an ounce of prevention better than a pound of cure"; therefore, they will make the forts of Virginia safe and bind you a little tighter—put on another handcuff and a few more ankle chains. No, no; Virginia is not yet exactly subdued—too many Wises, Goodes, Randolphs, Mortons, Daniels, and *Dispatches* there, to be thrashed yet—a few more soldiers and a few more cannons, and a little more grape and a few more chains, and a few more handcuffs, and a few more Black Republicans in your convention and legislature, and a little of the teat, if you please, and a few more social visits of your public functionaries to partake of the hospitalities of the Federal soldiers at Fortress Monroe, and "a little sleep, and a little slumber, and a little folding the hands to sleep," and you are then in the claws of your deadly enemy, betrayed there by Virginia's *bastards*.[17] But let it go; "let her rip."

Our soldiers will have a fight yet. If they cannot get it on their own "dunghill," they will help our little sister, Florida.

Virginius

CHARLESTON DAILY COURIER
March 16, 1861

CORRESPONDENCE OF THE COURIER

New York, March 12, 1861

The Black Republicans are having a good time cursing General Scott, ridiculing Old Abe, and quarreling with each other. A change, however, has come over the dreams of many, and they who a few days ago were most furious for a fight, now that Old Abe says so, think the abandonment of Fort Sumter a masterly stroke of policy. If the president were to say that vinegar was a healthier drink than water, I have no doubt the corner groceries would soon be exhausted of their stock in trade.

Some of the radicals, who were really spoiling for something to do,

17. Like a shotgun shell for cannon, "grape," or grape shot, was composed of iron balls sandwiched between two plates. When the round was fired, the balls dispersed. A similar round that was more widely used was "canister," which resembled a frangible tin can filled with musket balls.

and who would rather fight than starve, are extremely disgusted at the turn things have taken. They express their feelings in the coarsest and most ribald manner, d——g Seward, consigning Weed to a warm place, and expressing their belief that the devil was to pay in Washington.[18] The soreheaded malcontents will doubtless call a special meeting and ventilate their ideas on the cowardice of all compromisers. Lincoln, before being well seated in office, seems destined to meet with a degrading fall. I heard one crazy old man say that he would rather have his daughters go down and defend Major Anderson than the country disgraced by abandoning Sumter!

There is continued activity among the steamers chartered for special United States government duties. The *Star of the West* and the *Philadelphia* will both follow the *Empire City* and *Ariel*. The *Daniel Webster,* when she returns, will again be dispatched South. These rapid movements of the steamers, while the public mind is filled with exciting rumors of the abandonment of Sumter and the alleged conciliatory policy of Lincoln, may be but another Grecian horse about to enter Troy. (Since writing the above, I learn that the order for the *Ariel* to prepare for sea has been countermanded. It would take too long to get her ready.)

The blind preacher, Reverend W. H. Milburn, is here, lecturing on the fiery orator of the Southwest, the late Sargent S. Prentiss. The lecture is, of course, a very thrilling one, and the effect is heightened by an exhibition of Peale's great painting of the *Court of Death,* immediately after the sightless orator sits down. In these hard times it requires many rare combinations to attract crowds.

The arrangement entered into by the banks of New York on the 21st of November last, by united concert of action, to sustain the commercial interests of the city, expired on Saturday last, and the remainder of the outstanding loan certificates were all returned. The maximum amount issued of these certificates was $7,375,000, and having answered their intended purpose, they have all been paid off and canceled without the loss of a single dollar.

The news respecting the surrender of Sumter, which made the stocks jump up yesterday, is unconfirmed today, so they tumble back again. The brokers, as a general thing, haven't much of an opinion of Old Abe, believing that between Seward and Chase, he is merely a symbol of the ass between the two bundles of straw; consequently, their operations now are small and for a short time, until it is ascertained that "we have

18. William Seward, secretary of state (1861–69). Thurlow Weed, New York journalist and Republican politician.

a government."[19] Horace Greeley said we had, on the 4th of March, but like the office seeker's name which was sent to the Senate, that hasn't been confirmed yet.[20]

The occupants of most of the principal offices under the government have already forwarded their resignations, while all are ready to vacate at a moment's notice. Even Mr. Cisco, the subtreasurer, who was reported by Joe Scoville in the *Mobile Register* to intend to hold on to the national funds, is anxious and willing to hand them over to his successor. The superintendent of the Assay Office, Butterworth—Dan Sickles's friend—withholds nothing from the new custodian appointed by Lincoln.

The choice Federal offices in this city have been very profitable during the past four years. The incumbents have all held on through the entire term except poor Fowler, the postmaster. Collector Schell is believed to have pocketed his hundred fifty thousand dollars, and Surveyor Hart nearly as much more. Rynders, in the United States marshalship, has laid by enough to keep him snug and comfortable the rest of his days; besides, the valiant captain married a lady, who to her other charms united that of a substantial dowry.

Theodore Sedgewick, who was United States district attorney, died in office; Judge Roosevelt succeeded him and still holds on to the place. Messrs. Cisco and Butterworth are the only two government officials who have been in place for eight years.

There will be a clean sweep in the customhouse and all other places except, perhaps, the post office. It is believed now that Taylor, who succeeded General Dix, and who has been in the department for two or three score of years, will be retained. This will greatly please the merchants, but disgust the office seekers.

Pink

THE CONFEDERATE CONSTITUTION

Our space and engagements have not permitted comments on the plan of the Constitution adopted in Montgomery, nor do we now propose to consider it in detail.

It is a duty, however, to give utterance to our opinions on this topic, and in this case it gives us pleasure to record our full and cordial approbation that all essential features and provisions that were practically

19. Salmon Chase, secretary of the Treasury (1861–64).
20. Horace Greeley, abolitionist and publisher of the *New York Tribune*.

good and efficient in the United States Constitution have been wisely retained. The departures from that Constitution will be justified, we think, by events and experience and have been indicated or demanded by the practical developments under the late Union.

Beginning at the preamble—a more important portion than it was considered at the epoch of the Federal Constitution—we find and acknowledge a marked amendment in the distinct assertion of a federation instead of a consolidation, the omission of the vague and mischievous "general welfare," and the recognition of the Supreme and Almighty Ruler of men and peoples.

In the legislative department we are struck at once by the happy substitution of "delegated" for "granted" and by the comprehensive and simple remedy provided against the abuse of the elective franchise through any variations in the usages or regulations of any states concerning their state elections.

A vast improvement on the old Constitution will be observed also in the provision for impeachment; a measure of additional recognition and defense for the states severally, of additional guarantees for official fidelity, and of prevention against undue pressure from Federal patronage.

In the list of powers delegated or prohibited to Congress will be found several amendments and changes demanded by the abuses and corruptions we have renounced, and we commend to intelligent readers a comparison, clause by clause, with the old Constitution. We also respectfully suggest that for the convenience of the convention that will soon be called on to consider this Constitution, and for the information of citizens generally, it would repay an enterprising printer to issue, in good style, the United States and Confederate constitutions in parallel columns.

No part of the United States Constitution has worked, in practice, so much unmitigated evil as that referring to the executive, and to this portion of the "Confederate" plan we refer accordingly, with confidence, that the change will be approved and endorsed as great and important amendments. It may be questioned whether the change could not have been wisely carried further into the creation of the electoral body—a body which was originally designed to have elective discretion, but which in practice has only registered the votes of the primary electors. There was wisdom, however, in limiting the changes to such portions as had manifestly worked evil in practice. The shortness of term and re-eligibility have been the marked evils in the United States executive, rather than the mode of creating the electoral body, and these evils are avoided in the Confederate Constitution.

> How humiliating to every Mississippian to know that *after cursing and denouncing the people of the North,* as our citizens have been in the habit of denouncing them, *we are compelled to turn around and beg them for bread, and they in turn are trying to kill us with kindness* by treating our agent with the greatest respect and not only giving him more than he asked for but paying for the sacks to put it in. It certainly places us in a very humiliating position, and we hear Major Hawkins abused for going there and begging corn. But we say he has done right, and thousands of starving children, widows, and orphans will bless him for his efforts to keep them from perishing with hunger. Some narrow-minded, contemptible demagogues say that the citizens of Illinois give us corn because they fear us and wish to get on good terms with us again. We believe they are actuated by purely Christian motives and that they have purer and better hearts than those who make such charges. While we would rather labor day and night from one year's end to another than beg either of them or anybody else, we would not hesitate to beg if our little ones were starving.

The policy of thus "feeding the hungry" of the seceded states is plain, even if it were not dictated by higher considerations of human sympathy and benevolence. Every bushel of corn thus given loosens a prejudice in the mind of the recipient. Such "concessions," we trust, our suffering Southern brethren will receive in unmeasured abundance from the North and West. The gaunt image of Famine, as it rises in the imagination, is sufficiently pitiful to allay the fiercest antipathies of parties and sections; and everything given to save fellow beings from starvation is "twice blest."

NO DECISION IN REGARD TO THE EVACUATION OF FORT SUMTER—THE BOSTON POST OFFICE—THE POLICY OF THE PRESIDENT—OPPOSITION TO THE MONTGOMERY CONSTITUTION IN SOUTH CAROLINA—MOVEMENT OF U.S. VESSELS

New York, March 16, 1861

The *Times*'s Washington dispatch says the Cabinet has come to no decision on the question of evacuation of Fort Sumter, in opposition to which movement very strong arguments are made. Recent letters from Major Anderson resent, with indignation, the insinuations against his disposition to hold Fort Sumter to the last extremity.

Petitions have arrived from Boston, signed by merchants representing $50 million capital, in favor of Mr. Pangborn for postmaster.

A dispatch from Columbus, Ohio, announces that after twenty-nine ballots in the Republican caucus for candidate for senator, Mr. Sherman was withdrawn but will probably be brought forward again stronger than before.

The *Herald* has intelligence from Charleston which represents that there exists a pretty strong party in South Carolina opposed to ratifying the Montgomery Constitution, and who will resist it at every point.

The Confederate government has appointed W. L. Yancey, P. A. Rost, A. Dudley Mann, and T. Butler King commissioners to England and France, to obtain the recognition of the independence of the Confederated States and to make such commercial arrangements as their joint interests may inspire.

Steamers *Mohawk* and *Crusader* have gone to the Gulf.

Revenue vessels will be added to the fleet, which will augment it to a respectable Coast Guard.

Steamer *Philadelphia* will probably be used, in case of the evacuation of Fort Sumter, to bring the garrison to Point Comfort.

The *Tribune*'s correspondent says the shot fired at Fort Sumter was the result of a deliberate plan to try Major Anderson's temper, and the statement that it was accidental is an unblushing lie.

The *Tribune*'s Washington dispatch says Major Anderson's last statement to the War Department was that his stock of bread had been reduced to fourteen days' supply and of rice to twenty-three days'. With other supplies he might maintain himself a month.

The Montgomery correspondent of the *New York Tribune* says the South believes that the only thing that will satisfy the North is for the former to prove its ability to maintain its independence by force of arms, and it is willing to do so. The impost on Negroes imported from the border states will probably be 30 percent.

The *Herald* dispatch says that a member of the Virginia Convention called on the president today. The latter assured him that no vessel had been sent South with hostile intentions, that nothing would be done in regard to affairs in the South for sixty days, and that it was his purpose to restore peace and prevent the shedding of blood.

Doctor Thomas, of Dubuque, has been tendered the mission to Bogota.

Intelligence from Baltimore asserts that it is the intention of the secessionists there to resist any Republicans taking possession of government offices in Baltimore to the last.

NEW YORK TRIBUNE
March 16, 1861

FORT SUMTER

If the abandonment of Fort Sumter to the Rebels be indeed a military necessity, it must, of course, be abandoned. But the necessity must be so plain that people will all believe in it. If the abandonment of the fort be a present, pressing necessity, it seems probable that poor old Buchanan and his band of Cabinet traitors are not alone to blame. Some fault must lie at the door of Major Anderson for having so repeatedly declared (if, indeed, he has so declared, as we have constantly heard he has) that he required no succor, and especially for having done so about the time the *Star of the West* was sent to his relief. We give no credence to the insinuations alluded to by one of our Charleston correspondents as current there, to the effect that Major Anderson has a good understanding with the Rebels. But if he has failed to make known to the government the real exigencies of his position, he is greatly to be blamed. He has communicated with the government not only by letters but also by a special messenger, and it seems incredible that his real position was not made known. It must be assumed, then, that in stating his position to be secure for some time to come, Major Anderson stated the exact truth; and we must therefore conclude that there is no necessity for an immediate abandonment of Fort Sumter on account of a want of provisions. That the long delay in sending reinforcements and stores has given the Rebels great advantage, none can deny. Unquestionably, the danger to Fort Sumter from without is far more serious than it was a few weeks ago. The Rebels have had time to erect formidable batteries and to discipline their troops. Instead of being a mere state government, they are a confederacy of states, possessed of considerable means for carrying on war, mainly derived from the plunder of United States property and the treachery of United States military officers. From this state of things, however, there arises no necessity for an immediate abandonment of Fort Sumter, if that fortress be indeed sufficiently provisioned to prevent starvation and sufficiently manned to work its guns. But if the fort has no power to resist an attack, the discovery is made very late in the day, and all the labors of Major Anderson to put it in a condition to repel an attack will inure only to the benefit of the Rebels. The thought is far from pleasant.

But the real ground why Sumter is to be abandoned, if at all, is that the United States has not sufficient power at its disposal to hold it. We must reject the idea that the reason is because bloodshed and civil war will result; for to give that reason is only another way of saying that the secessionists are to have their own way in everything. It must be justified, if at all, upon the square, plump, and only tenable ground of want of power to preserve the fort from being captured. No other plea will ever satisfy the people, nor will that, unless it be a true plea. Thanks to honest Floyd and loyal Toucey, the army and navy are so disposed of, that it is difficult to say how far they are available for the protection of the coast defenses, but if they are sufficient for that purpose, the people will expect them to be so used. If they are insufficient, that is an excuse for giving up untenable forts before, instead of after, bloodshed—for no commander has a right by the laws of war to pretend to hold what is clearly untenable. Thus, then, stands the case:

1. There is no necessity for an immediate abandonment of Fort Sumter on the ground of a want of provisions to subsist the men.

2. There is no such necessity on the ground of want of men and provisions to make temporary resistance.

3. The United States have sufficient power to reinforce the fort and destroy the batteries opposed to it, and it is no good public reason for not exerting that power that blood would flow and civil war result.

4. But, although having the power, it is not at the present time available, and before it could be made so, the fort would fall into the hands of the Rebels.

5. If the last proposition be really true, the fort might better be given up at once.

We protest, however, against any acquiescence on our part in this humiliating and truly mournful measures being construed to mean that we are in favor of any other concessions of the kind. If the Gulf defenses all fall into the hands of the Rebels, they will acquire a military importance not to be despised and, perhaps, to be dreaded. After the alacrity they have shown in plundering mints, stealing arsenals, robbing creditors, thieving stocks, and prigging vessels national and private, he must be a confiding fool who doubts that our commerce would be preyed upon by the scoundrels who have instituted the Slave Confederacy if they could control our Gulf defenses and deprive our navy of any place of rendezvous near their own borders. With tears of indignation and sorrow, we may manage to acquiesce in the abandonment of Fort Sumter, but to go further is to overwhelm the nation with disgrace and cripple its resources in the war which will be sure to follow. For the men who have secession in hand, if they find us truckling, mean to exact concessions until they force us to take a stand somewhere and prove to the world by our own craven acts that we are unworthy to be called a nation. Rather than wait for that day, it were better at once to recognize the new Confederacy, let all who choose join it, and then sue for peace and mercy for ourselves.

1861

TIMELINE

April 1–7: A Union naval expedition is dispatched to Fort Sumter. The fort is put under blockade by the Confederates. Major Anderson is no longer able to communicate with Washington.

April 10: Before the relief ships arrive, Confederate General Pierre Beauregard is directed to "demand the evacuation" of the fort. In anticipation of relief, Anderson tries unsuccessfully to negotiate a delay.

April 12: Bombardment of the fort begins at 4:30 A.M. No serious casualties result, but Anderson, out of supplies and without recourse, surrenders the following day.

April 15: Lincoln issues a call for seventy-five thousand volunteers.

April 19: The 6th Massachusetts Regiment, passing through Baltimore on the way to Washington, D.C., is attacked by a mob of Confederate sympathizers; four soldiers and twelve civilians are killed. Lincoln orders a naval blockade of all ports in the Confederate states.

April 27: Though officially vacillating on the question of secession, Virginia effectively becomes a member of the Confederacy, and on this date offers itself as the site for a permanent capital. Antisecessionists in the western part of Virginia resolve to remain with the Union, and hold their own state convention.

May 2: Union General-in-Chief Winfield Scott proposes a total land, river, and sea blockade of the Confederacy, with the suspension of other military action, until the South is strangled into submission.

The press derides the scheme as the "Anaconda Plan." The Northern public clamors for action.

May 6: The Confederacy declares war.

May 13: Great Britain declares neutrality.

May 24: Federal troops occupy Alexandria, Virginia. Colonel Elmer Ellsworth is shot in an argument over a Confederate flag, becoming the first Union combat fatality.

At Fortress Monroe, Virginia, General Benjamin Butler refuses to turn over three slaves who escaped into his lines, and declares them to be "contraband of war," thus adding a new term to the American lexicon.

May 31: Postal service between the North and the South is suspended.

June 8: The U.S. Sanitary Commission is established. Its mission is to oversee the health and welfare of Union troops.

June 10: In the first land battle, at Big Bethel Church, Virginia, the Federals lose seventy-six men and the Confederates eleven.

June 15: The Confederates abandon Harpers Ferry, Virginia, to avoid capture by advancing Federal forces.

June 18: Inventor Thaddeus Lowe sends telegraph messages from a hovering balloon and will be employed as an aerial observer for the Union, with mixed results.

June 26: The *New York Tribune* begins exhorting, "Forward to Richmond!"

July 10–13: Minor victories in Virginia encourage the Union to move larger forces into the state.

July 18–20: The Confederates and the Federals engage in skirmishes leading up to the first major battle of the war, the First Battle of Bull Run (or Manassas), Virginia. Northern and Southern newspaper coverage on these dates prematurely hails these preliminary encounters as "The Battle at Bull Run."

July 21: The Confederates, under General Beauregard, score a resounding victory at Bull Run. The Union rout leads Lincoln to replace General Irvin McDowell with George McClellan. Confederate General Thomas Jackson earns the nickname "Stonewall."

August 10: The Confederates win at Wilson's Creek, Missouri. Engaged: North, 5,400; South, 11,600. Casualties: North, 1,235; South, 1,184.

August 14–15: Mutinies are reported in at least three Federal regiments; the soldiers' complaints center on lack of pay and furlough.

September 20: Northern newspapers incorrectly signal a coming victory. The week-long siege at Lexington, Missouri, forces the surrender of Federal troops under Colonel James Mulligan.

October 21: Battle of Balls Bluff, Virginia. The minor action at the Potomac River crossing near Washington fails to dislodge the Confederates from Leesburg, as reported in one newspaper. Ambushed, Colonel Edward Baker, Lincoln's friend and a former senator, is killed.

November 1: General-in-Chief Scott retires and is replaced by the thirty-four-year-old McClellan. It is not long before Lincoln begins to question his choice, as McClellan seems unwilling to take troops into battle.

November 2: Union General John Frémont, head of the forces in the West, is relieved of command. Henry Halleck assumes command on November 19. The removal of Frémont, the 1856 Republican candidate for president, is precipitated by his high-handedness and apparent reluctance to engage the enemy. Frémont resigns from the army eight months later.

November 7: Union forces under the command of Navy Commodore Samuel Du Pont and General Thomas Sherman (no relation to William Tecumseh Sherman) launch a seaborne expedition against Port Royal and Hilton Head, South Carolina, and win a permanent foothold on the coast.

November 8: A Union warship stops the British ship *Trent,* and the Confederate commissioners James Mason and John Slidell, en route to Europe to request recognition of the Confederate States from England and France, are removed. This illegal act becomes a diplomatic embarrassment, generating talk in some British quarters of declaring war against the United States.

December 20: Sixteen old sailing ships, loaded with ballast stones, are sunk in Charleston Harbor in an attempt to block traffic. The effort to enforce the blockade at the harbor will be ongoing until the fall of Charleston in February 1865.

APRIL 20, 1861

SOUTH

RICHMOND DAILY DISPATCH
April 20, 1861

FROM PETERSBURG
THE SEIZURE OF VESSELS AT CITY POINT—REJOICING IN PETERSBURG—MILITARY PREPARATIONS, ETC.

Special Correspondence of the *Dispatch*

April 18, 1861

The events of the day have been such as to render me almost unable to decide where to begin an enumeration of them. The excitement has certainly reached its climax, and events of the most extraordinary character would now be received with nothing more than comment. The prime cause, however, of the tremendous display of feeling today was the seizure of the three vessels at City Point. The originators of the plan to take possession of these vessels were certainly very ingenious, as well in the conception as in the management and execution of it. It was done almost secretly, I may say, for very few persons here had any idea of such a thing; and when the news of the success of the enterprise reached the city, the majority of our citizens were completely astounded. A company of twelve or fifteen men, commanded by Colonel E. L. Brockett, assisted by about an equal number from Richmond, headed by Captain Albert Akin, of Henrico County, were all that participated.

The first-class ship *Argo,* from Bath, Maine, was the first one taken. She is a large vessel, being of 1,080 tons' burden, and will undoubtedly render good service with an outlay of a small sum of money. No resistance was offered, though the officers thought it a little hard that they should so suddenly be deprived of their command and, consequently, of their means of support. Part of her crew, consisting of eighteen Negroes from different portions of the North, were put under arrest and brought to this city and lodged in jail. What disposition will be made of them I am not able to say, but I presume they will not be harmed, as Colonel Brockett pledged his word that they should not be troubled. They will be brought before the mayor tomorrow morning, and of course I shall keep you advised about them.

A U.S. surveying vessel was next boarded and seized and a sufficient force left upon her, as well as on the *Argo,* to protect and hold them.

The seizure of the *Jamestown* was accidental altogether, she happening to reach the wharf before the Petersburg train left, which would have brought all but the force necessary to guard the captured vessels, to this city. The *Jamestown* created general admiration as she proudly neared the landing with her flags floating gaily to the breeze. Nothing was said or done until she was firmly fastened to her moorings, when Colonel Brockett politely informed Captain Skinner of his intention to detain and take possession of her also. Objection was made by the gentlemanly captain, and a threat was made that he should clear away and proceed immediately back to New York. But by this time he found his ship being fastened by other hands than his own, and seeing it was to no purpose to longer object, he reluctantly yielded, and Colonel Brockett assumed the command. Arrangements were then made for the steamer to proceed on her regular route to Richmond, where I resign her further disposal to you.

Flags have been floating from many residences and public buildings today. A party ascended to the top of the new post office and flung a large and beautiful Southern flag to the breeze, in the presence of an immense assemblage of persons, who, already wild with excitement, cheered and hurrahed till their throats were hoarse.

Our city council sat with closed doors this afternoon, which action has caused a good deal of surmise and conjecture. Nothing in regard to their proceedings has as yet been divulged. It is generally supposed, however, that the members are engaged in discussing the propriety of arming the city, and otherwise preparing for her defense. I heard a rumor to the effect that an appropriation of $25,000 or $30,000 would be made for such purpose.

The Nottoway Rifle Guards, Captain Owen, arrived here in the one o'clock Southside train. This company had not been ordered to Norfolk, but merely came down to offer their services; it numbers forty-six fine-looking, determined men, who seemed much disappointed on finding they should have to return home.[1] They will go back tomorrow. The two companies from that county ordered to proceed to Norfolk today did not receive orders in time to assemble and come down.[2]

The Petersburg Riflemen were today ordered to proceed to City Point, to take charge of the vessels held there.

Four rifled cannons passed through here from Richmond this morning, en route for Norfolk.

Mon Coeur

CHARLESTON DAILY COURIER
April 20, 1861

EXCITING NEWS FROM BALTIMORE THE PEOPLE AROUSED—BLACK REPUBLICAN TROOPS SHOT—FOUR KILLED AND NUMBERS WOUNDED—RAILROAD TRACKS TORN UP—THE CITY IN ARMS—THE SOUTHERN BANNER HOISTED—MARTIAL LAW PROCLAIMED, ETC.

Baltimore, 19th—This city was today thrown into a perfect fever heat of excitement, occasioned by the arrival of Northern troops on the way to Washington, in obedience to the call made in Lincoln's late "Coercion Proclamation." When the first part of the Massachusetts Regiment was being transported through the streets of the city from the Philadelphia depot to the Washington depot, the horsecars were riddled with stones and missiles of every character. The windows of the conveyances were almost completely demolished, but luckily for the soldiers, no one was injured seriously, though many were badly cut with broken glass and bruised with the stones.

1. Norfolk, Virginia.

2. In general, Civil War armies were organized as follows: Four squads made a company, usually fifty to one hundred men; ten companies a regiment; five regiments a brigade; three brigades a division; and three divisions a corps. The term "corps" is derived from the French *corps d'armée*.

The remaining detachment of the regiment, while attempting to march through the city in order to arrive at the depot and proceed at once to Washington, met with a great deal of opposition. All along the route they were hooted at by the populace, and at the Pratt Street Bridge they came in contact with a dense crowd of reckless men, who opposed all further progress. Here a fight was commenced, and the assault was so vigorously made by the citizens that the Massachusetts soldiers fired upon them. On the part of the Baltimoreans, pistols and stones were plentifully used, so that many on both sides were killed and wounded, but it was impossible to learn the names of any of the parties. Four or five of the Massachusetts troops were killed on the spot, and others are badly wounded. Several dead bodies are now being hauled through the streets. The excitement is most intense. The whole city has flown to arms. Martial law has been proclaimed, and the Southern flag has been raised. The entire city has declared itself for states' rights and for the South.

[Private advices estimate the loss in killed and wounded at about one hundred thirty. Among the killed is Mr. Davis, of the firm of Davis, Painter, and Company.]

Later in the day an immense crowd, numbering ten thousand people, congregated around the Camden Street depot (depot of the railroad to Washington), and the Massachusetts troops were forbidden to depart. No troops will be allowed to proceed farther.

Soon after this, the tracks of the railroad from Baltimore to Washington were partly torn up by the people in order to prevent the departure of any force of men.

John W. Garrett, the president of the Baltimore and Ohio Railroad, has determined to allow the passage of no more troops over the line. Other railroads have come to the same understanding.

No more fighting is expected for the present. All our military force is under arms, and order will be preserved.

THE EFFECT OF OUR VICTORY

Our enemies have been stung to madness by the unexpected and utter defeat their arms have sustained in Charleston Bay. Their proud flag has been lowered at the bidding of a foe. They have been beaten by the very people for whom they cherish the most bitter hatred, and whom they affect to despise. They counted upon victory with absolute confidence. Their vile sheets have made them believe that Fort Sumter was impregnable to any attack our forces could make against it. These ingenious and unscrupulous papers had satisfied the credulous boasters that our men would fly before the bayonets of their brave regulars, that the reduction of our batteries would be attended with but small loss of life, and that, reinforced, the commandant of the strong fortress would bring the city a penitent suppliant at his feet. All this had been told them, and they had swallowed and digested it and grown fat and strong on the palatable fictions.

They had reasoned away all doubt as to the issue of the conflict, and with open ears and shouts on their tongues, they awaited joyous tidings. So confident were they of success, and so eager to receive the expected news, that the falsehood that passed over the wires and stirred up the fiendish delight of one of their reverend shriekers was received with hurrahs and tossing up of hats and every demonstration of unbounded joy in a temple consecrated to the worship of God. Never was a people so completely unprepared for bad news. The intelligence of the disaster which had befallen them shocked, stunned, maddened them. The calamity was at once a loss, a disappointment, and a humiliation. They had twitted us with tolerating the presence of a handful of hostile soldiers; they had abused us as windy braggarts.

Their scurrilous sheets had invented lying stories about our miserable weakness; their pictorial papers had exhausted all their venomous humor and artistic ingenuity in ridiculing us into an assault upon the strong fortification. But their filthy words and funny pictures failed to precipitate us into a premature and ruinous trial of strength. They imputed our delay to cowardice and delighted to imagine that the Palmettos, with all their reckless bravery, turned pale at the idea of provoking the wrath of the potent government by opening their batteries upon one of its strongholds.[3] How keen, then, must their mortification have been, how hot their fury, how black their wrath, when they were obliged to believe that we had struck the blow, that the hated flag waved over the battered walls of the renowned fortification.

We were prepared for the howls, and curses, and menaces the announcement of victory has called forth. We knew it would intensify their hate and envenom their malice. We knew it would wipe out party distinctions, change timid friends into avowed enemies, and make conservatism hide its bland and hopeful face. We knew also that we would hear the tramp of armed men hasting to obey the summons of their chief. We looked for all these demonstrations. The flag which, in their judgment, we have dishonored is more beautiful in their eyes than ever it was before, and as they look upon that symbol of their national glory

3. Palmettos: South Carolinians, the Palmetto State being the nickname of South Carolina. The palmetto is a low-growing fan palm.

and strength, their hearts burn with a livelier devotion. Their pride and patriotism have been aroused.

Under the impulse of those feelings, they have thrown out their banners and girded themselves for the conflict. Most signal and glorious have been the effects of that bloodless victory upon the states whose slowness and inaction we have felt obliged to chide. Virginia has thrown in her lot with us; North Carolina has committed herself to secession; Maryland has rushed impetuously to the embrace of her sisters, with the blood of her children upon her garments; Kentucky and Tennessee and the other slave states will soon place their symbol upon our banner.

The North and South are arrayed against each other. The fall of Sumter has finished the work begun by South Carolina. The two sections stand face-to-face in hostile array. The one is fired by a sense of wrong, sustained by the holy and potent inspiration of the justness of its cause—life, liberty, honor, all it holds dear is threatened by the ruthless aggressor; the other is actuated by a sentiment, maddened by mortified pride, blinded by diabolical rage. Who can doubt what the issue of the conflict will be? To doubt that we will be victorious were to doubt that justice is one of the attributes of the Almighty. The God of Battles makes our arms strong, and when we strike, the foe will fall.

DELAWARE DOES NOT SUCCUMB TO ABE LINCOLN!

From the *Savannah Morning News*

Friend Thompson:—The meeting held in Wilmington, Delaware, is not indicative of the real feeling in that gallant state. Wilmington just borders on Pennsylvania and was settled by Quakers; consequently, has in it quite a number of vile abolitionists. But, sir, the true and real feeling of the state we manifested in the last presidential election, when the state went by a considerable majority for Breckinridge and Lane.[4]

James A. Bayard, whom this meeting is said to have repudiated, has never failed to carry the state whenever he determined to do it. More, Delaware has *now* a governor who will *never* comply with the requisition of Lincoln.

Delaware, I assure you, will be found our friend through all the contest.

J. F. C.

4. In 1860, after two failed party conventions, Southern Democrats split from Northern Democrats over the latter's unwillingness to adopt a platform constitutionally guaranteeing the right to own slaves. They nominated Buchanan's vice president, John Breckinridge, for president and Senator Joseph Lane for vice president.

WAR MUNITIONS FOR THE SOUTH INTERCEPTED

Cincinnati, 17th—Thirty-five boxes of guns from Parkersburg were seized today on steamers destined for Little Rock, Arkansas, and Memphis.

A large shipment of powder has also been stopped.

A shipment of bacon for Charleston, via Nashville, was also disembarked, and owners of boats have been notified to take no ammunitions or provisions South. The police in boats search every passing steamer.

All the volunteer companies here are filled, and more are offering than can be accepted. Three companies start tonight to rendezvous at Columbus. Five hundred troops are in readiness at Newport barracks. The work of enlistment is progressing rapidly.

THE WAR FEELING

From the *Richmond Whig*

The indignation of the people of Virginia has been stirred to its utmost depths at the policy of the Black Republican administration in declaring war against the free men of the South. Yesterday it became almost necessary to station a guard at the door of the governor's mansion, to prevent the ingress of citizens from all parts of the state who desired to offer their services to the state. We attempted to get a list of the companies and regiments whose services in defense of Virginia had been tendered, but the only reply which the adjutant general had time to furnish was, "Everybody's volunteering."[5]

THE MILITARY MOVEMENT IN OHIO

From the *National Intelligencer*

Quartermaster General Wood of Ohio arrived here yesterday and made the necessary arrangements with the War Department for the disposition of the Ohio troops.[6] In addition to the thirteen regiments (ten thousand men) called for from that state, Ohio offers to raise twenty thousand more men, armed and equipped at her own expense. Two of the thirteen regiments called for set out immediately for this city, to be mustered into the service here instead of through the governor.

5. adjutant general: the chief administrative officer of the army; also, the administrative officer of a division.

6. quartermaster: an army officer in charge of providing clothing, food, and other provisions to a body of troops. "here": Washington, D.C.

NORTH

BOSTON EVENING TRANSCRIPT
April 20, 1861

THE DETERMINATION OF THE PEOPLE AND THE DUTY OF THE GOVERNMENT

The seven thousand conspirators who assaulted Fort Sumter have sown the dragon's teeth, which have instantly sprung up armed men. They have made the free states a unit, and such a unit! Intelligence, property, numbers, all "march one way." Since the landing of the Pilgrims, nothing has occurred on the American continent equal in grandeur and sublimity to the uprising of the people during the last seven days. The past week is indeed the great heroic week in our history. It realizes the magnificent image of Milton's vast and glowing imagination, of *"a noble and puissant nation, rousing herself like a strong man after sleep and shaking her invincible locks"*! In the War of the Revolution, there was a powerful minority; in the War of 1812, there was a powerful minority; in the war of 1861, the people are one and indivisible.

The first three requirements of government at this time are, first, energy—and, second, energy!—and, third, energy!! The character of the secession movement is now laid bare. He who runs may read. Its efficiency heretofore has come from the indisposition of honest men to believe it capable of the baseness and wickedness now proved against it. Let the government, therefore, avoid all half measures, all diplomatic chattering with treason and piracy, but strike with full force at the enemy's vital points. Backed up, as it is, by the whole people, let it give evidence that it appreciates the popular feeling and the popular power.

Let our rulers show that they have not only brain but blood, that they feel the impulse of the general sentiment as well as comprehend the instinct of the general intelligence. The dear old cause—the cause of liberty, of civilization, of human nature—is in peril. To save it the people are ready to pour forth their treasure and blood. Let the government understand the temper and the demands of the great people it leads.

[UNTITLED]

The glorious 6th has made a place for itself in history. Hereafter it will be read by posterity, as if written in letters of light, that the bravery of Massachusetts men on the plains of Lexington, April 19, 1775, was echoed by Massachusetts men in the streets of Baltimore, April 19, 1861, making of that day a double anniversary, to be commemorated as long as free men live. The 6th Regiment, on its way to defend the capital of the Union and maintain the cause of constitutional liberty, was attacked by a mob devoted to slavery and despotism. At first they showed the patient endurance that became them, under the circumstances. But when it became evident that they must fight their way through, they did it like men. All honor to the glorious 6th!

Massachusetts blood has besprinkled the streets of the Monumental City, but Massachusetts bravery has triumphed over mob violence, instigated by secession ruffians.[7] We mourn that any noble son of the Old Bay State has fallen, yet death could not find men better prepared than when battling to uphold the freest government upon the globe. We condole with the bereaved families, and the whole community unites in the tenderest sympathy for them in their affliction. The slain are the first martyrs to the cause of constitutional liberty in the present conflict, and their blood now cries to Heaven against their brutal and cowardly assassins.

NEW YORK TRIBUNE
April 20, 1861

THE RATTLESNAKE'S FANGS

The eighty-sixth anniversary of the fight at Lexington was signalized at Baltimore yesterday by the first bloodshed north of Charleston in the great proslavery disunion rebellion. The Massachusetts soldiery passing quietly and inoffensively through that city, in obedience to the orders of their government, were assaulted by a vast disunion mob, which first obstructed the railroad, then blocked up the streets through which they were compelled to march; and passing rapidly from hooting and yelling to throwing showers of paving stones, they at last wore out the patience of the troops by shooting three of them dead and wounding several others, when the soldiers fired back and stretched a few of the miscreants on the ground. The mob then gave way sufficiently to allow the defenders of their country's government and flag to push on to the depot of the Baltimore and Ohio Railroad, where they took the cars provided for them and proceeded quietly to Washington.

That the villains who fomented this attack are at once traitors and murderers, no loyal mind can doubt. There is no pretense that Maryland

7. Monumental City: Baltimore.

has seceded from the Union—on the contrary, the most desperate efforts to plunge her into the abyss of rebellion have proved abortive. She is among the states whose authorities, though sorely tried, stand firmly by the government and flag of the Union. Yet, in full view of this fact, the Baltimore secessionists held a great public meeting on Thursday morning and were harangued by their leaders in the most exciting and treasonable language. One of them, Wilson N. C. Carr, announced himself as ready and willing to shoulder his musket for the defense of Southern homes and firesides. His interrogatory whether the seventy-five thousand minions of Lincoln should pass over the soil of Maryland to subjugate our sisters of the South was answered with deafening shouts of "No, never." Such was the direct and calculated incitement to the murderous attack of yesterday. We rejoice to add that it resulted in the triumph of loyalty and the Union and in the necessary proclamation of martial law.

In every instance of collision between the Unionists and the secessionists up to this moment, the latter have not only been the aggressors, but the wanton, unprovoked, murderous aggressors. How much longer is this to go on? What can martial law in Baltimore be worth if the traitors who instigated this assassination be not dealt with according to law? If the authorities of Maryland do not suppress these murderous traitors, the United States will be compelled to occupy Baltimore with a force sufficient to preserve order and keep the way open to the city of Washington. This is no time for half measures.

PRIVATEERING

Jefferson Davis, in the face of the world, opens a bureau for the encouragement of piracy. No crime of the infamous Confederate States equals this in turpitude. To steal our money, to seize our arsenals, to bombard our forts, are trifling villainies in comparison with this master crime of piracy, under the name of privateering. Think of it for one moment! Think of the voyagers on the lonely seas exposed to all the atrocities practiced by pirates! The line between a privateer and a pirate is so narrow as to be only imaginary. The one plunders under color of law and the other without the hypocritical pretense of law. That is the whole difference, and even that is too broadly stated, for the privateer which fails to find an American ship to rob will not hesitate to plunder that of any other nation. The Confederate States have, therefore, engaged in the business of piracy, and they must be met by adequate remedies. What are those remedies? They are simple:

1. All the Southern ports must be blockaded to prevent privateers, alias pirates, from sailing out of and into them.

2. Whenever a privateer sailing under the letters of marque and reprisal of Jefferson Davis can be caught, all the men on board, from the captain to the cabin boy, should be at once run up to the yardarm without any further trial than an inspection of the ship's papers.

The government should attend to these things without delay.

MAY 18, 1861

SOUTH

RICHMOND DAILY DISPATCH
May 18, 1861

HONORABLE WAR NOT TO BE DEPLORED

It is not to be denied that the cost of war to all concerned will be very heavy. The pecuniary loss and the material destruction will be great. It will doubtless be far greater to the North than to the South; but it will be sore and grievous to each. It is in this form that the evils of war are most severely felt. But the losses of all honorable wars have their compensations.

War stamps a new character upon society. Prolonged peace brings into play all the sordid principles of human nature. War brings out the heroic qualities and gives them supremacy in the aspirations and in the conduct of men. The best casuists, while deprecating war in itself, have held that it would be well if every generation could have some experience of it. When a people devotes itself for two or three generations to the uninterrupted pursuit of wealth and to the enjoyment of the enervating and demoralizing indolence which wealth induces, it is only the exigencies of war that can recall them from lethargy and selfishness to sentiments of honor, patriotism, and glory. The sentiment of patriotism is one of the most ennobling in the human breast—but how little is it exercised in the dull and selfish routine of peace! The difference between peace and war in the impression they make upon character is the difference between Shylock and Othello; the thoughts of the type of one are upon Mammon, of the other upon glory. Avarice is the passion predominant in one condition, honor in the other. A nation could afford to sacrifice the gains of half a century of peace for the elevating sentiments of honor and patriotism which a single year of war will inspire. One year of self-sacrifice in a noble cause is worth more to the character of a man and of a nation than a lifetime of self-seeking, self-indulgence, and pecuniary thrift. Heaven mourns the growth of wealth and luxury; Hell delights in it. All the vices flourish in the time of prosperous peace; the privations and trials of war nip them all in the bud.

It is a mistake to suppose that peace alone is propitious to the growth of free principles. On the contrary, it is war which best fits men for freedom and self-government. Liberty flourished in Greece as long as the heroic character of that people lasted; when they ceased to be warriors, they ceased to be free men. The grandest days of Rome were those of the republic, when the temple of Janus was most rarely closed. The foundations of the greatness of Rome were laid in the ages of perpetual war, while the Romans were free men. It required many centuries to destroy the mighty fabric, but the decline began in the hour when the liberties of the people were taken away, and it was then that the legions ceased to be invincible.

Great Britain has been the theater of perpetual wars; and there it is that the fires of liberty have never been extinguished. Ireland has been the scene of but little organized war; and when was not Erin more or less in a state of subjugation? Switzerland has been the refuge of liberty in Europe through all modern times and has, during the whole period, furnished their best soldiers to its sovereigns.

It is not pretended that war does not often crush out all the vestiges of liberty, destroying it as effectually by force as does peace by undermining and corrupting it. But liberty flourishes no better in China and Japan, where they never fight in earnest, than it did in Europe while Bonaparte converted the continent into a camp. It was the perpetual wars of the aborigines of our own country that kept them stripped of all the comforts of life, but it was these very wars that kept them free. The Mexicans, subdued by Cortés, enjoyed a much higher state of luxury and civilization, but it is hardly a question whether the condition of the half-starved children of the northern forests was not more desirable than that of the subjects of Montezuma. The warlike Tartars are certainly a nobler race than the sordid Chinese, the abject Hindus, or the fetish Africans.

Whatever be the race of people, or their stage of civilization, or their progress in intelligence, peace will deprave, while war will ennoble them. Our own people constitute no exception to the general truth; nor is there anything in the prosperity of the country, or in the enlightenment of the age, to modify the rule in our peculiar case. War was necessary to elevate the American character. The heroic principle still had existence at the South, but it was extinct at the North. Butler is a specimen of the only type of hero which the North can furnish.[8] Sickles is another; Lincoln still another.[9] Seward the false, Seward the liar, is the best type of statesman that the North can boast. Paradoxical as it may seem, none who know him will deny that John C. Heenan has more of the higher qualities of character than any of the creatures we have named.[10] Heenan is a man of war in his way. Circumstances cast his lot in the lowest ranks of society; but even in the sewers he devoted his life to fame rather than to gain; and he is a better man today than Butler, or Sickles, or Lincoln, or Seward.

The South was far from being corrupted by the principles of gain and selfishness. With Davis, Beauregard, Pickens, Wise, Bragg, McCulloch, and thousands of their stamp, it would be a libel to say that her race of heroes was extinct. But war is the nursery of heroism, and it is doubtless for some great providential purpose that her sons have been invoked to arms. The thoughts of her people will be turned from self-aggrandizement and individual thrift to things beyond self and higher than personal ease and enjoyment. The very fact of men's abandoning the pursuit of selfish objects to devote their energies and their lives, if need be, to the cause of country lifts them above their old nature to a higher existence. The fact of deserving the love and thanks of man and woman elevates the character, ennobles the sentiments, and gives new incentives to honorable exertion.

CHARLESTON DAILY COURIER
May 18, 1861

CORRESPONDENCE OF THE COURIER

Montgomery, Alabama, May 15, 1861

In connection with the expedition of President Davis to the camp of General Bragg at Pensacola, much speculation exists as to the object of the executive. As I have before said, it is my belief that the visit is for nothing more than to inspect the works. The president was accompanied

8. Benjamin Butler, Union general, congressman, and governor of Massachusetts.
9. Daniel Sickles, congressman and Union general.
10. John C. Heenan, American bare-knuckle boxer and heavyweight champion.

by several distinguished army officers and civilians, among whom was Colonel Louis T. Wigfall.

It is a question whether we are yet ready to commence the fight at Pickens, though already this morning the city is rife with the rumor that the contest has begun. Indeed, I heard a gentleman say that he had it directly from one just arrived by the Pensacola train that the bombardment was commenced. He states that the engagement was commenced by the United States vessels, that they "opened the ball" by firing round shot into one of our outposts, and that within half an hour the fight became general.

Of course, there is not one word of truth in the report; but the people must have something to talk about, and the veil of mystery thrown around every movement of the government leads them to give credence to every idle rumor.

One thing, however, seems certain, and that is, we may look out for a contest in a very few days, perhaps in a few hours. All arrangements seem to be rapidly drawing to a close. Over 120 heavy guns have been put into position by our troops; 15,000 men are concentrated at the point; they have undergone rigid drill for many weeks; the most formidable batteries and defensive works have been thrown up; the force has been divided, subdivided, and organized; and, lastly, the president himself has gone to inspect and satisfy himself of the strength of the Confederate fortifications. His presence will inspire the troops with additional confidence, and conscious that they fight directly under the eye of the chief, they will emulate each other in deeds of noble daring.

I saw today about two hundred cases of "percussion altered" muskets taken out of the government buildings and carted off to the depot for transportation to Virginia. They were directed to E. K. Smith, Lynchburg, Virginia, and, I suppose, are intended to supply the sons of the Old Dominion.

The adjournment of Congress, and its reassembling at Richmond in July, continues as much a matter of speculation today as it was ten days ago. Whether purposely or not, I am unable to say, but it is nevertheless a fact that the greatest mystery is thrown about the determination of the Congress in this particular. One day we have it from sources that must be well supplied with knowledge that a removal has been decided upon; the next day a flat contradiction is given to the statement; and so from one extreme to the other we go, until we become thoroughly disgusted and the newspaper readers arrive at the sober conclusion that "correspondents," as a class, are a set of complete Munchausens, with revisions, corrections, and appendixes. Therefore, in order that I shall write myself down "Munchausen" as little as possible, I shall venture to say nothing in the future upon the subject of an adjournment of the Congress to Richmond until I procure a certified copy of the resolution, signed by Howell Cobb and Johnson Hooper, attested under oath before an Alabama justice of the peace, with the great seal of the sovereignty of Alabama thereto affixed.

Congress remained in open session but five minutes this morning after prayer. During that time, Mr. Smith of Alabama offered a resolution which was passed, instructing the Committee of the Judiciary to report a bill to establish federal courts in the state of Virginia. As a matter of course, the committee will report forthwith, though, as it will be a matter of local interest when Congress sits in Richmond, action may be deferred till that time, so as to give a chance to the Virginia delegation in the manufacture of bunkum for home consumption. It will be encouraging home industry and is therefore advisable.

Sprite

CORRESPONDENCE OF THE COURIER

Washington, May 14, 1861

It is confidently believed here that the Confederate army in Virginia is making gradual but certain and secure approaches to this Capitol, on the Maryland side, and also on the Virginia side. The troops at Harpers Ferry are expected to come down the railroad and dislodge the Federal troops from the Relay House and then advance to the heights in the rear of Washington, while the forces at Norfolk, Richmond, Winchester, etc., march against the city on its Potomac front. There was, at any rate, an advance yesterday at the Relay House, founded upon the rumor that the Harpers Ferry troops were coming down.

It has evidently been apprehended that by aid from Harpers Ferry the secession party in Baltimore would be enabled, ere long, to cut off the government communication with Pennsylvania by way of the Northern Central Railway, as the government could not, at this critical juncture, hazard that blockade.

General Butler was sent yesterday with a large force to occupy Federal Hill, which commands Baltimore. A very large force is to be sent to the Relay House and to Baltimore.

Fort McHenry has been again reinforced, and the number of men thrown into Fortress Monroe is equal to the full complement intended for that place. The defenses of the fortress on the land side, where it is weak, are in the course of rapid construction.

The Virginia troops have, with commendable vigilance, fortified the same important points on the Rappahannock, near Fredericksburg, for the reason that the Federal government may send a force to occupy the railroad between Aquia Creek and Fredericksburg and also command the river at Fredericksburg and Falmouth.

It has been said here that the Federal government would soon make a diversion of a very imposing nature in some quarter, with a view to deterring the meditated attack on this city. What the scheme is no one can imagine. The Cabinet keep their secrets. But if seventy-two thousand troops are to be brought here by the end of the month, it may be supposed that while some remain here to fortify strategic points, the rest will be sent on some expedition. The hint was thrown out in a quarter likely to be well informed, today, that the demonstration would be upon Harpers Ferry. That is, at least, quite probable. The objects, military and political, of such a movement are palpable.

Leo

NORTH

BOSTON EVENING TRANSCRIPT
May 18, 1861

THE UNION MEN IN THE BORDER STATES

The Union men in the border states have been "coerced" by the Rebels to such an extent that many of them declare their intention to remove to the North. A letter before us from one of the best citizens of Tennessee says: "I shall remove from the state if it goes out of the Union; for I shall never submit to any government but that bequeathed to me by Washington and recommended to my fidelity in his last words to his fellow citizens—or to any government which rejects the flag that has become famous as the emblem of liberty throughout the world."

Another letter from Nashville, dated May 14, thus speaks of the state of affairs in Tennessee:

> I am not at all surprised that you find it difficult to understand the desire to break up our government. It is equally inscrutable to the Union men here, and they are now, as they were on the 9th of February, largely in the majority, although it need not beget

wonder if the election, which is to be held on the 8th of June, should result in a vote for secession. When the vote of the 9th of February was polled, the legislature had refused to arm the state or to raise soldiers; now both have been resolved upon, and the people will be completely dragooned by the 8th of June and consequently will vote under mortal dread.

You have doubtless noticed the proceedings of our late session of the legislature. Of all the secession movements, they are the most illegal, extreme, and violent, and all in the face of the popular majority of near seventy thousand against secession.

In fact, the most remarkable—I might say wonderful—phenomenon of the times is the ineffable disregard of law and of consequences by the disunion men everywhere. They are utterly unplagued by scruples; they stop at nothing; they know no obstacles; and then, the impudence with which they complain at the measures of resistance and repression employed by the government is positively sublime.

The benefits of secession, so far as they have been realized, are enormous armies, overwhelming debts fixed upon the property of the country for a century to come, mob law, insecurity of life and property and whatnot.

FROM YESTERDAY'S EXTRA EDITION
FROM MISSOURI
ARREST OF SECESSIONISTS—SEIZURE OF MUNITIONS OF WAR

St. Louis, 17th—Several Union men having been driven from Potosi, on the Iron Mountain Railroad, a detachment of volunteers was sent Tuesday night to protect the loyal citizens there. They surrounded the town and took 150 citizens prisoner, formed them in a line, when the Union men were recognized and released. About fifty of the Rebels were released on parole and nine of the leaders brought to this city as prisoners of war.[11]

The lead manufactory belonging to John Dean was then taken pos-

11. For much of the war, both the North and the South, unable to manage and oversee large numbers of captured enemy soldiers, followed the European practice of releasing them "on parole," with the understanding that those released would not engage in combat until formally exchanged for an enemy captive of equal rank. In this the Confederates, with less manpower upon which to draw, had a distinct advantage. For that reason, from 1863 on, the Union began holding captured soldiers as prisoners of war, and the Confederacy followed suit.

session of and four hundred pigs of lead seized. On the return trip the volunteers dispersed a Rebel corps of cavalry at De Soto, capturing thirty horses, and hoisted the Stars and Stripes on a pole just raised to receive a secession flag.[12] Another prominent secessionist has been arrested in this city and another in Victoria, making twelve in all, who are confined at the arsenal.

Thirteen American families arrived here last night, having been driven from different towns on the Pacific Railroad for being Unionists.

General Price has issued orders instructing the brigadier generals to immediately organize the militia of their districts, to be in readiness for active service.[13] The officers and soldiers are enjoined to afford all the protection in their power to the persons and property of citizens, without reference to political principles. The object of this organization is said to be simply to protect the people and their rights under the constitution of the state, and Federal troops are warned to avoid a collision with any armed bodies unless absolutely required to protect the lives, liberty, and property of the people.

The state flag of Missouri is the only one to be used by the militia.

Nearly nine hundred Irishmen have been enrolled in the Federal service here and will probably be organized into a separate regiment.

NEW YORK TRIBUNE
May 18, 1861

THE WAR FOR THE UNION

Special Dispatch to the *New York Tribune*
Washington, May 17, 1861

THE RESPONSE TO THE CALLS OF THE TREASURY

To successfully wage war, money is a prime necessity. Mr. Chase has been abundantly cheered by the liberality with which the people of the country have responded to his call, but like a prudent man, he has begun to count the cost of that which government has undertaken.

12. Cavalry is composed of soldiers trained to fight on horseback. Only a few Civil War actions involved mounted troops.

13. While "brigadier general" refers to a commander of a militia district, the term originally referred to a general officer in command of a brigade. However, brigades were often commanded by colonels, while brigadier generals commanded other, larger units. The Union army had three grades of general officers: brigadier general (one-star), major general (two-star), and lieutenant general (three-star). The Confederate army had four general officer grades, adding "full" general officers (four-star).

THE ACCEPTANCE OF REGIMENTS

The expenses of the War Department are enormous; and with a view to reestablishing the army on a more economical basis, and of pruning extravagances, the advice of eminent military men, now here by invitation, is being considered.

It is evident from the decision of high military authorities that the recent action of New York and other state authorities is not endorsed by the government. Regiments that are raised by any competent person, if tendered to the War Department, will, without doubt, be accepted and all tedious state annoyance be thus obviated.

TROOPS AT HARPERS FERRY

The Cabinet held a long session this morning, and through Mr. Seward a report was made by the party who left Harpers Ferry yesterday afternoon. Generally, it corroborates our previous accounts. There were nine thousand troops there. Virginia troops have recrossed the river, retiring into their own state. Seven hundred insurgents occupy the Point of Rocks, and two mounted columbiads command the ferry and its approaches.[14] There are but few inhabitants remaining there, except those connected with the defense of the place, or whose business requirements are imperative.

GENERAL BUTLER AND THE BALTIMORE PAPERS

The Baltimore papers indulge in very harsh remarks and severe censures of General Butler. But Mr. Cameron stated today that General Butler had proved himself a soldier, and he thought well of him.[15]

THE BRIGADIER-GENERALSHIPS

Captain Hare of Massachusetts, one of the prominent actors at Annapolis and Baltimore, states that he was promised by the president a brigadier-generalship in case he raised two regiments, but that for some reason he now finds it impossible to obtain that position and gentlemen promised by him the command of companies are not accepted. He demands his promised position, but is willing to resign it if the government has no use for his services.

AFFAIRS IN MARYLAND

The troubles in Washington County, Maryland, grow apace, and at length, Mr. Lincoln has been called upon to interfere, unless he desired

14. columbiads: large cannons capable of firing a 320-pound shell 6,000 yards.
15. Simon Cameron, secretary of war (1861–62).

the people to take matters in their own hands and inaugurate civil war. Senator Stone, from that state, had a very earnest interview with the president on the subject this morning.

OFFERS OF CAVALRY

Offers of cavalry continue to be made to the president. S. H. Mix of New York today offered a regiment of a thousand mounted cavalry, but there is no likelihood that Mr. Cameron will accept it, as recruits for volunteer cavalry are apt to be unaccustomed horsemen.

THE TROOPS BECOMING RESTLESS

It is evident that something must be done with our troops—though drilled and exercised continually, they are beginning to be restless and somewhat undisciplined. In one or two camps, there is great complaint concerning the rations. The 7th Regiment last night had a mock funeral over their junk, which was buried near the camp, and over which were uttered mournful lamentations. Colonel Ellsworth's Zouaves complain terribly, and several serious troubles have already occurred.[16] The 3rd New Jersey Regiment complain that their quartermaster does not properly attend to his department. They breakfasted on sour bread and coffee minus sugar this morning. There are quite a number on the sick list in this regiment, attributable, they say, to eating too much salt meat. There can be no excuse for such abuses, and it is for the good of all that I mention these cases.

THE MICHIGAN REGIMENT

No regiment that has yet arrived has created such an excitement as the Michigan 1st. General Cass felt great interest in equipping and preparing its men and felt, as well he might, great pride in their appearance. With their band they paraded the avenue this afternoon and paid their respects to Mr. Lincoln, who expressed himself highly gratified with their martial air. Michigan may well feel honored in such representations. They number eight hundred and will probably quarter at the Patent Office.

16. The Zouaves were units in the French army, formed in 1830 and originally composed of Algerian tribesmen from Zouaoua. Though fierce fighters, the French Zouaves were best known for their colorful uniforms, patterned after the traditional garb of the Algerians. Before the Civil War, in both the North and the South, the Zouave motif was adopted by militia units and quasi-military social clubs, members of which later volunteered for active service. The movement was popularized by Colonel Elmer Ellsworth, whose "Fire Zouaves" were a unit of New York City firefighters.

DEATH OF A MEMBER OF THE 12TH

Thomas W. Benbon, member of the 12th Regiment, Company D, died this morning at half past ten. His remains will reach New York at 11:00 A.M. tomorrow. He has suffered from inflammation of the brain, caused by sunstroke on Tuesday last. Resolutions of respect were passed by his company.

FORTRESS MONROE

Senator Chandler, Secretary Nicolay, and two others went this morning to examine certain internal arrangements at Fortress Monroe. They will report probably tomorrow night.

ACCEPTANCE OF WESTERN TUGS

The president has accepted three fine tugs offered by Mr. Sturgis of Chicago some weeks since, and they will be detailed for service at Cairo.

ARRESTS OF TRAITORS

Arrests for treason continue to be made. Marshal Lamon has four under lock and key at the jail. Charles McCarthy, constable of this county, has been arrested, charged with using inflammatory language in the presence of and to the soldiers of government. A squad of New Jersey men overhauled a Virginian this morning as a spy, and by order of General Mansfield, he was added to the list of those charged with treason. Daily the lines are being drawn more closely.

APPOINTMENTS

George Dennison's commission as navy agent was made out today. Henry C. Beckwith is appointed surveyor of customs at Hartford, Connecticut.

THE ZOUAVES AND THE RECENT FIRE

The proprietors of Willard's Hotel, on behalf of themselves and guests, have presented a purse of five hundred dollars to the New York Zouaves for their noble conduct and efficient services in preventing the destruction of their hotel at the late fire.

THE REMAINS OF WASHINGTON

Mr. Herbert, superintendent of the Mount Vernon estate, and who resides on the premises, says there is no foundation for the report that the remains of Washington have been removed from their resting place.[17] This statement ends the controversy.

ARRIVAL OF POLITICIANS

Politicians are beginning to swarm hither, and already, despite the importance of graver matters, the speakership and its candidacy agitate their minds. But two names are prominently mentioned—Galusha A. Grow and Frank P. Blair, Jr.

THE CAMP JACKSON AFFAIR

The president has endorsed the action of the Missouri Brigade by issuing a commission of brigadier general to Captain Lyon.

QUIET AT CHARLESTON

A young man, resident of Newark, New Jersey, who has this evening arrived from Charleston, South Carolina, says that there is very little military activity there; that all the troops have marched for Virginia; that business of all kinds is absolutely prostrated; that he witnessed the bombardment of Sumter; that if any were killed at Moultrie or the batteries, they were buried there, and the fact is not known in Charleston; and that he has seen General Beauregard twice since the bombardment. He remained in Richmond one day. There, all is action. Troops are continually arriving and departing. Legitimate trade is stopped. The cavalry troops are good men, but poor horses seem to be very numerous; and perfect confidence as to the result of the conflict reigns everywhere.

A MAJOR-GENERALSHIP FOR THE HONORABLE D. E. SICKLES

The president has commissioned Mr. Sickles to raise a division of ten thousand men to report in sixteen days. Till then, he holds rank as brigadier general; from thence, as major general.

Colonel Austin, whose British Legion is to form part of General Sickles's division, will at once open recruiting offices at Detroit, Philadelphia, New York, and Boston and is to rank as brigadier general. On the banner of the legion are the words: "We come to redeem our forefathers," to which the president referred in his interview with Colonel Austin this evening as follows: "This legion has a political significance which we cannot overlook. It and its motto will be received with cor-

17. Mount Vernon, Virginia.

diality by this nation. Go ahead, Colonel, and recruit." Augustus Rawlings is General Sickles's private secretary.

THE 7TH AND 71ST

The 7th and 71st regiments are ordered home at the expiration of their thirty days. I am informed that forty-one officers and men have offered their services by letter to General Sickles.

JUNE 15, 1861

SOUTH

RICHMOND DAILY DISPATCH
June 15, 1861

GENERAL SCOTT

We have never been among those who regretted the determination of General Wingfield Scott to remain at the head of the Northern army.[18] We have long been accustomed to hear him styled, in the hyperbolical language so common in our country, the "great chieftain of the age," and have little doubt that he considers himself so; but have never yet seen any evidence of remarkable military skill, much less genius, in his whole career. His stand-up fights with the British in the late war were valuable exhibitions of game and endurance on both sides, but no generalship was attempted or required. In the Mexican War, General Taylor whipped the poor devils so often and so thoroughly before General Scott appeared upon the field that the latter, with the aid of Lee's engineering, had a comparatively easy task to accomplish. He made one or two awful blunders notwithstanding, though the patriotism of the country promptly threw its mantle at the time over the old man's shoulders.

General Scott once visited Europe and, having heard himself so often called the "great captain of the age," was intensely mortified and disappointed to find that his name was scarcely known by one in a hundred even of the military community. Andrew Jackson was known, the man who displayed, in fighting Indians and British, military genius as well as courage, but Wingfield (or Winfield, as he chooses to style it) was a man

18. General Scott was a Virginian by birth.

scarcely heard of. It is due to Scott's genuine courage to say that none of the wounds he received in the late war, and which he refers to on all possible occasions, ever gave him such a smart as the unaffected ignorance of the "great captain of the age" which he encountered in every military circle of Europe. Who but the vainest and most self-complacent of mortals could have supposed that in that Old World, where the bloody footprints of the Napoleons, Wellingtons, and a mighty multitude of the most magnificent military names ever known in human history were still fresh upon the earth, Wingfield Scott could have created a sensation as the most prodigious military comet that had ever blazed across the sky? We have never ceased to be grateful that this prodigious humbug prefers the command of the Northern army to loyalty and good faith to Virginia. The consequence is that the North gets the benefit of his imbecility, arrogance, and bad temper, while Virginia has at the head of her army that gentleman of real merit, and whose modesty is as great as his merit, Robert E. Lee.

The amazing vanity and petulance of Scott have involved him in innumerable difficulties with the civil and military authorities of his own government and even with persons in private life. Whom was he ever able to keep on good terms with? He quarreled with General Jackson, but Old Hickory soon brought him to his senses, and Scott fairly wilted beneath the wrath of that genuine man. Never was there a more complete back-down than Jackson forced upon Scott. He was foolish enough to pitch into old Marcy, and Marcy replied in a cool and excoriating epistle, which scarcely left a whole spot upon his body. He fell out with noble old General Taylor, a man so just, so self-poised, and so amiable as well as valiant that no one was ever before his enemy, except the enemies of his country. And last but not least, he tried the game of "Rebel," which now fills his soul with horror, against his lawful master, and intellectual, official, and military superior, Jefferson Davis, then secretary of war. The awful chastisement which he received on that occasion is undoubtedly smarting yet in his vindictive nature and prompting him to put forth all the energies of his impotent malice for the destruction of the Southern cause.

But Jefferson Davis has a rod still in pickle for this venerable ingrate, compared with which all the former scorchings of his vanity and egotism have been mere child's play. A long life of intense selfishness and successful pretension must soon end amid the sharpest pangs of disappointment and mortification. We shall not be surprised to see him soon discarded by his own government and his dear friend Wool put in his place—a punishment which is the only one we can imagine at all adequate to his deserts.

SUSPECTED PERSONS

As the law now stands, one of the most difficult problems of the times is to determine what to do with suspected persons. There are constant arrests of men considered inimical to the South and to the state in the immediate neighborhood of our armies. These persons are arrested by the officers in command and, in some instances, sent back to Richmond to be dealt with by the legal officers of the state and Confederate governments. In general, they have committed no overt act of treason, and while they are known to be inimical, no evidence can be found of positive treason or criminality. They can be arrested on no other ground than suspicion, and yet their arrest is almost essential to the public interests.

As yet, there has been no suspension of the habeas corpus writ, not by the Confederate president or the state governor, because neither has power to do so; nor by either the state convention or the Confederate Congress when they were in session, because the necessity of doing so was not then apparent.[19]

The result is that when suspicious persons are sent to Richmond by General Beauregard or General Magruder and they are taken before the officers of the law, it is impossible for those officers to do aught in their cases. There is no suspension of the writ of habeas corpus, and these officers have, therefore, no power to commit to jail on suspicion; and even if there be some evidence of abetting the enemies of the South, the witnesses are absent and the proofs of the charges imperfect. These officers are therefore either bound to discharge the prisoner for want of facts and of proofs, or, which is the utmost they can do, must stretch their powers so far as to send them to the governor to be held or sent out of the state.

Here is a subject which evidently requires some immediate legislation. The legislation required is a partial suspension of the provisions of the Habeas Corpus Act. It is competent under the Confederate Constitution for this to be done by the Confederate Congress, but the time yet to

19. In Latin, "habeas corpus" means "have the person." A habeas corpus writ requires that a prisoner be brought to court for a timely determination of whether the detention is lawful. President Lincoln quickly exercised a clause in the Constitution permitting the suspension of the writ in the event of an invasion or for the protection of public safety. President Davis and the Confederate Congress suspended and reinstated the writ several times between February 1862 and the end of the war.

elapse before that body meets is too long for the emergency. We suppose it is also competent for the state convention to pass such a law, armed as that body is with plenary powers. The conferring of this power upon the Confederate Congress does not, we take it for granted, render its exercise by the state legislature or convention illegal. The reason of the case seems to justify the exercise of the power by either the state or federal legislature in their discretion.

Certainly the power ought to be exercised by one or the other of these legislative bodies so far as to authorize judges, justices, and commissioners, to commit suspected persons until the condition of the country so changes as to render their running at large not dangerous to the public safety.

There is an ordinance of the convention, passed toward its close, authorizing the arresting of suspected persons and the carrying them before justices and judges, but it authorizes this to be done in order that the prisoners may be "dealt with according to law." If dealt with merely according to law, they must be discharged on failure to prove some overt act of treason; they must not be held or even tried on suspicion. If dealt with merely according to law, some of the most dangerous characters that ever infested a country must be turned loose to do their work of secret machination, correspondence, and treason, with impunity.

There is nothing to prevent the legislative authority of the country from interposing to provide a remedy for these evils. They have only to authorize the holding of all persons in confinement against whom there may appear reasonable cause of suspicion. When the suspicion is light and the character of the suspected person be such as to warrant mild treatment, the officers of the army, of the state, or of the law might be authorized, instead of sending them to the common jail, to confine them as prisoners of war in other places, or within prescribed limits on parole. In all times and in all countries, it has been deemed expedient and legitimate to curtail the liberties of citizens for cause, or on suspicion, during the pendency of invasion. The Constitution expressly authorizes Congress to suspend habeas corpus during such periods, and the present exigencies of the public imperatively demand that some legal authority should be vested in public officers, civil and military, over suspected persons.

FEDERAL OUTRAGES IN ALEXANDRIA

To the editor of the *Dispatch:*—Having just escaped from the vicinity of the "vandals" now occupying Alexandria, I cannot forbear giving you a few items with regard to their conduct and actions there, hoping it will not prove uninteresting. Soon after the Federal troops took possession, Colonel Wilcox, who by the death of Ellsworth was left commander of the whole forces, issued a famous proclamation, offering protection to all private property belonging to peaceful citizens and declaring his intention only to be the "putting down of all unlawful combinations." We will see how beautifully this magnanimous proclamation was kept.

No sooner were they fairly quartered on the town than the "Pet Lambs" began their lawless depredations. A party of them immediately broke into the depot; rifled trunks, boxes, and everything; and stole all the money to be found. This was their first step toward the "protection of private property"! They then proceeded to break into private houses and search for arms, Southern flags, etc. No house was sacred from their intrusion—stores were broken into and valuable property stolen. People actually buried their silver, their flags and arms, rather than let them fall into the hands of these ruffians. Finally they became so lawless that Colonel Wilcox thought it advisable to move them out of town. Accordingly, they were encamped on "Shuter's Hill," a beautiful grove about a mile from Alexandria and the property of Mr. Robert Ashby. The colonel coolly invited Mrs. Ashby to leave her house and grounds and give them up to a set of lawless hirelings. Mrs. Ashby's only remark on leaving her house was, "Sir, I can only say that if you have a wife, I hope she may never be placed in the position you have put me."

The troops are now throwing up entrenchments, tearing down the fences to build campfires, cutting down their beautiful trees, and otherwise "protecting private property."

Several instances of houses in the neighborhood of the Theological Seminary having been broken into, one of the ladies residing there, and knowing the colonel, requested him to send a guard to protect the neighborhood and seminary from these midnight marauders. A guard, ostensibly, was accordingly sent to the seminary; but what was the surprise of the good people, and some six students still remaining, to find themselves literally taken prisoner. When the detachment of Michiganders arrived, the students were on their knees in the Prayer Hall, attending their evening devotions. They were detained there full half an hour, while the seminary was strictly searched for "concealed arms." One sword and about six hatchets, their only utensils for cutting wood, were captured. Also two or three young ladies, who were enjoying the view from the cupola; the latter, however, were released finally by the lieutenant of the guard.

The Prayer Hall was then taken as quarters for the guard, and the seminary, once sacred to piety and learning, overrun by our so-called protectors. Sentinels were placed at every point, the students only released on parole; and man, woman, and child could not walk five steps without being challenged by a sentinel and required to show a pass. But the seminary proving rather a quiet locality, and finding time to hang heavy on their hands, a party of these valiant Michiganders suggested for amusement the capture of another Southern flag. Accordingly, they sallied forth about five miles from Alexandria and came upon a lonely country house, which they stormed and took—fortunately, "no one was hurt." It being rather early in the morning (the favorite hour of the Lincolnites), the poor man of the house was not up, but was soon roused. His flag they wrapped around him, and made him walk barefoot to Alexandria and then trample on it. Another party, some few days after, broke into the house of Dr. R. C. Mason, six miles from Alexandria; rummaged through the trunks, drawers, etc.; and then carried off a blanket as a trophy, reporting that "there were plenty more there." This also was done by the Michigan troops. Now, we were prepared for anything from the Zouaves, as the Northern papers had given us various kind hints with regard to them. But for the volunteers of those so lately called our "sister states" thus willfully to destroy private property and insult peaceful citizens was, we confess, more than we were prepared for. One of the lieutenants said they concluded all who "ran away" were secessionists, and so they had a perfect right to break into their houses and take what they could! Another soldier coolly remarked that Virginia was theirs now and they could do what they pleased! Various complaints being made to the colonel, he replied that these things were done without his orders. A poor compliment to a commander, verily, if, after issuing a proclamation, he should be so utterly powerless to enforce it.

The taking of the seminary, we must confess, looks very much like treachery on the part of the colonel, as he took the pains to write a note to the lady who requested the guard, "hoping she would be relieved from all anxiety," thus taking them completely by surprise, in order the more effectually to gain possession of any arms that might be in the neighborhood, unless the troops acted "without orders." But time would fail me to enumerate all the acts which graced this famous "taking of Alexandria"—the most unparalleled act of aggression that has yet characterized the corrupt policy of Lincoln and Seward, for they had not even the flimsy pretext of its being "Federal property" under the old Union. It now only remains for us to go forth, prayerfully and manfully, to repel these unprincipled invaders, who make the sacred name of

"Union" a pretext for their aggressions, and drive them ignominiously from our soil. But let us go forth in no revengeful spirit, our hearts filled with hatred and malice—only strong in the might of a good cause—and then the battle cry shall swell up from every Southern heart, "*Sic semper tyrannis*"—God and our native state![20]

A Lady of Alexandria

CHARLESTON DAILY COURIER
June 15, 1861

THE WAR

The war is begun. The North and the South have met on the battlefield, and Death has been there with his scythe. We do regret that our disagreements and contentions have at last taken on this complexion. It might have been otherwise. The cords that kept us together for so many years might and should have been unloosed, but wickedness and folly forced us to cut them asunder with the sword. We have shown that we desired to make the separation a peaceable one, but we were not allowed to do so. We waited long and, while we were waiting, used all honorable means to attain the ends we sought, but our protests only excited sneers, our arguments fell upon deaf ears, our promises were ridiculed, our courtesy drew down upon us insult, our stern defiances were called windy vaporing. During that long period, our patience was sorely tried. We were vexed by false promises, disgusted by unfair dealing, and goaded by huge and slanderous fictions. Our forbearance thus incontinently and studiously abused, it required all our watchfulness and self-control to refrain from making the issue before we had justified our cause in the opinion of all whose minds are sound and unbiased. But all our endurance and efforts have gone for nothing, and we now stand at the guns. As our course previous to the breaking-out of hostilities was marked by justice, moderation, and honor, so since the fall of Sumter, we have shown an energy and earnestness in preparation, and a spirit and intrepidity on the field, that have astonished and astounded our enemies.

The North has appealed to the sword, and the South is content to let the sword decide the question. Thus far the decision is in our favor. We have gained every important battle. Our troops have covered them-

20. *Sic semper tyrannis:* Latin, "Thus ever to tyrants"; motto of Virginia.

selves with glory. The victory at Bethel Church will shine among the brightest triumphs our arms shall win, no matter how long the war lasts and how glorious the victories.[21] On that occasion the enemy outnumbered Colonel Magruder's command over thirty-four hundred, and with this vast superiority of forces, they were miserably discomfited.

The signal successes that have crowned our arms are but the realization of our confident hopes. We would not imitate the bad example of our sordid and base enemies and vaunt our gallantry. And we would not be guilty of the great folly of underrating the might and courage of our foes. The campaign is only begun, and it may carry its evils and horrors through many years. We have just buckled on the harness, and we must not boast as if we had taken it off. And yet, when we consider the nature of our cause, the feelings and influences and purposes under which our soldiers fight, the spirit and courage of our volunteers, and the numerous and important advantages they possess over the enemy, we are emboldened to hope that the war will be a series of decisive and brilliant victories.

We see under our banners the sons of the soil defending their land from desolation, their homes from pollution, their honor from stain, their liberty and rights from destruction. Ranged under the flaunting symbol of despotism we see a vast horde, a large number of whom have taken up arms to escape starvation, a few of whom are moved by the weak inspiration breathed into them by their starred-and-striped piece of bunting; and the remainder includes the many thousands, who, dupes of the delusions that we are cowards and that there are many awaiting their coming to rise and crush out the new government, have gone forth at the beating of the drum to gratify their hatred and revenge, and lust and avarice. Here and there in the ranks of the invaders we recognize a gentleman, and perchance there may be a few who believe they are in the path of duty, but persons from the lowest walks of life and of the vilest character compose the strength of the opposing host. If the material of our army were vastly inferior to that of the aggressors, there are strong and numerous reasons for reckoning confidently on achieving success. The ground we fight upon is our own, and we fight for all that makes life worth having. But we are certainly as brave as our foes, and were the two sections unitedly waging war against some foreign power, the troops from the Southern states would win as many laurels as those from the Northern.

21. Big Bethel Church (Virginia), the site of a minor skirmish won by the Confederates on June 10, 1861.

The volunteers from the slave states fought quite as valiantly and as well in Mexico as those from the other side of the Mason-Dixon Line.[22] Aye, more gallantly did the Southern boys bear themselves. And if it were not almost too cruel a blow to inflict upon the nation that has set out to do such great things, we might remind Massachusetts that Caleb Cushing had to beat her affrighted and dismayed sons back into the ranks; we might remind New York that her sons wavered at an eventful moment and rallied not till the honorable work they were called upon to do had been gloriously accomplished with fearful loss by the Palmettos; and we might bid Indiana hush her blatant boasts and hide her face forever, for she was the greatest dastard of them all. But passing over these disagreeable facts which generations to come will read and ponder, for the reasons we have glanced at, we do not think we can be justly charged with vainglory and boasting if we daresay that we expect our troops to conquer in every battle.

THE FEELING IN NEW YORK

We learn from a gentleman who left New York on Tuesday of last week that the reaction of the commercial community in that city, of which mention was made in an extract published by us on Thursday from a private letter, has fairly set in and threatens to embarrass the action of the Lincoln government very seriously by cutting off its financial resources.

The Washington administration is now literally dependent upon loans, which must be offered and taken up to an extent unprecedented in our history, if the war against the South is to be prosecuted. The customs revenue at the port of New York for the month of May averaged a little less than $20,000 per day, which is equivalent to an annual income from that source of about $6 million—or less than one fourth of the income so received in the disastrous year of 1858. The revenues of the other United States ports, combined with that of New York, can hardly therefore put into the Treasury in all the rest of the year the sum of $15 million. Mr. Chase has already intimated his intention of asking for a loan of $50 million at the opening of the session of Congress, in addition to the $14 million now offered in Wall Street. To this we must add that the states of the North now asking for separate state loans have come into rivalry with the government for not less than $21 million.

22. The Mason-Dixon Line, a boundary line between Pennsylvania and Maryland, was originally drawn by the surveyors Charles Mason and Jeremiah Dixon to resolve property disputes between residents of the two states in the pre-Revolutionary eighteenth century. In the Missouri Compromise, the line served as part of the boundary between free and slave states.

United States securities, having declined from 94 on March 22 to 85 on May 24, are now offering at 84, and it is the calculation of the most sagacious financiers that the secretary of the Treasury will not be able to dispose of his next loan at rates above 75, if indeed he be not compelled to accept a lower figure still. As the actual expenses of the government, already incurred, will reach by the Fourth of July an amount at least equal to the whole sum which can be raised from the loans already projected, it is not at all surprising that intelligent men in New York, looking into the near future, should begin to tremble at the financial prospect before them.

Private subscriptions for war purposes, of which so ostentatious a parade was made after the 20th of April, have now almost entirely ceased. The sum of $50,000 being asked for early in May by Mr. F. P. Blair, of St. Louis, to equip a "Union regiment" in Missouri, no more than $9,600 had been subscribed by the 4th of June, and of this sum, by far the greater proportion had been offered by members of the "Union Defense Committee," customhouse officers, and other public functionaries. In explanation of the past "unanimity," as well as of the coming "dissension" in the war sentiment of New York, it should be remembered that between the 4th of March and the 20th of April, Mr. Lincoln's government had assiduously devoted themselves, through the vast Federal patronage of the New York Customhouse, Post Office, Subtreasury, and Navy Yard, to create a subservient army of opinion makers.

The eighteen hundred policemen of the city, appointed as Republicans under the Albany Metropolitan Commissioners, were also at the disposal of the administration, which further controlled no less than four of the leading journals, all of which were applicants in the persons of some of their staff for Federal office. Under the pressure of this tremendous organization, a "public sentiment" was created immediately upon the receipt of the president's proclamation, which swept everything before it. Little persuaded of the unity of Southern feeling, and anticipating a speedy reaction against secession South, from the display of force by the administration, the commercial community of New York bowed to the tempest of popular and partisan clamor. That tempest has now spent much of its force; volunteers are returning, dissatisfied and exasperated, to find their families suffering and their occupation gone, and the finance of the great city lifts up its head to see into what a gulf it is rapidly drifting.

The return of the 7th Regiment has contributed not a little to affect public opinion unfavorably to the policy of the government. The laboring classes not unnaturally begin to complain that the "gentlemen soldiers" first decoyed them into service for the war and then quietly withdrew and left them to bear the brunt of the business. However unjust this feeling may be, it exists, and is exerting a silent but powerful influence in favor of returning common sense.

NORTH

BOSTON EVENING TRANSCRIPT
June 15, 1861

FROM HARPERS FERRY
DETAILS OF THE EVACUATION—THE FLIGHT OF THE REBELS—GREAT DESTRUCTION OF PROPERTY

Frederick, Maryland, 14th—Evening—A special agent of the Associated Press has returned from Maryland Heights, overlooking Harpers Ferry, which place he left at seven o'clock this evening.[23] The Rebels have mainly left, only about two thousand men remaining. The route of the main body was by the turnpike leading to Charles Town and Shepherdstown, but their precise destination is unknown.[24] A rumor existed on both sides of the river that they had gone toward Winchester. Other accounts suspected they were going to Martinsburg to make a stand there.[25]

At five o'clock this morning, the great bridge of the Baltimore and Ohio Railroad over the Potomac was fired, and soon after, a tremendous report was heard, caused by the explosion of the mines under the center span. In one hour the entire structure was in ruins. The bridge was a thousand feet long and had six spans. The body trestling on which the road is supported from the bridge to the end is about a half mile long and is nearly all destroyed, as well as the upper bridge, which is one hundred twenty feet in length, over the government canal. The telegraph station and other railroad works were destroyed. The fire was raging all day in the government works. None of the national property remains, except a dwelling for officers on the hills back of the town and

23. In 1848, the high cost of telegraphy induced six New York newspapers to pool their resources and form a cooperative news service, the Associated Press. The AP material was made available to other newspapers for a fee. The war severed the news connection between the Southern press and the AP; the Southern newspapers initially used the Southern Associated Press and a "telegraphic news system" improvised by the Richmond press, but, finding neither satisfactory, established the Press Association of the Confederate States in 1863.

24. Charles Town (West Virginia), then part of Virginia.

25. Martinsburg (West Virginia), then part of Virginia.

two of the twenty armory buildings. The loss to the government in buildings must be $400,000 to $500,000, while the Baltimore and Ohio Railroad has suffered scarcely less.

The people of the neighborhood say that the company incurred the serious hostility of the Rebel troops by the supposed want of concert it had shown with them, and by the loyalty of its employees. The turnpike bridge at the mouth of the Shenandoah was also to be burned, according to report. Every night some further destruction may be done, as no U.S. troops are very near to prevent it.

Point of Rocks, Maryland, 15th—The obstructions on the Baltimore and Ohio Railroad this morning have been removed and the road reopened to Harpers Ferry. An immense boulder thrown on the road by the Rebels was removed last night by blasting, and the track now passes over its crushed fragments.

A mass of rock projects into the canal, but there is sufficient space for the passage of boats, and it can easily be removed by blasting. The culverts on the bridge, which the Rebels attempted to remove, are now fully repaired.

The Rebels' pickets of cavalry stationed on the Virginia side, within sight of this point, only number some half dozen.[26]

AFFAIRS IN MISSOURI
ARREST OF AN EDITOR FOR TREASON—MOVEMENTS OF THE UNION TROOPS—FEDERAL SOLDIERS FIRED AT IN BALTIMORE—APPREHENDED ATTACK ON WASHINGTON AND ALEXANDRIA—STRENGTHENING OF THE FORTIFICATIONS—MORE BRIDGES BURNED BY THE REBELS—A LOYAL VIRGINIA CAVALRY CORPS ORDERED TO LEAVE THE STATE—THE ELECTION IN MARYLAND A GREAT UNION VICTORY—THE DEFEAT OF HENRY WINTER DAVIS—ASSASSINATION OF A UNION VOTER

St. Louis, 14th—Joseph W. Tucker, editor of the *State Journal,* was arrested by the U.S. marshal today on a charge of treason. He was taken before Judge Treat under a writ of habeas corpus and admitted to bail in $10,000 for examination on Monday.

A dispatch from Hermann, 9:00 P.M., says that the steamer *Louisiana* embarked Colonel Boernstein's regiment, which will soon be ready to follow General Lyon. The advancing steamers had not passed St. Albans at eleven o'clock tonight—probably detained by a storm.

26. Pickets were composed of teams of infantrymen or, atypically, cavalrymen, sent out as an advance guard to signal the main body in the event of an enemy advance.

Baltimore, 14th—Two soldiers, members of Moorehead's regiment, were fired at from a house in Lombard Street this evening. One was slightly wounded.

New York, 15th—A dispatch of the *Tribune* says that General Schenck's brigade has been ordered across the Potomac. An attack from Beauregard is apprehended.

All the bridges on the Alexandria, Loudoun, and Hampshire Railroad between Leesburg and the Broad Run have been burned by the Rebels.[27]

The wives of unnaturalized Irishmen who have been forced into the Rebel army have applied to Lord Lyons for relief.

The British consul at Richmond is ordered to demand their release.

Captain Ball and a cavalry company, who took the oath of allegiance, have been ordered to leave Virginia.

Sherman's battery is to have two rifle cannons.[28]

The election of May over Winter Davis is not considered a disunion victory, and the president is reported to have said he was satisfied with the result.

It is rumored that Davis was defeated by the Republicans.

The ladies of Berkeley County are preparing a handsome reception for the Federal troops.

Edmund, who assaulted Hickman in Congress, is in command of the Rebels at Martinsburg, where a regiment is expected from Harpers Ferry.

Henry Winter Davis will probably be minister to Austria.

A dispatch to the *World* says that the election in Maryland has resulted in a grand Union triumph. Even in secession districts, heavy Union votes were thrown.

Dr. Ogden was assassinated in a disunion precinct within six miles of this city, in less than ten minutes after depositing a Union vote.

An escaped prisoner from Fairfax Courthouse states that seven hundred infantry and cavalry arrived there, and heard that Beauregard, with a large force, was to make an advance soon.

A large lot of 32-pounders was sent to the Alexandria fortifications today.[29] All was quiet there.

The probabilities of a march of the Rebels on Alexandria seem to in-

27. Leesburg, Virginia.

28. Battery may refer to an artillery unit equivalent to a company, or to a grouping of artillery pieces. The standard unit of field artillery was composed of six guns of the same caliber, each drawn by nine horses; support of perhaps six ammunition caissons, each drawn by six horses; and 155 officers and men. Actual unit strength varied.

29. The weight of the projectile of the largest howitzer used in the war was 32 pounds; artillery pieces were sometimes identified by weight of the projectile. Howitzers are medium-trajectory field artillery, as distinguished from the flat-trajectory "gun" and high-trajectory "mortar."

crease every hour, and extraordinary precaution has been taken to guard against a surprise. Additional telegraph lines to pickets fifteen miles off have been constructed, and operators report every half hour, night and day. Several additional regiments have been ordered to Washington.

Elmira, New York, 16th—The 26th New York Regiment has been ordered to Washington.

NEW YORK TRIBUNE
June 15, 1861

LO: THE POOR INDIAN!

The poor Indian is more worthy of commiseration than ever. Hitherto he has been ignorant; hitherto he has been savage, uncultivated, brutal, dirty, and drunken to a greater or lesser degree. But as yet, he has never been abandoned, badly as we have treated him, to his own foolish devices and left to throw himself into the arms of another race but a degree less untutored than himself, a good deal more cruel, quite as idle and unthrifty, quite as much given to the use of the pernicious "fire-water"—in short, not to put too fine a point upon it, the secessionists.[30]

This misfortune has befallen the Chickasaws. Disloyal, turbulent, and treacherous, as their nature is, they have hitherto given evidence of their sympathy with Southern treason; and partly for this reason, probably, and partly because the government needed nearer home all the available military force at its command, the United States troops within their territory have been recalled and the poor creatures left to take care of themselves for a season. That they should go on in the old way in which they have been taught was hardly to be expected; but with the thoughtlessness of children, on a level with whom the Indian intellectually is, and the ingratitude of a savage who can never remember a benefit the moment the benefactor is out of sight, they turn from those whose paternal care has saved them from annihilation long ago, and join their enemies.

30. The Confederates organized several Native American forces, promising to address the grievances of Native Americans if the Confederacy should prevail, but recruitment efforts fell far short of the goal of twenty thousand. Confederate Native Americans participated in only one major battle—Pea Ridge, Arkansas, March 7–8, 1862—and were typically employed as scouts and in raiding parties to harass Federal troops occupying Indian Territory. As a result of their Confederate service, existing Federal treaties were rendered null and void. Under pressure to open the western frontier to settlement, the Federal government used the war as a pretext to force relocations in New Mexico and Arizona, especially of Mescalero Apache and Navajos, of whom thousands died of abuse and starvation.

Cyrus Harris, "Governor Chickasaw Nation"—meaning thereby that he is governor of the Chickasaw Nation, but a little Anglo-Indian is to be expected—has convened an extra session of the legislature, and his message thereto is before us. We can only say that it is worthy of a Chickasaw. It announces that the government of the United States, which seems, in the mind of Cyrus, to have existed chiefly as a Chickasaw agent, exists no longer. Chickasaw has hitherto permitted that government to hold certain bonds and pay to it certain interests, but the usurping faction at Washington, called the "Lincoln government," failing to pay over these moneys on some absurd plea of not sending money South, the force of which Chickasaw doesn't see—Chickasaw now declares her independence. There is, however, a new government, which has arisen on the ruins of the old one, called the Confederate States of America, and it is proposed that five commissioners be appointed to enter into the same relations with that Confederacy that formerly existed with the late United States. These commissioners are also to have the little job put into their hands of demanding and receiving all the funds belonging to the Chickasaw, now in the hand "of a portion of the states formerly constituting the government of the United States."

Several other things are also suggested to the legislature by "Governor Chickasaw Nation," such as a military organization to defend themselves from the "lawless savages on our western borders," or "Northern troops," to make treaties with the savages, and to pass laws for the punishment of crime. But the most important suggestion, as well as the most sensible, is that Douglas H. Cooper, who has long been the Indian agent, should be appointed agent of this new independent nation, to assist the commissioners aforesaid; and it is proposed that his action may be independent and efficient and he properly accountable to the nation, that he be "adopted into the tribe as a Chickasaw." Whether this will require that Mr. Cooper be immediately painted, we do not know; but if the process be not altogether too painful, we trust he will submit to it and take care of these poor, half-civilized creatures. Floyd knows all about their bonds and would steal them without compunction if they got into the hands of the secession states.

TRAITORS IN THE DEPARTMENTS

Special Dispatch to the *New York Tribune*

Washington, June 14, 1861

The test oath has only been administered to about one third of the clerks employed in the Treasury Department, contrary to the general supposition. The public will doubtless be somewhat surprised to learn that the reason alleged by Mr. Harrington, the assistant secretary, for not administering the oath generally, is a fear that a stampede will take place from the different bureaus, as was the case with the Sixth Auditor's Office, the only bureau in which the oath has been administered so far. Twenty traitors were found here, and out of one hundred clerks, and doubtless the same percentage of treason exists in all the other auditors' offices. There is, however, a universal complaint among Republican senators and members that notwithstanding this condition of matters, they are utterly unable to get any of their friends accommodated there. It is certainly a pity if in the ranks of the great Republican Union party of the country there cannot be found competent persons enough to fill places now held, and which, we fear, will continue to be held by a gang of thieves, traitors, and spies. It can be proven that there are now employed in this department several clerks who have been heard frequently to say in the drinking houses of the city within the past week that it was a shame that Northern men would come here and join the armies of Lincoln for the purpose of waging war upon their Southern brethren, who were simply contending for their rights! A man employed in one of the auditors' offices has three sons in the Rebel army, and the fact can be substantiated that the father sends a portion of his monthly pay South for the support of these traitors. A man employed in the Interior Department wrote a book, winter before last, to prove that the assault of Northern abolitionists upon the institutions of the South would result as at the West Indies, in a raising of the blacks and a murder of the whites. Secretary Thompson, considering this book as constituting a claim upon the country, gave him the office which he still holds.

Clerks employed in the War Department are also in the habit of writing to places where agents of the South can hear things that should never be spoken out of the office. And correspondents of Southern journals and spies from Virginia have been known to boast that they were on intimate terms with clerks in this department.

JULY 20, 1861

SOUTH

RICHMOND DAILY DISPATCH
July 20, 1861

THE FIGHT AT MANASSAS[31]

Special Correspondence of the *Dispatch*

Manassas Junction, Virginia, July 18, 1861

Victory perches upon our banners. The Army of the Potomac, under the command of General Beauregard, gave battle to the enemy today at Bull Run, four miles from Manassas Junction in a northwest direction and three miles to the left of the Alexandria Railroad.[32] The enemy attempted to cross the ford at several points in great numbers, but were repulsed by our brave and determined troops three times, with heavy loss on the enemy's side. The enemy retreated about five o'clock in the afternoon in confusion, two of our regiments pursuing them. A large number of them have been taken prisoner. On our side the casualties are few.

Yesterday the enemy appeared in force at Fairfax Courthouse, when, after exchanging a few shots with them, our troops retreated to Bull Run, General Beauregard preferring to give them battle there. The general was hurriedly sent for and quickly came to the scene of action, when he ordered the retreat, which has proved to be a brilliant strategic movement. At first our troops were much displeased, believing the retreat had been ordered by some junior officer, but when they learned that the order emanated from their general in chief, they were perfectly satisfied, having in him unbounded confidence. The regiments engaged

31. The opening skirmishes were initially reported as "The Battle at Bull Run." The Battle of Bull Run (or Manassas) was fought several days later, on July 21. Bull Run is a stream just outside of Manassas.

32. The Federal and Confederate armies each had an operational organization known as the Army of the Potomac. The Union Army of the Potomac, operating between Washington and Richmond, was the focus of a great deal of military action and press coverage throughout the war. The Confederate version became the Army of Northern Virginia in 1862. Federal armies: the Cumberland; the Frontier; Georgia; the Gulf; the James; Kansas; the Mississippi; the Mountain Department; the Ohio; the Potomac; the Shenandoah; the Southwest; the Tennessee; Virginia; West Tennessee; and West Virginia. Confederate armies: Central Kentucky; East Tennessee; Eastern Kentucky; the Kanawha; Kentucky; Louisiana; Middle Tennessee; the Mississippi; Missouri; Mobile; New Mexico; Northern Virginia; the Northwest; the Peninsula; Pensacola; the Potomac; the Shenandoah; the Southwestern Army; Tennessee; the Trans-Mississippi Department; Vicksburg; the West; and West Tennessee.

in this brilliant and successful battle were the 1st Virginia, the 17th (Alexandria) Virginia, the Mississippi, and the Louisiana.

All of our men behaved with the utmost coolness and fought like the disciplined soldiers of a Napoleon. It would be invidious to single out the troops from any particular state as having exhibited qualities not found in all. The conduct of our gallant little army (never before under fire) on this occasion surpasses all praise. For steadiness under a most galling fire, indifference to their peril, good order and precision of aim, history may be ransacked in vain for a parallel. The enemy outnumbered them in the proportion of three to one. The Washington Artillery of New Orleans were at an early stage of the battle given an opportunity of displaying their high state of efficiency and marksmanship, and they abundantly justified the reputation of the battalion.[33] An eyewitness says at every fire they made a wide gap in the enemy's ranks.

The 1st Virginia Regiment, Colonel Moore, bore the brunt of the action, the killed and wounded on our side being chiefly in that regiment, as I have already informed you per telegraph. Colonel Moore himself was wounded slightly soon after the battle commenced, when, being unable to continue at the head of his men, the command devolved upon Lieutenant Colonel Fry, aided by Major Skinner and Adjutant Mitchell, who inform me that the bullets of the enemy came like hail. He saw eleven of his men wounded at one volley. Captain James K. Lee, Company B, of the same regiment, was mortally wounded. While I write, he is still in life, but not expected to survive the morning.

The following are all members of Colonel Moore's regiment:

Lieutenant H. H. Miles was mortally wounded.

Lieutenant W. W. Harris, slightly wounded.

Captain W. J. Allen, slightly wounded.

Private Reilly, Company E, mortally wounded.

Private Whitaker, Company C, mortally wounded.

Private Diaconte, Company K, instantly killed.

Private Wilkinson, Company G, instantly killed.

Private Mallory, Company C, instantly killed.

Private Allen, Company B, probably killed.

Sergeant Lumpkins, Company B, hand shot off.

Lieutenant English, Company C, slightly wounded.

I have not yet been able to learn the killed and wounded in other regiments. The enemy is variously reported to have lost from 500 to

33. artillery: cannon; also, an organization in an army that operates artillery.

1,500—the former probably being nearer the truth. Not having been on the field, I am unable to describe the ground, but am informed the enemy were strongly posted with numerous heavy guns on the embankment which slopes down to the ford, while our troops were in the hollow, disputing their advance to the other side.

It has been stated that the enemy threw chain shot and fired upon our hospital while the yellow flag, which secures immunity in civilized nations, was flying.[34] General Beauregard had a narrow escape, a ball having passed through the kitchen of a house where he was partaking of dinner. I need not say the general has displayed qualities of the highest order as a military commander, with, perhaps, the pardonable exception of indifference to his own life, now so valuable to the Confederacy. He exhibited great coolness during the engagement and was in all parts of the field.

The Alexandria Riflemen are said to have particularly distinguished themselves, having crossed the ford in the face of a terrific fire from the enemy's artillery and fought hand to hand with the Yankee hirelings.

Captain Dulany, of the Fairfax Riflemen, was seriously wounded. Lieutenant Javins, of the Mount Vernon Guard, of Alexandria, was also seriously wounded. William Sangster, of the Alexandria Riflemen, was killed. One of the enemy's colonels was killed by a squad of Colonel Kershaw's 2nd South Carolina Regiment, his horse shot, and seven hundred dollars in gold found upon his person.

The enemy will doubtless return tomorrow with reinforcements, being exasperated by their humiliating defeat.

I shall probably be able to ascertain additional particulars when the official reports come in.

D. G. D.

CHARLESTON DAILY COURIER
July 20, 1861

FROM RICHMOND

NEWS OF THE BATTLE AT BULL RUN—PRIVATE REPORTS

Richmond, 19th—The secretary of war and adjutant general informed me that they have no particulars as to the Confederate loss, or names of those killed or wounded in the battle yesterday on Bull Run Creek, near

34. chain shot: two cannon balls connected by a chain.

Manassas. Private reports so far refer only to small losses in Virginia regiments. The loss of the Confederates is vastly disproportioned to that supposed to be the loss of the Federals. We will send details as soon as received.

The secretary of war says he has no details of the fight at Rich Mountain or of Garnett's conflict.

OFFICIAL ACCOUNTS OF THE BATTLE AT BULL RUN—CONFEDERATE LOSS 60 KILLED—FEDERAL LOSS 500

Richmond, 19th—Official accounts received here at the War Department at noon today state that at the battle of Bull Run, near Manassas, the Confederate loss was sixty killed and wounded. The loss of the enemy is reported at over five hundred. There has been no appearance of the Federalists this morning. All is quiet in the Confederate camp.

FURTHER PARTICULARS OF THE RICH MOUNTAIN FIGHT—ARRIVAL OF THE MISSING GEORGIA COMPANIES AS PRISONERS ON PAROLE—MORE PARTICULARS OF THE FIGHT AT BULL RUN—TERRIBLE SLAUGHTER OF THE FEDERAL TROOPS—AN ARMISTICE ASKED AND GRANTED TO BURY THEIR DEAD

Richmond, 19th—An intelligent and reliable gentleman who left Staunton this morning says that all the missing companies of Colonel Ramsey's Georgia Regiment have arrived safely at Monterey. They were prisoners on parole. Colonel Stark, aide to General Garnett, says that on the day General Garnett was killed, there was no regular battle, but mere skirmish fighting. The enemy occupied the hill. Colonel Ramsey's Georgia Regiment was ordered to dislodge them. The Georgians moved up gallantly, four companies on the right of the stream near the mountain and six on the left.

The enemy made their appearance with such an overwhelming force that Colonel Ramsey gave the order to retreat. It is believed that four companies did not hear the order, but marched on, and probably were immediately surrounded. It is hoped, however, that four of the companies may yet reach camp. General Garnett's command only lost twenty killed, unless some from the above four companies were killed. No official details, however, have yet been received. The balance of General Garnett's command is safe.

Passengers from Manassas report 142 of the Confederates as either killed, wounded, or missing, and 986 of the Federalists left dead on the field. About thirty of their wounded have been brought here, also one dead today. The Federals this morning sent a flag of truce, asking an armistice for the purpose of burying their dead, which was granted.

NORTH

BOSTON EVENING TRANSCRIPT
July 20, 1861

THE BATTLE AT BULL RUN
FEDERAL LOSS 60 KILLED AND 40 WOUNDED—STRICT ORDERS TO RESPECT PROPERTY—REBEL ACCOUNT OF THE LATE BATTLE—HEAVY LOSS OF THE ENEMY

Washington, 19th—The following is from our reporter at Bull Run, dated four o'clock this afternoon:

From a careful inquiry and personal observation, the number of wounded on the Federal side amounts to sixty killed and forty wounded. Several amputations have taken place.

The greater part of the wounded are quartered in an old stone church, where every attention is paid to their comfort. Fourteen of the dead were buried this morning. There has been no firing at Bull Run today. The Rebels are still in possession of their principal batteries. Their pickets approach to within a hundred fifty yards of ours. With a spyglass, large bodies of Rebels were seen moving to the right and left, apparently extending their baselines of operations, not retreating.

Batteries are being erected on our side, commanding the enemy's works, which are of a substantial character. Owing to the slight repulse which we met, the movements against the Rebels will be more carefully planned and of greater magnitude than was at first contemplated.

Our troops are all eager for the fight. They have constructed tents with their blankets thrown over stacked arms. There is plenty of food, including fresh beef. The indications are that there will not be a general forward movement before Sunday morning, unless the Rebels provoke one.

Special attention is being paid to the Hospital Department in making preparations for the sick and wounded.

The batteries of the Rebels were scientifically worked.

This afternoon a general order was read to all the troops, prohibiting theft of every description and enjoining respect for persons and property and stating that the least penalty for violation will be incarceration in the Alexandria jail and for crimes of magnitude the severest penalties known to military laws.

The order also states that we have invaded Virginia to restore to persons their lawful rights and to secure their goodwill. Soldiers were not, at any time, to be judges of the acts of the Southern people; and to take upon themselves the office of awarding punishment would frustrate the designs of the government.

To this the troops acceded by clapping their hands and huzzahing for their commander.

Great pains have been taken by responsible men visiting the seat of war from Washington to impress upon the people that the government will protect them in the enjoyment of their rights and that the war is for the purpose of maintaining our nationality.

All rumors of fighting today are untrue. The Fort Pickens Battery, Major Hunt, arrived at Centreville this afternoon.[35]

New York, 19th—A special dispatch to the *Herald* from Baltimore gives a letter from a Rebel source, which says:

The artillery at Bull Run was in play all day from nine o'clock in the morning until five in the afternoon, except three intervals of about an hour each. The loss of the enemy was very heavy and ours very small.

Two of the Alexandria Riflemen were killed. A good many of the same regiment were wounded, among them Captain Dulany, severely. A Mississippi regiment fired into their own forces by mistake.

The enemy were repulsed three different times. A prisoner taken by our troops stated that the Federal troops were slaughtered like sheep, among whom were several field officers.

Baltimore has been excited all day by rumors, one of which was to the effect that the Federal loss at Bull Run was twenty-three hundred killed and four thousand wounded and taken prisoner.

FROM THE SEAT OF WAR

Correspondence of the *Transcript*

Washington, July 18, 1861

It was a glorious sight, and a rarely interesting privilege, to witness the moving of the advance of General McDowell's vast column of troops toward the "land o' Dixie" on Wednesday morning; and I send you the following details, devoid of all attempts at sensational news, directly from the seat of war.

35. Centreville, Virginia.

The evening of Tuesday, July 16, 1861, will long be remembered by all who were in this region on that day as one of the finest in the whole season—warm but clear and delightfully pleasant. During the morning, our little party secured the necessary passes to carry them across the river, and at 3:00 P.M. we reached the base of Arlington Heights, on horseback, this being voted the best mode of conveyance. We were, fortunately, well mounted, our animals were fresh, and we passed an hour or two moving around among the camps, where all was bustle and stir, preparatory to joining the march ordered "at any moment."

Horses were saddled, baggage was stored, rations for three or four days were got in readiness, forty rounds of ball cartridges were distributed, the evening parade was dispensed with, the sunset gun boomed forth its thunder upon the still, warm air, night fell upon the scene, and the soldiers slept upon their arms in readiness to start at the sound of the drum or bugle.

It was generally expected that the forward movement would take place during the night, but few of the regiments, however, were in motion upon the march till Wednesday A.M. During the night, our men were in most excellent spirits and only evinced a general anxiety to get started. So general was this feeling among the troops, and so universal was the desire to get a sight at the enemy, about whom they had heard so much, as being at Fairfax in force, etc., that few slept soundly and the majority certainly availed themselves of this luxury with one eye open, your humble servant among the latter.

At daybreak, after staying overnight each in a blanket upon the tent floor in one of the camps, we rose with the lark (or earlier) at the sound of the "long roll," and in a few minutes' time everybody was out. Horses were brought up, a hasty breakfast was swallowed, a little "parading" was done, orders rang forth from tent to tent and from regiment to regiment, and it was soon ascertained that the word had gone forth to move forthwith. At eight o'clock the column was being rapidly formed, the regiments and detachments of cavalry and artillery were forming into line, and at the signal we moved briskly forward toward Fairfax Courthouse, simultaneously from Arlington, from Alexandria, and from the space between those two points—leaving behind a sufficient force to protect and operate the fortified works at all points along the line.

The sun shone brilliantly, and the fresh morning air was highly invigorating. The troops on foot started off as joyfully as if they were bound upon a New England picnic or a clambake, and not the slightest exhibition of fear or uneasiness, even, as to what might possibly be in store for the brave fellows (thus really setting out upon an expedition from which, in all human probability, hundreds of them will never return!) seemed for an instant to occupy any part of their thoughts or their anticipations.

The huge column fell into line at last along the road. From an occasional elevation which we mounted, for the sake of enjoying the grand coup d'oeil, we could see this immense body of men, in uniform dress, with stately tread and glistening arms, move steadily forward—over twenty thousand strong at one point and nearly two thirds as many more at another—all marching on—on "to Fairfax."[36]

We pushed forward with our willing steeds, keeping pace with the extreme advance, as nearly as possible, with an eye constantly ahead and around us, of course, for "breakers" after we had passed a given point; for it had been hinted to us that a "masked battery" might open on us at any moment from some sheltered spot along the route, and we civilians had no particular wish to smell powder in this particular style, much less to get within range of any such demonstration, being (in the abstract) peace men, and only there as "lookers-on in Vienna."

Brigadier General Tyler's column, consisting of four brigades, under command of Colonels Keyes, Sherman, and Richardson, led the van, and on approaching Fairfax, the artillery fired a cannon, which unluckily served to notify the Rebels who were in the town that somebody was coming. There were between 3,000 and 4,000 Confederate troops there, and they were partially drawn up into line of battle when the gun rattled out its unfortunate note of warning. They quickly sent forth scouts, who returned more quickly than they came, informing the commander of the Rebel force that "McDowell was approaching with a *hundred thousand men* at his heels." A stampede followed this information, and before ten o'clock the town of Fairfax was evacuated by the cowardly rascals, who fled, leaving behind them many tents, tools, shovels, axes, grain bags, several quarters of fresh beef, cooking utensils, etc. When our advance guard entered the town, there was nobody and nothing to seize or to contend with at Fairfax Courthouse!

Our troops entered Fairfax—ten thousand of them—at early noon, the bands ringing out with cheering tones "The Star-Spangled Banner" and the boys cheering lustily for the Union and the Stars and Stripes. Six or seven thousand infantry blocked up the main street for a time; the courthouse building was taken possession of by the New Hampshire

36. coup d'oeil: French, "stroke of eye," meaning "comprehensive glance."

2nd, Colonel Gil Marston; a secession flag was hauled down and the banner of the regiment run up in its place; and then the foot soldiers opened right and left, or gave way, for the entrance of the cavalry and artillery. These dashed through the town at a gallop, and down the road out into the country beyond, in search of the fugitives. After going four miles beyond Fairfax and finding that the legs of the Rebels were evidently the longest—for they made the "fastest time on record" in this war, certainly—our troopers returned, with the cannon, and joined the van again.

Our party consisted of Honorables Schuyler Colfax, E. B. Washburn, Mr. Dixon of New Jersey, Judge McKeon of New York, and two or three reporters for the press. Mr. Russell of the *London Times* and Mr. Raymond of the *New York Times* were also together, with another party. Hundreds of persons arrived in Washington on Tuesday and Wednesday, who came expressly to see the battle. The hotels were packed full of human beings—the National alone turning away over four hundred guests, whom they could not lodge, for the crowd.

A few Union people lingered behind in the village, who were greatly relieved, so they said, to see our army coming. In a few places along the road from Ball's Crossing to Fairfax, trees had been thrown down, but our hosts soon cleared the way of these impediments, and there was no further obstruction to the triumphant entrée of the division of the United States army under General McDowell into the place about which so much has latterly been written and said.

Two or three random shots were fired from the woods as we approached the village, wounding an officer and two privates, but not seriously. These shots were discharged by Rebels who were mounted, and who fled before they could be reached.

The so-called fortifications of the enemy at Fairfax are about as much like those erected by Corcoran's Irish Regiment at Arlington, and those built at Fort Ellsworth by the New York Zouaves, as a peach is like a mule's head! They are entirely fabulous, comparatively, and are of no account whatever. If such be the character of *all* the Rebel entrenchments, they will occasion us little trouble. Guards of our troops were promptly stationed around the town, and especially about the "courthouse," of which you have heard so much. The two Rhode Island regiments, with James's rifled-cannon batteries, the New Hampshire 2nd, the New York 71st and 8th, five or six companies of regulars, and two other regiments took possession of Fairfax. General Bonham of South Carolina commanded the retiring Rebel force.

It was General McDowell's intention to follow the enemy up at midnight, but the boys were so much fatigued with the sharp march of the day that it was deferred till this morning. It is ardently hoped that the rascals will make a stand at Manassas, where Beauregard is now in command, with some forty-odd thousand men, it is said. But it is greatly feared they will run again. The Rebels have got the idea, evidently, that the Zouaves, and the Garibaldians, and Blenker's German Rifles, and DeKalb's sharpshooters, are so many "devils in human shape," and they will be disinclined to withstand a charge from these troops. If Beauregard does *not* give us battle at Manassas, his army will be thus thoroughly demoralized, and he is beaten, past a ray of hope.

From Fairfax our brave army moves toward Manassas, and thence—we hope, without delay—to Richmond! The fever's up, and our bold troops ask only to be led, and listen earnestly for the thrilling order—"Forward!" They remember that—

God, and our good cause, fight on our side;
Their wives will welcome home the conquerors.

There will be no yielding, no parley, no compromises now. The march is *onward,* and the willing hosts who have thus taken their lives in their hands for liberty, the Constitution, and the laws will halt no more, it is believed, until the back of this unholy rebellion is effectually broken. They meet the issue manfully, cheerfully, boldly, and their watchwords now are—

God, and the Right!
Richmond, and Victory!

Yours, etc.,
G. P. B.

NEW YORK TRIBUNE
July 20, 1861

SLAVERY—THE UNION—THE WAR

The advance of the Union armies into the heart of Virginia forces upon their commanders and the government the problem of slavery—its relations to the Union and its influence on the war. We propose to discuss them pointedly.

The doctrine we have always held sound and vital is that of the *incompetency* of the Federal government to intermeddle with the domestic or personal relations established by the laws of the several states between the inhabitants of those states respectively. Clay eating, for example, is a filthy, revolting, destructive practice, yet the Federal government has no power to prohibit it within the limits of any state—a Federal law against it would be operative only in the Territories. When, therefore, a Briton or Frenchman asks a citizen of a free state—"Why don't you abolish slavery in the Southern states and thus rid yourselves of a great trouble, shame, and danger?"—the proper answer is—"Why doesn't *your* government abolish slavery in Turkey and in Persia?" We cannot go beyond our rightful power.

But constitutions and laws are made for a state of peace and inevitably bend to the exigencies of war. A Rebel in arms against the authority of the Federal government and intent on its subversion must be treated as a Rebel—that is to say, he must be subjected to the fate to which he, in purpose, dooms the nation. If slavery, or anything else, says to the Union, "Your life or mine!"—the ready, necessary response is—"*Yours,* then; not mine!" The nation must live, though a locality or interest should have to die. When a great fire was raging in our city, the authorities ordered whole blocks of stores filled with costly goods to be blown up to arrest the devouring element. The owners of those stores, those fabrics, sued the city for their value and were beaten—the courts holding the public safety paramount to individual rights. Nobody pretended that there was any sentence in our Constitution that authorized the destruction of those goods—but a great public exigency had arisen which was a law unto itself. And it is this principle which impels conservative old lawyers like Mr. Browning of Illinois to admonish the slaveholders that they cannot plot and arm against the Union with safety to their peculiar interest—that the Union must live, though slavery should commit suicide. And thus it was that John Quincy Adams held that Congress could not (or should not) in time of peace disturb slavery even in the District of Columbia, yet insisted that in a critical exigency of war, not only Congress or the president, but even a commanding general might decree the extinction of bondage. If thus only could the nation be saved, he was bound thus to save it, and the act would be valid.

The Union armies advance into the heart of Virginia, where slaves are, unhappily, abundant. The government directs that those slaves be let entirely alone. It is no part of the business of our soldiers to liberate them; and those soldiers have nothing to do with hunting, capturing, and returning those who may have liberated themselves. The defenders of the Union are there to settle an account with white Rebels, not to mix or meddle in any way with Negro slaves. Such we understand to be the settled purpose of the government.

That our armies should be forbidden to encumber themselves with fugitive Negroes is a matter of course. Camp followers are always too numerous in the wake of a great army and are a hindrance even when they seem to be a help. They choke the roads, consume the provisions, and are perpetually in the way. Clear them out!

But an order that *no* vagrant Negro shall be allowed to enter the lines of the Union armies—if such has been or shall be issued—will prove at once mischievous and impossible of execution. An army advancing in a hostile region must procure information and cannot afford to be nice as to its sources and channels. A Negro offered to show our men a road by which to avoid the batteries of Great Bethel and take them in flank and rear; he was not heeded, and a disaster was the result. Central Virginia swarms with irregular cavalry and bristles with masked batteries. These batteries are easily dealt with if seasonably understood; but one opening unexpectedly on a marching column may do fearful mischief. The unknown is magnified by terror.

Our advancing columns in Virginia must be constantly gleaning information as to what is before them, and they are far less likely to obtain it from white men than from Negroes. But they cannot afford to reject it from whatever quarter.

We judge, therefore, that no order has been issued which forbids the admission of persons supposed to be fugitive slaves within the lines of the patriot armies. The mandate probably reads that none are to be retained there, which is quite another matter.

THE ENGAGEMENT AT BULL RUN

Special Dispatch to the *New York Tribune*

Washington, July 19, 1861, 2 P.M.

Mr. McClernand, member of the House from Illinois, brought General McDowell's dispatch. He was present during the action, spent the night at Centreville, and left there at seven o'clock this morning. We learn from him that the battle was as good as finished at the time your correspondent left yesterday afternoon. There was no firing after five or five-thirty last night upon either side. The action had not been renewed when Mr. McClernand left Centreville at seven, nor was any firing heard on the way, as it could have been, had the engagement recommenced up to ten o'clock at least.

The whole force on our side engaged was seven regiments, Colonel Richardson's brigade and Colonel Sherman's. Only portions of each were actually under fire. Sherman's battery was actively engaged. One gunner had his head shot off, another was severely wounded, and two or three horses were killed. Captain Carlisle's battery was also engaged.

Colonel Sherman's brigade, which the writer met on its way to reinforce, deployed through the woods on each side of the road, but did not fire or receive fire to any serious extent. Soon after this movement, the firing ceased on both sides. Other regiments came up before nightfall, and the hill where our shell struck was occupied, as well as the hither side of the creek, where the battle occurred, and the wood behind.

During the engagement, spectators with good glasses saw the enemy reinforced several times from the direction of Manassas Junction. The whole reinforcement was at least five regiments.

At about five o'clock General Schenck's brigade, which we left in camp a short distance this side of Centreville, received orders to move. The cheering, hearty and repeated, which we heard was in consequence of this order. The Ohio boys are represented to have been almost beside themselves with joy. General Schenck was ordered to the right by the Gainesville Road to flank the enemy's batteries.

In the course of the night, Colonel Hunter's division marched into Centreville, drums beating, colors flying, men shouting such a shout as was never heard in "Ole Virginny" before. The hill on this side of Centreville, which is crowded with the enemy's entrenchments, was occupied by our troops on both slopes last night, and the sight is described as a good one this morning.

A Negro reported to General McDowell last night, who belonged to Colonel Fontaine of the Rebel army. His master having been killed in the action at Bull Run, he concluded to seek the protection of the men who killed him. His story was that a thousand Rebels were killed. No doubt an exaggerated number, but indicating that great damage was done.

Several times they showed, what seemed to him, symptoms of giving way, but being reinforced, they held their ground, which was very strong, being protected by timber and the ravine, as well as ditched by the stream.

AUGUST 17, 1861

SOUTH

RICHMOND DAILY DISPATCH
August 17, 1861

EAST TENNESSEE[37]

Correspondence of the *Dispatch*

Morristown, Tennessee, August 10, 1861

Our election for governor, members of Congress, and the state legislature has passed off with but little excitement, everyone being satisfied beforehand as to what the result would be. The Southern Rights party has carried the state by a majority, which, in its effects, is overwhelming.

The Permanent Constitution has been carried; Harris is elected governor; and the legislature is so decidedly Southern that the traitor members from east Tennessee are talking largely about patriotism and loyalty to their state.

The quasi-rebellion vote of east Tennessee is again in the majority, though its numbers have been decreased from 10,000 to 5,000. It is thought Maynard, Nelson, and Bridges, rebellion candidates, are elected to the United States Congress from their respective districts. But I must say, in justice to the people of east Tennessee, that a majority of them will not raise the sword to strike down their own state, and if ever the time comes to test it, they will prove what I say to be true.

Unfortunately, the influence of demagogues and traitors has been great, and the people have been led astray. The world never before knew of a more ambitious man than Nelson, a greater demagogue than Johnson, or a more complete Yankee than Maynard.[38] The talents of these men combined have led the public mind of east Tennessee astray. But their work is now done; no more will their traitorous footsteps pollute the soil of Tennessee. Johnson is in Washington City, to him a congenial clime; for where else could he find enough corruption to fill his vora-

37. On February 9, 1861, a secession convention was rejected by Tennesseans by a margin of ten thousand, but on May 6, the state joined the Confederacy without a vote. Like West Virginia, eastern Tennessee had a heavy concentration of independent farmers and, accordingly, was pro-Union. Efforts by East Tennesseans to remain in the Union were suppressed by the occupying Confederate forces.

38. Andrew Johnson, Democrat from Tennessee, remained staunchly loyal to the Union. He served as congressman, governor and military governor of Tennessee, and senator and, later, as vice president (1865) and president (1865–69).

cious appetite?[39] Maynard has escaped through the mountains to Kentucky, on his way to Yankeedom, his native clime. Nelson is a prisoner. He was taken in Lee County, Virginia, a mile and a half from the Tennessee line, by Captain Daniel of the Home Guard.

We do not exult over the misfortunes of a fallen enemy; we deplore the necessity which caused his arrest; we admire his talents and character as a neighbor and personal friend. But ambition, that destroyer of our species, has led him to commit treason against his country and his people; therefore, we approve of his arrest and hope he may be dealt with as the merits of his case deserve.

We do not expect rebellion in east Tennessee—our people are not so fond of rushing into destruction. But even if the rebellious portion of them were willing to destroy their neighbors, their own preservation would cause them to desist from such an attempt, because they are unable to contend against the power of the state, much less that of the Southern Confederacy.

J. N. S.

CHARLESTON DAILY COURIER
August 17, 1861

OUR VIRGINIA CORRESPONDENCE
FROM RICHMOND

Correspondence of the *Courier*
Richmond, Virginia, August 13, 1861

The soldiers wounded on their way to Manassas have been brought to the city. Poor fellows, they left us so joyous and exultant a few brief hours before the sad accident, which sent some of them into eternity and left others maimed for life. There were eight cars precipitated down the embankment and splintered completely to pieces. The gentleman who was my informant, and one of the number, says they were reduced to kindling wood and nothing but the mercy of God spared any of their lives. They had each one of them their guns, and several severe bayonet wounds were inflicted. They were all Kentuckians, and large, athletic, splendidly formed men, full of life and spirit, and they were singing "My Old Kentucky Home" when the accident occurred. When they were told a few days before that they had received orders to go forward and that they had been promised a position in the front rank in the next engagement, their enthusiasm was unbounded. We may well give them credit

39. Washington City: Washington, D.C.

for enthusiasm when we remember that they have made themselves aliens from the home of their birth to aid us in our hour of peril. Their brave hearts revolt at the tyranny to which their fathers bow so meekly, and every pulse of their noble natures responds with sympathetic interest to our great struggle for constitutional liberty. They pledge us the aid of their strong arms; the benefit of their powers of endurance, which have been nurtured by their mountain training; the use of their unerring rifles, for which they have a worldwide reputation. They number within a fraction of a thousand and are all gentlemen. They have come here armed and equipped at their own expense. We give them a brother's welcome. If their patriot blood stains our soil, we charge it upon our sons who are native and to the "manner born" to avenge them five to one. If their mother state repudiates them, we will claim them for our own and give them such privileges in the land of their adoption that they shall forget but that it is the land in which they sported in the bright hours of infancy and childhood.

I went out yesterday evening to see the troops encamped near the reservoir and was present at the drill and dress parade of the 1st Georgia Regiment, Colonel Semmes. They bear the palm for drill. The universal testimony of all who have seen them is that they are the best-drilled regiment that has been in Richmond this summer. They moved with so much accuracy and precision, and so much ease, it was beautiful to watch them.

The country around the encampments, as everywhere else about Richmond, is replete with picturesque beauty. Sufficiently broken to be pleasant to the eye, it is not rugged or stern. Its plains and slopes are dotted with the richest verdure. The city lies like a bright panorama before the eye, while here and there, in all the woods around, pleasant, comfortable-looking dwellings peep out from embowing trees. The white, symmetrical tents which stud the plains in every direction as far as the eye can reach, and whose localities are manifest by the blue rising smoke, even where they are too remote for us to see the canvas, and which are numbered by the thousands, lend beauty to the landscape. Swarms of men around them present to the view a living, moving scene of animation which arrests the attention; and the thoughts involuntarily turn to the motive which has brought these congregated thousands together; made them willing to forgo everything which earth could offer in the way of interest or pleasure, and accept the hardships and privations of the camp. God does not send such a spirit of resistance to tyranny into the hearts of men, such hordes of men, without accompanying it with the power of resistance. These patriot heroes shall verily have their reward in their country's freedom from the invader's tread and the despot's rule.

Soon after the regiment had drawn up in line for the dress parade, our president rode up on his splendid iron-gray—almost white—horse. We rushed forward to be near him and heard his brief greetings to the colonel:

"Are your men all well?" he said.

"Only three on the sick list," was the reply. "But some are indisposed today in consequence of getting wet in the drenching rains of last night."

"What are your tents, linen or cotton?"

"Some of all sorts; part of them are only osnaburgs."

"You must present a requisition to the department for comfortable tents; our men must not be unnecessarily exposed. You can call on it for anything you need for the regiment. I hope you will not leave Richmond until the comfort of your men is secured as far as it can be."

Then, after a brief exchange of views as to the best material for tents, and a salute from the regiment, which was acknowledged by the president with uncovered head and a graceful bow, he replaced his hat and rode away.

There was among that listening crowd one heart which daily, hourly, throbs with anxious interest for the soldier's comfort, upon which those benevolent words of this peerless man were engraven, to be obliterated never, until death shall blur them. There is nothing too trivial for his attention, and nothing escapes his notice that can promote another's comfort. He seems to regard the people as his family, himself the patriarchal head. As soon as the word went around among the throng last evening, "Jefferson Davis is here," the band changed the air they were playing to "Ever of Thee I Fondly Am Dreaming."

As we turned from the encampment, the evening fires gleamed brightly, made conspicuous by the gathering shades, and added new beauty to the scene. We left them to their hard beds and harder fare, with the prayer arising from our hearts that He who rules among the armies of heaven and the inhabitants of earth would protect and comfort them and abundantly compensate them for their self-sacrifice by shedding the light of His presence around the encampment where they dwell. The scriptural meaning of "Manasseh" is said to be "God hath made me to forget my toil and all my father's house." Those who so long endured privations there were doubtless ready to yield a cordial assent to the sentiment when they gained their triumphant victory.

The Norfolk papers of yesterday say that an engagement occurred in the vicinity of Newport News between 120 of our cavalry and 65 Yankees, in which 50 of the latter were killed. The Congress of the Confederate States will adjourn on the 19th instant, to reassemble again the third Monday in November.[40]

I see by the papers that the Christian Association of your city, aided by the Ladies' Auxiliary Association, has made a noble offering to the sick and wounded here. May the promise be verified to them in having their own souls watered by heavenly dews.

We have some additional particulars of the burning of Hampton. Although it was directly under the guns of Fortress Monroe, and the Federalists had a regiment of infantry near the bridge, the troops which Colonel Magruder sent to burn it were scarcely molested. They opened fire once from the bridge, but as soon as our men advanced toward them and returned it, they took to their heels. Two companies of cavalry and one of infantry were detailed for the service.

I see the *Paris Moniteur* refuses to print the sentence in Mr. Lincoln's message which states that the rights of the United States are everywhere respected by foreign powers. I thought when I read this arrogant assumption that foreign powers would never accept it in the sense in which he evidently meant it to be received. The Northern papers are getting very sensitive on the subject of foreign relations. As soon as England and France are ready to enforce their decision, they will speak. Their large fleet in our waters and the active preparations to fortify Quebec are very significant.

Joan

Correspondence of the *Courier*

Richmond, Virginia, August 14, 1861

There is a great deal of sickness in our army. It is said that at Charlottesville and Culpeper there are over three thousand under the care of physicians.[41] A great many have been brought sick to this city, and at Norfolk and Yorktown there is more disease, according to the numbers, even than about us.[42] The measles have swept, and are sweeping, through every division of the army, and the exposure to which the men are subjected in their tent life makes it in its sequences a formidable disease. Then, this is our fall season, and the diseases incident to the climate at

40. instant: of or occurring in the present month.
41. Charlottesville, Virginia; Culpeper, Virginia.
42. Yorktown, Virginia.

this period prevail to some extent. But in my judgment, the cause of all this sickness lies further back than this; it is to be found in a defective and imperfect system of hygiene. Ample and wholesome rations are served to the men, but the food is in many instances, to my personal knowledge, so badly managed and cooked that it impairs the digestive organs and undermines the health. Rations are served out to the soldiers every three or four days, generally meat and flour. The meat is frequently fresh beef, sometimes very nice. They cook from it one day; then, from want of proper care, it is spoiled and thrown away. This brings them to their flour alone. This they mix up with water, and put it to bake. If well baked, it is perfectly unpalatable and indigestible, but three times out of five, it is raw or burned. Still, they must eat it; it is all they have. Is it any wonder that they are all the time ailing?

In Yorktown the soldiers trade away their rations of flour to the bakers for bread, pound for pound, so that the sickness there cannot be so much attributed to this cause; but then, these towns on the coast are always sickly at this time of the year. If our men could have bread instead of flour, I have no doubt it would very much promote their health; or, what would be better still, let them have cooks. One man could cook for fifty with the greatest ease such simple food as is given to them. Deduct from the soldiers' pay, if need be, the cook's wages; let each member bear his share pro rata; it would not amount to more than twenty-five cents a month each.[43]

Our soldiers are very different from the Yankee soldiers. All through New England and the western states, a man's kitchen is a part of his house, and it is a very common thing, particularly in winter, for people to eat in their kitchens and sit in them, with their food prepared immediately under their own eyes. There are few of them but what are competent, when an emergency arises, to prepare their own. Our cooking is done by Negroes, and in buildings entirely distinct from our houses. Our sons never see their food till they sit down to eat it. It is folly to suppose that they can commence learning to prepare it after they become men, and ever attain any proficiency in it. Now and then we see one who succeeds in gaining some insight into the science of cookery. There are some few people who claim to have a universal genius, but such are rare.

General Scott's army was far ahead of ours in the provisions made for the comfort of the men. They had cookstoves arranged on rollers

43. pro rata: Latin, "according to rate," meaning "proportionately."

that could be wheeled about, and cooking utensils of the most approved patterns. I do not say it complainingly. Our nation must not make herself bankrupt in the beginning of the contest by indulging in all manner of extravagances.

There is another point in the organization of the army which ought to receive more attention than it does; it is the appointment of surgeons. There are some most inefficient ones in office. Some of the soldiers complain that they cannot get medicine when they know that they need it; that they apply for it sometimes two or three successive days and are put off with the answer that it will be attended to after a while. If there was a drugstore accessible, this would not be so bad, but under the circumstances it is unpardonable. Delinquencies in this department are, of all others, most reprehensible. Men's lives are precious—precious to themselves and their families and, just now, *very precious* to their country. All possible care should be taken of them, and a surgeon negligent of his duty should become an abomination in the camp and be disgracefully expelled from it.

Some items from Washington say that there are not over thirty-five thousand troops in that city, that regiments are brought out and marched from one point to another to create the impression that new troops are arriving. It is said to be well understood there, notwithstanding the lying reports which have been promulgated about their losses, that the killed, wounded, and missing amount to twenty thousand.

One of the Zouaves, who turned up in New York, when asked if he had got leave of absence, said "he was ordered to fall back at Manassas and no one had told him to halt yet." I presume there are thousands equally glad to get themselves excused, in similar ways, from ever being found again in a position where they would have to act over again the scenes of that day.

As to their prisoners, there are thirty-six hundred in this city. It is well that provisions are plentiful.

One of the Pennsylvania regiments at Harpers Ferry is said to have mutinied and disbanded, and the army in Washington is thought to be in a state bordering on revolt. Yet, the Northern papers keep up their boasting tone, and the *Tribune* publishes that Garibaldi is coming to lead them, as if he would come here to overthrow what he was seeking to establish in his own land. What a humiliating confession to them that they have no leaders on whom they can depend, but rely on foreign aid.

Another item of Lincoln's impudent assurance has come to hand. Colonel Scott, of Pennsylvania, manager of the government railroads and telegraphs, just before the battle of Manassas, arranged a schedule for the running of three trains a day on the Alexandria and Manassas Gap Railroad and advertised on and after Monday, July 22, regular trains would leave Alexandria and Fairfax, regulating the maximum speed, etc.

Prince Napoleon, when present at a review of the Confederate troops near Centreville, expressed surprise at the apparent unanimity of sentiment among our people.[44] He was met on his arrival by a splendid escort of cavalry, headed by General Beauregard, and the same was tendered him on his return; but he selected as his return escort two officers from a Tennessee regiment. One of them, Captain Morgan, was consul at Messina when President Lincoln was elected, and resigned and came home, and his father fought in the Garibaldi campaign.

The line of soldiers formed for review extended several miles. The prince came up in an open carriage, attended by three gentlemen. The entire army saluted by presenting arms. The gentlemen all got out of the carriage, and the prince took off his hat and stood with General Johnston on his right hand, General Longstreet and Colonel Preston on the left.

The day was so excessively hot, and it would have taken so long to have reviewed the whole, that it was decided only one regiment should go through the form, and the 1st Virginia Regiment was selected. Virginia was, of course, entitled to the honor, as it was on her soil.

He is described as being about forty-five years old, six feet high, and rather corpulent. Very plainly dressed, he wore a straw hat, loose sack coat, and linen pants. He visited the battleground before the review. Immediately after, he returned to Washington.

Joan

44. Charles-Louis-Napoléon Bonaparte, or Napoléon III, the nephew of Napoléon I, was elected president in 1848, declared himself emperor in 1852, and fell from power as a result of the Franco-Prussian War (1870–71). In 1862, while the United States was enmeshed in the Civil War, Napoléon III sent French troops to Mexico, purportedly to restore the Mexican reactionaries to power. In 1864, he installed Austrian Archduke Maximilian as emperor of Mexico, but, yielding to U.S. as well as domestic pressures, withdrew his sponsorship in 1866. The following year, Maximilian was toppled by republican forces and executed.

NORTH

BOSTON EVENING TRANSCRIPT
August 17, 1861

AN IMPORTANT CAPTURE
ARREST OF A REBEL AGENT ON BOARD THE PERSIA—SEIZURE OF $200,000 INTENDED FOR THE ENEMY

From the *New York Evening Post,* August 16, 1861

Last Tuesday afternoon the surveyor of the port, with officers Isaacs and Bunn, boarded the steamer *Persia* at quarantine. On the way up to the city, intelligence was communicated to the surveyor to the effect that one of the passengers on board, named Thomas S. Serrill, was a violent secessionist and had stated to another passenger that he was returning from Europe with the proceeds of a loan which he had negotiated in Europe for the Southern Confederacy.

On the arrival of the steamer at Jersey City, officers Isaacs and Bunn made a thorough search of the person and baggage of the passenger designated, and succeeded in finding forty thousand pounds in Bank of England notes and a large number of letters and other important papers, the contents of which leave no doubt that the information given to the surveyor was correct.

Surveyor Andrews at once communicated with Secretary Chase, who was in the city, and the secretary commended the proceedings already taken and advised the arrest of Serrill. The matter was also communicated to the Federal government at Washington.

Meanwhile, the money, amounting to forty thousand pounds, and the letters were taken to the surveyor's office. The letters have been read and are discovered to be strongly secessionist in tone, and some of them suggest plans for breaking the blockade and supplying the Liverpool market with cotton. These dispatches leave no doubt as to the character of the bearer and render it probable that the forty thousand pounds was a loan to the Confederate States, as he represented.

Several passengers by the *Persia* have voluntarily come forward and have made affidavits respecting the secession talk of Serrill on board the ship.

Friday morning, the United States district attorney put a warrant for Serrill's arrest in the hands of an officer.

Mr. Serrill is a New Orleans man, who has been for years engaged in the cotton business. He is about fifty years of age and is represented to be wealthy.

Some of the affidavits of passengers, made this morning, state positively that Serrill said that the money in his possession was "a loan for the Confederate States."

At a quarter past one o'clock, Mr. Serrill called upon Surveyor Andrews by appointment and had a brief interview with him. He was then introduced to a deputy of the United States marshal, who arrested him and took him to the marshal's office.

The vigilance of the surveyor of the port in causing this important seizure and arrest, and his general watchfulness over the character of passengers arriving by the steamers, cannot be too highly commended.

The forty thousand pounds and the letters taken from Serrill have been handed by the collector to the United States district attorney, together with the surveyor's statement respecting the seizure.

SERRILL IN THE TOMBS[45]

Immediately after his arrest, Mr. Serrill was taken to the marshal's office, and from there was sent to the Tombs.

His commitment to the Tombs is probably only temporary, until the United States district attorney decides whether to proceed against him, with the evidence at hand, for treason, or whether he will hand him over to the War Department, to be confined at Fort Lafayette, till instructions are received from Washington as to his disposal.

Serrill was arrested at two-twenty and conducted immediately to the office of the United States district attorney. The intelligence was immediately telegraphed to Washington. Mr. Clarkson N. Potter appeared as counsel, but no commissioner was to be found; matters remained in abeyance till our reporter left.

The prisoner remained in the office, holding communication with no one, but studiously reading the papers and awaiting the action of the authorities. The prospects are very indubitable that he will spend the night at the Tombs. Whether he will be proceeded against for treason or delivered to the military authorities is still an open question.

SOUTHERN "NEWS"
ALLEGED SERIOUS LOSS BY GENERAL BANKS—REPORTED BATTLE AT LEESBURG—300 UNION TROOPS KILLED AND 1,400 TAKEN PRISONER

New Orleans, 16th—General Evans, with the 17th and 18th Mississippi regiments and the 8th Virginia Richmond Howitzers, passed Leesburg

45. The Tombs: the nickname of a New York City jail whose original motif was inspired by that of an Egyptian mausoleum.

on Tuesday morning, in pursuit of seventeen hundred of General Banks's division, who were depredating on this side of the Potomac. General Evans probably captured them, as the river was swollen, thus preventing their escaping to the other side.

Richmond, 15th, via New Orleans, 16th—In the absence of real battles the public is considerably exercised about a fight at Aquia Creek, and a battle is said to have taken place at Leesburg on Wednesday, in which three hundred Federals were killed and fourteen hundred taken prisoners. Neither report is confirmed.

Nothing was publicly done in Congress today.

The reported battle at Leesburg gradually assumes an air of plausibility. It appears that seventeen hundred Federal troops forded the Potomac near or opposite Leesburg, but during the night, the river rose and the Confederate troops surrounded them. The Federals lost about three hundred killed and wounded, and fourteen hundred were taken prisoner. The Confederate loss was small. Several passengers from Manassas this afternoon report this news as current there and generally credited. Some say that a large number of wagons sent up to convey property down were captured.

The reported affair at Leesburg is said to have occurred on Wednesday, but intelligence from General Banks's headquarters up to Thursday night makes no mention of any such thing, and we are led to the belief that the story is a gross exaggeration, to say the least. The following is all the telegraphic intelligence we have from General Banks up to Friday night:

Baltimore, 16th—A letter from Sandy Hook, Maryland, today says a gentleman from Martinsburg yesterday reports that small parties of irregular Rebel cavalry were scouting in that section of country and daily firing on our pickets and Union fugitives, as well as paying frequent visits to the town. Yesterday a party approached within two miles of Harpers Ferry and fired on the pickets and retreated. It was reported last night that a party of one hundred thirty Rebel cavalry captured three men of our 2nd Cavalry picket, stationed just outside of Harpers Ferry. The camp remains very quiet. All appear to have perfect confidence in General Banks and staff, as well as the brigade officers.

Parties from Winchester report only four thousand militia rendezvoused there for drill and discipline, also that there are two Rebel regiments at Lovett's Mill, only eight miles distant.

NEW YORK TRIBUNE
August 17, 1861

[UNTITLED]

The name of Beauregard, the Rebel general in chief, having penetrated to Mexico, the *Diario de Mejico* furnishes some biographical information concerning him. This authority states that the grandfather of Beauregard was a Mexican bandit, called Boregallio, who acquired great wealth by his depredations in the mountains of Sierra Madre. At his death the gang broke up, and his son, Boregallio, Jr., emigrated to New Orleans, where he bought two large estates; the first he called Touton and the second Beauregard—hence his name of Touton Beauregard. Subsequently he was fortunate enough to marry a lady of high parentage and at once acquired great influence among the foreign population of Louisiana. As with his property, so with his offspring: The first child was named Touton, the second Beauregard, and so on with all the children alternately. In the year 1831 or 1832, he obtained for his fourth son an admission into the Military Academy at West Point, under the appellation of G. T. Beauregard. This fourth son is the man now general in chief of the Rebels.

FROM FORTRESS MONROE
THE CLAIMS OF UNIONISTS FOR PROTECTION—FAMILIES IN THE BUSH—A MISSIONARY SPY IN CAMP—MUTINY IN COLONEL HAWKINS'S REGIMENT—SHAMEFUL NEGLECT OF THE SOLDIERS—EXPECTATIONS OF GENERAL WOOL

From Our Special Correspondent
Fortress Monroe, Old Point Comfort, Virginia
August 14, 1861

I believe I but reflect the general idea when I express the hope that it will be among the first acts of General Wool, who is looked for every day, to throw all the protection in his power around the Union men residing between Hampton and Back River, who are now exposed to the ravages of the Rebels and live in continual danger, not only of having their houses and barns, with their crops, burned, but of being seized and dragged to Yorktown or Richmond for the crime of being Union men. I am assured that there are a good many families who have taken to the woods since the burning of Hampton. The grain crop has mostly been secured, but is liable to be burned any day. The case of this class of inhabitants appeals forcibly to General Wool. They have a right to demand protection. The Rebels should be driven back and the district restored to security and quiet.

The inference naturally drawn from the appointment of General Wool to this department is that this is to be made the base of active operations in the ensuing campaign.[46] General Wool's extraordinary capacity for making good soldiers out of volunteers has for some time caused him to be pointed to as peculiarly needed in this war. His large experience, prudence, and sagacity qualify him to command a department where important operations are to ensue. We may therefore assume that General Wool's presence has a meaning and a significance equally interesting to the supporters of the government and the disunion conspirators.

On Saturday a rather queer-looking as well as queer-acting party made his appearance at General Butler's headquarters and announced himself as a preacher of the gospel, pretty much on his own hook, from somewhere near Petersburg, in Virginia. He exhibited a certificate, purporting to be signed by some of his neighbors, which set forth that he was a Union man, and "sound on the goose" generally. He furthermore had passes that took him through the Rebel lines. He said that he thought he had a call to preach, and proposed to deliver one sermon here and then proceed to Washington and preach another discourse there. General Butler thought it quite likely he had a call to preach, and proceeded to inform the man, in whose madness he conceived there was some method, that he had a congregation ready for him and, as their spiritual welfare might be in a suffering condition, he could enter on his labors at once. The general therefore gave him permission to repair to the Rip Raps. Now, it should be known that the Rip Raps is a sort of penal colony, where prisoners and all doubtful characters are quartered, and over whom Captain Leach, with his company, keeps guard. It is an immense mass of stones, upward of a mile from shore, and out of which Fort Calhoun has commenced to rise. A more uninteresting place can scarcely be imagined, especially in dog days, when the sun has heated the stones so as to remind one sensibly of the place against which our friend the preacher informed General Butler he conceived it his duty earnestly to warn him. Our traveling missionary went willingly to the Rip Raps. The next day was Sunday, and the venerable and sober Cap-

46. department: the basic territorial division of forces, into which an army and subsidiary military bodies were organized; not to be confused with governmental departments, such as the War Department.

tain Leach, who lives as nearly as possible up to the golden rule, thought it was well to have preaching; indeed, nothing could be more proper. The preacher was therefore invited to commence his labors; for this was his flock, and there was his fold. He readily assented, and wanted to know if Captain Leach had a preference for text or subject. The worthy captain had none, so it was sound doctrine and the text from the Bible. Our missionary friend finally concluded that he would not preach a regular discourse, but would entertain his select audience with the history of man. Whatever else the discourse was, as a literary performance, taken in connection with his conduct, it confirmed the suspicion that he was nothing more nor less than a spy. Captain Leach concluded that the fellow should at least earn his rations, which are likely to be served out to him for some time. Indeed, the captain was of the opinion that the missionary from Petersburg would not proceed to Washington, or travel elsewhere for the present, but that he might consider himself as permanently settled, with a regular though somewhat shifting congregation, and that, though the salary might be rather small, the place was remarkably well suited for meditation. I have since learned that the fellow appears to have improved his opportunities for meditation. This morning he sent for Captain Leach, who found him stretched out, clasping his head with his hands. He said he thought he was just coming out of one of the turns to which he was subject, which turns, he informed the captain, were insanity that came upon him by spells. But the new dodge didn't work with the captain. He assured the fellow that what he most needed was rest, and expressed the opinion that by the time he emerged into the world again, he would be quite restored. The fellow probably begins to smell a rat.

The *Harriet Lane* has again made her appearance in the Roads, where she is ever welcome.[47] She will proceed along the Southern coast as far as Savannah and, in the course of the trip, will probably have an opportunity to try her new armament on some of the Rebel privateers and batteries that abound in that direction.

Thirty of the 9th Regiment, Colonel Hawkins, have been placed under arrest for mutinous conduct. There is much bad feeling in this regiment, as well as in the 2nd and 10th, because they are not paid or furnished with clothing. The complaint is well laid. The payrolls have long since been sent to Washington, and in one case, I believe, acknowledged correct, but no pay has been forthcoming. Thirty thousand dol-

47. Hampton Roads (Virginia), a channel through which the James River flows into the Chesapeake Bay.

lars have been lying here for three weeks awaiting the appearance of a paymaster, who probably is little worthy of the place. I am forced to say that if our volunteers elsewhere are not better cared for than those we have here, then there can be no possible hope for our cause. To rely on men in the condition they are suffered to remain in is worse than idle—a criminal delusion. Half-naked, unpaid, unofficered men cannot be expected to win your battles. The truth may as well be known. If the Rebel soldiers are no better off than some of our New York regiments, then I should confidently count on victory with odds of three to one against us. Though mutiny cannot be excused, the men are not so much to be blamed for complaining in strong terms.

I improve the opportunity to remark once more that there are between thirty-five and forty vacancies in New York here awaiting the action of Governor Morgan. Some of them have existed for nearly two months, and the regiments are greatly disorganized on account of the failure of His Excellency to act.

SEPTEMBER 21, 1861

SOUTH

RICHMOND DAILY DISPATCH
September 21, 1861

COLLECTING OFFICERS OF THE CONFEDERATE TAX

As a matter of interest to the people and to the revenue officers of the different counties, it may be well for us to state the determination of the secretary of the Treasury in regard to the agents who will be appointed for making the assessments and collecting the taxes of the Confederate government. It is known that under provision of the Confederate law levying a direct tax, any state which shall pay its quota of the same into the Confederate Treasury by the first day of April next will be entitled to a discount of 10 percent on the amount assessed against it. This discount is probably rather more than the expense which will attend the collection of the tax from the people, and therefore, any state paying in its quota by the date specified may save a small percentage of the amount to its people.

As this saving, however, cannot be great enough to afford much temptation to the states to undertake the collection of the Confederate tax, the government will doubtless have to appoint assessors and collectors of its own in many of the states for the purpose. Looking to this probability, we understand that the secretary of the Treasury is maturing instructions to the Confederate marshals on this subject. We understand that an important feature of these instructions will be a requirement upon the marshals *to appoint for the assessment and collection of the Confederate tax the same officers in all the counties which perform similar duties for the state governments*. We understand that these instructions will be *mandatory* and that the marshals will be left no option in the matter.

We throw out this piece of information in order to relieve the department here, and the marshals in all the districts of the South, from the swarm of applications for appointments in the Excise with which they would otherwise be overwhelmed. The measure resolved on by Mr. Memminger takes away from this prolific source of patronage every feature of partisanship and, considering the immense patronage thus voluntarily relinquished by the Confederate government, reflects great credit upon the president and the secretary of the Treasury.

While the policy thus resolved upon avoids the invocation of a countless swarm of office seekers throughout the land, it removes in great measure the most odious feature of direct taxation—in relieving the people from the annoyance of two sets of tax gatherers dinning their demands into each ear at the same time. In the great majority of cases, the officers who will assess and collect the Confederate tax will be men of the people's own selection, and whenever not of their own choosing, they will be the appointees of their own county courts. We look upon this determination of the president and the secretary of the Treasury as one of the most important and happy that has attended the administration of our new government.

In regard to Virginia, we suppose that the late period at which our legislature meets will preclude any effort on the part of the state to collect this tax itself and that instructions will have gone out from the Confederate government, and the work of collection entered upon, before the legislature will meet.

UNPARALLELED BRUTALITY

The outrages perpetrated upon helpless women in Maryland by the brutal soldiery of Lincoln are the darkest and most infernal features of this cruel and wicked invasion. We are aware that in all armies may be found men capable of any crime and that in the sack of European cities, rape and murder have often run riot through the streets; but we venture to say that the history of civilized countries does not afford a solitary parallel to the conduct of the Yankees in proclaiming in advance "Beauty and Booty" as their deliberately selected mode of carrying on war.

When we pronounce the wretches who are capable of such crimes as those committed in Maryland and upon the Virginia border baser and more degraded than the sepoys, we do not give utterance simply to the honest indignation that must swell every human heart, but proclaim a literal fact, entirely free from exaggeration and as capable of demonstration as any proposition in Euclid. The sepoys are heathen and barbarians; these people not only profess to be a Christian nation, but the cream of Christendom, thanking God that they are not as other men and holding immense Fulton Street prayer meetings—duly reported in the *New York Herald*—for the conversion of the rest of mankind. We do not wonder that the journals of all civilized Europe cry, "Shame! Shame!" upon these enemies of humanity. How long can such hypocrisy and wickedness defy the face of Heaven and convert the earth into a hell?

CHARLESTON DAILY COURIER
September 21, 1861

KENTUCKY

Kentucky is at last forced to open her eyes to the realities of her condition. She has been sleeping sweetly under the opiates administered by traitors in the pay of Lincoln, dreaming all through the deep slumber of neutrality. She fancied that the thunder of battle would fall on her ears from a distance and that her heart would not be wrung with anguish at the sight of her dead and bleeding children. She has awaked out of sleep, and the pleasant delusion has vanished.

There are now two hostile armies within the borders of that state. The Lincolnites occupy Paducah; Hickman and Columbus are held by the Confederates. The legislature has ordered the Southern army to leave the state and refused to adopt the resolution for the expulsion of the Yankees. That corrupt body has furthermore evinced its partiality for the wicked and base cause by passing a bill "making the waging of war against the United States, the enlistment of troops for the Confederates, a felony, with one to ——— years' imprisonment; the invasion of Kentucky by any of her citizens as a Confederate soldier to be punishable with death." Major General Polk has been waited upon by the commissioners of the state and served with a copy of the unfriendly resolutions and bill. The general expressed a willingness to comply with the command, but refused absolutely and emphatically to evacuate the important points he held unless the Lincolnites were forced to retire from Paducah.

It was the purpose of the Confederate government to respect the neutrality of Kentucky. President Davis's reply to Governor Magoffin's letter expressed this intention with clearness and force. The despot's reply to the inquiries and entreaties of the government was in strong contrast, in language, sentiment, and tone, to the noble production of our pure and able president. In that communication the artful tyrant discovers his base designs, questions with characteristic rudeness the statements and assertions of the high-minded gentleman and pure patriot, and treats his just and courteously preferred solicitations with evident contempt. He had worn the mask till the fitting time had come to take it off, and now the imperiled and distracted people who have believed his lies and been imposed upon by his plausible arts behold the open face of the despot in all its native hideousness.

Kentucky is committed by the action of her legislature to the cause of tyranny and oppression. Does that body represent the people of that state? Are those Unionists the exponents of their sentiments and determination? Will that brave and high-minded people bow their necks to the yoke of the meanest despotism the world has ever known?

The state has been driven by Lincoln from her neutral position. She can no longer hope to be permitted to sit a mere spectator of this terrible war. She has now to decide whether she will fight for or against us—whether she will draw her sword in defense of liberty or despotism. We cannot doubt which side she will choose.

That people are now aroused. Their eyes are opened to the deceitful arts of Lincoln and the traitors on their own soil. They see that neutrality was a snare and that it was the purpose of Crittenden, Guthrie, and the whole party of Unionists to bind them hand and foot and give them over to the tyrant. The treachery has discovered itself, and the people will arise in the might of their wrathful indignation; denounce the traitors who have thus tampered with their dignity, abused their confidence, and imperiled their liberties, their honor, and their lives; and drive the hireling soldier from their borders with a sword of fire.

It is well for the state that these infamous designs have been exposed. The cup of bitterness which Maryland is drinking in her disgrace and anguish has been mixed for that noble and gallant people. The chains that were intended for the limbs of these free men are already forged. But, thank God, they will not have to drink the chalice of woe and disgrace, and their sinewy limbs are still unfettered. They have awaked from their stupor in time to ward off the blow which would have lain them in the dust. They have heard the clanking of the chains, and, alarmed and indignant, they will rush by the thousands to protect their liberties, their property, and their homes. Our cause is their cause. We are of the same blood, our institutions are one, our interests are identical. They will be with us. They will cast away Unionism as a filthy garment, and their corrupt and traitorous leaders will be forced to flee with the hireling soldiery of the vulgar and bloody despot. The day of their redemption has dawned, and they welcome the light with exultant hearts. They are ready to strike for liberty and honor and to endure with heroism the evils they may have to suffer in working out their deliverance.

NORTH

BOSTON EVENING TRANSCRIPT
September 21, 1861

[UNTITLED]

A vigorous policy on the part of the national government is now demanded by the people of the loyal states. Very nice legal distinctions, mere political considerations, in a party sense, and narrow, hesitating policies are not agreeable just now to the temper of the great mass of the honest and earnest people—especially if that mass are to be looked to for a zealous support of the government. The day for these has gone by, and that must be a singular blindness that does not perceive that it has. We have got thoroughly into a civil war—face-to-face with a great rebellion. And the directest path toward ending that war—crushing that rebellion—is what the popular voice demands. Consequently, some of the questions which seem to be troubling the authorities and occupying their precious time are questions about which the people care very little, except to have them laid upon the table until the conflict is over. Sincere earnestness and indomitable activity in carrying on the conflict is about all that is asked for at present. The squabbles of individual officials and the exhibitions of their rivalries and competitions are of little account with the public mind, intensely engrossed with the one great issue, in the presence of which all other issues seem petty, impertinent, and intrusive.

The proof of this is in the all-but-universal applause with which every vigorous blow struck at the rebellion anywhere and by anybody has been hailed and rejoiced over. If ever men in power had the clearest expression of the will of their constituents, irrespective of party, to guide them, the men in power at Washington and all serving under them have such an expression today. Take one point, for example, where there seems to be a difference, arising from the diverse and hesitating action of the authorities, in feeling and policy, between them and the great body of the people.

We do not understand that we are fighting to overthrow the "peculiar institution." We agree entirely with the administration that the object of the contest on our part is the preservation of the Union. But if the administration does not mean to preserve the Union unless it can preserve the institution of slavery also, wherever it has heretofore existed, then we imagine the administration does not understand the wishes of its supporters. It is true, no doubt, that many in arms to sustain the government would not fight directly to put down slavery; but it is equally true that many in arms for the same patriotic purpose have not the slightest intention of fighting, directly or indirectly, for the upholding of slavery as a national concern. The time has come for the "peculiar institution" to take care of itself as best it may. The conflict with loyal people is neither for it nor against it, in itself considered. If, however, it gets itself in the way of the march of the forces seeking to defend the national government from all assailants, then it must abide the fortune of war. We might as well talk of respecting and sparing rifled cannons in the batteries of Beauregard as talk of respecting and sparing slavery when enlisted in any way on the side of the rebellion.

NEW YORK TRIBUNE
September 21, 1861

THE LATEST WAR NEWS

The war news this morning is very meager. From Washington we have absolutely nothing of special importance. Concerning the reported battle at Lexington, Missouri, we receive only some fragments, from sources not too trustworthy or intelligent. It is said that on Tuesday General Price made a movement to obtain three ferryboats on the river near Lexington, but that he was repulsed with considerable loss; he appears, however, to have subsequently secured the boats.[48] On Wednesday, according to the same narrative, Price attacked Colonel Mulligan in his

48. Confederate General Sterling Price.

entrenchments at Lexington and was driven back with the loss of 300 or 400. This statement is in a measure confirmed by reports from other sources. The attack on Wednesday was determined, and lasted nearly all day. Reinforcements had reached the vicinity of Colonel Mulligan, but it was not certain that they could find boats in which to cross the river. McCulloch, with two thousand men, was at the last accounts on the Osage River, about seventy miles from Jefferson City. It was thought that an attack would soon be made by him. We have news of a variety of skirmishes in Missouri and western Virginia, in the course of which the Rebels are always signally defeated, but the engagements are not of sufficient magnitude to attract special attention.

DYED IN THE WOOL

We have often, when curiously observing certain politicians, thought this to be rather a tame characterization. There are some men who are dyed not simply in the wool, but in the skin, flesh, bones, and viscera—men to whom prejudice, education, and habit have given a certain indelible tint, in comparison with which the leopard's spots are evanescent and the cuticle of the Ethiopian washable—men who are the prisoners of past and petty experiences, and who never learn, never forget, and never forgive. A "narrow-minded Democrat" one would have supposed to be a contradiction in terms. Democracy should be large, expansive, and catholic. Democracy should adapt itself to the will of the people, or it is an absurdity. A Democrat who opposes his personal notions to the expressed and unmistakable voice of the masses is not merely a mad Don Quixote, but he is substantially that which he professes the most bitterly to hate—he is an aristocrat, because he thinks himself to be the best of all the world. He stuffs his stomach with his own creed and then goes into a political dyspepsia. "Democrat," as he calls himself, he flouts at majorities, undervalues the intelligence of the people, derides the ballot box, mocks the Constitution, and throws dirt at the government which, by his own theory, he has helped to create. While the majority are of his mind, all goes well, but when the same majority dares to differ from him, he discards his confidence in constituencies and bawls out that most men are fools. The war has proved very mortal to this breed of Democrats, common sense in most neighborhoods prevailing; but here and there, maugre the excellent and patriotic exertions of Messrs. Dickinson and Hallett, we may descry some monument of human absurdity, overrunning with self-importance, loudly announcing that he is not for sale. Experience has shown that men who are fussiest upon this particular are always to be bought; and mighty bad bargains they would be, no matter how little the price paid for them. Thus, in the late Democratic state convention in Massachusetts, a certain brisk little gentleman, of whom we never heard before, and of whom we never expect to hear again, announced that he was not to be sold by Benjamin Hallett, as if even that veteran tactician could sell him, could even give him away. Evidently, all this man's democracy was in the personal pronoun. So respectable a person as Dr. Childs of Pittsfield was not afraid of being sold, and appeared to have marvelous confidence in his power of taking care of himself; it was only those who wanted a bid who were boisterous against venality.

Against the advice of its oldest and most respectable leaders, the convention, by a trifling majority, determined to nominate a state ticket and, with a cruelty really sickening, compelled Mr. Isaac Davis of Worcester—who is a respectable man—to run, or rather to creep, for governor, with that ancient Democrat and ex-postmaster, E. C. Bailey, for his lieutenant. Mr. Davis, when this sweet little honor was thrust upon him, had also the misfortune to be present and was forced to make a speech. Now, the speech of a gubernatorial candidate may fairly enough be considered as an expression of the views of the men who have placed him in nomination, and, therefore, Mr. Davis's speech was the voice of the convention. Was it? Let us see! Mr. Davis said that "he went for a vigorous prosecution of the war until the rebellion is crushed out; and he held, for the preservation of liberty, that our patriotism ought to rise above party"—what a severe slap at the majority of the convention!—"so far as the support of the present administration in all its *just* measures is concerned." Now, Mr. Davis did not, in his speech, point out any *unjust* measures of the administration; and as the presumption is that he would have done so if any had occurred to his mind, we think we have a right to ask him what his grounds of opposition to the administration are. He must have some, for he is a candidate in hostility to the government. If he has reasons for his hostility, let us have them! If he has none, why is he a candidate? Now, let us go to the resolutions—to the platform upon which Mr. Isaac Davis is reclining. He is a sensible man, we believe, and if we had him on the stand, under oath, and were permitted to subject him to one of those unlimited cross-examinations which lawyers love so well, we would put into his hand the resolutions of this convention and would ask him:

Do you believe, Mr. Davis, that the national administration wishes to interfere with the right of every state to regulate its domestic affairs in its own way? with the freedom of the press? with the right of personal liberty? with the right of trial by jury? Oh, you do not! Well, your convention is of the same mind. Your delegates say that they do not believe that the administration will do anything of the kind. Oh, no! Not at all! Then where was the necessity of saying anything, and of this specification of high crimes and misdemeanors which delegates did *not* believe the administration would commit? Suppose that they had passed the following resolution concerning you and your nomination, Mr. Isaac Davis:

Resolved, That while we will support Mr. Isaac Davis for governor, it is in the belief that he will not embezzle the public funds—that he will not take bribes—that he will not appoint blackguards to office—that he will not tell lies, and that he is quite above any knavishness whatever; and that should he be elected, and should he embezzle the public funds, take bribes, appoint blackguards to office, tell lies, and turn out a knave (which the Lord forfend!), we hereby caution him that our support will be withdrawn.

—There, Mr. Davis, how would you like to go to the people with a backing of that variety?

But let us descend from the platform to the benches and see of what materials this convention was composed. There was a certain delegate, Samuel Wells of Boston, who was moved in his serene mind to offer a resolution recommending a sort of Hartford Convention to consist of delegates from the New England states, to suggest constitutional amendments, "furnishing ample guarantees of protection to the rights of the South, so that the states now in arms against the government may be induced to return to their allegiance to the Constitution." We do not know Mr. Wells, and we do not want to know him, for in spite of his name, we do not believe that he is very deep. At any rate, the bucket came up empty on this occasion. Gentlemen rose at once to protest against committing the convention to any such absurdity, and well they might. Delegates had just voted with entire unanimity that the rebellion must be "crushed" and the war "vigorously prosecuted"; and, lo, the astute Wells proposes to substitute compromise for crushing, constitutional amendments for campaigns, and gammon for gunpowder! Well, now, what did this wise convention do with this resolution? Rejected it, of course, for they could not do otherwise without writing themselves down, forever and forever, asses. But will the intelligent reader believe that upon the question of indefinitely postponing this idiotic resolution, one hundred twenty-five delegates, actually and without a joke, voted in the negative? A change of five votes would have given Mr. Wells the ignominy of success.

But if we Republicans did not get any cakes in this precious Democratic convention, the Constitutional Union party—our old friends the Bell–Everetts—did not get any ale.[49] A committee of this party sent to the convention "a communication proposing a union of all parties in nominating state officers." It was a mild and modest suggestion, and such as became a minimum party—but how was it treated? With a coldness equivalent to contempt. Oliver Stevens told the Democrats that the communication was entitled to "respectful consideration"; and so it was referred to the Committee on Resolutions, from which time the poor thing was no more heard of than if it had not been sent at all! It might as well have been buried in the deep bosom of the ocean. "Be off about your business!" said this Democratic body to the ill-treated Bell–Everetts; "we will have nothing to do with you!" We have heard of eccentric people who, when in the article of death, desired to be left entirely alone, so that the serenity of their passing might not be disturbed by a rustle or a whisper. The Democracy of Massachusetts has evidently a prejudice in favor of this quiet style of exit. Let them be gratified! Who wants an entangling alliance with the sepulcher? The high-minded and honorable men of the late Democratic party will take care of themselves. Let the residuum go out of sight and to the bottom, where it belongs!

OCTOBER 19, 1861

SOUTH

RICHMOND DAILY DISPATCH
October 19, 1861

ENGLAND'S OPPORTUNITY

There is not an interest nor even a passion of Great Britain, if governments can be supposed to be influenced by passions, which is not involved in the present contest in America. If she fails to avail herself of this golden opportunity, it is because her statesmen are incompetent to the guardianship of her affairs. We do not believe that. The dullest perception cannot fail to see that the commercial, navigation, and manufacturing interests of England must all be placed beyond the reach of

49. Founded in 1859 by former Whigs, the short-lived, moderate Constitutional Union party was pro-Union but neutral on the slavery question. In 1860, John Bell ran for president, and Edward Everett for vice president, on the Constitutional Union ticket.

human rivalry by the success of the Southern Confederacy. Nor is this all. The Monroe Doctrine will no longer interpose even a nominal barrier to the progress of European colonization on this continent, and the colonies which England already possesses will no longer be in danger of absorption by the mammoth republic. The influence of radical principles, which, with every year of the progress of the United States, must continue to grow until it gradually undermines existing institutions in Europe, will not only be checked but annihilated by the overthrow of the United States government. The only considerations which can be adduced in opposition to giving "aid and comfort" to the South are the abolition sentiments of Exeter Hall, the fear that Canada may be invaded, and, what the North has threatened, that $500 million of British property within its borders will be confiscated.

Exeter Hall, however, has not yet become such a power in the British Empire as to influence its policy where pounds, shillings, and pence are concerned. Moreover, it is not sufficiently assured of the purposes of the Federal government in this war to give that active sympathy which it always yields to impracticable and destructive measures. If the war is one simply to put down what the *London Times* has styled an insurrection of Southern planters against their commercial masters in the North, Exeter Hall, of course, feels no interest in such a strife. It must be such a war as Frémont has proclaimed in Missouri to enlist the sympathies of Exeter Hall; but Frémont has been recalled.[50] When we consider the enormous war debt which the Lincoln government is running up, with no earthly prospect of ever paying the interest upon it, except by obtaining command of the cotton crops of the South, Exeter Hall may well conclude that the public creditors of the United States have not advanced their money upon the theory that an institution which is essential to the cultivation of cotton shall be destroyed. It is therefore idle to suppose that the pseudophilanthropy of Great Britain will be stimulated to any special paroxysm in behalf of such a cause; nor, if it could, has it ever yet been able to control the policy of England in any point affecting her commercial interests and national power.

The security of Canada is, of course, a subject which no British ministry could overlook, and doubtless affords a reason for the caution which that government has exercised upon the American question. The colonial possessions of England on this continent are nearly as great as the territory of the late United States and have been constantly increas-

50. In 1861, Union General John Frémont issued an emancipation proclamation in Missouri, freeing the slaves of anti-Unionists. The proclamation was later revoked by Lincoln.

ing in wealth and importance. Canada, in proportion to her population, is a more profitable customer of England than the United States, and large amounts of British capital have been invested in public works and private enterprises in that growing portion of the British Empire. The government has aided in the construction of magnificent improvements —of railroads, canals, and bridges—which are intended to develop the vast resources of Canada and to enable her to compete in trade and prosperity with her republican neighbor. The Canadian people, always among the most loyal of British colonists, have become more than ever attached to their institutions since the disruption of the American Union. They point with pride and confidence to the solidity and safety of their own government, to the permanent security of property and life, and to its vast superiority, even on the score of civil and political freedom, to the lawless military despotism which has triumphed over the American Constitution. We cannot, of course, expect that England should abandon such a colony to the risk of a Yankee invasion, which has been openly menaced by the profligate and shameless journals of New York. We must give her time to put Canada in a state of defense before she assumes a position that must bring her in direct collision with the American government. This she is doing as rapidly as possible, both in the construction of fortifications and in such large reinforcements of men as to excite the jealous outcries of the Northern press. It is only for the South to hold its own a little while longer, and we shall be in close alliance with the most powerful empire of modern times.

The Northern menace, in the event of British recognition of Southern independence, to confiscate the $500 million of British property in the North is a mere *brutum fulmen,* which the British government will know how to value as it deserves.[51] If, as the Northern press alleges, the control of Southern commerce is worth the expenditure of $500 million a year for a series of years, the same Golconda would be purchased ever more cheaply by Great Britain if the North should confiscate every dollar of her property within her borders. But the North would never venture on such a step, with the prospect of having all its cities on the Atlantic Coast knocked about their ears by British squadrons in twenty-four hours after the decree of confiscation should go forth.[52] Nothing is more absurd than the gasconading threats of the Northern press against Great Britain. What could the United States do in the event of a war with that country? Privateering she has herself denounced as piracy,

51. *brutum fulmen:* Latin, "unfeeling thunderbolt," meaning "mere noise."
52. squadrons: organizations of naval forces made up of two or more ships.

and at this moment has our Southern privateers in prison cells, about to try them for their lives on that charge.

The successes of the last war with England afford no standard by which to estimate the results of another conflict with that gigantic power. The United States went to war with England when England was at war with all the rest of the world, and, besides, was herself united when she ventured upon that hazardous enterprise. She would now find England unoccupied with any other combatant and able to bestow the undivided attentions of a thousand ships of war, most of them steamers, and some of them iron-plated vessels, upon the handful of ships in the United States navy and the populous and inviting towns upon their seacoast. Hence, we come to the conclusion that if England cannot obtain cotton in any other way, she will not be deterred by apprehension of any damage the United States can inflict upon her from opening the Southern ports without ceremony and at such time as her convenience dictates.

CHARLESTON DAILY COURIER
October 19, 1861

OUR VIRGINIA CORRESPONDENCE FROM RICHMOND

Correspondence of the *Courier*

Richmond, Virginia, October 16, 1861

The probability of another attack upon our army in front of Washington seems to increase with fresh advices from our camp and that of the enemy. In the latest papers received here from the North, I observe that the impression prevails among all the journalists and correspondents that McClellan will shortly make another forward movement.[53] The very latest rumor in the Baltimore papers, of the 11th, was that Banks had crossed the Potomac with twenty thousand men. The next fight is not likely to result in a Bull Run blunder on the part of the Federal generals. They have learned by disaster to estimate the fighting qualities of the men they have to contend with, and they will guard against an overwilling confidence in their own invincibility. The Federals, as they advance upon our lines, are throwing up fortifications. If they are repulsed in the next battle, they will not be compelled to retreat over the whole

53. Union General George McClellan, Democratic presidential candidate (1864) and governor of New Jersey (1878–81).

distance between Manassas and Washington. They can easily fall back behind their earthworks and throw before our troops successive obstacles during the pursuit.

I am pleased to learn from members of the medical staff that our Army of the Potomac has been greatly strengthened within the past few weeks by the return of convalescent soldiers from the hospitals. It has recovered nearly its original effectiveness. One instance is related. A regiment from the cotton states at one time had only two hundred sound and effective men in the ranks; the balance were in the hospitals. Last week the same regiment had nearly eight hundred men on dress parade. Its ranks were being augmented daily. This regiment is now thoroughly effective, for, besides its efficiency in drill, its members are "seasoned" to the war.

The most significant feature in the recent advices from the North is the growing discontent of the northwestern states. The immediate cause of trouble is the withdrawal of so many regiments from the West to protect Washington. The western editors affect to believe that Beauregard has sent at least fifty thousand of his best troops into Kentucky, and they are really alarmed lest the Rebel Johnston should attack Cincinnati and overrun the states of Ohio, Indiana, and Illinois before the winter is over. The western people, too, generally take sides with Frémont in his quarrel with the administration. Some of the journalists are very severe. They indulge in threats which in Kentucky or Maryland would result in the suppression of the papers by the Federal authorities. One Republican organ published in Indiana even hints at the possibility of a disruption between the eastern and western states. It thinks the war is taking a turn which looks solely to the benefit of the commercial and manufacturing interests of the Atlantic states. The West is ignored, and Cincinnati and Chicago left defenseless, so that the eastern cities may be secured against invasion. The persecution of Frémont, the "western general," is denounced.

The editor even adverts to the vast expenditure occasioned by the war, and grumbles over the figures. Why should the West be burdened with a large proportion of this heavy debt if the war is so palpably for the benefit of the merchants and manufacturers of the East? There is a vast deal of meaning and mischief in these editorial reflections. They indicate the rising of a sectional western party. The interests of the agricultural West are almost as much opposed to those of the speculating and trading North and manufacturing East as the interests of the Confederate and Northern states. Why should the West continue to pay tariff duties to support the nabobs of Fifth Avenue and Lowell?[54] These questions have been hidden by the war furor, but now that the difficulty of conquering the South becomes apparent and reason is beginning to take the place of passion, the impracticability of a union between the East and West on the old terms excites the observation of the suffering section. A great defeat of the Federal army at Manassas, or in Kentucky, would strike a terrible blow to the "Union." If the western people are ripe for revolt, occasion could speedily be found, and if some popular man, like Frémont, should have the daring to attempt a coup d'état, he could easily elevate himself to the dictatorship.

The new five-cent postage stamps were sold for the first time today. I have a specimen before me. The stamp is colored green and bears a tolerably good engraving of President Davis. The principal defect of the engraving is its indistinctness. It is the best, however, offered to the inspection of the Post Office Department and will have to answer until the war is over.

General Henry A. Wise had a relapse a few days ago, and his friends really despaired for his life. To their joy, however, he has shown symptoms of recovery today, and they are quite sanguine that he will henceforth improve. His son, Captain O. Jennings Wise, returned to the city yesterday from the West.

Poor Calvin Huson, the Democratic politician, who, like Ely, came out to Manassas to "see the fun," and who fell into the hands of the funny Rebels, expired on Monday at the residence of a Virginia gentleman, whose hospitable mansion is not far from the city. Huson has had the typhoid fever for some weeks. A few days before he died, by permission of General Winder, he was removed from the prison to the private residence I have alluded to. He was a clever, good-humored fellow and used to protest that his feelings were not inimical to the South. He was caught, however, in company with black sheep and had to pay the penalty.

The underground railroad is again in operation and runs three times a week. Letters are taken through to a point in the North where they are mailed. The freight is fifty cents. The conductors are making a small fortune. The agents receive letters only from persons known to be responsible and who would not be likely to communicate information to the enemy.

Among the recent arrivals here is a company from Vicksburg, Mis-

54. Lowell, Massachusetts.

sissippi, rejoicing in the euphonious appellation of the "King Cotton Guards." Military nomenclature in the Southern Confederacy must afford considerable amusement to foreign lookers-on. The ancient "Grenadiers," "Fusiliers," and "Light Infantry" are very often abandoned for the more extravagant and striking titles of "Rebels," "Invincibles," "Tigers," "Rough-and-Readies," etc. A Virginia company which suffered severely in the battle of Manassas was the "Grayson Daredevils." Two Georgia companies here call themselves the "Miller Wildcats" and "Jackson Avengers." Another has adopted the name of the "Joe Browns" in honor of the governor of Georgia. The oddest title is that borne by an Arkansas company, to wit: the "Muddy Bayou Heroes."

The first concert of the South Carolina amateurs came off at the African Church on Monday night. The occasion was made interesting by the debut of the daughter of a prominent and wealthy planter of York district. The young lady has been for nearly two years a pupil of Torriani, the well-known *chef d'orchestre*.[55] She has a really fine voice, and it exhibits the most assiduous cultivation. Aside from the not unexpected nervousness of the amateurs, they all acquitted themselves admirably and won the most flattering applause. After giving two more concerts here, they proceed farther south, Charleston in due time being visited. The proceeds of the concerts, you will recollect, are appropriated to the Soldiers' Relief societies.

The theater here has been secured by a Professor Hewitt, who will open shortly with a brand-new sensation drama founded on the battle of Manassas and called *The Scout*. This is the New York way of attracting the public. The theaters are fighting all the battles of the second revolution over again. The Bowery manages to produce an authentic version of each great Northern victory within three days after the first report appears in the reliable columns of the *Herald*.

Sumter

[UNTITLED]

On looking more closely into the narratives of the naval engagement near New Orleans, we are gratified at finding that South Carolina was represented on that glorious occasion not by one only but by two of her gallant sons.

The monster that did the grand deed with her prow of steel, crashing through the wooden sides of the man-of-war and smiting the hearts

55. *chef d'orchestre:* French, "head of orchestra," meaning "conductor."

of the Lincoln seamen and soldiers with dismay and terror, was commanded by Lieutenant A. F. Warley, a native of Pendleton, in this state.

Lieutenant Warley was one of the first officers who resigned from the United States navy after the secession of South Carolina.

He was a lieutenant aboard the U.S. steamer of which Captain Duncan N. Ingraham was commander. He was in Genoa in December last, where, hearing that his state would probably secede, he immediately left and traveled with all possible speed toward home. He stopped in England on his way hither but a single day, so intense was his desire to participate in the opening scenes of the fearful struggle.

On reaching Charleston, Governor Pickens gave him a commission, and he was placed in command of the Dahlgren Battery on Morris Island, where he remained till after the reduction of Fort Sumter, when he received his commission in the Confederate navy, and has been ever since superintending the fitting up of the *Crao,* of which vessel he has command. He also commanded one of the batteries in the Ship Island affair.

This gallant soldier is a son of the late Jacob Warley, an officer of the Revolution, and he belongs to one of the oldest families in the state.

NORTH

BOSTON EVENING TRANSCRIPT
October 19, 1861

ABANDONMENT OF LEESBURG CONFIRMED—FEDERAL RECONNAISSANCE TOWARD FAIRFAX COURTHOUSE—IMPORTANT BALLOON VIEW OF THE REBEL FIELD—THE BALLOON SHOT AT BY FEDERAL TROOPS—THE REBEL TROOPS OBJECT TO MIGRATING SOUTHWARD—DISCONTENT IN THE INSURGENT CAMP—RUMOR OF REBELS CROSSING THE POTOMAC—FAVORABLE DISPATCHES FROM EUROPE

New York, 19th—The *Herald*'s Washington dispatch says that the abandonment of Leesburg by the Rebels is confirmed, and it is reported that the Rebels have proceeded to the nearest point on the Manassas Gap Railroad, but some surmise they have gone toward Harpers Ferry.

Colonel Stapel made a reconnaissance on Little River Turnpike this morning to Annandale and toward Fairfax Courthouse. Annandale was not deserted, the inhabitants stating that several regiments of Rebels had left yesterday morning. He went within two miles of the courthouse, leaving his force at Coyle's Tavern; and having satisfied himself that nearly all the Rebels had disappeared from that vicinity, he returned, much to the dissatisfaction of his small force, who expected to go to the courthouse.

Professor La Mountain made a balloon reconnaissance this afternoon, the wind carrying him some six miles over the Rebel camps to Fairfax Station and Courthouse, and landed at Blenker's headquarters. He saw their encampments at Manassas, but no Rebel force was seen this side of Fairfax Courthouse, at which place were only a few companies, with appearances of a recent evacuation. There was a larger force at Fairfax Station.

Other valuable information was obtained, which is in the possession of the government. When landing, our German troops fired on him several times, thinking he was a Rebel. Several bullets perforated his balloon.

It is stated that the Rebels object to going into winter quarters in Virginia and insist on wintering either in Kentucky or Maryland, and the men from the extreme Southern states insist on going home and murmur loudly at the present inactivity.

It is presumed that a large force has been sent from Virginia to Kentucky, as there is now no prospect of their invading Maryland.

A stand of colors from California to the Rhode Islanders was presented by the president to Colonel Wheaton's 2nd Rhode Island Regiment today.[56] Governor Sprague addressed the troops; also Bishop Clarke and a large number of distinguished personages witnessed the ceremony.

It is supposed that the Rebels are crossing from Aquia Creek, but will be handsomely received if they make such a movement.

A Cabinet meeting was held this morning, at which our foreign relations were discussed. The tone of the latest dispatches from abroad indicates a more favorable feeling, and the whole diplomatic corps in Washington evince more cordiality.

REBEL BARBARITIES—APPEAL OF SOUTHERN CITIZENS FOR PROTECTION—IMMEDIATE CONFISCATION OF REBEL PROPERTY

New York, 19th—The *Tribune*'s dispatch says that during the reconnaissance of Colonel Stapel today, a family was found who had had three sons impressed into the Rebel army as servants, their cattle and crops destroyed, and their property confiscated.

56. stand of colors: a flag or flags carried by a military unit.

While the place was occupied by the Rebels, the family was taken sick with measles, but the Rebel surgeon refused to attend them. The only eatable they had was a cabbage, on which they were dining. The German soldiers sent them good rations and subscribed liberally. It is needless to say they were Unionists.

It is stated that one hundred fifty voters of Chincoteague took the oath of allegiance on the 14th, in the presence of Lieutenant Murray of the steamer *Louisiana*.[57] The inhabitants are represented as being loyal and request the continued presence of a war steamer to prevent their subjugation by the Rebels, who have assembled on the opposite shore for that purpose. The American flag is kept flying by the Chincoteaguers.

The *Times*'s dispatch states that Marshal Murray has arrived on important business and that the government has determined to commence confiscatory proceedings forthwith of all real and personal property of the Rebels.

NEW YORK TRIBUNE
October 19, 1861

THE LATEST WAR NEWS

The gallant fight which took place the other day at Bolivar, where our troops were so brilliantly successful, was yesterday followed by a second battle. In the morning the Rebels appeared on the heights and attacked the national troops under Major Gould, using artillery alone. Major Gould returned the fire by canister from the gun captured from the enemy himself; the Rebels were beaten back, but not till they had wreaked their vengeance by burning a mill from which our troops had taken a great quantity of wheat, and making the miller a prisoner. At the latest accounts, the firing was going on between the combatants; Major Gould was throwing shot and shell after the enemy who was in retreat. Great terror prevailed among the women and children of the neighborhood, numbers of whom were hastening to Maryland.

It is reported that the Rebels who retired from the Potomac in the vicinity of Harpers Ferry on the approach of the sickly season are now returning to the river, that they were at Charles Town within a few days, and that they will shortly make their appearance at the several fords along the stream. Stirring work is looked for by the troops in that neighborhood.

57. Chincoteague, Virginia.

From Missouri we learn that General Price has, as was expected, made a stand in Cedar County, twenty-five miles from Osceola, with twenty thousand well-armed and well-disciplined troops and a large force of irregular militia. It is stated that Hardee, with a large body of troops, is expected to join him by next Sunday.[58] General Frémont has reached Warsaw and had on Wednesday begun preparations to lay a pontoon bridge across the Osage River. When he arrived at Warsaw, the opposite bank of the river was lined with Rebel cavalry, who were dispersed with a few rounds of canister. It has been stated in several ways that for want of adequate means of transportation, and because of the muddy state of the roads, Frémont would not be able to move his army; but in an incredibly short time, he is almost in face of the enemy, ready to push on with a vigor as great as if his way were perfectly smooth and pleasant in every particular. We have news also of a fight which occurred at Pilot Knob, Missouri, on Wednesday. Major Gavit of the 1st Indiana Cavalry made an attack on the enemy at the place named, but, finding them too strong for him, retired until he met a reinforcement of six hundred; then, forming an ambuscade, he led the pursuing Rebels into it, and in a short time they were completely routed.

We hear by way of Cincinnati that General Sherman on Thursday sent by telegraph to Washington urgent requests for reinforcements. Secretary Cameron and Adjutant General Thomas, who reached Cincinnati yesterday, at once sent orders to Pittsburgh, Indianapolis, and Chicago for eight thousand men to be sent to his aid. It is thought that sharp work may be very soon expected in that section.

[UNTITLED]

Great exultation has been long felt and shown by the Rebels over their determination to pay none of their debts to Northern creditors. They have complimented each other on the patriotism of this course and have with keen satisfaction sold their stolen goods at blockade prices, regretting only that they had not made heavier bills when they had the confidence of the "damned Yankee traders." On the other hand, the Northern merchants have long since resigned all hope of ever receiving a dollar toward the payment of their dues from the South and have in weariness and disgust closed the ledger on whose pages is inscribed the unsatisfactory record. A letter which we this morning publish from Alexandria, however, is promising. Through the healthful influence of the advancing national arms, Southern repudiators may yet be compelled to pay their

58. Confederate General William Hardee.

debts. The "dead horses" of the slave states may revive, and again may speculation show itself in their fixed and stony eyes. Not by the voluntary honesty of the debtors will this be done, though; a court of summary proceeding and of efficient power will be the instrumentality used. The case reported by our Alexandria correspondent was simple enough: Southern debtors, there doing business, refused to pay a merchant of New York, then ran away, leaving their work to be done by another, and betook themselves farther South, where they joined the Rebel army. They left behind them some of the goods they bought on a long credit, as well as other property. A suit was brought against them in the provost court, and in less than an hour, the evidence was put in, the arguments made, and the decision announced. The latter was that all the property of the absconding debtors should be taken possession of by the court; held for five days to allow their friends, if such persons there were in existence, to redeem the goods; and that then, the claims being still unpaid, the property should be sold for that purpose. There are many things to commend this rapid form of proceeding to the hearts of Northern creditors. It is a good thing to have a court of original and exclusive jurisdiction following the advancing army and settling the estates of defeated Rebels. Let the precedent stand firmly and be sharply followed.

NOVEMBER 16, 1861

SOUTH

RICHMOND DAILY DISPATCH
November 15, 1861

[*The* Dispatch *did not publish an issue on November 16. The following articles are drawn from the Friday issue.*]

FAST DAY

The solicitude of both North and South for the countenance of Europe is alike disgraceful to both. The time has come when the South, at least, owes it to her self-respect to forget, if practicable, that Europe is in existence. If two champions of the "ring" get together in the court green and, instead of devoting their whole attention to each other, turn continual and wistful glances to the bystanders for sympathy and assistance, they are voted at once "bad game." It behooves us to learn a lesson of pluck from its primitive schools. We are fighting for independence. We are engaged in an effort to separate our political fortunes from a loathsome and corrupt companionship; we are resisting the attempt of a cowardly community, presuming upon a strength of four to one, to reduce us to their infamous rule. We are able, alone and unassisted, to maintain our stand. We have abundant resources and resolution to withstand the invasion and the onslaught of the Northern barbarians. We can help ourselves, unaided, out of the contest, and we owe it to our self-respect and our future standing among nations to fight this battle through alone, hand to hand, with the enemy.

What further alliance do we need but that which we already possess? Our cause is righteous, and "thrice is he armed who hath his quarrel just." The plainest manifestations of divine favor have been vouchsafed us. Our people are honest, moral, and religious, their enemy infidel, debauched, and utterly depraved in principle. We have all the attributes and auxiliaries requisite to success. One thing only must we possess to render these circumstances effective: We must have the resolution to conquer success, and an implicit confidence in our cause. Hercules is only the friend and ally of him who helps himself. Fortune favors the brave. Providence waits on the steps of the persevering, resolute, and bold.

Independence won by the sword and the musket will be ten times more precious and valuable than independence wrung from our enemy through the aid secured by cotton. We can whip the enemy. We will defeat all the schemes of the North. We should long ago have driven back the invader from our borders if it had not been for the traitors within our own boundaries. We commenced the struggle under every disadvantage. We could not induce the submissionists among us to take up arms until they had turned over the common government, with its army, its navy, its treasury, its ships, its munitions of war, its vast stores of arms and supplies, and its strongest fortresses into the hands of the enemy. We first stripped ourselves naked of every resource; we first armed our enemies to the teeth and provided them with every advantage; we turned over to him the government and its prerogatives; we first put a rope around our necks and handed it to that government; we armed it with the semblance of regularity and of legal right and authority; we furnished it with the brand "Rebel" to burn into our foreheads—and then we began the fight. All that folly, timidity, hesitation, and disloyalty could do to defeat a cause in advance we did, and then we commenced the struggle.

But we had right on our side—and courage, morality, and religion; public honesty and Providence. The people have risen spontaneously, and done all that patriotism and self-sacrificing public spirit could do to redeem and retrieve the criminal faults of their politicians. No country ever had fewer Ananiases or fewer Sapphiras. Our brave young men have rushed to the field; and our braver women have cheered and encouraged them in all their steps; have tenderly dressed their wounds and softly waited at their sickbed sides.

Our rulers had deprived us of, or refused to provide us with, arms at the beginning. This was all that we needed to secure success, and arms have seemed to drop down to us from heaven. Within a week past, many thousands of them have been brought into our shores, as if piloted through blockading fleets by an angel. Our machinery for their manufacture, also, is all now in full play, and our country is now in a better state of defense than it has been since the discovery of the continent.

What need have we for an ally in Europe, when we enjoy the aid of such potential ones at home? In our own right, arms are our sole defense, and the God of the brave, honest, and faithful is our all-sufficient ally. In our trusty muskets and rifles have we a much more perfect security than in our cotton and tobacco, and when we look beyond these for countenance and support, let us cast our view above into the benignant skies and not abroad into the dens of European tyranny and corruption. Such is the invocation to which the president invites the good people of our Confederacy today.

EAST TENNESSEE

The Confederate government has hitherto exhibited the greatest leniency and toleration to the Unionist faction in east Tennessee. These dissatisfied and turbulent men were bound by every obligation of duty and gratitude at least to desist from acts of resistance and insurrection against the constituted authorities. The sovereign voice of the people of Tennessee had proclaimed her an independent state and had also united her with the Southern Confederacy. Their first outbreaks of discontent, and even of treason, were not visited by the government with the punishment it might justly have inflicted. On the contrary, their leading organ, Brownlow's incendiary paper, was permitted week after week, and month after month, to court in vain the crown of martyrdom.[59]

This humane and paternal forbearance, instead of softening their ob-

59. Brownlow's incendiary paper: the pro-Union *Knoxville Whig,* published by William Brownlow, who later served as governor of Tennessee (1865–69) and senator (1869–75).

duracy, has only emboldened them to open acts of ferocity and resistance, until at last they are in armed and organized insurrection. Hereafter they will be recognized in the character of traitors and enemies, which they have themselves chosen, and be visited with the chastisement and retribution due to their crimes, the only treatment they are capable of understanding. Open enemies we may respect, but secret, bridge-burning incendiaries, assassins, and traitors are as despicable in the eyes of those who make use of their baseness as they are detestable in the opinions of all honest men.

THE GERMANS OF CHARLESTON

The gallant conduct of the Germans of Charleston in the late action on the coast is worthy of special honor. The characteristic courage of their race was never more brilliantly and gloriously displayed. From beginning to end, against heavy odds, they fought like heroes, and entitled themselves to the everlasting gratitude and admiration of their adopted country. Worthy brethren-in-arms of the native chivalry of South Carolina, they have covered themselves with glory and given a noble illustration of the fidelity and valor of the Germans of the South.

CHARLESTON DAILY COURIER
November 15, 1861

[*The* Courier *did not publish an issue on November 16. The following articles are drawn from the Friday issue.*]

FROM BLUFFTON
MOVEMENTS OF THE ENEMY ON OUR COAST—PINCKNEY ISLAND IN THEIR POSSESSION—YANKEE THIEVES STEALING THE NEGROES

Bluffton, South Carolina, 14th—The enemy is in possession of Pinckney Island. They have seized all of the able-bodied men on the plantations and carried them aboard the fleet. This has created a panic among the others, who are anxious to get away, but are prevented by force.

The enemy has made no attempt as yet to land on the main. Yesterday our pickets at Buckingham were fired upon by a party in a launch at long tow without effect.

We have not been able to ascertain their force, but it is represented by the Negroes to be large.

FROM NASHVILLE

TROOPS POURING INTO KENTUCKY

Nashville, 13th—Yankee troops continue to pour into Kentucky. A regiment from western Virginia arrived at Louisville on the 4th instant. Two Ohio regiments started for Louisville on the 5th instant. Ten regiments from Ohio, Indiana, and the North were expected to arrive at Louisville last week.

Madisonville, Hopkins County, was occupied by one thousand Lincolnites on the 10th instant. Gentlemen are compelled to fly to avoid arrest.

FROM RICHMOND

LATE NORTHERN NEWS

Richmond, 14th—The *New York Herald,* of the 8th instant, contains the following summary of news from Washington to the 6th instant:

General Meigs has been mentioned as the successor of General Frémont. General Halleck will probably be sent to Kentucky.

The reported resignation of General Wool is unfounded.

Colonel Hawkins, commanding at Hatteras, advises that the troops be returned to Fortress Monroe, in consequence of the untenable conditions of the place. In severe storms, much damage has been done, and during the recent storm, the troops were obliged to retire from the forts.

The smallpox has broken out among the crew of the *Harriet Lane*.

The *Baltimore Sun,* of the 6th instant, says there was no truth in the report that General Beauregard was en route to Charleston.

The *News* sheet says that eleven thousand troops will be sent south as soon as the transports of the armada return.

Robert S. Bunker, ex-mayor of Mobile, and Andrew Low, a merchant, were arrested at Cincinnati and taken to Fort Warren in Boston Harbor by order of Secretary Seward. Both of these gentlemen had recently returned from Europe and were arrested on suspicion of having important information for the Rebels.

A Washington correspondent of the *Philadelphia Bulletin* asserts that he has received assurance from the most authentic source that Lincoln informed several gentlemen, high in authority, that the army will not go into winter quarters but that a forward movement had been determined on, which would take place at the proper time.

The *New York World,* in speaking of the great naval expedition, says it is manifestly not the intention of the Lincoln government to attempt the capture as yet of any large Southern seaport. It thinks that New Orleans, Mobile, or Savannah could be taken without any great expenditure of blood, but the retention of all, or rather one of those cities, would be a much more serious matter. It also says that the lodgement on an island, or a series of islands, commanding important harbors, with a view to future operations, is manifestly the object of the expedition.

One of General Cheatham's staff reports an engagement on Monday last beyond Mayfield between Bowen's, Benham's, and Martin's regiments and two thousand Lincolnites. The latter were routed and pursued to Paducah. No particulars are given. The Confederates are in position beyond Paducah.

LATEST NORTHERN NEWS—
LATE EUROPEAN INTELLIGENCE

Richmond, 14th—The *Norfolk Day Book* of this morning publishes a summary of the news in the *New York Herald,* of the 12th instant.

The following is a dispatch from Rolla, Missouri, of the 11th instant: "All the sick and wounded at Springfield have been sent to St. Louis. General Price has fallen back, moving south, evidently with a view to lead and not to fight the Lincolnites."

The general opinion is that St. Louis will soon be in the hands of the Confederate forces now at Columbus, Kentucky.

Advices from Fortress Monroe to the 10th instant state that the steamer *Spaulding* had arrived from Hatteras with the 12th Indiana Regiment. The officers say it is almost impossible to remain any longer at Hatteras Inlet. The regiment suffered severe privations. Colonel Hawkins's New York regiment goes to Hatteras on the *Spaulding*'s return. About a hundred of the regiment were sick.

A party of Confederates numbering about six hundred attacked the town of Guyandotte, Cabell County, western Virginia, on the 11th. They killed and took prisoner about one hundred; then burned the town and retired with a trifling loss.

The Richmond Convention barely had a quorum today at the time of adjournment. Nothing new from the camps, but exciting times looked for.

Dates from Liverpool to the 26th ultimo have been received.[60]

The Paris papers of the 25th say that England, France, and Spain have come to a complete understanding in reference to the Mexican expedition. The convention is to be signed in eight days.

Willmer and Smith's *Times* says the cotton market for this week has been much excited and was daily advancing.

60. ultimo: of or occurring in the previous month.

Liverpool Cotton Market—Sales for the week 145,800 bales. The market advanced ¾d on American, and 1d on the other grades.[61] The decrease for the week in the stock of American was 20,000. Fair Bowed 12⅜d; Mobile 12½d; New Orleans 12¾d; Middling Orleans 12d; Mobile 11⅞d; Uplands 11¾d. No American cotton was known to be at sea for Liverpool.

A quantity of East Indian cotton, supposed to be about 166,000 bales, was at sea, to arrive about the end of January.

Havre Cotton Market—Sales of the week 24,000 bales, at an advance of from 1 to 2 francs. Stock on hand 163,000 bales.

Liverpool Provision Market—Rice had advanced 2 shillings.

London Money Market—Consols are quoted at 93@93¼ for money.[62]

NORTH

BOSTON EVENING TRANSCRIPT
November 16, 1861

THE GRAND CAMPAIGN

The navy will undoubtedly follow up the work so gloriously begun by Commodore Du Pont, by attacks upon other places open to assault, while the army is to bear down upon the Rebels at all points where they are collected in force. Du Pont will soon occupy Fernandina, Florida, or the other end of the railroad on the Gulf of Mexico. Our ships will then probably open upon Pensacola. A second fleet will go to New Orleans, which must be before long in our possession. We shall thus have a complete line of military posts all around the coast side of rebellion. The western army will assail the Rebels on the Mississippi wherever they can be reached, while Tennessee, rising in the rear of Zollicoffer, opens the passes of the mountains to the Kentucky divisions, which will thence be able to advance their columns into Georgia.[63] A simultaneous movement from Fortress Monroe upon Norfolk and from Port Royal upon Charleston and Savannah will give the Rebels rather more than they can do, and show them that they have only compassed their own destruction in endeavoring to destroy the United States government.[64]

61. d: an abbreviation of the Latin *denarius,* meaning "pence" or "penny."

62. consols: a type of bond issued by the British government. 93@93¼: shorthand for "between 93 and 93¼."

63. Confederate General Felix Zollicoffer. On January 19, 1862, he was killed by Federal troops at Logan Cross Roads, Kentucky. Middletown, Tennessee, was renamed Zollicoffer in his honor; after the war, it reverted to its former name, and is, today, Bluff City.

64. Port Royal, South Carolina.

The reinforcements to be sent to General Sherman number fifteen thousand troops. Accounts from Washington state that these regiments will be on board ship before sunrise tomorrow. The Navy and War departments are surprised at the small number of soldiers found at Beaufort and Port Royal by the expedition.[65] As the Rebels know its destination and had direct railway communication with Charleston and Savannah, the fact that no more troops were sent to the forts to resist our fleet leads to the inference that the fighting population has been drained for service in Virginia. This circumstance gives us an immense advantage when other expeditions are precipitated upon difficult points on the Southern coast.

During the past week, the advices from all quarters have been of the most cheering nature and afford convincing proof of the strength of the government, now that it is fully roused to an apprehension of its duties and evinces a determination to omit no effort for the complete restoration of the Federal authority over the entire Union.

REVEREND H. W. BELLOWS AND THE SANITARY COMMISSION[66]

We have received a printed copy of the discourse delivered in New York, on the day of the National Fast, by the Reverend Dr. Bellows. It is entitled "The Valley of Decision." The sermon is worthy of being selected from other sermons relating to the same occasion, because its author is preeminent among the clergymen of the country for the practical part he has taken in the contest now raging. As the organizer, as the head and heart of the Sanitary Commission, he holds position to which no other clergyman can lay claim. When the history of the war is written, we feel confident that he will have an honorable precedence among those thoroughly practical Christians who were foremost in devoting themselves to the cause of their country.

He has not, like the perjured and renegade bishop of Louisiana, become a leader of armed men. To all the laurels which Bishop Major General Polk may attain he lays no claim. He has simply thrown himself into the service of his country in a way which no Christian of any church or sect can contemplate with any other feelings than those of delight and admiration. Impelled by a holy instinct of benevolence, he has succeeded in interesting in his scheme the skill of the most advanced med-

65. Beaufort, South Carolina; not to be confused with Beaufort, North Carolina.

66. The Sanitary Commission was organized to assist with the care of sick and wounded Union soldiers and their families. Involving as many as seven thousand local aid societies, it was headed by medical professionals and prominent business and civic leaders and funded by donations.

ical science. The health of our army on the Potomac is, under God, due in a great degree to the ceaseless exertions of Henry W. Bellows.

The opinions of such a man are entitled to great respect. He does not announce abstract propositions independent of facts, but builds his practical argument on a foundation of facts which he has himself explored. He has earned the right to have his opinions fairly considered by all parties, and we therefore commend his sermon to the charitable construction of every patriot and Christian in the land. He is more conservative and constitutional than most of his brethren, but then, it should be remembered that he has done more than any of them for the cause to which they all are pledged.

NEW YORK TRIBUNE
November 16, 1861

TRAITORS' EXCUSES FOR DEFEAT

The fertile ingenuity in falsehood which the Rebels have displayed from the outset of the present struggle receives a fresh illustration in their variegated excuses for their Port Royal discomfiture. Their pretenses that they inflicted serious damage on our fleet—that their guns were dismounted by their own recoil—that they beat off the Union fleet on the occasion of its first attacks, etc.—are utterly disproved by the facts. They had been for months preparing for this encounter and had erected and finished two first-rate forts, which they had mounted with new, heavy, and excellent guns. They had ample and official notice of the coming of the expedition and had all South Carolina and Georgia to draw upon for troops, Charleston and Savannah being each within three to five hours' steam, with abundance of navigable inlets behind the islands, and a railroad a few miles inland. They met with no disaster, such as the explosion of a magazine, but were simply and throughly shelled out of all their forts and chased out of reach, leaving everything behind but their clothes and making the very best Bull Run time until they had rushed aboard their boats and put on all steam for their distant hiding places. Never were men more thoroughly whipped, and their acts confess what their words belie.

[UNTITLED]

The *Independent,* with reference to its recent remarkable paragraph affecting Messrs. Seward and Weed, says:

> If our memory serves us, the insane cry "On to Richmond," which appeared in the *Tribune,* not once, by accident or through an irresponsible officiousness, but day after day, and week after week, was at length disclaimed by the editor as never having had his sanction.

The *Independent* does utterly and grievously mistake, as we trust both it and the *Express* (which has eagerly reprinted the above) will inform their respective readers by copying this paragraph. The exhortation "Forward to Richmond!" expressed what was, is, and ever will be an intense conviction of the responsible editor of the *Tribune.* He believes that a well-appointed army of one hundred thousand men should have been collected at Washington or Fortress Monroe so early as the 1st of June and sent "Forward to Richmond" by the most practicable route. He believes that thus the back of the rebellion might have been broken and the border states restored to the Union before the Fourth of July last. He believes that refusing volunteer regiments whose services were eagerly urged upon the government, rejecting every proffer of cavalry, with the simple remark that the government didn't want cavalry, giving the traitors time to organize, fortify, collect arms, munitions, provisions, etc., until the term of our three months' men had all but expired—they, meantime, loafing about Washington, undrilled, unbrigaded, unexercised in army movements, unacquainted with the generals who were to lead them against the enemy, but squandering their energies and means in drunkenness and debauchery—were crimes, whereof the country has reaped the bitter fruits at Bull Run and elsewhere. The editor of the *Tribune* never doubted, and never intimated a doubt, that "Forward to Richmond" was the dictate of the truest wisdom, the noblest patriotism, and the tenderest humanity and that the only mistake was in making it so late and in such slender force, and in not taking care that Patterson's column should fully and promptly cooperate in it.

It is quite true that the particular phrase "Forward to Richmond" was not inserted in these columns by the responsible editor and that its frequent iteration was, in his deliberate judgment, a mistake. It was unwise for the *Tribune,* because it enabled the false-hearted and halfhearted to say, when a blundering, pointless, unconcerted movement had been made neither in time nor in force such as we desired, that that movement had been impelled and constrained by the *Tribune;* and thus a disaster, invited by the treachery of some and the cowardice, incapacity, or indisposition to act of others, was most falsely charged to our account.

But the patriotic zeal of our associate which impelled a repetition in these columns of the cry "Forward to Richmond" counseled no movement which was not in strict accordance with the emphatic judgment of the responsible editor.

DECEMBER 21, 1861

SOUTH

RICHMOND DAILY DISPATCH
December 21, 1861

ARMY OF THE POTOMAC

Our Own Correspondent

Manassas, Virginia, December 17, 1861

Those who love to read Shakespeare will remember in *King Henry V* the grand expedition into France, and the plans formed by Bardolph, Nym, and Pistol, to better their condition. Each had his hopes and wishes and saw before him the ambition of a lifetime almost as surely realized as if France were indeed partitioned between the three. But ancient Pistol exceeded them all in those qualities which indicate the shrewd man of business, for he chose the position which in all ages has been more profitable than any other—that of sutler to the army.[67] He saw in the future all his own wants supplied, and so much did the prospect soften his heart that he began to look out for the fortune of his friends. "Ah!" says he to Corporal Nym, "a noble shalt thou be"; and then, after promising him a bountiful supply of worldly goods, plenty to eat, and wine from his own cellar, he continues: "For I shall sutler be unto the camps, and profits will accrue; give me thy hand."

No person can fail to admire the sagacity of ancient Pistol, and especially those who have been for the past three months in the Army of the Potomac can realize fully the feelings which prompted him in his choice of the spoils of the expedition. Who wonders, after seeing the tradesmen of our army coining money day by day by a system of most unmitigated swindling, that the position is desirable to men who, like Pistol, are determined to make a fortune? One by one, for a long time back, small

67. sutler: an authorized civilian purveyor of food, beverages, and other items to the troops.

shanties have been erected in the vicinity of the junction, which, even before completion, have been filled with goods purchased at a low price, to be retailed to the soldiers at most exorbitant profits. Every one of these places has been crowded from morning until night with men anxious to purchase at any cost some of the luxuries of life they are accustomed to have at home. I have previously spoken of the meager stock contained in a majority of these shops, and need not repeat it; suffice it to say, none of them contained a first-class article of any kind, but yet the prices in every instance were prodigious. Two or three hundred dollars is enough to purchase a stock of goods upon which twelve hundred can be realized. I have heard one sutler boast that he had made one thousand dollars' clear profit in a single month, and another, who came here with nothing and purchased his stock on credit, that he had a large bank account after paying his debts. The proprietor of one of the smallest establishments here told a friend not long since that he had taken in fifteen hundred dollars since opening, and he might have added that he had taken one half that amount out of the pockets of soldiers fighting for their country at eleven dollars a month. Since the provost marshal has forbidden any more sutler shops in the place, large sums have been offered for partnership and interest in old establishments.[68] On Monday of this week, an order was issued by General Johnston closing every sutler shop in Manassas but two. This made a great scattering among the speculators, but a few yet remain here trying in some way to get a chance at the money of the volunteers. Some of these men are honest and fair in their dealings, and, I presume, it was on account of this that all the shops were not closed by a general order. Sitting at dinner in the Warrenton Hotel a few days since, I overheard a short conversation between two men, in which one of them boasted that he had now got the thing fixed to his satisfaction, and that he could not make less than one hundred dollars a day off his contract to supply bread to the army, and that he should be much disappointed if he did not clear two hundred a day. Who the speculator was I am unable to say, but it is right that attention should be called to such things in the beginning, for we all know that the corrupt system of speculating in the old government was the primal cause of its destruction. It was the conversation mentioned above that caused me to speak of army sutlers and speculators.

A few nights ago, while sitting in my tent enjoying a fragrant Havana, from which the smoke floated upward in blue wreaths, forming

68. provost marshal: the head of the military police in a camp or district.

the web and woof of many pleasant fancies, a small box was handed me upon which was the following note:

> Martinsburg, Virginia, 1861
>
> Bohemian:
>
> In your letter of November ———, you say "my candle admonishes me to draw my letter to a close." Knowing how disagreeable it is to have the candle go out while one is engaged in writing, and not having another near to replace it, I take the liberty of sending you a small box of homemade candles and hope they will answer every purpose.
>
> I have read all your letters with pleasure and, while in Centreville, endeavored to find out who you were, but failed. Woman's curiosity!

The candles were packed very nicely in a small box, and I am sure they will do me very good service. One of them illuminates the page upon which I am now writing. For some time past I have looked with envy upon the boxes containing so many nice things from home and friends that have been received in camp, and my sleep has been disturbed by dreams of smoking caps, dressing gowns, slippers, comforters, and all sorts of worsted things wrought by female hands. Now, however, I am as fortunate as anyone, for when I get envious and sad, I look at my little box of candles and think that someone is interested in me, or at least in the labor of my pen. My fair friend has ten thousand thanks for her splendid gift.

Some time ago a box containing a lot of clothing for the 1st Maryland Regiment was forwarded from Pittsboro, Chatham County, North Carolina. The ladies of that town have been very patriotic and have furnished the troops from their own vicinity with every necessary article of clothing. Their own people being provided for, the young ladies of Pittsboro responded to the call made in behalf of the Maryland boys, and at once forwarded them a large box of wearing apparel. The box was sent to Mr. Zimmerman, at Manassas, who delivered it to one of Colonel Stuart's men. Since that time, nothing has been heard from it, and the ladies fear it may have been mislaid. There is little doubt but the box was received by the regiment and that although there has been no formal acknowledgment of it, the Maryland boys have been benefited by the present from the kind ladies of Pittsboro.

The certainty that the army will winter somewhere in the vicinity of

Bull Run has caused quite an increase in the number of buildings in Manassas. Our friends of the Southern Express Company are erecting a new building which promises to be very convenient for their extensive business. The railroad company also is building a new freight depot, and several hospitals have been erected a short distance below the junction. Manassas now looks more like a town than ever before. Prominent among the new buildings is the telegraph office, a small wooden house about twenty feet square, containing two large rooms, a battery room, closet, and, above, a sleeping room for the operators. It is immediately opposite the depot and post office and in full view of the passengers as they arrive on the trains. In the room are four instruments connected with the wires running to Richmond, Lynchburg, Winchester, and Dumfries. Across one end is a counter to keep out loafers and a shelf for writing messages.

The second room is for private business and contains a few chairs and tables for the use of newspaper correspondents, as the office is a place of habitual resort to three or four special individuals who remain here. At present, I am sorry to say, the tables are vacant, as our best and readiest writers are on a trip to Richmond and are enjoying the hospitalities of that city. The plan of this new office is a good one, as it combines convenience with all the elegance that plain pine boards will furnish. The architect was Mr. J. T. Coldwell, the superintendent of the line and of the field corps, and it was built under his direction. Quite a novelty here is the new sign, black letter on a white ground, looking, in comparison with others in the city, so very gay that it is positively gorgeous. The chief operator here is Mr. C. C. Clark, assisted by Mr. C. M. Barnes, for some time connected with this office. The change from the old car so long used as the telegraph office is quite an improvement.

Preparations are being made as rapidly as possible to put the army into winter quarters. Yesterday the Louisiana brigade moved this side of Bull Run.

Bohemian

CHARLESTON DAILY COURIER
December 21, 1861

THE FIRST YEAR OF SECESSION

Friday, 20th instant, was the first anniversary of secession—the Ordinance of South Carolina, the first on the seceding list of states, having been passed in St. Andrew's Hall and afterward ratified and published in the Institute Hall, on the 20th of December, 1860. The day was honored in good form and with respectful memory.

The Confederate and state flags floated over the customhouse, the Old Exchange—which connects Charleston of this day with the Charleston of colonial history and with the names and services of Laurens, Gadsden, Pinckney, and their compeers of 1776.

The Charleston Hotel, Mills House, and other places gave also to the breeze flags which had been exhibited during the memorable epoch of December 1860.

The merchants' flagstaff, at the west end of Hayne Street, showed the flag which was unfurled to prove that the merchants of Charleston have not forgotten the example and teachings of Henry Laurens, the patriot merchant and imprisoned diplomatist of the revolution. The "secession" gun, which has been the special charge of a committee of gentlemen since it was planted at the north of the exchange, was fired, and other demonstrations of respect and memory were generally and heartily exhibited.

Citizens conversant with our history recalled and mentioned the fact that South Carolina achieved, in 1719, the first revolution on American soil for the vindication and assertion of a great principle of constitutional government, that South Carolina in 1776 was the first of the American colonies to declare independence, and that South Carolina is the only state whose secession takes date in 1860.

A noble sisterhood of states has rallied to the sacred cause, and several of them have been enabled, and are now ready and able and willing, to do more in means and men and efforts and sacrifices than the leading state.

The question was proposed to many citizens by friends meeting on this anniversary day, "Do you regret the action of this day?" and the answer was in almost all cases an emphatic and decided "No." In other cases the answer was—"I do regret that South Carolina had not seceded earlier and that other states had not gone with or soon after her."

Secession has been tried for one eventful year, and the dawn of approaching success now brightens the horizon, beclouded as it is with the smoke of disaster and conflagration. We look around and see a portion of our beloved city in ruins, but we see also much left, and we see cheerful faces beaming forth unchanged and unchangeable resolution.

We thank God for what has been spared and what we have enjoyed, and we thank Him no less devoutly for the lessons of His apparently afflictive dispensations. We take courage and "go forth to meet the future."

THE YANKEE STONE FLEET OFF CHARLESTON

On Thursday last, Federal vessels kept arriving off this harbor during the entire day, and on Friday morning not less than twenty-three of all classes were in sight. As well as could be noticed with a spyglass from a distance of three or four miles, there were some four gunboats, one large steamer which looked like a frigate, and the balance appeared to be mostly sailing vessels. One of their steamers was stationed to the northeast of the bar, near the Rattlesnake Shoal, and the remainder of their fleet was near the old ship bar. During Thursday night and Friday morning, with the weather calm, the sea smooth, and a moonlit night, they succeeded in sinking some seven hulks, consisting of two ships and five barks.

This is the first step in the Lincoln program to try and permanently blockade this port. The hulks lay on their sides with a list aport, some of them having already been stripped of their canvas, and others had their sails flying loose. A small steamer of very light draft was seen moving actively about, and she was supposed to be the tug used to place the vessels in position previous to sinking. They had, it is thought, about fifteen old vessels to sink, of which, if placed in single file, and allowing the large amount of two hundred feet obstructing capacity to each vessel, the whole will blockade about three thousand feet.

The latest reports from the bar last evening say that the enemy had sunk fifteen vessels, and from appearances it is inferred that all their hulks which have been brought here up to this time have been made use of and that those now remaining outside are blockaders.

NORTH

BOSTON EVENING TRANSCRIPT
December 21, 1861

[UNTITLED]

The news from Missouri proves how loose is the organization of the Rebel army in that state and how easily its various portions are captured or defeated. The number of the killed and wounded in the late affair is ridiculously small, when we consider the tone of bravado and defiance which has characterized the proclamations of Jackson and Price and the resolution to "conquer or die," which, we were assured, the soldiers had taken. The truth seems to be that Price's men have been demoralized by being compelled to support themselves by pillage. Habits of pillage destroy the possibility of discipline among raw levies and prevent what perverted public spirit they originally possessed from taking the form of martial courage and self-devotion. To plunder the houses of Union men, to destroy crops, to burn railroad bridges, to cause the greatest possible misery among noncombatants, with the least possible risk to themselves —this has been the occupation of Price's ruffians. His army is essentially a mob and is losing courage as it relaxes more and more in discipline and becomes more and more depraved in character. The qualities which make efficient robbers and murderers are not those which make intrepid soldiers.

[UNTITLED]

The rebellion, unless it receives foreign assistance speedily, is in a fair way of obtaining that treatment which its heinousness deserves. General Sherman is pressing the South Carolina and Georgia traitors to the wall. Colonel Brown has just administered to Bragg's troops, at Pensacola, a rebuke of shot and shell, which the latter will long bear in remembrance. Another powerful expedition is nearly ready to sail from Annapolis, to increase the well-grounded fears of the defenders of the Southern Confederacy. In Missouri, General Pope's army has achieved a memorable success, the effect of which will be felt in the restoration of order in that state. General Buell's magnificent command of seventy-five thousand Indiana, Illinois, Ohio, and Kentucky troops is almost ready to strike a blow in Kentucky which shall free the home of Henry Clay from Rebel contamination and open an avenue through which relief may reach the gallant Unionists of Tennessee.[69] As we turn to survey the Potomac, General McCall's cheering victory on Thursday last is only the precursor of more brilliant triumphs by the youthful commander to whom the American people have entrusted the highest military power within their bestowal. The cordon of bayonets which is to subdue the conspiracy against the general government is rapidly encircling the area of armed opposition to Federal authority, and without outside interference it will soon be apparent that the traitors have only one recourse, and that is to submit to the beneficent rule they have so wantonly outraged.

69. Known as the "Great Pacificator," Henry Clay (1777–1852) had a long, distinguished career as congressman and senator and was the architect of the Missouri Compromise (1820) and the Compromise of 1850.

COTTON AND SLAVES

The *New York Commercial Advertiser,* referring to the amount of cotton obtained at Port Royal, and the conduct of the Negroes, remarks:

> The value of the cotton brought by the *Atlantic,* at New York, is about fifty thousand dollars. When the vessel left, others were loading and under sailing orders. The *Webster, Oriental, Matamoras,* and *Empire City* have been ordered home and will be here in a few days, some of them with cargoes of cotton. The officers of the *Atlantic* state that the Negroes are very fond of the exchange of masters—they like their "new masters," as they call the troops, better than the old ones. They bring into the camps, for a slight consideration, an endless variety of poultry and fresh meat, so that the gallant defenders of our flag on Southern soil are enjoying a continual series of thanksgiving dinners at a small expense. The Port Royal Negroes do not bear out the general idea of Negro laziness. They are very industrious and are willing to do all they can to gain the goodwill of their new employers and earn the wages given them for their labor. The soldiers are not employed in cotton picking, as their time is sufficiently occupied in arranging their camps and building fortifications.

REBEL AGENTS ARRESTED

Baltimore, 21st—The deputy provost marshal this morning overhauled the steamer *George Weems* as she was leaving for Patuxent River Landing, and arrested an Englishman named W. T. Wilson.

He had secreted in his clothing and in a bladder in his hat a quantity of morphine and quinine.

He also arrested a suspicious man named Hanua, of Chester County, Pennsylvania, formerly of California. Both are supposed to be Rebel agents.

General Dix holds them in custody. The steamer was permitted to proceed with a guard of troops.

DISTRESS IN THE SOUTH

The Fortress Monroe correspondent of the *Philadelphia Inquirer* transmits the annexed items:

> Rumors from passengers arriving here on the *Spaulding* give an idea that many of the inhabitants of Charleston are now in a

starving condition. Relief is going forward from all the Southern cities.

Great distress prevails throughout the South for want of the actual necessities of life. Everything like grain, potatoes, and meat has been taken for the army now in the field, and many families acknowledge that they are consuming their seed corn and wheat.

FROM PORT ROYAL

A letter from Port Royal says that an English overseer and his wife came in from an interior plantation to seek the protection of the Federal army.

They represented that a universal panic had seized the white inhabitants and that Negroes were running riot with their masters' property.

Everything conduced to establish the opinion that but a word of encouragement from our government was needed to plunge the whole state of South Carolina into the horrors of a servile insurrection.[70]

NEW YORK TRIBUNE
December 21, 1861

LATER FROM NEW ORLEANS
DEFEAT OF COMMODORE HOLLINS—HIS SHIP SUNK BY THE MASSACHUSETTS—DESTITUTION IN LOUISIANA—NOTHING TO FEED NEGROES UPON—SLAVE INSURRECTION IN MISSISSIPPI—DESTRUCTION OF THE QUITMAN ESTATE

From Our Special Correspondent
Port Royal, South Carolina
December 14, 1861, 10 P.M.

I have just been aboard the *Wabash*. I write this on the steamer *Spaulding,* to leave at daylight tomorrow. I suppose the *Connecticut* will carry the news of Hollins's defeat, and the sinking of his ship by the *Massachusetts,* and also the Pickens business; but I have had some conversation with an officer of the *Wabash,* who conversed with a deserter from the Confederate navy—an intelligent man. He says there is universal depression throughout the South and that the whole game is up. New Orleans is particularly despondent. The sugar planters are Union at heart,

70. servile insurrection: an insurrection by slaves.

and if we take New Orleans or Mobile, the cotton planters would all bring their cotton in for sale.

There is great destitution, and planters have nothing to feed their Negroes on.

There has been a great Negro insurrection in Mississippi, and an immense quantity of property destroyed—a hundred fifty thousand dollars on the Quitman estate alone.

THE TALK OF TREASON—BROWN OBFUSCATED

Brown, who plays at governing the ungovernable state of Georgia, is, we sadly suspect, an ass. Why do we suspect this? Because, in his inaugural, Brown says: "Sooner than submit, let the last man in the Confederacy die nobly at the point of the bayonet, and let our wives and children, and all the property we possess, perish together on one common funeral pile; and let the winds that pass over our graves and chant our funeral dirge tell to other generations, in other climes, that we lived free men and we died free men."

The folly of this fustian will be apparent to all who seriously calculate the chances that in case of the return of Georgia to her constitutional allegiance, Brown will commit suicide with a bayonet. Who believes that Brown will do it? If Brown had no legs, Brown might do it, though then it would remain an open question whether Mrs. Brown would consent to mount, with her little Browns, the "common funeral pile." Especially as Mr. Brown, with a bayonet through his vitals, would not be in a condition to enforce his igneous requests and compel Mrs. Governor Brown "to perish" with his other "property."

By the way, Brown, for a man bent upon such uncommon exit, shows a singular ignorance of suttee. Brown says, "Let the Union pass over our graves." Now we hope that Mrs. Brown will fully understand that if she does mount the "common funeral pile," she will be reduced to ashes; and though she may, in her condition of cinders, be preserved by her friends in an urn, yet if all her friends are also, according to the Brunonian plan, reduced to ashes, with the exception of George Brown, who will have a bayonet through his midriff, who, we should like to know, will bottle up the remains of Mrs. Brown and her pulverized progeny? And though the winds may be perfectly willing to pass over her relics and to chant the funeral dirge of the family, yet in their pulverized condition, the Browns may get mixed up with the "niggers"—who are also to be burned—so that the best-intentioned wind in the world will not be able to tell to other generations whether this particular dust was that of a "free man" or not. On the whole, we think that Mrs. Brown had better not burn, and we know that the little Browns will fully agree with us in this opinion, and if Brown himself could be persuaded to give up his notion of dying nobly at the point of the bayonet, it would be better for his family and perhaps for himself, if not for the state of Georgia. Still, if worse comes to worst, we hope that nobody will hold him.

The governor seems to take it for granted that if the arms of the Union prevail, it will be all up with the Browns. He sees ahead, in such an event, burdens, taxation, military despotism, standing armies, insolence, insult, bondage, degradation! No wonder that he is bent upon suicide (with a bayonet) and is determined to calcine his family. But does he not, after all, take too dark a view of the future of his beloved Georgia? To be sure, the Browns might commit felo-de-se—that, perhaps, is settled—but then the Smiths might not, and even the Joneses might be persuaded to live.[71] Personally, we should prefer to have them step out, and so no longer break our peace; but will they step out? Will funeral piles be erected all over Georgia? Will suicide (with a bayonet) and suttee become epidemical in that state?

"Were we disposed to yield," says Brown, "it is now too late to calculate the cost of submission." It being thus "too late," of course Brown falls, as we have seen, to calculating, and that, too, in rather a blue way. We beg of him to cheer up a little, for we do not really think this "Sorrows of Werther" style just the thing in a governor. The particular injuries upon which these Rebels are mounted we do not, to this day, know; nor do we expect to know until the governors and editors of the fugitive states suspend their general ejaculations and treat the world to a bill of particulars. Brown tells us of the aggravated cruelties which the general government, should it secure an opportunity, *will* commit; but Brown doesn't tell us what wrongs this same general government *has* committed. This puts the loyal states in a pretty predicament, for how can we plead to the indictment before hearing it read? We do not think it, at any rate, fair to try us not for what we have done but for what we may do. If it will be at all sedative to Governor Brown's nerves, and if he will promise not to kill himself (with a bayonet), we believe that upon the return of the state of Georgia to her legal political position, the president will so make easy the final settlement that Mrs. Brown and her children will not feel obliged to perish upon "one common funeral pile" with Brown's "property." In all seriousness, when one reflects upon

71. felo-de-se: Latin, "felon on oneself," meaning "suicide," suicide having been a felony in Great Britain.

the horror of this wicked war, the money it will cost, the morals it will debauch, the terror which it will inspire, and then read Brown's inaugural, so utterly flimsy and meaningless, one is tempted to ask why Providence did not inspire Brown with the idea of using that bayonet upon his person a great many years ago. And so much for Brown!

THE WAR FOR THE UNION

From Our Special Correspondent

Port Royal, South Carolina, December 14, 1861

The sanitary condition of the troops has assumed a special interest in connection with the proposed building of a temporary general hospital for the division. A disagreement as to its necessity, between the medical officers of the Expeditionary Corps and Surgeon General Finley, and the gravity of the question on which they are at issue make it most important that the facts should be known. The surgeon general considers a hospital unnecessary, because the climate is mild and the condition of the troops, on the whole, good. Reports to the same effect have gone North. A New York paper of November 29 is before me, in which it is said that the troops at Port Royal are all in good health and spirits. Similar statements, I understand, have been generally made and believed. Now for the facts.

Ninety-eight soldiers have died since the expedition left Annapolis, October 21; eighty-four since it landed at Port Royal, November 7. The whole number of sick from its arrival to the end of November, exclusive of the 8th Michigan, was 4,282. Of this number there remained at the end of that month 634 requiring hospital treatment. The 8th Michigan, not included in the above because its returns have been sent back for correction, has suffered more than any other regiment and would swell the total of sick to nearly five thousand. The returns for December are not made up. More than three hundred patients are now in hospital; a still-larger number requiring hospital treatment are left in quarters for want of hospital tents, and the sick list daily enlarges. A complete list of deaths, copied from the official record, is herewith sent.

The division was landed at Port Royal before the frost had destroyed the deadly growth of marsh and swamp, and malaria fell with its most fatal effect on the exhausted systems of soldiers who have been obliged to work in the water and to go to their tents at night wet, chilled, and tired, with no change of clothes or means of warmth. The influence of such hardships is shown by the fact that no officer has been attacked by any disease peculiar to the climate, in malignant form or with fatal result, the only explanation of which is their comparative freedom from exposure and the greater warmth and comfort of their quarters. The fatal diseases have been, with the exception of smallpox and typhoid fever, almost entirely those incident to the climate, and caused in this climate by overwork and exposure, especially in the water. These diseases are congestive and remittent fever, acute dysentery, and malarious pneumonia, all of the most malignant and dangerous type. Six cases of smallpox have resulted fatally, every one of which would have been saved by proper hospital accommodation. Eighteen cases are now in hospital, some of which will be fatal for the same reason. The sudden change of weather and fall in the temperature, December 3, was followed by instant increase in the number of deaths. That night three men were literally frozen to death—two cases of smallpox and one of congestive fever, all in a fair way of recovery, but unable to resist the cold, against which there was no protection. The almost equally sudden change of last Wednesday night brought with it great increase of suffering to all the sick, and two other men ill with the congestive fever, who would otherwise have recovered, were killed by the cold. I have for these statements the authority of one of the ablest surgeons attached to the division, who said to me that he would risk his professional reputation on the accuracy of the assertion. The sick suffer constantly from the cold, the nights being always chilly, and they suffer also from the deficiency of almost everything necessary for their comfort and rapid recovery.

A two-story building, about eighty feet by thirty, occupied by the Rebels as barracks, has been used as a temporary hospital since the landing. It is in every respect unfit for the purpose, unfurnished with medical supplies, without proper officers, and wanting even the most ordinary comforts and conveniences. The hospital is, in fact, destitute of everything that makes a hospital; has no bedding, no spoons, knives, forks, or dishes; no kitchen, not even a stove or a place for a stove, nor any protection whatever from the cold but its shattered walls and roof. Into this building, which has room for not more than 70 patients, from 150 to 200 are crowded, in berths piled one over the other, in a manner which makes it a pesthouse rather than a hospital. There are no medicines for this hospital. Medical supplies for the army are of two kinds—for general hospitals and for field service. In the latter are included only such as are wanted for regimental use while troops are in camp. The hospital system divides itself, accordingly, into regimental and general. The former are for mild cases. To the general hospital are sent all patients seriously ill or likely to recover slowly. The medicines supplied to regiments are therefore wholly inadequate to the necessities of a division, many kinds indispensable for general practice not being furnished at all, others only in very small quantities. For this division there were no general supplies whatever, and not even the usual regimental supply at the start. Fifteen regiments left Fortress Monroe with supplies for only ten. On the passage three regiments lost all their stores overboard, and most of the others lost a portion. But two lots out of the ten remain undistributed, and these two are immediately wanted. No medical officers but brigade and regimental surgeons having been attached to the expedition, the medical director, Dr. Cowper, has found it necessary to leave the sick in this temporary hospital to the care of their respective regimental surgeons; and whatever supplies, conveniences, and comforts they have had have been from the same sources. The patients for whom no room could be found have necessarily been cared for in the regimental hospital tents, where, however, they cannot have suffered more than in this wretchedly built, unfurnished, and comfortless barracks, which does hospital duty for fifteen thousand men.

In these circumstances—in a climate where diseases become fatal by exposure, and whose severity is continually greater for months to come, with nearly a hundred men already dead, who might have been saved if the means of care and comfort had existed, with a sick list steadily increasing in numbers and mortality, while suffering and deaths are both augmented by the want of proper protection, with no hospital deserving the name—on the recommendation of the medical director of the division, the order was issued by General Sherman for the immediate construction of a temporary general hospital. The building was designed for three hundred patients; will be 1,200 feet long, on three sides of a square, 31 feet wide, 14 feet high; and was planned in the most economical manner consistent with the comfort of the sick, attention to hygienic laws, and general fitness for its purpose. The estimate of three hundred was made for only two brigades, in the expectation that the third would soon go elsewhere. Its departure being still uncertain, and reinforcements having since arrived, the capacity of the building is likely to be insufficient. Requisitions had previously been made by the medical director for supplies, which should have been furnished when the expedition started, and of which, whether any hospital is built or not, there is urgent need. The neglect at the outset was not the fault of the Medical Department at Washington but of the medical officer who was originally detailed as medical director of the expedition but is not now connected with it. Officers for the hospital are indispensable to its organization and successful operation, and medical men of wider experience in the diseases of this climate than surgeons of Northern regiments can often have are especially needed. There is no bedding except a few blankets, not a bed sack, sheet, or pillowcase in the division, outside of the regimental supplies.

Plans for the building as above described were prepared by Captain Saxton, chief quartermaster, and orders for its immediate construction went to New York by the *Illinois,* December 11, the building to be shipped in parts, ready to be put together on arrival here. This information was communicated to Quartermaster General Meigs. An answer has been received from him, saying that he has conferred with the major general commanding and with Surgeon General Finley, who are of opinion that the climate does not require the erection of a building for hospital purposes. This opinion is given, although full accounts concerning the climate, its diseases, the suffering from cold, the want of every comfort, the increasing sickness of the troops and severity of the weather, and the almost total deficiency of hospital accommodations have been sent sometime since to the Medical Bureau at Washington. The decision of such questions is properly the office of the surgeon general, and relying on his opinion and that of General McClellan, Quartermaster General Meigs urges on Captain Saxton the necessity of economy by dispensing with the erection of unnecessary buildings. To anyone who has ever heard Captain Saxton's name, it is needless to say that his department has been conducted with rigid economy and scrupulous fidelity in all respects. In the plans for the hospital, all unnecessary expense has been avoided, but the necessity for the hospital itself was too plain to admit of hesitation. In a matter vital to the health of the division, an unwise economy is profligate extravagance, for the saving of money is the waste of life. It is not in such a direction that retrenchment is to be attempted. The letter of General Meigs did not countermand the orders that had been given, and the building must be more than half finished already. It does not seem probable that its transportation should be forbidden; it must be impossible after the publication of these facts. I am sure they will also do much to supply deficiencies in other respects and relieve suffering from other causes. I ask especially for this letter the attention of the Sanitary Commission. No statement is here made that is not made on the best authority. There is not one which can be contradicted or questioned. I have no comments to offer; the facts are too sorrowfully eloquent.

Port Royal, South Carolina, December 15, 1861

Sunday, for once, is comparatively quiet; at least there is a noticeable difference between this and all previous days. Less hurry and noise, less business of all kinds, disturbs the stillness of the morning, and there is an attempt at remembrance of the day by closing the post office and the more crowded express office beneath it and postponing at headquarters whatever can be put off till tomorrow. Services are held, I believe, in the various regimental camps, and the contrabands have a meeting which I wanted to attend but cannot find time.[72] Not more than 200 or 300 men are busy on the beach and wharf; the carpenters have struck work on the half-dozen buildings which are in all stages of unfinish; most of the Negroes are idle; and but for the debarkation of the troops that came yesterday on the *Ericsson,* there would not be much more noise and bluster than is common in New York on weekdays. The soft air from the sea scarcely ripples the water, and the warm sunlight streams into the open windows, out of which I can only half-enjoy the beauty of the perfect day.

Much the most important news in a military way is the final abandonment of the expedition hitherto expected to move south from this point, often postponed and always preparing. It was decided yesterday to give it up. In other words, so much of the Expeditionary Corps, as was originally destined for a point farther south, with its stores, transports, and accompanying naval force, is to remain at Port Royal and share in the operations which have this station for their base. The decision is a wise one—if an opinion on military matters is permissible. Experience has shown that the original plan was a mistake, and that a separate expedition can be fitted out from New York easier than here, until a sufficient permanent dock is built. Stores intended to be discharged here and those to remain aboard were mixed together in the same ships, and necessarily caused confusion and delay in unloading, not to speak of infinite distraction to quartermasters. Some vessels designed for the second expedition were heavily laden with freight for Port Royal; others, not intended to go, have more or less cargo that must be transshipped. The style in which the ordnance stores are stowed on board the *Ocean Express* has been before described.[73] There are other cases not much more creditable. Still, all these difficulties might have been overcome by energy and time. A more serious embarrassment was the disagreement between Commodore Du Pont and General Sherman as to the point of

72. contrabands: slaves who escaped into or entered Union lines.
73. ordnance: military supplies; also, cannon, artillery.

attack, and worst of all was the want of troops. The occupation of Beaufort, Tybee, Otter Island, and Seabrook required more troops than have yet been supplied by reinforcements, and to reduce the remaining force by sending off the regiments originally assigned for this service would have left the command without the means of doing the work that lay nearer to its hand. I believe circumstances to which I shall refer by and by have changed the plans and purposes of General Sherman to such an extent that more troops are wanted here than have heretofore been thought necessary. Beside this, the stores for the 2nd Division are needed onshore and cannot well be spared till the arrival of supplies from New York—a very uncertain period indeed. Lumber, nails, ordnance stores, tents, and many other things are wanted at once and, now that the long-pending question is settled, will be immediately landed. In fact, the whole division, half crippled by its necessities and the prospect of separation, is set on its feet again and begins to hope the winter will not pass idly away. We know that reinforcements are coming in considerable numbers, but there is work for all government will send, and more than we shall get. They are urgently and immediately needed; for what purpose this is not the place to state, but I have before said, and every man knows, that with the means of improving its advantages the value of this position cannot be overestimated. If General McClellan thinks the North is impatient for a movement, let him spare us a tenth of the troops he has concentrated under his eye at Washington and send them here with fighting orders, and he may continue to review and maneuver the rest at his leisure. The surprise and dismay of the South at the success of this movement are not confined to this vicinity. But there is no extremity of despair from which they may not recover in time, and here especially, "every inch of delay is a South Sea of" opportunity and possibility to them. Its effect upon our new troops I need not describe. They came here to fight and, so far as their work hitherto is concerned, might nearly as well have hired themselves out to dig a canal or build a railway embankment. Admitting the importance of fortifications and unloading ships, it may yet be asked why laborers were not sent before, or why some of this work was not given to contrabands, of whom any number might have been had. Nothing depresses the spirits and destroys the discipline of troops like fatigue duty—a remark as true of regulars as of volunteers. A portion of this work will be done in future by the two hundred laborers who arrived yesterday on the bark *Fanny Ealer*. This vessel was only three days on the passage from New York, while the *Magnolia,* which arrived at the same time, was twelve days.

The *Alabama,* Captain James, came in on Friday with an English ship, the *Admiral,* loaded with coal and salt, from Liverpool for Saint John, New Brunswick, ninety days out and captured trying to get into Savannah—not exactly the usual route from Liverpool to Saint John. The *Rhode Island,* which arrived on the 11th from New York via Fortress Monroe and Hatteras, overhauled near the latter place the British schooner *Phantom,* said to be from Antigua to New York. The captain of the schooner, like a true Briton, objected to being searched or having his papers endorsed, or, in fact, being in any way interfered with. When first hailed, he answered with emphasis that he was an Englishman, but complied with the order to back his sails and come on board the *Rhode Island* in a boat. Papers and schooner were looked at, suspected of irregularity, and the captain ordered to report to the *State of Georgia,* blockading Ocracoke Inlet—an outrage on British sovereignty of the seas which he resented so far as to remark that he supposed the next thing the United States would do is to annex England itself. The captain of the *Rhode Island* undauntedly assured him that he thought it very probable, sent him aboard the *Phantom,* and the *Phantom* to the inlet. The naval reconnaissance by Captain Rogers of the *Wabash,* in the *Seneca, Ottawa, Pembina,* and *Andrews,* had no very important result. The squadron went to Ossabaw Sound, next below Wassaw, and found it deserted like the rest of the coast.[74] No fortifications were discovered.

A few days ago I spoke of the arrangements for the embarkation of the troops that were sent to Beaufort as an illustration of the want of such attention to details as is indispensable to their comfort and health. Somebody ought to have taken care that the 5th Michigan—a regiment which has suffered more than any in health and left one hundred fifty men behind unfit for duty—did not lie on the beach all day and half the night, unprotected against the heat of the one and cold dew of the other. Today the *Ericsson* is landing her troops, which arrived yesterday afternoon from Fortress Monroe. It was high water about seven this morning. The wharf is now built out so far—though from its cobhouse construction and the nature of the sand, it has sunk a foot and a half on one side for nearly its whole length—that for two hours before and after high water, boats can discharge alongside without difficulty. If they had begun in good season, the whole regiment might have been landed before the tide had fallen. Instead of this, the debarkation commenced about noon, at nearly low water. The heavily laden boats could only

74. Ossabaw Sound, Georgia.

approach within fifty or a hundred yards of the beach, and as some of them carefully selected the shallowest water, the distance was often greater, through which the soldiers waded ashore, part of the way up to their waists in water, and sometimes getting an unexpected plunge into a hole. As the day is warm and the water not very cold, the men enjoy it well enough for the time; but when night comes on, and the air grows chilly, and clothes are wet, the fun will be considerably diminished. This is not a climate in which *unnecessary* exposure and risk can be afforded. If a wetting is a trifling affair in itself, it must be remembered that its consequences may be very serious, especially if no precautions are taken against its probable effects. Nobody who has seen a case of congestive fever brought on, perhaps by equally slight exposure, can think any caution excessive against such a danger.

Seabrook Landing, where a guard has been hitherto stationed to protect the wharf, is now occupied by a strong force. Until the dock is finished, the heavy stores will be unloaded at this point. Vessels can carry up twenty-four feet of water at high tide. The stores have to be brought six miles to camp over very heavy roads, but at present this is the best, and for some purposes the only, means of getting them where they are wanted. Seabrook is on the west side of the island and is approached by the channel which rejoices in the cheerful name of Skull Creek. Immediately after the arrival of the troops, and probably from an apprehension that a further advance was contemplated, the town of Bluffton was deserted. The news of this latest Southern hegira was brought, as almost all news is, by the contrabands; in this case, by two intelligent articles of property, who reported that the cotton in town and vicinity had been burned and the frightened inhabitants had fled to Hardeeville, the present rendezvous of the fugitive white population of the island, and of the new-levied militia—in other words, of those who have run away and those who will.

The number of contrabands is rapidly increasing. Including those at Beaufort and Otter Island, there cannot be less than a thousand good and true Union men who have responded to General Sherman's proclamation and claimed the protection of the flag. Was there anything in the terms of that proclamation which excluded from its appeal any complexion or color of fidelity? I have no copy and cannot say, but if there were, then so much the more credit to the Negroes who came without being asked and are faithfully serving the government which never particularly served them. But the proclamation was addressed to citizens of a rebellious state. Who ever questioned the loyalty of the Negroes or their readiness to fight and work under the Stars and Stripes? Yet, are not the Negroes a majority of the inhabitants of this rebellious state, and why is a state permitted to be rebellious when four hundred thousand of its citizens are loyal and only three hundred thousand, at most, are traitors? Or, to put the question a little closer: Why are a minority of traitors still aided and encouraged by the Federal government to control, imprison, and shoot the only men loyal to that government, which prefers to be striving to reduce traitors to submission and protect loyal citizens? Perhaps some reflection would not be wasted in the honest endeavor to answer that question, instead of giving hard names to those who honestly ask it.

A thousand men, whose fate seems to depend in a measure on the will of one, are for the present emancipated from the immediate operation of the laws of South Carolina. As these laws, however, are deemed to exist for some purposes even on conquered soil, possessing, perhaps, a suspended vitality, it must be considered in violation of their sovereignty that an effort is made to do what can be done meanwhile for the Negroes in camp. A school is to be immediately established, and a part of the three hundred who are in the charge of the superintendent at this point will begin their education as soon as any materials for the work can be procured. There are no books, and not even the simplest means of instruction for teaching the alphabet—a process with which few of the blacks of any age can dispense at the outset. The number who can read a little is very small—a fact not to be wondered at when the severe penalties of Carolina laws against teaching Negroes to read are remembered. In default of other resources, it has been recollected that in the schoolhouse at Beaufort—there known as a college—two or three blackboards are still remaining.

On these the alphabet can be chalked out and, with the help of reading and talking, a rude beginning made. There is no room yet to be had for the school. When the new hospital is finished, perhaps the barracks now used for that purpose can be had, or some other accommodation may be sooner furnished. General Sherman has given his consent to the plan. Captain Saxton, whose position as chief quartermaster makes his cooperation especially important, gives his sincere interest and best efforts in its behalf, and Mr. Lee, the superintendent, is actively engaged in the work. There will be no obstruction here, therefore, in the way of success. Beginning in the open air, without books and without regular teachers, with no other immediate object than the elementary instruction in letters and morals of the few Negroes who can be reached at first, I yet cannot help thinking that this attempt may be the basis of wider efforts and, I hope, of some general plan of education for the slaves whom this war *must* free—some, if not all. Something has been tried, I have heard, at Fortress Monroe, but I know nothing of the results or the present condition of the school, if there be one. Whatever it be, the position can hardly be so important as this. Monroe has never passed from Union control. Carolina, about a year ago, asserted her independence, and it is less than two months since her territory was reoccupied by Union power. She is the peculiar representative and champion of slavery and the fountain of rebellion. The district of Beaufort contained 32,000 slaves and 5,000 whites, a larger proportion of the former than any other county in the state. It is to Carolina what the state is to the South. This citadel of slavery is the spot selected, with singular felicity, for the first landing of what is called the invading force. An army large enough to hold, and soon to be large enough to extend, its conquests is established on this central point of the slavery-cursed soil. As it was the heart of the system, no blow can be struck here that is not felt at the extremities. The questions of emancipation, relation of the government to the institution, military necessities as affecting the slave, are here most forcefully presented, and require immediate answer of some sort. Furthermore, they are questions which will not wait the leisure of vacillating generals and ambitious politicians, but will presently, in default of other response, answer themselves in sufficiently decided terms. Meanwhile, if the influence of educational efforts upon the Negroes in the camp lines is great, their influence on those who are not yet freed, and also upon the general future policy involved by the progress of the war, will not be less. Let us accept our responsibilities, not evade them; and when the slave rallies under our flag, let us say to the world that we dare not only free but educate him—that into this heathen state, Christian civilization shall accompany our arms with equal step.

Teachers and books are wanted. No means exist to pay or support the one or supply the other. The means for the present may perhaps be expected from private liberality. The only teachers at first will be volunteers who have other regular duty. With the school fairly started, the help of those who come here for the purpose will be wanted, since the number of pupils and the corresponding increase of labor will require all the time of many persons. I have already heard of men anxious to come out. My hope is, however, that the obligation of the government to the slave will be recognized and discharged; that if no funds exist that can be drawn from, they may be immediately supplied, enough at first for temporary purposes. When the limits of the effort enlarge, let the means be increased by a general appropriation for this specific purpose, and that will be the best evidence of the desire of the government to manage and sustain the schools.

1862

TIMELINE

January 10: General Grant manages to conceal from the press a planned move along the Tennessee River, from Cairo, Illinois, to Fort Henry, Tennessee.

January 11: Corruption within the Union War Department forces Secretary of War Simon Cameron to resign; Edwin Stanton is appointed to the post. (The Confederacy will change its secretary of war four times.) Federal troops, under General Ambrose Burnside, set sail for North Carolina aboard a fleet of ninety ships and a month later capture Roanoke Island.

February 4: The Confederate House of Delegates debates—for the first but not the last time—whether free African Americans should serve in the army.

February 6: Grant is delayed, and Fort Henry is captured by a Union gunboat flotilla. The Confederates shift their forces to Fort Donelson on the Cumberland River in Tennessee.

February 12–16: Grant follows the Confederates to Fort Donelson. The battle ends when Confederate General Simon Buckner accepts "unconditional and immediate surrender." Grant is promoted. Confederate Generals John Floyd and Gideon Pillow, who abandoned Buckner, are roundly criticized.

February 21: Union forces approach Nashville, Tennessee; the Confederates destroy their own supplies and withdraw from the city.

February 26: The Federal government creates the first national paper currency, to supplement coinage and paper issued by state banks. In July, postage stamps will be authorized as small change.

March 7–8: The Federals are surprised by Confederate and Native American troops at Pea Ridge, Arkansas, in the largest Trans-Mississippi battle. The Confederates are forced to withdraw. Casualties: North, 1,384; South, 800.

March 8: The Confederate ironclad *Virginia* (formerly USS *Merrimac*) disables three Union warships at Hampton Roads, Virginia. The next morning the Union ironclad *Monitor,* just arrived from New York, engages the *Virginia* in the first significant naval battle between ironclads. During the three-hour duel neither vessel is able to inflict any significant damage. The *Monitor,* described as a "cheesebox on a raft," lends its name to a new class of ship.

March 11: McClellan is removed as general in chief and is now to command only the Army of the Potomac; Halleck is later given the senior position. A week after his demotion, McClellan launches the Peninsular campaign, with the aim of seizing Richmond.

March 14: Burnside captures New Bern, North Carolina.

April 5: McClellan is stalled at Yorktown, Virginia, for a month.

April 6–7: Battle of Shiloh, Tennessee. Confederate General Albert Johnston attacks Grant near Shiloh Church in the bloodiest engagement to date. The Federals lose 13,047 men, with 1,754 killed; Union General Benjamin Prentiss and 2,200 men are captured after a six-hour standoff in an area dubbed the "Hornets' Nest." The Confederates lose 10,694 men, with 1,723 killed, including Johnston, and withdraw to the railroad center of Corinth, Mississippi, the scene of several future actions.

April 11: The Federals capture Fort Pulaski, Georgia.

April 16: The Confederates authorize a draft of white males between the ages of eighteen and thirty-five.

April 25: The Union navy, under Admiral David Farragut, captures New Orleans. Troops under General Benjamin Butler are dispatched to occupy the city; Butler's draconian rule will earn him the nickname "Beast" from the Southern press.

May 15: Federal gunboats shell Drewry's Bluff, eight miles from Richmond. In a panic, the Confederate government makes plans to defend the city.

May 31–June 1: Part of the Peninsular campaign, the Battle of Fair Oaks and Seven Pines (Virginia) ends as a draw, each side numbering about 40,000. Casualties: North, 5,031; South, 6,134. Robert E. Lee is appointed commander of the Army of Northern Virginia.

June 6: The Federals capture Memphis, Tennessee.

June 12: General J.E.B. Stuart's Confederate cavalry makes a four-day detour around McClellan's forces.

June 25–July 1: The Seven Days' Battles, along the Chickahominy River (Virginia), ends McClellan's attempt to capture Richmond. Federals outnumber Confederates, 115,000 to 88,000, but are repulsed. Casualties: North, 15,849; South, 20,733.

July 15: The Confederate ram *Arkansas* moves downstream toward Vicksburg, wreaking havoc on the Mississippi River, but on August 6, with its engines compromised, is cornered and scuttled.

August: From Tennessee, Confederate General Braxton Bragg launches an invasion of Kentucky. Ultimately, he advances as far as Louisville, but is forced to withdraw from the state in October.

August 29–30: In the Second Battle of Bull Run (or Manassas), the Confederates prevail again. Richmond is saved; Washington appears vulnerable.

September 4: Lee takes advantage of Federal confusion and disorganization and begins moving across the Potomac River into Maryland.

September 5: The Confederate commerce raider *Alabama* claims its first Union ship. In the course of two years, it will sink, burn, or capture sixty-nine ships.

September 17: Battle of Antietam (or Sharpsburg), Maryland. Lee's forces concentrate at Sharpsburg, outnumbered two to one. This one day will become the bloodiest in U.S. history. Some twelve thousand Federals and fourteen thousand Confederates are killed, wounded, or missing in action. McClellan is the nominal victor, but because of his failure to pursue Lee, he will soon be removed from command and replaced by Ambrose Burnside.

September 22: Lincoln announces the Emancipation Proclamation, effective January 1, 1863.

September 27: The Confederates broaden the draft to include white males between thirty-five and forty-five.

October 8: In the only significant battle fought in Kentucky, General Don Carlos Buell's Federals best a retreating Bragg at Perryville.

October 25: Grant assumes command of the Department of the Tennessee and, a week later, begins the Vicksburg campaign. Securing Grant's reputation as a brilliant strategist, the campaign ends the following year, on July 4, 1863, in a resounding Union victory.

December 13: In the Battle of Fredericksburg (Virginia), Burnside is routed by Lee. Casualties: North, 12,700; South, 5,300.

December 31: Bragg, with thirty-eight thousand men, attacks forty-seven thousand Federals under General William Rosecrans, initiating the Battle of Stones River (or Murfreesboro), Tennessee.

JANUARY 18, 1862

SOUTH

RICHMOND DAILY DISPATCH
January 18, 1862

FROM NORFOLK

Our Own Correspondent

Norfolk, Virginia, January 15, 1862

"Do you call this money?"

Leaning over the counter, a puzzled volunteer was endeavoring to reckon up the change just paid out by the sleek-haired clerk. Before him lay a quantity of mutilated bills, ragged and dirty pieces of paper, bits of cardboard, printed checks, a few copper pennies, milk tickets, postage stamps, and other interesting specimens of the present outrageous "coin of the realm." Over and over again the puzzled volunteer essayed to count the pile of villainous currency, and over and over again he failed to find it satisfactory. It was too much for his rustic arithmetic: The problem was too difficult to solve upon only ten fingers. The bystanders laughed. The money was spread out upon a showcase, as young ladies lay cards upon a table in telling fortunes, and the soldier stood before it searchingly examining every piece. "Do you call this money?" he asked, taking up a small yellow parallelogram looking very like the brass card on the top of a sardine box. "Do you call this money?" holding up an advertisement of fine Havana cigars. "And this?"—a bill for fifteen cents, in which some weak-minded printer had gone raving mad in different kinds of type. *"Good for one shave"*—reading slowly—*"Dick, the barber*—do you call this money?" The sleek-haired clerk was puzzled also. "It'll pass all over town; indeed it will, sir." Once more the soldier scrutinized the ragged and incongruous pile and, grasping it in one hand, soliloquized: "So, this is money—money? Ha! I call it 'stuff.' Why, a man might hold his hand full and then have but thirty-seven and a half cents' money!"

A few days ago I spoke of the currency in the "days of '76." Allow me to recapitulate a little for the purpose of going more into detail. To carry on the revolution, colonial bills of credit were issued to the amount of $200 million. For six years this was almost the circulating medium of the country and was exclusively used in domestic trade. After a time, owing to the presence of the French army and trade with Spanish smugglers, specie became plentiful, and the colonial notes grew valueless and went out of circulation. Hundreds of private individuals and companies, especially in New England, issued notes upon their own responsibility, and these, too, became worthless. No one thought of redeeming them. The whole history of this Continental paper money is a history of an immense fraud, originating with Boston speculators, who patriotically shouted, "Down with the king," and clamored loudly for revolution and war. As soon as peace was declared, the paper issues entirely ceased to circulate—the specie was sent off to pay for foreign goods, and the importation being large, the country was soon drained of its gold and silver. Once more, the people began to cry out for want of change, and many of the states had recourse again to the same wretched expedient to supply themselves with money. This, after a short time, impoverished the merchant and embarrassed the planter by driving all the specie beyond his reach. A shinplaster would not be noticed when coin could be had, and every possible plan was resorted to, to keep it in circulation.[1] The state of Virginia tolerated a base practice of allowing people to cut dollars and smaller pieces of silver for the purpose of making change without recourse to paper note of small denominations. Georgia followed, and speculation soon became the rage. A piece of silver was cut into five parts, each part passing for a quarter, the owner making one by the operation. When there was no silver to speculate on, everybody went to making paper money again, until the country was completely

1. shinplaster: a privately issued paper currency.

flooded with vile shinplasters. The consequence was that when foreign trade was established, the states found themselves in an indescribable prostrate condition. Half the people were utterly ruined, only the bankers making money.

The same necessity for change exists now that existed eighty years ago; there is the same mania for speculation, which, if not checked by timely legislation, will be attended by the same results. Hundreds of corporations and even individuals, regardless of the law, are engaged in the pernicious business of issuing private money, not for public convenience, but that profit may accrue. Banking has become a rage. The notes of "Dick, the barber" circulate the same and lie in the same portemonnaie beside those of "Gunny Bags, the ship chandler." Norfolk is disgustingly full of these personal shinplasters. Men advertise their wares on a bit of paper, sign their names to it, and out it goes as good as "legal tender." We have boat money, bridge money, river money, road money, store money, and dry goods money. We have bills "good for one copy of the daily *Dispatch,*" "good for one cigar," good for this, that, and the other thing, of a market value equal the figure stamped upon the note. All people inquire about is the signature. A printed piece of paper with a name in the corner is good—and I really believe one could pass the label from a bottle of olive oil. Strangers coming here are apt to look with suspicion upon some of the issues that pass perfectly well, and oftentimes ask, like the puzzled volunteer mentioned above, "Do you call this money?" A week's residence, however, cures them of all scrupulous feeling.

The use of postage stamps is getting somewhat out of fashion, as they wear out with little handling. A short time ago the newsboys used them considerably and were accustomed to give as change stamps from which the gluten had departed, and so dirty that no one could tell whether the figure was intended for Jeff Davis or the eagle bird. It was out of the question to use them on a letter unless they were pinned on as the backwoodsman attached his stamp a few years ago.

When the new three-cent U.S. stamps were first put in circulation, a letter was dropped into one of our post offices that at the time attracted attention. It appeared to have been written with the greatest care; the envelope was nicely ruled, so that the address might be perfectly straight; it was sealed to a nicety and directed in a cramped but careful hand to a Miss in the country. Only one thing remained—a stamp! The writer was evidently a tyro in the art of paying postage, and his nice white envelope attested the fact. The stamp appeared to have been soaked, and the letter licked from one side to the other. In vain endeavors to make it stick, the stamp had been pressed here and there, leaving in each place a spot of dirt and gluten. The trial seemed to have been a severe one. But at last the tyro conquered and, running a pin through the letter, stamp, and all, wrote underneath, seemingly in a fit of desperation, "Paid, if the d——d thing sticks."

Moral: Beware how you use post office stamps for change.

The fact exists that the country is being rapidly flooded with shinplasters and worthless personal notes. How the pernicious evil can be stopped I leave wiser heads to determine. I have spoken of the matter as it exists—in a spirit of levity, maybe—but nevertheless have called attention to some patent truths. But joking aside, this is a matter that calls at least for an examination, not so much on account of its being a present outrage as on account of the evils it entails upon the future.

About the Burnside fleet.[2] Like "his illustrious predecessors" (intended for sarcasm, as Artemus Ward says), Burnside went to sea in a storm after allowing six weeks of lovely weather to escape him. Soon after the expedition sailed, a huge wind arose, and from that time to this, old Boreas has kept out his scouts in the shape of storm clouds, which scud rapidly across the sea. The ocean has been rough and turbulent. It must have been amusing to have seen the condition of these transports yesterday and day before and to have seen 8,000 to 10,000 soldiers paying their devoirs to Hatteras as the ship rounded the cape. Old seamen say the storm was very severe outside, and we have been piously hoping that every vessel may go to the bottom before it is over. If the expedition escapes the Scylla of the sea, it has a Charybdis of land to encounter. I believe its destination to be either Wilmington or to reinforce General Stevens on the Carolina coast, but something must be heard from it before this supposition reaches you.

In the local line there is little to relate. An incident or two, a furious storm, the promise of a hop at the "Huger Barracks," and a fair for the benefit of the 50th Virginia, which opens tonight, are about all, I believe.

The question of the collectorship is exciting some talk, especially as the Yankee prints are making a great handle of Mr. Garnett's advertisement. It is fortunate that the fault of an exposé does not rest on some honest and hardworking newspaper reporter, or a civil "Aunt Betty" or a

2. Union General Ambrose Burnside led a successful naval expedition, February–July 1862, against Confederate coastal installations in North Carolina, capturing Roanoke Island, New Bern, and Beaufort.

military "Grandmother" might issue an edict of excommunication against him. The true state of the case I believe to be this: An appointment was made here which, whether justly or not, gave rise to some complaint. After that, no person came forward to take the place. And why? Because the salary is only eight hundred dollars and a bond of forty thousand dollars is required. In these military times there are few persons who care to give such monstrous bonds for the paltry sum of eight hundred dollars a year.

Bohemian

CHARLESTON DAILY COURIER
January 18, 1862

LATEST NORTHERN INTELLIGENCE RESIGNATION OF CAMERON—THE BURNSIDE EXPEDITION—CHASE'S FINANCIAL EMBARRASSMENTS, ETC.

Richmond, 17th—The *Examiner*'s special Norfolk reporter sends the following items of intelligence, taken from the *New York Herald* of the 15th:

Cameron has resigned and, it is said, will go as minister to Russia. T. M. Staunton, of Pennsylvania, is named as Cameron's successor.

McClellan is again up attending to business.

It is rumored that Secretary Chase intends to resign to accept a seat in the Senate.

Colonel Kearney is dead.

The Yankees claim a victory at Prestonsburg over General Marshall. Colonel Garfield's report says: "Marshall was repulsed, his forces fleeing in great confusion and carrying off the dead and wounded. The Federals found twenty-seven dead on the field and took twenty-five prisoners. The Federal loss was two killed and twenty-five wounded."

Commodore Goldsborough left Fortress Monroe in the steamer *Spaulding,* with the 13th Massachusetts Regiment on board, bound, it was said, for Port Royal. Goldsborough commands the fleet and Burnside the land operations.

Thirteen vessels at Hampton Roads went to sea on Thursday. The steamship *Constitution,* with the Maine and Massachusetts regiments on board, arrived at Fortress Monroe on Thursday.

The United States House of Representatives has passed a bill abolishing the franking privilege.

The appropriations for the Yankee army for the year ending next June amount to nearly $450 million.

A board of bankers from the principal Northern cities met the Finance Committee of the Lincoln Congress at Secretary Chase's residence on Monday last, followed by no satisfactory result. After four hours' conference, Chase wound up by threatening the country with high taxes.

The bankers remained inexorable.

The Federal Senate, on Tuesday, passed a bill discharging all fugitive slaves jailed in the District of Columbia.

Nothing has been heard officially at Richmond of General Marshall's Prestonsburg fight.

Postmaster General Reagan has decided that postmasters ought to receive Confederate Treasury notes on deposit in payment of postage and that there can be no objection to making change for such notes in postage stamps when the parties will accept them.

The following appointments of brigadier generals have been confirmed: Henry Heth, of Virginia; Johnson K. Duncan, of Louisiana; S.A.M. Wood, of Alabama.

Ex-president John Tyler is very ill.

Nothing made public in Congress today.

THE COTTON CROP OF 1862

The cotton planters of Natchitoches Parish have, in public meeting, resolved that no planter, no matter what may be his force, should plant or raise more than five bales of cotton of five hundred pounds each in 1862 unless the blockade is raised before the 1st of March next.[3]

The following were appointed delegates to a state convention of cotton planters: Henry Hertzog, Jules Sompayrac, Joseph Henry, L. L. McLaurin.

SALE OF NEGROES

The *Alexandria* (Louisiana) *Democrat* of the 8th, speaking of the sale at auction of the property of Judge Ogden, says:

> The Negroes sold at enormous prices; several young lads brought $1,700. The mules, furniture, etc. all brought proportionate prices to the land and slaves. We must not forget to specify

3. Natchitoches Parish, Louisiana. Louisiana, once a possession of France, is divided into parishes instead of counties.

one special instance of a rare bargain. A venerable friend of ours purchased Jack, aged 157 years, and his wife, Patience, aged 116 years, for $480.

NORTH

BOSTON EVENING TRANSCRIPT
January 18, 1862

THE SINEWS OF WAR

From the *New York Evening Post*

We must ask the patience of our readers while we say a few words on a most important and pressing subject. The discussion of financial questions is dry to most readers, but we will make ourselves as clear and be as little tedious as we can.

There is a large class of persons in this country who are always ready to favor any scheme for giving us a currency the value of which shall grow less and less. These are the speculating gentry—men whose brains are teeming with projects to make their own fortunes at the public expense. The present time seems to them a most favorable opportunity for accomplishing their object. The country has great need of means to carry on the war, and they make haste to suggest schemes which shall finally lead to the unlimited issue of notes representing no stable or fixed value—lying promises, made to be broken. The moment we reach that stage in our financial administration, the credit of the nation is annihilated; there can be no more loans; nothing can be done on the security of our future resources; the war in which we are engaged must suddenly stop, simply for want of means to carry it on; and we shall be forced to patch up an ignominious peace with the Rebels. Shameful as these consequences may be, they are certain.

We earnestly hope, therefore, that Congress will proceed with the utmost caution in deciding upon the plans of finance before it. Congress must not take counsel of ingenious and plausible projectors, who have only in view a large expansion of the credit system, by means of which they hope to pay large debts with but little money, or build towering fortunes for themselves. Neither is it quite safe to take the advice of capitalists already largely interested in the public securities, however experienced they may be, and however shrewd their judgment in regard to such subjects. They have a personal interest in the matter and may ingeniously seek to reconcile that interest with measures not the most likely to promote the public interest. What Congress wants is the judgment of men intelligent and experienced in the laws of trade governing the money market and yet entirely unembarrassed with any personal interest beyond that which every good citizen has in public measures. The counsels of such men are the only ones to which the legislative body can safely give heed.

For our part, we must confess that in our judgment, the haste shown to get out a new and large issue of Treasury notes payable on demand is a bad omen. There are other measures which should come before the issue of these notes. Taxation for the purpose of raising means to pay the interest of our national debt and provide for current expenses ought to be the first thing thought of by Congress. For this measure the nation is fully prepared; the same spirit which has filled our armies with volunteers and made every neighborhood in our country a voluntary association for contributing to the comfort of our soldiery will lead our people to submit to a direct tax with the utmost cheerfulness. We have said "submit"—the word is too weak for the meaning in our minds—they ask, they demand, they require to be taxed—they only stipulate that the money raised shall be honestly applied and that the war shall be energetically prosecuted to the complete putting down of the rebellion. Taxation is needed to secure for the Treasury bonds running for a long period a fair price in the market; taxation is needed to prevent the notes payable on demand from depreciating in value. Allow large issues of Treasury notes and postpone taxation, and by and by the unanimity in favor of taxation will no longer exist. Objections will be made and obstacles thrown in its way, and it may be found difficult to get a tax bill through the two houses of Congress.

Again: It will be a deplorable mistake to rely, as many seem disposed to, on the issue of demand notes or short bonds as our main resource for carrying on the war. Beyond what we can raise by taxation, we must rely principally on the sale of bonds which have some years to run, brought into market with a proper judgment as to the times and occasions after our plan of finance is matured, and disposed of at the best prices we can obtain. This should be done before we have recourse to any large issue of notes due on demand. The bonds will bring better prices if we keep that resource as a reserve. Suppose we first exhaust the issue of Treasury notes, pushing it to the utmost limit to which we can safely go, and then come into the market with our long bonds, as they are called. We shall come as a government in sore need, a government driven to extremity and with no other means of raising money at its command. The capitalists at home and abroad will take advantage of our necessities and will only give their own price. We must make a hasty bargain with them at such rates as they are pleased to offer.

If, on the other hand, we leave the resource of short loans, notes due on demand, and short bonds unexhausted, we shall have something to fall back upon; we shall be able more wisely to choose the occasions of bringing our long bonds into market.

This emission of Treasury notes for currency should be fortified in such a manner as to make the public satisfied that it represents a real and stable value. The government should be obliged to receive it for all payments to its agents; there should be a certain mode fixed for its redemption; and the holder should be allowed to convert it into public funds at a good rate of interest. If any other method can be hit upon to raise its credit with the people and induce them to receive it voluntarily, it should be adopted. The expedient of making it a legal tender, however, is the last thing that should be thought of. That is the rock upon which paper currencies have been wrecked again and again. Make its acceptance compulsory on the people, and it begins to depreciate the very day the order is given. Capital will slip away like quicksilver through a sieve; foreign capitalists will receive the measure as a notice to get their investments out of the country as soon as possible; and all the American stocks they possess, including those of the government, will be immediately in the market.

Nor can we see any wisdom in pledging the revenues of the government for any special part of the public debt. All parts of that debt have an equal right to be defrayed out of the public income. If the pledge be general, so as to cover all the obligations to pay money which the government has undertaken, it amounts to nothing; if it be partial, covering only specific issues, it is unjust, and a fraud upon the creditor whose claims are not included in it and must consequently suffer depreciation.

FRIENDS AMONG ENEMIES

It is gratifying to learn from time to time that the good conduct and patriotic purposes of the Northern troops dispel in a measure, as they become known, the bitter prejudices entertained toward them. The Massachusetts 13th, it would seem, have been honorably useful in this way and won respect for New England, where New England has been regarded with dislike, not to say hatred. There is some secession and not a little conditional Unionism in the portion of Maryland where they have been serving. But the intelligence of the corps and their gentlemanly deportment have made them almost welcome to many of the people as pleasant guests and trustworthy protectors.

We have seen, among other proofs of this, a poetical tribute to the regiment, breathing the warmest regard and the best of wishes. The young men thus eulogized by the representative of fair ladies must be proud of these praises from strangers, on their own account, and on account of the justice it renders to the patriotism of the Old Bay State. It is not necessary to disturb their modesty by publishing the kindly lines. It is enough for them to know that their services are appreciated, even in Maryland, and that they have done a good work in putting to rest the absurd error that Northern troops are either invaders or blackguards.

NEW YORK TRIBUNE
January 18, 1862

FROM CAIRO
THE GREAT "NASHVILLE EXPEDITION"—HOW THE REPORTS ORIGINATED—GATHERING OF THE JOURNALISTS—LIFE AT CAIRO—PROGRESS OF PREPARATIONS FOR ATTACKING COLUMBUS—LATE MEMPHIS PAPERS—A CINCINNATI PAPER "FRIENDLY TO THE SOUTH"

From Our Special Correspondent
Cairo, Illinois, January 13, 1862

The telegraph has been advising you these three days that 25,000 soldiers were on their way here from St. Louis and that a great expedition, 60,000 or 70,000 strong, was about starting from Cairo for offensive operations, with Nashville as its probable destination.

The report has excited intense interest throughout the West. The Cincinnati, St. Louis, and Chicago papers speak of the expedition as one of the most formidable movements of the war and, at our latest advices, were waiting with bated breath for further intelligence from it. Correspondents come flocking here by every train, until the "Bohemian Brigade" at Cairo already musters twenty strong and several of the leading journals of New York and the western cities have each two or three representatives here.[4]

But they find that the dispatches which brought them thither rest upon a very slight basis of truth. There are probably no troops whatever on their way from St. Louis to Cairo. There are certainly no 60,000, or 30,000, or 15,000 men about starting from Cairo for anywhere; and

4. Northern war correspondents called themselves, collectively, the "Bohemian Brigade."

as for an early attack upon Nashville from this point, why, one upon Keokuk, Iowa, is quite as probable, at present writing. The first dispatches as to the size and destination of the expedition were not written by the representatives of the press, but by an officer of General Grant's staff, and transmitted at his request, by order, it is understood, of General Halleck.

All the facts upon which they rest, as yet, are that seven thousand men have left Cairo and been transported by river to Fort Jefferson (not a fortification, but an old Indian post), on the Kentucky side of the Mississippi, seven miles below here, where they are now encamped, except two thousand who have advanced two miles to the eastward; and that six thousand left Paducah two days ago, destination unknown. For the last two days, it has been given out that General Grant (who commands here) was just about embarking, with his staff, to join the Fort Jefferson expedition and lead it—nobody knows where. Meanwhile the journalists, in their woolen shirts and other camp habiliments, with blankets and portfolios packed, have been waiting in a state of great expectancy, holding themselves in readiness to join the general and his staff at a moment's notice.

But the notice doesn't come, and they give vent to their indignation, if not their impatience, in maledictions upon Cairo, which is the dreariest, the muddiest, and the most unlovable town on the North American continent; and upon its only hotel, which, six stories in height, and crowded with unhappy guests, is certainly one of the noisiest, most confused, and most uncomfortable in the civilized world. Of course, the proprietors are "polite" and "gentlemanly"—as what landlords are not? —and anywhere else, probably, they could "keep a hotel"; but in Cairo all general rules fail. Its atmosphere seems to destroy the connection between cause and effect. You sit down to a palatable-looking meal and find the chicken ligneous, the beef spongy, the coffee bitter, and so on to the end of the list. You pull away at your bell cord for half an hour, in the delusive trust that it will produce a result. So it does, too, but the result is only the breaking of the cord or the loss of your temper. You commit your boots, with their two-inch coating of the free soil of Illinois, to the bootblack and even cross his palm with silver. You may not see either the boots or the servant again before you have broken the fourth commandment for two hours, but if so, you will be more happy than an unfortunate roommate of mine yesterday. He looked like an exemplary, decorous, father-of-a-family style of a citizen, as no doubt he is; but even Job, with all his trials, never stopped at a Cairo hotel.

But the expedition. When it is to go, where it is to go, or whether it is ever to go anywhere are mysteries which the journalistic vision fails to penetrate. It may go for a short distance into Kentucky; but the reports which have been sent abroad about it, and perhaps the affair itself, are evidently a feint. Perhaps they are designed to draw Rebel troops from Bowling Green—perhaps from southwest Missouri.

The great expedition down the Mississippi cannot start at present. The ten gunboats will all be ready for service in a few days, but the thirty-eight mortar rafts are by no means prepared, and there is no such concentration of troops here as the expedition will require.[5] The Rebels have eighty guns at Columbus and have added much to the great natural strength of that point. They have evidently determined to make their great stand there. If our forces succeed in taking Columbus, Memphis and New Orleans will fall of their own weight. This, of course, presupposes that the expedition will start sometime, though, in view of the general lethargy in the Union armies, loyal men here are not disposed to be sanguine. The inexplicable and apparently criminal neglect to throw a force into east Tennessee, which would have cut the Southern Confederacy into two parts and saved those loyal men of the mountains from being hunted down and hanged like malefactors, is very severely commented upon. The fresher news of the course of treatment which has compelled General Sigel to resign is also spoken of with a good deal of bitterness. As Sigel is the only general in our armies who ever commanded forty thousand men before the war broke out, and has shown himself one of our most able and efficient officers, this policy is perplexing to those who suppose that we are at war in earnest.

Memphis papers from the 2nd to the 10th, inclusive, have been received here. They do not contain much news of interest. A dispatch from Richmond states that W. H. Hulburt of New York, who has been for several months under arrest, has been set at liberty by order of Governor Letcher. An editorial in the *Memphis Appeal* reasserts that the Rebels will never give up the war until our government not only recognizes their independence but also gives them Kentucky and all the other slave states. They recognize the fact, you perceive, that slavery has something to do with the war. The *Memphis Avalanche* of the 2nd states that the *Cincinnati Enquirer* is regarded as "friendly to the South" and, since the suppression of the *Louisville Courier* by the Union authorities,

5. A mortar is a high-trajectory, short-barreled artillery piece that fires a fused "bomb" shell over enemy fortifications or at distant enemy targets. Heavier mortars were mounted on railcars or floating rafts. Mortars, classified by bore diameter, ranged from 4 to 13 inches; the largest could lob a 220-pound bomb more than 4,000 yards.

is largely taking the place of that journal among the Rebels of southern Kentucky. The *Enquirer,* you are aware, is just now engaged in its old cry of "abolitionist" at everybody who believes in conducting the war effectively, and was one of the most unscrupulous, persistent, and malignant leaders in the crusade against General Frémont. The traitors evidently know who their friends are.

FEBRUARY 15, 1862

SOUTH

RICHMOND DAILY DISPATCH
February 15, 1862

FROM THE SEACOAST
ACTIVITY OF YANKEES AT SAVANNAH—A SAWMILL—BOAT BUILDING—OUR PREPARATIONS—BATTLE FLAGS, ETC.

Our Own Correspondent

Savannah, Georgia, February 10, 1862

Misfortunes never come singly, but, like friends in the hour of prosperity, in troops. The reverses which have been reported in Kentucky have caused general gloom and regret; and today the telegraph reports the loss of Roanoke Island, with twenty-five hundred troops surrendered, to add to the foreboding admonitions of the wise and the never-ending requiem song sung by the croakers.[6] The rumors that find circulation in this city, from whatever source they originate, would appall an honest, guileless heart who could conceive and disseminate only truth. We have not received a Richmond mail for four days past and have begun to believe that the Yankees had obtained possession of the route; but the active efforts our foes have put forth lately no doubt have caused the occupation of all available transportation on the lines between here and the capital city of the South. I trust the Postal Department of the government can avail itself of that excuse and may have always so proper a rejoinder to any future complaints.

The Yankees are still actively engaged in our vicinity. Their gunboats are to be seen to the number of ten in Wall's Cut, with a steam dredging

6. Roanoke Island, North Carolina.

machine at work, striving to deepen the channel. Nothing has been done in some time to molest them at their work. But Fort Jackson is being rapidly strengthened and the other batteries finished, and so much has been effected that I have great hopes that in the event of their reaching the Savannah River, they will speedily wish themselves out of it.

I will here give you the various items of information gleaned from our advanced posts in regard to the movements and doings of the Federalists in this neighborhood. They have, with the energy of their Puritan progenitors, set up a steam sawmill and are working out large quantities of timber on Wassaw Island. They can obtain but little pine of any value on that island, and the oak will not need a steam saw to cut it up, as it is only the crooked arms which are available for the knees of ships and such work. It has been surmised that boats were being built; but it is probable they are about to erect huts for the shelter of the large force they have had on shipboard for some time, awaiting the most favorable moment to attack.

We are anxious to know how much longer General Sherman will wait for reinforcements and when they will come. In the meantime, we are prepared for the worst. All are on the qui vive, and our officers have been expecting daily an attack; but so far it has not been made.[7]

The enemy is as busy as possible, and we shall not look long in vain for their expected advance. They may resolve to push on now, when so many movements of their other columns have been made, with the effect to distract our energies and cause a mistrust of our own future success. This feeling, I am aware, finds little encouragement from the brave and resolute hearts which now are enlisted in our cause, and to which are entrusted the hopes of all their countrymen; but nevertheless, it weighs upon the hearts of the weak and despondent.

It is rather astonishing that though Savannah, a large and populous city, a wealthy community, in ordinary times a thriving port, and one which now gives much solicitude to our enemy, is in danger from a foe near enough to exchange signals with, and the sound of whose drums can frequently be distinguished from our lower batteries; yet we are apparently more anxious about the positions in Kentucky and Tennessee than our own. There is something wrong in all this; the people have gone to sleep and want to be roughly awakened by some calamity, to teach them the urgent, the absolute necessity of rousing all their energies to meet the onset of our enemy. They must be taught not to despise

7. qui vive: French, "(long) live who?" (originally a sentry's challenge), meaning "alert or watchful state."

their power or to decry their courage; it is the worst foe we now have, that overweening self-confidence in our own prowess and ability to match with strong arms and valiant hearts all the inequalities of the present struggle. It has lulled our people into a false security, and time, which has been well employed by our enemy in effecting a more thorough organization, has not found us improved in many respects. Should all the news be true that has this day reached us, the fall of Roanoke Island and surrender of so many of our best troops, it will prove a rough shake and awakening to our slumbering energies. If all our people gave their utmost attention to the foe at their own doors, I believe we would have fewer mishaps to chronicle, more energy would be infused into the conduct of our defense, and we should soon have the proud satisfaction, I am convinced, of witnessing the desertion of their fruitless attempt at subjugation.

A presentation of a battle flag took place a few days since at Camp Harkie, a few miles from the city, on which occasion I availed myself of the opportunity to go incognito to take my notes, though I have no fear that the subjects of them will at all object to seeing themselves in print. The banner, very tastefully wrought by fair hands, was presented by the artist in person, who accompanied it with a speech quite ornate and of the usual length of feminine epistles. The speech in response was also worthy of the theme. But I wish to jot down the most singular feature that I observed on the occasion, and that is the large number of the wives of both officers and men who had come from the up-country to follow their "better" halves in the fortunes of war. To them seem to have been delegated all the household duties of their new ménage, and apparently the inconveniences of camp life and the camp kitchen did not incommode or disturb the placidity of their dispositions. It was a novel sight, and peculiar to the countryfolk of upper Georgia to inaugurate so easy a transition from home to the comforts of camp. But I believe it was a progress in refinement, notwithstanding, and will tend to render all more anxious to advance in the new road to refinement.

The men are all, without exception, the denizens of the piny woods, and plain and unvarnished, even unhewn; but they are the right grit and will not let the Yankees see their coattails in any event.

A good move has been made here toward freeing the city from the numbers of disorderly, or rather drunken, soldiers who have frequented the streets. The city has been placed under the military government of General Walker, who has issued an order prohibiting the sale of any liquor to a soldier, under penalty of the store being closed and the liquor emptied into the street. It will produce great good and tend to remove the many complaints which are made of the disorderly soldiers found in our thoroughfares daily. Richmond is not the only place which needs the strong head and firm hand to carry out municipal improvement and correction, and you have received your wonted share of magisterial attention within the three months past.

Some cotton is being pressed, and some little change in the product has taken place just to that amount. Everything else quiet here. Markets pretty well supplied—even strawberries occasionally to be seen.

Mercury

CHARLESTON DAILY COURIER
February 15, 1862

FROM NEW ORLEANS
GLORIOUS NEWS—ARRIVAL OF 15,000 STAND OF ARMS—FURTHER FROM FORT DONELSON

New Orleans, 14th—The steamer *Victoria* ran the blockade of this port this morning. The blockading steamer fired two hundred shells at her, but she arrived safe with a cargo of fifteen thousand stand of arms, ammunition, and coffee.[8]

A private dispatch received from Nashville says a dispatch has been received here from Cave City, Johnson saying we had eighteen killed and fifteen wounded in the last fight. The enemy's loss in killed is estimated at from 400 to 500—General Pillow whipped them. The enemy's gunboats were materially damaged.

FROM RICHMOND
FURTHER DETAILS OF LATE NORTHERN AND EUROPEAN NEWS

Richmond, 13th—In the Lincoln Congress, on Tuesday last, Senator King of New York presented a petition in favor of the immediate passage of the Treasury Note Bill, pledging the merchants of New York to the support of the government.

A resolution has been adopted by the Northern Congress that that body will assemble in the House of Representatives on the 22nd of Feb-

8. Technically, a stand of arms is the full weapons kit of an infantryman: rifle, cartridge belt, ammunition box, and bayonet. Often the term referred to only the rifle and cartridge belt.

ruary, and that the president, Cabinet, foreign representatives, officers of the army and navy be invited, and that Washington's Farewell Address be read.

Senator Hale, of New Hampshire, said it would be better as a preliminary step to hang some of the public robbers and shoot some of the cowardly officers.

Mason and Slidell arrived at Southampton on the 29th.[9] The *Rinaldo* could not reach Halifax on account of the gale and proceeded to Bermuda. No public demonstration was made on the arrival of our ministers in England. They were received by the officers of the Confederate steamer *Nashville* and other gentlemen, in the presence of a large crowd that had assembled upon the dock.

The *Tuscarora* has left Southampton.

McCuffa, president of the Civil Tribunal at Rome, has been assassinated.

The stock of coffee at Rio on the 8th of January was 320,000 bags.

A dispatch from St. Louis, the 11th, says the Confederates are being rapidly reinforced and are confident that they can hold their position.

The French steam sloop of war *Gazand* arrived in Hampton Roads on the 10th instant. Commander Gautier and two of the officers arrived in Richmond today.

Napoleon, in a speech in the French Chambers, said the civil war which desolates the American country compromises the commercial interests of France; nevertheless, the rights of neutrals must be respected; and he must confine himself to the utterance of his wishes that the American dissensions should be terminated.

A Federal force took possession of Edenton yesterday morning. The inhabitants had nearly all left. It is reported that they proceeded up the Roanoke to Plymouth.

ARRIVAL OF THE REMAINS OF CAPTAIN WISE, LIEUTENANT SELDEN, AND CAPTAIN COLES

Richmond, 14th—The bodies of Captain O. Jennings Wise, Lieutenant William Selden, and Captain Coles arrived here this morning from Currituck, whence a boat with a flag of truce went to Roanoke Island.

9. On November 8, 1861, the Union warship *San Jacinto* intercepted the British ship *Trent,* and the Confederate commissioners James Mason and John Slidell, who were en route to London and Paris to plead for recognition of the Confederate States, were removed. Although this action was met with enthusiastic approval in the North, it was patently illegal and created an uproar in Great Britain. The commissioners, held in Boston, were released and allowed to continue their journey on January 1, 1862.

Captain Wise received three wounds in the body; Lieutenant Selden was struck down by a ball through the head. General Wise, when he saw the body of his son at Currituck, was much moved.

A portion of the enemy's fleet at the south end of Albemarle Canal shelled the Confederate troops stationed in that vicinity under General Wise.[10] Various conjectures continue to be made as to the movements of the enemy.

ARRIVAL OF FLAG OF TRUCE—THE REPORTED CASUALTIES AT ROANOKE ISLAND

Richmond, 14th—The flag of truce from Roanoke reports the Confederate casualties as 8 killed and 30 wounded. The Federal loss is reported to be 2 colonels, 35 other commissioned officers, and 175 privates killed and 400 wounded. The bodies of Captains Wise and Coles reached Richmond this evening.

LATEST FROM NORTH CAROLINA—DEPREDATIONS OF THE ENEMY—NORTHERN NEWS

Richmond, 14th—A letter from Suffolk today containing information from there states that late last evening the Federals reembarked at Edenton and went to some other point. The number of horses landed was overestimated. The Federals assured the citizens that they did not come to harass or rob. Notwithstanding this, while the officers were giving this assurance, the soldiers were filling their gunboats with cotton found on the wharf.

Elizabeth City has been partially deserted by the Federals.

The latest information from Winton reports that nothing further has been seen of the gunboats which started up the Chowan River from Edenton. It is thought they were perhaps only reconnoitering.

Dr. Cohen, a wealthy citizen of Elizabeth City, now at Suffolk with other refugees, says they remained at the former place until the enemy had possession. They were invited back and assured they would not be harmed, but our people were afraid to trust them.

The Reverend Shaddock Worrel, of Gatesville, had a cargo of corn captured in Albemarle Sound.

A Mr. Elliott saved seventy-nine thousand pounds of government pork, which was at Hertford. A large number of young ladies from Murfreesboro College have reached Suffolk.[11] The people of Murfreesboro

10. Albemarle Canal was part of the inland water route connecting Albemarle Sound, North Carolina, to Norfolk, Virginia.

11. Murfreesboro, North Carolina; not to be confused with Murfreesboro, Tennessee.

are apprehensive of an attack. Suffolk is crowded with North Carolina refugees. The next depredations of the enemy are expected at Plymouth and other towns on the Roanoke River.

The *New York Herald,* of the 13th instant, commenting on the European news, says certain parties in England have resolved to object to every measure taken by the government for the restoration of the Union.

The Paris correspondent of the *Herald* says that in French circles the opinion was almost universal that France and England would interfere in the American difficulties in less than a month. He says the ministers of the government, the people, and the government papers of France are all ready for intervention.

In the Northern Congress the Senate has passed a bill appropriating $7 million to the completion of various fortifications.

Cotton in New York is less active and commands 29@30 cents.

Bennett of the *Herald* crows lustily over the Federal victories in North Carolina and Tennessee and says the Rebel leader has no idea of holding Virginia, Kentucky, or Tennessee.[12]

The news of the capture of Roanoke Island was sent to Europe by the *New York Herald* on the steamer *Africa,* which sailed on the 12th.

The Lincoln Senate has inserted a clause in the Treasury Note Bill requiring the interest of bonds, which are to be sureties for the notes, to be paid in coin.

There is nothing of importance from any part of the Army of the Potomac.

A dispatch from Cincinnati says the Federal army in central Kentucky is in motion.

Intelligence from Cairo to the 12th says passengers report eleven transports, filled with troops, passed Paducah that day.

Leavenworth, Kansas, intelligence to the 11th states that there is great activity of preparations observable for Hunter's expedition.

Washington is wildly jubilant on the news from Burnside. Stanton is quite sick.[13] The Senate Naval Committee is considering a bill to reorganize the army. Two more bureaus are to be added.

12. James Bennett, publisher of the *New York Herald.*
13. Edwin Stanton, attorney general (1860–61) and secretary of war (1862–68).

NORTH

BOSTON EVENING TRANSCRIPT
February 15, 1862

FURTHER PROGRESS OF THE BURNSIDE EXPEDITION—GENERAL WISE'S MOVEMENTS—COMMODORE PORTER'S MORTAR FLEET EXPECTED AT NORFOLK—EDENTON OCCUPIED BY FEDERAL TROOPS—HERTFORD CAPTURED—THE DEFENSES OF RICHMOND

Fortress Monroe, Virginia, 14th—The propeller *Jersey Blue* arrived from Annapolis this morning with about two hundred fifty troops belonging to various regiments, who were sick and left behind when the Burnside expedition sailed. The *Jersey Blue* will proceed as soon as the weather moderates.

The *Stars and Stripes* is still here and will probably sail tomorrow afternoon with a large cargo of ammunition.

A flag of truce went out this morning and, returning, brought several passengers, mostly ladies, to go North.

We find the following in today's *Norfolk Day Book:* "A rumor reached this city yesterday by passengers from Suffolk that the enemy had taken possession of Edenton and also of Plymouth. Later in the day it was rumored that a couple of the enemy's vessels had proceeded on a reconnaissance as far as Colerain."

The *Norfolk Day Book* gives a sketch of the new flag adopted by the committee of the Confederate Congress on the subject. It is a blue union on a red field, and four stars in the form of a square are in the union.

The *Richmond Enquirer* says that four hundred prisoners of war are expected to leave Richmond for Newport News in a day or two, in exchange for an equal number of Confederates released by the Federal government, and who reached Norfolk on Monday.

The 11th Pennsylvania Cavalry Regiment, Colonel Spear commanding, went out on a scouting expedition to New Market Bridge today. Nothing was discovered by them.

The *Richmond Dispatch* of Friday has the following: "General Wise is near Currituck Courthouse and sent down a flag of truce to Roanoke Island on Thursday."

A Norfolk telegram says that it is believed that the mortar fleet is intended for this place.

Petersburg, Virginia, 18th—The editor of the *Express* has received a letter from Suffolk, dated Thursday, which says that Edenton and Hertford have been captured. Five gunboats moved slowly to the wharf at Edenton yesterday at nine o'clock and landed their troops. Very soon afterward fifteen more gunboats arrived. The citizens raised the white flag. Between 3,000 and 4,000 troops landed at Edenton. The population of Edenton is about two thousand and is distant from Suffolk about fifty miles.

In the afternoon two gunboats went up the Chowan River toward Winton and several others toward the mouth of the Roanoke.

A gentleman just arrived from Gatesville says that several hundred horses were landed at Edenton last night and also that a large number had been landed at Elizabeth City.

Hertford, the capital of Perquimans County, was taken by the Federals yesterday.

Captain Goodman of the North Carolina Rip Van Winkles, with fifty-two of his men and seven of the Wise Legion, have reached Suffolk.

Baltimore, 15th—A passenger from Old Point states that some workmen in the ironworks at Richmond, who came by the flag of truce, say that they left there for the want of work. So great was the scarcity of iron and coal that the works there were being suspended. Coal was enormously high. These men say there are few, if any, cannons left at Richmond, all having been sent away to other points. Very few of the defenses there have any cannons mounted.

NEW YORK TRIBUNE
February 15, 1862

THE LATEST WAR NEWS

The joy which the glorious news from the Burnside expedition caused throughout the city yesterday was greatly heightened by learning the smallness of the losses on our side. Forty-two killed and about one hundred forty wounded comprise our casualties. The full and able letter of our special correspondent, which we print this morning, contains a complete history of the affair and will be read with lively interest. It would be difficult to decide which to praise more warmly for intelligent bravery—the army or navy as represented at Roanoke Island. The vessels in action were served vigorously, and with great precision, against a land force and a hostile fleet. The troops, when opportunity was offered, went into the fight with a forgetfulness of self which was truly splendid. The charge of the Hawkins's Zouaves is spoken of as worthy to rank with similar exploits which have become historical. The whole affair, from the first steady advance toward the enemy's batteries, on Friday morning, to the taking of Edenton, on Wednesday, was indeed brilliant. Blow after blow was struck, the Rebels becoming more and more bewildered each hour, till a general and long-continued panic seized them and sent those of them who could escape flying into the interior, leaving their arms, equipment, and baggage along the road and carrying most exaggerated stories of their own losses. The Southern papers are now scolding right and left, laying the blame of the disaster on various shoulders. We have taken an island and two towns; have captured three thousand prisoners; have destroyed a hostile fleet; have sent panic and dismay through the Rebel country; have placed ourselves in a position to move with ease to even more important points; and have inspired our armies with courage, the whole loyal nation with hope and confidence.

From Missouri we have also good news. Price has once more declined to make his stand and has fled from Springfield. The Union troops now hold that town and are in pursuit of the retreating Rebels.

We have authentic information that the various columns of General Buell's great army are at last in motion upon the enemy. General Nelson's division, about fifteen thousand strong, crossed Green River, Kentucky, about eight miles east of Munfordville, on the 7th, 8th, and 9th instant, and was at latest advices on its march to Glasgow, Metcalfe County, over the turnpike from Bardstown to that point. General Mitchell's division, twelve thousand strong, marched from Bacon Creek to Munfordville, crossed over the bridge on the morning of the 10th, and advanced over the turnpike in the direction of Bowling Green. General McCook's division, sixteen thousand strong, encamped about Munfordville, had also marching orders on the 11th and has probably followed Mitchell's before this. The greater portion of General Buell's army is concentrating upon a line of operations only forty miles in width. In conjunction with General Grant's forces on the Tennessee and Cumberland, the advance of Buell's divisions upon Glasgow secures the flanking of the Rebels on both the right and left.[14] General Buell feels confident that in less than three weeks, the last Rebel will be driven out of Kentucky. On Tuesday last, information reached him that the center of the secession army is preparing to evacuate Bowling Green and fall back on Clarksville. This was expected by General Buell, as the dispersion of Zollicoffer's army and the planting of General Grant's division on

14. Cumberland River, Kentucky and Tennessee.

the banks of the Tennessee and Cumberland had rendered this position untenable. It is presumed at headquarters in Louisville that the Rebel forces will be distributed so as to defend the two railroads from southern Kentucky to Nashville. All the newly organized regiments in the western states have been ordered to Kentucky, and forty thousand additional troops will be in that state in less than ten days. Eight Ohio regiments left Cincinnati since the 7th instant, bound as stated. The reinforcements will mostly be used to strengthen General Grant and for operations against Columbus. Documents captured at Fort Henry revealed the fact that General Polk really has but about twelve thousand effective men, and these demoralized and restive. Altogether, we may expect a succession of stirring news from Kentucky during the next three weeks.

FORT DONELSON ATTACKED[15]

We are moving now in earnest! At a late hour last night, we received the exciting news, which will be found in another column, to the effect that the attack upon Fort Donelson was begun on Thursday and that a vigorous fight had been kept up through the day, at the close of which the fort in one part showed signs of weakness and the Rebels had gained not an inch of advantage.

On Wednesday, General Grant, his staff and bodyguard, the artillery, and the whole force of infantry left Fort Henry for Fort Donelson. This branch of the army numbered forty thousand. On the same day eleven regiments left Paducah, under convoy of gunboats, to go up the Cumberland, making in all an attacking force of over fifty thousand men.

On Thursday morning, this force invested the fort, almost entirely surrounding it. A heavy cannonading and skirmishing immediately commenced. The Rebel force within the fort was supposed to number fifteen thousand. They were cut off from all possibility of reinforcements. Generals Pillow, Floyd, Johnston, and Buckner were said to be with them—great booty for us to capture, if this be so. Early in the day only one gunboat was in the fight, but near noon all of them came into play. The *Carondelet* received a 10-inch ball through her hull, which wounded some men but did no material harm to the vessel.

During the day's fight, which was suspended at nightfall, our troops vied with each other in displays of valor. They charged up to within less than a hundred yards of the walls, and that, too, in face of a heavy

15. Established by the Confederates in 1861, Fort Donelson (Tennessee) guarded the Cumberland River and was captured by Union forces on February 16, 1862.

fire. The 25th Indiana Regiment is spoken of with particular commendation. The losses are not stated with any accuracy of detail, but the regiment just named had forty wounded; the 7th Illinois and 7th Iowa also suffered some losses, being well forward in the fight. It was thought that the left redoubt had given way, but this was not certain. The fort would be stormed after the second day's bombardment, if it did not then surrender.

Of course, the intelligence from this battle is not full, nor very explicit. Such as it is, however, it is authentic, and we look with confidence to have news within a few hours of the downfall of this Rebel stronghold and the final discomfiture of treason in that section of the country. The day is breaking!

MARCH 15, 1862

SOUTH

RICHMOND DAILY DISPATCH
March 15, 1862

DEATH OF BISHOP MEADE

The whole religious community of the South will be deeply grieved to learn of the death of the venerable Bishop Meade, of Virginia, which took place in this city yesterday morning. A Virginian of the olden time, descended from one of our most ancient families and united by close ties of consanguinity with others illustrious in Virginia's historic annals, he was as fine a specimen of the Virginia gentleman of the olden time and of, what is better and nobler, the conscientious Christian minister as we have ever seen. A man of more exemplary and almost austere virtue we never knew. A man of loftier moral and physical courage never led armies to victory. A more generous, humble, and self-sacrificing character is not recorded in the annals of our country. The signal and remarkable proof of this will at once recur to those who are acquainted with his private life. In the exalted sphere of a Christian bishop, he was unblamable, and in the character of a Christian, above suspicion. All religious denominations of the South held him in profound reverence and honor. Of the fifty years of his ministry it may be said with truth, "He has fought a good fight—he has kept the faith." His last ecclesiastical sermon was on Thursday of last week, when he assisted in the consecration of Reverend Dr. Wilmer to the episcopate of Alabama. He was then in such feeble health that he could with difficulty get through that portion of the services which fell to his lot. It was evident that while the consecrating hands of the presiding bishop of the Episcopal Church in this country were laid on the head of a new leader of the Christian host, the consecrating hands of the Angel of Death were descending upon his own white locks and preparing them to receive that crown of glory which is the reward of him who is faithful to the end.

THE GREAT WORK TO BE DONE

The Southern people have a great work before them, a work in which every man, woman, and child can cooperate—the achievement of their independence. In order to accomplish that result, the country must be divided into two classes—without respect to age, sex, or condition—the class who fight and the class who assist by their labor and self-denial those who are offering their lives for the cause. To prevent the grand desideratum of our independence, a result which will deprive the Yankees of what is dearer to them than life itself—the profits derived from the products of Southern industry—they have determined to put forth all their energies and resources to subjugate us, and to perpetuate the tributary relations of the South to the North, which have existed since the foundation of the old government.

To meet and to defeat the Yankees in the struggle for what is dearer to us than life itself, our liberty and independence, is the great work which the Southern people have to do. But to accomplish this grand consummation, we must show at least as much energy and self-denial as our enemies have in endeavoring to reduce us to subjugation. We must give ourselves to the great work, heart and hand and soul. We must relinquish everything in our daily life, and our daily habits, and our daily occupations, which will retard the grand object we have in view; and give ourselves up with entire and unreserved devotion to those objects and those occupations which will contribute to the main end of the revolution. All unnecessary pursuits, all idle extravagances, all luxurious indulgences, all follies and vanities, all untimely and festive entertainments and celebrations—all, all, must be discarded and abandoned. The horde of speculators and extortioners must be reduced in number and restricted in their operations by a combination of government measures and public opinion and policy. We must not buy a single article of any kind we can do without. The ladies, who have been our exemplars in patriotism, who have given their sons, brothers, and husbands to the battle, should make the smaller sacrifices, to the cause, of everything that ministers to display and luxurious living. They should eke out their wardrobes, deny themselves the fashions, and thus give us indubitable proof of their devotion to the cause of their country. They should refuse to encourage the speculators who are smuggling costly goods into the country to deprive it of the means which should support the cause, for the purpose of swelling their own individual gains. Except for the army, there is clothing enough in most families to last a year without further purchases. If the amount which is spent in finery and folly, in fashion and vanity, in a twelvemonth could be given to the cause, it would immensely strengthen the sinews of war and, perhaps, of itself accomplish the deliverance of the country.

Let industry and economy, then, be the universal watchword throughout the South. Let those who do not fight deny themselves for the cause, and work for the cause. Let us universally resolve not to buy anything, nor make anything, which is not indispensable for the use of the army or for those engaged in clothing and feeding it. Let those who are not engaged in fighting labor to clothe and feed those who are. Let the women of the South bring out the old spinning wheels and the old looms and set them to work. They were used in former days by the grand old matrons of the first War of Independence, and they will not derogate from the dignity of those who are engaged in the second. Let every farmhouse make enough clothes, and knit enough socks, to supply at least a corporal's guard. Let our men of practical sense, and genius, apply themselves to the production of saltpeter, ammunition, weapons, and to the improvement and multiplication of the means of defense.

Again we say, let the whole nation be divided into the army and into those who feed and clothe the army and furnish it with weapons and ammunition. In this way, everybody will help the common cause. It cannot be expected that all should fight, but the least that those who do not fight can do is to provide for and make efficient those who are in arms. The man who thinks of himself at this time is a public enemy. The man who is using the present troubles to fill his purse deserves as much to be put under arrest as anyone now in prison. The men and women who will neither fight nor deny themselves are traitors to their country. Maintained in a spirit of patriotic labor and generous self-sacrifice, the Southern cause must triumph. Thus, and thus only, can we gain our independence, our freedom from Yankee domination, our right to manage our affairs in our own way, and all the numberless blessings which follow in its train. For these great benedictions of a benign Providence we ought to be willing to make any sacrifices. Without them we must be a subjugated, degraded, ruined people. Once triumphant, we can turn our attention to our own little personal matters, with the gratifying assurance that a people who have first secured the safety of their country merit the blessings of individual happiness and prosperity.

EMBALMING

The Yankee nation is introducing the fashion of embalming its deceased notorieties, beginning with one of the sons of the American pharaoh, who lately died and whose body has been preserved by that process. The late General Lander has also been embalmed. They are also engaged in embalming the Union, which has long ago been defunct, but which they fancy they can restore by preserving the externals of life. In due course of time, we suppose, Lincoln, Seward, and the Cabinet and military chiefs will also be embalmed, if the world can produce aromatics enough to save such a mass of moral and physical corruption.

GUNBOATS

We have already chronicled the fact that the ladies of Mobile, Charleston, and other points in the Confederacy are contributing with liberality and enthusiasm to the fund for the construction of gunboats. We are glad to learn that the example has animated the men of Charleston to set afoot a movement for the speedy completion of an ironclad gunboat of the most formidable character, intended to put an end to the imperfect blockade of Charleston Harbor now maintained by the war vessels of the enemy. The success of the *Merrimac* has given a wonderful impetus to this very proper enterprise, which will undoubtedly be pushed forward with all possible dispatch.

CHARLESTON DAILY COURIER
March 15, 1862

FROM ATLANTA
ENGAGEMENT ON THE TENNESSEE RIVER—A GUNBOAT DISABLED—MARTIAL LAW IN MEMPHIS—PRESIDENT DAVIS EXPECTED IN THE WEST—MESSAGE OF GOVERNOR HARRIS

Atlanta, 14th—Passengers report an engagement at Chickasaw, on the Tennessee River, near Eastport, Mississippi. On Wednesday four Federal gunboats attempted to ascend the river, but were repulsed several times by the shore batteries of the Confederates. One gunboat is believed to have been disabled. None on our side were injured.

Memphis has been placed under martial law. All cotton, sugar, and molasses stored in the city, with the exception of enough for family supplies, have been ordered to be removed to the interior.

The *Memphis Appeal* publishes a dispatch from Richmond stating that President Davis is going west and urging all to rally to his standard.

The Tennessee legislature has succeeded in getting a quorum. Governor Harris presented his message. In reference to the surrender of Nashville, the governor says, "Immediately after hearing of the fall of Fort Donelson, I called upon General Johnston, to tender him all the resources of the state which could be made available, with my full cooperation in any and all measures to defend our state and capital.

"General Johnston informed me that under the circumstances which surrounded him, and with such small force under his command, he regarded it as his duty to the army he commanded, and the government he represented, to fall back with the army south of Nashville, making no defense of the city, and that he would do so immediately upon the arrival of the army from Bowling Green."

The governor urges the legislature to provide ways and means to sustain the troops and calls out the entire military power of the state to sustain the Confederacy.

NORTH

BOSTON EVENING TRANSCRIPT
March 15, 1862

THE NEW INDIAN WARFARE AND ITS HERO

A report of the recent glorious battle of Pea Ridge states that there were two thousand Indians in the fight upon the Rebel side and that eighteen of our men were scalped by them. It is some time since we have heard of the cruel Indian warfare within the United States, except in the case of the wild Comanches and Apaches of the frontier. But the history of the country is full of fireside legends of Indian massacre in New England, at the hearing of which the blood yet grows cold.

When men lived in garrisoned houses and went to their labor in the fields always accompanied by a loaded musket, and women retired at night clasping their children, in fear that, before morning, they might hear the yell of the savage and behold the deadly tomahawk and scalping knife, their houses in flames, and themselves, if living, in captivity—it was a time of fear, of which all but the remembrance has passed away. Since then have come the bloody forays upon the infant settlements of the West—there have been Tecumseh and Red Jacket and, last of all, the indomitable Billy Bowlegs of the Everglades of Florida. With him, people have supposed, all regular Indian warfare came to an end.

They were mistaken. Southwestern advices stated sometime since that Albert Pike was stirring up the Indians of the Plains to fight against the United States.[16] An example of the result of his efforts has come to the world through the battle of Pea Ridge. There were Mr. Pike's copper-colored allies, with their scalping knives, in all their original merciless ferocity. It is hard to believe that such a miscreant could have existence—as one who was willing to reopen the war of the savage, and that upon his own blood and upon his own countrymen. But renegades are always loathsome creatures, and it is not to be presumed that a more venomous reptile than Albert Pike ever crawled upon the face of the earth.

The meanest, the most rascally, the most malevolent of the Rebels who are at war with the United States government are said to be recreant Yankees. Albert Pike is one of these. He has been called Albert Pike of Newburyport, as he emigrated from that place, but he was born in Boston. His father was a journeyman shoemaker, but he never did his duty to the son, or he would have *strapped* him into a decent observance of the commands of God and the regards of man. There is no pit of infamy too deep for him to fill. An eminent French novelist once said of suchlike wretches—

The carrion crow, with croakings low,
Claims for his prey the renegade.

Certainly, the language has no term of reproach, the mind has no idea of contempt and detestation, which might not fairly be applied to Albert Pike and be exhausted in its application.

The subject is disagreeable. It is not pleasant to speak of the renegade or of his misdeeds. But this one will go down to "the vile dust from whence he sprung," with every mark of ignominy upon his head. His "poetry" will help preserve the record of his infamy.

16. Confederate General Albert Pike, a noted poet and writer, headed the Department of Indian Territory and, several months after the Battle of Pea Ridge (1862), resigned from the army over differences with Commanding General Thomas Hindman.

NEW YORK TRIBUNE
March 15, 1862

THE EVACUATION OF MANASSAS AND STORIES OF THE CONTRABANDS

From Another Correspondent
Headquarters of General Heintzelman,
Within Two Miles of Alexandria, Virginia
March 12, 1862, 8 A.M.

When I left Washington on the afternoon of the 10th, I expected nothing so little as to find myself two days afterward stranded in inaction. The city was all astir with excitement and expectation, its streets almost blockaded by slowly moving trains of artillery and departing soldiers. Horsemen spurred and splashed hither and thither through its muddy streets; its windows were thronged by spectators; its Long Bridge was a mere procession of troops and cannons, their faces and muzzles turned steadfastly and with animus toward Dixie.

Hurried off by the fever of the occasion, I quitted the capital under an aspect which I shall long remember, and which for excitement and interest could only have been paralleled by the morning of the disastrous day of Bull Run, anticipating a night ride of twenty or thirty miles in order to overtake the division reportorially assigned to me. I had been told that "Heintzelman's" was moving, and though I might have distrusted the assumed celerity in connection with such a body of men, I floundered and splashed down the dirty mile that lies between Pennsylvania Avenue and the Alexandria Ferry at good speed, arriving just in time to ship myself and horse for the disloyal side of the Potomac and to be, five minutes afterward, agreeably undeceived as to the necessity of such exertion by a friendly quartermaster.

ALEXANDRIA

Accordingly, I rode leisurely through that admirable sample of a third-rate Virginia city, Alexandria, which loves the Union no better at this hour than on the morning of Ellsworth's assassination, albeit it is now obliged to mutter its hate covertly, or, at most, like the superannuated ogre Pope in *Pilgrim's Progress,* to scowl in impotent defiance at the passersby.[17] Its streets were in their normal aspect of spring filth, in its

17. In Alexandria, Virginia, Colonel Elmer Ellsworth was shot by James Jackson, a hotelier, on May 24, 1861, for removing a Confederate flag from the roof of the latter's establishment. Jackson was then killed by a Union soldier. Both Ellsworth's and Jackson's deaths were denounced as murder by their respective side.

main thoroughfare a great gap of smoldering and smoking ruins indicated the past locality of a batch of its few really handsome stores, and around the provost's office there clustered a handful of idlers, desperately sympathetic in behalf of a dozen newly captured Rebels within. Making a slight detour to enjoy the spectacle of the ruined slave pen of which we have heard so much—where certain of Uncle Sam's blue-coated "Yankees" were gymnastically disporting themselves and laborers at work tearing down the building (may it prove symbolical of the result of the war!)—I gladly left decayed, dingy, and depressing Alexandria behind me and rode out into the wild country, turning my horse's head in the direction of Fort Lyon and "Heintzelman's."

THE COUNTRY UNDER MILITARY OCCUPATION

It was sunset, on a moist, dull March day, and a red glare on the western horizon lit up the landscape. Can the readers of the *Tribune* imagine the look of a country under military occupation? I will supply a few details.

In the first place, all the fences are gone—used up for firewood. Many of the farmhouses ditto—destroyed piecemeal, either for the building of shanties, barracks, or for fuel. Then, the crops—all indications of them have disappeared—there is no more "bourne filth and tillage" evident than in Gonzalo's imaginary kingdom in *The Tempest*. Trees, also, and brushwood are sparse and scanty, plenty of recently hewn stumps suggesting the past existence of the former. There is no vegetation, no grass, no very accurately designed roads, only earth, for the most part just emerging from its two months' condition of mud—all intersected, cut up, and crossed by innumerable tracks of men, horses, and vehicles. Suppose a country so hilly as almost to deserve the title of mountainous, with attendant declivities and ravines, a monstrous area of earthwork fortifications, still in progress, named Fort Lyon (after our Missouri hero) upon a breezy elevation, its cannons commanding the vicinity for five or six miles in every direction. Add hundreds of white tents most picturesquely situated on the summits and sides of the surrounding hills, and you have the general aspect of my present locality.

"HEINTZELMAN'S"

The headquarters from which I write is, or *was,* a pretentious Virginia house of the modern sort, built of wood, with a piazza in front, marble mantelpieces in the parlor, and unusually spacious rooms. Constructed for, and abandoned by, a Virginian of strong secession sympathies, named Bellenger (now resident in Alexandria), it, in common with much of the surrounding territory, has lapsed informally into the possession of our national Uncle, as represented by his loyal soldiers. They have sojourned here for something like twelve months, enduring both the summer's heat and the winter's cold and, worse than either, the abominable mud, rhapsodically designated the sacred soil of Virginia. Happily, under the blessed influences of sunlight and wind, it is fast disappearing. What it must have amounted to a month ago it is fearful to think of. Any number of mud Pythars, inclusive of the old original one addicted to turning up adjectively in the pages of Thomas Carlyle, could certainly have been comfortably accommodated within it.

The two front parlors of our "headquarters" are occupied as offices. That to the left is used by our general (who returned from Washington about an hour after my arrival in camp, with the assurance that we should hardly receive marching orders for a day or two). I write in the other, devoted to general official business. It stretches from front to rear; is accommodated with a stove, sundry desks, campstools, maps, and a telegraph apparatus, which furnishes a ticking accompaniment to all that is occurring. Out of doors the sun shines gloriously; the morning breeze blows fresh and free over the hilltops, fluttering our newly hoisted Star-Spangled Banner in front of the door and affording delicious greeting to the sun-browned cheeks within. A group of officers converse on the piazza, others are busy enough indoors, horses stand picketed around, sentries pace to and fro, soldiers come and go, and everything is as cheery as may be—and decidedly unlike an advance. We hear of movements on the part of other divisions, but suppose that the evacuation of Manassas and the falling back of the Rebels for sixty miles to ——— has effected a change in the plans of General McClellan, and incidentally in our disposition.

NEGRO FUGITIVES FROM MANASSAS

Contrabands and stragglers have been coming in all day yesterday, all confirming the unlooked-for flight which seems less improbable than had been supposed in view of the masterly outflanking process to which the Rebels have yielded.[18] Doubtless the telegraph has already flashed the general particulars to you, yet the details obtained viva voce may claim some interest.[19] I talked yesterday with half a dozen of these emigrants from Secessia, now dispatched to Washington, to repeat what they here volunteered, to the proper authorities.

18. stragglers: soldiers who wander away from their assigned units.
19. viva voce: Latin, "by the living voice," meaning "orally."

They were a picturesque group—six sturdy "boys," whose net value may have averaged a thousand dollars each, as "God's image, carved in ebony," is rated in the rapidly lessening dominions of Davis. Roughly but stoutly clad in homespun garments, and, with one exception, well shod, the eldest might have seen forty years, the others averaging little more than thirty. Thoroughly African in appearance, their black faces and white, glistening teeth (the latter irresistibly suggestive of huge, closely set grains of Indian corn) beamed with satisfaction at the successful result of their hegira as they leaned sunning themselves against the side of the house, answering the questions put to them, and laughing gleefully at the expense of their recent "owners."

When I approached, the elder, a thickset, heavily built Negro, was displaying an old revolver, a "five-shooter" of Colt's pattern, duly capped and loaded, and declaring that he had made up his mind before leaving Manassas to escape or die. He and his party reckoned they had ten shots among 'em. Directly they see how things was a-goin', they determined to clear right out, and they done it, too. They quit at night, took to the woods, and had to wade Occoquan Creek twice, "up to here"—pointing to the waist. They heard the dogs after 'em, but wasn't afraid of them—not "nigger" dogs, you know such as they hunts us with 'way down South—only sport dogs. They got through the pickets easy—(through our pickets, too, they might have added, for we heard nothing of them until they presented themselves at headquarters)—knowing the country. He, the principal speaker, quit on Thursday night. Then our side—the Rebels, sir—was busy leavin'; he reckoned they had all gone now. They was all kinds, Mississippians, Virginians, North Carolinians, and Georgians. They had taken the cannons away, too. Most of 'em was pretty well armed with Enfield rifles or shotguns, but some had only knives and hickory clubs. An Arkansas company fought only with bowie knives —"them choppers, you know—they went right in with 'em." They were pretty well clad and fed, had fresh pork and bread, but no coffee for a long time, and no salt. Nearly all on 'em, even the privates, had niggers to wait on 'em—they couldn't get along nohow without *us*. The colored people knew what was goin' on, but they had to keep mighty quiet about it. Everybody said the rebellion was gone up—caved in, though the "secesh" thought a good deal of Beauregard and Davis—'specially Beauregard.[20] They got news of all the movements of the Union troops and obtained the Northern papers regularly.

20. secesh: secessionist.

I mentioned the tenor of President Lincoln's recent Emancipation message and asked whether the speaker thought it probable under any circumstances that the South would attempt the abolition of slavery. The answer was emphatic: "No, sar! Dey dig us under de ground fust!" There were some black regiments, composed, my informant believed, of free Negroes, but not at Manassas; plenty of them down South, guarding the coasts. All the colored folks were for the Union: "Of course, sar. Dey believe God's goin' to set 'em free." They had heard of John Brown and of the song about him; he was the bravest man that ever lived.

Humanely apprehensive for the well-being and future prospects of this dusky chattel—who, as he stated, was a Kentuckian born, a Mississippian by compulsory adoption, and, four days ago, a slave of one John Calhoun of Claiborne County, in that repudiatory state—I inquired how he proposed to maintain himself. He smiled—his smile rippled into a grin—and he responded: That he was *all right;* that he had raised garden truck, and perfectly understood carpentering. And, really, he seemed quite ready to launch himself upon the untried experiment of individual responsibility, on the strength of these ridiculous accomplishments. I wonder if his ex-master could get along in the world as well, were he cast adrift in a similar manner.

I have seen few pleasanter things than the afternoon sun shone upon immediately subsequent to this conversation: the six escaped slaves sent off under escort of a single soldier; not, as an officer humanely explained to them, to prison or punishment, but that they might be fed and cared for and, after they had retold their story, receive their first vital experience of God's truth—that He created all men free and equal.

APRIL 19, 1862

SOUTH

RICHMOND DAILY DISPATCH
April 19, 1862

A YANKEE LIE BELIEVED IN ENGLAND

The *London Times,* in an article devoted to the exploits of the *Virginia,* says, "The two vessels [the *Virginia* and *Monitor*] engaged each other at close quarters for five hours, after which period, but then only, was the armor of one of them *perforated by shot*. It was *the* Monitor *which thus drew the first blood, and the* Merrimac *then retired.*"[21]

Of course our readers are aware that the *Merrimac* was not "perforated by shot," that the *Monitor* did not "draw the first blood," and that the *Virginia* "did not retire." The whole is a Yankee lie out of the whole cloth. Of course our papers never reach London; but we should have thought that any man who has sufficient pretensions to entitle him to a seat upon the editorial tripod of the *Times* would have had sense enough to entertain some doubt in such a case as this, where the person or persons had not been on board the *Merrimac* and could not possibly know the extent of the damage sustained by her. The fact is that although the vessel in question received at least one hundred shot of the heaviest weight—some of them rifled, and one weighing upward of one hundred sixty pounds—fired at very short distances, sometimes not more than fifteen feet—they affected nothing more than so many indentations upon her armor. In some places—from the heat and weight of the shot—the plates were welded together. In other places the plates were broken, but not broken through, and the damage was repaired by simply taking off the injured plates and putting on others. Her prow, which was made of cast iron, was broken when she ran into the *Cumberland,* but she supplied herself with a better one. So far from flying herself, she made the *Monitor* tuck tail and run into shoal water, under the protection of the guns of Fortress Monroe, and there she still lies, not daring to poke her nose outside, in spite of the *Virginia*'s insults and challenges.

In the whole course of the war, there has never been baser or more palpable lying on the part of the Yankees than that in connection with this fight. And yet Yankee mendacity has been unbounded and continues to be so. We have before us the dispatch of General Beauregard announcing the capture of three thousand prisoners and fourteen guns at Shiloh; and yet the Yankees are offering up thanks to Heaven for a splendid victory! What they say or do is a matter of very little importance to us, but it is a little hard that foreign journals, knowing their mendacious propensities and often commenting upon them in terms of just indignation, should yet give them currency.

21. The Confederates refitted the steamer USS *Merrimac* (originally spelled *Merrimack*) as an ironclad ram and renamed it the *Virginia*. The *Monitor–Merrimac* duel, fought on March 9, 1862, in Hampton Roads (Virginia), ended as a draw, with little damage inflicted.

CHARLESTON DAILY COURIER
April 18, 1862

[*The* Courier *did not publish an issue on April 19. The following articles are drawn from the Friday issue.*]

FROM RICHMOND
CONGRESSIONAL PROCEEDINGS—THE ENEMY AT MONTEREY, VIRGINIA

Richmond, 16th—In the Senate today the Committee on Postal Affairs reported a bill to increase the rate of postage on single letters after the 1st of July to ten cents. The bill was placed on the calendar.

The Committee on the Flag have not finished their report, but the chairman informed the Senate that it would be ready on Friday; also, that the ensign had been already agreed upon.

In the House a voluminous report was presented from the committee appointed to investigate the disaster at Roanoke Island.

The enemy have taken possession of Monterey, Highland County, Virginia, on the Staunton and Parkersburg Turnpike, with a force of about four thousand.

All was quiet in the Valley, and General Jackson's force was increasing daily. There are indications of an early engagement. Fierce skirmishing on the Peninsula is reported to be going on today.

The French minister has arrived here.

THE FIGHTING ON THE PENINSULA—THE ENEMY REPULSED WITH HEAVY LOSS—CONFEDERATE CONGRESS

Richmond, 17th—Official dispatches received last night from Lee's Farm, on the Peninsula, state that the enemy commenced a furious bombardment of our lines at half past eight o'clock yesterday morning, continuing their fire until 7:00 P.M. Their attack was made upon our center, but they were splendidly repulsed. The enemy tried to force and occupy General Cobb's position, between Lee's and Wynn's mills, and for that purpose waded a creek. Some of our rifle pits were occupied for a moment by the enemy, but they were soon driven out and repulsed with a heavy loss. Our troops behaved nobly. At ten o'clock all was quiet. Our loss was twenty killed, including Colonel McKenny, of the 15th North Carolina. Not over seventy were wounded. Eight artillery horses were killed and one howitzer disabled.

The report of the Roanoke Disaster Investigation Committee was read in the House yesterday. It concludes by saying that whatever of blame and responsibility is justly attributable to anyone for the defeat of our troops on Roanoke Island, on the 8th of February, should attach to Major General Huger and the late secretary of war, J. P. Benjamin.

COINS OF THE CONFEDERATE STATES—AUGUSTA A PORT OF DELIVERY—CONJECTURES ON FRENCH MINISTER'S VISIT

Richmond, 17th—The Senate today passed a bill making provision for coins of the Confederate States, to bear such devices as the secretary of the Treasury may suggest or think proper.

The House bill making Augusta a port of delivery for goods imported into Charleston was also passed by the Senate.

Nothing is positively known of the object of the visit of the French minister. Among various conjectures is one that he has come to ascertain what commercial treaties with France are contemplated, whether the independence of the Confederacy can be maintained, and to report thereon to the emperor.

MILITARY TRANSPORTATION—OFFICE OF CHIEF OF TRANSPORTATION CREATED

Richmond, 17th—The House today passed a bill providing for the safe expedition and transportation of troops and munitions of war by railroad. The bill passed by six majority. It creates the office of a military chief of railroad transportation, with a salary of five thousand dollars.

ALL QUIET ON THE PENINSULA— GALLANTRY OF OUR TROOPS

Richmond, 17th—An official dispatch, received this evening from General Magruder, makes no mention of any subsequent fighting on the Peninsula. He refers in terms of high commendation to the behavior of our troops in the affair of Wednesday last.

NORTH

BOSTON EVENING TRANSCRIPT
April 19, 1862

FROM YESTERDAY'S EXTRA EDITIONS
BATTLE AT YORKTOWN

Washington, 18th—The following is from General McClellan today:

Headquarters of the Army of the Potomac, April 18, 1862

About half an hour after midnight, the enemy attacked General Smith's position and attempted to carry his guns. Smith repulsed them handsomely and took some prisoners. I will forward details as soon as my aides return. The firing was very heavy, but all is now quiet.

Second Dispatch

My position, which was occupied yesterday by Smith, was extended last night, so that we have been able to prevent the enemy from working today and kept his guns silent. The same result has been accomplished at Hogan's Mills.

Yorktown was shelled by our gunboats and some of our barges today, without effect. There was a good deal of firing from the Yorktown land batteries.

PARSON BROWNLOW'S RECEPTION IN PHILADELPHIA

Philadelphia, 18th—Parson Brownlow was received at Independence Hall by the city authorities this morning and was greeted by the president of the council with the heartiest welcome. Parson Brownlow replied at some length and recited the tribulations which the Unionists of east Tennessee have undergone. One time he was saved from being hanged by the vote of one drunken secessionist in a drumhead court-martial.

He said he wanted to go back to east Tennessee with a cocked hat, sword, and a coil of rope. He alluded to his wife and children, now held as hostages in Rebeldom, and spoke of the joy and exultation with which the Union army would be greeted in east Tennessee.

President Lincoln has invited him to the White House.

OFFICIAL REPORT OF THE CAPTURE OF FORT PULASKI[22]

Washington, 18th—An official report from General Hunter of the capture of Fort Pulaski has been received at the War Department.

22. Fort Pulaski, Georgia.

The firing was continued thirty hours, when, as our troops were about to storm the fort through a breach, the Rebel flag was struck. We captured 47 guns, 7,000 shot and shell, 40,000 pounds of powder, 360 prisoners, with their small arms and accoutrements and a good supply of provisions. One of our men was killed, none wounded.

NEW YORK TRIBUNE
April 19, 1862

OPENING OF THE HIGHWAY TO SAVANNAH

We have now sufficiently ample accounts of the siege and capture of Fort Pulaski to enable us to judge at once of the nature of the enterprise, of the worth of the labor employed, and of the measure of success achieved for the national cause. The reports which we publish this morning embrace our special correspondent's narrative (which we can safely recommend for its clearness as well as its completeness); the telegraphic announcement of the capture of the fort by General Hunter; and the admissions of Rebel journals as to the essential facts of the campaign and its prospective results. Altogether, the reports of but few of the expeditions which have marked the progress of the war so well bear examination as this; and those who may be disposed to regard the work accomplished as having been performed with superfluous caution, or even too tardily commenced, will find ample compensation for any such misgivings in the energy which characterized the operations during the month immediately preceding the surrender.

It was so long ago as the beginning of last December that Captain (now General) Gillmore made his first reconnaissance in the vicinity of the fort from Tybee Island. Immediately thereafter a plan for the reduction of the place was submitted to the commanding general. This plan, however, had to be sent to Washington for approval, and the middle of February had arrived before the ordnance necessary for the commencement of operations had reached Port Royal. After this, not an hour was lost in proceeding with the work. On the 19th of February, Captain Gillmore was ordered to Tybee Island, and was there invested with the powers of general commanding. The Savannah River having been blockaded on the 11th, the blockade was rendered complete by the 22nd, and on that day the landing of ordnance on Tybee was commenced. In the extraordinary labor required for this task, in the performance of which a whole month was consumed, we are reminded of the labors of the Allies at Balaklava before the tramroad enabled them to move their trains to the high grounds in front of the Malakhov and Redan—the difference being that General Gillmore had no means of constructing a railway, while the heavy guns and mortars of the besieging army had to be dragged over the sand ridges on the north side of the island. And, as our correspondent informs us, the ground over which the heavy ordnance was carried was a mere crust of sand on a bed of mud. Through the heart of this slough, mortars weighing seventeen thousand pounds had to be forced by the sheer muscle and endurance of the brave Northern lads, in some instances as far as three miles. And to add still further to the difficulty of the task, the movements had to be so conducted as to conceal, as far as might be, the nature of the operations from the Rebels. Inch by inch such passage as could be made on such soil was cut out by the energy and perseverance of the men. In this way eleven batteries, mounting in all thirty-six guns, were ultimately planted where the commanding officer desired. And special record is most surely due in these columns of the fact that the labor, not only of transporting the ordnance but of constructing the earthworks, was done in great part by the 7th Connecticut Volunteers, under Colonel Terry. Other regiments receive honorable mention in our correspondent's narrative, but Connecticut appears to have carried off the honors which belong to the hardest and most enduring labor.

On the morning of the 10th instant, the usual formal demand was made by General Hunter—now at the head of the department—for the surrender of the fort by the Rebel commander, Colonel Olmstead. The reply was sufficiently spirited to be met, as it was, with a vigorous and prompt attack by the national forces. Early in the morning of the same day (the 10th) the order was given to fire, and the guns and mortars were worked on our side with more than ordinary vigor until late in the afternoon, when the fire began to slacken; and after sunset until daylight on Friday, only a few shells were thrown on either side. Friday's work opened with even greater spirit than that of the previous day, and at 2:00 P.M. of the 11th, Pulaski, with its garrison, had surrendered. The services of Lieutenant Porter are spoken of with special and deserved commendation, and the fleet appears to have vied with the land forces in pursuing the enterprise to a thorough and decisive result.

A positive view of the importance of this siege and the surrender following it is seen in the Rebel correspondence from Savannah, which we publish in other columns. "I can give," says a writer in a Richmond paper, "but a faint idea of the consternation the capture produced. The blow has been sudden and totally unlooked-for. The enemy will not wait long to attack the batteries about Fort Jackson. Their heavy ships have entered the river above Pulaski and are in plain view of the defenses of the city of Savannah." This is the testimony of the besieged, and it throws more distinct light on the result of the expedition than any surmises offered through more direct and loyal channels. If it should comport with the general plan of the campaign, General Hunter, having had prescience of the state of surprise and terror into which the Rebels have been thrown, may see the importance of an early advance. When he shall have reached Savannah, should that be his next movement, he will find—if the correspondent whose words we have quoted is to be believed—a large body of the citizens ready to receive him with open arms. The city is under the despotism of a military mob; juveniles in Rebel uniform are forcing the best of the people into camp; and the helpless are fleeing from the military tyrants. Surely, these facts may well help to speed the national arms, as they plainly herald the approaching national triumph.

[UNTITLED]

Beauregard, in his letter to General Grant asking permission to bury his dead, has the audacity to say, "I deem it proper to say that I am asking only what I have extended to your own countrymen under similar circumstances." How little warrant he had for such an assertion is shown by the savage conduct of his command toward our dead at Bull Run; nor can the heartless reply of this same general to the sister of Colonel Cameron be forgotten, when she pleaded with him for the remains of her dead brother.

MAY 17, 1862

SOUTH

RICHMOND DAILY DISPATCH
May 16, 1862

[*The* Dispatch *did not publish an issue on May 17. The following articles are drawn from the Friday issue.*]

VIRGINIA NOT TO BE SURRENDERED

Two gratifying papers were communicated to the Virginia legislature yesterday—a message from Governor Letcher and a communication from the president of the Confederacy, giving the assurance that the army will not leave Virginia until every means has been exhausted in her defense. The language of the president is clear and emphatic.

We are proud of the spirit of our governments, Confederate and state, relative to this question of holding and defending this state to the last. The army will not abandon the adored soil of Virginia. That has been made the battleground, and on that must the enemy establish his superiority in a fair fight before it will be abandoned to him. The evacuation of the seacoast positions and cities became a necessity. There was no avoiding it, in consequence of the immense advantage enjoyed by the enemy in his possession of the entire navy of the United States and the material and mechanical skill for the rapid construction of ironclad gunboats, while we had neither a navy, nor the material and the mechanical force, to enable us to compete with him in any sense. It is true, we had the *Virginia,* but, besides her, nothing. Her destruction, and the questions it involves, suggests matters of debate which afford neither satisfaction nor benefit now to discuss. Our inability to meet the enemy on the water, as a general question, was clear and indisputable and the withdrawal from the sea unavoidable.

Second to Virginia is the defense of this city, for manifold reasons, and it is in keeping with the general purpose of both governments that they should resolve to the uttermost to defend Richmond. All the means in the power of the state and the Confederacy are pledged to this, and we may be assured that the enemy will not be allowed to gratify the prominent desire of his heart, to hector and domineer over the inhabitants of this far-famed and beautiful town, until every means is exhausted.

The president nobly takes the stand that though Richmond should fall, there are plenty of battlefields yet in Virginia to fight for the cause for twenty years! The sentiment is as truthful as patriotic. The Confederate government assures us that the Old Dominion is not to be given up. God forbid that it should! It would be giving up much more than Virginia. The cause would be, indeed, itself well-nigh surrendered in that event. The government is not only just but wise in its determination to stand by Virginia to the last.

THE DEFENSE OF RICHMOND

Though late in commencing our preparations for the defense of the approach to this city by the James River, and though the enemy's "infernal gunboats" caught our obstructions at Drewry's Bluff hardly in readiness, we have the satisfaction at least of having repelled his first assault. He went away yesterday, we have reason to hope, smartly damaged after two and a half hours of fearful cannonading of our batteries. His withdrawal gives time for further preparation for his next essay, which will certainly be made. Our loss is slight, but more than in some instances where important positions have been surrendered. We trust that this beginning is an earnest of the determination to keep the gunboats back. They have been felt by our artillerists, and some idea may be formed of their real capacity and power for evil. The men who man our guns are somewhat more reliable than the militia who have been entrusted with guns at some points where it was most important we should make good our defense. Seamen are the best of gunners, and it has been a great mistake to leave them nothing to do while the cannoneering in many cases has been left to men who were not at all to compare with them.

The public spirit here is the best imaginable. The people are ready to make any sacrifice to defend the place and are entirely averse to surrendering it at all to the gunboats. They will cheerfully submit it to destruction first, according to the disposition of both the governments.

The successful resistance thus far has been highly encouraging. But this encouragement should only be to put forth increased exertions. We should strengthen and increase the number of our obstructions, and we should strengthen our batteries and increase the supporting force.

Nothing is wanting in disposition. It is only necessary for the leaders to give the proper direction to the labor and the defenses. This being properly done, it may yet be proved that gunboats are not invincible, nor can they go where they please.

THE DEAD AT THE BATTERIES

We think it would be an act proper and creditable to the city to vote a pension to the families of the dead who perished in the special service at the river batteries to defend this city. Also, to pension any who may be permanently disabled in the same way. We are sure it would meet the unanimous approval of our people. The service is especially for the protection of this city from an invading foe whose impelling motive is greed and gain, and whose policy is designed to humiliate and crush the pride and spirit and erase the nationality of the South. In this temper, what might we not apprehend were they to get possession of the capital of Virginia and the Confederacy? Therefore, every motive of patriotism and honor should stimulate our people to resist to the last the most efficient and dreaded form of the invasion, which aims at the cities of the

South, and which is directed at this with all possible malignity and power. In this especial act of resistance we should enlist every feeling sacred to the cause. Honor to all who shall distinguish themselves in it, and let none suffer from the death or disability of any of our gallant defenders who are killed or wounded at the batteries in protecting the city.

GENERAL JOHNSTON'S ARMY

The *Petersburg Express* learns from a gentleman who left the army at ten o'clock Tuesday forenoon that General Johnston's vanguard was only one mile this side of New Kent Courthouse—General McClellan's advanced forces were at the courthouse, but the impression seemed to prevail that he was retiring. New Kent Courthouse is twenty-eight miles from Richmond; and were McClellan defeated at that point, the greater portion of his forces would be compelled to retreat in the direction of Yorktown, before reaching which they would be captured or cut to pieces. It was thought not improbable that General Johnston would render the young Napoleon battle.

THE FATE OF RICHMOND

The next few days may decide the fate of Richmond. It is either to remain the capital of the Confederacy, or to be turned over to the Federal government as a Yankee conquest. The capital is either to be secured or lost—it may be feared, not temporarily—and with it Virginia. Then, if there is blood to be shed, let it be shed here; no soil of the Confederacy could drink it up more acceptably, and none would hold it more gratefully. Wife, family, and friends are nothing. Leave them all for one glorious hour to be devoted to the republic. Life, death, and wounds are nothing if we only be saved from the fate of a captured capital and a humiliated Confederacy. Let the government act; let the people act. There is time yet. If fate come to its worst, let the ruins of Richmond be its most lasting monument.

NEGRO INVADERS

The people of the South have been unwilling from the first to admit the startling fact that the Yankee government even contemplated the invasion of her borders by the armed colored population of the slave states in the prosecution of her plans of subjugation. This fact, humiliating as it may be to humanity and shocking to civilization, has at last been demonstrated by the organization, in Washington, D.C., of two regiments and, in Charles Town, Virginia, of one or more companies, who are drilled daily after sundown and instructed in the manual of shooting down their owners. This is the secret of the running off of the male slaves of the Valley. It is a pity that Virginia's eyes have been closed so long to the real designs of the Lincoln government. They are now opened. Blindness is no longer an excuse for suicide.

CHARLESTON DAILY COURIER
May 16, 1862

[*The* Courier *did not publish an issue on May 17. The following articles are drawn from the Friday issue*.]

FROM RICHMOND
REPULSE OF THE TERRIBLE IRONCLAD GUNBOATS—THE GALENA FIRED—RETREAT OF THE REMAINDER—OUR MEN IN HIGH SPIRITS

Richmond, 15th—The following intelligence is posted on the bulletins of the newspaper offices of this city:

> This morning about eight o'clock several Federal gunboats, two of them supposed to be the *Monitor* and *Galena,* opened fire upon our batteries at Wilton, at a distance of about five hundred yards. The enemy fired with great rapidity and violence. Our batteries replied deliberately.
>
> 1:00 P.M.—We have just fired the *Galena,* and the other gunboats have retired down the river.
>
> Our loss is four killed and eight wounded. The *Galena* was on fire when she retired. Our troops are in high spirits and confident of success.

PROCLAMATION OF GOVERNOR LETCHER—
RESOLVED TO DEFEND THE CITY TO THE LAST

Richmond, 15th—The following proclamation was issued today by Governor Letcher:

> The General Assembly of this Commonwealth having resolved that the capital of this state shall be defended to the last extremity, if such defense is in accordance with the views of the presi-

dent of the Confederate States, and having declared that whatever destruction and loss of property of state or individual shall thereby result will be cheerfully submitted to, and this action being warmly approved and seconded by the executive, therefore I do hereby request all officers who are out of service from any cause, and all others who may be willing to unite in defending the capital of this state, to assemble this evening at the City Hall at five o'clock and proceed forthwith to organize a force, etc.

Prompt and efficient action is absolutely necessary. We have a gallant army in the field upon whom we fully and confidently rely, but no effort should be spared which can contribute to this noble object. The capital of Virginia must not be surrendered. Virginians must rally to the rescue.

Given under my hand under the Seal of the Commonwealth at Richmond, this 15th day of May, 1862, in the eighty-sixth year of the Commonwealth.

John Letcher

In accordance with the above proclamation a large assemblage met at the City Hall in the evening at five o'clock. A fine spirit prevailed. Brief addresses were made by Governor Letcher and the mayor. Both declared they would never surrender the city.

The latest report from the river states that the *Monitor* and *Galena* are steaming down the river.

OFFICIAL FROM DREWRY'S BLUFF

Richmond, 15th—The Navy Department has received the following official dispatch:

Drewry's Bluff, Virginia, May 15, 1862, 11 A.M.

Sir:—We have engaged today five of the enemy's gunboats, the struggle lasting two and a half hours. We fired the ironclad steamer *Galena*. She has withdrawn and is going down the river, accompanied by three wooden vessels. Our loss in killed and wounded is small.

Respectfully, your obedient servant,
E. Farrand

P.S.—The *Monitor* has left.
Honorable S. R. Mallory, Secretary of the Navy

NORTH

BOSTON EVENING TRANSCRIPT
May 17, 1862

[UNTITLED]

The present abnormal financial state of our country has baffled the theories and calculations of the most astute financiers of the day. Gold is virtually demonetized and has become simply an article of merchandise, varying in price from day to day with the fluctuations in the volume of currency and in conformity to the laws of trade.

American gold is now selling at about 103¼ and sterling exchange at about 113½ to 114. These two items must for the present be in near approximation to each other in regard to relative market value. Exchange at 109½, sixty days' sight, is near the point at which our bankers can remit gold at par; therefore, any additional premium on gold must be added to the price of exchange. Consequently, the present rate of foreign exchange is simply par, and the market rate of coin added thereto. We hope that our banks will not be induced to part with any of their specie—as the fact of their holding so large a specie reserve acts beneficially upon the public mind, and the confidence inspired among the community as to the soundness of our banking institutions is of far more importance than the realization of any immediate gain from the sale of their coin.

The redundancy of paper currency naturally leads to inflation—real property and commodities of every description rise in nominal value, and thus a spirit of speculation is induced among all classes of individuals, which hitherto has led to general bankruptcy and ruin. In order to check as far as possible this state of things, it is of the highest importance that the banks should keep a sufficient amount of coin in their vaults to enable them to return to the payment of specie at the earliest moment practicable.

The government stocks of every description are commanding a high premium and are finding a ready market among the capitalists of our country, thus evincing the confidence of the latter in these securities and the ability of the government to meet the interest as it becomes due. The amount originally subscribed by the Boston banks to the government loan—with the exception of the first issue—is now held by those institutions and is sufficiently large to yield them a handsome profit, should they think proper to sell at the present market rates. But with the great ease in monetary affairs and the scarcity of good business paper, together with a reasonable prospect of a further advance in this class of securities, we presume they will not be inclined to dispose of this item of their loans until the calls upon them for business purposes are more pressing than they are at present.

The demand Treasury notes, dated August 10, 1861, are selling from ¾ to 1 percent premium; being receivable for government dues, they will, in the course of a few months, command the same premium as gold. These notes are not fundable into stock. The demand notes of the new issue, which will amount to $150 million, are convertible into twenty years' six-percent stock, redeemable at the pleasure of the government anytime after five years, and are known as the 5-20 six-percent stock. Should this stock be at a premium of 1 to 2 percent, a withdrawal of the demand notes, which are fundable into this class of securities, will, to a certain extent, take place, and whether under such circumstances it would be sound policy to reissue them is somewhat questionable.

The 73-10s are fundable into the twenty years' six-percent stock at any time up to the date of their maturity.

The circulation of the Boston banks has *decreased* since March 10, the date of the legal tender notes, $1,155,200, and the deposits have *increased* during the same time, $4,086,913—showing an increase in the volume of currency of $2,971,713. Caution and sound judgment should now, more than ever before, be called into action by our financial men and bank managers. We are passing through a phase in monetary affairs wholly without precedent in this country, and although so far successful beyond our most sanguine expectations, we must be careful not to allow that very success to prove ultimately ruinous.

NEW YORK TRIBUNE
May 17, 1862

[UNTITLED]

The *Boston Courier* urges that upon our theory that secession was originally condemned and opposed by a majority of the Southern people, the Republican party ought to have done its best to keep that majority from plunging into the abyss of crime and misery which the original traitors were preparing for the entire South. To which we respond: *They did.* President Lincoln's inaugural was a full, clear, authentic message of peace from the loyal states in refutation of the frauds and falsehoods of the traitors. It could hardly have been more explicit in statement on the vital points involved; kinder in tone it could not have been. Had those of the South been generally a reading, reflecting people, that manifesto alone ought to have stopped this rebellion at the outset. Here is what the *Courier* thinks the Republicans ought to have done:

> To us it seems clear that, taking every necessary step to suppress the rebellion and to meet actual force with force, the wishes, the feelings, and the supposed interests of that majority thought to be loyal at heart should have been carefully and frankly consulted. In language, the meaning of which admitted of no possibility of mistake, and expressed with a warmth of good feeling which would have been a warrant for its hearty sincerity, these well-disposed citizens should have received every executive, congressional, and popular assurance, through the press and in every practicable mode, that no wrong whatever would be done to them, or countenanced toward them; that so far as any persons resisted the lawful authority of the United States, they would be compelled to submit; but otherwise we were their friends and fellow citizens, seeking nothing but their good and the good of the whole people, under the Constitution and laws of the land.

We have already cited the "executive" assurance that was actually given, and whoever can turn to it will see that it exactly meets the *Courier*'s requirements. Congress (then Republican in both branches) did its part fully in passing by a two-thirds vote in either House the joint resolve initiating an amendment of the Constitution whereby the nation should forever be debarred from abolishing slavery in the states. And never was the North freer, whether through its press or its popular meetings, from menacing or irritating language toward the South than during the memorable five months that intervened between the election of Lincoln and the bombardment of Fort Sumter.

How, then, was a majority of the Southern people driven into the rebellion, against its own judgment and convictions? We answer: Just as it had been previously driven into so many acts of injustice and aggression—by raising the mad-dog cry of "abolitionist." Tens of thousands in the slave states were forced to join in the chorus of commendation of Brooks's brutal and cowardly assault on Sumner by the fear of being branded abolitionists if they spoke as they felt.[23] And when it was determined that the South was to be plunged into revolution and civil war by its traitor chiefs, hundreds of thousands of such men as the *Courier* supported for president in 1860 rushed into treason from fear of being left behind in the general race for safety, and then robbed, abused, tortured, and butchered, as the east Tennessee and other unshrinking loyalists have actually been. The rebellion being notoriously a war for slavery, those who refused to unite in it felt that they would be plausibly accused of a lack of heart in support of the "peculiar institution" which so curses the South and debases the *Boston Courier*. Hence the general deluge of treason.

THEN AND NOW

A contemporary thinks us inconsistent in maintaining that the rebellion was the work of a minority of the South, yet that nearly all the whites of the revolted states are now Rebels. Let us see:

We hold, on the strength of their own votes, that a majority of the Southern whites opposed the rebellion at the outset. We know not where to find higher or more conclusive testimony. The states of Virginia, North Carolina, Maryland, Missouri, Kentucky, Tennessee, and even Arkansas gave majorities against secession when the question was first submitted to them. North Carolina, while she chose a Union majority to her convention, voted at the same time that said convention should never meet. Louisiana was barely carried for secession. The other cotton states gave majorities for secession, but on a very moderate poll, with all the excitement and all the denunciation and violence on the side of treason. No man in any slave state feared to vote for the rebellion, but he who dared vote against it often did so at the peril of his life. Hence thousands of Union men were restrained from voting at all, while all the timorous and trimming were made to vote for secession. And yet the Union received a majority in the aggregate vote of the slave states, proving the rebellion the work of a minority.

Afterward, however, the buying up or subsidizing of the Union press, the systematic lying by letter, public address, and telegraph, and, finally, the actual clash of war transformed thousands of Union men into secessionists. Men who had stood by the Union up to the bombardment of

23. On May 22, 1856, South Carolina Representative Preston Brooks stormed onto the Senate floor and beat Massachusetts Senator Charles Sumner with a cane, rendering him bloody and nearly unconscious. Brooks had become incensed over what he deemed libelous remarks directed at his home state and his uncle, South Carolina Senator Andrew Butler, in Sumner's antislavery "Crime Against Kansas" speech, delivered on May 19–20.

Sumter concluded to "go with their section," since the breach had become inevitable. Hence, counties which at first gave majorities for the Union have since been wholly given over to secession.

JUNE 21, 1862

SOUTH

RICHMOND DAILY DISPATCH
June 21, 1862

OUR PROSPECTS FOR PAPER

We have reason for believing that we shall soon be able to get an ample supply of paper to enable us to print the *Dispatch* on a whole instead of a half sheet, as at present. During our short supply of paper, however, we will issue a whole sheet once a week, to enable us to publish the large amount of advertisements which we are compelled to leave out in issuing a half sheet. We feel confident that in a week or two, at furthest, we shall be able to print the *Dispatch* on a whole sheet.

A CHARMING PROSPECT

Among the letters picked up on the battlefield of Shiloh was one from an Illinois soldier by the name of Donnelly, addressed to his wife, his "dear Sue," as he affectionately calls her, in which he tells her that he has already picked out a fine house and farm and that after the war is over, he expects he and his "dear Sue" will be supremely happy in their "sweet Southern home."[24] The women of that region, he says, can be employed to perform the domestic duties of Mrs. Donnelly's household and the men to plow and plant corn, while "you and I, dear Sue," exclaims Mr. Donnelly rapturously, "will be as happy as kings." Ah, hopeful Donnelly! He has got his "sweet Southern home" a little sooner than he expected. The men who were to plow his land and plant his corn have performed their duty, we trust, to his entire satisfaction. They have plowed up his little farm and planted him in. Like thousands of other Yankees who came in quest of Southern farms, he has secured a small homestead where no one will ever distress him for rent and taxes. His

24. The Confederates were forced to withdraw from much of Tennessee after the Battle of Shiloh, April 6–7, 1862.

"dear Sue" can have the consolation of reflecting that she is the widow of a Southern landed proprietor.

It is not difficult to comprehend the feelings which prompt such ebullitions as those of the lamented Donnelly in his last letter to the adorable Susan. It is a not uncommon boast among the Yankees that they not only intend to occupy the Southern farms, but that the Southern men shall do the work and, while "the Northern matron presides in the mansion, the Southern lady shall bend over the washing tub." We care not to enumerate the difficulties which would embarrass the execution of this project. They would be undoubtedly of a somewhat serious character. The Yankee men and women who would endeavor to play master and mistress over a Southern white family would soon be gathered to their fathers. The hypocritical wretches who profess to be overwhelmed with grief at African slavery and then propose to make white people their slaves would soon be disposed of with steel and strychnine. But a menace of this kind, a threat to degrade the men and women of the South to such a condition, could only proceed from natures which are in themselves inherently servile and brutal. It develops in the most unmistakable manner the rankling envy and jealousy which have as much to do as any other cause with this atrocious war. We do not desire to involve in such a charge the whole Northern people. We are well aware that there still exists in that section some remnant of the social worth and excellence of former days. But the great mass of the population are simply the peasantry of the Old World transported to the shores of the New and fighting out that quarrel with their betters in this hemisphere, which they had begun and carried on unsuccessfully in another. Like a bull, who has only to be shown a red rag to excite his combativeness, this Old World peasantry, no matter whether it has lived in America two centuries or two years, has only to be shown something that is conservative, venerable, and dignified to make war at once upon it. This was the prompting motive of the anti-rent disturbances in New York, and it lies at the foundation of the whole fierce outcry against slavery. It is not the sorrows of the slave, but the comfort and dignity of his master which stir to the very bottom their philanthropical bile. They can find no parallel in Southern society to their own condition, except that of the Negro, and *hinc illae lacrimae.*[25] The master reminds them of the feudal lords to whom their forefathers once paid homage, and whose dominion they were only able to escape by flying, like fugitive slaves, to

25. *hinc illae lacrimae:* Latin, "hence those tears."

America. The idea of gentlemen and ladies in a country where they had never expected to find either fills them with horror and rage, and hence they determine to exterminate them, or, what has always been a favorite scheme of revenge by inferiors toward their superiors, of degrading them, making them exchange places with their subordinates and be transformed into "servants of servants and slaves of the devil."

But the degradation of a people, fortunately, is an achievement beyond any power to effect but their own. A race of men may be beaten in battle; their arms may be taken away; their country subjugated; their political, civil, and religious rights sacrificed; but they can never be degraded except by their own hands. Even the French Revolution—that leveling, irresistible tornado—failed to humble the aristocracy which it hated with such malignant hate. The lineal descendants of houses noble before the Crusades were chased to the scaffold by a howling mob, let loose upon them by the fierce tyrants of the Convention, but maintained to the last their equanimity and self-respect. The demoniacal exultation of the bloodhounds, in witnessing the uncertainty of human greatness, as exhibited in the death agonies of their superiors in station, never disturbed the composure of the dying men. Even those of them whose frivolity and licentiousness first evoked the storm of popular fury are said to have been the first to display the most chivalric courage in the terrible face of the guillotine. Beautiful women, too, in all the pride of their loveliness, met the inhuman stare of the mob undismayed. "Nor were these traits," says one who describes these scenes, "without their fruits. This noble spirit—this triumphant victory of the wellborn and the great —was a continual insult to the populace, who saw themselves defrauded of half their promised vengeance, and they learned that they might kill but *they could never humiliate them*. In vain they dipped their hands in their red lifeblood and, holding up their dripping fingers, asked, 'How did it differ from that of the canaille!' Their hearts gave the lie to the taunt, for they witnessed instances of heroism, from gray hairs and tender womanhood, that would have shamed the proudest deeds of their newborn chivalry."

It will prove as impossible for Black Republicans in America as for Red Republicans in Europe to degrade those whom nature and Providence have made their superiors. They may kill but they cannot humiliate those Southrons whom they so envy and hate. We are no admirers of European royalty or European aristocracy, but still less are we admirers of an ignorant mob. Of all tyrants, save us from King Demos. And, whatever we may think of European social institutions, one thing is certain: Aristocracy, in some form or other, always has existed and always will exist, till the end of time. The assertion of the Declaration of American Independence that "all men are born free and equal" is, in its Northern acceptation, the most stupendous and audacious fiction that was ever uttered by human lips. Men are neither born equal, nor can they be made so by any process which philosophers or statesmen have yet discovered. Society must have leaders, men who guide it in intelligence, refinement, humanity, and civilization, or it will relapse into barbarism. It is not necessary that these leaders should be hereditary, but leaders there must be. The South has always recognized the fact; it is itself a nation of gentlemen, and so long as the Northern masses were guided politically by Southern statesmen and socially by their van Rensselaers, Clintons, and Livingstons of their better days, the country prospered, and they were themselves a happy and orderly race. But the coachman is off the box, and the horses have taken the reins in their own keeping. Hatred and vengeance against their betters more intense than that of the French Revolution has seized upon the Yankee mob. With an ex-rail-splitter and -boatman at their head, they are threatening not only to overrun the fair territories of the South but to convert the masters and the mistresses into their servants. Let them not lay the flattering unction to their souls. They may destroy our country, they may exterminate our race, but *they cannot humiliate us.*

CHARLESTON DAILY COURIER
June 21, 1862

SALE OF NEGROES AT THE BROKERS' EXCHANGE

Wilbur and Son sold on Friday, the 20th instant, for cash, a gang of twenty-two Negroes for $15,865, average $721 each.

Two fellows, 19 years, brought $1,030 and $1,005 each; one fellow, 24 years, brought $970; two fellows, 18 and 20 years, brought $965 and $960 each; two fellows, 20 years, brought $925 and $900 each; one fellow, 18 years, brought $810; one fellow, 30 years, brought $730; one fellow, 40 years, brought $605; one boy, 10 years, brought $640; one girl, 16 years, brought $925; one woman, 24 years, brought $970; one girl, 18 years, brought $800; one woman, 50 years, two women, 22 and 25 years, and an infant, brought $1,800, average $450; one woman, 20 years, and infant brought $820, average $410; one woman, 35 years, brought $600; one woman, 30 years, not warranted sound, brought $410.

MOVEMENTS OF THE ENEMY'S SHIPS

On Thursday night several heavy guns were fired from the fleet off this port, and which were heard with great distinctness in the city. It is thought that their shots were aimed at several schooners which left here that night to pass the blockade, and one of which, it is supposed, they captured, as a schooner-rigged craft was seen in company with the fleet on Friday morning. Some ten blockaders are constantly near this bar and are at times very close in to the shoals.

AFFAIRS ON JAMES ISLAND[26]

The latest news from the island, on Friday, reports everything quiet. A flag of truce was sent to the enemy's lines in relation to the prisoners on both sides. The Confederate prisoners taken by the enemy have been sent to Port Royal. It is understood that the Federals will be allowed to send in supplies of medicines, clothing, etc., to the wounded prisoners in our hands.

We learn that the Federal officer riding the cream-colored horse, and who was brought down in the fight at Secessionville, Monday, was Colonel Graves of the 8th Michigan Regiment.

The firing heard Friday afternoon was from the discharge of some heavy guns and the trial of some new ones.

A GRIEVANCE WHICH OUGHT TO BE REDRESSED

We learn that numerous articles arrive at our railroad depots and at the office of the Southern Express, directed to our gallant soldiers, without indicating where they are to be found, and remain there unclaimed. The consequence is that such articles as are perishable decay and become utterly lost to those to whom they are sent. A box of hams, for instance, arrived a short time since by the Southern Express and remained at the office uncalled for until the meat rotted away. We would call attention of the military authorities to the fact and urge an immediate remedy. It is respectfully suggested that proper persons should be detailed for the special duty of attending the various points of delivery and seeing that the soldiery speedily obtain whatever may be sent them on their own account or as friendly or benevolent donations.

MEDICINES FOR OUR SICK AND WOUNDED

Ought we not to seize the occasion which has put us in possession of numerous wounded prisoners to insist that the blockading enemy shall

26. James Island, near Charleston, South Carolina.

allow necessary medicines to reach our port, so that both their and our wounded may be duly cared for?

EXPRESS LIST

We invite attention to the list giving the names of persons for whom packages have been received at the Southern Express office, meeting opposite Hayne Street.

All persons expecting parcels by Express should examine this list daily, or as often as it appears, and should inquire at the Express office.

The list will always be found on our fourth page with the railroad consignees.

FRUIT AND VEGETABLES

Ample and well-arranged measures should be taken in season to procure a supply of fresh fruit and preserved vegetables for the use of our army.

Farmers, planters, and gardeners who are raising good crops of any fruits or vegetables which are not convenient to market for fresh supplies cannot do better service for the South and the comfort of the army and citizens than preparing such supplies. Apples, peaches, etc., can be easily kept by drying in the way familiarly known to all good housekeepers, and many of the most important vegetables can be preserved by drying, compressing, sealing, etc.

Will some friend of experience give our readers, through our columns, plain directions in this matter?

NORTH

BOSTON EVENING TRANSCRIPT
June 21, 1862

FROM CORINTH
THE OPENING OF RAILROAD COMMUNICATION—
MOVEMENT OF THE FEDERAL ARMY—UNION
SENTIMENT IN WESTERN TENNESSEE—
THE REBEL ARMY AT OKOLONA

Corinth, Mississippi, 19th—The telegraph line north was prostrated in the early part of the week by heavy rains.

Our army has returned from Boonesville and now occupies a more northern position.

General Pope has gone North on a furlough. The Memphis and

Charleston Railroad is in running order from Tuscumbia to Cypress Swamp, fifty miles west of Corinth.

The Mobile and Ohio Railroad is in running condition north to Jackson, Tennessee, and railroad communication is open to Grand Junction via Jackson. The road west from the junction is reported to be badly damaged. All the railroads and telegraphs north are in good condition.

Generals Ord, Sullivan, and Hamilton have arrived.

There is considerable Union sentiment displayed in western Tennessee, especially in Bolivar and Jackson counties.

Beauregard's army, at last accounts, was at Okolona, eighty thousand strong; Kirby Smith was at Chattanooga with twenty thousand; Price was at Fulton with fifteen thousand; and Van Dorn, with a small cavalry force, was at Grenada.

FROM MEMPHIS
REMOVAL OF OBSTRUCTIONS FROM WHITE RIVER—A SEVERE FIGHT—BOILER EXPLOSION AND LOSS OF LIFE

Memphis, 19th—An expedition composed of the gunboats *St. Louis, Lexington, Conestoga,* and *Mound City,* with transports carrying the 43rd and 46th Indiana regiments, under Colonel Fitch, were sent hence some days since to remove the obstruction from White River.

On the 17th, the expedition reached St. Charles, eighty-five miles above the mouth, where the Rebels had erected a battery. An engagement ensued lasting an hour and a half.

While the gunboats engaged the batteries, the troops, under Colonel Fitch, landed a short distance below and proceeded to storm the place.

During the cannonading, a ball entered the boiler of the *Mound City,* causing a fearful explosion and loss of life.

The crew consisted of 175, of whom 125 were killed and wounded. The following officers are among the killed: John Kinsil, James Scoville, John Green, Henry R. Brown, Joseph Nixon, John Cox; Captain Kelty, flag officer, was badly scalded, but it is thought he will recover.

Colonel Fitch's charge upon the battery was a perfect success, driving the enemy out at the point of the bayonet. The Rebel loss is 125 killed and wounded and 30 prisoners.

General Halleck has occupied Holly Springs.

NEW YORK TRIBUNE
June 21, 1862

REBEL DESERTIONS

The *Richmond Dispatch* of June 16 says: Desertion has become far too frequent in the Confederate army. And yet the habit is not peculiar to Confederate soldiers. There must be desertions from all military service where there is no punishment for desertion. We mean no punishment adequate to the offense, none which a coward or a vagabond had not rather encounter than endure the service or the peril of a battle. Death is the proper punishment, and it is the punishment prescribed in our laws—the punishment meted out to the deserter by governments generally. We anticipate that our own government will be forced to resort to it. With a creditable humanity and forbearance, the policy of appealing to the pride of the soldier by advertisement, by disgraces, has been pursued by our commanders, but there is little pride in the deserter, and the fear of disgrace will not deter him from absconding. The penalty of death will. An example or two would have a fine effect.

"DRAWING IT MILD" IN MEMPHIS

We are ready to make our solemn affidavit that there is nothing in this world like that divine philosophy which is succinctly expressed in the great command, "Grin and bear it." The conductor of the *Memphis Avalanche* has so gracefully melted into this mild mood that, secessionist as he is, we consider him to be a credit to the craft. He owns up like a man. He admits that he is "humbled and downcast." His "pride has been wounded." What then? Does he wriggle and roar? Does he inefficiently flounder like a fish out of water? Not at all. He quietly concludes to make the best of a bad matter. Like Archimedes at Syracuse, he involves himself in his virtue and goes on with his studies, though the Union foot is upon the neck of Memphis. "Let us," he says, with an originality and power which are alike admirable, "—let us bear with manly fortitude what we are unable to avoid." "This," he concludes, "is true philosophy—a philosophy suited to our condition." Now, this calm, godlike, serene, and unimpassioned acquiescence appears to us to be something in itself so exquisitely beautiful, and something, moreover, so much needed in Memphis, that our hope is that our editorial brother will consent to erect in that city a school for the express dissemination of his doctrine, which is much needed there—a kind of portico, lyceum, or academy—in which, like Aristotle or Plato, he may rub his true philosophy like an emollient ointment into the tender frames of the fevered youth of Memphis, in which he may teach them that the grace of submission is better than bowie knives and "barkers" and a stern stoicism infinitely preferable to peach brandy and peppermint. There are wild ones in Secessia who clearly need this medicinal indoctrination and sagely sanative treatment. There are ferocious old fools and young ones there who talk with maniac energy of dying in the last ditch; who prattle grimly of the combustion of themselves and of their cotton; who itch to make a new Moscow of Memphis—who conceive it to be quite necessary, should worse come to worst, to blow up the universe generally and to put an end to themselves, playing Cato of Utica with a real sword, in particular. These perturbed spirits need laying, or they will do themselves a mischief. For our part, unless the new Memphis philosophy can be brought into high fashion, we look for an unpleasant superfluity of arson and suicide in Confederate regions—squads of disgusted chevaliers popping themselves off after the high Roman fashion—piles of patriarchs, who, having first slaughtered all their niggers, cows, sows, horses, dogs, wives, sheep, and daughters, will be found wrapped in the Confederate flag as in a winding sheet, as dead and as dignified as Julius Caesar, with the remains of their former greatness gloomily heaped around them. To be sure, in the cities already "subjugated," we don't hear of these patriotic diversions. The most rampant patriots appear to subside with a wonderful facility and to disregard quite contemptuously the injunction to destroy themselves in which some of their newspapers abound. We suppose, however, that they are waiting for a General Proclamation of Suicide by their mock president Davis. They are desirous of dying according to law, and of destroying themselves constitutionally. It becomes their Davisian Jefferson—the best Jefferson they have, poor fellows!—himself to set an example. When all is lost, we hold that it will be his duty to blow out what brains he may have left—his remainder cerebrum, so to speak. To make the whole preceding more sublime, he might announce that upon the 14th instant, at high noon, he intended to consummate his felo-de-se and request his friends and admirers to hang or shoot themselves, or to take big morphine pills, at the same identical moment. Then, with simultaneous kick or quiver, or firing their own salvo over their departure for Hades, the chiefs of secession might secede from this wicked world and enter upon another from which, however hot, secession will be impossible. We throw out these hints merely from an ardent passion for seeing things done neatly. If we are to have no Confederate States, we shall need no Confederate statesmen. In a restored Union, it will be impossible to put Mr. Jefferson Davis and his crazy cronies to any sort of use. Will they have the grace to step out? Will they have the goodness to leave an unappreciative world and betake themselves to those places which from the beginning have been prepared for them?

We do not know. We confess that we are by no means assured and the new Memphis philosophy somewhat staggers our confidence in the desiderated stampede. What if the secessionists, as the *Avalanche* would seem to indicate, should turn capital Christians—models of forgetfulness and forgiveness—after all? What if it should suddenly dawn upon the secession mind, the smoke of battle no longer, in conjunction with extra whiskey, befogging the brain, that a big plantation and plenty of "niggers" and slavery guaranteed by the Federal government will be more pleasant than the neatest and most impressive and historically correct suicide? What says the *Avalanche* man? Is he not ready to go on, letting slide innumerable and endless *Avalanches,* even under the accursed Federal banner? And if he, cream of Confederate cream—the guide, philosopher, Mentor, and Palinurus of the rebellion in those parts—is so submissive, why, who can tell how many others will follow his loyal lead? What are we to do? If these great ones, when they are "humbled and downcast—their pride wounded," etc.—are to betake themselves to "a philosophy suited to their condition," must we forgive them for the sake of science? It is a question for jurists. Such clear evidence of a penitent disposition is certainly worthy, in these wicked times, of a charitable consideration. That impulse which we all feel to spare the sick and the sorry is one of the best feelings of our common nature.

JULY 19, 1862

SOUTH

RICHMOND DAILY DISPATCH
July 19, 1862

STRAGGLERS FROM THE ARMY

We have just gained a series of brilliant victories. Our enemy lies prostrate beneath the powerful blows which we have inflicted upon him. It is of the utmost consequence to maintain the ground we have gained, and, of course, in order that we may do so, to retain our present force in full.

Under such circumstances, we appeal to the public to frown down those soldiers who have straggled from their colors and are now wandering through the country, whose defense they have abandoned, and to whose cause they are a disgrace. We call upon all men who love their country, and who desire to see it emerge from its present difficulties with honor, to unite in this duty of every patriot. Let them show the straggler no quarter. Let their houses be closed against them. Let them not approach their firesides. Let them be banished from their society as foul and loathsome lepers, whose very breath is pestilence, whose lightest touch is contamination. Turn your backs, fellow citizens, upon the wretched who desert their country in the hour of her peril—upon the coward who leaves his comrades to face the enemy in the field of battle, while he is skulking in safety—upon the villain who, for a mess of pottage, is willing to surrender, like Esau of old, the precious inheritance bequeathed to him by his fathers, and by them won on many a field of death. You do not reflect, fellow citizens, when you take these men to your houses and extend to them the right hand of fellowship, what it is that you are encouraging. Of all felons whom it is possible for the law to describe, there is none so dark, so loathsome, so foul, so steeped in disgrace as the coward who deserts his colors when his country calls for his services. Yet the crime of which this man is guilty is the crime which you unwittingly encourage when you receive him in your houses and entertain him as an honest man.

To our countrywomen—more especially to the younger portion of them—we appeal, to treat the renegades with the scorn they deserve; to drive them back to their colors with the scorn which nobody but a woman knows how to manifest. Women are all-powerful in this matter, as they are in everything else. They are the truest of patriots, and though their physical strength be weak, their souls are infinitely stronger than those of the men. They all hate cowards and renegades. Let them show it in the plainest manner that they can possibly fall upon. Let them not speak to, nor honor with so much as a look (unless it be a look of contempt), the recreant who skulks in the chimney corner when his country's banner is in the field and his country's foe is striving to tear it down. The country owes a debt to its women which it can never repay. Let them add this one other obligation, and they will find that it is the greatest of all. They have everything in their power. What renegade dare stand before the united scorn of all the women he knows?

We do entreat the people of the country to take this matter up, if they ever expect to beat the Yankees—if they ever expect to be free—if they do not wish their homes to be pillaged, their daughters to be outraged, their sons to be made bond slaves, by the most detestable race that God ever permitted to breathe the air of life.

CHARLESTON DAILY COURIER
July 19, 1862

FROM MOBILE
GOOD NEWS FROM THE WEST—CAPTURE OF MURFREESBORO, TENNESSEE—GENERAL T. L. CRITTENDEN TAKEN PRISONER

Mobile, Alabama, 18th—A special dispatch to the *Mobile Advertiser and Register,* dated Knoxville, July 17, says:

> We have positive information that Colonel Forrest took Murfreesboro on the 13th instant after severe fighting and with considerable loss on both sides. The Federal general Crittenden is a prisoner.

[We have this capture reported by mail elsewhere.]

FROM JACKSON
THE BOMBARDMENT OF VICKSBURG—RESULTS OF THE ARKANSAS'S FIRST TRIAL

Jackson, Mississippi, 17th—The enemy continue shelling Vicksburg, apparently feeling for our troops. The lower fleet has moved up about a mile. The ram *Arkansas* has proved to be a troublesome customer, and the Federals say they will capture her if they lose half their fleet in the attempt. Nine gunboats are said to have passed down the river, running the gauntlet of our batteries, but they were badly damaged.

It is thought the enemy will make a desperate effort to capture the *Arkansas*. Their loss in the late encounter is supposed to have been five hundred.

Captain John Kerr has been assigned to the command at Jackson.

FROM ATLANTA
COLONEL FORREST'S CAVALRY EXPLOIT—THE FIGHT AT MURFREESBORO—CAPTURE OF PRISONERS, STORES, FIELD BATTERY, ETC.

Atlanta, 18th—A gentleman direct from Murfreesboro says Colonel Forrest, with two thousand cavalry, entered Murfreesboro, Tennessee, last

Sunday, at 5:00 A.M. A fight immediately took place, which lasted five hours. Over one hundred Yankees were killed and a large number taken prisoner. Among the latter is General Thomas Crittenden. Our loss was about twenty-five killed and a few wounded.

Colonel Forrest burned up 3 locomotives and trains attached, 65 wagons, all laden with the enemy's stores; burned the depot filled with commissary stores; captured 465 mules and horses and a battery of 4 brass pieces.

The Yankee soldiers were paroled and the officers brought to Chattanooga.

NORTH

BOSTON EVENING TRANSCRIPT
July 19, 1862

WAR ON THE PRINCIPLES OF WAR

The time has come when the Confederates should be treated as enemies as well as Rebels. As long as they resist the government, the latter should exercise against them, under the War Power, all the rights of war. They are too powerful to be safely indulged with their so-called "rights under the Constitution" they abhor and have rejected. By their control of the state governments of their Confederacy, every man and every dollar of property of the hundreds of thousands of square miles over which they wield uncontrolled dominion are at their disposal, and this advantage they are determined to push to the uttermost before they succumb. We are fighting not merely for national existence and the recovery of national territory now occupied by their armies, but to prevent the invasion of the border states and the transfer of the seat of war to Ohio and Pennsylvania. Were all the nations of Europe banded together for our destruction, they could not do us half the evil which the Confederates are capable of doing. If they are not enemies in the full sense of the word, we shall never have enemies during the full course of our future history; and if we cannot act toward them as enemies, but are constitutionally bound to treat them as we would treat a few hundred malcontents engaged in a treasonable riot, we are placed at a frightful disadvantage in carrying on the contest.

Those who are most earnest in defending what they call the "rights of the South" are really playing into the hands of Jefferson Davis and his crew of conspirators. Davis has repeatedly put on the livery of the Constitution to serve the devil of rebellion in. At first he argued, with

Buchanan, that states could not be constitutionally coerced, even if their acts of secession were unconstitutional. Since he has raised armies and fought battles, he has favored us in his messages with many arguments intended to prove that the whole action of the United States, since the war began, has been unconstitutional and that the Constitution had not in it the means of its own preservation. The government, he contended, was bound patiently to submit to overthrow, or exercise arbitrary power. In either case, the South was justified, on his logic, in seceding.

Our present champions of Southern rights do not go so far. They admit that the rebellion should be put down, but they seek to deprive the United States of those rights of war by which alone it can not only be put down but be prevented from ever again rising up. By opposing the most moderate schemes of emancipation and confiscation, they practically tell the Rebels that they may fight until they are utterly exhausted, and then be received back into the Union without punishment.[27] If they succeed, we are lost; if they fail, they lose nothing but the expense to which they have been in carrying on the war. This is called a conciliatory and constitutional policy, but it certainly ignores every principle of common sense. Practical sagacity teaches that while the war lasts, we should strike the enemy's vital points and end the war by the sharpest and quickest methods. To attempt conciliation while the war is in operation, and while our government is opposed by half a million of armed men, is to assist the enemy and dampen the ardor of our own troops. After the war is over is the time for conciliation.

The true, manly, and sensible ground to take is this: that the War Power under our government is constitutionally as vast and as undefined as the War Power of any other nation. When we are fighting an enemy, that enemy has no rights under the Constitution. If he is a Rebel as well as an enemy, his rights under the Constitution begin when he has laid down his arms. If we intend to punish him, we must do it by the process of weakening him during the progress of the war. After the war is over, all his supporters may, we suppose, successfully resist every attempt to confiscate their estates or take their lives. Each will be entitled to a jury trial in the district where his crime was committed, and this will be equivalent to an acquittal. If Jefferson Davis himself is not punished during the war, he will surely not be punished after it. While the war is in operation is the time to confiscate and emancipate. These are war measures and find their justification in "military necessity."

27. The Northern Congress passed two Confiscation acts (1861, 1862), authorizing the appropriation of property, including slaves, belonging to Southern slaveholders.

LETTER FROM NEW YORK

New York, July 18, 1862

The event of the week here has been the great gathering of the people in Union Square, to testify anew their devotion to government as the guardian and representative of free institutions and to pledge again their lives and property for the suppression of a rebellion that seeks their overthrow. In numbers it was all that could be desired; the square was crowded with a dense mass of human beings; the sentiment prevailing was less demonstrative and buoyant than it was a year ago, but probably none the less resolute and determined. The feeling, however, was much less hopeful. Since the meeting a little more than a year ago, the government has called out nearly 700,000 men and has expended, probably, nearly if not quite $700 million, while only slight progress has yet been made in putting down the rebellion.

We are now called upon to recruit our ranks, decimated by disease and the sword, by new levies to the amount of 300,000 men, involving a further outlay of $500 million. In the meantime the feeling between the North and South has been developed into one of intense antagonism, if not hatred. There is no possible basis left for amicable reconstruction. Whatever we hold we must hold by main strength. The moment we withdraw our armies from any portion of the seceded states we have occupied, the population rises almost to a man against us. Where we retain possession, we are everywhere threatened and menaced by armed bands of marauders and guerrillas, who destroy our communications, cut off isolated and detached bodies of troops, and wear out the patience and endurance of our armies by constant alarms and fruitless efforts to attack and destroy these pests which are swarming on every side.

In such a dilemma the question necessarily presses itself upon all —cannot we divide the South so as to neutralize the elements now directed with so much energy and force against ourselves? To divide and conquer has been the most universal and successful maxim in all warfare. Our efforts so far have tended to create enmity instead of dividing the South. It is now very gravely asked whether we can conquer a united people numbering ten million souls, for at present a slave counts as much as a white man, as the labor of the former enables the whole male adult population capable of bearing arms to take the field.

The confidence of our people in a successful future has not yet deserted them, but since our reverses before Richmond, it expresses itself in a much more subdued tone.[28] In truth, the spirit of any other people might sink under an equal disaster. We cannot long afford to spend a year in creating an army to have it worsted in its first great encounter. The effect of this defeat has shown itself in an unwillingness to enlist. Drafting may have to be resorted to in this state—a necessity greatly to be deplored.

The Rebels, in initiating the rebellion, counted upon a divided North, as assuring their success. In this they have not been mistaken, although the division and aid came in a very different form from that anticipated. No one can go from New York or Boston to Washington without being painfully impressed with the difference in sentiment and purpose of the government and that of the people of the Northern states, who bear the whole burden of the war. The problem at Washington has been restoration, the meaning of which is to put down the rebellion and save slavery—not for any love of the institution, but from the legal position taken by government—so that it was only a conservator of the peace and had nothing to do with the domestic institutions of the revolted states.

"The restoration of the Constitution" is an admirable motive, but it is not one fitted to inspire that earnestness and lead to sacrifices necessary to all great achievements. The heart must be touched with a live coal. It cannot be raised to white heat by intellectual propositions. Having no adequate motive, we have had but few brilliant actions or results. The vast army collected on the banks of the Potomac was kept in a state of listless idleness for nearly a year, during which its morale was greatly weakened, its numbers reduced probably one-half by sickness, while the end is a reverse which will require one hundred thousand men and six months of precious time to repair.

Hamilton

NEW YORK TRIBUNE
July 19, 1862

BATTLE IN ARKANSAS

ROUT OF THE REBELS WITH HEAVY LOSS

Springfield, Missouri, July 17, 1862

An expedition recently sent from here under Major Miller of the 2nd Wisconsin Cavalry, consisting of one section of Davidson's battery and

28. Refers to the Seven Days' Battles, Virginia, June 25–July 1, 1862. These engagements terminated General McClellan's Peninsular campaign, the aim of which was to capture Richmond.

detachments of the 10th Illinois, 2nd Wisconsin, and 3rd Missouri State Militia, numbering about 600 men, attacked the combined forces of Rains, Coffey, Hunter, Hawthorne, and Tracey, about 1,600 strong, eight miles beyond Fayetteville, Arkansas, early Monday morning, and completely routed them with heavy loss. Major Miller's command marched seventy-five miles in two nights and took the Rebels by surprise. Our loss was very small. Colonel Hall of the 4th Missouri Militia, stationed at Mount Vernon, reports the killing of 21 guerrillas and the capture of 1,200 pigs of lead during the past few days.

ANOTHER VICTORY BY THE "INDIAN COUNTRY" EXPEDITION

Fort Scott, Kansas, July 8, 1862

A messenger from the Indian expedition near Fort Gibson, in the Indian Territory, arrived last night and reports that a detachment of the 6th and 9th Kansas regiments had surprised Colonel Coffey's command of from 500 to 600 Rebels and captured all their munitions, camp equipage, etc. Thirty Rebels were found dead on the field. McGuire, the notorious half-breed commander of the Rebel Indians, was taken prisoner. Our forces, under Brigadier General Blunt, have penetrated south as far as the Arkansas River, where they will make a halt for the present.

Fort Scott has been made a military post during the war.

NORTHERN TRAITORS

New York, July 12, 1862

To the Editor of the *New York Tribune.* Sir:—Armed rebellion at the South receives the armed attention of the government. Unarmed treason at the North should receive the unarmed but nonetheless summary attention of that same government. We are in a great rebellion. The existence of our national government is in imminent danger. Treason has armed hundreds of thousands for its destruction. These thousands in arms are all in *one section* of our country. Another section is in arms for its maintenance. In this last-named section are hundreds, perhaps thousands (among twenty million), whose political antecedents and hopes or desire for the trade of the rebellious section lead them to sympathize with that section. Not daring to subject themselves to the penalties of offended law, or to the bitter contempt of their fellow citizens, by open and avowed acts against their government, yet being determined to do all they can with personal safety, cowardlike, and with diabolical malice, they resort to the apparently more safe and just as efficacious mode of aiding the rebellion by attempts at dividing the North against itself—

and hence the traitorous cry of "Hang abolitionists and secessionists together." The odium that should center on and burn deep into the hearts of armed Rebels, these peace-preaching Judases try to divide and place on a great portion of law-abiding, government-upholding citizens by demagogue howls and grogshop-party catchwords that appeal to the baser passions and lower prejudices of the lowest of the discontented scum that curses society with its presence. These semigalvanized corpses of a once great political organization know from past experience the power of union and the weakness of disunion and, fearing that the unity of the North will speedily and thoroughly crush the most infernal rebellion that ever outraged a nation or disgraced mankind, coolly and deliberately set about dividing the loyal people of the North by any and every means within their reach. To divide the North is to weaken the North. To weaken the North is to strengthen the rebellious South. These Northern traitors desire to aid the rebellion, and hence their efforts to stir up division among us of the loyal North. Any party or any man, be he a city mayor out of office or a renegade editor in full feather, who attempts, by word or deed, to render any part of the people of the loyal North odious to any other part of that people is a traitor at heart, and the love of his country is not in him or in that party. Loyal men should shun all such as moral lepers, whose touch brings death, and whose very breath breeds pestilence. Government should mark them. State and city authorities should proscribe them. Officers of the law should indict them. Courts should punish them as promoters of disorder. Whosoever is not for the government is against it. These traitorous dissensionists of the North are not for the government. They had rather see the Union destroyed than to see it saved if its salvation caused them the loss of party influence. With these men, party is all; Union, government, country, are naught. Hence their attacks on the personnel of the administration. They intend to make the present government of the people odious in the sight of the people, thus weaken it, thus cripple its power, thus help the rebellion, hoping, in the confusion of divisions thus created among us, to ride into power and then hastily patch up a speedy and dishonorable peace, at the cost of the loyal states and to the disgrace of the nation.

Peace-preaching, dissension-creating treason is as dangerous as treason in arms. Beware of it! Strangle it! Treason in this form attacks Cabinet ministers while lauding the president. Why? It desires to weaken the government, and not daring to openly attack the people's chosen head, it covertly stabs the president through the bodies of his recognized advisers. This kind of treason hopes and aims to tie the hands of the government by false accusations and intolerable abuse of particular members of the national administration; thus weaken it and, by this hoped-for weakness, aid the Rebels. No good citizen will depreciate the efforts of the government, nor of its authorized officials, in this trying time. When men are talked of for position, it is proper to discuss their merits. While a proposed measure is not yet decided on, discussion is proper, but when men are in place and do their best, and when a plan has been decided on, let discussion end and action begin. The unity of the people of the loyal states is their salvation. Their diversion is their death.

AUGUST 16, 1862

SOUTH

RICHMOND DAILY DISPATCH
August 16, 1862

BASENESS OF OUR ENEMIES

A matter has recently occurred which exhibits in its most repulsive aspect the rascality and baseness of our enemies. Among the paroled prisoners who had been confined in Fort Delaware were a number who, when they reached Southern soil, were so debilitated from harsh treatment, improper food, and other causes that it was found necessary to send them to hospitals. One of these, a member of the 8th Alabama Regiment, was taken to the South Carolina hospital at Petersburg, and the next day variola developed itself. He stated to the surgeon in charge that, while confined in Fort Delaware, the prisoners were exposed to smallpox by the Yankees with the hope, it is presumed, that they would bring it hither. The case, however, happened to be of a very light form, and no danger is apprehended from it.

EAST TENNESSEE

The engagement at Tazewell last week, which was so grossly exaggerated, we are satisfied, was but the beginning of active operations in that quarter. The public may safely calculate upon receiving information of a much more important movement in the same direction before the expiration of another week, and it is not improbable that they will have a confirmation of the result anticipated by the dispatch already published. We are assured by a gentleman recently from that section of the Confederacy that our officers and men are fully alive to an opportunity of striking an effective blow to the minions of Lincoln and that stirring news must reach us, before many days, of the operations of our forces.

MEETING OF CONGRESS

The Confederate Congress will reassemble at the capitol, in this city, on Monday next. Among the many matters of importance claiming the early attention of this body is one that has already been brought to the notice of the grand jury of Richmond, and which brings up an issue having no little influence over the future conduct of the war. We allude to the cases of persons known to be guilty of stealing and arming our slaves and inciting them to rebellion and insurrection. We have laws imposing the severest penalties upon our citizens who are guilty of stealing their neighbors' Negroes, and we cannot see why it should be a palliation of the offense that the thieves are dressed in the garb of Federal soldiers. Surely some policy ought to be adopted by the government for the severe and summary punishment of every captured Yankee against whom proof can be brought that he has been in any way instrumental in despoiling Southern men of their Negro property, and we earnestly invoke the attention of Congress to the subject.

THE YANKEE FAILURE AT VICKSBURG

A gentleman recently from Vicksburg informs us that General Van Dorn estimates the number of shot and shell thrown by the enemy during the bombardment at 300,000! Yet, with this stupendous expenditure of ammunition, nothing was accomplished, save considerable damage to buildings in the city, many of which are perforated by the iron missiles, and a very slight destruction of human life. The Yankees, it now appears, did not withdraw their whole force from opposite Vicksburg on the late retirement. They left about six hundred fifty men, strongly entrenched in bombproof ditches and under orders not to move until the archangel sounds the last great reveille for all the nations of the earth. Some are victims of fever and some of the *Arkansas;* but in plain words, they all died.

CHARLESTON DAILY COURIER
August 16, 1862

BRITISH SENTIMENT

The *London Times,* in an article of which the Yankee papers furnish only a few detached sentences, calls upon the British people to give their "whole moral weight to the South, who have so gallantly striven so long for their liberties against a mongrel race of plunderers and oppressors." In contrast with this "mongrel race," the Southern people are spoken of as "our own English kith and kin," and their struggle characterized as the "gallant defense which brave men are making for their liberties," while the attempts of the enemy are denounced as acts of "robbery and oppression by alien hirelings."

From the *London Times,* July 23, 1862

Such an overthrow as the Union army has received before Richmond cannot but have had an instantaneous effect throughout the whole of the South. Wherever in that vast area the news of the great success has been conveyed, by telegraph or steamboat, by horseman or runner, we may be sure that the exultation has been wild and frantic. Even to our sober English eyes, the battles on the Chickahominy seem like a crowding victory; to the excitable Southerner, burning with rage and hate at the invasion of his soil and the atrocities with which it is accompanied, the description of the six days' fighting and the successive "stampedes" of his enemies must have been so inspiriting as to make inaction impossible.[29]

We may, then, it seems to us, expect movements of the highest importance all through the South. It is not easy to discover what is passing in that convulsed but silent region. The Confederates have learned to unite the most fervid enthusiasm with a secrecy which not even Russia has realized in modern warfare. Their enemies never see them till they feel them; never know what is their strength, their position, or their resources, until the dawn of some morning brings an irresistible attack, or reveals the fact that a whole Confederate army has made off without the loss of a man, or a gun, or a barrel of powder. So we ourselves can know little for certain of their plans, but we may yet make a very shrewd guess.

29. The Seven Days' Battles were fought along the Chickahominy River, Virginia.

There is every reason to believe that the western Confederate states will become in a week or two—perhaps have already become—the scene of new struggles, far wider and fiercer than that of the past spring. The news received yesterday of the capture of Murfreesboro by the Confederates shows that the work has already begun in Tennessee, and unless the Unionists are reinforced far more largely than we think them likely to be, it is possible that before the month of July is over, the whole of Tennessee will be in a blaze. The situation of this state is, indeed, most unhappy. It had to bear the brunt of the best-planned and most energetic Union movement that has been made during the war.

While the Confederates were unwisely dispersing their force along the coast, or massing them on the Potomac, they left unguarded this important state, relying, perhaps, on the protection afforded by the extent of the country and the sympathy of the Kentuckians. But by a series of operations which no impartial observer will desire to depreciate, the Unionists, supporting their army by their gunboats, gained possession of the principal places in Tennessee and may be said to have almost conquered the state. But the contest is far from an end. The battles before Richmond have come just in time to rouse Tennessee to the new campaign, for which its leaders are said to be preparing.

The white people of Tennessee number about a million; they are throughout nearly the whole state bitter secessionists, the only Unionist section being the eastern, where a certain number of Union sympathizers are to be found, though from the silence of the Northern press on the subject we are inclined to think that even here the number of Union men has been greatly overrated. Tennessee is represented to have suffered more than any other Southern population from the tyranny of the Union commanders and the rapine of the mercenaries who form so large a portion of the Union armies. It may be that now the time of retribution is at hand and that the Federal government will expiate by serious disasters its faults in allowing such atrocities to be practiced on a people which it still affects to consider as its own.

The capture of Murfreesboro is an event of considerable importance, if we look upon it as the prelude to a general renewal of the western campaign. Murfreesboro is almost exactly in the middle of the state and less than forty miles from Nashville, the capital, where the Federal military governor has been putting clergymen in jail for refusing to take an oath of his own dictation. The fact that Murfreesboro should be in the hands of the Confederates shows that the rising must have made great head, and it is quite within probability that the threatened attacks on Nashville may succeed in throwing the Union corps, which holds it back, on to the frontier of Kentucky and in restoring central Tennessee once more to the Confederacy.

NORTH

BOSTON EVENING TRANSCRIPT
August 16, 1862

FROM CUMBERLAND GAP[30]
FEDERAL VICTORY AT TAZEWELL—LARGE AMOUNT OF REBEL PROPERTY CAPTURED—REPORTS OF REBEL VICTORIES AUTHORITATIVELY DENIED

Louisville, Kentucky, 15th—Captain J. H. Terry, division quartermaster, has just arrived from Cumberland Gap, which he left on the 12th instant, at noon. He reports that General Decourcy's brigade was attacked by Stevenson's Rebel division on the 9th instant, at Tazewell, and that Colonel Cochran, of the 14th Kentucky Regiment, whipped four Rebel regiments. Colonel Cochran held his fire until the Rebels were within one hundred fifty yards, and then checked their advance.

The Federal loss was 3 killed, 15 wounded, and 57 of the 17th Regiment taken prisoners. The Rebel officers admitted a loss of 250 killed and wounded. We took 113 wagonloads of forage and 70 horses. We lost the knapsacks of two regiments.

There has been no fight at Big Creek Gap, as reported, or any other engagement in the vicinity of the Gap or at Tazewell than the foregoing. All reports of other engagements and of the cutting to pieces of General Carter's and Colonel Byrd's forces by the Rebels are utterly false.

General Morgan has issued a special order thanking General Decourcy and Colonel Cochran for their gallantry.

Knoxville papers give a list of one hundred nine Rebels killed at Tazewell.

30. The Cumberland Gap is the pass through the Cumberland Mountains, located near the junction where the boundaries of Virginia, Tennessee, and Kentucky meet.

FROM WASHINGTON
THE NEW POSTAL CURRENCY—MARYLAND SECESSIONISTS LEAVING FOR THE REBEL SERVICE—PROMOTION OF SOLDIERS FROM THE RANKS

New York, 16th—The *Times*'s Washington dispatch states that the new postage-stamp bills for small change were expected to begin arriving from the engravers in New York tomorrow, but it is understood now that they will not come until about Tuesday next.

The secessionists in Maryland are leaving at several points in large numbers, going South to enter the Rebel service to avoid the draft. Advices from Poolesville say that on Tuesday night nearly one hundred persons left there for that purpose.

The *Herald* dispatch says the feeling increases among the army to promote privates for meritorious service. Colonel Marston, of the New Hampshire 2nd, who was here a few days since, says that the vacancies in his regiment must be filled from the ranks with men who are entitled to this reward for their service.

NEW YORK TRIBUNE
August 16, 1862

LET US REASON TOGETHER

It is every day becoming more and more the conviction of our best minds that there can be no permanent settlement with the South short of a general act of emancipation. It is the earnest desire of our most truly conservative men to see the responsibility assumed of declaring a general law of freedom, accompanied by such provision for the remuneration of loyal persons as may be deemed advisable. The welfare, no less than the safety of the country, is believed to require such action, and the only question which we can ask ourselves is, Shall it take place in an orderly manner, under the sanction of authority and as an act of highest national necessity, or be brought about through infinite throes, foreign wars, and the destruction of a whole generation of the youth of the land?

The question is one of the greatest seriousness and importance. The probability amounts almost to a certainty that unless we not only subdue the South but establish order there within a reasonable time, we shall be necessarily involved in the additional burdens of some outside war. The confusion and derangement which have already taken place are too great and too radical to admit of anything but a positive cure. So soon, therefore, as we can realize that order can only result from emancipation, instead of believing that the restoration of order can *precede* it, that moment we shall first begin to draw near the end of our troubles.

It is true a declaration of emancipation might not now keep us from the probability of a participation in a general war. This chance has become so imminent that it behooves us to look it fairly in the face, in any event, until our crisis is past. But if it should not avert, it would enable us to meet it with confidence and equanimity. If a foreign contest be indeed inevitable, we could have no safeguard so sure as the sense of our having acted up to our best conceptions of duty and statesmanship, while casting aside the burden of a divided and halting purpose.

The practical sense of the nations of the world is more than disturbed by the want of precision and result with which we have treated the slavery question during the present year. After all is said, it is probable that the emancipation element in our civil war has been what has thus far kept European peoples from interfering in a contest which has been so prejudicial to their economy and industry. In spite of their own suffering, they have looked on with folded hands, so that we might have every chance to remove forever the hated thing from the face of the earth. Let us never disappoint the forlorn hope of the best men in Europe. Let us not end the war with the burden of slavery still on our soil, to paralyze and benumb our reviving energies. Let us away with it without peradventure, and then we shall have acquired something better than the sympathy of Europe—we shall have the sense of deserving it.

There are points in the history of every republic where an effort has been made, and a responsibility taken by individuals, more searching and stringent in its character than any legislative action can possibly be made to reach. This necessity is recognized so fully in all free states that a liberty of action withheld from senates is accorded for times of emergency to the executive power. Such, from the beginning of this contest, have been the responsibilities which the government has assumed, and which the country has supported and applauded it in doing. Every step has already been taken in emancipation but the last. The last step but includes those already taken—each of which has implied and foretold it.

It is a great error to believe that a sudden uprising and revolt of the Negroes would follow the declaration of an act of emancipation. Such an act would be progressive and gradual in its practical working, not instantaneous and revolutionary. The general history of the race would teach us this, did we need to go beyond the facts of the present war. We have only to remember that several acts of partial emancipation have been passed since the present war began, each more or less general in its character, while the effect of each and all of them has been no more perceptible in the form of insurrectionary tumult than if they had not been executed. Emancipation, if intelligently inaugurated, has acted, and will act, like the tide rising upon the beach, which silently lifts up and floats off every obstacle in its way.

We shall all be surprised, when emancipation is actually declared and at work, to observe how soberly and steadily it will operate. Its destructive quality will have been swallowed up in the magnitude of the war. On the other hand, its constructive power, its power as an arm in the war and an element in any peace, cannot be yet comprehended or estimated. It alone will render peace safe, enduring, or possible. We shall come to it through great travail, but we shall certainly come to it, and the end will be a permanent peace.

THE QUESTION OF EUROPEAN INTERVENTION

The steamship *Glasgow,* which arrived yesterday off Cape Race, brings us several important items of news respecting the question of intervention. Russia, as was to be expected, officially denies having joined France in a proposition of mediation. In the English Parliament, Earl Russell stated that no communication had been received with regard to this question from any other power. He admitted, however, that if mediation were to be offered, he wished to see it offered by all the great powers of Europe conjointly. We regard all this as a confirmation of the views expressed by us in previous articles that there is no probability of immediate interference in our war on the part of any power in Europe.

The *London Times* shows itself very anxious that all appearance of any design of intervention be avoided. The *Times* evidently expects to hear by one of the next mails that the Federal government has found it impossible to raise three hundred thousand volunteers and has therefore given up the contest as useless. When it shall learn that the whole force called for is to be raised without difficulty and the war is about to be renewed with fresh vigor, we must, of course, expect to see its tone again change.

SEPTEMBER 20, 1862

SOUTH

RICHMOND DAILY DISPATCH
September 20, 1862

CAPTURE OF HARPERS FERRY—THE BATTLE IN MARYLAND

From the moment that our armies testified their great superiority to the Yankees at Bethel and Manassas, we saw and said that their true policy was to assume the offensive and never to depart from it. A contrary policy produced a series of disasters which brought the Confederacy to the verge of destruction, and had it not been abandoned at last, we are not sure that we should not, in the end, have become a subjugated and an enslaved people. From the moment the defensive system was abandoned, we began to reap the fruits of our superiority in valor and endurance. Victory followed victory in such rapid succession that the whole civilized world stood amazed at our successes. Each successive victory seemed to rise above the last in brilliancy and importance. Kernstown was eclipsed by McDowell, McDowell yielded to Front Royal, Front Royal was surpassed by Winchester, Winchester gave way to Port Republic, Port Republic bore no comparison with the seven battles around this city, and they, in their turn, were overshadowed by the second battle at Manassas. We have this day to record an achievement which throws them all in the shade. An army besieging another army in a position strong by nature and strongly fortified has been assailed at the same time by a third army and has not only succeeded in defeating that third army with great slaughter, but has on the same day compelled the besieged army to surrender at discretion. We remember but three exploits similar to this. One of them was that of Julius Caesar at Alesia—incomparably the greatest of all that mighty general's achievements—where, with 60,000 men, he kept in an equal number who were besieged in the town, and defeated, with enormous slaughter, 250,000 who attempted to relieve them. Another was that of Marino Falier at the siege of Zara, where he kept in the besieged, and defeated a Hungarian army of 80,000 men. The third was that of Prince Eugene at Belgrade.

As far as we can understand the operations, from the very imperfect accounts which we have received, they were somewhat as follows: Our army in Maryland is divided into three corps, commanded by Generals Jackson, Longstreet, and Hill. Of these corps, Jackson's was engaged in the siege of Harpers Ferry, and the other two covered his operations.

Conceiving it to be of great importance to raise the siege and to relieve the beleaguered forces, which amounted in numbers almost to a *corps d'armée,* McClellan resolved to make a powerful effort.[31] He left Washington, it is said, with a force of eighty thousand men. From the correspondents of the Yankee papers, we heard of him at Rockville and other places on the National Road, sometime last week, from which we conclude that his army marched upon that road in the direction of Fredericktown. The road passes through Fredericktown, but whether McClellan kept it that far we have no means of ascertaining. The first we hear of him is at Boonsboro, in Washington County, which is nearly equidistant from Fredericktown, Harpers Ferry, and Hagerstown, being between twelve and fifteen miles from each and lying a little north of west from the first, nearly due north from the second, and nearly southeast from the third. At this place, on Sunday, he fell with his whole enormous force (eighty thousand men) upon the corps of General D. H. Hill, which was the rear guard of the army. The battle was long, furious, and bloody, but General Hill, although attacked by vastly superior forces, stood his ground without yielding an inch. In the night General Longstreet's corps arrived, and on Monday the two combined attacked McClellan and totally defeated him, driving his forces before them for five miles. But for the intervention of night, it is said that the rout would have been complete. At ten o'clock, while the battle was still raging at Boonsboro, General Miles, with his whole army, variously estimated at 8,000, 10,000, and 12,000 men, surrendered to General Jackson. Vast quantities of stores, 12,000 small arms, 50 pieces of artillery, and at least 1,000 Negroes (some say 2,500) were captured. Having disposed of Miles and his army, General Jackson was marching rapidly down the Potomac, with the intention of crossing below and getting in the rear of McClellan, thus cutting him off effectually from Washington. These operations shed an almost unparalleled luster on the Confederate arms.

In the battle of Boonsboro, or in the operations before Harpers Ferry, (it seems to be uncertain which), General Samuel Garland was killed. He was but thirty years old and was one of the most promising young officers in the army. His education was military, he having graduated at the Virginia Military Institute, and from the time the war commenced, he adopted the profession of arms with an ardor that amounted almost to a passion. He was possessed of fine talents and was as fearless as the sword he wore. While in command of a regiment, he was severely wounded at the battle of Williamsburg, but refused to quit the field. He was in all the battles around Richmond, in which he lost 840 men out of

31. *corps d'armée:* French, "army corps."

1,700, the strength of his brigade. In private life he was a most agreeable and a most amiable man. He was the only son of a widowed mother. We have heard of no other officer of high rank who was killed in the late actions.

VIOLATION OF PAROLE

It becomes a matter of importance that the question should be promptly and rigidly investigated whether or not Federal prisoners, paroled during the last few months, have in many cases, as is alleged, violated their pledged faith and again taken up arms against the South. Under the rules of war, such perfidy is punished with death, and it should be unhesitatingly visited upon all offenders. There must have been some forty thousand Federal prisoners, all veteran soldiers, discharged upon their parole within the last few months, and if the unscrupulous Federal government, which is vile enough to stoop to any crime, has again compelled these men to take up arms, it is time our military leaders should adopt some stringent measures to prevent the repetition, in the future, of a species of villainy unknown in honorable warfare, and which deprives us of some of the most valuable advantages of victory, purchased at the cost of precious Southern blood.

ARRESTS

William Barrett has been committed to the military prison of the Eastern District for acting as a substitute agent.[32] A man in his employ, named William McNiven, was put in on the same charge. Edward A. Foran, a member of the 14th Regiment Louisiana Volunteers, was also arrested and locked up for trying to sell himself as a substitute. A. Doobar, a Yankee member of the 1st Maryland Cavalry, has been placed in Castle Thunder, as also James Smith, arrested for selling liquor.[33]

32. Men whose names were drawn for the draft and who were not otherwise exempt because of health, personal circumstances, or, in the South, occupation could avoid military service by hiring a substitute to serve in their place for a fee ranging from a few hundred to a few thousand dollars. In the North, one could also avoid service by paying a "commutation fee" of three hundred dollars. The process was quickly corrupted by cheaters and unscrupulous brokers. Noting that healthy men were avoiding service just when they were needed the most, the Confederate Congress ended legal substitution in 1863. The Federal law authorizing commutation was repealed in 1864. Allowing substitutes was not a Civil War expedient, but had long been practiced in both Europe and the United States. Despite cries of "rich man's war and poor man's fight," evidence, at least on commutation, shows that paid exemption from service was not predicated on wealth.

33. Castle Thunder was the nickname given to two tobacco warehouses converted to Confederate prisons, one in Richmond and the other in Petersburg. Castle Thunder in Richmond housed political prisoners, traitors, and spies, while the one in Petersburg housed Union prisoners of war.

ESCAPED

The soldier named W. H. Wright, arrested a few days since by Detective Boyd for passing a hundred-dollar counterfeit note on the Bank of Mobile and for having in his possession two other bogus notes purporting to be issued by the Manufacturers and Mechanics Bank of Columbus, Georgia, escaped from Castle Booker, corner of 6th and Cary streets, on Thursday night. Had he not succeeded in giving the guard the slip, it was the intention of the provost marshal to have turned him over to the mayor for examination.

CHARLESTON DAILY COURIER
September 20, 1862

FROM RICHMOND
GREAT BATTLE IN MARYLAND—CONFEDERATES AGAIN VICTORIOUS—THE FIGHT AT HARPERS FERRY CONFIRMED

Richmond, 18th—The report of the fight at Harpers Ferry and capture of eight thousand prisoners is confirmed.

On Sunday, General D. H. Hill's division was attacked in Maryland by eighty thousand of the enemy. The fight continued all day with heavy loss on both sides. On Monday General Hill was reinforced by General Longstreet, the battle renewed, and the enemy driven back three miles.

General Garland, of Virginia, was killed in Sunday's fight. His body arrived here this afternoon.

SURRENDER OF HARPERS FERRY—10,000 PRISONERS, 51 CANNONS, 12,000 STANDS OF ARMS, 1,500 SLAVES, HEAVY STORES, ETC., CAPTURED

Richmond, 19th—On Sunday last, Generals Jackson and Longstreet attacked the enemy at Harpers Ferry. After a severe fight, the Yankees surrendered. Ten thousand prisoners and twelve thousand stand of arms, fifty-one cannons, and fifteen hundred slaves were captured, with heavy stores.

The same day, General D. H. Hill's division met McClellan's forces near Poolesville, Maryland. Generals Hill and Longstreet drove the Yankees five miles with great slaughter.

FURTHER FROM HARPERS FERRY
THE GREAT BATTLE BETWEEN BOONSBORO AND MIDDLETOWN, MARYLAND

Richmond, 19th—Governor Letcher today received letters from Winchester, dated September 16, confirming the report of the unconditional surrender of ten thousand Yankees at Harpers Ferry on Monday without the loss of a man on our side. Jackson captured fifty pieces of artillery, ammunition, stores, etc.

The letter also mentions an engagement having occurred in Maryland between Boonsboro and Middletown, in which the enemy were repulsed, with a reported loss of five thousand killed and wounded. The Confederate loss was heavy. No further particulars have been received.

FROM CAMP MOORE
YANKEE DEPREDATIONS

Camp Moore (Line of the New Orleans and Jackson, Mississippi, Railroad), 17th—The Yankees, two hundred strong, came up the railroad to Ponchatoula on Monday, 15th instant, and burned seven or eight cars. In a fight which ensued, the Yankees lost five or six killed, about the same number of wounded, and a few taken prisoners. Our loss was one killed and a few wounded.

FROM IUKA
DETAILS OF THE CAPTURE—THE ENEMY'S LOSS—VANDALISM OF THE YANKEES

Special to the *Mobile Advertiser and Register*

Iuka, Mississippi, 16th—This place was captured Sunday morning last. The enemy evacuated it during the night, and but for a premature attack, we should have captured the entire garrison. We have taken over a million dollars' worth of stores. The enemy were strongly entrenched. Our loss was five; that of the enemy thirty, of whom ten were left dead on the field. Our forces arrived in time to save the town from destruction. The citizens were found with their household goods packed and out of doors, awaiting the application of the torch by the vandals to their dwellings.

The enemy carried off two hundred Negroes, thirty of whom were afterward released by our scouts. Twelve houses and three mills were destroyed on the line of the enemy's march from Marietta to Iuka. They retreated in the direction of Corinth, making a demonstration on our lines on the night of the 15th, but which is believed to have been only a feint to cover their retreat. It is also believed that they are crossing the Tennessee River at Hamburg.

The *Chicago Times* of the 13th says: "Stonewall Jackson left Baltimore and Washington to the right and is marching on Harrisburg, Pennsylvania. Jackson's cavalry advance is on every road, creating consternation, it not being known upon what point he will make a demonstration. Governor Curtin had called on the mayor of Philadelphia to furnish twenty thousand men in twelve hours for the defense of the city."

The hour of retaliation has come.

FROM KNOXVILLE
EVACUATION OF CUMBERLAND GAP—
OUR TROOPS PURSUING THE ENEMY

Knoxville, Tennessee, 19th—The enemy evacuated Cumberland Gap, Wednesday night, blowing up their magazines, destroying all their property, and blasting rocks to block the roads. They retreated by way of the Harland Road to Kentucky. Our forces were pursuing them by Cumberland Ford and Baptist Gap.

Andy Johnson's family, who were at Greenville, east Tennessee, within our lines, were permitted, by order of the secretary of war, to return to the enemy's lines.

FROM WARRENTON
WOUNDED SOUTH CAROLINIANS IN
WARRENTON, VIRGINIA, HOSPITALS

Warrenton, Virginia, 18th—The following is a list of wounded South Carolinians at Payne, Wewby, and Cas hospitals, Warrenton, Virginia:

W. Jones, thigh, Company A; H. A. Lockwood, knee; H.H.C. Walker, knee; F.W.D. Fogle, leg; A. H. Ewidier, hip; W. J. Dibble, thigh; A.S.L. Airs, leg; H.O.F. Gregory, leg; H.J.B. Plowden, face, severe; H.J.D. Felder, leg; H.N.E. Brown, leg off; B.F.P. Hughes, thigh; A. J. Early, arm off, bad; G. A. Woodson, arm, severe; E.J.J. Fowley, leg off. All of the above are of the Hampton Legion and doing well.

Wounded, since dead: Charles H. Atkinson, James McGee, Thaddeus L. Cay.

For the want of clothes, many of the men are nearly naked.

NORTH

BOSTON EVENING TRANSCRIPT
September 20, 1862

LET THE WORD STILL BE "ONWARD"

The nation was driven by the audacity of rebellion to engage in war and incur all its casualties and calamities. Of the unavoidable disasters attending sanguinary conflicts, even when the result is for the right, we are now having another heavy and heartrending installment. Patriotism is to be tested in the very presence, as it were, of our own dead and wounded, and many are called upon, in the trials of private sorrow, to adhere resolutely to their convictions, to maintain unflinchingly their principles. The cry has been that the rebellion must be put down at all costs and at any sacrifices. When the hour comes for the payment of those costs and the making of those sacrifices, the cry must be the same —equally stern and unswerving.

Of the forces in the field, courage in the face of danger, courage in the midst of carnage, courage as friends and companions fall or are borne wounded to the rear, is demanded. They are expected to be all the braver the greater the peril and never to falter or cease fighting so long as there is the slightest chance of maintaining their ground, the slightest hope of defeating the enemy.

This same spirit must be manifested at home—however sad in many respects the circumstances under which it is called for—and manifested with all the more steadiness when it seems as if the bloody path through the battlefield was the direct way to victory; that out of individual suffering is to come the great boon not only of peace, but of a rescued nationality and the freedom it guarantees.

Not a tear for the loved and lost need be kept back; not a sigh of mourning affection need be hushed; not an effort to assume the appearance of unmoved stoicism need be made. The troubled heart may have its rights; the bereaved affections may lament their losses; honor may be rendered to the heroic dead; and fullest sympathy may be sincerely tendered to distress visited upon the living. But in and through all the exercise of the sad and hallowed privileges of the finest sensibilities, there should be no faltering of the great purpose which has roused a great people and made them almost welcome the sword, rather than allow their government to be overthrown and all that is dear to them subjected to the rule of heartless despotism.

If rebellion, in its desperation, can endure hardships, throw away life as a worthless thing, beggar its communities, send grief into thousands of households, squander the prosperity of a generation, to secure its bad end—if rebellion can do this, surely intelligent and high-souled loyalty can, in its devoted earnestness, endure and bear all that it is summoned to do and bear in the defense and maintenance of its priceless trusts.

At this moment, then, with all the seriousness widespread affliction must bring, as part of the price paid for success, let there be expressed the unconquerable determination to follow up all advantages gained, until the final and complete conquest of the foe shall permit an honorable return, beneath the folds of a vindicated flag, to the pursuits of peace.

IMPORTANT RUMORS
STONEWALL JACKSON DEAD—
HARPERS FERRY IN OUR POSSESSION

New York, 20th—A special correspondent of a morning paper has the following:

> A chaplain of the Rebel army taken prisoner in Gibbon's brigade told Lieutenant Sexton of the 2nd Wisconsin Regiment that Stonewall Jackson was certainly dead.[34] He declared that he had himself seen him brought off from the field.
>
> A telegram was seen today at Frederick purporting to come from a surgeon at Harpers Ferry and asking another surgeon to send some medical supplies to that place. If this fact may be relied upon, and it is certified by General Hartsuff's aide as of his own knowledge, Harpers Ferry is ours. Such also is the general opinion in our army at Sharpsburg.[35]

[This telegram may have been received, but does *not* prove that Harpers Ferry is in our possession, as Drs. Vosburg, Hoyt, and others were left at that place in charge of the wounded in the hospital.]

The *Herald*'s correspondent also has the following:

> Stonewall Jackson relieved Longstreet in the latter part of the day and is believed to have been killed during the engagement. A

34. The rumor is false. General "Stonewall" Jackson died a year later, on May 10, 1863, as a result of a wound received during the Battle of Chancellorsville.

35. Sharpsburg (Maryland), the site of the Battle of Antietam (or Sharpsburg), September 17, 1862.

shout went along the whole line that Jackson was killed, and a number of prisoners state that he was missing and supposed to be lying dead upon the field within our lines.

A Rebel chaplain captured late in the action made the same statement and assured an officer that Jackson had been missing for some time. No intelligence relative to his death had reached General McClellan last night, but as Jackson wore no distinguishing marks, it is probable that he lies unrecognized somewhere upon the field.

50,000 REBELS STILL IN MARYLAND—RUMORED CAPTURE OF GENERAL LEE—20,000 DEAD AND WOUNDED REBELS IN OUR HANDS

New York, 20th—A Baltimore special dispatch states that there was considerable skirmishing yesterday.

It is the general impression that fifty thousand Rebels are still on this side of the Potomac River and must yet be captured.

There is a rumor here tonight that General Lee has been captured. It is believed that at least twenty thousand wounded and dead have been left in our hands. Many are still unburied.

It is thought to be impossible for the Rebels to retreat through Virginia.

1,200 REBEL PRISONERS ARRIVE AT BALTIMORE

Baltimore, 20th—Twelve hundred more Rebel prisoners arrived this morning from Frederick. They were captured by General McClellan. They are being sent to Fort Delaware. Another train is on the way. They are in all sorts of garbs and are dirty and ragged.

[UNTITLED]

New York, 20th—The steamer *Haze* sailed for New Bern, North Carolina, today with two hundred recruits for Massachusetts regiments.

[UNTITLED]

New York, 20th—Albert Potter, Company B, 22nd Massachusetts Regiment, died in the hospital at York, Pennsylvania, on the 8th instant.

NEW YORK TRIBUNE
September 20, 1862

THE LATEST NEWS IN WASHINGTON

Special Dispatch to the *New York Tribune*

Washington, September 19, 1862, 11:50 P.M.

Up to eleven o'clock there was nothing from General McClellan later than this morning's dispatches.

Several of our wounded officers arrived in this city from the battlefield near Sharpsburg tonight, among them Lieutenant Colonel Thomas S. Allen of the 2nd Wisconsin, wounded in the right arm by a rifle ball. He also suffers weakness in the left arm from a wound it received at Bull Run. Captain D. W. Gibson, wounded in the foot; Captain George B. Ely, wounded in the arm, both captains of the 2nd Wisconsin; and an aide of General Hartsuff have also arrived.

All agree that no battle, since the rebellion broke out, has engaged more men or been fought with more desperation. Our soldiers behaved like heroes, new recruits fighting as well as old ones. If there was faltering anywhere, it was the fault of the regimental officers, some of whom exposed their men unnecessarily but rarely exposed themselves.

The impression among the wounded officers here is that the victory of Wednesday would have been a much more complete one had not General Hooker, whose leadership was having a wonderful effect in inspiring our army, been wounded. As he was being borne from the field, General Hooker exclaimed that he would rather have been shot in the head at the close of the battle than in the foot at that time.

There are at least three thousand Rebel prisoners at or near Frederick.

We held the field, these men say, after the battle of Wednesday, along the whole right and center, and brought off all our wounded and buried our dead. They were told that we possessed the same advantage on the left at the close of the fight.

Rebel prisoners captured acknowledged that they had been terribly beaten.

These officers left Keedysville, which is about two miles from the battlefield, at eight o'clock this morning. There was sharp artillery firing from the time they started until their arrival at Frederick, two hours. There seemed to be no musketry, and it was impossible for them to form an opinion as to whether the cannonading indicated a renewal of the conflict, or a retreat and pursuit, as it probably was.

They understood at the time of leaving that no practicable ford was open to the Rebels and that they were surrounded by our army, drawn up in the shape of a crescent, stretching from Antietam Creek below its ford and bridges around on the right to the Potomac.

Yesterday afternoon the Rebels sent in a flag of truce; for what purpose it is not known. Immediately after their return, they drove in our pickets by concert along the whole line, which would seem to have been intended to cover a retreat.

A chaplain of the Rebel army, taken prisoner in Gibbon's brigade, told Lieutenant Sexton of the 2nd Wisconsin that Stonewall Jackson was certainly dead. He declared that he had himself seen him brought off from the field.

The town of Sharpsburg, inhabited mostly by Union citizens, but in possession of the Rebels, was burned on Wednesday night.

An aide of General Hartsuff's, who arrived here this evening from Frederick, where he has been taking care of his general, says that his wound, which is from a minié ball in the fleshy part of the thigh, is painful but not serious.

General Hartsuff's brigade, which went into the battle nineteen hundred strong, lost half its number in killed and wounded.

A telegram was seen today at Frederick purporting to come from a surgeon at Harpers Ferry and asking another surgeon to send medical supplies to him at that place. If this fact may be relied upon, and it is certified by General Hartsuff's aide as of his own knowledge, Harpers Ferry is ours. Such also is the general opinion in our army at Sharpsburg.

ANOTHER ACCOUNT OF WEDNESDAY'S BATTLE

From Our Special Correspondence

Battlefield, Evening, September 17, 1862

The enemy, as usual, concealed and sheltered his forces as much as possible in woods. His baseline ran along an almost unbroken stretch of timber for at least two miles. He had some troops besides in advance on the summits of the numerous undulations, in open ground, on the line of Antietam Creek. We were the attacking party and, of course, were obliged to go to the enemy. Our way lay across open fields. The position we occupied early in the morning was perhaps a mile in the rear of where we commenced our attacks. Richardson's division was separated from Sumner's corps and added to Hooker's on the right of the center, to strengthen Hooker for the opening movement in the fight. Mansfield's corps also supported Hooker. Franklin's corps, which in the morning lay at the extreme left, was sent around to the extreme right, and Porter's corps occupied the center, and Burnside with Reno's and Stevens's divisions on the left. That is the order in which the army went into the fight. The enemy lay on and before a wooded ridge between Antietam Creek and Sharpsburg.

The field was full of points of view from which the battle in its whole length and breadth could be witnessed by a single eye.

The day opened hazy, but by ten o'clock had cleared up, leaving a flecked sky with a gentle breeze to temper the burning heat of the sun a little.

By nine-thirty the fighting had become general and close between the infantry of General Hooker's corps leading, supported by General Mansfield's corps, and Richardson's, followed by the corps of General Sumner, on the right of our line of battle. Meantime the batteries of General Fitz-John Porter's corps, situated about the center of our lines, assisted the advance of our right by firing across at the enemy in its front.

At ten-thirty General Burnside was ordered to advance on the left and attack with vigor.

Eleven-fifty. As Meagher's Irish Brigade was advancing over a plowed field on a brigade of the enemy, a shell from our center burst among the Rebels and started them back on a run. The Irish Brigade could hardly keep its line of march in its eagerness, every man going as fast as he could individually after the skedaddlers.

General Burnside's command was composed of Reno's and Steven's divisions. General Burnside was ordered to take the bridge crossing Antietam Creek, a strong, heavy stone structure, most formidable for defense, and one of the necessities for crossing over to the enemy's ground. The 5th New York Duryee's Zouaves were first sent out to skirmish. The bridge was held by one Rebel regiment. The 2nd Maryland was first sent to dislodge them and did good work, but failed of the object. The 51st Pennsylvania and 51st New York were then sent, and succeeded after a desperate resistance and at an awful cost of life to us. About five hundred of our brave fellows fell killed and wounded in that exploit. The struggle lasted full three hours.

The 21st Massachusetts was also engaged and suffered severely. General Rodman succeeded in fording the creek about a mile below the bridge with his brigade, consisting of the 4th Kentucky and 8th and 11th Connecticut. The Rebels were driven from the front of their line, which was the western bank of the creek up to and beyond the hill in the rear of the Rebel right and held by General Burnside at the close of the day. A battery was also captured and retained, while, on the other hand, General Burnside lost nothing but so many of his brave men, together with General Rodman; Colonel Kingsbury, 11th Connecticut; Lieutenant Colonel A. H. Coleman, 11th Connecticut; and other of his valuable officers. General Rodman and Colonel Kingsbury were mortally wounded, and Lieutenant Colonel Coleman killed outright.

General Burnside had perhaps the hardest work of the field. The bridge was the enemy's strongest defensive position. And not only that, but in the course of the day, the strength of the enemy wore around to our left and concentrated considerably upon Burnside's wing, and one corps was all he had to stem the current. The terrible onset made upon the enemy's left by Generals Hooker and Mansfield, and the sharp cannonading of our center, had the effect, no doubt, to discourage the Rebels from any sanguine hopes in that quarter, and the later opening of the ball on our left invited them in that way as the least desperate chance. The bridge, too, was a great point with them.

They had some idea of turning our left before we developed our force there, and at one time made a very respectable attempt to do so, but although they fought to admiration in the attempt, our troops, on discovering their purpose, foiled them at the first movement and drove them before them.

This is the greatest battle of the war, and the most stubbornly contested on the part of the Rebels of any general engagement of great magnitude. The splendid work of our brave boys is past praise. To see them, as I saw them, walking up to the blazing batteries and the rapid musketry would explain any degree of enthusiastic admiration. Several veteran officers told me they never saw such magnificent fighting.

It was not all plain sailing with us, however. We were more than once temporarily driven back; we very nearly lost the battery we captured by a sudden reinforcement of the point from which it was taken. A whole Rebel division was brought up. Our brigade fell back, but retained their captured battery. Some notion may be obtained of the sharpness of the enemy's fire at times, through which our boys marched without faltering, by the fact that Captain Clarke's battery had every commissioned officer—captain and three lieutenants—shot down before it was even brought into position to be used, and it was afterward fought by its noncommissioned officers!

General Burnside and staff occupied a point of observation within range of the enemy's artillery, but partially protected by haystacks. Shells burst repeatedly near them.

Some of our batteries on the left fired away all their ammunition by sundown, or a little after; but more had come up ready for a renewal of the ball in the morning. An addition also had been made to the number of the batteries for the left. The Rebels stopped firing a little before positive darkness obliged them, and after a few rounds from one gun on our side, darkness closed the awful scene.

J. E.

OCTOBER 18, 1862

SOUTH

RICHMOND DAILY DISPATCH
October 18, 1862

FURTHER FROM KENTUCKY
CONFIRMATORY ACCOUNTS OF BRAGG'S VICTORY

Mobile, Alabama, 17th—A special dispatch to the *Advertiser and Register* from Holly Springs yesterday says:

> Lieutenant General Pemberton has assumed command of the department. Our burial party of three hundred, sent to Corinth, were seized and returned as prisoners.
>
> The Cincinnati papers, of the 11th, are filled with accounts of the great battle between Generals Bragg and Buell. The tenor of their account is that Buell is badly defeated and driven across the Kentucky River and that Bragg is pursuing vigorously.
>
> Three hundred paroled prisoners arrived here this evening.

Chattanooga, Tennessee, 17th—The *Rebel* has the following dispatch from La Vergne, today:

> All is uncertainty. I believe the Yankees are leaving Nashville. In addition to the above, I am satisfied there is something on hand.
>
> Letters from Bragg's army say that Buell's army is the worst-whipped and most badly cut-up army of the war. There is no doubt but that we gained a most glorious victory.

Mobile, Alabama, 17th—A special dispatch to the *Advertiser and Register* from Senatobia says:

> Dispatches, dated the 12th, from Indianapolis to the *Chicago Tribune,* say that intense excitement prevails there, caused by dispatches from General Boyle saying that General Bragg was in rear of Buell, marching on Louisville. He urges Governor Merton to send him reinforcements, as there were only two thousand troops in Louisville. The impression prevails at Louisville that Buell was badly whipped. The excitement in the city was intense. The *Cincinnati Commercial,* of the 13th, claims a victory, but the dispatches are very conflicting.

CHARLESTON DAILY COURIER
October 18, 1862

THE WAR'S COMPENSATIONS

No war ever waged has been more fruitful of evils and miseries than the contest at present going on between the United States and the Confederate States. Blood has flowed like water, tender bosoms have been torn with grief, fair and fertile districts have been visited upon with desolation and ruin, and the constancy and fortitude of our people have been most severely tried by multiform and grievous hardships and woes. Our loved lie in unmarked graves on the field of battle where they fell, and languish in beds of suffering in our hospitals. Every day adds some noble spirit, the joy and pride of some household, to the long list of the untimely dead, and every battle causes thousands of hearts to swell and throb with anguish.

In the midst of this confusion and mourning, we find it difficult to procure food for consolation and strength. Ills and sorrows press so heavily upon our souls that we are oftentimes at a loss for considerations that afford relief and comfort. The compensations for all this trouble seem vague, uncertain, and unsatisfactory, while the calamities are real and terrible. The one overshadows the other, and so deeply dark is the shadow of the evil that we see but dimly the good observation reason and faith tell us is present. The one has obtained ample possession of the soul, and the other cannot enter and bestow the blessing it would impart.

But it is our bound duty—a duty we owe ourselves and the righteous cause in which we are engaged—to avail ourselves of the influence of every fact and consideration that will help to lighten the burden of our woes. It is wrong, and foolish, and harmful in the last degree to shut our ears obstinately to the pleasant voices that sing songs in this night of affliction. The dreariness of the waste is relieved with sprays of grass and lovely flowers, green and blooming here and there. Common sense and piety alike enjoin us to open our eyes, and ears, and hearts to everything that will yield solace and strength, and we shall find that these times, so troublous and calamitous, have already been productive of great benefit and are still dispensing blessings which would not have been bestowed, or at any rate not accepted, were we not passing through the furnace of affliction.

The effects of this war upon the people at large have been most signally beneficial. Forced to contend against an enemy far superior to ourselves in numbers, wealth, and the matériel of war, we have realized thoroughly the great truth of a superintending, directing, and controlling Providence. The greater power and resources of the enemy have caused us to lift our eyes to the source of wisdom and might, and with humble, trustful hearts we have besought the help of Heaven. And in times of rejoicing, under the influence of brilliant victories, dismissing pride and vainglory from our exultant minds, we have bowed in adoring gratefulness before the God of Battles, sung praises to His name, confessed our transgressions, and promised to amend our ways. The worship and the repentance were sincere, for we felt in our heart of hearts that God had given us the victory and that we could prevail over our enemies only by the aid of His right hand and holy arm.

These open and hearty acknowledgments of our dependence upon the God of Heaven and of our belief in His universal sovereignty have had a most wholesome effect upon the feelings and character of our people. The comprehension of that sublime truth has in many instances led to a change of life, but even when the effect has not extended thus far, it has in a measure purified and elevated the moral nature and prepared the heart for the effectual working of the spirit of grace.

The softer and gentler feelings of our nature have been called into unwonted exercise. Our hospitals have developed their fine and noble traits and qualities, which are the most beautiful ornaments men or women can wear, in comparison with which gold and gems lose all their luster and attractiveness. The largest amount of good yielded by this source has been experienced by our women. Clothing themselves in plain apparel, expelling from their minds all frivolous thoughts,

Southern women, impelled by the promptings of humanity and patriotism, have taken their seats beside the couch of the sick and wounded soldiers and ministered with tenderness and skill to the noble sufferers. And not content with administering to the diseases of the body and alleviating physical pain, transformed into angels by the holy work, they have shown these languishing ones the way of salvation and, with gentle voice and tear-filled eyes, guided their feet into that pleasant path. More lovely wives, more faithful mothers, more obedient daughters, better women, are they for having labored in this sphere of benevolence.

We have acquired a reputation for bravery, constancy, and fortitude which we could not have hoped to attain under ordinary circumstances. The qualities we gloried in possessing, but which those ignorant of our character refused to accord us, have been made to shine with wondrous brightness. We have suffered with a degree of patience and resignation which has elicited plaudits as warm from neutral nations as the heroism and gallantry we have manifested on the field of blood. Though still unrecognized in our national capacity by any member of the family of nations, those powers have not failed to mark and admire the high and noble qualities we have exhibited, and there is not one of them who deems these Confederate States unworthy of alliance. No nation ever claimed independent existence on better grounds; no nation ever began its existence with so transcendent a display of power, valor, resolution, and wisdom.

NORTH

BOSTON EVENING TRANSCRIPT
October 18, 1862

[UNTITLED]

Skulking and straggling are not confined to the army. These cowardly movements can also be seen at home. Just as mean-spirited soldiers, enlisting only for the pay and rations, the fun of camp life, and a little holiday festival, or from other unmanly motives, hide and run to save their petty lives as they are summoned to encounter the stern realities of battle; just so the patriotism of some civilians oozes out of the end of their shaking fingers as they are called upon to show the sincerity of their professions by firmness in meeting unanticipated perils, or sacrifices in responding to demands to secure the safety of the country.

At the outset, when the rebellion was not regarded as very formidable, and all felt sure that its resources were wholly insufficient for the execution of its iniquitous designs and that it would be destroyed by the first heavy blow of the Federal government, everybody was loyal—in speech, at least. It was easy then to render all the support which seemed to be needed to preserve the nation one and undivided. But as the contest deepened and, in its expensiveness and risks and magnitude, has tried men's souls, pockets, pluck, and honesty, more or less of hesitation, shrinking, and retreat from the warfare has become visible. Fear of taxation, fear of serious disturbance of business, fear of diminished incomes and consequent loss of luxuries and the downy comforts of ease, fear lest old associations may be dissipated past recovery and old positions, political or otherwise, lost—fear of these and other discomforts and losses as likely to fall to their lot has affected some nerves and caused some whispered inquiries whether it is not best to stop the dangerous and costly work of fighting, crawl out of the conflict somehow, and submit to any terms that promise to give quiet sleep of nights and reduce the war prices.

It takes a big fight to bring out the many heroes and the few cowards in a regiment of volunteers. And it takes a similar process to separate true and sturdy from halfhearted and pusillanimous patriotism. The former becomes only the more earnest and determined the greater the exigency, while the latter shows the white feather in proportion as things look serious. The one, in its clear convictions and truthful purposes, knows that the issue is the same, however the difficulties in the way of deciding it for the right may accumulate, but the other trembles before these difficulties and prates about them as a sufficient reason for a sneaking desertion of noblest principles.

There is nothing alarming, therefore, in the apparent increase of skulking and straggling from the gigantic and hot contest for the honor of the Stars and Stripes. It is only the sifting of the tares and the wheat under the winnowing of the stormy hour of danger and making the difference between them, which has always existed, a little more distinct. This is no matter for regret. It is not a moment too early to know precisely how much unconditional loyalty there is in the land to bravely meet the crisis, formidable as it now is, or still more formidable as it may become. Upon the amount of that unconditional loyalty the existence and future prosperity of the republic depends. Let it be seen, then, just what invincible might the freedom of a continent has at its command.

BOSTON AND NINE MONTHS' MEN[36]

The quota of Boston under the last call of the president, according to the latest statement, is 3,738. From this is to be deducted 569 three years' men, enlisted here since the state's complement for the war has been completed, which would leave 3,169 as the number of recruits to be furnished for nine months.

Official information has been received at the statehouse of the mustering in of 1,488 men for the short term of service. Four hundred ninety-four have been added since Wednesday by transferring persons from other places, without counting the enlistments in the city, which have been quite numerous. One or two hundred more, to be ultimately computed in Boston's quota, are in camp and have not been inducted into the army of the Union.

There is no doubt that the number of nine months' troops now to be raised in the city does not exceed fifteen hundred. If the city government performs its whole duty with respect to the bounty and uses due diligence in obtaining the surplus of towns overrunning their complement, and the community takes proper interest in the matter, Boston may yet be able to say that no real draft has occurred within its limits.[37]

NEW YORK TRIBUNE
October 18, 1862

REMINISCENCES OF THE BATTLE OF SHILOH—SERENADE TO BRIGADIER GENERAL PRENTISS—ACCOUNT OF HIS CAPTIVITY—SUFFERINGS OF THE MEN TAKEN WITH HIM—WHAT HE THINKS OF THE PROCLAMATION—COLONEL MULLIGAN ON REBEL SYMPATHIZERS

Special Dispatch to the *New York Tribune*

Washington, October 17, 1862

General B. M. Prentiss of Illinois was serenaded this evening at Willard's Hotel; some fifteen hundred people were assembled. He was introduced as the "man of the West" and spoke as follows:

36. The periods of enlistment in both the North and the South varied widely and from state to state. At first, the service could be as short as ninety days, but the period was later expanded, ranging anywhere from six months to the duration of the war.

37. To encourage voluntary military service, national, state, and local governments in the North offered bounties ranging from $25 to $400. At the start of the war the Confederate government offered a $10 bounty; the amount was later raised to $50.

My Friends:—This ovation, if intended for me, is a high compliment, for which I thank you. As a soldier, permit me to say, if it is your pleasure, it is my will to recount to you some of the scenes through which I have passed with my fellow officers in captivity in the "Land of Dixie." [*Cries of "That's what we want."*] In doing so, my friends, permit me to say that I may use some harsh language. If I do, don't blame me, for I have cause. For six long months I have been kept in close confinement by those demons of the South. Permit me to commence with my capture on the 6th of April last on the field of Shiloh, at five o'clock in the morning, with those officers that were afterward in captivity with me. We were fighting the enemies of this government. We continued to fight them until fifteen minutes of six in the evening, when, being completely enveloped by the entire Rebel force, we had to succumb; and it was a bitter moment for us. It was on that field that I beheld Illinoisans, Iowans, Missourians, and some from Indiana battling for their country. It was there that I saw the noble Stars and Stripes trailed in the dust by these demons of the South. Yet, after having been persecuted during my entire captivity, I come home to the North and am told that there are men with us not willing to sustain the government. Let me say to you, as a soldier, as a man, as a loyal citizen, if you have traitors among you, send them South. [*Cheers, and cries of "Good, good."*] I trust it is not so. I trust you have not got them at the North. I go on an early train to the West as an officer. It is not my duty to assail persons, but that man who is not willing to defend his government at this hour of trial is my enemy. [*Loud cheers.*] And I claim the privilege everywhere of assailing him. [*Applause, and cries of "Bully for you."*] My friends, I was taken at Shiloh with twenty-two hundred others, brave and gallant men. We were marched the day after our capture, both wounded and well soldiers (some three hundred of them badly wounded), a distance of twenty-two miles without food, they having taken their last meal on the morning of that fight. We were marched to Corinth, placed in boxcars, all together, and sent to Memphis, arriving there on Tuesday night. Twenty-two hundred of these men were placed in one building. After I had pleaded and begged that they might have provisions, I went into the hall, called the colonel commanding the post, and told him that these men had been without provisions from Sunday until Wednesday morning. None could be furnished. Perceiving the goddess of Liberty painted upon the end of the hall, I said to them, "Soldiers, rise to your feet." The poor men were lying upon the floor. They got up, and every one of them joined in singing in one grand chorus "The Star-Spangled Banner" and "Columbia, the Gem of the Ocean." An immense assembly of people came flocking around the building; after we had taken our position in the train for the South at ten o'clock that day, having received only a few hard biscuits from the Southern Confederacy, women, yes, loyal ladies of Memphis, furnished us something to eat. Had we depended upon the men there, your soldiers would have suffered longer. As the cars were leaving, the ladies would step up to the windows and throw us bread, meat, and crackers, as we were passing, which they had purchased themselves. We were taken next to Jackson. The passenger train which preceded us had given notice to the citizens that several thousand Yankee prisoners would arrive that day. We were kept on the track on Wednesday night so as to be taken into Jackson by daylight. Citizens had assembled at the depot, and great cheering was heard upon our arrival. The question was asked, "How many are there of you?" Twenty-two hundred twenty-nine, I replied. "Well, seven thousand of you devils went into Memphis on Tuesday night," was the response. We were taken the next day to Meridian, Mississippi, where we were paraded again as a menagerie on the street. "How many Yankees have you got?" says a citizen to the conductor. "Twenty-two hundred twenty-nine" was the answer. "That's right, seven thousand in Memphis, twenty-five hundred in Jackson, and twenty-two hundred here today—pretty good haul." Mobile was our next stopping place, where an immense concourse witnessed the arrival of "live Yankees." "How many have you on board?" "About two thousand." "Glorious haul for Shiloh. Hurrah for Beauregard! Two thousand shipped to Meridian and placed in quarters there yesterday; seven thousand at Memphis, two thousand at Jackson, and now two thousand here. Pretty good haul for Shiloh." Wherever the train stopped, people ran to see the Yankees, and the same sort of arithmetic went on. They manifested a great desire to see a live Yankee general. Some of the many stories these people have published concerning me were true, for I was a little saucy for a prisoner. I used to go to the window to show myself. Every now and then I found a Union man, and began to give him instructions on what to do. The colonel in charge, seeing me so conversing, would exclaim, "Take your head in; you must not talk with these men." "Sir," I replied, "I have fought for my country. I am a live Yankee. You have the power to punish, but God alone can stop this tongue from wagging." [*Applause and laughter.*] At Mobile we were placed on transports and there, for the first time, learned that we were to be separated from the private soldiers. They were sent to the prisons of Alabama, at Tuscaloosa. I learned that we officers had to go to Talladega. Having in my possession from Colonel Jordan, an aide to General Beauregard—who, permit me to say here tonight, and you may herald it throughout this country, is the only man wearing a secesh uniform that I have received the least particle of courtesy from since I have been with them—drew me aside. [*Cries: "What is his name? What is his name?"*] His name is Colonel Jordan, assistant adjutant general of General Beauregard. That man had given me a letter to his brother at Mobile to assist me if I needed food. He also wrote to General Jones, commandant there, authorizing him to parole me if I wished. I went with that letter to the headquarters of General Jones, who, by the way, is a renegade Yankee. I extended my hand. He said, "No, sir," and bowed me to a seat. I said, "No, sir," and asked him to proceed to business. While the adjutant general was writing my parole out, I talked with General Jones so plainly that he began to respect me. When the adjutant handed me my parole and bid me good-bye, Jones arose and extended his hand. I said, "No, sir," and bowed. I went up the Alabama River. No accommodations for the officers, but we were told that we were to be treated as gentlemen. We knew enough not to be disappointed. We were sent to Talladega, in northern Alabama, which is a very healthy and pleasant locality—[*Voice: "Not for the Yankees, however"*]—and there I met Lieutenant Colonel Hurnley, a renegade Illinoisan, who said, "General, have you any Chicago men in your crowd?" "Yes, sir, we have; the officers of one regiment—the 58th Illinois." He said, "I, too, once lived in Chicago, but I was compelled to leave there, because I was persecuted for my sentiments. I could not go with the abolitionists, and I could not sustain your government because it was so corrupt." "Yes, sir," I responded, "you were no doubt compelled to leave because you were guilty of some crime for which you feared an arrest. Don't trouble me with your presence." [*Laughter.*] I asked a special favor of that gentleman: that he would not approach us again and trouble us by his presence. We remained a week at Talladega. There, one hundred fifteen of us were confined in a room thirty by fifty feet, well ventilated, but secesh soldiers had been quartered there. It was a lively place, I assure you; our rations were a quarter of a pound of musty bacon and a piece of corn bread, said to be the Southern soldiers' rations. We were soon sent to Selma, where we were put under the charge of Colonel Kent. If you ever see Kent, serve him as he served us. I cannot advocate a war of extermination, but a record is made. If this persecutor of me and the other officers falls into my hands, he shall suffer as we suffered. He attempted to torture me about my son, who, he said, had been taken and hanged as a spy, if their papers could be believed. But I had a paper in my pocket to give him the lie with, and this is how I got the paper: A lady was passing in the street beneath the window. She had passed several times before and had attracted the attention of the officers confined; some of them suggested that she was a Union lady. We tore off one of the curtains which hung in the hotel where we were imprisoned, and in large letters wrote on it with chalk, "God bless the prisoners' friend." She nodded assent and bowed to us when we showed it. She went to a house some hundred fifty yards distant, and I sent a Negro boy who cooked in the kitchen—and let me tell you that they are the best Union men in the South. [*Loud applause. Voice: "That's what you are fighting for."*] Yes, sir, I am fighting for the freedom of every man on earth. [*Cries of "God bless you," and loud applause.*] I sent him, the Negro, to the house where this lady went for a pitcher of milk. When he reached there, I observed her take a newspaper out of her pocket and place it in the pitcher which she had already filled with milk. We were two months at Selma. At Montgomery, whither we were taken—now, listen—our bread at Montgomery was made of corn and cobs ground up together. The Richmond and Columbia prisons are palaces as compared with those at Tuscaloosa, Talladega, Madison, and Montgomery. Before we left Montgomery for Atlanta, I asked the privilege of visiting our hospitals, where I found a hundred gallant men who had fought with me at Shiloh, without nurses, medicines, or clothing. They cried as I entered, and I cried with them. I found some good Union women, from whom I borrowed money for these poor men. Arriving at Atlanta, we noticed a procession coming up the street, consisting of two or three wagons. We could not make out what it meant. We had heard of their hanging and lynching Union men, but we did not suspect that this procession had anything to do with a matter of this kind. But we afterward learned the sad facts. Eight privates of an Ohio regiment were hanged at Atlanta. They had been sent by General Mitchell to do a little work on the railroad and telegraph lines of Alabama. Coming back, they unfortunately forgot to cut the telegraph lines, by the use of which a force was ordered from Chattanooga to intercept them. The gallant Ohioans were whiling away their leisure hours in prison with a game of euchre when the guard led them out to be hanged. What do you think, Mr. Rebel Sympathizer, of Southern chivalry now? [*Voice: "D——d poor stuff!"*] I think so. I think I speak the sentiments of two hundred thirty-two commissioned officers, and also the privates who were taken with me at Shiloh, when I tell you that we are not any longer ashamed of being called Negro sympathizers. [*Cries of "Good, good," and prolonged applause.*] We are not afraid of the cry of "abolitionists." [*"Good," and cries of "No, not now," and applause.*] We are not afraid of any cry. We will take by the hand each man as a brother who will fight for and defend his government. We despise altogether every man who refuses aid and comfort to his government in this time of our danger. The Rebels are determined. It is a perfect reign of terror in the South. I have found Union men bearing arms against our government. Let me tell you who are afraid of the cry of "abolitionism." The white race in the South are today more in the condition of slaves than ever were the blacks before this war commenced. White men, free, intelligent, educated, dare not say that they will part with this government, dare not find fault with the leaders in public. They have more men in the field than the people of the North imagine, fight better than they have credit for doing, because their cause is desperate, and because they are in earnest.

My friends, go to work, and persuade your officers and men that it is time for them to fight without gloves. [*Loud applause.*] Tell them that now is the time to strike. The Rebel army is somewhat demoralized. We met thousands and thousands of men going home on parole, taking their dead and wounded with them. Let me tell you, furthermore, that at the battle of Antietam, you hurt them a great deal more severely than you think you did.

> Train after train of their dead and wounded were sent South. When we arrived at Richmond, we were placed in what is called Colonel Corcoran's hotel, or the Libby Prison.[38] In Richmond I met an old schoolmate, the second renegade from Illinois, named Warner, who is quartermaster there and takes charge of the prisoners; and I have a hundred dollars in my possession which he handed me, with the request to deliver it to his family, now residing in Illinois. Being a Yankee, I would lead them into conversation concerning the war. They always said, "You never can conquer us; we shall whip you." After hearing them awhile, I directed their attention to Lincoln's Proclamation. "That Proclamation you never can enforce. It will be the ruin of you." I replied, "Why do you find fault with it if you are going to whip us?" I find this—and I want to say it boldly and have it proclaimed everywhere—that more than all the battles that have been fought, more than all that has been said and done, Lincoln's Proclamation is ending the rebellion. [*Loud and prolonged applause*.]

Colonel Mulligan, of Lexington memory, followed with a few impassioned remarks, in the course of which he gave Northern sympathizers with the rebellion the castigation they deserve.

General Prentiss has been presented with a gold-headed cane by officers of the 8th Iowa, with a $250 watch by other prison messmates, and with a sword by officers of the 23rd Missouri.

NOVEMBER 15, 1862

SOUTH

RICHMOND DAILY DISPATCH
November 15, 1862

FROM NORTHERN VIRGINIA

There was an alarm at Winchester on Sunday last, caused by the report that a body of Federal cavalry, numbering some three thousand, supported by infantry, were at Bunker Hill, and moving on that town. The

38. Libby Prison, located in Richmond, housed only officers and was originally the warehouse of the ship chandlers Libby and Sons.

citizens, as is usual on such occasions, commenced preparations to leave, and many of them did evacuate the place. But on Monday morning the report was ascertained to be without foundation, and everything quieted down.

The enemy made a dash into Martinsburg on Saturday evening last and captured *one* wounded Confederate soldier. On Sunday they made an advance in considerable force on General A. P. Hill's division from the direction of Charles Town, shelling the woods on each side as they advanced, but their fire was not responded to by our troops. They did not approach nearer than five miles of our forces.

On Saturday last, 11 members of White's cavalry of Loudoun County captured 130 stragglers of the enemy's forces at Snicker's Gap. They belonged to various regiments and, at the time of their capture, were unarmed. In addition, two sutlers' wagons were captured, containing a valuable lot of shoes and clothing. One hundred twenty-six of these prisoners were brought down by the Central train last evening, three took the oath of allegiance to the Confederacy, and one was left in Winchester, too sick to travel. The three who took the oath are shoemakers and volunteered their services in that capacity.

Passengers by the train state that a report reached Staunton from Winchester yesterday morning to the effect that General A. P. Hill had had an engagement with the enemy on Wednesday, in which he captured a large number of prisoners and a wagon train of great value, estimated at not less than two hundred thousand dollars.

Along the line of the Rappahannock, everything is quiet, and no indications of an advance of the Yankees.

THE HIGHLAND REPORT AGAIN

It is difficult to arrive at the truth with reference to the report of the existence of a body of Yankees in Highland County. Yesterday we stated, upon what was deemed good authority, that there had been a Yankee raid upon Monterey, and last evening a gentleman direct from Staunton assured us that no such raid had ever taken place. How these unfounded reports originate we are unable to state, but it is now a question for others to solve: Are the Yankees in Highland or not?

"THE FEELING AT THE NORTH"

Under this heading a paragraph has been going the rounds purporting to be from the pen of Reverend J. R. Graves of Nashville, author of *The Great Iron Wheel,* giving a description of the intense war feeling at the

North. Mr. Graves is not the author of the article, as we learn from a letter, though it was written by a Reverend Mr. Graves, a Presbyterian minister of the North Carolina synod, who has returned from a visit of six weeks to the North, having succeeded in getting a passport from the authorities at Richmond to visit his relatives and friends there. What importance is to be attached to grave opinions formed in so short a visit we are not prepared to state, but as the supposition that these opinions were entertained by Reverend J. R. Graves gave them additional weight with the public, it is proper to place the authorship where it belongs.

CHARLESTON DAILY COURIER
November 15, 1862

FROM RALEIGH
THE ABOLITION FORCE IN THEIR LATE EXPEDITION

Raleigh, North Carolina, 13th—The Yankee force which lately threatened the line of the Wilmington and Weldon Railroad consisted of the following regiments of infantry, viz: 5th, 23rd, 24th, 25th, 27th, and 44th Massachusetts; the 5th and 10th Connecticut and 5th New Jersey; 5th Rhode Island and Hawkins's Zouaves, with three others not known. They had thirty pieces of artillery and five companies of cavalry—the whole under the command of Major General Foster. These forces were drawn from New Bern, Fort Macon, Roanoke Island, and Washington, North Carolina. It is believed they have returned to their old posts, as all fell back toward Plymouth, destroying all the bridges on their retreat.

FROM RICHMOND
NORTHERN AND EUROPEAN NEWS

Richmond, 14th—Northern papers of the 8th, received here, furnish the following items of news:

Insurance rates on American ships in Liverpool had advanced from 3 to 5 percent under the influence of the *Alabama*'s doings.

Sir Benjamin Brodie, an eminent surgeon, died on the 21st of October.

At a public meeting in Oldham, England, resolutions were offered calling on the government to recognize the Confederate States. An amendment was offered declaring such recognition impolitic and likely to result in a war with the North. After some further proceedings the original motion was declared carried, although the meeting was equally divided.

It is stated from Paris that Persigny and Fould will remain in the

Cabinet, the emperor having assured them that there is nothing reactionary in his present policy respecting Italy, but that he declined to take any hurried step with regard to Rome.

The accounts of Garibaldi's health excite much apprehension.

The Prussian Chamber of Deputies, by a vote of 308 to 11, refused to grant supplies for a large increase in the army which the government had already effected. A royal decree terminated the parliamentary session of the ensuing day.

Commodore Garrett J. Pendergrast died in Philadelphia on the 7th instant.

The *Washington Star* has a dispatch from Chicago indicating that Lovejoy, the abolitionist, was not reelected to Congress.

The town of Haymarket, Virginia, was fired by two men of General Steinwehr's command.

The Washington correspondent of the *New York Post* says the president will not retract from his Emancipation Proclamation because of the results of the election. The government fully realizes that what it has to do must be done with dispatch and that going into winter quarters means disgraceful peace—consequently the army will not go into winter quarters, unless it is possible for the commanding general to overrule the president.

LATEST FROM THE NORTH
McCLELLAN TAKES FORMAL LEAVE OF THE ARMY—
GREAT DISSATISFACTION AT HIS REMOVAL

Richmond, 14th—Northern dates of the 13th have been received.

The *New York Times* and *Tribune* approve of McClellan's removal. The *Tribune* says, "Though done at the last hour, it is not too late, it trusts, to save the country." The *Herald* and *World* are down on the removal. They say the president has again yielded to a radical pressure.

The reports in regard to dissatisfaction in the army growing out of the removal of McClellan are pronounced unfounded by the government agents at Washington.

In Philadelphia the removal of McClellan has met with no sort of favor. His friends condemned it, while the radicals said it was no time to change commanders in the face of the enemy.

At a Democratic jubilee in New York, Monday night, John Van Buren said that Lincoln had made McClellan next president of the whole Union, though it would be under an amended constitution.

Ira Harris, Republican senator of New York, denounced the removal in an open speech.

McClellan, in quitting Warrenton, said to the troops, "Stand by Burnside as you stood by me, and all will be well." He took formal leave of the different army corps last Monday. On Sunday night the officers assembled at his headquarters to bid him adieu. He has gone to Trenton, New Jersey.

Gold in New York on the 10th instant was quoted at 133.

FROM MOBILE
REMAINS OF GENERAL VILLEPIGUE

Mobile, Alabama, 14th—General Villepigue's remains arrived here last night. The body lies in state at the headquarters of General Forney. All the flags in the city are at half-mast.

FROM CHATTANOOGA
AFFAIRS IN MIDDLE TENNESSEE

Chattanooga, Tennessee, 14th—Fresh reinforcements are reported to have reached Nashville.

Andy Johnson made a speech on the 12th in welcome of the first arrival of relief. He said the western campaign was now all right and the Rebels are driven closer and closer on the confines of Hell.

Our forces are arranging some very pretty traps, which will be heard from soon.

Major Strange of General Forrest's staff was wounded on the 12th instant.

FROM OXFORD
MOVEMENTS OF THE ENEMY

Special to the *Mobile Advertiser and Register*

Oxford, Mississippi, 14th—The enemy continue to advance. General Grant's whole force is believed to be at the south of Grand Junction. His cavalry occupied Holly Springs yesterday. Their advance skirmished with our forces eight miles south of that place. We captured six prisoners. Our army is anxious to meet them.

NORTH

BOSTON EVENING TRANSCRIPT
November 15, 1862

THE HUMANITY OF PATRIOTISM

The war has its very bright as well as its sadly dark side; and when the history of it is fully written, many will be the illuminated pages recording heroic deeds and many the golden-lettered chapters telling the story of timely, diligent, thoughtful, and tender benevolence—much of it benevolence that was ready for service almost before its services were required.

Its quick, intelligent, and foreseeing activity has to a large extent prevented or mitigated terrible distress that would otherwise have met with unavoidable neglect. For, with honorable exceptions, it cannot be denied that the official provisions to guard against the perils of the camps and the weariness of the march, to lessen the horrors of the battlefield, and to assuage the sufferings of the hospital have not been sufficiently ample and systematic to meet the emergency. The imperative haste to have an immense army equipped as a fighting force led to hurried arrangements that left many needful things for the proper care of that army in other respects undone or entrusted to inexperience and incompetence. The charge, therefore, of these needful things fell into the hands of volunteers. And if those hands had not been outstretched and wide open to receive the trust, the consequences would have been most lamentable, as anybody can readily imagine by seeing how much earnest labors have accomplished outside of, or in cooperation with, the direct action of the government.

The efforts of the Sanitary Commission; the thousands of soldiers' aid and relief societies; the superabundance of supplies freely given to the Medical Department, without waiting in many cases for any requisition; the numerous offers of personal attendance as nurses; the free hospitals in our cities; the refreshments regularly and gratuitously bestowed in Philadelphia and elsewhere upon regiments and recruits on their way to their posts of duty—these and many like things show how hosts of noncombatants, the loyal women being the greater number of the foremost of them, have been mercifully engaged with their whole hearts in the grand struggle to save the life of a republic.

Reviewing these beneficent movements, it is especially pleasant, for obvious reasons, to note what has been so nobly done in Baltimore—enough to conceal by its brightness the blot which the momentary outrage of a few malignant and vindictive conspirators cast upon its fair escutcheon.

The first Annual Report of the Executive Committee of the Union Relief Association, made last June, has recently been put into our hands. This society came into existence as a part of the reaction by which loyalty asserted its rightful superiority in Maryland and defeated those who tried "to manipulate the state, against the will of the majority, into the wickedness of rebellion." It began its philanthropic operations on a small scale, but soon enlarged them, so that its year's work amounts to a goodly sum of well-doing. It has taken care of the sick, fed the hungry, given drink to the thirsty, clothed the naked, welcomed and cheered and hospitably entertained the Federal troops both going to and returning from the seat of war. It has done this bravely and thoroughly according to its means, in the midst of unconcealed and scowling sympathy with the treasonable slave power, and thus at once performed its deeds of charity and vindicated the good name of the Monumental City.

In this respect the Baltimore association is a striking example of a fact common to all the voluntary benevolent agencies alluded to.

Their humanity is the product of patriotism. Love for the republic and the free institutions of the republic has moved them to undertake and continue their unwearied and unstinted labors in behalf of the defenders of the republic. These labors come of unconditional and unswerving loyalty. Those who could not fight to drive back and destroy the invader and usurper have rushed forward to encourage and succor the brave men who have bravely faced the foe.

The assertion may be safely ventured that not one of the tens of thousands of men and women who have been most eager to help the sufferers from the hardships of the campaigns has been otherwise than true as steel to the cause of freedom. Nay, more: Ever ready and zealous as they are to soften the horrors of the conflict by gentle and humane ministrations, they are the last who desire to see it ended by any short-lived pacification and yielding to the ungrateful and perjured domestic traitors. They would have the contest go on until the wrong is defeated and the right prevails. How the patriotism that is thus allied to tenderest humanity, without losing anything of its resoluteness and unyielding spirit, shames the selfish coldness and cowardly indifference that would ignobly make terms with rebellion!

CONFEDERATE ALLIES IN THE NORTH

In the intercepted letter of General Beauregard, just published, that arch-Rebel advises General Bragg to issue an order directing his subordinates to call the Union forces "abolitionists" instead of "Federals," assuming that this odious name will have a "stinging effect" on portions of the Northern forces. In connection with this recommendation of the little Creole, it is instructive to observe that the journals and orators in the "submission" interest here in the North have adopted the name, and every man who is in favor of a vigorous prosecution of the war, according to the ordinary rules of civilized warfare, which consist in striking the enemy where he is most vulnerable, is stigmatized as an "abolitionist."

We ask our readers to note the closing paragraph of General Beauregard's letter to General Bragg, published on the first page, and compare it with the current columns of such papers as we have alluded to and the tone of such speeches as that of John Van Buren at the last Cooper Institute meeting in New York, and see the inspiration of these flings at the abolitionists. These men are simply issuing Rebel proclamations here in the North.

THE ELECTIONS

The reports from Pennsylvania indicate that the "Hughes Democracy," as it is called in that state, has been thoroughly beaten. Mr. Henry has been reelected mayor of Philadelphia by from 3,000 to 5,000 majority. He is a Republican, supported by all Union men. Thaddeus Stevens, the leader of the administration party in Congress, has been reelected by a majority reported at three thousand.[39] In what have heretofore been some of the most Democratic portions of the state, the "Regular Democracy" appear to have been broken down by imputed sympathy with secession, which was charged upon them by their political opponents. The election in Pennsylvania is of great importance, as members of Congress and a legislature which will choose a senator of the United States are to be elected.[40]

From Ohio we have a few scattering returns, not very definite, but reporting the defeat of Mr. Gurley, the present member from one of the Cincinnati districts, and that the notorious Vallandigham has been shelved. Additional election returns will be published in the telegraphic columns as soon as received.

39. The Radical Republican Thaddeus Stevens was an influential Pennsylvania congressman (1849–53, 1859–68). After the war he called for the expropriation of Southern plantations and for part of those lands to be divided among freedmen. He also played a prominent role in the attempt to impeach President Andrew Johnson, whom he considered too conciliatory toward the South. In accordance with his wish, Stevens was buried among the graves of African Americans in Lancaster, Pennsylvania.

40. At the time, senators were chosen by state legislatures; popular election of senators was established in 1913 by the Seventeenth Amendment.

NEW YORK TRIBUNE
November 15, 1862

ARREST OF TWO OF GENERAL McCLELLAN'S STAFF OFFICERS—OTHER MEMBERS OF HIS STAFF TO BE ARRESTED—THE CHARGES UNKNOWN

Trenton, New Jersey, November 14, 1862

Lieutenant Colonels A. P. Colburn and J. C. Duane, of the Engineer Corps, both belonging to the staff of General McClellan, were sent to Washington this morning under arrest.

It is said that the orders were received by an officer of the United States army in this city and that the persons named repaired at once to Washington to place themselves at the disposal of the authorities.

A report prevails here that other members of General McClellan's staff are to be put under arrest.

The charges against them are unknown.

SHALL THE REPUBLIC DIE OF TRAITOROUS CALUMNIES?

The president of the United States, after long hesitation and listening to all manner of counsel, has taken two important steps toward the crushing out of the slaveholders' rebellion: He has proclaimed the freedom of all persons who may be held as slaves within the states which shall persist in the rebellion after the first day of January next; and he has appointed General Burnside to the command of the Army of the Potomac, whereof General McClellan is relieved.

Does any man on earth doubt the sincerity of the president's conviction that these steps are calculated to secure an early and favorable termination of this most devastating struggle?

Does any even pretend to doubt the president's absolute right to appoint whomsoever he pleases to the command of the respective Union armies?

If none—and the Constitution and laws are so plain as to leave no loop to hang a doubt upon—then why do journals and politicians professing loyalty persist in assailing the president's exercise of discretion of a trust expressly reposed in him by the country?

Why are licentious and traitorous journals like the *Herald* permitted from day to day to assail the president, demoralize the army, and mislead the people into sedition by falsehoods so black and villainous as the following:

> Like Henry Clay, who said he would rather be right than be president, McClellan prefers to be right than to be general in chief even of the Army of the Potomac, which had "grown up under his own care." Had he shown the servile, sycophantic nature of other men and violated the dictates of conscience—his obligations to God and his country—he would have been retained in the chief command today. But like Aristides the Just, for whose banishment his envious opponents admitted they voted because they hated to hear all men praise him, or like the Roman general Fabricius, who declined to be a party to the taking of the life of the hostile general by treacherous poison—Fabricius of whom it was said that he was like the sun, who could not be turned from his course—McClellan was resolved at all hazards to "support the Constitution of our country" as well as the "nationality of its people." For this he became obnoxious to a dominant fanatical faction in temporary power, who would sacrifice not only General McClellan, but the army and the nation itself, in order to carry out their one idea. There is no amount of blood and treasure which they are not prepared to expend in the vain and impracticable attempt to elevate the Negro to an equality with the white man, or, rather, to drag down the white man to a level with the black. Because McClellan would not become their pliant, supple tool in this visionary scheme, involving hideous horrors and cruel barbarities from which humanity revolts, they compelled him to "walk the plank."

There can be no mistaking the drift of this villainous concoction. It tends directly—as is doubtless intended—to excite mutiny in the army and insurrection among the people, thus insuring the triumph of the slaveholders' rebellion. If the traitors at Richmond could have directly written for their organ here, they could have written nothing more thoroughly in the interest of their foul rebellion.

Now let us contrast the secession falsehoods of the *Herald* with some undeniable truths:

1. It is utterly false that General McClellan has done or said anything in conflict with the president's Proclamation of Freedom and is relieved on that account.[41] On the contrary, his order based on that proclamation

41. On September 22, 1862, Lincoln issued the Proclamation of Freedom, announcing that slaves in the states in rebellion would be declared free by a more formal process (the Emancipation Proclamation) on January 1, 1863. The Proclamation of Freedom did not apply to the 800,000 slaves in the border states.

was promptly issued and was all that could be desired. No one could doubt his perfect conformity to the president's policy, and no one desired his removal on any assumption or suspicion that he would not fully sustain that policy.

2. General McClellan's removal was directly based on charges preferred against him by his immediate superior, General Henry W. Halleck, commander in chief, implying a lack of energy and efficiency in pursuing and attacking the Rebel Grand Army after its flight from Maryland and while that army was still far away from its base of operations and supplies. General Halleck, in politics, was never anything else but an ultra-proslavery Democrat and has *not* publicly or officially endorsed the president's Proclamation of Freedom, as General McClellan has done.

3. The salvation of the republic absolutely demands signal energy and activity in the movement and management of our armies. It is vitally necessary that our soldiers should be led by generals who are not afraid of beating the Rebels too decidedly, nor of hurting them too much. A capable general of this stamp would have routed the traitor host at Antietam and run it into the Potomac, minus its guns and baggage. Such a one would have relieved Harpers Ferry at least two days before its surrender, saving *twelve thousand men* with their arms and trains. Such a one, if balked of a decisive victory in Maryland, would have followed up the Rebels vigorously and compelled them to fight a month ago near Winchester, with immense advantage in numbers, arms, supplies, and prestige on the national side. Peremptory orders so to follow and fight were given to General McClellan directly after Antietam, and by him disregarded, on grounds deemed entirely frivolous or unreal by his superiors. One consequence of that disobedience is a renewed disposition of foreign powers to interfere in our domestic quarrel to our prejudice; another is the escape of the Rebels to positions far nearer their own resources and much farther from ours. Another was a defeat of the friends of the administration in several states, through popular disappointment and disgust at the slow progress of the war, for which they held the president responsible. These defeats are direct contributions to the Rebel strength. They encourage the traitors to hope that *their friends* are coming into power in the loyal states—those whom they have always bent to their will, and who will say to them, with John Van Buren, "Wayward sisters! Depart in peace!" The defeat of the administration at the polls thus strengthens and encourages the Rebels; and it is the direct result of the preceding inaction and inefficiency of our armies under McClellan and Buell—an inaction which stubbornly defied orders

and could only be overcome by placing new commanders at the head of our forces.

That those who have held the president and his supporters responsible for the failure of the late campaign should now decry a change intended to secure greater energy and efficiency in the future was to be expected. Dreading a complete triumph of the national arms, they clamor against any step calculated to secure such triumph. But in times of grave peril like these, there should be some limit to their calumnious and treasonable assaults on the president, who clung to General McClellan to the last and only with the greatest reluctance finally gave him up—not because others distrusted him—not because he had done or refused to do anything respecting slavery or emancipation—but simply because he had fully proved himself one of those "augers that won't bore."

DECEMBER 20, 1862

SOUTH

RICHMOND DAILY DISPATCH
December 20, 1862

PROFESSOR LOWE AND HIS BALLOON

The idea of calling a balloonist a professor could never have originated with any but a nation of humbugs. And the balloon itself, from a military point of view, seems to be as great a humbug as "the professor." On the eve of every battle, up goes the balloon, and at the close of every battle, down go the Yankees. It may be doubted whether Lowe ever gets as high as the army gets low. The ascension of this Professor of Gas to the heavens is an invariable signal for the descent of the Yankees to the shades. Lowe and his balloon, soaring to the skies, is an admirable emblem of the towering expectations of Yankeedom before a fight; the balloon collapsed is a faint image of their condition afterward. The Professor of Gas made a good many ascents in the Peninsula, and he made another on the eve of the battle of Fredericksburg.[42] Long may he soar! He is the only Yankee who has ever yet been able to look down upon the Confederates. We may be consoled for that when we remember that he is the only Yankee who has yet exhibited a heavenward tendency

42. The Battle of Fredericksburg, Virginia, December 13, 1862, was a Confederate victory.

during this war. If the blue empyrean can tolerate his presence, we can afford to let him soar over our heads like buzzards and other obscene birds, especially when his appearance is always a signal of victory to our arms.

YANKEE CRUELTY

A gentleman from western Virginia states that two or three young ladies are imprisoned in the jail in Wheeling, and *tied to the floor,* on the charge of disloyal sentiments and practices. Such outrages upon humanity call for the prompt action of our generals in the West, not upon women, but upon the first male subjects, of Pierpont and Lincoln, who fall into our hands.[43] They should tie up the first dozen Yankees they capture to the trees, and keep them tied till these young ladies are released. No measure short of this will ever teach the brutal enemy the first principles of civilization.

CHARLESTON DAILY COURIER
December 20, 1862

GENERAL JOHN H. MORGAN'S KENTUCKY EXPEDITIONS

We had the pleasure of an interesting conversation on Thursday with Major R. A. Alston, formerly adjutant of General John H. Morgan. Major Alston accompanied General Morgan in his late expeditions in Kentucky and is therefore enabled to state facts which came under his own observation.

When General Bragg's army arrived at Lancaster, Kentucky, on their way back, General Morgan was ordered to bring up the rear. In carrying out this order, he discovered that Buell had given up his pursuit of General Bragg and was pushing him out of Kentucky with only one division (Crittenden's) of his army. In the meantime Buell was concentrating the main body of his forces at Franklin, with a view of marching upon middle Tennessee, for the purpose of securing Chattanooga, regarded as the most important point in the Southern Confederacy. Upon the discovery of these designs, Morgan immediately sought and obtained permission from the commanding general to move back and make a detour through

43. In 1861, representatives of the pro-Union western counties of Virginia held the Wheeling Convention, to repudiate the ordinance of secession adopted at the Richmond Convention and to establish a rival state government. Francis Pierpont was elected governor of Virginia by the Wheeling delegates on June 20, 1861.

western Kentucky and destroy both lines of railroad to Bowling Green. On Friday, October 17, Morgan left his encampment near Glades Church, and reached Lexington the next morning about two o'clock. After resting an hour, he surrounded the town and succeeded in capturing twelve companies of the 3rd and 4th Ohio Cavalry, under the command of Colonel Kenney. Not a man escaped of the entire garrison.

From this point Morgan moved to Versailles, and thence to Schryocks Ferry, where he met General Dumont, who had marched from Frankfort to intercept Morgan. The meeting, however, was rather unexpected to Dumont, who, after a slight demonstration, fearing an ambush, ordered a retreat, and Morgan continued his march to Bloomfield. At the latter place he captured a captain and his forces, who were acting as garrison. Leaving Bloomfield, he moved in the direction of Bardstown, Kentucky, where the enemy had a large force. By threatening Bardstown he caused the enemy's forces to be drawn up and remain in line of battle all that afternoon, while Morgan sent out a company toward Louisville and succeeded in capturing 350 prisoners, with a train of 158 wagons. He destroyed the latter and the next day paroled his prisoners. He then took up his line of march to Elizabethtown, where his men destroyed the railroad and bridge over Valley Creek. While thus engaged, a long train of cars loaded with Yankees came up. Morgan retired to the other end of the town and built some 3,000 or 4,000 fires, thus creating the impression of a very large force with him and keeping the Yankees from making an attack.

The next place he reached was Litchfield, and from thence moved forward to Morgantown, where he was again intercepted. From Morgantown they marched to Rochester; crossed Mud River on a hastily constructed bridge of flatboats, which they sank after crossing; and next day went forward to Greenville, Kentucky, from there to Hopkinsville, making the latter place a base of operations.

Here General Morgan halted his command for the space of five days, during which time he was occupied in sending out expeditions in various directions. A portion of his command went to Owensboro on the Ohio River, for the purpose of diverting the Yankee troops from Bowling Green; another portion of the command marched to within five miles of Bowling Green and destroyed the railroad from Bowling Green to Russellville, including a bridge, etc. Another portion of his forces started out and destroyed all the water tanks within reach. A large trestlework near Springfield was destroyed, and all the bridges from Springfield down to Gallatin. The march was then continued to Trenton and Keysburg back to Springfield and Gallatin. These successes brought the Yankee army to a halt for want of supplies and the interruption of communication. It has already caused Rosecrans a delay of over two months in repairing the roads over which his supplies must reach him. For greatness of conception, daring, and rapidity of execution, this expedition of Morgan's has not been surpassed since the commencement of the war.

PLEASING INDICATIONS

Having resolved by the help of Heaven to conquer our independence, we are prepared to suffer all the miseries our foe is able to inflict upon us, and so deep-seated is that resolve that no discomfiture, no matter how disastrous, can at all shake our resolution. We would rejoice at the return of peace, but that peace must be an honorable one; otherwise, we would reject the proffer with scorn and defiance.

While we are ready and willing to make any sacrifices the triumphant vindication of our cause demands, and to oppose force to force so long as our enemy continues to pursue his present policy, it does not in the slightest measure impair the strength of our determination to recognize those indications of inability to prolong this contest to a much greater period which a limited acquaintance with the affairs of Yankeedom presents to our view. For if these signs prove delusive and our enemy presses upon us with larger numbers, more determined valor, and greater military skill, we shall do our utmost to frustrate his designs and to compel him to give up the impossible undertaking.

Financial troubles are brewing which must soon sweep with fury through the communities of Lincolndom. The reckless issue of currency by Secretary Chase has already produced distrust and confusion, which go on increasing until the makeshift system of the ingenious financier has caused universal bankruptcy. Steadily have the government notes been depreciating in value for months, and in the face of that woeful and rapid depreciation, bills are thrown off as fast as they can be printed and signed; and notwithstanding the immense number now in circulation and the additions made daily to that unparalleled issue, the supply falls far short of the demand. The government is largely in arrears with its employees; and contractors, clerks, and the hirelings who are fighting its battles are clamoring for their wages. And not only are they calling with a loud voice for the payments due, but they are insisting, with an earnestness not at all agreeable to the powers at Washington, on allowance being made for the actual depreciation in their currency.

The laws of finance will assert themselves; and when the mischievous effects of the measures that have been resorted to are clearly apparent, no longer able to sustain a war which is costing them $3 million daily, our boastful enemies will have to retire with ignominy from the contest.

The North was sanguine of the success of Burnside's attempt to reach Richmond. They gave him a numerous and splendid army, regardless of cost. The plans of the newly made chieftain were well considered and thoroughly matured. And when the hero of Roanoke marched his immense and eager host in the direction of our capital, the whole land rang with praises of his dash and enterprise. Despite the fact that their best general had refused to accede to their wishes and that their ablest military men had pronounced the onward movement improper, the press and the people shouted vociferously the cry, "On to Richmond."

The attempt has been made. The Rappahannock has been crossed and a battle has been fought in the fields and woods in front of Fredericksburg. The fight was fierce and bloody. The invading army assaulted and resisted with impetuous daring and determined courage. The ground was drenched in blood. But life and limb were given in vain to the cause of the Union. The enemy sustained a complete and severe discomfiture and was fain to retire to the other side of the river.

The result of that sanguinary contest has grievously disquieted the mind of our foe. Those papers friendly to McClellan will be sure to give a truthful account of that battle, and the disappointment, mortification, and rage the terrible defeat has given rise to will lead to fierce disputes and rancorous contentions. And the heavy loss they sustained on that field of carnage may open the eyes of multitudes to the real nature of the work they expected Burnside to do, and the felt impossibility of taking Richmond may change their opinion of the war and lead to consequences of a most beneficial character.

From two sections of the North, far distant from each other, we hear notes of discontent and an emphatic condemnation of the policy their government is pursuing. The members of Congress from New Jersey are about to propose an armistice, and the governor of Michigan has issued a proclamation calling home the troops of that state, in case there is not an amnesty in the course of the present month.

And we are not surprised at this action by the executive of Michigan. Lincoln's infamous ukase proclaiming the emancipation of our slaves has had a most injurious effect upon his cause throughout the West, and the brave and hardy men of that region are aware that they have been made to do the most arduous work and the hardest fighting, while they have been denied a share of the plunder. They have been so hard used, and have suffered so severely, both in battle and from the inevitable effects of the war, that they are heartily sick of the contest and ripe for revolution. That significant proclamation expresses the sentiments of thousands of frontiersmen, and we may look for something even more startling from that region of the despot's domain.

NORTH

BOSTON EVENING TRANSCRIPT
December 20, 1862

THE VICTORY AT KINSTON, NORTH CAROLINA—COMPLETE FEDERAL SUCCESS—SEVERE FIGHTING AND HEAVY REBEL LOSS—ACTION BETWEEN FEDERAL GUNBOATS AND REBEL BATTERIES—MASSACHUSETTS REGIMENTS ENGAGED—ADVANCE OF GENERAL FOSTER ON GOLDSBORO

New York, 20th—The details of the victory at Kinston, North Carolina, show that the march was a continued series of fighting in which all distinguished themselves. Several bayonet charges took place.

The Rebels are reported as having 15,000 men, and their loss in killed and wounded is heavy; 500 were taken prisoners.

The lieutenant colonel of the 96th New York Regiment was killed.

Our total loss will not exceed 150.

The principal fight was a few miles from Kinston, where the Rebels were entrenched; but after three hours' fighting, they retreated toward Kinston, endeavoring to destroy a bridge leading to that place; but the 9th New Jersey charged over it and saved it. Our division rapidly crossed when the Rebels retreated, one Rebel brigade toward Goldsboro and the other toward Weldon, our shells helping them along.

Captain Wells and Lieutenant Perkins of the 10th Connecticut Regiment were killed. Their regiment fought till they got out of ammunition, then went in with bayonets.

The 23rd Massachusetts Regiment, Major Chambers commanding, captured seventy officers and privates, including a lieutenant colonel of the 23rd South Carolina Regiment.

The march was taken up on the 16th instant for Goldsboro.

New York, 20th—A New Bern, North Carolina, letter states that the gunboats and flotilla acted in conjunction with General Foster. The gunboats, however, could not proceed far up the Neuse River on account of a low stage of water, and the Marine artillery, under Colonel Manchester, aboard the flotilla, was obliged to proceed without them.

On arriving within two miles of Kinston the flotilla suddenly came upon an eleven-gun battery, which opened very effectively on the *Allison;* but she finally backed out, having been pierced in many places, her smokestack cut away, pilothouse torn away, and the steam safety pipe cut away.

The flotilla retreated, and the next day were fired upon from the banks by guerrillas, who used balls dipped in verdigris and with copper wire attached. A shell from the *Allison* did great damage to the battery, and some thirty Rebels were killed on the way down the river.

One of the flotilla, the *Ocean Wave,* struck a stump on returning, sinking in three feet of water. Her guns, cargo, etc., were all saved, and she will be got off soon.

Another New Bern letter states that deserters and prisoners from the enemy, as well as dispatches to General Evans, captured, show that all the calls by General Evans for reinforcements from Petersburg, Weldon, and Goldsboro were refused on the grounds that each place needed all the troops available to protect its own positions.

Dispatches have been received from Richmond at Weldon and Raleigh, as well as Wilmington and Goldsboro, urging the necessity of reinforcements.

The Rebels say that General Burnside is advancing and all is lost if they are not aided at Richmond, even at the expense of giving up North Carolina. They are greatly frightened at the capital.

NEW YORK TRIBUNE
December 20, 1862

FROM GENERAL ROSECRANS'S ARMY
A BATTLE IN PROGRESS AT CORINTH—THE REBEL FORREST ENGAGED WITH GENERAL DODGE—MORGAN MOVING AGAINST THE LOUISVILLE AND NASHVILLE RAILROAD—VAN DORN WITH 50,000 JOINS BRAGG—THE STORY DISCREDITED—PURGING OUR ARMY OF INEFFICIENT OFFICERS

Special Dispatch to the *New York Tribune*
Headquarters XIV Army Corps, Department of the Cumberland
Nashville, Tennessee, December 18, 1862

General Sullivan, at Jackson, Tennessee, telegraphs General Rosecrans that General Dodge telegraphs him from Corinth today that his cavalry have been fighting Forrest all day in that vicinity, with 2,500 cavalry and 5 pieces of artillery, having left Waynesboro on Tuesday.

Colonel Napier, with 2,000 or 3,000 cavalry and 4 cannons, crossed the Tennessee River to Carrollsville on Monday to join Forrest. It was reported that they would strike Jackson first, and Bethel next, to stop Grant's supplies.

Second Dispatch

Nashville, Tennessee, December 13, 1862

Forrest and his four thousand cavalry have turned up in the vicinity of Corinth, Mississippi. A telegram received at headquarters tonight reports fighting with him going on in that vicinity all day today. Morgan is reported moving northward to cut off the Louisville and Nashville Railroad.

It is reported from Kentucky that Van Dorn, with fifty thousand men from the Army of Mississippi, has arrived at Stevenson, Alabama, to join Bragg. Our own trustworthy advices contradict the report. The move is too hazardous to be attempted. No important movements in our front today. Hardee's corps has moved to Trion. Kirby Smith is reported moving toward Lebanon, supporting Morgan.

The whole force of Rebels in Tennessee is variously estimated at 70,000 to 80,000 men—an exaggeration. Their old regiments are filled with conscripts. The force at Murfreesboro yesterday was 25,000 men. Rains's division is at Hollow Tree Gap. Rebel outposts were about eleven miles from Nashville, on various roads.

The *Herald*'s dispatches about the commander of the Rebel army misled the public. Bragg is in active command. Official letters are received from him almost daily. The *Herald*'s story that the enemy had advanced all along our front and driven in our pickets last week was entirely fabricated.

Major Schuyler Hamilton is relieved from duty in this department, at his own request, on account of ill health, and left for New York today.

The resignation of Colonel Norton, 21st Ohio, has been accepted. Captains Dougherty, Langley, and Myers, Lieutenants Wilson, Huston, and Holt of 1st Tennessee Infantry, were dismissed from service today for disobedience of orders. Lieutenant W. Freer, 44th Illinois, will probably be dismissed for drunkenness and disobedience of orders. General Rosecrans has dismissed about twenty others since he assumed command.

1863

TIMELINE

January 1: The Emancipation Proclamation goes into effect. Lincoln calls for the creation of the first African-American regiments. Although Congress had authorized the enlistment of African Americans in July 1862, Lincoln vetoed ad hoc local efforts in South Carolina and Louisiana. By the end of the war, more than 200,000 African Americans are in the Union army.

January 1–3: Stones River fighting ends with a Confederate withdrawal. Rosecrans claims victory and occupies nearby Murfreesboro, Tennessee. Casualties: North, 12,906; South, 11,739.

January 25: Ambrose Burnside is replaced by Joseph Hooker as commander of the Army of the Potomac. Burnside is transferred to Ohio, where he participates in the Vallandigham trial and the capture of the Confederate raider John Hunt Morgan.

March 3: Lincoln signs the Conscription Act, covering men between the ages of twenty and forty-five. Voluntary service and legal exemptions limit the number actually drafted to about forty-six thousand.

April: The Confederates lay siege to Washington, North Carolina. Unable to retake the town, they withdraw.

April 7: Launched from the sea, the Union assault on Charleston proves unsuccessful.

May 1–4: Battle of Chancellorsville, Virginia. Hooker's Army of the Potomac is routed by Lee's Army of Northern Virginia. Strategically almost flawless, this battle will be known as "Lee's masterpiece," later serving as the backdrop for Stephen Crane's novel *The Red Badge of Courage* (1895). Engaged: North, 134,000; South, 61,000. Casualties: North, 17,278; South, 12,821.

May 3: Three reporters are captured by the Confederates at Vicksburg. Richard Colburn, from the Democratic *New York World,* is quickly released; Albert Richardson and Junius Browne are held, because of their affiliation with the abolitionist *New York Tribune*. Richardson and Browne escape after twenty months of difficult captivity and walk four hundred miles to freedom.

May 5: The Ohio Copperhead politician and former congressman Clement Vallandigham is arrested. He will be tried for treason and sentenced to two years' confinement, but will be later banished to the South. The Confederates do not welcome him and hold him as an "alien enemy." Ohio Democrats nominate him in absentia as the "Peace Democrat" candidate for governor.

May 10: "Stonewall" Jackson dies of wounds accidentally inflicted by his own troops during the Battle of Chancellorsville.

June 3: Lee begins the Gettysburg campaign, moving troops north from Fredericksburg, Virginia. The South believes that a major victory on Northern soil would encourage the Northern peace movement and prod the European powers to recognize the Confederacy.

June 9: Federal cavalry surprises Confederate General J.E.B. Stuart at Brandy Station, Virginia, provoking the largest cavalry action of the war. Some twenty thousand mounted soldiers fight to a draw.

June 15: Lincoln calls for one hundred thousand local militia as Lee continues north. Preparations are made to relocate government offices from Harrisburg, the Pennsylvania state capital.

June 22: West Virginia is admitted to the Union.

June 28: In a dispute with General Henry Halleck over strategy, and with Confederate units occupying much of southern Pennsylvania, Hooker asks to be relieved of the command of the Army of the Potomac. He is replaced by General George Meade. Lee assembles his forces at Gettysburg, Pennsylvania.

July 1–3: Battle of Gettysburg. Southern hopes for a decisive victory are dashed. After sustaining heavy losses, Lee is forced to retreat. Casualties: North, 23,049; South, 28,063. The Confederates never recover from this setback, and the momentum shifts irrevocably in favor of the Union, whose superiority in resources and manpower will decide the outcome of the war.

July 4: After a year-long assault by the Union army and navy, the Confederates unconditionally surrender Vicksburg, Mississippi.

July 9: In the wake of the loss of Vicksburg, Port Hudson (Louisiana) is surrendered. The full length of the Mississippi River is now under Union control.

July 9–16: Union General William Tecumseh Sherman follows Confederate General Joseph Johnston to Jackson, Mississippi, and during these dates puts the city under siege. The Confederates abandon the city and retreat.

July 13–16: Draft riots erupt in New York City; Boston; Portsmouth, New Hampshire; Rutland, Vermont; Wooster, Ohio; and Troy, New York. The riot in New York City, lasting four days, is by far the largest and has distinctly racist overtones. The mob, numbering fifty thousand at its peak and composed largely of Irish workingmen, attacks the offices of the *New York Tribune* and terrorizes the city's African-American population.

July 18: Union forces, including the African-American troops of the 54th Massachusetts, attempt another frontal assault on Charleston. The offensive is unsuccessful, and the siege of the city is resumed. In August, the sieging Federals introduce the "Swamp Angel," a muzzle-loading cannon capable of throwing a 200-pound shell.

July 26: The Rebel cavalryman John Hunt Morgan is captured after a spectacular but inconsequential twenty-four-day raid through Indiana and Ohio. He is imprisoned in Columbus, Ohio, but later escapes and is killed in action a year later in Greenville, Tennessee.

September 2: Knoxville, Tennessee, is captured by Union General Burnside.

September 8: A Federal gunboat attack on Sabine Pass, Texas, proves unsuccessful, resulting in the loss of the Union ships *Sachem* and *Clifton*.

September 9: Outflanked by Union General Rosecrans and awaiting reinforcements, Bragg evacuates Chattanooga, Tennessee. Maneuvering and skirmishing continue as the city is put under siege.

September 19–20: The Battle of Chickamauga, Georgia, is nominally won by Bragg, but Rosecrans retains control of Chattanooga. Casualties: North, 16,170; South, 18,454. The North orders emergency reinforcements.

October 9–20: Lee fails in an effort to flank Meade and threaten Washington. Desultory skirmishing continues until Meade goes into winter quarters in December.

October 23: At Chattanooga, Rosecrans is replaced by Grant, who bides his time waiting for reinforcements.

November 16: Confederate General James Longstreet, failing to provoke a battle, lays siege to Burnside at Knoxville. In December, after an unsuccessful offensive, Longstreet takes up winter quarters.

November 19: Lincoln delivers the Gettysburg Address during the dedication of a new Federal cemetery in Gettysburg.

November 24–25: Battle of Missionary Ridge, Tennessee. Union General Hooker captures Lookout Mountain as Bragg's troops retreat to the valley below. Grant defeats Bragg at Missionary Ridge. Bragg's army remains intact, but is forced to withdraw, leaving the state in Union hands.

JANUARY 17, 1863

SOUTH

RICHMOND DAILY DISPATCH
January 17, 1863

CONSERVATISM IN ILLINOIS

The movement of the conservatives in Illinois is one of the most important events which has transpired in the Federal Union since the rupture of the old Union. Mr. Richardson was nominated by a legislative caucus of that state, which adopted a series of resolutions denouncing the Lincoln despotism in the most decisive language for its suspension of the habeas corpus; its outrageous and cruel imprisonment of its citizens in its bastilles without accusation and without trial; its usurpations of the powers of the Constitution in many respects, but especially in the proclamation abolishing slavery; and "its perversion of the war into a war of abolition." They further favor a restoration of the Union by peaceful means and, with that object, propose a cessation of hostilities and the assembling of a convention. These resolutions we publish today, together with a speech from Mr. Richardson himself, taking very strong grounds against the despotic acts of Lincoln.

These resolutions are in themselves important, but their consequence is greatly strengthened by the intelligence that Richardson has been elected to the Senate by the Illinois legislature, receiving *sixty-six* out of a *hundred*—the entire number of both houses. We hope this may be true. The blow, coming from Lincoln's own state, is a heavy one to him and will probably suspend his jokes longer than they have been at any time since he has been in Washington.

Illinois is a powerful state of the great Northwest, whose real interests are just as hostile to Puritan New England as are our own. That she should take this decided stand against the abolitionism, the fanaticism, and malignity of New England is a sign of the times at the North, full of significance. It cannot but be regarded as the outgiving of the impatience of the Puritan rule that must ultimately terminate in a more formidable resistance to it and a separation from that detestable portion of the Union which has been the source of all the troubles among the states, as it has been of all the new schools of philosophy and religion which have so fearfully demoralized society at the North.

It is true that the men who are making this bold movement in Illinois, and Mr. Richardson at their head, studiously persevere in the idea of that impossibility: the restoration of the old Union. They could do nothing less than this. But they propose with this view a *cessation of hostilities*. It can hardly be doubted that the ostensible cessation of the war must be its permanent denouement. It cannot be renewed—at least by the present parties to it.

These conservatives can do no less than praise the old Union and pray for its restoration, but we doubt whether they dream of a renewal of this war even if the overtures for the restoration of the Union fail. It is a political sequence of the dissolution that has taken place that there shall be another dissolution—that the Northwest shall split off from the Northeast.

We are satisfied that there has been among northwestern men a growing hate for New England and a growing respect, at least, for the Southern states. The generous exhibition of our disposition for a fair and liberal arrangement with the inhabitants of the upper Mississippi, and for commercial intercourse, deprives them of the only real apprehension of injury from the dissolution of the Union which disturbed them. To fight hopelessly for a restoration of the Union, when they can enjoy all the commercial advantages they ever had without it, is a folly to which their eyes must be gradually opening. On the one hand, these benefits are proffered by the South; on the other, they behold endless taxation to maintain the wasteful Lincoln despotism in an unsuccessful war and the disgusting and arrogant rule of Puritanism while they remain tributary to the opulence of the maritime power and grandeur of those eastern states and cities in which they cannot share. Three years of unavailing war, with all its extravagance and horrors, ought to suggest to them this train of reflection, and we shall be disappointed if a brief time does not prove as much. Indeed, we need not look to the upper Mississippi altogether for the signs of this effect. The Phillipses and the abolition presses of New England have already become the accusers of the Northwest.[1] Their own minds have led them to apprehend a secession of the Northwest, and they have transformed their own speculations into open accusation of that section, imputing to it such a purpose. Their speculations are just, and so, no doubt, are their accusations.

These signs are agreeable, of course, to the people of the South, but it would be in the last degree unfortunate for us if, relying upon them, or any other extraneous indication, we relaxed in the least our own zeal, our own energetic and brave measures of self-protection from the hordes which the beastly and rapacious power of the North is throwing upon the Southern Confederacy. The only means of securing our own independence is the sure one of increasing the discord among our enemies and rendering certain the breaking up of the Federal Union. This event is necessary to the just completion of that horrid drama now being enacted, by the punishment, the isolation in misery, of that race of men whose villainies have conjured up all the national woes which now fill this continent.

CHARLESTON DAILY COURIER
January 17, 1863

THE BATTLE OF FREDERICKSBURG

Camp near Fredericksburg, Virginia

Dear Uncle:—Today gives me an opportunity of writing the third letter since I received one from you. I wish to know what is the matter with you, if you have run out of something to write. I thought a few days ago we would have a dull time about Christmas, but I think the Yankees have quite enough of us to do them until we can spend Christmas, anyway. I wish you could only see the battlefield. On the morning of the 11th, before day, the signal guns were fired; and by daylight we were under arms and took our position in line of battle, and laid out six days in sight of nearly all the fighting that was done, but did not get a chance

1. Wendell Phillips, abolitionist and reformer.

to fire a gun during the fight. This was the first time we were ever held in reserve.

I have never seen men lie so thick as they did on the outskirts of the city. In one little garden, not more than two thirds of an acre, there were one hundred forty-seven lying dead, and all over the city they were lying dead, where it seemed that balls could not have gotten to them. The city is torn to pieces, houses plundered, furniture destroyed, books torn from the libraries and scattered over the floor; even ladies' dresses were taken from their wardrobes and packed in Yankee knapsacks. The houses that were on our line of breastworks were torn to pieces by their balls. I think there is a bullet hole for every four inches in the houses. Our men let them come up within thirty paces of them, and then would fire into them, and would sweep them off as far as the balls could reach for the houses. There was a plank fence they would dodge behind that was shot entirely away by our riflemen. The planks were torn in splinters. We had four 32-pound rifle cannons that did great execution. I saw some of the best shots made by them I ever saw in my life. There was one company of Yankees that would come up in a railroad car and fire at our men, and I saw a shell from a 32-pound ball fall among them and explode, killing several. On the right of our line, where General Hill's division fought them, we could see their line advancing on ours, but they would not stand long before they would break and run like frightened sheep. There is scarcely a house in Fredericksburg but has the mark of cannonballs—many of them torn to pieces and some burned. We had but one man from our regiment wounded, and he belonged to our company. The Yankees are said to be leaving and going back toward the Potomac, where they will go into winter quarters. The river is our picket line. Our sentinels and theirs are close enough to each other to talk. We were on picket day before yesterday, and relieved the 11th Virginia Regiment. They informed us that the Yankees had been making inquiries about our regiment, and Sergeant McKinstry asked one of the Yankees why he was making inquiries about the 6th South Carolina Regiment. His reply was that they were such d——d fools they were afraid they would shoot at them. It is an understanding between Generals Lee and Burnside that the pickets shall not fire on each other unless one or the other advances. The river is about one hundred yards wide. Some of the Yankees came over and traded coffee for tobacco the day before we went down. Thus you will perceive that they are deprived of some of the pleasures of the earth as well as we are.

General Lee, however, has ordered all talking and passing to be stopped; but we were compelled to talk a little on the sly with them anyhow. We took one of the Bucktail Rifles a prisoner. He asked for our regiment and said it was the first fight he had ever been in, that he didn't want to fight our regiment. We have six regiments in our brigade, and the Hampton Legion, which has been recently attached to it. Our regiment has nearly armed itself with Enfield rifles; got most of them at Manassas. Our army is in better spirits than I have ever seen it. We commenced, as soon as we got here, to fortifying and are now well fortified. You must write me all the news from the coast, and if there are any Yankees about there. If there are not, I expect there will be soon, as General Lee has made Burnside *take water*. I am afraid, however, the next time we fight the Yankees that McClellan will be at their head. We have had some of the coldest days I ever felt—wood being scarce and no prospect of moving from here very soon. Our general is a strong believer in drilling his men. When we are not marching, we are drilling twice a day: regimental in the forenoon and brigade in the afternoon. This consumes the greater part of the day. We drill in an old field about one mile square and run all over it twice a day. A gun in hand on a cold day is not pleasant, as you are aware. But we should not murmur, but take it all in that way in which Southerners should do. I trust the day is not far distant when I shall meet you in a home of peace and a land of independence.

Your nephew,
J. C. R.

THE DELUSIONS OF THE ENEMY

The months that have been drenched by the bloodshed during this terrific war have turned many of our hopes into miserable delusions. We have not only been called upon to suffer the mortification of disappointment, but the indulgence of those confident hopes has been the fruitful cause of great calamities.

Those evils have sorely tried our fortitude, but having been furnished with the necessary strength, we have been enabled to bear the burden of woes, and we are at the present time more strong and determined and brave than before we endured those grievous afflictions.

These hopes have gone out, but pursuing the course we have marked out for our feet, guided by our own wisdom, illuminated with light from Heaven, and resolved to accomplish our high purpose by the vigorous use of the means God has placed in our reach, we are assured that success, complete and glorious success, will crown our efforts and endurance.

But while we no longer imagine that cotton will compel England and France to open our ports and that these mighty nations, yielding to the demands of precedent, of justice and of humanity, will admit us into the family of nations, our enemies still continue to hug to their bosoms the vain hopes they embraced at the beginning of this war. Events have demonstrated their fallaciousness, but still they cling to them with a firm grasp and refuse to give them up.

They prated earnestly concerning the Union element in the seceded states and announced that it was one of the prime objects of the war to extend protection to the thousands who still professed allegiance to the old government. They have, by the conquests they have made, given those loyal ones opportunity to choose the side they would fight with, and not only have they afforded them encouragement to express the sentiments of their hearts, but they have made use of every means suggested by ingenuity and a base, cruel spirit; and yet a few only—and they, for the most part, of the same blood and nature with themselves—have taken advantage of the presence of their armed hosts and sheltered themselves under the folds of their flag.

They still believe that it is possible to restore the Union to its former power and grandeur; and in the discourses put forth by their journals on the subject of intervention and recognition, they admonish foreign powers to be careful how they proceed in these momentous matters, and threaten them with a war on an unparalleled scale if they should wound the tender sensibilities of this nation, openly declaring that if the United States is treated with indignity, the latent feelings of national pride in the bosoms of the Southerners, aroused into vigorous action, will cause them to come out as one man to the defense of the country and the insult will be avenged by the united power of the sections now engaged in bloody war.

They refuse to believe that it is impossible to reconstruct the Union, and in the face of our declarations and deeds—despite the hatred and abhorrence we profess to entertain for them, and the resolution we have formed—they still imagine that we love the old flag and that when their arms have triumphed and we are in bondage to the states of the North, we will be the most exemplary citizens in the borders of the Union.

Have not these people been bereft of their senses? Did ever a people cling so tenaciously to a foolish hope? What could we have done that we have not done to convince them that the Union is a stink in our nostrils? What care we for their troubles and dangers, for the insults they may receive from foreign governments, for the distresses that may be inflicted upon them? Do we not consider them disgraced forever—the basest, vilest, and most wicked people the sun ever shone upon? We would rejoice in their calamities; and calling to mind the evils we have suffered at their hands, the outrages they have committed in the course of this war, their groans and cries would be music to our ears. We would laugh at their humiliation and sing songs of joy over their downfall and destruction.

The enemy confidently reckon upon overcoming us by force of numbers. They boast loudly of their numerical strength, and contrasting their twenty million with our eight, they have never ceased, even when suffering under the most disastrous discomfiture, to promise themselves eventual success. The seventy thousand called out by Lincoln was to make short work of the rebellion. That mighty array of illustrious chieftains and intrepid warriors was to march through the length and breadth of the rebellious states, hang the leaders of the movement, desolate the land, blot out the Confederacy, and restore the country to quietude and prosperity.

And when that force was found insufficient for the tremendous work, an army of three hundred thousand men was organized. That host was scattered by the steel and lead of Southern boys, and soon the army of the vulgar usurper numbered six hundred thousand, and when that splendid and powerful army failed to accomplish the great work, the army was augmented by over a half million. That immense force is now moving upon our lines. But we contemplate the armed million without apprehension. We shall have to fight with valor and skill and to suffer with all the fortitude we can command, but we have no fear of the result. Their ranks were thinned at Fredericksburg, Murfreesboro, and Vicksburg; and with such generals and such soldiers to plan and fight our battles, and with God to bless their skill and valor, we shall triumph gloriously in spite of the numerical superiority of the foe, and of all the other great advantages he possesses.

NORTH

BOSTON EVENING TRANSCRIPT
January 17, 1863

[UNTITLED]

New England, which is the especial object of the attacks of disloyal Democrats at the present time, is defended by the *New York Times* in a long article, of which the following is an extract:

As regards slavery, New England undoubtedly has been less tolerant toward the institution than any other part of the country. She has discussed its character and tendencies with an earnestness nowhere else displayed. If slavery has suffered from this, it speaks but very poorly for slavery, for it is only the false and the evil that discussion can damage. But even if New England had erred in this respect, the present would be the last time in the world to denounce her for it, when the republic is engaged in putting down the most hideous and wicked rebellion the earth ever saw, which this same slavery has engendered. The worst that New England ever said against the institution does not come up to the enormity of the crime it has actually committed. When slavery succeeds in purging itself from all responsibility for this rebellion, then, and not until then, may New England be held to answer for her hate.

But let the Rebels and the factionists howl on. Nothing will come of it. They may as well bay at the moon.

At a meeting held in Chicago a few evenings ago, to protest against the traitorous tendencies of the submissionists in the legislature, the Honorable Stephen A. Goodwin made the following eloquent remarks:

> The recent attacks upon New England are to pave the way for this deep and damnable design. I am not a New England man, nor am I a Republican, with preconceived attachments to New England politics. But as a born New Yorker, and a New York Democrat, too, with six generations of New England blood in my veins, both on father's and mother's side, I deem it my right to brand with infamy these foul aspersions upon the fair name of New England. She needs not my eulogy here. The successive waves of her population have carried the virtues and the intellect and the enterprise of New England over every rood of free soil from western New York to the Pacific Ocean. Her fame in arts and arms and literature is bright upon every page of our country's history.
>
> Our own great Northwest is the proudest monument to her statesmen. It was Nathan Dane of Massachusetts who, in the old Continental Congress, drew up, introduced, and procured the passage of the celebrated Ordinance of July

1787, for the government of these northwestern states.[2] Wise in all its provisions, it forever excluded slavery from this wide domain. To a New England lawyer, and a New England statesman, belongs the credit of the ordinance in advance, so that through all the seven great empires of the Northwest, her virgin soil should never be polluted by the footprint of the slaveholder, nor the crack of the Negro-driver's whip be heard either in her solitudes or her peopled cities.

The great Northwest herself—in every valley and prairie and hilltop—is New England's monument, as enduring as her bordering Alleghenies—as perpetual as her mighty lakes and ever-rolling rivers.

It is this great West that is now asked by Northern- and Southern-born traitors and New England renegades to part from the Mother of States—and to accept the destructive embraces of slavery, endorsing the foul calumnies of Jefferson Davis and his hellish crew upon the land of their ancestry.

Such, my countrymen, is the character and object of this opposition to the Proclamation of the president. The time is fast maturing when the loyal people of the Northwest, imitating the example of their revolutionary fathers, may be driven to organize committees of safety, whose duty it shall be to see that the Union cause shall take no detriment from Rebel sympathizers and traitors.

NEW YORK TRIBUNE
January 17, 1863

THE DISASTER IN GALVESTON BAY

We present some additional particulars respecting our recent disaster in Galveston Bay. The attack was unexpected, according to this statement. The *Harriet Lane* was aground and fought, accordingly, under the greatest disadvantage. She sent some well-directed shots into one of the attacking steamers and caused the vessel to sink. Her gunners and officers were then picked out by the Texan sharpshooters aboard another

2. The Ordinance of July 1787 is more commonly known as the Northwest Ordinance.

steamer, protected with cotton bales—and Lieutenant Wainwright thus fell. This heroic officer was the son of the late Bishop Wainwright of this city, and his father's family here doubtless will find in the splendor of his defense of the country's flag some assuaging circumstances to their dark bereavement. It was a magnificent defense—one of the grandest in human history, rivaling Marathon and Salamis, Waterloo and the Lakes. Of a crew of a hundred twenty aboard the *Harriet Lane,* but seventeen survived. We do not recall to mind any more terrible encounter in history, the forces engaged considered. We feel impelled under the sublimity of such a death as Commander Wainwright's the virtue of the venerable apothegm, *"dulce et decorum est pro patria mori."*[3] Then, how the superb nobility of the end of Commander Renshaw stirs the blood! His vessel aground, he determined not to surrender and blew her up, himself and the lieutenant, Zimmerman, being hurled into eternity by the act which saved the honor of the dear old flag.

With such men—such officers—such sailors—such soldiers—the republic cannot die. Their proud demises cannot be forgotten. They will be as a rushing tide of glory bearing the youth and courage of the land on to victory, and to such a victory, not simply for a technical Union—but for liberty, liberty for all—and not a sign of oppression left, the scourge raveled for want of use—the chain rusted for need of a wearer—the fierce bloodhound to become an extinct breed, through having no victim to hunt—the overseer, with his knife and revolver, having seen the heavenly light of conversion—and the nation jubilant in her newborn dignity, achievement, and hope.

ARMY AND NAVY PAYMENTS

A joint resolution providing for the immediate issue of $100 million legal tender Treasury notes, to be applied to the payment of the army and navy, has passed the House and Senate, meeting no opposition in the latter except the factious and disloyal negatives of Messrs. Powell of Kentucky and Saulsbury of Delaware. We hope to hear at an early day that these notes have been issued and that the soldiers and sailors have thereupon been promptly paid the amounts hitherto withheld. Meanwhile, a word on the condition of the army and of the finances which made this extraordinary measure necessary may not be amiss.

The efforts of the Federal government to subdue the rebellion are directly dependent, for their success, upon the army and navy. The War

3. *Dulce et decorum est pro patria mori:* Latin, "It is sweet and seemly to die for one's country."

Department has called into service, partly by draft but mainly by volunteering, more than a million men. Every one of the private soldiers composing this immense army is entitled to be paid by the government thirteen dollars a month, and to be paid at least as often as once in two months. Upon the promptness and regularity of these payments depend in a great measure the morale of the army, the zeal of the soldier, his comfort, and the security of his family from suffering and want. He entered into the service of the government, often relinquishing more profitable situations, and in many cases doubtless from considerations of loyal devotion to his country; but he nonetheless became a party to a contract by which he was bound to perform military service, the government, on the other hand, being equally bound to pay him his stipulated wages.

If the government fails to perform its share of the contract, the soldier is not legally nor practically released from his. He remains in service for the full period of his enlistment unless sooner discharged by illness or death. But he remains there by compulsion, by force of military discipline. Whatever enthusiasm once inspired him has vanished with the protracted failure of the government to discharge its obligations. His only inspiration arises from a sentiment of loyalty. How can he be expected to retain it if the government for whose support he offers his life to the chances of disease and battle is so careless of its pledged faith and of his welfare and comfort as to neglect the payment of his wages? It is obvious enough that it is for the interest, as it is for the honor, of the government to take care that its soldiers are punctually paid. An ill-paid army is often mutinous, seldom contented, never enthusiastic.

The arrears of pay now due the army amount probably to not less than between $50 million and $60 million. There are many regiments which have not received a dollar of pay for three, five, six, and even eight months. Not a few of our defeats might be traced in some measure to the discouragement, discontent, and general dissatisfaction occasioned by this unreasonable and inexplicable delay. If there is any satisfactory reason or excuse, we have failed to hear it suggested. It ought not to be deemed unreasonably exacting to require from the government an adherence to the principles of commercial morality which are recognized among merchants in private life, and which form an unwritten code for the regulation of mercantile affairs. When the government makes a contract, or when it comes into the market as a borrower, it is not easy to see why it ought not to conform to the rules which govern individuals in similar relations and necessities. If, then, it undertakes to pay its employees, which the soldiers are, a certain sum per month and fails without adequate excuse, how shall it expect to preserve its credit? It was easy to calculate how much would be due to the army and what means were provided to pay it. If more money was needed, more should have been raised. If it were not raised in season, it is a positive delinquency for which somebody is responsible.

We may congratulate ourselves on the low rate of interest at which the public loans have been obtained. But it should be remembered that the interest which the government saves a class of its creditors loses, whose claims are practically loans to the government just so long as their payment is deferred. On these debts no interest will ever be paid—not even on the arrears to the soldiers, to whom the amount thus due is computed at not less than $1 million. A much larger item may be obtained from the debts to contractors, few of whom are so fortunate as not to know practically the difficulties in the way of receiving payment of the principal of their claims. There are scores of cases in this city where the adjustment of undisputed claims on accomplished contracts has been delayed for months without reason or excuse; and when a settlement is finally made, the best terms the government has to offer are one-third cash and the remainder in six-percent certificates of indebtedness, which are worth from ninety-five to ninety-eight cents on the dollar. Suppose *these* interest accounts were added to the exhibit of the Treasury. What would then be the average rate?

It would have been far better for our national credit, and immeasurably so for our national honor, if the government had, from the outset, fairly estimated its accruing liabilities and sought to provide for the whole of them at maturity by well-regulated measures of finance, early adopted and honestly adhered to. The resolution which has anticipated so large an amount of the loan or note issue to be finally adopted was an act of necessary but only partial justice. What we need, and what the government ought to announce its determination to adopt, is some plan which shall not merely make late payment of long arrears, but which shall restore its solvency and its credit by creating a belief in its purpose as well as its ability to pay its debts when they become due.

FEBRUARY 21, 1863

SOUTH

RICHMOND DAILY DISPATCH
February 21, 1863

A TRIP THROUGH THE UNITED STATES

A gentleman who has recently visited several of the principal cities of the North has furnished us with an account of his trip and sojourn among the Yankees. Leaving Richmond two days before Christmas, he arrived in Maryland on Christmas Eve and was warmly received in that portion of the state where he landed, where the Southern sentiment is almost unanimous. Every facility was afforded him in making his way to Baltimore. He arrived in that city in the middle of the day on Sunday, and, being well-known there, found it necessary to observe great caution in his movements. He remained in Baltimore one week, during which time he kept himself carefully secreted during the day, making his perambulations through the city after night by gaslight. While he remained in the city, he saw a number of its prominent businessmen, with whom he conversed freely. They all seemed hopeful of the result of the present struggle and believe that Southern independence will be the inevitable consequence of the present revolution. There was no public expression of opinion, all parties appearing to be awed by, and subdued on account of, the presence and unwarrantable acts of the military stationed in their midst. They express deep mortification at the present humiliated condition of their state, and great regret that the real sentiment of her people is not properly understood and her embarrassment appreciated. The usual lively aspect of affairs in the city at this season of the year is painfully changed, and sadness and gloom hang over everything. Few ladies are to be seen on the street at any time.

From Baltimore our traveling friend made his way to the city of New York. Here he remained for more than a week, and during that time circulated freely in all quarters, affording himself an opportunity of hearing expressions of opinion with reference to the present crisis from all classes of the population of the city. None of the restraint felt in Baltimore is experienced in New York, and those who oppose the Lincoln administration talk with great freedom and act independently, without apparent apprehension of consequences. Of the war they declare themselves heartily tired, and with its management completely disgusted. He heard Lincoln and his supporters openly denounced as traitors in the public houses in New York. In favor of an honorable adjustment of the present difficulties there is a very strong and rapidly growing sentiment. Little, if any, hope is entertained of finally subjugating the South by the thinking portion of the community, but there is still a lingering hope that the states of the Confederacy may yet be induced to return to the Union. It is everywhere openly and boldly proclaimed that no more troops can be raised for the prosecution of the war under present auspices. The Negro policy of the Republican administration at Washington is violently condemned, and the bone and sinew of which Northern soldiers are made swear they will fight neither for nor with the Negro. General Lee is spoken of publicly as the greatest military genius of the age, and incomparably superior to any general upon the Federal side. Not only is he spoken of as a great commander, but as a polished gentleman, devoid of that braggadocio for which their own officers are characteristic. "Stonewall" Jackson is greatly admired for his daring and brilliant achievements, and others of our general officers are talked of in terms of warm commendation. The health of "Jeff Davis" is not unfrequently drunk in the public barrooms. During his sojourn in Gotham, our friend stopped at the St. Nicholas Hotel. General Wool and his staff were guests of the house at the same time. There were very few soldiers in the city, and not many on the route between New York and Baltimore. All the places of amusement in the city were open nightly and pretty generally thronged. Business was not active, many of the merchants declaring their determination to retain their goods on the shelf in preference to disposing of them for "greenbacks."[4] Very few "greenbacks" are in circulation, the principal currency being state bank money, and postage currency for small change. No specie is seen or circulated.

Leaving New York, the gentleman alluded to proceeded to Boston, where he arrived in the midst of a heavy snowstorm. Being on a sightseeing expedition, he determined, however, not to be deterred by the inclement weather. Procuring a hack, he visited Charlestown, Cambridge, and the Bunker Hill Monument. He does not recollect to have heard a word said about the war during his stay in Boston, and the people there seem scarcely conscious of the stupendous struggle that is in progress. There seemed to be a general spirit of gaiety, the Yankees in that local-

4. The Federal government first issued paper money in early 1862, as an emergency measure to provide currency in place of gold. The bills, which were printed on one side in green ink, were soon nicknamed "greenbacks." Because of their great popularity and functional convenience, the original plan to retire the notes at the war's end was never put into effect.

ity apparently feeling little of the pressure resulting from the troubles which are afflicting other and more deserving sections of the country. He soon tired of the city and left it in disgust, returning to New York by the "Stonington route," where he remained several days longer.

From thence he came on to Philadelphia, and put up at the Girard House, intending to spend several days in that city. On the night of his arrival, Senator Wall of New Jersey, who was en route for Washington, addressed a large gathering of the people from the front balcony of the Girard House. Our friend says that no idea can be formed from the newspaper reports of the enthusiasm created by this speech. From beginning to end it was received with tumultuous applause by the Philadelphians. After the speech was concluded, our traveler, in passing through the hall of the hotel, met with a detective whom he had formerly known in Baltimore, and by whom he was afraid of being recognized. This unexpected meeting of an old acquaintance—with whom he had no desire to hold an interview—determined him to make his sojourn in the Quaker city very brief, and as the cars were about departing southward, he at once engaged passage.

After more than a week of tedious journeying, over a route which we do not deem it entirely prudent to mention, he arrived safely in Richmond, much gratified with his trip and firmly impressed with the belief, from all that he could see and hear, that the 1st of July will witness the termination of the war.

CHARLESTON DAILY COURIER
February 21, 1863

PEACE AND THE NORTHWEST

We have been so often deluded by hopes of peace, and have suffered so severely from those false expectations, that we are admonished not to lend a willing ear to those reports and statements which promise deliverance in a short time from the calamities caused by this terrible contest. All these statements concerning the disaffection in the army threatening Vicksburg may be true, and it may likewise be true that Indiana, Illinois, Kentucky, and Ohio are prepared to solicit admission into the Southern Confederacy and, in the event their request is refused, to establish a separate independency. All these statements may be true —true to the letter—and yet it is dangerous to bottom our hopes of a speedy termination of our troubles on those advices.

The people of the Northwest are in a bad humor because, after having done the most brave and bloody fighting, they are suffering for the want of a market for their grains and bacon. The Emancipation Proclamation has also a great deal to do with the mutinous spirit of the inhabitants of that region. But though they have given expression to their just and sensible sentiments in terms so plain and forceful and have even gone so far as to call a convention for the purpose of adopting measures for the adjustment of the momentous questions at issue, before the date set for the assembling of that body, events may transpire that will change the tone of their feelings.

For these demonstrations and designs do not in any measure impair the vigor and weaken the determination of the men in power at Washington. They are as bitter and as resolved as they were before the muttering of these murmurs and complaints and curses reached their ears. In truth, so far from making them less earnest and determined, those words of menace and denunciation have intensified the fierceness of their wrath and aroused the more deeply all their mighty energies.

The feeling in the Northwest, which may break out into revolution, only serves to hasten the prosecution of the campaigns now in progress. And if any one of those campaigns is successful, the victory may hush these notes of disaffection and cause the war to be waged with more fury and obstinacy.

The course of the Northwest depends upon the result of the battle at Vicksburg. The dwellers in that region are uncomfortable and mutinous because they cannot avail themselves of the navigation of the Mississippi. If we can keep that river closed, we can maintain and increase their opposition to New England and the Yankee administration. They will grow more and more disloyal to the government, they will continue to devise means to deliver themselves from their galling and disgraceful bondage, they will adopt measures in harmony with their greatness, and those measures will be executed with a spirit and energy that will secure success.

But if the many-hilled city falls before the guns that will in a short time thunder upon its earthworks, that victory may arrest the movements afoot and give a different complexion to matters in that quarter. Having been relieved of their heavy load of woes, the people of the Northwest may abandon their intentions, submit with grace to the usurpations of the government, and cooperate with renewed ardor in the wild scheme of reconstruction. If disaster befalls our arms at Port Hudson and Vicksburg, the convention may fall to the ground, and those powerful states now on the verge of revolution, and inspired by high motives of patriotism and honor, may retire from the position they have taken and, swallowing the infamous Proclamation and the stupid and cruel Negro Regiment Bill, give their earnest support to the party they at present so detest and denounce.[5]

These tidings that have come to us over the wires are pleasant, but it is dangerous to build our hopes of an early peace upon them. If the Northwest does carry out its purposes, we may expect the war to terminate at no distant day. But the execution of their designs depends upon events which are yet in the womb of the future, and we should not suffer those movements to abate our vigilance or relax our energy. The expeditions that are now ready, the attitude of foreign powers, the advantages possessed by the enemy, warn us not to give place for a moment to seductive influences. If guided and strengthened by divine wisdom and might, we are equal to the demands of duty. Without human help we are able to achieve independence. Let us be more earnest, and patient, and valiant, and we shall conquer an enduring and honorable peace when it seems good in the eyes of Him whose approval and assistance we have invoked.

NORTH

BOSTON EVENING TRANSCRIPT
February 21, 1863

FROM RICHMOND
EXTREMITY OF THE REBEL ARMY—
CONDITION OF THE REBEL CAPITAL

From the *New York Evening Post*

We have seen a gentleman who has been lately in Richmond and spent some time there. He had good opportunities for seeing how the affairs of Rebeldom are getting on. He gives us the following interesting particulars:

5. Several bills introduced into Congress to enlist African Americans as soldiers were debated toward the end of January 1863. Democrats hoped to stall action on the legislation until that session of Congress expired on March 4, but the Negro Regiment Bill, authorizing the enlistment of African Americans up to a maximum of 300,000, was passed, 83 to 55. More than 200,000 served in the Union army. While the debate raged, a large number of African-American sailors were already serving in the navy, which had been traditionally integrated; by the war's end, 29,000 African Americans were in the Union navy, comprising about 25 percent of the enlisted force.

He says in the most positive manner that the Rebel army "has done growing." *Every man in the South* between eighteen and forty who can possibly bear arms is now in the service. There is a bill before the Rebel Congress conscripting even foreigners and Marylanders. The latter have been hitherto exempt.

Even at present they give "foreigners" ten days to leave the country, but they issue no passes; and all who escape the clutches of the conscript officers hereafter will have to get away secretly and without a pass.

The supplies of the Rebel army, with the exception of its shoes, are better than they have been. Above one half of the soldiers are supplied with overcoats, and it is said that three out of every four of these are "Yankee overcoats" captured from us.

Shoes are scarce. A great many soldiers wear canvas shoes and moccasins. Cavalry boots are worth seventy dollars in Richmond. Some of the men our informant saw were absolutely barefooted; even officers of the lower grades had marched and fought in bare feet.

The troops are very deficient in camp equipage. But in the matter of clothing the Rebel army is now better supplied than it was a year ago. Much gray cloth is manufactured now in the South and sold only to the soldiers.

Horses are getting scarce. There is not a good horse in the country, except those now in the army. Cattle, too, seem to be getting scarce. In the droves collected for the army, one sees the greater part yearlings or two-year-olds, such animals as we do not think of killing here.

AMMUNITION

The Rebels are reported to be somewhat short of powder. They get the most of this from England, by way of Charleston and Mobile.

Forage, too, is getting scarcer. General Fitzhugh Lee has command of the cavalry on the line of the Rappahannock, from Fredericksburg to the mouth, and he has eaten the country bare of provisions and everything which can be consumed for twenty miles back of our line. The unfortunate people who live in that region are at the point of starvation.

PRICES IN RICHMOND

Old bacon is sold at $1.25 a pound. There is no new bacon, as there is not salt enough to cure it. They pickle pork lightly, but it will not keep in warm weather.

Lard is sold at $1.25 a pound. There is no oil for lights and for lubricating purposes to be got in the South, and lard is used instead. For this reason, this article is rapidly rising, as much is consumed for machinery, in the coal mines, as well as for lights.

Butter sells for $2.50 a pound, molasses $15 a gallon, sugar $1.25 a pound, oak wood $25 a cord, pinewood $20. Luxuries are at fabulous prices. Hairpins are not to be had in the South. White kid gloves alone are sold at reasonable rates, because no one wears them. Calico sells at $2.50 a yard—this for the commonest quality. Whiskey brings $40 a gallon, and poor at that, and dram drinkers must pay often $1 a glass.

Ladies' shoes, such as one buys here for $1.25, cannot be had for less than $20 the pair. Common pocketknives bring $9. Common soft hats, price $3 here, sell there for $25. It is believed that there is not fine black cloth enough in Richmond to make a frock coat.

Beef sells for $1 a pound; flour sells at $28 the barrel in Richmond. The poorer people live chiefly on corn, and now and then a little rusty bacon. Salt is held cheap at 25 cents a pound. This has fallen in price, and this is the only article of consumption which has gone down. Everything else constantly rises in price.

Substitutes for the army cost $2,500, but it needs much influence to get leave to hire a substitute. Often, when a soldier has engaged and paid a substitute, the authorities catch him and conscript him.

Our informant is certain that but a few days ago, there was a formidable Rebel force in front of Hooker. He laughs at the assertions and reports in the Richmond journals that part of Lee's army has gone to Vicksburg. He says—and here he but repeats what every man we have seen returned from the South has told us—that the Rebel papers never speak the truth about army movements. They dare not tell, even if they happen to know, for the Rebels stand no nonsense.

RICHMOND

Richmond is surrounded with earthworks. The James River is completely defended by fortifications at Drewry's and Chapin's bluffs, which command the channel so that no vessel could get up. There are rows of piles, too, driven in the channel.

At the Drewry's Bluff fort the bombproofs were found not to work, so that now it is said the guns are without cover, but "rat holes" have been constructed for the gunners to take refuge in to avoid shells.

There are guards on the corners of all the streets who demand exemption papers of any passerby whom they may not know to be exempt. All who have not these are at once arrested and sent out to camp and put under arms. Applicants for railroad tickets must show a pass, and if none is shown, the unfortunate is sent to Castle Thunder.

There is no gas in Richmond to light the streets with. Coal is at such extravagant prices that a man could wheel off in a barrow twenty dollars' worth. Potatoes are sold at eight dollars a bushel.

The aristocracy have no longer fine carriage horses, but are pulled about by lanky, slab-sided jades and in shabby carriages. There is not much party-going. There are no young men to take the ladies out. In the Richmond theater the leading attraction is a young woman who formerly danced in a lager-beer saloon in the Bowery.

The enforcement of the conscription law has made life and property safer than they were before in the Rebel capital. The roughs have been sent to the army.

Smallpox is almost epidemic in Virginia, at the capital as well as in the country.

UNITED STATES TREASURY NOTES

"Greenbacks," as they are called, are hoarded as much as gold in Richmond. Three hundred twenty dollars of Confederate money is now needed to buy $100 in gold, and $100 of Confederate money buy $40 in United States Treasury notes—that is to say, $250 of Rebel Treasury notes are readily paid for $100 in United States Treasury notes. Virginia state money, even, is sold at from 35 to 40 percent premium over Confederate money. North Carolina money is also at a high premium.

Charleston is reported to be thoroughly fortified. They can bring a hundred guns to bear, it is said, on a certain point which it is necessary to pass. It was also rumored that the harbor was blocked up, and only a passage left wide enough to pass a vessel out. These were the reports about Richmond.

NEW YORK TRIBUNE
February 21, 1863

THE TECHE EXPEDITION
NEGROPHOBIA—CRUEL TREATMENT OF THE COLORED SOLDIERS—AFFAIRS AT BATON ROUGE—THE REPORTED CAPTURE OF THE BROOKLYN

From Our Special Correspondent
St. Charles Hotel, New Orleans, Louisiana
February 12, 1863

Contrary to the anticipations expressed in my last letter, I have nothing to communicate respecting General Weitzel's proposed expedition into the Teche country for the purpose of "cleaning out" the Rebels there. As the general was in this city yesterday (I write at early morning), I suppose one of those apparently inevitable delays attendant on military operations has supervened. From up the river, however, I derive the particulars of Colonel Paine's movement, designed to act in conjunction with that of General Weitzel from below, as heretofore related. They are as follows:

Colonel Paine, acting brigadier general, left Baton Rouge on the morning of Saturday, the 7th, with three transports—the *Iberville, Continental,* and *Che-Kiang*—conveying the 4th Wisconsin, the 8th New Hampshire, the 133rd and 173rd New York. These troops disembarked at Plaquemine, thirty miles below, on the west bank of the Mississippi, and marched straightway inland to a place denominated Indian Village, at seven miles' distance, comprising about half a dozen miserable cabins. Arriving at sunset, the troops bivouacked for the night, the *Iberville* following with the stores and tents and a guard of cavalry by way of Plaquemine Bayou. There our troops are temporarily encamped, at no great distance from a crevasse which has already submerged some adjacent woods. Two weeks ago this Indian Village was occupied by a band of guerrillas, who were driven off by a company of United States cavalry.

The *Iberville* took on board, in lieu of her military stores, upward of four thousand dollars' worth of sugar and molasses from the neighboring planters, who professed themselves rejoiced at the opportunity of transmitting their produce to New Orleans. It lies now at the levee of this city.

General Amory left here for Carrollton yesterday, to proceed with the following regiments to the reinforcement of Colonel Paine: the 38th and

49th Massachusetts, 156th New York, 16th New Hampshire, and a section of the 18th New York Battery. With these there may be others. Combining with the four regiments under Colonel Paine, the entire force will push for Bute la Rose, there to effect a junction with General Weitzel.

At Baton Rouge, things are quiet, but hardly satisfactory. I am informed that two epidemics, indigenous to this department, have appeared there—that they are, indeed, horribly prevalent. I allude, in the first place, to the plague of speculators, akin to that of Egyptian locusts; secondly, to the disease "negrophobia"—a moral blindness through which our nationality may yet grope its way to the pit of destruction. In a former letter I have surmised that perhaps the only effectual cure for the first evil would lie in a big crevasse, deservedly drowning the whole of us. With respect to the second, I have hitherto preserved a reticence, which I shall now break.

Three weeks ago there was sent up to Baton Rouge the 3rd Louisiana Native Guards—a colored regiment, commanded by Colonel J. A. Nelson, formerly a captain in the 31st Massachusetts and provost marshal of Ship Island. Having previously mustered in two colored regiments, this officer became satisfied of their usefulness and efficiency, and himself accepted command of a third. The men were principally recruited in New Orleans and did good service in the Bayou Teche fight, ending in the destruction of the Rebel gunboat *Cotton* and the death of Commander Buchanan—particularly in throwing up defensive earthworks, a kind of labor always unwillingly performed by white troops. So satisfactory was their behavior that it is known to have won the approval of General Weitzel, himself anything but a believer in the military capacity of the race. Well, the men were sent to Baton Rouge, the regiment being full a thousand strong; ten colored persons—four captains and six noncommissioned officers—forming part of the command. They drilled well, marched well, kept themselves clean, performed all their duties as soldiers—nothing in the world is alleged against them but that they are Negroes and have Negro officers; hence the ill will, the detestation, with which they are regarded.

I am informed that General Grover will not "recognize" the regiment; that he has asserted that in case he shall be officially required to do so, the United States government is welcome to his commission; that the regiment can neither draw clothing, blankets, nor pay in consequence; that the officers of certain white regiments vindicate the purity of their cuticle on every possible occasion by insulting the colored ones; that some (of the former) have resigned; that the colonel of the 133rd New York—an Englishman—has distinguished himself by issuing an address exhorting his men "to continue in the performance of their duty until such time as the regiment is brought into contact with" the Negroes "by guard duty, drills, or otherwise, when he trusts that his men have that confidence in him to believe that he will not suffer their self-respect or manliness to be lowered by contact with an inferior race," etc.; and, generally, that the Union soldiers, rank and file, are doing their meanest to induce the Negroes to regret their old normal state of chattelism and their Southern owners.

"Between the devil and the deep sea" is a nautical conception of a dilemma. Between Jefferson Davis's threats of hanging and the wicked prejudice, hatred, contempt, and ill-usage experienced at our hands, the poor Africans are evilly entreated. General Hunter encountered just the same difficulties in organizing colored regiments in South Carolina and —God bless him for it!—squelched them. I hope General Banks will do the same; Colonel Nelson is here to request it. This stone that the builders so persistently and contemptuously reject is yet to become the head of the corner, or we, with it tied about our necks, sink to deserved oblivion. I hold that God's meaning in this war is to free the slave, and woe be to him who fights against it and Him, directly or indirectly!

From the report of an individual who was recently allowed to pass outside our lines at Baton Rouge and those of the Rebels "on business," and who journeyed some fifteen miles inland, I am informed that the country is very quiet and food plentiful. He remained for a day or two, regaling on chickens, wheat and corn bread, fresh butter, and coffee, the presence of which excites little surprise in those who know how things are managed in that vicinity.

A week ago the Rebels at Port Hudson hanged an ex-resident of Baton Rouge, known as "Monkey Joe," for spiking, or attempting to spike, one of their guns—it was alleged, in consequence of a great reward offered to him by one of our generals![6] Two other persons were under arrest suspected of similar intentions. All the pickets in the neighborhood are Tennessee cavalry, excellently mounted.

At Baton Rouge, Southern Confederacy shinplasters are generally taken by our sutlers as money, at the rate of forty cents on the dollar. Any paper bearing the endorsement of Pike, President of the Branch Bank of the State of Louisiana, circulates freely. One hundred dollars of

6. spike: to disable a cannon by driving a spike into its vent and breaking the tip off flush with the surface of the cannon.

Confederate notes are considered equivalent to half that amount in New Orleans bills, and twenty-five dollars in gold.

A Mr. Benjamin, brother of the Rebel secretary of war, came to this city from Baton Rouge on the *Iberville* during her last trip. I know nothing distinguishable about him except this relationship and a general physical resemblance to Count Fosco in Wilkie Collins's novel.

In my last letter, or the one preceding it, I sent Commodore Farragut, on board his flagship *Hartford,* to Galveston, Texas. He got no further than the bar at the mouth of the Mississippi this time, then returning. It is understood that he will start in earnest soon, that he is impatient to do so.

Yesterday's and today's New Orleans papers will bring you a report of the stranding of the *Brooklyn* off Galveston; also, of her capture by the *Alabama,* the *Harriet Lane,* and some other Rebel craft. This story is discredited in every particular by the navy.

Another contraband schooner, laden with medicines, was captured yesterday in the attempt to cross Lake Pontchartrain to the northern shore.

The secessionists here have a wild story about the assassination of General Butler by Bouligny, in New York, and much more of an equally probable character—very much more than I care to particularize.

T. B. G.

THE NEED OF VICTORY

The intelligent Washington correspondent of the *Independent* thus speaks of the prospect of foreign intervention in our civil war:

> As it has always been since the war broke out—*the issue is with us.* If we act with stupidity and pusillanimity, intervention may come, but even in that event there is a great deal more danger that the Rebels will, without aid from abroad, achieve their own independence. It is a stand-up fight, and if we are true to ourselves, we can win it, and before next June, too. We have come at last to the hour when it will do to talk of "ninety days." The backbone of the rebellion *can* be broken in the next ninety days, and it must be done. Two or three wholesome victories now, and the country is saved.

We know well that army movements in the Northern slave states are simply impossible amid the frequent rains of such a winter as this, and we do not assume to indicate where or when blows for the Union should be struck; but in the spirit and essence of the above we heartily concur. One or two staggering Union victories would do more to ward off the danger of foreign intervention in our troubles than all the clever dispatches that have been or could be written. It is not a case for rhetoric, but for rifled cannon. If we can demonstrate our ability to crush the rebellion, Europe will say amen. But if all that our war practically amounts to is an interruption of trade and a privation of cotton, we shall have intervention at no remote day, and as we have ostentatiously repelled it, there is now a moral certainty that it will take a shape unfriendly to the restoration of the Union. This prospect should not discourage us, but simply incite our chiefs, civil and military, to strike so soon as may be, and strike hard. Delay is perilous; inaction is death. In victory is our only safety.

MARCH 21, 1863

SOUTH

RICHMOND DAILY DISPATCH
March 21, 1863

THE TRUE PATH TO INDEPENDENCE

It is not alone by chivalrous and gallant deeds that the independence of our country is to be secured. If it were, we should have no doubts of the future. There never has existed yet a people who surpassed the South in its heroic and self-sacrificing devotion to country. But it must be admitted that we are too fond of ease and pleasure, and it has been even doubted whether we should not now be in a better condition if the glorious victory of Manassas had never been achieved. That wonderful success tempted us to lie on our laurels, and it was only when routed from our perilous repose by the sharp sting of adversity that we recovered our equanimity and put forth the full energies which the magnitude of the contest and the persevering and implacable character of the enemy demanded.

If we will consider in what the strength of the enemy lies, we shall derive some instructive lessons for ourselves, for it is lawful to learn from an enemy. That strength does not consist in his numbers alone, nor even principally, great as those numbers are; nor, still less, in any superiority of fighting qualities. We do not question the courage of the Yankees, or any other race of men, but we do not believe that they have the military aptitude of the Southern people, and we know that they have not as lofty and inspiring motives in this contest as our own. But there are qualities by which they have always been distinguished—system, caution, labor, thorough attention to details, and dogged perseverance. They are made more vindictive and persistent by defeat; and their revenge seems to sharpen their faculties and clear their understanding, while they make the most of their victories and turn them at once to practical account. Mechanical labor is in abundance among them, and they are employing all its appliances in the present war. It is undeniable that we need more system and practicality in all the departments of our government and in every field of operations. We must make a business of war and conduct it with the same thoroughness and attention to detail that a successful businessman exhibits in the conduct of his business affairs.

The South could not have a better model to fashion itself after, both in war and peace, than the illustrious founder of its civilization, Captain John Smith.[7] In him we see how the loftiest chivalry and the most infallible common sense may be united in the same person. The present war, fruitful as it is in examples of the most magnificent courage, has not produced a more glorious warrior than Captain John Smith, nor has Yankeedom ever boasted a mind more practical, energetic, and patiently laborious. Europe and America resounded with the praises of his chivalry, and yet no man, reared to labor with his own hands, ever more highly appreciated mechanical industry, or had a more exalted estimate of the dignity and value of labor. His letters to the London commissioners were full of indignant denunciation of the indolence and effeminacy of men who expected to lay the foundation of a state with gloves on their delicate hands. If the South would ever fulfill her grand destiny, she must act upon the maxims of this truly great man. She is at this moment suffering from the absence of manufacturing industry—a misfortune and not altogether a fault—for, though fond of ease and leisure, she has been deprived by the policy of the Federal government of those inducements and advantages for manufacturing and commercial enterprise which have been extended to the Northern states. But under these disadvantages she no longer labors. With the establishment of her independence she will no longer be forced to pay tribute to Northern

7. Captain John Smith founded Jamestown, Virginia, in May 1607.

taskmasters. Her noble harbors will be available for her own commerce; and her unrivaled advantages in climate, and waterpower for manufacturing purposes, will then be at her own disposal. It depends upon her use of these advantages whether the glories achieved by her arms will be of practical value and her independence be established in fact as well as in name.

CHARLESTON DAILY COURIER
March 21, 1863

THE NEAR FUTURE

Diverse causes have delayed the execution of the stupendous military plans the enemy has been devising and maturing for many weeks. His generals in command, urged by the clamorous demand of the people, would doubtless have attempted to carry out their programs long before this, had not circumstances made the postponement of them an absolute necessity or a clear duty. There are influences of a most potent kind in vigorous operation that have been and still are exerting all their power upon the leaders of their great armies, which will force them to adventure battle at no distant day. The strongest of these is the great need of an important victory. The North is famishing for a grand success on some extended battlefield. The winter campaign closed disastrously for their arms. They have not yet recovered from the depression consequent upon those checks and reverses. A large portion of their population have come out openly for peace on any terms, and all would rejoice over a final cessation of hostilities. Trouble is brewing in the Northwest; and unless the Mississippi is opened, and that right early, the threats and denunciations of those rough and brave men of the frontier states will shortly become more fierce and fiery, and their bold words will be changed into bloody deeds.

The government and the politicians who support the administration are aware of the importance of a great military success, and they are willing to incur the hazard of defeat in order to accomplish the important ends nothing beside a signal victory will enable them to attain. They know that if any one of their armies is successful in the performance of the work assigned it, the wave of joy that will roll over the Yankee heart will submerge all dissatisfaction and murmur and that while the song of victory is fresh and sweet, the voice of opposition will not dare to mar the rapturous melody with its discordant notes.

And a decisive and glorious success would so delight the souls of that fickle and foolish people that for a while they would cease to curse Chase's financial scheme. They would not be conscious of the burdens imposed upon them by the depreciation of their redundant currency, and the enforcement of the unlawful draft would excite no dangerous complaint or serious opposition.

For these and numerous other reasons we may apprehend some movement, at an early day, of some portion of the vastly extended line occupied by the forces of the enemy.

The country has for some time been listening for the deep roar of the enemy's guns in this quarter. Port Hudson has again repulsed the iron-clad monsters with complete success, inflicting upon the presumptuous squadron, from its batteries on its cliffs, severe damage and loss. Fort Pemberton has given the confident invader so harsh a reception that he has disappeared from its frowning walls. It was expected that the two armies would have decided, weeks ago, the question of the possession of middle Tennessee. But the enemy still hesitates to expose his cheese boxes to the terrific fire of the guns that guard the entrance to Charleston and Savannah. It is likely he will let Fort Pemberton and Port Hudson alone for a season, and there are no symptoms of a conflict shortly between Rosecrans and Johnston.

There is a point, however, from which indications justify us in reckoning upon hearing startling news before another week completes its course. The bloody drama at Fredericksburg is about to be repeated, with all the horrors that marked its first performance in an aggravated form. Hooker is prepared to attempt the achievement that has been the death of all his predecessors. He is compelled to obey the "On to Richmond" cry the North is bellowing forth again with its millions of brazen throats. The movements which look to another struggle on the line of the Rappahannock have already begun. The usual orders that precede the opening of a campaign have been issued. And we may with confidence expect in a few days to hear that the grand Army of the Potomac and the noble veterans who have discomfited the foe on so many fields of blood have joined battle.

And it is not improbable that before this month has passed away, battles will be fought at other vital points. On the day set apart by the president for humiliation at the shrine of prayer, we may have to deplore some disaster, or rejoice over some splendid success.

Let us contemplate the future with penitent, tranquil, trustful hearts. Defeats may await us in quarters that we look not for them. Our souls may be grievously afflicted. We should prepare our minds for reverses. For it is not reasonable to expect that we shall come off victorious from every one of the conflicts now impending. If we nerve our spirits for the endurance of defeats, victory will thrill our spirits with a higher rapture. If our apprehensions are realized, we shall bear the calamity with a heroic fortitude. To God we commend our cause.

[UNTITLED]

If the New York papers report truly, more than five thousand bales of American cotton have reached New York in one week lately, from Liverpool. Are the English spinners so well supplied with cotton that they can afford to let cotton go to New York? Is this cotton purchased in Liverpool for New York? In connection with the fact that, at our latest accounts from Liverpool, American cotton was advancing and other descriptions declining, this return of cotton may be noted as one of the results of the war and a practical comment on the Yankee talk about an early suppression of the rebellion.

It may also suggest the question whether there is not cotton enough now extant, under present circumstances, and whether, even apart from immediate necessities of the army and our citizens, it will not be the best policy to secure a full crop of provisions.

NORTH

BOSTON EVENING TRANSCRIPT
March 21, 1863

THE ATTACK ON NEW BERN

Army Correspondence of the *Transcript*
Camp Peirson, New Bern, North Carolina,
March 15, 1863

Mr. Editor:—Events in this department during the past fortnight have forcibly illustrated the uncertainty of a soldier's life. Two weeks ago it seemed very probable that we should have a long period of quiet here. General Foster's force had been so much reduced by the withdrawal of troops to Charleston that it was not expected he would engage in any operations except such as were needed for promoting the security of his position, while the attention of the Rebels was so much occupied in other quarters that it was not thought that they would attempt any movement against this well-fortified stronghold. But these anticipations have not been realized, for during the last ten days there have been continued movements of the Federal troops, hurried departures, hasty marches, and reconnaissances in force; and at the present time a Confederate force is threatening the city, while on our part all is bustle and activity in preparing to repel an attack.

On the 5th instant, orders were received by Colonel Horace C. Lee's brigade (5th, 25th, and 46th Massachusetts regiments) to prepare three days' cooked rations and be ready to march at one hour's notice. Early on the morning of the 6th, the 25th started out on the Trent Road, proceeding about seven miles beyond our main picket camp, where they remained several days, watching the movements of the enemy. In one of their reconnaissances, they surprised a small Rebel camp which was occupied by one company of Confederate troops, and charging upon it, the Rebels fled, abandoning all their camp equipage, which was destroyed by our troops. Two New York regiments also left on the 6th, for a reconnaissance toward the coast, and returned after an absence of several days, having thoroughly scoured the country between this and Swansboro, without meeting any large force of armed Rebels, and finding the inhabitants in a state of extreme destitution. Two Pennsylvania regiments were also dispatched on the 7th instant on an expedition into Hyde County, to look after guerrillas.

On the 9th instant, the "marching orders" under which our regiment had held itself in readiness for several days were revoked, and on the evening of the 10th, the 24th Massachusetts Regiment returned to their camp, near our own, having left four of their companies out on picket duty. Our regiment assembled on the margin of the pond which separates the two camps and, at the suggestion of Colonel Peirson, vociferously cheered the 25th men on their return, while our regimental band came out and added their music to the welcome. The 25th heartily responded to the greeting. Our men subsequently repaired to Colonel Peirson's tent and gave three enthusiastic cheers for our popular commander, who came out and briefly thanked them for the compliment.

Information having been received at headquarters on the 13th that a large Rebel force was threatening our outer pickets on the Trent Road, General Foster ordered Colonel Horace C. Lee's brigade (5th, 25th, and 46th Massachusetts regiments), with Belger's Rhode Island battery of six pieces and Lee's New York battery of six pieces and a small cavalry force, to proceed up the road immediately on a reconnaissance. Our regiment received its orders at 5:30 P.M. and immediately began preparations for the march, taking such scanty rations as were at hand, and at six o'clock the regiment was in line, and started to join the other regiments of the brigade.

The expedition, under command of General Palmer, entered the woods beyond Fort Totten at sundown and marched rapidly during the evening, over the wretched road already made familiar to us on the Goldsboro expedition, halting for the night at nine o'clock in a cornfield seven miles distant from New Bern. The 25th and 46th Massachusetts regiments occupied the advance. The left wing of our regiment was posted as a support to Belger's battery, one platoon of Company I being thrown to the woods on the left as a picket guard.[8] Our right wing was placed a short distance ahead, supporting Lee's battery. The night air was keenly cold, and as it was deemed imprudent to light fires, our troops, who had taken no blankets with them, were much pinched by the severity of the weather. Huddled together in groups, crouched under the scanty shelter of rail fences, or running about to keep ourselves warm, we passed a sleepless night, whose dreary hours went by with tedious slowness.

Morning dawned at length, and at the first approach of light, fires were built in our camp, and our men succeeded in keeping themselves comfortable until the line was formed for starting at seven o'clock, at which hour the troops began to move onward. Just before the column was put in motion, the report of heavy guns was heard in quick succession from the direction of New Bern, and it was at first supposed that the forts and gunboats were firing salutes in honor of the anniversary of the capture of New Bern one year ago that day. But the long continuance of the firing induced a belief that the Confederates had commenced an attack on the defenses of the city.

The march was continued until the advance reached Deep Gully, eight miles from New Bern, when intelligence reached General Palmer that the enemy had attacked our forces on the north side of the Neuse, opposite New Bern, and were also shelling the gunboats lying in the river. No considerable Rebel force appearing in our front, and it being apparent that the real designs of the enemy were directed against New Bern itself, the army was ordered to retrace its steps, and commenced the return at eight o'clock, proceeding without a halt until it reached New Bern, our regiment entering its camp at 11:00 A.M., just seventeen hours from the time of leaving it. Our main pickets were withdrawn

8. platoon: a subdivision of a company, composed of two or more squads and commanded by a lieutenant.

as the army returned, and such of the camp equipage as could not be conveyed by the wagons at hand was destroyed. On reaching camp, our regiment stacked arms on the parade ground and were ordered by Colonel Peirson to hold themselves ready for action at a moment's notice.

It appears that a brigade of Confederate troops, numbering about three thousand men, with fourteen pieces of artillery, appeared before the fortified camp of the 92nd New York Regiment early in the morning and summoned the garrison to surrender, informing them that they knew the strength of the garrison and that resistance would be useless against the overpowering force under General Pettigrew. The gallant commander of the 92nd could not see the propriety of surrendering the fort before the Rebels had begun to try their strength in assaulting it, and after a short parley, the enemy opened a heavy fire upon the garrison.

Our troops had no artillery, and as the enemy were beyond musket range, the Federal soldiers could do nothing but remain under the shelter of their breastworks and await the onset of the enemy. But the Confederates made no attempt to charge over the deep trench and formidable earthworks, upon the besieged garrison. For several hours the Rebels poured a fire of shot and shell upon the fort, completely riddling the tents and destroying much of the camp equipage, but injuring none of its defenders.

Shortly after the fire opened, the Federal gunboat *Hunchback* commenced throwing shells over the Federal fort upon the Rebel battery assailing it, and also directed a portion of the fire against a Rebel battery planted near the river's edge, farther up the stream. The enemy replied to her fire, twice striking her without doing serious injury, and many of their shells exploding in close proximity to the vessel.

Other gunboats speedily arrived to aid the *Hunchback,* and two schooners, with guns worked by Negroes, also took part in the action. The colored men worked their guns nimbly and behaved admirably, exhibiting much pleasure when they succeeded in getting in six shots to the Rebels' five. Measures were also speedily taken to reinforce the Federal garrison by troops taken across the river in flatboats.

The Confederates soon found their position too hazardous, and their fire almost wholly ceased at about 9:00 A.M. They had succeeded in inflicting but slight damage upon our forces and had suffered a loss of five men killed and several wounded by the explosion of one of their own guns. Several men of the 92nd New York Regiment were wounded by fragments of shells thrown over the forts by our gunboats. Our boats continued to shell the woods occasionally, in various directions, during the day. A reconnaissance late in the evening found the enemy in considerable force on the Trent Road, about five miles out.

Toward evening four brass field pieces, two 24- and two 32-pounders, were brought to our camp and placed in the embrasures. A detachment of Captain Angell's 3rd New York Battery was detailed to serve them.

During the evening two large mails arrived in camp from the North, from which we had had no regular mail for a fortnight, and the arrival of this large budget of letters was most gladly welcomed. Patient waiters were no losers in this case, for the number of letters was larger than ever before brought into camp at any one time. They came into the companies by the peck, and one "mess" (thirteen men) of the Somerville company received *ninety-three* letters.

The night passed without an alarm. The 43rd and a part of the 46th and 25th Massachusetts regiments were out on picket duty during the night.

Reconnoitering parties were sent out this morning on the north side of the Neuse, and reported that the enemy had retreated a considerable distance up the river. A large Rebel force is reported between the Trent and the Neuse, and appearances indicate that the Confederates are concentrating their strength directly in our front. One of our gunboats has been up the river nearly all day, shelling the woods, to ferret out any of the enemy who might be concealed there.

March 16—All is quiet today. General Foster is closely watching the movements of the enemy, and the greatest confidence is entertained of our ability to withstand any attack. The wildest rumors are afloat, and it is difficult to get at the exact truth.

Company D of our regiment, Captain Howard, are now at Plymouth, North Carolina, doing garrison duty; Company G, Captain Grammar, still remain at Hatteras.

Corporal Finney, of Company E, died on the 12th instant, at the General Hospital in New Bern, of inflammation of the brain.

The 3rd and 8th Massachusetts regiments remain here encamped in and near Fort Totten. The 17th still has its camp on the south side of the Trent. The 23rd and 24th are at or near Charleston, South Carolina. The 27th is in garrison at Washington, North Carolina. The 44th left last night for the same place, at short notice. The 45th is still doing provost guard duty in New Bern.

Prescott

NEW YORK TRIBUNE
March 21, 1863

HEAVY ENGAGEMENT IN TENNESSEE COLONEL HALL'S BRIGADE ATTACKED—HE HOLDS HIS GROUND UNTIL REINFORCED—SEVERE FIGHTING AT LAST ACCOUNTS

Murfreesboro, Tennessee, 20th—Colonel Hall's brigade of General Reynolds's division was attacked near Milton today by a large force of Rebel cavalry.

Colonel Hall sent word he could hold his own until reinforcements could arrive. Colonel Wilder went to his aid with a mounted infantry force.

At last reports quite a heavy engagement was going on.

The Rebels have lately been making serious demonstrations from General Morgan's position at Liberty, feeling our lines on the left.

VAN DORN REINFORCED AND COMING FORWARD AGAIN—OUR FORCES READY TO MEET HIM

Franklin, Tennessee, 20th—A considerable force of the enemy's cavalry recrossed Duck River and advanced toward Franklin yesterday, but were driven back by Colonel Walker's cavalry brigade.

The bridge at Columbia has been rebuilt, and General Van Dorn is said to have been largely reinforced.

Cavalry skirmishes occur daily.

We have vast advantage in position.

THE ATTACK ON CHARLESTON—OUR GUNBOATS SAID TO HAVE PASSED FORT SUMTER—THE CITY BOMBARDED

Philadelphia, 20th—The *Inquirer*'s special dispatch from Washington says Rebel prisoners report that six or eight of our gunboats passed Fort Sumter on Monday and Tuesday and that Charleston was being bombarded.

This needs confirmation.

LATER FROM VICKSBURG A LARGE FORCE GONE UP THE YAZOO— SUCCESSFUL EXPEDITION TO TUSCUMBIA AND FLORENCE, ALABAMA

Cincinnati, 20th—Advices from Vicksburg report the health of the army improving. The troops are enthusiastic with the prospect of an immediate engagement.

It is thought that the Lake Providence Canal, opposite Vicksburg, will prove successful.

There has been a large movement of transports and gunboats up the Yazoo Pass.

The *Atlantic Confederacy* contains a detailed account of a brilliant and successful raid in north Alabama by the Union brigade under Colonel Corwin. The expedition, accompanied by gunboats, reached Tuscumbia, February 22. The gunboats destroyed two ferryboats at Tuscumbia, another at Florence, and afterward dropped down below Tuscumbia.

Soon after dark, the Union advance guard dashed into Tuscumbia and dispersed the Rebel cavalry, who fled to the mountains. Colonel Corwin occupied the town and issued a proclamation levying assessments on wealthy Rebels.

On the 25th instant, Colonel Corwin proceeded into the interior, taking considerable plunder with him.

Nothing is published concerning the further progress of the raid.

The same paper complains bitterly of the numerous atrocities committed by the Yankee troops.

LATEST FROM RICHMOND
THE HIGH PREMIUM ON GOLD—EXTRAORDINARY EDITORIAL OF THE EXAMINER ON THE OPERATIONS OF GENERAL HOOKER—DISASTER TO THE REBEL ARMY ANTICIPATED

Headquarters, Army of the Potomac, 20th—Notwithstanding the quotations of gold in the Richmond papers, it is known here that from $6 to $6.50 in Confederate notes have been offered for $1 in gold within the past two days in Fredericksburg and, moreover, $2.25 in Virginia bank notes and $3.50 in Confederate notes are freely paid for our national currency.

The *Richmond Examiner* of yesterday has an extraordinary leader, the tone of which is evidently intended to prepare the public mind of the South for serious reverses to the Confederate arms on the line of the Rappahannock. It commences with the following significant language:

> The active operations of the chief Union army, under Hooker, are now commenced, and either a decisive battle or the retreat of General Lee must be the speedy consequence, and the latter contingency is possible but not probable; and another heavy struggle over the line of the Rappahannock may be safely anticipated.

After speculating upon the supposed plan of General Hooker and the strength and probabilities of success of General Lee's forces, the editor remarks: "If, however, the Confederate general's force is not sufficiently numerous to prevent the completion of the maneuver, it is supposed that no course remains but to fall back upon some point nearer Richmond and give the enemy battle at a greater distance from his base."

There is nothing of importance from any scene of active operations in the field.

There was a heavy fall of snow here during the day and last night. It is cold now.

APRIL 18, 1863

SOUTH

RICHMOND DAILY DISPATCH
April 18, 1863

FROM SUFFOLK

Our intelligence, derived through an officer who left Suffolk on Thursday, contradicts the reports that our troops had "completely invested" Suffolk. They have not yet invested it, nor have they gotten between the enemy and Norfolk. What movements are afoot it would be improper to state. In a skirmish on Monday the Fayette Artillery, of this city, lost Sergeant James Clarke, killed, four wounded, and seven horses killed. The body of Sergeant Clarke has been brought to Richmond. Intelligence received at the War Department confirms our information about the condition of affairs at Suffolk.

PROGRESS OF THE SIEGE OF WASHINGTON[9]

We have news from Washington, D.C., as late as the 15th instant. Heavy cannonading was going on there then and had been heard during the two days previous. As several heavy guns had been mounted by the Confederates, it is supposed the bombardment had commenced. The reprise of the Yankee forces at Blounts Creek, while attempting to reach Washington, seems to have been an utter rout. The Yankees admit having had

9. Washington, North Carolina.

12,000 men there, but deny that more than three regiments were engaged. They put down their killed and wounded at 300. They had 18 horses and 2 men drowned by the foundering of a boat in crossing the Neuse from Barringtons Ferry to New Bern, on the retreat from Blounts Creek. It is reported that they are 25,000 strong at New Bern and are being still further reinforced.

CHARLESTON DAILY COURIER
April 18, 1863

FROM JACKSON
LATEST FROM VICKSBURG

Jackson, Mississippi, 17th—Eight gunboats passed the Vicksburg batteries last night. One was burned, two disabled, and five were successful. It is rumored that the Yankees are digging a canal from Millikens Bend to reach the Mississippi River near New Carthage. It is believed the enemy has banished the constructing of his batteries opposite Vicksburg.

The attack upon Vicksburg will be made within the next ten days. All officers absent from their commands have been ordered to report immediately.

Sixty-four steamers left Memphis for Vicksburg, crowded with soldiers and Negroes. No papers are allowed to come below Cairo. The Yankees are fortifying the Rolla Railroad, north. The *Memphis Bulletin* and *Argus* have been suppressed and their editors arrested.

FROM RICHMOND
CONGRESSIONAL

Richmond, 17th—In the Senate today the House bill to displace from the quartermaster's and commissary's departments all clerks liable to military duty, and to detail for clerical duties disabled soldiers, was passed. The House bill passed early in the session, repealing certain clauses of the Exemption Act, was taken up and amended by substituting the clauses of the Senate Exemption Bill, relative to overseers on plantations, and further amended by incorporating all the provisions of the Conference Committee bill rejected yesterday, except one paragraph in relation to overseers. In this shape the bill, after a long debate, was passed.

The House passed the Exemption Bill reported Wednesday last from the Committee of Conference; also a bill to allow hospital accommodations to sick and wounded officers at one dollar per day.

The House adopted the following device for a seal of the Confederate States: "An equestrian portrait of Washington, copied from the monument at Richmond, surrounded with a wreath composed chiefly of agricultural productions of the South." Motto: *"Deo Duce Vincemus."* "God being our lead, we will conquer."

The House then went into secret session.

FROM CHATTANOOGA
ARRIVAL OF FEDERAL OFFICERS

Chattanooga, Tennessee, 16th—Nothing additional has been received from the front today. Eleven Federal officers captured by Wheeler reached here this evening. Captain Maple and Lieutenant Spencer of General Rosecrans's staff are among their number.

NORTH

BOSTON EVENING TRANSCRIPT
April 18, 1863

NAVAL ATTACKS UPON FORTIFICATIONS
CONSTRUCTED TO RESIST THEM

Some sanguine people who, in the light of all naval and military experience, gave credence to the belief that Charleston and its great defenses could be beaten down and captured by an untried squadron of iron-defended ships are disconsolate at the repulse and withdrawal of the Federal attacking squadron from before the city where rebellion first hung out its treasonable flag. Let them look at history for a moment, and they will find an example even in the very place where their hopes were so recently concentrated. The attack of Sir Peter Parker upon Charleston during the war of the American Revolution, and his signal repulse, is a story known to every American schoolboy, and at that time the defenses of Charleston were mainly the natural obstructions of the harbor.

The successful defense of Gibraltar by General Eliott, against the mighty Spanish and French flotillas which bombarded it, has always been a great source of pride to the British nation.[10] The subject formed the groundwork of a great national picture, copies of which, upon huge canvas, are to be seen in this country—the highest honors were be-

10. George Eliott, British governor of Gibraltar during "The Great Siege" (1779–83).

stowed upon Eliott, and Gibraltar furnished a new noun in the English language, signifying something impregnable. Yet the strongest fears were exhibited in England with regard to the event, and the besiegers believed that the fortress could easily be subdued by the tremendous force which they were able to bring against it. But we have not to go back ten years for an example of successful defense, which is in the minds of everyone who remembers the Anglo-French war upon Russia in 1854–55.[11] The British were as sure of capturing Kronstadt, and thereby of having St. Petersburg and the Russian fleet at their mercy, as many of the Northern people were satisfied that it would be easy to capture Richmond before the battle of Bull Run. Even Admiral Napier, whose skill and bravery are not to be questioned, was full of boast and bravado before he entered upon the work of reducing Kronstadt. "Sharpen your cutlasses," he said in his address to his fleet, before commencing the great undertaking. The cutlasses of the British man-of-war's men might as well have been dull as sharp, so far as the Russians were concerned, for they never came within three miles of the latter.

The British and French squadron, in their great but friendly rivalry of force, show, and equipment, cruised up and down the Gulf of Finland from Seskar Island, which is about thirty miles to Toll Beacon, which is about three miles from Kronstadt, but they struck no decisive blow. It was, apparently, death and destruction to any ship which might attempt to pass the narrow channel on each side of which Kronstadt was defended. The sinking of a single ship would have stopped the passage of all who should attempt to follow her. The expedition was fruitless. And it was not only in Great Britain that its success was confidently prophesied by unconsidering people. The reduction of Kronstadt was confidently expected in this country even by military men. A merchant of this city, who was formerly a shipmaster and was well acquainted with the Baltic and its defenses, expressed the opinion at that time that Kronstadt would not be captured by the allied fleets, in the company of some distinguished gentlemen who were very sanguine of its capture; and his practical opinion was borne out by the event.

Admiral Napier returned home and shifted the blame of inaction—if blame there was—off upon the French admiral, who, he said, was not willing to cooperate with him. We have never heard that Commodore Du Pont has made any threats or promises with regard to the reduction of Sumter or Moultrie and the bombardment of Charleston. He made

11. The Crimean War (1853–56), fought between Russia and Britain, France, and Turkey.

the attempt, and to the practical mind it cannot be made clear that his force was in any wise strong enough to subdue the immense fortifications which the Rebels have been erecting at Charleston within the last two years. Nature has given to Charleston that great defense which is enjoyed by Kronstadt—shoal water. When the admiral's flagship, the *Ironsides,* came too near the bottom, the undercurrent affected her steering so much that she would not obey her rudder, and she was twice obliged to anchor. Nautical men understand these difficulties very well, although landsmen do not.

The attempt on Charleston is, we are informed, to be renewed. Of course, this will be done with an adequate land as well as naval force. Admiral Du Pont's reconnaissance simply proves that eleven hundred men and thirty guns are not competent to take a city whose approaches are lined with four miles of fortifications and defended by a covering army of fifty thousand men.

NEW YORK TRIBUNE
April 18, 1863

DISCOVERY OF A NEST OF TRAITORS IN NASHVILLE

The *Nashville Dispatch* of the 14th instant gives the following particulars of an extensive system of operations to aid the Rebels, which the detectives in the employ of General Rosecrans have brought to light:

John Trainor, a clerk in the Ordnance Department, has been arrested on a charge of smuggling arms, munitions, and medicines through the lines and conveying information to the Rebels.

A careful and thorough investigation has been made in this case. The guilt of Trainor of the highest crime recognized in either civil or military law is fully established. His operations extend back over a period of two years. He has occupied a position which gave him unusual facilities for carrying out his designs, and he has not failed to take advantage of them to the best of his ability. Having had greater or less control of wagon trains since he entered the service, he has, if his own statements are trustworthy, on several occasions attempted to place trains in positions where they might be easily captured. In addition to his own admissions there is absolute proof of his treason.

Connected with this case is that of the parties in Louisville concerned in the sale of nearly nine thousand dollars' worth of quinine and opium to Mrs. Trainor. It is shown that those most interested in this sale must have known that the medicines were purchased for the purpose of being smuggled South. Edward Wilder, of Louisville, the wholesale druggist from whom the medicines were obtained, is shown to be strongly in sympathy with the Rebels. He has sold large quantities of drugs since the opening of the war to persons who were to take them through the Union lines. By this last transaction he has involved his whole stock of goods. The evidence adduced in this matter, with other evidence obtained, shows that other merchants of Louisville, and also merchants in New Albany, Indianapolis, and Cincinnati, have been largely engaged in the sale of drugs and other goods for a Southern destination.

THE ARMING OF NEGROES SPEECH OF ADJUTANT GENERAL THOMAS AT LAKE PROVIDENCE, LOUISIANA—THE PRESIDENT'S POLICY UNALTERABLE

Fellow Soldiers:—Your commanding general has so fully stated the object of my mission that it is almost unnecessary for me to say anything to you in reference to it. Still, as I come here with full authority from the president of the United States to announce the policy which, after mature deliberation, has been determined upon by the wisdom of the nation, it is my duty to make known to you clearly and fully the features of that policy. It is a source of extreme gratification to me to come before you this day, knowing, as I do full well, how glorious have been your achievements on the field of battle. No soldier can come before soldiers of tried valor without having the deepest emotions of his soul stirred within him. These emotions I feel on the present occasion, and I beg you will listen to what I have to say as soldiers receiving from a soldier the commands of the president of the United States.

I come from Washington clothed with the fullest power in this matter. With this power I can act as if the president of the United States were himself present. I am directed to refer nothing to Washington, but to act promptly—what I have to do, to do at once—to strike down the unworthy and to elevate the deserving.

I can only speak briefly and cannot enter into the details of the subject at present. It may be that some of you are better acquainted with this country than I am, but all my early military life was spent in the South. I know this whole region well. I am a *Southern* man and, if you will, born with Southern prejudices, but I am free to say that the policy I am now to announce to you I endorse with my whole heart. You know full well—for you have been over this country—that the Rebels have sent into the field all their available fighting men—every man capable of bearing arms—and you know they have kept at home all their slaves for the raising of subsistence for their armies in the field. In this way they can bring to bear against us all the strength of their so-called Confederate States, while we at the North can only send a portion of our fighting force, being compelled to leave behind another portion to cultivate our fields and supply the wants of an immense army. The administration has determined to take from the Rebels this source of supply—to take their Negroes and compel them to send back a portion of their whites to cultivate their deserted plantations—and very poor persons they would be to fill the place of the dark-hued laborer. They must do this, or their armies will starve. You know perfectly well that the Rebels had an opportunity offered them under the Proclamation of the president in September, to lay down their arms and come back into the Union. They failed to do it. Not but that the hearts of many men in the South were with us and against the rebellion. The leaders of the rebellion, Jefferson Davis and his satellites, would not permit it; therefore, they are still in arms against us.

On the first day of January last, the president issued his Proclamation declaring that from that day forward all the slaves in the states then in rebellion should be free. You know that vast numbers of these slaves are within your borders, inside the lines of this army. They come into your camps, and you cannot but receive them. The authorities in Washington are very much pained to hear, and I fear with truth in many cases, that some of these poor unfortunates have on different occasions been turned away from us and their applications for admission within our lines have been refused by our officers and soldiers. This is not the way to use freedmen. The question came up in Washington, "What is best to be done with this unfortunate race?" They are coming upon us in such numbers that some provision must be made for them. You cannot send them North. You all know the prejudices of the Northern people against receiving large numbers of the colored race. Some states have passed laws forbidding them to come within their borders. At this day, in some states, persons who have brought them have been arraigned before the courts to answer for the violation of state enactments.

Look along the river and see the multitude of deserted plantations upon its banks. These are the places for these freedmen, where they can be self-sustaining and self-supporting. All of you will someday be on picket duty, and I charge you all if any of this unfortunate race come within your lines that you do not turn them away, but receive them kindly and cordially. They are to be encouraged to come to us. They are to be received with open arms; they are to be fed and clothed; *they are to be armed.*

This is the policy that has been fully determined upon. I am here to say that I am authorized to raise as many regiments of blacks as I can. I am authorized to give commissions, from the highest to the lowest, and I desire those persons who are earnest in this work to take hold of it. I desire only those whose hearts are in it, and to them alone will I give commissions. I don't care who they are or what their present rank may be. I do not hesitate to say that all proper persons will receive commissions.

While I am authorized thus in the name of the secretary of war, I have the fullest authority to dismiss from the army any man, be his rank what it may, whom I find maltreating the freedmen. This part of my duty I will most assuredly perform if any case comes before me. I would rather do that than give commissions, because such men are unworthy of the name of soldiers.

I hope to hear that in this splendid division, as I know it to be—"veterans," as Napoleon would call them—for you are veterans—I hope to hear before I leave that I shall be able to raise at least a regiment from among you. I don't want to stop at *one,* nor at *two*. I must have two at least. It is possible that I can procure four. I would like to raise on this river twenty regiments at least before I go back. I shall take all the women and children and all the men unfit for our military organizations and place them on these plantations; then take these regiments and put them in the rear. They will guard the rear effectively. Knowing the country well, and familiar with all the roads and swamps, they will be able to track out the accursed guerrillas and run them from the land. When I get regiments raised, you may sweep out into the interior with impunity. Recollect, for every regiment of blacks I raise, I raise a regiment of whites to face the foe in the field. This, fellow soldiers, is the determined policy of the administration. You all know full well, when the president of the United States—though said to be slow in coming to a determination—when he once puts his foot down, it is there and he is not going to take it up. He has put his foot down. I am here to assure you that my official influence shall be given so that he shall not raise it.

THE WAR NEWS

The studied silence as to movements by General Hooker's army is broken at last. Our Washington correspondent states that our forces, comprising cavalry, infantry, and artillery, under General Stoneman, the chief of cavalry, after making a feint of crossing at Kelly's Ford, crossed the Rappahannock some distance higher up and rapidly pushed on to Culpeper and Gordonsville.[12] They now occupy the latter place, having driven out the enemy. This movement took place the day before yesterday, we presume. What more might have been done but for the inopportune storm—the third or fourth that has fallen upon the Army of the Potomac at a most critical moment—we can only guess. By the occupation of Gordonsville, the Rebels lose the use of the Virginia Central Railroad and are practically flanked at Fredericksburg. Perhaps this movement may account for the otherwise unaccountable suspension of the grand Rebel effort to capture Foster and retake New Bern, Suffolk, and the Sounds.

The Navy Department has received an account of a little fight in the Nansemond River on Tuesday last. (The Nansemond is the stream running into the James, next above Elizabeth River, and is the regular water communication with Suffolk, in which neighborhood the Rebels have been operating all the week.) The report states that on Tuesday morning some of our vessels came down—from Suffolk, probably—the *Mount Washington,* steamer, being disabled. About noon the Rebels opened, and our vessels at once got into action. At one o'clock the *Mount Washington* got around, and the Rebels made her a special target at only seven hundred yards. At high water the steamer *Stepping Stones* hauled the *Mount Washington* off, and at 5:00 P.M. the Rebel batteries were silenced. Our loss was slight, only five killed and eighteen wounded. Our vessels were to anchor for the night just where they had fought all day. The object of the enemy was to cross the river, so as to get in the rear of Suffolk; but at the date of this report they had not done so, and it was thought that they were in retreat. Our letters from Suffolk are up to the 16th. No important military events had taken place. It was supposed that a fight would come off very soon, unless Longstreet's Rebel force should withdraw.

From Richmond papers of the 16th, we learn that all was quiet at Charleston (on the 15th, we presume). Union troops occupy Coles, Kiawah, and Seabrook islands. Seabrook lies at the mouth of the North Edisto River. Kiawah lies immediately above Seabrook, from which it is separated by a narrow creek. Coles Island lies at the junction of the Folly and Stono rivers, separated from Kiawah by Stono Inlet. Coles Island was occupied before the late attack by two or three Union regi-

12. Gordonsville, Virginia.

ments, who advanced inland some distance, driving the Rebel pickets before them. The Richmond papers also report that the Rebels have destroyed two gunboats and three transports on the Cumberland River. This is evidently an enlargement of an old story.

By way of St. Louis, we have a word from Arkansas. A dispatch from Colonel Phillips, dated the 11th, at Park Hill, in the Cherokee Nation, states that he has cleared the Rebels from the north side of the Arkansas River, and part of his command now holds Fort Gibson. Park Hill is on the road from Fayetteville to Tahlequah, and Fort Gibson is an old government post beyond Tahlequah, on the Neosho, near its junction with the Arkansas. Colonel Phillips had received overtures of loyalty from the Creek Indians. The Rebels were in force on the south side of the Arkansas and held all the fords.

MAY 16, 1863

SOUTH

RICHMOND DAILY DISPATCH
May 16, 1863

THE "WILDERNESS" AND CHANCELLORSVILLE[13]

Accounts of the great battles on the Rappahannock continue to come in—each one adding something to our previous knowledge of the events which occurred, or correcting statements made in the hurry of writing soon after the event. Our attention has been specially called to one point not hitherto dwelt upon by any correspondent, though the fact has been alluded to by nearly all. We refer to the question, who commanded the corps of the immortal Jackson when he was rendered *hors de combat* and forced to leave the field?[14] We have received from authority which places the statement beyond question the following particulars, which we briefly put on record for the information of our readers:

General Jackson made his great flank movement against the right and rear of the enemy on Saturday. Getting into position, he attacked

13. Located in a region known as the Wilderness, Chancellorsville (Virginia) was the site of the Battle of Chancellorsville, one of General Lee's greatest victories, fought on May 1–4, 1863. The Wilderness was also the site of the Battle of the Wilderness, May 5–7, 1864.

14. *hors de combat:* French, "out of the fight."

with his corps about an hour before sunset and, driving the XI Corps of the Federals before him, routed and pushed them nearly to Chancellorsville. His assault was made at the well-known locality of the "Wilderness"; and this contest will be known in history as the Battle of the Wilderness. Soon after nine o'clock at night, General Jackson received the wound which caused his death, and about the same time General A. P. Hill, the ranking major general of his corps, was also disabled. General Rodes, whose heroic conduct made him a major general on the battlefield, and who succeeded Hill in command, immediately dispatched a messenger to General J.E.B. Stuart, who had proceeded with a detachment of cavalry toward Ely's Ford, and on the arrival of that general formally turned over the command to him, with the full approbation of General Hill, whose wounds disabled him from further participation, even by conference, in the battle. It was then too late to renew the battle, and General Stuart busied himself in reorganizing the command, hurrying up ammunition, and preparing everything for the struggle next morning. Riding upward and down the lines, he scarcely closed his eyes throughout the night and saw in person that all was ready.

At daylight in the morning he formed his line of battle, gave the order for his right to advance, and soon engaged Hooker with the entire corps, driving him from all his defenses, huddling his shattered troops in upon Chancellorsville, and finally routing him completely and sending him thoroughly defeated back to the river. This desperate contest, in which Jackson's unfinished work was completed, to the full satisfaction of the illustrious soldier, took place in close vicinity to, in, and all around Chancellorsville. It will be known as the Battle of Chancellorsville. These details of the battles which terminated in the defeat of Hooker and his inglorious rout are noted down for the satisfaction of our readers, for whom the late occurrences on the Rappahannock still continue to possess a paramount interest.

MATTERS IN MISSISSIPPI

Information was yesterday received, and is stated to be reliable, that Jackson, the capital of Mississippi, had fallen into the hands of the enemy. We were prepared for this when we learned that Raymond, which is in the same county and only fifteen miles distant, had been occupied by the Yankee forces. There was no confirmation of the reported fall of Jackson at the War Department late in the afternoon of yesterday, as we are informed.

THE NORTHWESTERN EXPEDITION

From the last information received we are led to believe that our forces are returning from their expedition in the Northwest. The *Staunton Spectator* mentions, as one of the results of the expedition, that 1,200 horses, 500 head of cattle, and a considerable number of sheep have been sent back and are now near Mount Solon, in Augusta County. A portion of the expedition were at last accounts in Pocahontas County, and a portion were in pursuit of some retreating Yankees. About 700 prisoners were captured by our troops while on this expedition.

FROM THE SOUTHWEST

Tullahoma, Tennessee, 15th—All quiet in front. The *Louisville Democrat* of the 10th has a special dispatch from Murfreesboro, which says that three thousand contrabands have been organized, in companies of thirty men each, loyal Tennesseans commanding each company.

The *Democrat* says that the Supreme Court of Minnesota has decided that the law passed by the legislature suspending the privilege, to persons aiding the rebellion, of action in the courts as unconstitutional and void.

The *Nashville Dispatch* of the 10th says that the Federal loss in the battles on the Rappahannock was over fifteen thousand.

MURDER

Mr. Terisha W. Dillard, of Amherst County, Virginia, was brutally murdered by some of his servants on Saturday last. He was superintending some work which he was having done on an island in James River, near his residence, in which six hands were employed—four women and two men—when the murder was executed. He was caught and held by the men, and the women inflicted the fatal blows. His body was horribly cut and mangled, presenting a shocking spectacle of mutilation. After the deed had been performed, the remains were covered up in sand, but soon two of the women made confession of the crime and, with the two men, were arrested. The others are yet at large.

GONE WEST

Six hundred Confederate prisoners, fresh from Camp Chase, exchanged and sent to Richmond, arrived at Chattanooga last Sunday night. They are all officers.

CHARLESTON DAILY COURIER
May 16, 1863

CORRESPONDENCE OF THE COURIER

Gadsden, Alabama, May 3, 1863

We had a number-one sensation in our hitherto quiet village yesterday. Being remote from the scene of action of bloody conflict, we little dreamed that a Federal force would enter our peaceful village. But like a clap of thunder on a clear day, a regiment of Yankee cavalry, under General Strait, entered our town about eleven o'clock yesterday, the 2nd instant. The citizens had no intimation of their approach, and consequently were not prepared for them, and lost many valuable horses and mules. The party seemed more bent upon plunder than anything else, save that of eluding General Forrest, who was in close pursuit. He would have engaged them at this place, but two miles from here they burned the bridge on Black Creek and thereby impeded General Forrest's progress. A slight engagement took place at the bridge, which resulted in the loss of one of our men.

The enemy remained in town perhaps two hours, breaking open houses, stealing bacon, clothing, etc., and even taking the silver plate from some of our ladies. They inquired particularly for Captain R. B. Kyle, who is the government agent for the distribution of salt in this district and formerly quartermaster of the 31st Alabama. They had been informed he had large amounts of money and government stores on hand, and sought him diligently, but found him not. He and your humble servant had pressing engagements in a dense thicket some mile or so from town.

When they first entered our town and commenced taking horses, we supposed they were "bushwhackers" on a general stealing expedition; and when they approached Captain Kyle's horse and untied him, he in a very authoritative manner ordered the party to "tie that horse back where he found him," but upon a Federal's presenting a dubious-looking fusee, or carbine, the captain very complacently remarked: "Ah, Federals, is it? All right, gentlemen, just take him along." Having uttered this compulsory speech, he passed through his store and from thence sought refuge in the woods, where many a scared brave was anxiously awaiting the issue which was to exile him for months, or return him home to his family within a few hours, which latter soon took place—upon the advance of General Forrest, whose advance guard entered the town as their rear guard were going out. Colonel Roddy was sent across the mountain to intercept them between here and Rome, Georgia, and as he had four regiments of men, we expect soon to hear of him and General Forrest capturing the whole of them. General Forrest had about a thousand men and three small cannons, the Federal force about the same. The enemy is between the Coo, a river, on the east and the Lookout Mountain and Colonel Roddy on the west.[15] Runners have been sent to Rome, who will doubtless reach there six or eight hours in advance of the Federals. We see no chance for them to escape and hope soon to announce that all have been captured and shot.

A. G. P.

P.S. There was an engagement last night *twelve* miles above here at Mr. Blount's. Colonel Hathaway, of New York formerly, and *four* other Federals were killed. None killed on our side.

B.

NORTH

BOSTON EVENING TRANSCRIPT
May 16, 1863

FROM WASHINGTON
GENERAL BUELL'S CASE—THE COMMAND OF THE POTOMAC ARMY

Washington, 15th—The record in General Buell's case has arrived here. There is reason to believe that the findings of the court are such as to show that the president had ample reason for removing General Buell from the command of the Department of the Cumberland and that the government only erred in postponing his removal so long.

It is said that the dying words of Stonewall Jackson were a request that General Ewell might be assigned to the command of his troops.

The *World*'s dispatch says, from what I can learn, General Hooker returned to retain his present command, and conduct the army, unaided by General Halleck, through another advance movement, whenever such shall be determined on. This you may consider as reliable at the present writing.

15. Lookout Mountain (Tennessee), the site of the penultimate battle (Battle Above the Clouds, November 24, 1863) of the Chattanooga campaign.

The Honorable Preston King is named as the probable successor of J. Madison Cutts in the second comptrollership of the Treasury Department.

The *Washington Republican* says it is understood that Bayard Taylor, the secretary under Mr. Cameron, allowed his name to be used against Minister Clay in the Senate, which is probably the cause of his removal.

THE FUNERAL OBSEQUIES OF THE REBEL GENERAL JACKSON

New York, 16th—A Richmond paper gives full accounts of the wounding, death, and funeral of Jackson, the former leaving no doubt that the wound was inflicted by a mistake of their own men. One of his aides was killed, another wounded, and two couriers killed. Jackson was struck by three balls in the left arm and hand. This occurred after dark on Saturday evening. He had given orders to fire at anything coming up the road. Before he left the lines, Federal skirmishers approached ahead of him, and he turned to ride back. Just then someone cried, "Cavalry charge," and the Rebel regiment fired.

The result is as stated above. The funeral is said to have been a most tumultuous outburst of mourning. It was attended by President Davis and Cabinet and all the members of the state, Confederate, and city governments and an immense throng of citizens. The body lay in state at the capital until the morning of the 13th, when it was sent to Lexington. A statue of Jackson is to be erected in the capital.

NEW YORK TRIBUNE
May 16, 1863

SHALL WE HAVE A WAR OF EXTERMINATION?

In repeated instances the Rebels have evinced a desire to render the war now in progress one of extermination. Thus, in one of the early conflicts in Louisiana, some of our men (white citizens of Louisiana) were taken prisoners, three or four of whom had formerly served in the Rebel camps—they said as conscripts. These men, it is reported, were denied the character of prisoners of war and ignominiously put to death. So when Galveston was recaptured by the Rebels on the 1st of January last, certain Texans who were found serving in our ranks were butchered without formality—so the Rebel sheets exultingly proclaimed. Prior to this, Mr. Jefferson Davis had proclaimed that white officers of black Union regiments who should be taken prisoners should be turned over to the states, to be by them hung as inciters of servile insurrection, while the black privates were to be sold into slavery. We are not aware that this threat has been carried into effect—possibly, because none of its subjects have been captured—but it has not been publicly withdrawn and is this day an obstacle to the organization of black regiments which our government is bound to remove or countervail.

A Rebel dispatch from Vicksburg, printed in our last, reads as follows:

> Among the Yankees captured by Forrest are many citizens or natives of Southern states. *We hope the governors of the several states will promptly make a demand for the retention and trial of these traitors under the state laws.* It will be worse than idle mockery to turn them loose on exchange.

This is tolerably cool, considering that we have had thousands at a time of Rebel prisoners who were citizens of nonseceded states, and who were treated and exchanged exactly like other prisoners of war. There was General Buckner—who had most villainously abused the confidence of the authorities of Kentucky by employing the power and influence accorded him as commander of the "State Guard" to urge thousands into the Rebel ranks and finally absconded to lead them to defeat and capture at Fort Donelson. Kentucky wanted him to try and hang as a traitor, but he was regularly exchanged and is again in arms against his state as well as the Union. At least twenty thousand Kentuckians have entered the Rebel armies—all of them "traitors under the state laws"—laws of a "Southern state," too, mind you! All the best officers in the Rebel service, including their commander in chief, are renegades from the Union service, fighting against the government that liberally educated and long generously subsisted them. Maryland and Missouri have many soldiers in the Rebel ranks; even New York and other free states have sent volunteers to fight for disunion and slavery. Can the Confederacy afford to initiate the punishment as traitors of prisoners of war taken in fair fight? Will it not lose thereby more than it can gain?

These questions demand immediate answers. Colonel Ludlow, our commissioner for the exchange of prisoners, should be instructed at once to ascertain what exceptions, if any, to the general rule of exchanging all who are captured in open warfare the Confederates propose to make, so that our action may be conformed thereto. We trust a simple demonstration of the purpose of our government to stand firmly by its soldiers will answer every purpose. Retaliation would be a fearful necessity; yet if captured Union soldiers are to be slaughtered in cold blood because they were born in Southern states, what alternative is left? Again, we pray our government to give this subject the very earliest attention, and so act upon it as befits its own dignity, the safety of its defenders, and the majesty and righteousness of its cause.

SLAVERY—EMANCIPATION—THE WAR FOR THE UNION

We print on another page a letter from Mr. Orson S. Murray, widely known as an original, extreme, and uncompromising abolitionist. Like most men of his school, he regards everyone who does not see exactly as he does as a knave or fool—oftener both—and treats him accordingly. Mr. Murray is a thinker and vigorous writer, but seems to us to have very inaccurate conceptions of some grave matters that he discusses with great volubility and self-confidence. Paying little attention to his misconceptions and imputations concerning the *Tribune*, we proceed to review with all possible brevity the leading points made in his letter:

1. Mr. Murray regards the Federal Constitution as a very imperfect and ill-contrived affair and points triumphantly to the present state of our country as establishing his position. Well, suppose we concede that the Constitution *is* radically vicious or fatally defective—what then? What has that to do with any matter on which he is in controversy with the *Tribune*? Bad or good as it may be, that Constitution is "the supreme law of the land," and we must all submit to and respect it until it shall have been amended or replaced by a better. And just now, when we are in a death grapple with a formidable and bloody rebellion, wherein our great advantage inheres in the fact that we are upholding the government which was deliberately framed and adopted by the fathers of all of us, it does seem that we who stand for the Union cannot afford needlessly to disparage and discredit the Constitution.

2. But we deny that the simple existence of the rebellion proves the Constitution defective. Bad men have in all ages revolted against good governments. Most Christians believe that there was once a rebellion in Heaven, wherein a third of the angels participated, but they do not thence infer that the divine government was defective or vicious. It is slavery, which existed before the Constitution—which would have continued to exist in the absence of the Constitution—which the Constitution simply acquiesced in as a fact beyond its control—that impelled and still sustains the rebellion. Were slavery dead today, there would be no

subsisting rebellion next month. And then, we think, "the Constitution, as it is," would very well subserve its purpose.

3. Mr. Murray holds that slavery *of right* has no existence anywhere, and therein we heartily agree with him. Yet he knows as well as we do that slavery *in fact* does exist in fifteen states of our Union—in five of them not opposed by the Federal government; in eight under its ban; in two (Virginia and Louisiana) partly tolerated and partly condemned by the Federal authority. Mr. Murray knows just as well as we do that the slaveholder in Georgia or Texas holds his slaves by as firm a grip as his brother in Maryland or Kentucky holds *his* slaves, though the former holds them in defiance of the Federal government, while the latter holds his with its acquiescence and implied permission.

4. But, it is said, the slaves in the Rebel states are held by sheer brute force, contrary to law. Grant it—and what then? Is not the supremacy of brute force the essence of slavery? See what Blackstone or any other elementary writer on law says of the essential nature of law—of the invalidity of flagrantly unjust, oppressive laws—of the lack of power in legislators to give the sacred character of law to the contrivances of fraud and oppression—and you will hesitate long before you award the name of law to the enactments whereby slaveholders conspire to sustain each other in compelling other men to work for them all their lives for nothing and in selling those men's wives and children. In a narrow, technical sense, those enactments may be laws; in the higher and better acceptation, they are not.

5. "Then the president's Proclamations of Freedom amount to nothing." Who told you that? We certainly never did, and never thought anything of the kind. It is a great, an immense fact that the government of the Union, for generations the accomplice and convenience of the slave power, has become its active, avowed, determined enemy. That government has done very much to uphold, strengthen, and diffuse slavery. It is now doing—not *all* it might and should, but still very much—to overthrow and abolish the giant iniquity. Every day that the war for the Union continues weakens slavery in its strongholds and sees many of its victims liberated. Let the war simply go on, with such alternations of fortune, such steady advances in public sentiment, as have marked the past year, and slavery must gradually die. And slavery once dead, the rebellion will be left without ailment and the Union restored by a force resistless as gravitation.

What, then, is there to quarrel about? Wherein does Mr. Murray and such as he find occasion to quarrel with us?

1. We contend that the war is purely defensive on the side of the Union—that slavery is the aggressor and has been throughout—that, whether in the loyal or in the revolted states, every essentially slaveholding community (say, St. Marys County, Maryland, or Howard County, Missouri) is in heart and purpose on the side of Jefferson Davis and secession, while every substantially *non*slaveholding community (witness Sevier County, Tennessee, or Harrison County, Virginia) is instinctively, determinedly loyal and Union-loving. Even in the nonslaveholding states, the communities, classes, or individuals who have been closely and profitably identified with the slaveholding interest are at heart with the rebellion and would rejoice to learn that its banners waved in triumph over Washington, Baltimore, and St. Louis.

2. The Union government, in simple, naked self-defense, has been compelled to recognize this grave fact and to strike at slavery to preserve its own life. It ought to have done so with entire consistency by decreeing the downfall of its archenemy in Tennessee, Missouri, and those parts of Virginia and Louisiana under its control, and we think also in Delaware, Maryland, and Kentucky. There was ample "military necessity" for this, and it would have contributed immensely to our success in the pending contest. President Lincoln's proffer of compensated emancipation to the loyal border states was wise, prudent, statesmanlike, and the plan ought to have been pressed to instant consummation.

3. It seems to us of vital consequence to keep this whole matter right end foremost—to convince loyal Democrats, ready to fight for the Union but not for emancipation, that the war is waged on our side exactly and truly on their ground and for the ends they approve. We wish them to believe and feel what we know to be true, that the president has from first to last made the preservation of the Union and the restoration of the rightful constitutional authority of its government the polestar of his course—that whatever he is impelled to do against slavery is done expressly to save the Union and because slavery is an obstacle to its restoration. We insist that his power over slavery flows entirely from the rebellion and will die with it—that each Rebel state will recover all the power it ever had over the *status* of its own people by the simple and salutary process of ceasing to be Rebel and becoming once more loyal. We believe and hold, moreover, that the president has always had the power to accept the submission of any revolted state to the Union and (with the consent of the Senate) to remit any penalties of confiscation or other disability which it has incurred by the rebellion. What he *will* see fit to do in any supposable case we have never inquired and do not pre-

tend to know, but we *do* insist—for we hold it imperatively necessary that Democrats who may be drafted shall understand and believe—that *he* is not enslaved by his Proclamations of Freedom, but is today, ever has been, and ever will be at perfect liberty to accept the submission of the revolted states on whatever terms shall be deemed by him consistent with the integrity, the perpetuity, and the honor of the United States.

4. That honor, as we understand, imperatively requires our government to guarantee liberty and protection to every person who shall, because of the Proclamations of Freedom, have come over to us from the enemy and served, or tried to serve, the national cause. But we do not feel that we are under equal obligation to those slaves who (most reluctantly, we doubt not) serve the Rebel batteries at Vicksburg, Port Hudson, etc.—their masters watching them from places of safety in the rear, ready to shoot down anyone who shall flinch. We trust the progress and event of the war will secure liberty to all, but we think the obligation to these is not the same as to the others.

And now, having given this whole subject a pretty thorough ventilation, allowing those who dissent from our view far more space than we have taken for our side, we propose to stop the discussion right here and devote our columns to matters of more imminent and practical concern.

JUNE 20, 1863

SOUTH

RICHMOND DAILY DISPATCH
June 20, 1863

THE NEWS FROM THE POTOMAC
OUR FORCES REPORTED TO BE IN MARYLAND—
REPORTED CAPTURE OF MILROY

The reports which reach us of the operations of our forces in northern Virginia are of the most interesting and encouraging character and, if reliable, transfer the scene of military operations from the soil of Virginia to the enemy's own territory. There is nothing official as to the movements of our army, but well-attested reports represent that a portion of it crossed the Potomac a few days since, near Point of Rocks, and at last accounts were in possession of Maryland Heights, overlooking the town of Harpers Ferry, cutting off the escape of the Federal garrison at that point. The same reports state that a brigade of Confederate cavalry had advanced as far as Hagerstown, Maryland, but five miles from the Pennsylvania line. While we cannot vouch for these rumors, we have faith in their accuracy in the main.

The news with reference to our victory at Winchester, already published, is fully confirmed, and there is little reason to doubt that our captures there are nearly equal to any since the commencement of the war. One statement is that Milroy, finding himself unable to defend the town with success, evacuated it on Sunday night, taking with him the main body of his forces, leaving only a small force to defend the works and retard the advance of our columns, and attempted to escape on the Martinsburg Road. This movement, however, was anticipated by General Ewell and the retreat of the Yankees intercepted at some point between Martinsburg and Winchester, when they surrendered without offering battle. (There is nothing improbable in this statement, though it does not exactly correspond with our previous accounts of the capture.)

There is yet nothing certain in regard to the capture or escape of the notorious Milroy. Rumor has it that Mrs. Ewell, wife of General Ewell, now in Charlottesville, received a letter from the general on Thursday stating that Milroy had been captured near the Potomac. There may be some truth in this rumor, but of course we have no means of verifying it.

There are other rumors numerous and interesting, but we cannot decide upon their accuracy.

In addition to the above, we have some facts about the capture of Winchester:

From Our Own Correspondent

Staunton, Virginia, June 18, 1863

Several days ago I could have written you quite an *interesting* communication, had I been willing to receive half the stories brought to this place from the lower Valley. I preferred to wait for such details as could be relied on. I have this morning conversed with a gentleman who was with the army during the late important transactions, and who left Winchester Tuesday morning, and I will give you a few items derived from him.

Our glorious Ewell—under whom I served during last year's campaign, and for whom I often felt jealous (though he never felt jealous for himself)—has indeed caught the mantle of the ascended Jackson. Brilliantly has he reenacted the scenes of the spring of '62, on the same theater.

Having first occupied every road approaching Winchester, Jackson-like, he *made* a road leaving the Valley Turnpike near Kernstown and stretching across the Romney Road and, for six miles farther on, bearing toward the Martinsburg Road. By means of this road, he led his army half around the town and attacked the enemy, who were expecting an attack from forces on the Martinsburg Road, on the flank and rear. The surprise was complete. So little were they anticipating an attack from the direction in which it came that they had placed there all the wagon trains, which thus actually were between us and them.

It seems that skirmishing all around was going on during Saturday, the enemy's pickets retiring. It also continued Sunday, and on that day Ewell, with great secrecy and with painful toil, conducted his army over the new road, getting them into position about 6:00 P.M., when the cannonade commenced. It continued for two and a half hours, during which the Louisiana brigade gallantly charged, with cheers, the enemy's outer works and took possession of them. Here darkness closed active operations, but on Monday morning the enemy, utterly disorganized, evacuated the town, leaving horses, wagons, commissary and medical stores, and artillery.

They seem to have destroyed nothing. Some 300 or 400 wagons were secured; also, 60 pieces of cannon and 2,800 horses, among which a large number were unusually fine animals.

Three miles above the town a brigade en masse was captured, principally, I believe, by the immortal "Stonewall Brigade." Besides this, during today large numbers of prisoners, in squads, were being brought in.

The avenues of exit from the place were strewn with the knapsacks and clothing of the fugitives.

It was feared the brute Milroy had escaped, but if so, it was after the style in which his master Lincoln entered Washington.

Our whole loss in killed and wounded does not exceed two hundred. Of course we lost none in prisoners. The enemy's loss in killed and wounded was comparatively small, but we appear to have captured nearly the whole force, amounting to 6,000 or 7,000. Probably at least as many muskets as prisoners were taken.

Is not all this a noble achievement for our maimed Ewell? Right glad am I that he rides as of old.

From this place and from everywhere else, refugees from the lower Valley are flocking thither. Merchants and speculators, male and female,

Jew and Gentile, are also crowding to Winchester. But it will be no go, as there are few, if any, goods there. I learn that the town is in a filthy condition. As you know, a slaughterhouse had been established in the center of the place. The market and some of the principal buildings had been used as stables. The Yankees had been the principal sufferers from the "chotted fever," though a kind of typhoid fever had prevailed among the citizens.

I was pleased to hear that the country this side of Winchester is less desolated than last year. Many fences are up, enclosing luxuriant grass or corn or wheat. The season there has been better than in this region.

I learn that on Tuesday morning our army was three miles below Martinsburg and ordered to march at eleven o'clock with three days' rations.

Massanutten

CHARLESTON DAILY COURIER
June 20, 1863

LATEST FROM THE WEST
VICKSBURG AND PORT HUDSON STILL
HOLD OUT—GRANT AND BANKS BUSY FORTIFYING

Jackson, Mississippi, 18th—This morning, for the first time in four days, heavy firing has been heard in the direction of Vicksburg. Last accounts from there represent Grant as busy fortifying and cutting down trees beyond the Big Black to impede General Johnston's movements. They also represent great distress prevailing among the citizens inside the enemy's lines. The Yankees have robbed them of all their provisions, and numbers are in a starving condition.

Oscar, Louisiana, 16th, via Mobile, Alabama, 19th—Officers from Port Hudson report all safe and our men in good spirits. They have provisions enough for three months. The enemy has made twenty-seven assaults and each time was terribly repulsed. His loss is fully five thousand. Our loss is about three hundred.

Jackson, Mississippi, 17th, via Mobile, Alabama, 18th, via Montgomery, Alabama,19th—Numerous couriers from Vicksburg have arrived within the past few days. They bring the same stereotyped reports and bring nothing new beyond the fact that Grant's sappers and miners are at work to blow up our works.[16]

16. sappers: military engineers whose function is to undermine enemy fortifications.

A courier from Port Hudson, with dispatches to General Johnston, arrived last night. He reports the garrison there in fine condition and spirits. Banks's force is estimated at twenty thousand strong. He also has abandoned the idea of storming the place and has gone to ditching.

Official dispatches from Millikens Bend state that our attack at that place was a failure. The enemy had three lines of works. He was driven out of two, but made a desperate stand at the third, when, with the assistance of his gunboats, he repelled our forces. Nothing is known, outside of official circles, of Kirby Smith's movements. Advices from Memphis state that the wounded, on transports, are still arriving from Vicksburg.

OUR VICTORY AT WINCHESTER
IMMENSE AMOUNT OF PROPERTY CAPTURED—
HARPERS FERRY REPORTED TAKEN—GENERAL EWELL
MARCHING ON MARYLAND, ETC.

Richmond, 18th—Passengers by the Central train this evening bring but little additional news from Winchester. The number of prisoners taken is fully 7,000, the number of horses from 2,000 to 3,000, and an immense number of wagons. It is also reported that the wife of General Milroy was captured on Sunday at Martinsburg.

Before the capture of Winchester, Milroy notified the Rebels he would burn the town if an attempt was made to storm his position. Ewell replied he would hang every Yankee captured.

It is reported that Ewell has taken Harpers Ferry, with immense stores, and is en route to Frederick City, Maryland.

Heavy explosions have been heard in the direction of Aquia Creek. It is believed that the enemy is blowing up the wharves and buildings at that point.

The Yankees have entirely disappeared from Stafford County. The buildings at Aquia Creek were not destroyed. The citizens of Fredericksburg, so long exiled, are preparing to reoccupy their homes, and the good people of the place are reaping a rich harvest of spoils from the enemy's deserted camps in Stafford County.

Nothing official has been received today from northern Virginia.

Richmond, 19th—The serious apprehensions entertained of a drought in this vicinity have been relieved by a copious and refreshing rain last night.

The *Sentinel* of this morning says it has received a number of communications indignantly denying that our cavalry were surprised at Brandy Station.

IMPORTANT FROM THE NORTH
GREAT PANIC IN LINCOLNDOM—CONFEDERATES MARCHING ON PENNSYLVANIA AND MARYLAND—LINCOLN CALLS FOR 100,000 MILITIA, ETC.

Shelbyville, Tennessee, 18th—All quiet in front.

Nashville papers of the 17th received contain Lincoln's proclamation calling out one hundred thousand militia for six months' service.

The following are the latest Northern dispatches in the Nashville papers:

Loudon, Tennessee, 16th—The Rebels are in heavy force in Cumberland Valley.

Bedford, Pennsylvania, 16th—Scouts report six thousand Rebel cavalry at Cumberland, Maryland. The inhabitants are flying for safety.

Harrisburg, Pennsylvania, 16th—Business is suspended and all important documents have been removed from the capitol. Milroy telegraphs, officially, his repulse from the fortifications at Winchester by 15,000 Rebels, with the loss of 2,900 men. Governor Curtin calls on Pennsylvanians to defend the state, saying that Philadelphia has not responded while the enemy is in Chambersburg, and reproaches Pennsylvanians for sniffling about the length of service when such an exigency exists.

Other dispatches state that everything looks gloomy and there is no saving the country south of the Susquehanna.

Baltimore, 16th—Governor Bradford calls on the people of the Valley to the defense of Maryland.

Rhode Island, 16th—Governor Smith convenes the legislature Thursday for the purpose of raising troops.

Philadelphia, 16th—The mayor has issued a proclamation, closing all the stores and ordering the occupants to join military organizations to defend the city.

New York, 16th—All the regiments are getting ready under arms. In Brooklyn the bells were rung at midnight, summoning the men to their regiments, which were leaving immediately for Philadelphia. Governor Andrew, of Massachusetts, tendered Lincoln all the available force of the militia.

Shelbyville, Tennessee, 19th—Further Northern accounts have been received. The Rebels had advanced six miles beyond Chambersburg on the 16th. General Tyler telegraphs officially his retreat and the capture of the Federal forces at Winchester.

Latest—Shelbyville, Tennessee, 19th, 6:00 P.M.—Nashville papers of the 16th received. The *New York Times* says: "Lee and his army, ninety thousand strong, are marching northward. Hooker's army is marching on to prevent Lee's advance."

The governor of Ohio calls for 30,000 troops, and the governor of Pennsylvania calls for 50,000, to prevent the invasion of each of their respective states.

Washington, 15th—Lincoln has issued a proclamation for 100,000 men, to repel the invasion of Maryland, northern Virginia, Pennsylvania, and Ohio.

Harrisburg, Pennsylvania, 15th—Dispatches from Chambersburg and Hagerstown state that the Rebel cavalry were at Berryville and Martinsburg on the 14th. Hard fighting was going on. The Rebels had driven General Reynolds from Berryville and were advancing on the capital. Several other towns and cities throughout Pennsylvania were in danger.

Later private dispatches state that on the 16th the Rebels were at Chambersburg in force. The Federals were removing the railroad machinery, stock, and stores. Great excitement and alarm prevailed.

Vicksburg, Mississippi, 10th—The Federal lines were contracting. Kirby Smith, with six thousand men, came up the Washita River, making demonstrations on the Louisiana side. The Federal troops at Millikens Bend had been reinforced.

LATER FROM EUROPE
ARRIVAL OF THE SCOTIA—THE ALABAMA AND FLORIDA BUSY

New York, 16th—The steamship *Scotia* has arrived with Liverpool dates to the 10th instant.

She reports that the C.S. steamer *Florida* had burned the bark *Ira* and ship *Oneida*.

Captain Lambert of the whaling schooner *Kingfisher* has arrived and reports that his vessel was captured and burned by the *Alabama*. He has published a card of thanks for the kind treatment he received from "the officers of the Rebel pirate."

The brig *Arabia,* which has arrived from Aspinwall, reports that she was boarded by "the pirate," taken as a prize, and released on giving a bond of forty thousand dollars. The pirate captain reported that he had destroyed two other vessels on the 12th ultimo, and intended to destroy all he could.

The English and Austrian consuls arrived in New York on the 16th, having been driven out of the Confederacy by the Rebel authorities.

Gold in New York, on the 15th, was quoted at 149, cotton 58 cents.

NORTH

BOSTON EVENING TRANSCRIPT
June 20, 1863

GENERAL LEE'S PLANS

The telegraph this morning gives the opinion of competent military men in Washington that the Rebel army, under General Lee, is marching against General Hooker's force, with the purpose of attacking the latter. The number of men under General Lee is reported at one hundred thousand. If the Rebel general falls upon the Potomac Army, it will not probably be with columns numerically inferior—especially as the Federal troops will have the choice of position and may be speedily reinforced. Only in one contingency can such a supposition be entertained. General Lee may underrate both the numbers, bravery, and skill of the Federal force, and the generalship of its leader, and, in that case, pay dearly for the mistake.

Perhaps the Rebel commander does not propose a decisive battle with General Hooker. He may be massing his forces with the design of invading Maryland and getting between Baltimore and Washington. This would be a desperate expedient, in keeping, however, with the motives which prompted the march into the Shenandoah Valley.[17] A very few days will determine which of these courses the Rebel general will take, as every hour's delay strengthens the power of the general government to resist Lee's offensive movements. No one seems to think that Lee will slink back to his old haunts without attempting to accomplish something worthy of an enterprise so ostentatiously announced in advance in the Richmond papers.

The enemy is thought to have been baffled thus far by the rapid marches of General Hooker and the bold cavalry attacks made by his direction. The Rebels made a dash in force upon Winchester and carried that place, with considerable loss to their troops; pushed on to Martinsburg and captured the town and then sent a small force into Maryland to produce consternation among the people of Maryland, Pennsylvania, and the whole North. They intended this demonstration to divert the attention of General Hooker away from their real purpose, but Hooker was not so easily deceived. He kept an eye upon Lee himself and not upon his raiders. General Hooker knew very well that General Schenck was strong enough to take care of all the Rebels that had left Lee to go

17. The Shenandoah Valley, Virginia, was a critical supply and invasion route for the Confederate army and lies between the Allegheny and the Blue Ridge mountains.

toward Pennsylvania. Finding that he made a mistake, Lee is contracting his lines again, and drawing in his cavalry from Maryland and Pennsylvania, and concentrating his forces in the valley between Winchester and Strasburg. The strategy of General Hooker is thus referred to by the *New York Evening Post:*

> General Hooker, whom the Copperhead press are attacking so fiercely now, just as he is busied with meeting and foiling Lee's plans, has done more injury to the Rebels since he assumed command of the Potomac Army than was accomplished by all the generals who commanded it before.[18] He has organized a cavalry force which has twice whipped the enemy's and once ridden within the defenses of Richmond, and which has performed even more brilliant deeds than those which made Lee and Stuart famous and dreaded while the Potomac Army was on the Peninsula. He has fought a battle against many disadvantages, in which he inflicted an irreparable loss upon the enemy in the death of Stonewall Jackson. And within two weeks he has met Lee at every point and, as it now appears, has forced him, by timely dispositions and unexpected attacks, to put off and to re-form the plans he was about to execute. A general who has done so much deserves further trial. He may not prove a great commander, but he has already shown Lee that he is a more formidable opponent than that Rebel general has had since Rosecrans beat him in western Virginia.

The *New York Evening Express,* which is a McClellan print, is obliged to make the following admissions:

> The objects of the Rebel general, we guess, were first to scatter, or gobble up, our forces at Berryville, Winchester, Martinsburg, Harpers Ferry, and all along the upper Potomac; second, to force Hooker back from the Rappahannock by threatening Maryland and Pennsylvania and by the same movements to divide and scatter the Army of the Potomac; third, to overwhelm the new state of West Virginia about the time her new constitution goes into effect; and fourth, while doing this, to take advantage of all the chances for a dash on Washington, Baltimore, Harrisburg,

18. The militant, openly pro-Southern Peace Democrats were called Copperheads, after the venomous snake of the same name. As a badge of defiance, some Peace Democrats began wearing copper Indian-head pennies.

Pittsburgh, or elsewhere, as may best suit his purpose. In most of these objects he has been foiled. While Hooker has retired from the Rappahannock, his army remains intact; and although we have lost Winchester and the upper Potomac, the dash into Pennsylvania availed him but little, and Baltimore and Washington are, we may hope, safe beyond doubt.

THE MOMENT FOR ENERGY

It is the part of sagacious leadership to seize upon and use favorable conditions of public sentiment—to see when the iron is hot and strike accordingly. Within a week the government has had a fresh opportunity to test the resolute purpose of the people to put an end to the rebellion. Even the opposition journals have spoken of the vanishing of the Peace party before the uprising, in consequence of the threats of invasion. The patriotism of sentiment—impulsive loyal feeling, the patriotism of principle—the farseeing and right-seeing political sagacity, the patriotism of the counting room—carefully calculating what the interests of business demand in regard to the country's future—these have separately and together once more shown their readiness and their determination to save the republic from disunion.

Does not this fact indicate the duty of the government to use the opportune hour with promptest decision? Does it not require at its hands the boldest action? Does it not command it to take, as it were, the initiative and meet the wishes of the people by the alacrity of its onward movement? It can have the sufficient support of all parties except traitors now, if it will proclaim the rally with no uncertain sound, and charge home upon the enemy. Let us have life—earnest, electric life—at Washington—the clear, sharp ring, in word and act, that indicates one end and aim—the strain of every nerve, to accomplish the overthrow of the conspiracy, and this policy will be responded to, so as to speedily put matters in a shape to defy opposition in the loyal states and make the national power victorious in the disloyal states.

COPPERHEAD BOOKS

The manner of men who buy Copperhead books is indicated in the following order from Illinois, for "copyes" of Mahony's *Prisoner of State*. The *New York Evening Post* gives it verbatim, bad spelling and all:

> June the 1863—Concord Buda Bureau Co Ill—Dear sur pleas send mee to copyes off mahony's great book. The democrats are agitting waked up out here, give me liberty or give me deth.

direct to Concord Buda Burea Co Ill
yours with due respect, Elbrdge Stevens
Ps you wish agents iff I can due eney thing for you I will due it.

NEW YORK TRIBUNE
June 20, 1863

COPPERHEAD REBELLION IN OHIO
ORGANIZED RESISTANCE TO THE ENROLLMENT—TROOPS FIRED UPON BY THE INSURGENTS—THE FIRE RETURNED AND THE MOB DISPERSED—TIME GIVEN THE INSURGENTS TO YIELD THE LEADERS

Cleveland, Ohio, June 19, 1863

Troops have been sent to Holmes County, in this state, to break up an organization to resist the enrollment. They arrived at the scene of disturbance Wednesday. As the troops advanced, a number of shots were fired by the insurgents without effect, when the soldiers under Colonel Wallace fired a volley and then charged bayonets, scattering the insurgents, who fled to the woods.

Eight prisoners were taken and two slightly wounded. The number of the insurgents was reported at 500 or 600, chiefly armed with shotguns. They are now roaming about the woods without leaders or any concert of action. They relied on reinforcements from the surrounding country, but were generally disappointed.

The military commander gave notice that the troops would remain quiet Thursday and give the insurrectionists an opportunity to surrender the originators of the movement and disperse. If this was not done by Friday morning, severe measures would be taken.

Another report states that four soldiers were killed and ten Vallandigham Democrats killed and wounded and that reinforcements were sent for by the commander of the Union forces. This report is considered exaggerated.

RESISTANCE TO THE ENROLLMENT IN INDIANA
AN ENROLLING OFFICER PELTED WITH EGGS—ANOTHER MURDERED WHILE RIDING ALONG A ROAD

Cincinnati, Ohio, June 19, 1863

The enrolling officer in Boone County, Indiana, was captured by several persons on Monday. The men held him while the women pelted him with eggs. Fourteen of the most active partisans have been arrested.

Fletcher Freeman, the enrolling officer of Sullivan County, Indiana, was shot dead yesterday while riding along a country road.

THE DISCONTENT IN NORTH CAROLINA AND VIRGINIA—PERMANENT SECESSION OF THOSE STATES NOT TO BE EXPECTED—IMPORTANT DECLARATION BY A REBEL COMMITTEE—ORGANIZATION OF POWERFUL UNION FORCES—20,000 INSURGENTS READY TO JOIN THE UNION ARMY ON OCCUPYING RALEIGH

Fortress Monroe, Virginia, June 19, 1863

The United States transport *Emilie* arrived today from New Bern with our advices from our correspondent there to the 17th. He reports as follows:

The Rebel Committee on River Fortifications reports that the Union forces are in possession of a belt of country 300 miles long by 150 wide, with inland seas and rivers filled with Union gunboats, reaching through North Carolina and Virginia, which prevents fortifications' being constructed; that while this continues, the permanent secession of North Carolina and Virginia cannot be expected.

The Unionists in eastern Tennessee and western North Carolina have organized powerful forces and joined the thousands of deserters and conscripts from the Rebel army, to whom protection is guaranteed, for the purpose of holding the mountain region against the Rebel government.

Rebel citizens have petitioned Governor Vance for protection against this organization. Vance replies that he has no troops to send; they must protect themselves. Twenty thousand insurgents have already offered to join the Union troops as soon as a military post is established at Raleigh.

JULY 18, 1863

SOUTH

RICHMOND DAILY DISPATCH
July 18, 1863

FROM GENERAL LEE'S ARMY THE ENEMY ALSO ACROSS THE POTOMAC— FIGHT NEAR CHARLES TOWN

From a gentleman who came down on the Central train last night, we gather the following particulars of affairs in the lower Valley:

On Monday evening it was ascertained that the enemy were crossing the Potomac in heavy force, at a number of different fords between Williamsport, where the right of our army rested, and Edwards Ferry, near Leesburg. During the afternoon of Monday, a portion of their forces which had crossed at Harpers Ferry engaged the 12th Virginia Cavalry at Halltown, four miles from the river. In this engagement Colonel A. W. Harman, who commanded the 12th, was severely wounded. Finding themselves opposed by a vastly superior force, the regiment fell back, and the enemy advanced as far and occupied Charles Town that night.

At the same time a heavy column of the enemy crossed the river at Shepherdstown, twelve miles above Harpers Ferry, and another column at Point of Rocks, nine miles below. It is also reported that a considerable force was thrown across the river at Edwards Ferry.

On learning that the enemy were thus attempting to gain his rear, General Lee at once commenced the passage of the river at Williamsport and Falling Waters, and throughout the entire night of Monday, his army was engaged in crossing the Potomac, still somewhat swollen by the recent rains. Early the next morning the last of our troops reached the Virginia shore and moved on in the direction of Winchester. The last heard from our army, it was in line of battle at Bunker Hill, midway between Winchester and Martinsburg.

THE ENEMY IN THE RIVER

The two Yankee gunboats which came up the James River Wednesday went down again Thursday to City Point, where they now lie with the rest of the fleet. Our pickets are now within three miles of Portsmouth, Virginia. Nearly all the troops have been removed from Fortress Monroe, Norfolk, and Old Point. About fifteen thousand Negroes are now in Portsmouth.

THE SIEGE OF CHARLESTON

The fact that no telegrams have been received in the city from Charleston during the week has led croakers to give forth the mournful predictions of the "impending fall" of that place with stupid pertinacity. They were quite sure that the government had news of terrible import, which it refused to divulge. We have from the Charleston papers a partial answer to these jeremiads. The Yankees are as busy as beavers on Morris Island, but Charleston has not fallen yet. On Monday two wooden gunboats commenced shelling Battery Wagner. The three monitors, which were lying behind a point near the lower end of Morris Island, kept very quiet throughout the day. Our batteries (Gregg and Wagner) and Fort

Sumter responded slowly and at long intervals to the enemy's fire. One shot from Sumter is reported to have struck the enemy's observatory, erected on Craig's Hill, Morris Island. The Yankees have an immense derrick and are reported placing more guns in position, fortifying Craig's Hill, and also Black Island, between Morris and James islands, of which they are reported in possession. About eight o'clock in the evening, the steamer *Gabriel Manigault,* lying in a creek between Morris and James islands, was burned by the enemy's shells. Of the operations on Tuesday the *Courier* gives the following summary:

> The exchange of shots between the Yankee gunboats and our batteries on Tuesday was kept up at long intervals until the afternoon, when the firing became more rapid. Fort Sumter continued to throw shells with effect at the Yankee working party on Craig's Hill. An officer from Battery Wagner, who arrived last night, reported the enemy throwing up rifle pits and entrenchments. Their working parties are plainly visible, both on Craig's Hill and Black Island. Four mortar boats were observed for the first time Tuesday inside the channel, one of them seemingly placed in a position to cover their working parties. The monitors, four in number, were lying close inshore, apparently receiving a fresh supply of ammunition. An additional number of transports are reported to have arrived Tuesday. There were no casualties at the batteries yesterday.

The governor of South Carolina has issued a proclamation calling for three thousand Negroes to work on the fortifications. He says the need for them is pressing. The *Charleston Courier* thinks the city is in imminent peril, and to save it, the Yankees must be driven off Morris Island. From an interesting editorial in that paper on the "situation" we make the following extracts:

> We mean not either to censure our military authorities or to dictate or embarrass their movements. On the contrary, our honest and earnest desire and purpose are to encourage, stimulate, strengthen, and sustain them. With all proper deference and respect, then, we say to them that our people are fully up to the exigency of the times, and stand ready, at any and every hazard and cost, to second them in a brave and determined effort to drive the enemy back into the ocean from their strongholds on Morris and Folly islands. If the safety of Charleston be involved in such a

movement, there should be no hesitation in making the attempt. Let us do all that may become men whose liberties and lives, whose homes and altars, and all that is dear to them as fathers, brothers, and husbands are staked on the momentous issue.

The fall of Charleston involves consequences which we shudder to contemplate. With her capture, the whole state would soon be at the mercy of the foe, and the great cause of Southern independence would be put in fearful jeopardy. Nothing but a guerrilla warfare for the southern and southwestern portion of the Confederacy, if not for its whole extent, would then be left us in manifestation of our undying and unconquerable determination never to submit to Yankee rule. Let us, then, resolve to defend our beloved and time-honored city to the last extremity. First, let us make every possible human effort to wrest the adjacent islands from the enemy and enable Sumter and our other harbor fortresses, with our steam rams, to keep the vandals at bay. Failing in this, and even should Sumter become untenable, then let us resolve on a Saragossa defense of our city, manning and defending every wharf—fighting from street to street and house to house—and, if failing to achieve success, yielding nothing but smoking ruins and mangled bodies as the spoil of the ruthless conqueror. Should Charleston fall, life will be no longer worth living. Let us, then, freely peril life in her defense and resolutely devote her to destruction sooner than yield her undemolished, as a trophy and flourishing seaport, to the accursed foe. We once advocated a different policy—we were once for capitulation, in preference to self-sought or self-inflicted desolation. But we then mistakenly thought we had to encounter an enemy bound by the rules of civilized warfare. The mask is now thrown aside. New Orleans, Nashville, and Memphis have taught us what we have to expect from the tender mercies of our unprincipled foe, and we know that our subjugation involves submission to a vile and atrocious despotism, to worse than savage barbarities, to degradation and insult (sparing neither age, sex, nor condition), and to the galling infamy of servile domination. Let us, then, bid destruction and extermination welcome, sooner than succumb to Yankee dominion and all its nameless enormities; and if Charleston must fall, let her, although in ruin, yet live as the most glorious monument of self-defense ever recorded in history, covering her defenders with immortal glory and her vandal conquerors with undying infamy.

We are among those who cherish the confident hope that the

enemy will be miserably unsuccessful in executing the plans he is at present working so vigorously and resolutely to carry out. We expect him to be punished severely if he persists in the undertaking. But we may be disappointed. Our hope may prove a delusion. The result the timid and despondent predict may transpire. The capture of our city may perchance delight his base and corrupt heart. In case that frightful calamity fall upon us, they who remain here must suffer grievous evils. The woes they will have poured out upon them will be far heavier than those under which the citizens of New Orleans and Nashville and Memphis have groaned; for the vile foe hates the people of this state with a tenfold more bitter hatred than he entertains for the inhabitants of any other section, and he will not spare us when he comes as conqueror.

On the supposition of the foe's success, it is our duty to avoid incurring his fiendish malignity. All who can be of no service in the work of defense should betake themselves to places of shelter. And it were well not to defer removal to a late day. We may be compelled to remain, or, if we make good our escape, circumstances may oblige us to leave all our personal effects behind.

We should also consider that our city is going to make a fierce and determined resistance. If the enemy gets it, he will have to take it. No flag-of-truce boat will meet him midway between the wharves and Fort Sumter in order to effect a surrender. We are going to fight till we are driven from street to street, and continue to fight while we are retreating. So determined a resistance involves immense injury to our fair city at the hands of the enemy. It will be little better than a heap of ruins, even though the work of destruction is not ensured by military order.

We repeat that we are of the opinion that the present attack will result as the other attacks have done, and even more disastrously to the mean and wicked foe. But is it not proper to prepare for the worst? If we are forced to defend our city after the manner we have resolved to defend it, the women and children and aged men who tarry too long would suffer miseries infinitely greater than they will have to bear during their temporary exile.

It behooves us to give this subject serious and profound consideration. If the enemy is forced to abandon the effort he is making to gain possession of our city, we can return to our homes in a short time. If he is successful—which God forbid!—we will have avoided privations and woes of which we can now form no adequate conception. Let us take counsel of prudence.

The citizens of Charleston are furnishing cooked rations to the troops on Morris Island. The foreigners in that city who refuse to fight are not sent North to their Yankee friends. Here is the way they are served:

> We learn that not more than six or seven of all the employees at the arsenal refused to join any company, and Major Tresevant, commandant of the arsenal, quickly sent these, with their "foreign protection papers," to Major Perryman, our new enrolling officer, who as quickly forwarded them to Morris Island, where "ditching" is going on and "foreign papers" are not respected.

CHARLESTON DAILY COURIER
July 18, 1863

A CAUTION TO WRITERS

There have recently appeared in the columns of the Southern press—and the *Courier* is probably not exempt from the list—various statements calculated unintentionally to do injury to our cause. At this time especially, the enemy is watching our journals to take advantage of every hint that conveys information of our points of strength or weakness. It therefore behooves every writer for the press, and not less every private correspondent, to exercise extraordinary prudence in making current the facts at his command. It should be their aim to give to the public a record of the past alone and to let the future take care of itself. Our generals require no information from the press on the subject of strategical warfare, and any allusion to the manner in which certain things may or may not be done, or when and how certain places should be occupied or evacuated, only serves to weaken our cause, frustrate our plans, and fortify those of the enemy. Let every man, then, be cautious, even in his conversation, and remember that silence is now our safety and strength—"silence is gold."

We propose for adoption the following rules:

1. Never allude to the number or position of our forces.

2. Never describe points likely to be occupied by the enemy, or utter doubts as to their strength.

3. Never refer to the arrival or departure of troops.

4. Never discuss the events of the future, or hint at enterprises to be undertaken.

5. In describing a battle, avoid details of our strength, and confine the narration to things done.

THE CALL TO ARMS

While the Army of Northern Virginia was advancing into Pennsylvania; while Bragg continued to confront his wily and active antagonist from his fortified position at Tullahoma; while Vicksburg and Port Hudson stood proudly defiant, beating back every assault of the powerful foe; while General Taylor and his worthy coadjutors went on capturing city after city and town after town in Louisiana, the race of the Yankees was downhearted and unnerved, and the South was exultant, hopeful, and active.[19] Providence smiled brightly on our cause, and the end of this terrific contest seemed to be drawing near.

But the failure of the great Southern captain to discomfit and destroy the Army of the Potomac, the retrograde movement of the Army of the West, the loss of Vicksburg and Port Hudson, with the apprehension of the direful evils these disasters involve, have sorely tried the fortitude of our people and raised the Yankees to the highest point of confidence, flooding their base souls with a sea of joy.

If these events produced no other effect than to fill the Yankee mind with joy, there would be sufficient grounds for increased energy, activity, and determination. But they have not only made the Doodles glad, they have also reinspirited and reassured them; and encouraged by those successes, they will put forth all their strength and power to accomplish the ends they vainly imagine they can speedily attain.

The administration at Washington are taking advantage of the change in the public sentiment and sent forth the enrolling officer. The call for four hundred thousand men is pressed with earnestness; and under the influence of the delusive hopes excited by these reverses to our arms, the draft will be complied with; and in a shorter time than we suppose, that vast army will be added to the host now threatening our rights and liberties and all we hold dear.

Our army must be increased. It is probable the next Congress will so alter and amend the Conscription Act as to embrace in its limits persons of forty or forty-five years of age. But the number included in the extension of the liability to bear arms will not meet the demands made upon us. There will yet remain a large number who should never have been exempted from military duty, who must be made to come forth and perform their portion of the great work we have enterprised.

Foreigners will have to take part in this struggle. We might urge this

19. The Army of Northern Virginia was the principal Confederate army in the east, commanded by General Robert E. Lee from June 1862. Before then, it was known as the Army of the Potomac.

claim our country has a right to make upon this class of our community, on the ground that, having partaken of the benefits and blessings the citizens of our country enjoyed in times of peace, they should, while war is desolating our land and imperiling our precious heritage of independence, aid in the defense of that country that has enabled them to procure so many blessings. And that consideration is made the stronger when we consider that many of those who have kept aloof from the battle under the plea of foreign nationality have been foremost of that execrable crew of extortioners and speculators whom every patriot loathes and abhors. Happy in the immunity purchased for them by consular certificates, they have had ample opportunity to amass fortunes and, now rolling in wealth, fancy they are free to enjoy it without molestation from the enrolling officer.

But whether or not they have taken advantage of the times to enrich themselves at the expense of the worthy and honest, of the families of our noble soldiers, and the widows and children of those who have laid their lives on the altar of liberty, judicial authority has decided that all who claim allegiance to foreign powers are come within the bounds of the Conscription Act. Judge Magrath of South Carolina and Judge Jones of Alabama have both ruled with distinctness and emphasis that alien residents are liable to military duty. These decisions are supported by reason and sound sense, and we trust they will be acted upon.

It is gratifying to know that a large number of foreigners are now in the ranks of our army and that they have fought as valiantly, suffered as grandly, and done as good service as our own sons and brothers. But there are others who, while their brethren have shown the sincerity of their attachment for our form of government and our institutions and manifested their gratitude for the protection afforded them by our laws, have refused to have anything to do with the struggle, and who, in place of giving us their help in this, our time of danger and distress, have augmented the sum of our evils and rendered success more difficult to obtain.

Those who have availed themselves of substitutes should also be required to take their places in the ranks. He who has more money than patriotism is a pitiable object. They should never have been permitted to fight by the hand of another. But the crime they were guilty of in sending a man to take the place they should have felt it an honor to fill was not nearly so great when the act was committed as it is under present circumstances. The cause needs every man who is able to carry a musket. He who refuses to meet the call now made by his country is unworthy of that country—unworthy of its gallant men—unworthy of its noble women. The call is to each one of us, and each must obey it for himself and in his own person. He who answers the demand by furnishing someone else is as despicable as he who, under any false plea, evades the solemn duty now devolved upon every man in this Southern land. We need both the substitute and him who has bought his services with his money. The perils that encompass our country render it necessary that both go forth to the battle.

The crisis through which we are passing does not admit of the indulgence of those tastes and habits which it was lawful to encourage in the days of white-winged peace. The cloud of war grows blacker. The enemy is putting forth all his great power. His armies march and fight under the inspiration of recent successes, and army and people work and suffer in the confident expectation that they will speedily reduce us to submission. Frightful woes await us if the foe is successful. If we are made to succumb, we will account them happy who have fallen on the field of blood. Death in any form, a thousand deaths in any form, were preferable to Yankee rule. If we would save ourselves from so terrible a fate, we must stir our strength and go forth resolved to conquer or die. Let every man do his duty, and God will vouchsafe us deliverance and victory.

NORTH

BOSTON EVENING TRANSCRIPT
July 18, 1863

DESTITUTION OF INDIAN TRIBES

Washington, 17th—The Indian agent for the upper Arkansas district, in an official communication, dated Colorado, 30th ultimo, speaks of visiting the Caddos and other Indians, thirty miles south of Fort Sound. They were destitute of both clothing and provisions, having been robbed of everything by the Rebels before leaving Texas. But for the abundance of the buffalo herds, they would have starved.

The agent ministered to their necessities. They say they will always remain loyal and celebrate the Fourth of July, as has been their custom. Other Indians from Texas soon join them. Those remaining in Texas are in a deplorable condition, having been plundered of all their stock to feed the Rebel troops, a large body of whom were on the Red River, moving northwest. Governor Doty has made important treaties with Indians in Utah, thus additionally securing safety to emigrants.

THE WAY THEIR SINCERITY IS EXHIBITED!

There are those who emphatically assert that their sympathies are entirely with the Union. The way they express those sympathies is to attack every agency and instrumentality—"all the measures and all the policy"—seeking the preservation of the Union. They sneer at and libel those portions of the free states which have been unconditionally loyal. They support the men who from the outset have avowed their alliance in opinion with the Rebels. They eulogize Jefferson Davis as the statesman and Lee as the general of the crisis.

They predict reverses to Federal troops, always doubt the success of Federal arms, whittle down and belittle Federal victories. They pronounce the entire administration either imbecile or corrupt, object to the use of colored soldiers, and at the same time set their faces against the drafting of white soldiers. They rail at the confiscation of the property of traitors or the emancipation of their human chattels, although in this property and these chattels lies their war strength.

They maintain that the chief peril of the hour is at Washington, and the chief enemies of the republic are the loyal people who are endeavoring to save it. They praise Pierce, the old and the present confrere of Jefferson Davis; Seymour of Connecticut, always ready to yield everything to the slave power, and always averse to anything but "moral force."[20] In a word, their entire argument is to create distrust and disaffection at the North and weaken the power of the existing government. And still they assert that their sympathies are entirely with the Union.

They belong to a faction which has always been contending that the inexcusable authors of all our political woes were none of them south of the Mason-Dixon Line; who have always believed in the superior chivalry, generous hospitality, and all the graces of the aristocracy of the plantation, and in their hearts despised the honest, industrious democracy of free commonwealths! The statement of the position of this faction ought to be enough, for it enables every true man, every true American, to decide where he will stand and what principles he will stand by.

[UNTITLED]

The *New York Herald* appears to have been apprehensive that the mob would miss some of its victims, or overlook some place where the property of the United States was stored.[21] It therefore volunteers the following information:

20. Franklin Pierce, Democrat, president (1853–57). Jefferson Davis served as his secretary of war.
21. Refers to the New York City Draft Riots, July 13–16, 1863.

There is but one quarter where these unfortunates, the blacks, live, which has remained unharmed—Sullivan Street, in the Eighth Ward. . . . There is a United States storehouse in Worth Street, where there are upward of fifty thousand muskets.

NEW YORK TRIBUNE
July 18, 1863

THE RIOT

The rioters, after the terrible punishment they received on Thursday at the hands of the military, subsided during the night, the main body dispersing and retiring to their homes. Numbers of them, however, in gangs of from three to five, roamed through every street in the city except where there was a patrol, attacking indiscriminately all well-dressed persons whom they found abroad, first knocking down their victims, then beating and robbing them.

Professional thieves also took advantage of the absence of the usual police force from the streets and hunted the city in search of plunder. Every point at which it was thought the mob might gather was guarded by the military. Yesterday morning the east side of the city, between Eighteenth Street and Yorkville, was comparatively quiet, although there was no evidence that the rioters were not awaiting some signal from their leaders to again assemble and renew their acts of violence. The presence of the 7th and other regiments has given a greater feeling of security to our citizens. A number of factories resumed operations yesterday, under the protection of the military and police, but with only a portion of their hands, the remainder probably keeping away from fear of the mob.

Through the low groggeries on the avenues and side streets, groups of men lounged about the doorways and stoops, ready for any mischief. The bitterest feeling was expressed against both police and military. Large numbers are in possession of arms, stolen from the armories and various gun stores, with which they threaten to shoot from their windows at night every obnoxious person who may pass by. Many have laid aside their arms for want of ammunition and instead have filled corners in their rooms with stones and bricks.

About nine o'clock yesterday morning, as Captain John H. Howell, of the 3rd New York Artillery, U.S.V., was passing up Seventh Avenue to Thirty-second Street in his private carriage, to examine the Wednesday's scene of action, a gang of six or eight of the rioters, spying his uniform, cried out, "There's the man who fired on us here. Let's hang him."

The outcry which they made soon swelled the crowd to about fifty, who at once made a rush upon the carriage and ordered the driver to stop. Captain Howell drew his revolver and told the driver to turn down Thirty-first Street at once, or he would shoot him. The mob then stoned the carriage, breaking the windows and panels. One of the missiles struck an old wound in the captain's side, paralyzing his arm for a few moments. The driver started on a gallop as directed, the crowd, with yells and shouts, pursuing the vehicle. Captain Howell fired five shots from the back window of the carriage into the midst of the crowd, emptying his revolver, which had the effect of halting the mob until the carriage got beyond their reach. He is unable to say positively whether anyone was killed, although he saw the mob bearing away one of their number. One of the rioters who attempted to climb in at the window lost his hold and was run over.

Captain Howell won the indignation of the rioters in that district by firing upon them, on Wednesday morning, with the 8th Regiment Artillery, of which he had command. He says that the story circulated by the *Daily News* that he fired into an innocent crowd of women and children is an "infamous lie" and that the facts are as follows: The troops, under command of General Dodge and Colonel Mott, proceeded on Wednesday morning, at daylight, to Thirty-second Street, where the rioters were hanging colored men and sacking houses. No less than three Negroes had already been killed by the rioters when the force arrived upon the ground; the lifeless body of one of the Negroes was cut down by Colonel Mott himself, with his sword. This appeared to be the signal for the rioters to commence their attack upon the troops, with stones, brickbats, and slungshots. Colonel Mott then ordered Captain Howell to bring his piece into battery at the corner of Thirty-second Street and Seventh Avenue, but he was only enabled to do so by the aid of the infantry and cavalry, who charged down the street with fixed bayonets and drawn sabers, driving the insurgents as far as possible. Captain Howell at this time approached the mob alone and warned them to disperse, or he should fire upon them with grape and canister shot. General Dodge and Colonel Mott did the same in other parts of the street and avenue. These cautions were repeatedly given, and it was not until the rioters had rallied and again attacked the military with stones and made a rush to take the pieces that Captain Howell gave the command to fire. About half a dozen rounds of grape and canister were then fired in earnest, which soon cleared the street. The military now broke into column and marched over the district, arresting a large number of the rioters, who were locked up in the station houses. As soon as the military had left the scene of action, the lifeless bodies of the Negroes were taken in hand by the mob and again suspended to the lampposts.

Captain Howell is stationed at New Bern, North Carolina, and had been home on a furlough. He was, at the time the riot commenced, en route for his battery and was detained here by order of General Wool and placed in command of two batteries of artillery. He is now acting on General Ledlie's staff, but hopes to be relieved today, when he will proceed at once to his command. Captain Howell was formerly a lieutenant in Colonel Bailey's celebrated artillery and was wounded at Fair Oaks, where Colonel Bailey fell. Upon recovering from his wounds, he was promoted to a captaincy in the 3rd Artillery and made chief of artillery on General Negley's staff. He passed with that general through his campaigns in North and South Carolina, and upon General Negley's being relieved by General Hunter, he was returned to the command of a battery in the 3rd Artillery, which he now holds.

HOW TO ENFORCE THE DRAFT

It has been intimated that the suppression of the insurrection in New York should be left to the city and state authorities and that the national government has no immediate duty in the premises. Such an opinion is a perilous, and may be a fatal, mistake. For—

1. The mobs were nominally there in order to resist the draft, which it is the business of the national government to enforce.

2. They were really originated and fomented by Northern traitors, in aid of the falling fortunes of the rebellion at the South, the draft being the occasion, not the cause, of the insurrection. And the national government must crush treason at the North not less than at the South.

3. The city authorities were without a force to subdue the mob, inasmuch as that the police—who have bravely done all that police could do against a mob, but who cannot be expected to control a continuous insurrection—are independent of them. The state authorities, in the person of Governor Seymour, assumed the leadership of the riot, at first, and only hung back when it seemed to be getting beyond their control. Governor Seymour's disgraceful speech should have been ample warning to the president that no honest effort to enforce the draft was to be expected from him. Moreover, Governor Seymour has done what he

could to disgrace and undermine the national authority by seeking to prevent the draft after, as well as before, it had been begun.

4. The president has announced that the draft will not be suspended but enforced. How does he expect to enforce it? Will he trust the city authorities? They aver that they have no power to keep the peace. Will he trust Governor Seymour? He avows himself opposed to the enforcement and, by his address, encouraged a mob to resist it. Will he trust the mob? Let him hearken to the muttered threats in the streets, and the insolent menace in the *World,* the *News,* and other organs of riotous treason, that the renewal of the draft shall be the signal for a renewal of the insurrection. It is unequivocally proclaimed by a powerful and desperate faction that the draft shall *not* be enforced. The president assures the country that it shall. Again we ask, how does he expect to keep his promise and compel obedience to the law?

5. There remains but one answer—the military power of the national government must enforce the draft. We tell the president plainly—if it is possible he can need to be told—that unless vigorous measures are adopted in season, he must expect to witness another—and, beyond doubt, a better-organized, more extensive, and infinitely more dangerous —insurrection than has yet occurred. Martial law and the means of enforcing it, soldiers, and a general of courage and capacity will secure the execution of the draft, and they only will secure it. Will the government be warned in time?

THE RIOT IN BOSTON

Boston, Massachusetts, July 16, 1863

The mob spirit in this city appears to have been effectually squelched, and there are no indications of its renewal.

As a precautionary measure, however, a strong military force and police patrol will guard the city tonight and, if deemed necessary, for several nights to come.

The Constitutional Democratic Club have voted to test in the courts of law the legality of the Conscription Act.

Bernard Doge has been arrested for haranguing a crowd in opposition to the draft. He was locked up in default of $5,000 bail.

From the *Evening Traveller,* July 15, 1863

The exciting scenes of yesterday afternoon at the North End were continued, and assumed a more formidable appearance last night. Late in the afternoon the storekeepers near the scene of the riot, apprehensive of further trouble, closed their stores, as a general thing, and barricaded the entrances.

At the request of Mayor Lincoln, Governor Andrew summoned a number of military men to the aid of the civil authorities, and before eight o'clock in the evening, about a thousand men were under arms.

At six-thirty, Companies B, C, and D of Heavy Artillery from Fort Warren arrived in this city, under command of Major Cabot; a detachment of about a hundred men from the 2nd Regiment of Heavy Artillery, under Colonel Frankle, and a detachment of dismounted men from the 2nd Regiment of Cavalry reported at the statehouse, and quarters were assigned them in various parts of the city. Brigadier General Richard A. Pierce was placed in command of all the troops. Orders were also issued to the 11th Battery, Captain Jones, to the 44th Regiment and battalion of dragoons; and they were in readiness at their armories.[22]

Shortly after seven o'clock last evening, crowds of people began to assemble in Endicott, Hanover, Prince, and other streets, and the numbers continued to increase.

ATTACK UPON THE ARMORY IN COOPER STREET

Matters looked so threatening that at eight-thirty, a signal was given by the fire alarm telegraph, which brought all the military men under arms to their feet and ready for duty.

A large crowd assembled in front of the armory in Cooper Street, inside of which were Captain Jones's battery, Company D of the Heavy Artillery from Fort Warren, and a detachment of the 11th U.S. Infantry. For a while, the mob contented themselves with shouting and yelling at those inside of the building.

A portion of the crowd tore up the sidewalks in the vicinity and threw the bricks into the street, from which they were speedily conveyed to the armory in Cooper Street and thrown against the doors and windows.

The garrison had positive orders from Mayor Lincoln to use all means to hold their position, and cannons had been placed to command the two doors. Finally the mob succeeded in battering one of the doors in, and in an instant the order was given by Captain Jones to fire, and a good round of canister burst into the close ranks of the rioters. The men then used their side arms freely. The casualties, as far as known, were as follows:

22. Similar to a cavalryman, a dragoon is an infantryman who uses a horse for transport but normally dismounts for battle.

An unknown man was instantly killed. He appears to have been a laboring man, thirty years of age, perhaps, and about five feet three inches tall. His body was pierced by the canister in eleven different places and frightfully shattered.

John Norton, a boy about ten years of age, residing at 166 Endicott Street, was shot in the heart, dead.

Michael Gaffy, fourteen or fifteen years of age, residing at 31 Cross Street, was shot in the abdomen, causing a protrusion of the bowels. He was sinking rapidly at midnight and, in the physician's opinion, could not live.

P. Reynolds, about twelve years of age, residing at 12 Bolton Place (off Hanover Street), was shot in the hip, making an ugly wound. He was taken to the hospital.

John McLaughlin, a boy about ten years old, residing in Hanover Street, had his left arm shattered to pieces. He was borne away by some of the mob upon a blind. It is doubtful if he recovers.

A young man named Norwood, who said he was passing quietly by the building, had two or three of his fingers of his right hand badly mangled, and his left hand was also injured.

A man named Dennis Hogan received quite a severe wound in his left arm. His friends took him away in a carriage.

Two or three other boys received slight wounds, but were able to go home without assistance.

A woman in the crowd was shot in the neck and is reported to have since died.

Mr. William Locke, provision dealer, 12 Salem Street, corner of Prince Street, received a musket ball through his right thigh, near the bone. He was standing in the crowd as a spectator.

A young woman named Henniman, residing in Cross Street, was injured by a musket ball, which entered under her chin, passing backward and producing a serious wound.

A woman named Moore, also residing in Cross Street, was injured by a charge of shot, which must have been fired by the rioters; and a ball also struck her in the shoulder, but glanced without doing serious injury.

Inside of the armory, Lieutenant John P. Sawin, of Jones's battery, was seriously hurt about the head by bricks.

Private Dexter McIntyre of Company D, Heavy Artillery, was injured about the foot. Another, named Day, was struck in the forehead and injured pretty severely. He was sent to the hospital.

There was no further disturbance at the armory. Later in the evening the battalion of dragoons proceeded to Cooper Street and formed in line and made preparations to resist a renewal of the attack.

Mr. William Currier, a venerable and widely respected citizen of the honored age of seventy-two years and father of officer William W. Currier of the First Station, residing at 23 Cooper Street, was killed by a shot from the rioters while he was entering his house.

ATTACK UPON GUN SHOPS

The mob next visited the new and well-stocked hardware and arms store of William Read and Son, 13 Faneuil Hall Square. Apprehensive of some such visitation, a guard had been placed inside, but for some reason the rioters did not make an attack. One of the rioters was seen brandishing a musket, and after a fierce struggle, he was captured by Sergeant Dunn of the police, but not until the rioter had been shot by another officer.

He was wounded severely. His name is James Campbell, and he is in the employ of Michael Doherty in North Street.

The rioters next turned their attention to the hardware and arms store of Thomas P. Barnes, 28 Dock Square, and, having broken in the door and window, entered and helped themselves to rifles, pistols, and knives. They took about a hundred guns, seventy-five pistols, three or four dozen bowie knives, and all the fine cutlery in the showcases.

Mr. Barnes estimates his loss at about three thousand dollars. Among the property stolen from his store was a lot of valuable cutlery.

A guard of regulars was placed before J. Hapgood's gun store, 26 Washington Street, but no assault was made upon it.

The military soon arrived upon the spot, and squads of armed men were placed at different points in Dock Square and cannons placed to command the approach to both.

At midnight all was as quiet as could be expected.

The fire alarm was sounded two or three times during the night, the mob having broken open the boxes. The rioters attempted to set fire to the armory in Cooper Street about midnight, but were prevented. A large crowd again gathered at this spot between twelve and one o'clock, but were driven off by a detachment of police under Sergeant Dunn, who were afterward reinforced by detachments from the heavy artillery companies.

ATTACK UPON A BREAD STORE

Between two and three o'clock this morning, the bread store of Jabez F. Hewes, 140 Prince Street, was broken into by a gang of men. A squad of soldiers was sent from the armory in Cooper Street to protect the place and one or two arrests made. One of the men was rescued from two soldiers who were left to take charge of him, and escaped. During the melee, several shots were fired.

Michael A. McNamara, a young North End rough, was arrested about eleven o'clock, near Dock Square, by the police, and in his possession was found a carving knife about a foot long, with which he boastingly asserted that he had cut two men during the night.

John Keneford was arrested by the Second Police, half an hour later, while attempting to create a disturbance, and a knife stolen from Mr. Barnes's store was found in his possession.

AUGUST 15, 1863

SOUTH

RICHMOND DAILY DISPATCH
August 15, 1863

BOMBSHELLS AND ARISTOCRACY

We see it stated that Admiral Porter, during the bombardment of Vicksburg, availed himself of the agency of bombshells to transmit a large number of handbills inside, addressed to the private soldiers of Vicksburg, endeavoring to excite their prejudices against their officers as aristocrats, who would get all the glory, while they did all the fighting, and who would never permit their names to be given to the world, no matter how great their valor and self-sacrifice.

We had supposed that Admiral Porter was an honest fighting sailor and not a dirty demagogue, but it seems we were mistaken. We should like to know if he ever heard of an army or a navy in which it was possible to publish all the names of the rank and file and if so, why he, the aforesaid admiral, has never published the names of the sailors under his command, or Grant those of the rank and file of his army. He must think the soldiers of the South are dolts and idiots. He doesn't know the men he is fighting against. They are not mercenaries and agrarians, but patriots, and many of them persons of education and wealth, who had a higher motive for taking up arms than to get their names in the newspapers. They took up arms to deliver their country, not for glory and emolument. As to aristocracy, we have yet to see a country where an aristocracy does not exist, and the only question is what it shall consist of—men endowed by the Creator with qualities which fit them to become leaders of society, or whether they shall be a vulgar, pinchbeck imitation of good society. Nowhere is there a more tyrannical and heartless aristocracy than that of the North, and as to their officers, the men have often complained of the contrast which their brutal tyranny presents to the gentlemanlike conduct of Southern officers to soldiers. No great merit is due Southern officers for this; for many of the privates are gentlemen by birth and station as much as their officers, and all are held in as high esteem by their country. All are engaged in the same holy cause, and if either class, as a class, have won superior honors, it is the privates, because they have no conceivable motive but patriotism to govern their conduct.

The reproach of aristocracy is an old one against the South, but it comes with a poor grace from the stiff and starched upstarts of Yankee society. The gentlemen and ladies of the South, like true gentlemen and ladies everywhere, are kind and unpretending in their manner to all and not afraid of compromising their dignity by courteous treatment of all classes. The Northern aristocrat, on the other hand, can be told a mile off by his stiff and icy demeanor and his ridiculous attempts to be lofty and exclusive. Such a person cannot generally go back many generations without stumbling over some of those mechanical callings which he professes to hold in such supreme contempt. From such aristocrats may the South long be delivered! Admiral Porter will have to send a good many more handbills before he can undermine the confidence which our rank and file have in their officers and the respect which they have for themselves.

CHARLESTON DAILY COURIER
August 15, 1863

FROM THE SOUTHWEST
CAPTURES ON THE BIG BLACK—YANKEE PLANTERS SENT TO TEXAS—AFFAIRS IN THE TRANS-MISSISSIPPI DEPARTMENT

Morton, Mississippi, 13th—Yesterday the 4th and 6th Texas Cavalry captured, on the other side of the Big Black River, some twenty-two Yankees, four wagons, eighteen mules, and brought them safely to this point. The prisoners belong to General Steele's division, of the V Army Corps. The enemy has withdrawn his pickets from this side of the Big Black.

General Dick Taylor captured thirty-five Yankee planters, who were engaged planting cotton for the Lincoln government. They have been sent to Texas for safekeeping.

The health of this army is improving finely and rapidly. Only six sick soldiers were sent off yesterday, and large numbers are returning from the hospitals daily. Absentees are also returning to their commands. The weather is excessively dry and warm.

A staff officer of General Kirby Smith's, who has just arrived here, says four transports laden with troops passed Rodney going up Friday. The troops sent down by Grant were to replace the troops whose term of service had expired in Bank's army.

General Price is at Pine Bluff, Arkansas, and General Dick Taylor's army at Berwick Bay. General Taylor, on last Tuesday, sank two transports near Donaldsonville, Louisiana.

General Kirby Smith's headquarters are at Shreveport, Louisiana. He has issued a call to the governors of the Trans-Mississippi Department to meet him at Marshall, Texas, on the 15th.

The governor of Texas has taken the field with ten thousand state troops.

General Magruder's headquarters are at Galveston.

NEWS FROM THE ISLANDS

During Thursday night a continued fire was kept up between the land batteries and at intervals became very rapid and heavy. On Friday morning the enemy fired a few shells at Fort Sumter from the two mortar hulks which they have grounded on the beach, opposite their nearest battery to Fort Wagner. The shells, however, fell far short of the mark. After this exhibition the enemy remained quiet the rest of the day, our side still sending them an occasional shell from Battery Simkins. About half past eight o'clock last night another fierce cannonade opened between batteries Gregg and Wagner and the Yankee batteries on Craig's Hill. This firing was unusually rapid. It was reported that Battery Wagner gave the enemy the benefit of some new guns of heavier caliber, the fire from which is believed to have been very effectual. The cannonading was still going on with some rapidity at the hour of writing, viz: twelve o'clock at night. We could hear of no casualties.

[UNTITLED]

There are persons who seem to take a malicious pleasure in circulating evil reports. They hear the bad tidings, and altogether regardless of the character of their authority, they go forth and spread them far and near.

They are assisted in their bad work by another class of newsmongers composed of brainless, conceited creatures, who delight in giving utterance to bad news, simply because it makes them appear to know more than others. There are others who try the patience of everybody with sense and courage by proclaiming every unpleasant rumor that reaches their ear for no other reason than that they cannot keep their tongue still. If they did not open their mouth and let the thing flow out, they would burst.

No matter what the motive that prompts to the promulgation of groundless rumors, their circulation should be condemned by public sentiment. Whether the report be concerning military movement, or some reverse, or some unfavorable circumstance, or the conduct of officers or men while in the discharge of important and dangerous duties, the wise and true patriot will not aid in disseminating it until satisfied it is true, and in many cases, though convinced of its truth, judgment and generosity will restrain the right-minded and generous from repeating it.

NORTH

BOSTON EVENING TRANSCRIPT
August 15, 1863

LETTER FROM WASHINGTON

From an Occasional Correspondent

Washington, August 13, 1863

A timely east wind, accompanied by rain, has so far reduced the temperature as to enable one to write. The "heated term" through which we have passed has exceeded anything of the kind known for the past thirty years, at least so say those reliable people, the oldest inhabitants. One remarkable feature of the torrid (or horrid) spell has been the persistency with which the heat has pestered us during the entire twenty-four hours, being just as bad, and often seeming worse, at night than in the daytime, thereby preventing any sleep and provoking much imprecation. We had all taken to prophesying epidemics, thoughts of the attacks of which, though not creating so much panic, were acknowledged to be worse than the raids of Rebels. But at last, thank heaven, we have a change of regime and the rain reigneth.

I don't suppose your readers will object to learning what is thought in Washington of the present aspect of affairs. At no period during the war has government felt so hopeful and confident. The lull which is taking place is but the time of preparation for earnest work. The government is beginning to feel its own strength and is determined to exercise it. This is seen in the retaliatory measures for the officers condemned to death by the Rebels and for the Massachusetts colored troops captured at Charleston; in the firmness with which the president informs Governor Seymour that the draft will be proceeded with; and in the vigor with which the authorities have commenced the prosecution of cases of fraud against government, and which till now have been supposed to pass by —not unnoticed, however—because there was enough else to do.

The siege of Charleston is looked upon as a matter of time. Preparations have been and are still making, which cannot but ensure the success of the undertaking. There will be no underrating the strength of the place besieged, no rash attempt to achieve a brilliant success, but steady, solid work and hard fighting. If Lee sends reinforcements, so can we— if they have heavy guns, we have or will get heavier ones. The fall of Charleston has been decided upon, and the people may rest assured *it will be accomplished*.

Certain movements are taking place in the armies West, which have a much wider significance than it would be proper to publish. When another campaign opens, the victorious troops of Grant may have opportunities of winning new renown upon another field. The Army of the Potomac is to be reorganized, and the work has already been begun. The refilling of the old regiments with conscripts is regarded as equivalent to sending double the number of raw troops into the field in new regiments. The freshness of the new troops, whose minds are not warped by idolatry of this or that general, will exercise a healthy influence upon the morale of the army; and from the skill and experience of the veterans the recruits can readily learn the manual and how to adapt themselves to circumstances.

The canards started by the *New York Herald* about war with England and trouble with France are mere bubbles blown from the pipes of the children who play on the doorsteps of that paper's editorial rooms in this city. The children have hardly time to admire their bubbles before they break over their heads and the lies hidden in the vapory globes fall at their feet.

The condition of our foreign relations is not considered as affording cause for apprehension. The policy adopted by the secretary of state is the result of mature deliberation, and arrived at by throwing aside all feeling and prejudices and simply asking what is for the best good of the country at the present time. Mr. Seward has been accused of figuring for a political future. A remark of his made recently may be introduced here, which is at least a happy statement of the present state of affairs. The remark was to the effect that "it would be quite as reasonable and profitable for a man to undertake, in the existing state of the country, to speculate upon any political schemes for the future as it would have been for Noah and his sons to have attempted to lay out and speculate in corner lots on Mount Ararat while floating around in the ark."

The financial condition of the country is, as has been stated, much better than the former accepted estimates of the public debt showed. The return of Mr. Chase brings the assurances of the moneyed interests of the North that there will be no difficulty in obtaining whatever means may be required for the use and support of the government.

Reports to the General Land Office show a rapid increase of settlements in the far West, which seems almost incredible, with such a war raging. The indications now are that Puget Sound will become the Mediterranean Sea of America and that a direct trade with China and Japan will make the extreme Northwest a golden field for enterprise.

The returns of the state of crops for July to the Agricultural Bureau show very favorable. They will soon be made public.

It seems to me this is quite a hopeful and cheering letter. Now, don't let us have any more hanging down of heads and moanings of "Tomorrow and tomorrow; and tomorrow never comes," but let us all rejoicingly sing—"It will all be right in the morning"—for it will.

NEW YORK TRIBUNE
August 15, 1863

NEWS OF THE DAY: THE WAR

We learn from James Robson, who recently made his escape from Mobile, Alabama, that every available man has been impressed into the service to defend the place. He calculated that the Home Guard numbered about eighteen thousand men. The Rebels, he says, have three floating batteries with four guns on each—four rams, two of which mount four guns, and two, six guns each. One of these rams was incomplete when he left, yet a large number of men were at work thereon, ten dollars a day being paid each for this labor. They have also one big steamer, cotton-lined, carrying two or three guns, and three side-wheel steamers alternately keeping watch between Fort Morgan and the city.

Mr. Robson says that the Rebs are building an enormous ship up the Alabama River, with which they calculate to raise the blockade. She was nearly finished when he left, and was pierced for thirty or forty guns of large caliber. Beside this fleet, they have two torpedo vessels. Robson made his escape in a blockade runner, being secreted in the hold by a friend. The steamer wouldn't employ him in his capacity as fireman, for fear that he would leave at Havana, whither they continually went; nor would the provost marshal take him as a conscript, because he was a native of England.

Judge Advocate General Waterbury stated to the Board of Councilmen yesterday that the draft would commence in this city on Wednesday next. He also stated that he should go to Albany today to get the governor to telegraph to the president to allow men to volunteer to be substitutes immediately, so that recruiting substitute offices may be opened, and thus prevent men from being taken away, as is now constantly the case, to fill orders from other cities.

The bark *Growler* cleared yesterday from Boston with a cargo of ice purchased by the government for the soldiers and sailors at Charleston.

General Dodge is still quite sick at Memphis, but no danger is apprehended.

We have New Orleans dates to the 7th instant. No news of importance.

The Rebel general Holmes died of delirium tremens a few days since.

TERMS OF PEACE

Most intelligent readers are aware that in a confidential letter to Mr. Colorado Jewett last winter, in hearty response to his solicitations that we should do our best to restore peace to this afflicted land, we warned him that there must be no negotiations or conditions on the side of the Union save by the Federal government and its agents duly accredited to this end. Although, when that letter was written, we did not expect it would ever be published, its suggestions were founded in settled convictions, which we shall not lightly depart from. When, therefore, we are asked to enter publicly upon such discussions as we then pronounced contraband, our response is already indicated. Months ago, when it seemed proper and useful to do so, we fully expressed and defended our conviction that the president of the United States has not enslaved himself by his humane and glorious war edict of emancipation; that he is and ever has been at perfect liberty to accept the submission of the Rebels on such terms as he shall at the time judge expedient and right. The necessary effect of that war edict on the legal *status* of those whom it declared free is a question for the courts and will doubtless in due time receive their profoundest consideration. If—as good men have held—it has made them all legally free, then no future stipulation of the president, no action of the Federal government, can possibly affect that consummation, for no man has ever yet contended that the power to enslave freemen is among those conferred on that government or any part of it. And it seems to us very clear that popular and journalistic discussion of hypothetical terms of "reconstruction" in the loyal states can do no good. Whenever those now or hitherto in rebellion in any state, territory, county, district, or city shall propose unconditionally to return to loyalty, we trust that they will be unconditionally welcomed; if any shall propose to submit on certain specified terms, we undoubtingly trust that those terms will be promptly and earnestly considered by the government, with an anxious desire to find them consistent with national safety and public faith. Those who see how they can do good by urging or opposing the acceptance of these conditions will do so, but we shall probably see fit to leave the question to the unembarrassed action of the president, in whose sagacity, humanity, and patriotism we implicitly confide. This position does not satisfy the *World,* which in its last issue assails us as follows:

> **THE TRIBUNE AND THE SOUTH**
>
> The *Tribune* preserves an obstinate silence in the midst of the renewed general discussion of "terms of reconstruction." It has nothing to say upon the subject of the policy proper to be pursued toward a reduced and relenting rebellion. That the *Tribune* should shrink from the thought of seeing the Union reconstructed as of old is natural enough. This everybody can easily comprehend. But that the *Tribune* should be equally indifferent to the prospect, in which the scathed soul of Sumner rejoices, of beholding the defeated South led in chains by Negroes, a company of conquered territories, each ancient state shorn of its sovereign honors, may appear to require explanation. The explanation is ready and obvious. The *Tribune* wishes to have no further political connection of any kind with the South. It is now what it always has been, the firmest ally of the party of secession.

Before we begin to answer this tirade, let us ask the *World* why, if the *Tribune* "has always been the firmest ally of the party of secession," Mr.

Jefferson Davis still keeps our two correspondents—captured months ago while running his batteries at Vicksburg—in his Richmond prison, while the *World*'s man was speedily released and allowed to come home?[23] There is no pretense that our correspondents have specially offended him in any way; their sole crime, in his eyes, is their connection with the *Tribune*. If, then, he thus treats "the firmest ally of the party of secession," who would not rather be that party's enemy?

And now, as to "seeing the Union reconstructed as of old," let us make a statement of naked facts:

A prominent Democrat who lives and does business in our city (and whose name, not for publication but for the verification of this statement, is at the service of the *World*) was induced some years since to buy an estate in eastern Virginia reputed rich in gold. He employed a foreman to develop it, hired twenty-five or thirty of the poor whites residing upon or adjacent to it to assist as laborers, and came here to attend to other business. But a few weeks had elapsed when he received a dispatch from his foreman, urging him to hurry back to Louisa County and help the said foreman out of trouble. He promptly obeyed and, soon after reaching his estate, was waited upon by three gentlemen, who proclaimed themselves a committee from the neighboring proprietors, appointed to notify him that he must not employ white labor on his estate but must hire or buy slaves. He ventured to remonstrate—urged that he had imported no laborers into Virginia, that his men were all natives of the state and fixed residents of the vicinage, etc., but was cut short by the spokesman (now the Rebel general Jenkins), with a curt reminder that they had not proposed to argue the point—that it was not the policy of Virginia to encourage white labor where slaves were to be had—and that they only desired to know whether he proposed to comply with their demand or take the consequences of refusal. Here one of the white laborers—a respectable, worthy citizen, over fifty years old, who happened to be present or passing—ventured to interpose the query: "But what are we to do to support our families?" "Don't you know enough to hold your tongue?" responded the scion of chivalry, with such a look as he might have bestowed on a toad who had undertaken to

23. On May 3, 1863, while attempting to follow a reported move by General Grant toward Vicksburg, Mississippi, the *Tribune* correspondents Albert Richardson and Junius Browne and the *World* correspondent Richard Colburn were captured by the Confederates. Colburn was released, but Richardson and Browne were imprisoned because of their affiliation with the *Tribune*. After twenty months' captivity, the pair escaped from Salisbury Prison in North Carolina on December 18, 1864, and walked some four hundred miles to reach the Union lines in Tennessee.

lecture him on trigonometry. The poor white was cowed into abject silence; the New Yorker said that he had no choice, so he submitted with the best possible grace, dismissed his white Virginians to their sorry huts and ragged, unschooled children, and proceeded to hire the Negroes of his domineering neighbors, as he needs must. He was paying the whites eighty cents in cash per day; they told him they would gladly work for sixty cents rather than be thrown off; but though he wanted their work and they wanted his money, they were all under the yoke of an iron despotism and had to succumb.

Such is the infernal, God-defying, man-debasing system which the white laborers of this city are now being goaded by Fernando Wood and Horatio Seymour into treason to uphold and perpetuate—and all because those reckless aspirants believe their own chances of political aggrandizement will thereby be promoted![24] May the lightnings of divine justice blast their fiendish ambition!

Now, the *Tribune* does *not* desire that this country shall now or ever be divided, but *does* most anxiously, fervently labor and strive that the whole and every part of it shall be freed from the blighting curse of the diabolical "institution" which robbed those poor white Virginians of their right to labor, of education, competence, comfort, and self-respect—and has probably ere this driven them into the Rebel armies to suffer hardships and risk their lives for their own deadliest foe, the chief cause of their lifelong degradation. And we undeniably cherish the hope that this gigantic, wicked rebellion, fomented and inaugurated by the slave power for its own aggrandizement and fortification, may result in its most signal, righteous, utter, beneficent overthrow. Yet we do not say, and have never said, that no peace must be made that does not stipulate for and secure the immediate abolition of slavery. The fortunes of war do not always enable the righteous party in a great struggle to insist on every iota of justice. But this we *do* say: Any peace which attempts to restore to slavery the consideration, respect, and power which it enjoyed before it rushed into rebellion and civil war will prove an illusion and a snare—will be regarded by the baffled, mortified slave power as but a truce, a breathing spell, an opportunity for preparation in view of a new struggle wherein to wipe out the remembrance of its defeats, its losses, and its humiliations; and will inevitably subject the sincere Unionists of the entire South to systematic tyranny, abuse, out-

24. Fernando Wood, Tammany Hall politician and Peace Democrat, served as congressman and mayor of New York City. Horatio Seymour, a Democrat, served as governor of New York and was defeated by Grant in the 1868 presidential election.

rage, robbery, maiming, and murder, until the last of them shall have been hunted out or exterminated. Such are the inevitable results of a proslavery "reconstruction"—and such is the consummation toward which Wood, Seymour, their confederates, and their dupes are now drifting our country. May a merciful God yet avert the catastrophe!

SEPTEMBER 19, 1863

SOUTH

RICHMOND DAILY DISPATCH
September 19, 1863

FROM TENNESSEE

Special Correspondence of the *Dispatch*
Salem, Roanoke County, Virginia
September 15, 1863

We arrived here in the pleasant village situated in the fertile Roanoke Valley today at noon, and as we shall be detained till night, I have concluded to indulge in a few jottings, which, if they do not prove interesting, may serve to while away time. Almost everyone has heard of the famous Roanoke Valley, noted, among many other things, as the birthplace of the eccentric and widely known John Randolph of Roanoke; but no one who has never been here can form the faintest idea of the beauty of this serene and quiet spot—surrounded on every side by lofty mountains, now clothed in living green—the fields around divided in farms, on which are generally neat farmhouses, inhabited by a generous and hospitable people, who seem to live and move amid plenty. A feeling of envy cannot fail to rise in the heart of the man of the thickly inhabited city, who is continually bent on the everlasting chase of the almighty dollar. The contrast is so great that it may be said to be indescribable.

O. K.

Wytheville, Virginia, September, 16, 1863

This morning we find ourselves at the county seat of Wythe, but hear of nothing in the vicinity which would prove interesting to your readers. The down-mail train passed us at 6:00 A.M., and from passengers, many of whom are refugees, we learn that apprehensions exist at Bristol of an

genuine. Mr. Memminger's eyes appear in the counterfeit rather popped instead of sunken, as in the genuine. The date of this counterfeit is September 2, 1861.

CHARLESTON DAILY COURIER
September 19, 1863

THE EVIL OF THE DAY

From the *Richmond Whig*

It is painfully evident, as a Southern contemporary says, that the degrading passion of avarice has been developed, during this war and among our people, on a scale of unprecedented magnitude. It has not been limited to interests or classes. It has not been the vicious peculiarity of the trader. It has not been the characteristic only of the money changer. It has spread its deleterious influence to the producer. It has even seized for its prey some of the gentler sex, and not entirely omitted the ministers of Him who had not where to lay His head. It has thus been a moral epidemic that has diffused its poison through nearly all the veins and arteries of the body politic. The restoration of healthy moral functions to the diseased social constitution has been an office vainly exercised by pulpit and press.

The general cause of this evil has no doubt been bad legislation. It has been stimulative, instead of repressive, of this base passion. The war would under any state of circumstances have brought out moral irregularities that are always produced by the suspension of regular habits of industry and trade, but our system of legislation furnished additional incentives to the civil tendency that only required the hand of the legislator to perfect the work.

The creation of a scheme of redundant paper money has been the chief source of this moral iniquity. Our people have been seduced into the channels of illegal enterprise—of spurious adventure. They have become speculators and extortioners by the deceptious bait—which has put on the semblance of riches—of paper money. It has proved a delusion, because the imagined wealth has taken to itself wings and flown away. With every addition to the gains of traffic in a constantly depreciating medium there has been a correspondent loss in the rise of prices. At the close of the struggle to become wealthy without increase of thrift or exertion, what were deemed stores of opulence will leave the parties no richer than before.

But it may be alleged that paper money was our only instrument of deliverance—that it was a financial necessity. Our reply is that it became a necessity—an imperative, sad necessity from the neglect of sound principles of legislation. If, instead of making paper money the basis of our system of finance, this basis had been taxation, we could have created a superstructure of paper money of such proportions as would not have threatened the overthrow of the whole edifice. To speak without metaphor, we reversed all safe principle. Instead of commencing with a scheme of taxation that would have a solid foundation for such emissions of paper money as would have been the *auxiliary* and not the *principal* means of the treasury—we delayed our system of direct and internal taxation until the sources of wealth had been largely impaired, the currency had been almost irremediably depreciated, and public credit greatly weakened. That which ought to have been done at the commencement we have been compelled to do in the sequel. We have thus inverted the order of financial proceedings. We have made our floating debt, instead of our funded debt, the bulk of our engagements. We have, in consequence, proceeded from one stage of depreciation to another and inflicted an irreparable blow on the public morals.

NORTH

BOSTON EVENING TRANSCRIPT
September 19, 1863

FROM THE DEPARTMENT OF THE GULF
NEWS OF THE LATE EXPEDITIONS—
FEDERAL DISASTER AT SABINE PASS

New York, 19th—The *World*'s New Orleans letter of the 11th instant contains important intelligence. It states: Last week, from 10,000 to 15,000 men were conveyed by the Opelousas Road from Algiers to Brashear City and to Bayou Boeuf, the whole force under the command of General Washburn.

Almost simultaneously Herron's men moved up the Mississippi toward Red River; General Franklin's division, in the meanwhile, embarked in transports here and at the camps above near Carrollton and moved down the river toward the Gulf. It was therefore a combined movement by three distinct columns and by three routes.

The three routes, this correspondent suggests, were: Franklin's corps, going by transports by way of the Gulf, would advance to Sabine Pass, the boundary line on the Gulf between this state and Texas; Herron's men, going by way of Red River to Simmesport, would march from thence to Opelousas or to New Iberia, while Washburn's column crossed Berwick Bay and made the old movement via Pattersonville, along the Teche.

When Franklin's men went down the river and Washburn's corps moved by the railroad to Brashear and Bayou Boeuf a week ago today, the two Federal gunboats *Clifton* and *Sachem* moved down Berwick Bay to the Gulf. Franklin's transports were accompanied by three gunboats, the *Arizona,* the *Quaker City,* and the *St. Charles,* I think.

Herron's column was taken by steamboats to the mouth of the Red River to go to Simmesport.

Until today, beyond rumors we have heard nothing definite from the movement. This evening it was well-known in the city that a number of vessels, chartered as transports for the movement, had been discharged or released from the engagement.

LATER

We know of thc arrival of one or two of General Franklin's transports from Sabine Pass and learned that others were coming up the river. At the same time some of the vessels that went in the expedition came back to Berwick Bay and landed the troops at Brashear City.

The 12th Connecticut Regiment, which was lately withdrawn from Brashear to Algiers, was ordered back again today, and two regiments only of General Weitzel's division, under command of Acting Brigadier General Brig, of the 18th Connecticut, remained in camp near Thibodaux.

From various sources tonight we gain the following authentic information about the movement:

The *Clifton,* at Brashear, took aboard two companies of the 75th New York Regiment, and when she and the *Sachem* moved down the bay, the Rebel colonel Majus's force at Camp Brisland, watching the movement, immediately moved to Vermilion Bay to repel the entrance of the Federal force at that point. In the event of their not entering that bay, it is known to have been Majus's intention to push on to Sabine Pass.

Day before yesterday the gunboats arrived at the pass, the *Clifton* taking the lead and the *Sachem* following. When they got in, they were exposed to a raking fire from both sides of the bay. It is not known that Majus had arrived, but Sabine Pass was well fortified, and the armament consisted of the heaviest siege guns.

Captain Crocker of the *Clifton* fired a broadside, and in turning to fire the other broadside, his boat grounded and stuck fast on the flat. He was exposed to a very heavy fire. Some of the soldiers or sailors on board ran up a white flag without Crocker's orders. In view of his hopeless condition, Captain Crocker turned one of his largest guns and fired through the machinery, completely disabling the gunboat. He then spiked his guns.

In the meanwhile, two Rebel gunboats came down and captured the *Sachem*. Franklin's gunboats and transports entered the pass just in time to see the last of the brief action. One or two soldiers escaped from the *Clifton* and swam toward Franklin's transport and were taken aboard. They say there was not a man in the aft part of the *Clifton* who was not killed or wounded by the Rebel fire. Those remaining on board were, of course, taken prisoners.

Captain Johnson and his men of the *Sachem* were also taken prisoner. The *Clifton* is believed to be a wreck, and useless to the Rebels.

This disaster, the low stage of water, and the quite unexpected formidable resistance no doubt induced General Franklin to run back again and abandon that part of the expedition.

The news first reached us by a gunboat arriving from Sabine Pass at Brashear City and thence by telegraph to this city.

Herron's men have not been heard from today. Up to this evening not a regiment had crossed the bay from Brashear.

The arrival of the transports here today should give us full details of the Sabine Pass affair in time for the *Columbia*'s mail tomorrow. It is believed that the movement will now begin de novo—General Franklin's corps going to Brashear and the army there moving across the bay to follow the old track along the Teche.[26]

DISTRICT COURT OF THE UNITED STATES

The grand jury of this court, for the September term, made their report this afternoon. They returned twenty-six indictments against various parties. William Cooke was indicted for presenting to a United States paymaster a paper with the false signature of Assistant Adjutant General Thrall, of the Army of the Cumberland, for the purpose of obtaining pay alleged to be due him as a soldier.

Isaac Brown was indicted for carrying on the business of a lawyer in Lynn, without a license from the proper officer under the Internal Revenue Act.

26. de novo: Latin, "from new," meaning "from the beginning."

Barnard Doyle was indicted for aiding and counseling resistance to the draft. Doyle was arrested by the police for haranguing a mob in South Street during the day of the Cooper Street riot, stating that he would give all he was worth to prevent drafted men from being taken out of Boston.

James Gibbens, Henry McLanglen, John West, Patrick Sweeney, and others were indicted for aiding resistance to the draft. These are the parties who in Prince Street, it is charged, began the assault upon Messrs. Howe and Wilkins, the enrolling officers engaged in distributing the notices to drafted men, requiring them to report to the headquarters of the provost marshal. This assault was the initiative of the occurrences which culminated in the attack upon the Cooper Street Armory.

Thomas Murphy and Miles Lee were indicted for enticing and procuring soldiers to desert from the conscript camp at Long Island.

Edward Pratt and Joshua Daniels were indicted for endeavoring to induce two United States soldiers—enlisted in Pittsfield—to desert from the service.

Thomas Eckels was indicted for carrying on a retail liquor business without a license under the Internal Revenue Act.

Besides these indictments, others were found against officers of different vessels for illegal punishment of sailors, and one against a person for the destruction of certain letters confided to his care.

Before separating, the grand jury passed the following resolution:

"*Resolved,* That the members of the grand jury hereby tender their thanks to Assistant District Attorney Lothrop for the uniform courtesy and consideration which has marked his intercourse with them, and for the excellent manner in which he has conducted the causes which the jury have investigated with his assistance."

Resolutions were also adopted complimenting the foreman and clerk of the jury for the way in which they had performed the duties devolving upon them.

NEW YORK TRIBUNE
September 19, 1863

BARBARITIES IN WAR

The *Daily News,* in the course of an essay on "The Barbarities of War," says:

> There seems to be literally at the North an entire oblivion of the ordinary instincts of a common humanity. It is only when the

> poisoned chalice they have extended to others is lifted to their own lips that they cry out with well-simulated horror. The town of Lawrence is sacked and many of its inhabitants brutally murdered.[27] It is clearly unjustifiable by all the rules of modern warfare. It is directly in violation of those laws of civilization, an observance of which can alone exalt a nation. It is attended, however, with no *grosser acts of atrocity and brutality than the burning of several Southern cities we might name,* and we remember full well that Northern Republican presses justified these acts of Northern vandalism. The burning and sacking of Lawrence is but the result of the wicked lessons we have been giving to the South.

The *News,* though to all intents and purposes a Rebel organ, is published in New York and edited by a Democratic member of the last and of the next Union Congress. Its assertions will therefore be accepted in Europe, not as the Rebel calumnies they truly are, but as *Union admissions*. In behalf, therefore, of our country, her defenders, and of truth, we brand the assertion placed above in italics as a wanton, wicked, atrocious calumny and demand its specific retraction. It is not merely a lie with circumstance, but a lie inspired by treason, such as should subject its author and his backers not merely to disgrace but to punishment.

Lawrence was an interior city, totally unarmed and ungarrisoned, and possessing no shadow of strategic or military importance, utterly unsuspicious of danger, when a Rebel guerrilla band, raised entirely and far within the Union lines, among a population ostensibly loyal, in a region where no Rebel flag had openly floated for months, stole across the Missouri border unobserved and, being well mounted and moving rapidly by night, fell upon the sleeping inhabitants just at daylight, surrounded their several dwellings, dragged or drove out the inmates, and murdered in cold blood every adult male, and then burned the houses after plundering them of all that could be carried off. There was no resistance, no military array in defense of the doomed city—nothing but the base and cowardly murder of civilians dragged from their beds.

Now, if the Union forces have ever burned "several Southern cities" under circumstances rivaling these in "atrocity and brutality," the *News* would have given names and dates instead of dealing in vague generalities. It is indefinite because it is consciously false. Its only approach to a specification imports that Charleston was shelled unwarrantably

27. On August 21, 1863, William Quantrill and his Confederate bushwhackers killed 150 residents of Lawrence, Kansas. Quantrill trained the outlaws Jesse James and Cole Younger and was mortally wounded by Federal troops in Kentucky on May 10, 1864.

by General Gillmore. But Charleston is a strongly fortified seaport—a place of the greatest strategic importance—and had been formidably blockaded for many months and earnestly besieged for some weeks before a shell was thrown into it. It had not merely been forewarned by General Gillmore of the shelling, but its commander had publicly ordered noncombatants to quit it days before. So the Welshman's parallel between Monmouth and Macedon ran on all fours in comparison with any that can be instituted between the sack of Lawrence and the shelling of Charleston.

GENERAL ROSECRANS'S CAMPAIGN

General Rosecrans's advance since the occupation of Chattanooga has been steadily pushed. His plan for the seizure of that stronghold was conceived and developed in such a way as to make the possession of what was really his first objective point incidental to the progress of the comprehensive campaign which contemplates the complete military occupation of the mountain regions of northern Georgia and the final capture of Atlanta. The columns which flanked Chattanooga on the south and west were in the direct line of advance to Rome, which is itself a long step toward Atlanta, connected with it by railroad, and of very great intrinsic importance as the site of extensive powder mills and other manufactories. It will be remembered as the point aimed at, and nearly reached, by the ill-fated expedition under Colonel Streight, the destruction of its mills being then the chief object in view.

Like the campaigns which General Rosecrans has previously executed, the present is gigantic in extent and beset with inconceivable difficulties. He operates in a mountain region, over roads nearly impassable, and often over mountains which no road has ever crossed, putting great distances between his separate columns, and still greater between them and their bases of supplies, and confronting at every step obstacles which to a less resolute commander would seem insurmountable. It follows, of course, that such a campaign is a work of time, and its progress is with difficulty traceable until its object is attained. For general information, it is sufficient to indicate its purpose and to explain the value and relation of the points toward which the Army of the Cumberland is pressing forward. Moreover, concerning the forces, movements, and plans of the Rebel commanders, there has been little trustworthy intelligence since the evacuation of Chattanooga. It is only known—at least it is positively stated—that Bragg and Johnston have united and that a stubborn resistance to Rosecrans's advance is still contemplated.

Atlanta is the last link which binds together the southwestern and northeastern sections of the Rebel Confederacy. Break it, and those sections fall asunder. The two systems of southwestern railway communication centered at Chattanooga, and the conquest of that place and Knoxville severed the northern line. Between the former and the present capitals of the Confederacy, Montgomery and Richmond, there is now no railway communication, except by the road which turns east at Atlanta and runs to Augusta, thence by two lines reaching northwardly into Virginia; and even portions of these are held by the most precarious tenure. Of course, with the capture of Atlanta, this system is also broken up, and since the capture of Atlanta involves also the subjugation of northern Georgia, the present campaign of General Rosecrans aims at nothing less than the military isolation of Mississippi, Alabama, and Georgia from the remaining states of South Carolina, North Carolina, and Virginia. The southern portion of Georgia indeed cannot be affected by this success, but may speedily find itself threatened from another quarter.

It is with reference to the results of this campaign of General Rosecrans, not less than to the movements of General Meade, that the defensive attitude of the Rebel army in Virginia has been maintained. Over territory so vast as that of Mississippi, Alabama, and Georgia, railways are the only possible means of connected operations on a large scale, and the loss of their last railroad is therefore to the Rebels the loss of the states for all purposes of military cooperation. They have lost Kentucky, lost Tennessee, and if these other three go with them, the resources of the rebellion, whether of men or supplies, are too much contracted to support a military establishment of such magnitude as the present. And since Lee, with his present forces, is able to hold General Meade at bay, it seems more than ever probable that the decisive battle for the possession of Richmond is to be fought neither on the Rappahannock nor on the Rapidan, but in the heart of Georgia, five hundred miles to the south and west.

It is too soon to express an opinion on the probable strategy of Bragg and Johnston, for there is nothing to show decisively whether their campaign is meant to be strategically defensive, or whether the preservation of their army has become their principal object. In view of the considerations already suggested, the utter abandonment of Atlanta is not probable, nor do we believe it will voluntarily occur. Whether it may not fall as Chattanooga fell is another question; but its remoteness is so great, and its topographical features so materially different, that General Rosecrans can hardly be expected to repeat his former strategy. He is more likely to direct his attention in the first place especially to the Rebel army, with the purpose of compelling a battle, and postpone until after a decisive victory the occupation of Atlanta. If he means to force Bragg to fight, the features of the campaign may undergo many changes before our general finally sets his face southward. But it is to be always kept in mind that any strategy on the part of the Rebel leaders which does not cover Atlanta, and which is not meant to hold that place to the last moment, is for them as significant a confession of defeat, and is as pregnant with disaster, as if their standard went down on the battlefield and their arms were piled in front of a victorious national army.

OCTOBER 17, 1863

SOUTH

RICHMOND DAILY DISPATCH
October 17, 1863

THE ENEMY IN BRISTOL—OUR FORCE FALLEN BACK

Special Dispatch to the *Dispatch*

Lynchburg, Virginia, 16th—The enemy occupied Bristol, Tennessee, Wednesday evening, and our forces fell back to a point in the vicinity of Abingdon, where there was fighting this evening—the result unknown.[28]

The enemy's force is estimated at between 6,000 and 8,000, composed of Foster's brigade of cavalry and four or five regiments of east Tennessee Tories.

They are all doubtless endeavoring to get possession of the salt-works, with the intention of holding Bristol as a base for future operations.

O. K.

FROM EAST TENNESSEE

Lynchburg, Virginia, 16th—The *Lynchburg Virginian* has the following from east Tennessee:

> Before the battle of Chickamauga, twenty-seven regiments of Yankee cavalry and mounted infantry, estimated at fourteen thou-

28. Abingdon, Virginia.

sand, passed Greenville, Tennessee, bound eastward, with the intention of making a raid on the Virginia and Tennessee Railroad. Upon receiving intelligence of the defeat at Chickamauga, they retreated west, to reinforce Rosecrans, and were met by our forces at Loudon and Sweetwater, and here driven back. A portion of this force attacked our forces at Bible Ridge, six miles west of Greenville, on Saturday, the 10th. Our men fought gallantly, defeating and inflicting severe loss on the enemy—our loss in the engagement, fifty killed and two hundred wounded. Apprehensive of a flank movement, our force withdrew to Henderson, ten miles east of Greenville. Another engagement took place there, and at Rheatown on Sunday, in which our forces fought desperately, cutting their way through four regiments of the enemy, who, supported by artillery, had succeeded in reaching our rear. Our men fell back to Zollicoffer until the Yankees, heavily reinforced, advanced upon them, when they were withdrawn to Bristol.

Our loss in both days' fights is estimated at 300 killed and wounded. Numbers of the wounded fell into the hands of the enemy. Captain Battle and several others, wounded at Rheatown, have arrived here. The Union men of east Tennessee say the Yankee loss is estimated at 1,200 killed and wounded.

On Wednesday night the enemy arrived at Bristol, and are reported to have advanced toward Abingdon yesterday with a heavy force, supposed to number 8,000 or 10,000. Joe Hooker commands in east Tennessee. Burnside has left, having been dismissed or resigned. Three regiments of Tennessee renegades have been organized, and four thousand refugees are following the Yankee army. The enemy destroyed no property in east Tennessee, as they expect to hold the country permanently.

FROM GORDONSVILLE

Gordonsville, Virginia, 16th—A severe battle is reported to have taken place near Catlett's Station on Wednesday. The enemy retreated toward Occoquan, where ten thousand of Sedgwick's corps were suddenly attacked by General ———, and it is reported that three thousand prisoners were captured. Further particulars not yet received.

Seventy-five more prisoners were brought here last night from Steppin's Springs, captured in the affair at Jefferson on Monday last.

Small squads of the enemy are frequently picked up in the country recently occupied by them.

Five Yankee conscripts hailed the returning cars from Rappahannock on Wednesday and voluntarily came aboard.

FROM CHARLESTON

Charleston, 16th—This is the ninety-eighth day of the siege.

A grand review of the troops by General Beauregard will take place today.

Nothing new this morning. Weather fair.

Second Dispatch

Charleston, 16th—General Beauregard, accompanied by General Pierre Soulé and staff, reviewed the troops of General Taliaferro's division this morning on James Island. The display was magnificent, and the troops presented an imposing appearance. The length of the line was about three miles. The banners of many of the regiments were inscribed with the names of battles in which they have been engaged.

Our batteries are firing about as usual today, the enemy making no reply. It is rumored that the Yankees have refused the French vessels outside permission to communicate.

NORTHERN NEWS

Petersburg, Virginia, 16th—The *New York Daily News* of the 14th, received here, says that the Pennsylvania and Ohio elections are still in doubt. The *News* believes both have gone Democratic, the former by seven thousand majority.

Five hundred of the wounded in the fights of Saturday and Sunday on the Rappahannock have reached Washington. Also six hundred sick.

Advices from New Orleans to the 3rd state that in the fight at Morganza, on the Mississippi, on the afternoon of the 29th, the Federals were repulsed and driven to the river, with a reported loss of between 1,500 and 2,000. Franklin has gone toward New Iberia or Vermilionville with the XVIII and XIX Corps, and bloody work is expected.

CHARLESTON DAILY COURIER
October 17, 1863

THE MILITARY ASPECT

While we are suffering under great and manifold evils, the result of insatiable greed for gain, if we can turn our eyes from these grievous ills and contemplate the aspect of military affairs, we shall find abundant reason why we should be of good cheer.

When the president of the Yankee states, after one of the most bloody battles of this war, and one in which his dead were numbered by thousands, alarmed at the boldness and power of his antagonist, made a peremptory call for 450,000 men, it was feared by not a few, and those persons of courage and judgment, that the large accession to his fighting force that draft would make would render it necessary for us to do battle against large and almost overwhelming odds. No one apprehended that the measure would augment the Yankee army by more than a third of the number specified. But even that addition furnished ground for some degree of uneasiness. Instead of swelling the hosts of the enemy to that formidable figure, we learn on the authority of his own hireling journals that the high-sounding proclamation has placed in the ranks of his army not more than between 35,000 and 40,000 men.

Disappointed, chagrined, and alarmed at the failure of that draft, the tyrant, firmly resolved to accomplish his iniquitous purposes, has made another call upon his subjects for twice the number demanded for the former instrument. In all likelihood, that tremendous conscription will be evaded to the same extent as the other. The former has not furnished a sufficient number of recruits to fill up the gaps made by the battles of Gettysburg and Chickamauga, and by the time those conscripts under the latter call are qualified to perform military service, the army will be so diminished by battles, disease, desertion, and the expiration of the periods of enlistment that they will barely suffice to bring the army up to its present numerical strength.

Though no race of people ever lived who loved money more ardently than the people who are doing their utmost to subdue and enthrall us, they whose names are drawn by the conscripting officer gladly parted with a portion of their substance in order to save themselves from Southern bullets. Most cheerfully did they pay the price required, and so general and intense was the desire to remain at home that associations were formed all over Yankeedom for the payment of the fines of such as were not able to purchase exemption. The miserable wretches who were compelled to clothe themselves in martial habiliments have no stomach for the contest and will certainly desert or take to their heels at the first opportunity.

The Irish and Germans, who at the first offered themselves so willingly as volunteers and substitutes, under the influence of lying promises and delusive hopes, weary of the hardships and miseries of a soldier's life, and satisfied that Southern soldiers are as brave and as constant as themselves, chose rather to labor in their accustomed vocations, and enjoy the comforts of home, to marching, digging, and fighting for wages that do not purchase as many potatoes as their family consumes daily.

The foreign population has determined to stand aloof from the quarrel, and the genuine Yankee must now come forth and make good his intemperate boasts and execute his direful threats. But the sons of the soil are not disposed to imperil their precious persons, even to gratify the venomous hatred and malice they delight to cherish against the South. They would like to have the work done for them—they would be pleased exceedingly could they see the brave, high-toned Southerner conquered, humiliated, enslaved—but they themselves are not disposed to perform their due share of this extremely difficult work. Having discovered that the foreign element is averse to fighting battles for them any longer, they have turned, in their extremity, to the Negro. Already they have several thousand ebony warriors, and if it be possible, the entire number called for by the Negro Regiment Bill will be forced into the army. They will get them, doubtless, for they have the power to compel "Americans of African descent" to enlist in the army. According to their most influential journals, the hope of consummating the great work in which they are engaged is grounded upon the courage and martial powers of their black-skinned soldiery. These redoubtable warriors, under Yankee officers, are to finish the work the Irish and Dutch began. Well, we shall see.

It is manifest, despite their accounts of the magnitude of their armies, that the men at present fighting under the Yankee banner compose a number far below the figures set down by their editors and correspondents. Before the battle of Chickamauga was fought, their papers represented Rosecrans's army as of sufficient strength to overwhelm and scatter the opposing force. That mighty host was to wipe out Bragg's small and contemptible force and march to Atlanta and overrun the state of Georgia. The subtle-minded captain failed miserably in attempting to carry out that magnificent program, and in the Yankee narrative of that conflict the defeat of their army is attributed to our large numerical superiority. The vast army that was to do such great things was suddenly placed in jeopardy by reason of its inadequate numbers, and Meade was obliged to send large reinforcements to his brother in distress, while he himself, who was to have marched upon Richmond, had to flee in hot haste toward Alexandria. Thus, their two largest and best-equipped armies are powerless: The one is fleeing before an antagonist whom he dreads; the other can neither advance nor retreat.

These facts are most pleasing to the patriot. Let us consider them with sentiments of gratitude and hope. God is working for us, and if we will only cooperate with Him to the extent of our ability, with cheerful earnestness, unflagging energy, and undaunted spirits, we shall triumph gloriously.

OUR ARMY CORRESPONDENCE

Lookout Mountain, near Chattanooga, Tennessee
October 7, 1863

In connection with the battle of Chickamauga, nothing has been written concerning one of the most gallant brigades in the western army and two of the best of South Carolina's regiments. I refer to the command of General Arthur Manigault, formerly the colonel of the 10th South Carolina Volunteers. A portion of this letter is therefore devoted to a narrative of its achievements, during and prior to the battle.

The brigade, as at present constituted, is composed of the 10th and 19th South Carolina regiments (consolidated), Colonel J. F. Pressley commanding, Lieutenant Colonel Julius T. Porcher, Major J. L. White, and Adjutant Ferrell; the 24th Alabama, Colonel N. M. Davis; 28th Alabama, Colonel J. C. Reid; 34th Alabama, Major J. N. Slaughter; and Waters's battery of artillery.

After leaving MacFarland's Spring, at the foot of Missionary Ridge, a few miles from Chattanooga, which for some time had been the camping ground of the brigade, the first active movements of the campaign commenced.[29]

On the 8th of September, the brigade moved under command of General Hindman, who, with his own division and the corps of General Buckner, had been ordered to make a reconnaissance in force, learn the position of the enemy in McLemore's Cove, and attack them. The latter, it is supposed, under the command of General McCook, of Ohio, had, by orders of Rosecrans, crossed the Lookout Mountain through one of its passes, with a view to making a left flank or rear demonstration, while Crittenden, with a similar corps, was advancing on our right toward Ringgold and Lafayette, to make a similar movement there and burn railroad and other bridges. General Thomas, with Rosecrans and the main body of the Federal army, remained in our front, doubtless watch-

29. Missionary Ridge: an Appalachian ridge overlooking Chattanooga, Tennessee; the site of the final battle of the Chattanooga campaign, October–November 1863.

ing for an opportunity to swoop down upon Bragg and destroy his army in detail.

After a march of fifteen miles, the enemy was discovered on the afternoon of the 10th instant. Our artillery was immediately brought forward and opened fire, preparatory to a general attack; but the Federals, evidently aware that our force was superior to their own, hastily retreated to a mountain pass, from which they could not be dislodged—one of the thousand strong positions in this Switzerland of our continent, which must be seen before their military value can be appreciated.

Failing to cut the Federals off, Hindman was now ordered to Lafayette and, on the evening of the 11th, received instructions to join General Polk, who was with Cheatham's division and the corps of General W.H.T. Walker, who were in the line of battle near Rocky Spring Church, not far from Pea Vine Ridge, and eight or ten miles directly north of Lafayette, on the Chattanooga Road. A long night march ensued, and at sunrise the destination was reached.

The wary enemy, however, had changed his position and, when sought for in the morning, was not to be found. Thus he had eluded his pursuers a second time, on both occasions having been offered battle with very nearly equal forces.

[The reader will properly surmise that it was the object of Bragg not less than that of Rosecrans to meet and whip his adversary in detail.]

On the 13th, Hindman's division, and probably other portions of the Confederate army, returned to Lafayette, where they remained until the night of the 17th. Orders were then again received to advance to the Chickamauga Creek, where, on arriving, the enemy was found in strong force posted on the opposite side in the vicinity of what is known as Lee's and Gordon's Mill. Hindman's division was there formed in line of battle. During that and the following day, skirmishing took place along our entire front, the troops on both sides being subjected to an annoying artillery fire from the contending batteries. Hindman's division at this time constituted the extreme left of the army.

On the 19th, battle was joined by the two armies, the firing commencing on the right and rolling steadily toward the left. About two o'clock the division commander received orders to push forward to General Polk's command. Marching about four miles, he crossed the river at Hunt's Ford and about five o'clock got within range of the enemy's artillery near that point. Soon after, the line was formed, and advanced to the front. Before getting fairly under the musketry fire, orders came to retire, which was done, and this portion of the line was then reformed in the following order—Hood on the right, Buckner on the left, and

Hindman in the center. The brigades of Hindman's division stood in the following order—Deas on the right, Manigault on the left, and Anderson supporting the two.

[The object of the present narrative being only to show that portion of the picture in which Manigault's brigade had a place, I have not attempted to give the general outline of the whole battle, which is reserved for another communication.]

On Sunday, Hindman's division, with Buckner's corps, was placed under General Longstreet, who commanded the left wing of the army. The battle commenced on the right, and the orders were that each brigade should move forward as the fight progressed from right to left. The tide of musketry was thus rolling on at half past eleven o'clock, regiment after regiment and brigade after brigade having previously gone into the bloody surge with varying success. The animating yells of our men mingling with the steady, ceaseless rattle of musketry and the heavy detonations of artillery told that the battle was at its flood, while floating above all, and enveloping the combatants until they were almost obscured from view, was a huge shroud of dust and smoke. Such was the contest into which Manigault's brigade—all true and trusty men—now that their time had come, plunged with a battle shout.

The three right regiments advancing found the enemy strongly posted in a dense wood, the two left regiments and Waters's battery being exposed in an open cornfield, but with a thick wood upon their left. The ground was uneven and ascended gradually in front, partaking of the broken and irregular character of the country.

The first notice of the position occupied by the Federals was on finding them confronting our line on the right at a distance of only eighty yards, the thickness of the woods and the recumbent attitude of the men preventing the discovery at an earlier moment. Instantly a fringe of fire leaped from the muzzles of our rifles, and then the fearful whir of bullets and the falling of the dead and wounded bespoke the fray commenced.

Manigault was now fighting on the extreme left of the entire army, a post at once of honor and of danger, but nobly maintained throughout. As far as he could see—to the length of a full brigade—the Federal line overlapped him and stretched away to the left. The firing from this superior force was harassing in the extreme, as well as that from a battery posted on the summit of the hill in our front, and required the strongest nerve and the best discipline to withstand. For a moment our men flinched before its fury; the line wavered and reeled like a broken ship in the grasp of a whirlwind, but, finally recovering, pressed forward.

The breastworks were carried, the artillery captured, and that portion of the field won.

General Manigault, however, finding that his left was still entirely exposed, the regiments there being overlapped by the Federal line and suffering severely from an enfilading fire, ordered the brigade to fall back about three hundred yards for the purpose of reforming his command and awaiting his support.[30]

Meanwhile, Deas and Anderson had likewise driven the enemy before them, and the latter, finding themselves about to be flanked on their left, also retired. There was now a brief breathing spell, during which Manigault advanced and rejoined the remainder of his division. After proceeding about half a mile, the enemy were again encountered —as before, admirably posted upon a ridge of commanding hills, and General Bushrod Johnson industriously engaging their attention. Manigault was at once ordered to his support. It was now about half past two o'clock. Again the battle raged thickly in the little brigade, and again it won new titles to honor.

At half past three o'clock, the order having been given to make a right half wheel for the purpose of enfilading the right of the Federal line, Manigault came in collision with a heavy force of fresh troops, and now ensued the most desperate struggle in which that brigade, or any other on the field during the day, were engaged. The enemy outnumbered us and held every advantage of position. Whipped elsewhere, they struggled like men who had cast their last die in the balance and were resolved "to meet the shuddering battle shocks until their lives ran ruddy rain." But they were encountered by braver soldiers than even they—by men whose banners were stirred by old battle memories —whose hearts held royal throbbings and beat with nobler blood, and in whose eyes was already flashing the light of another victory. Such troops were not to be conquered.

Time after time they were driven back by the overwhelming forces in front, yet, rallying, each fresh attack drove the enemy farther from his original position than before. Large numbers were here killed or wounded, and owing to the nature of the country, it being thickly wooded and much broken, it was almost impossible to preserve a regular line of battle. Nothing but the gallant conduct of the officers and men, individually, enabled them to sustain the heavy fire to which they were exposed. The different regiments became mixed with each other, and here and there the fainthearted were stealing to safer positions in

30. enfilading: raking (with gunfire) in a lengthwise direction.

the rear; still, there was no thought of defeat. Men fought from behind trees and coverts, loading and firing while they dodged from point to point, but always gaining ground. In short, the character of the battle at this juncture was that of skirmishing on a grand scale. Eventually the enemy were thus driven a distance of three fourths of a mile.

During this stubborn resistance, the colors of one of our regiments fell into the hands of the Federals. The flag of the 10th South Carolina was also captured during one of the attacks of the enemy, and its bearer, Sergeant Glysson, was killed, but the regiment rallying promptly in this emergency, the Federals were in turn attacked and the colors recaptured.

Such was the intensity of the fire that our cartridges were exhausted in the very heat of battle, but many of the brigade, unwilling to fall back, abandoned their own muskets and, seizing the rifles of the dead Yankees and stripping the ammunition boxes from the corpses, thus supplied their wants and, with the enemy's own guns and bullets, whipped them from the field.

About sunset the Federals were drawn from their last position, and a large number who had been partially surrounded by Manigault's brigade were captured by fresh troops just entering the field. Properly they were the prize of Manigault and his men, who had fought them during the most desperate hour of the day, but it is one of the fortunes of war that the trophy was snatched from his grasp by those not entitled to it, at the very moment it seemed ready to fall into our own grasp.

The battle ceased about sunset, at which time the Federals had been driven from every position on the left, a distance of two and a half miles, and that, too, not merely over an open plain, but across ravines, and from ridge to ridge, and wood to wood, where positions were almost impregnable to attack by an army less determined than our own.

General Longstreet subsequently paid a compliment to the division by saying that troops who could carry such points were capable of winning a victory on any field.

On the following morning, skirmishers were thrown out to discover the position of the enemy, but Rosecrans was then many miles distant on his way to Chattanooga. The loss of the brigade was 539 killed and wounded, out of 1,850 men. Among the noblest spirits who fell was Captain D. E. Huger, the inspector general of Manigault's brigade—one of the most promising officers in the entire army.[31] While gallantly rallying a portion of the command about an hour before sunset, he was struck by a ball, which killed him instantly.

31. inspector general: a military officer who investigates and reports on organizational matters, such as discipline, morale, and supplies.

In the language of another, "there was none whose judgment was more reliable, decision more prompt, or energy more untiring. He had won the esteem of the whole brigade, and his loss is one that cannot well be replaced."

In connection with the battle, the names of Colonel Pressley, Lieutenant Colonel Porcher, Major White, Captain White, Captain Ferrell, Colonels Reid, Davis, and Major Butler of the 28th Alabama; Captain Walker, the present adjutant general; and others are conspicuously mentioned for their splendid bearing on the field.

It is a significant fact, although it has been noticed in former letters from other localities, that nearly all the officers who went in on horseback were either killed or wounded, while a considerable proportion of those on foot were unhurt. General Manigault himself had a narrow escape. His horse was shot diagonally through under the saddle, the bullet coming through one of the legs of the general's pantaloons, and his sword was nearly cut in twain. On dismounting, other bullets perforated portions of his clothing, but, fortunately, not one inflicted a personal injury.

In this connection, I may add that officers and men attached to brigades other than his own speak in the highest terms of General Manigault, as one of the ablest, coolest, and most gallant commanders in the western army.

All quiet today along the line, except occasional shelling of Lookout Mountain by the enemy's batteries. We make no response. Weather cool at night, balmy by day, and admirably suited to the work in which we are engaged. Fever and ague and dysentery prevail throughout the army, especially in Longstreet's corps, who are unused to the water and climate, but the mortality thus far is comparatively slight. There are no evidences of an immediate change of our present attitude, though we are still in the line of battle.

Personne

NORTH

BOSTON EVENING TRANSCRIPT
October 17, 1863

RECRUITING SHOULD BE THE ORDER OF THE DAY

The great elections are over. There is no longer a question what is the popular will and purpose of the North. Compromisers, peace men, and the conservators of the letter of fossil precedents which have no affinity with live principles have utterly failed in their attempts to stay the work of putting an end to the rebellion. The victories at the polls have been grandly won.

But these victories, to bear their full and most glorious fruit, must be followed up, and that quickly, by victories in the field. In the midst, therefore, of exultation, there should be mindfulness of duty—the immediate, the next duty; the duty, indeed, always predominant and present until the Federal arms are everywhere and wholly triumphant. An army engaged in active service always needs reinforcement—should be constantly replenished by an ever-flowing stream of fresh men. At this moment the question as to the duration of the struggle depends mainly on the rapidity and extent with which this fact is heeded. The question is almost entirely a question of numbers.

We recur to this subject not to deal in general exhortations, but to urge work directly here at home. There seems to be a singular fatuity only too prevalent in the community. It is too generally forgotten that the strife is to be ended and the country saved by men—armed men—full regiments swelling armies till they reach a might equal to the overwhelming of the foe at every point. The North might be twice as populous as it is, but if it failed to send, and to keep sending, its hosts to the seat of war, its power would be no better than weakness. The point is not what we are able to do, but what we are actually doing to crush the forces of the rebellion.

Massachusetts has nobly met the calls upon it heretofore. Experience has shown a necessity, as great as at any former time, for the renewal of those calls. The fresh summons must be answered, and *active* measures must be taken to make the response prompt and adequate. The business of the commonwealth should be very extensively and zealously to aid recruiting. The war will go on, and the difficulties of ending it and restoring peace to the country will be increasing, until the military strength of the Confederacy is annihilated.

What is necessary to accomplish this result every schoolboy knows. And yet loyal and patriotic men are passive, as if the hour for action in promoting enlistments had gone by. It has been stated that the Federal exceed the Rebel armies only by about a hundred fifty thousand men. Does anybody imagine that the conflict is soon to cease, unless the nation swells its serried ranks far beyond their present numbers? The duty of the moment is to get soldiers, and that duty is to be done in every neighborhood.

It will be seen, by reference to the general order of the adjutant general of the state, in another column that the governor has organized a plan by which recruiting can be made immediately efficient. The plan is to fill up certain regiments of infantry and artillery therein named, and the bounty for those recruits who have been before in the military service of the United States is the large sum of $452. We trust that an immediate effort will be made in all the localities of the state, similar to that made a year ago, to recruit the nine months' regiments, to meet the requisitions of the state. Every person who has any influence should exert it to promote this object. If successful, it will save Massachusetts from another draft and tell with great effect on the issue of the war. Instant action in all the villages, towns, and cities of the state would fill up these regiments and batteries in less than a month, and we cannot too earnestly urge that action on the patriotism and public spirit of the community.

"PECULIAR"

This is the title of the new American novel by Epes Sargent, to be published by G. W. Carleton, New York, early in November. As we have already announced, it is founded on some of those interesting facts respecting white slaves in New Orleans which General Butler has to tell about, and which were fully authenticated by Governor Shepley and others. "Peculiar," one of the principal characters of the novel and an escaped black slave, having been christened by his master, in a drunken freak, "Peculiar Institution," retains the name. Inasmuch as the novel reveals some of those more recent phases of slavery which have been unveiled since *Uncle Tom's Cabin* was written, and which the civil war has verified, the title of the book, odd as it is, must be regarded as felicitous. There is already a call for the work which is premonitory of a large sale.

NEW YORK TRIBUNE
October 17, 1863

FROM THE ARMY OF THE POTOMAC
SKIRMISHING ALL ALONG THE LINES—NO FURTHER GENERAL ENGAGEMENTS—THE BATTLES FOUGHT ON WEDNESDAY—THE REBELS TWICE REPULSED—THEY MEET WITH HEAVY LOSSES—THEY LOSE FROM 700 TO 900 PRISONERS—WE ALSO CAPTURED SIX PIECES OF ARTILLERY

Special Dispatch to the *New York Tribune*

Washington, October 16, 1863

Your correspondent Beta, who arrived from the front at two o'clock this morning, brings in the following report of Wednesday's fighting:

About daybreak on Wednesday morning the corps of A. P. Hill made a desperate assault upon the rear of our wagon train, under guard of the II Corps and Gregg's division of cavalry, consisting of the 6th Ohio, 1st Rhode Island, 10th New York, 1st Massachusetts, and 1st Pennsylvania, the 10th New York acting as rear picket. Our forces were on the country road leading into Centreville, a little to the northeast of Catlett's Station. From the manner of Hill's assault it is evident he deemed our retreat from Sulphur Springs a panic-stricken rout. I shall not deny that special efforts were made to induce this belief. The enemy opened upon us with shell, followed up by a spirited dash of his cavalry. But our boys were prepared. Getting the teams to the rear, General Gregg charged his men upon the Rebel battery, capturing five guns, two colors, and about five hundred prisoners—all North Carolinians.

This unexpected repulse had the effect to keep our assailants at bay for a season, but it was apparent that they were bent upon some flank movement. Our forces continued to fall back in good order, exchanging compliments with their pursuers, until reaching Brentsville, at about three o'clock, where the rear of our trains had halted. The enemy's infantry was discovered in heavy force emerging from a line of woods skirting the north bank of the railroad. Here it was that the II Corps, under General Warren, dashed in and displayed the most commendable heroism. The discovery of either force at this juncture was a mutual surprise, and a rush was made by both parties for the cut of the railroad, our boys getting in first and receiving a terrific volley of musketry over their heads. Springing to the crest of the bank, we returned a most deadly fire, which mowed down their ranks like grass and left their dead and wounded lying in heaps in our front.

A portion of Hill's corps was still pressing our rear, but so admirably were our troops handled by Gregg and Warren that they were kept at bay, while we administered the most terrible punishment for his audacious attack on our flank. We also captured six pieces of artillery and a large number of prisoners, estimated in the aggregate at 700 to 900, the most of which were sent to Washington this afternoon.

Just at dusk General Sykes came to General Warren's support with his V Corps, but the enemy had retreated in confusion to their covering of woods and took good care not to exhibit themselves again.

While this desperate encounter was going on, our cavalry scouts discovered that Ewell's forces were attempting a flank movement to the west of Fairfax, but the timely discovery has thus far prevented any demonstration from that quarter, and all has remained quiet up to nine o'clock tonight, with the exception of unimportant picket skirmishing. In the extreme front of our lines, beyond Centreville, the 6th New York, the 1st Pennsylvania, 1st Rhode Island, and 1st Regular Batteries were also engaged, and to the skillful management of their pieces are we indebted for the remarkably few casualties on our side, considering the desperate character of the contest.

Our surgeons in charge, and other officers, say our entire loss in killed, wounded, and missing will not reach four hundred. In their skedaddle back to the woods, the Rebels left large numbers of their dead and wounded behind. Three trains left Fairfax for Alexandria about nine o'clock, conveying ninety-four of Buford's and Kilpatrick's men, mostly wounded in the Sulphur Springs fight, and forty of Gregg's men, wounded yesterday, together with the remainder of the infantry wounded of the II Corps.

In addition to the names already forwarded are the following: Captain Bowe, 6th Ohio Cavalry, mortally wounded; Lieutenant Brigham, 6th Ohio Cavalry, dangerously; Corporal Stroup, Company I, 6th Ohio Cavalry, killed; Private Tyler, Company B, 6th Ohio Cavalry, killed; Captain Richards, Company I, 6th Ohio Cavalry, wounded; Corporal Chaffe, Company I, 6th Ohio Cavalry, wounded; Private O'Brien, Company C, 6th Ohio Cavalry, wounded; Privates O'Brien, Company C, and Hike, Company G, 6th Ohio Cavalry, seriously wounded; Lieutenant Scranton, 14th Connecticut, wounded.

Our present lines are well chosen, and no doubt exists of our ability to maintain them. In short, General Meade is ready and anxious for a fight in his present position.

General Sickles and staff arrived at General Birney's headquarters about four o'clock and were most enthusiastically received.

Headquarters, Army of the Potomac
October 16, 1863

Our lines of battle were maintained throughout yesterday and today, but the enemy have made no further demonstrations, and all has remained quiet. The Rebel pickets appear close to our front, but whether, after having been so completely foiled in all their recent endeavors to gain an advantage, they will try another flank movement, or risk a general engagement, is as yet undeveloped by any discoveries we have been able to make.

A reconnaissance on our right has disclosed a heavy body of infantry occupying the passes of the Bull Run Mountains, while Ewell's corps is believed to be still hovering upon our left. A squad of mounted Rebel raiders dashed in upon the headquarters supply train of the VI Corps, between Chantilly and Centreville, about midnight last night, capturing the teams of only four wagons. All rumors of a fight having taken place at Fairfax Courthouse, or that our army had all retreated thither, are fabrications.

General John Cochrane reached Fairfax Courthouse this afternoon. Between fifty and sixty more Rebel prisoners were brought in today and were this evening dispatched to Washington. The remainder of our wounded in Tuesday's fight were also sent in. All sutlers and other attachés of the army likely to embarrass active movements have been ordered to Alexandria, and the Army of the Potomac, reduced to light weight, awaits its Southern friend.

NOVEMBER 21, 1863

SOUTH

RICHMOND DAILY DISPATCH
November 21, 1863

BURSTING OF THE RUSSIAN BUBBLE

The *New York Herald*, which lately led on the Russian furore and blew its trumpet till the welkin rang again in glorification of the Great Bear, has turned into lampooning the late objects of its idolatry; says they might just as well have been feasted on lard and train oil; calls them barbarians and denounces them for their long oppressions of Poland, which it seems just now, for the first time, to have heard of.[32] We thought at the time of the Russian glorification that it was only in fact a self-glorification by the New York mob, who seize upon every celebrity that visits their shores to make themselves conspicuous. But we had no idea the humbug would be so soon confessed. What does it mean? Have they found out that the Russian card will not play well in Europe, where Russia is a synonym for all that is despotic, cruel, and barbarous? Taken in connection with Henry Ward Beecher's late admission at Exeter Hall that they had only been coquetting with Russia and that they really loved the English a great deal better than the Russians, we are

32. furore: Italian, "frenzy" or "enthusiastic admiration."

satisfied that the Yankee–Russian fraternization has come to an untimely end and that the czar will not be likely to regard with much respect and affection the people who have been paying him so many compliments at their firesides, only to ridicule him before he is well out of their house.[33]

The *Herald* complains that its Yankees have always made fools of themselves over foreign lions and that when the lions had feasted themselves at their expense, they have turned to, and endeavored to rend and devour, their entertainers. It instances the cases of Marryat, Dickens, the Japanese, the Prince of Wales, etc., who, after being obsequiously courted and caressed in America, went home and abused the Yankees, wrote libels and begot rams, and endeavored to lie and butt the whole race of Yankee-Doodles out of existence. We don't know that there is any truth in this accusation as far as the Prince of Wales is concerned, but if he was not disgusted with the servility and flunkyism he was treated to in America, it was because he had not the discernment to discriminate between genuine good feeling and gross flattery and to perceive that it is to gratify their own vanity, not to evince any respect for merit, that the Yankees go mad over foreign celebrities. No man ever failed of securing the respect of others who respected himself. And the same is true of communities. The Americans have set themselves up as a great republican people, who judge all men by their personal merits and not by the rank they hold in society, and who have preferred contempts for the distinctions of rank and title in Europe. Yet, there never has been, and never will be, such a title-worshiping race in the world, and European visitors, seeing this at a glance, seeing how these boasted republicans are never so happy as when they are tuft-hunting and licking the dust from the feet of lords and ladies, naturally jeer and laugh at them, and let them see that they understand them, and not only regard them as inferiors, but are aware that they are themselves conscious of this inferiority. Of course, all this is very galling to Yankeedom. That all the plum puddings and sparkling champagne and honeyed compliments should not be able to melt the obdurate hearts of the foreign patricians and exalt the snobs of the Yankee cities in the esteem of others, or even in their own esteem, is a dreadful thing. And they become very vituperative and more vulgar than ever in consequence. But we see no help for it. They have never, for excellent reasons, been able to respect themselves, and they cannot expect others to respect them.

33. Henry Ward Beecher, abolitionist, reformer, and brother of Harriet Beecher Stowe, was a Congregationalist preacher of national reputation.

Now, the South, we are willing to concede, has as few friends in Europe as the North; but we have the satisfaction of knowing that we have never humbled ourselves at the feet of foreign lions, nor sought to propitiate their favor, nor cared a groat for their good or bad opinions. They hate our institution of slavery; but though they may hate us also, we have taught them to respect us, and the present war has wrung from them many an emphatic testimony to that effect. We are not sure but at this very moment even Russia, especially in view of the disclosures of Beecher and the *New York Herald,* has more respect for the South, which has never given the czar so much as a compliment, than the North, which loads him at one moment with sickening adulation and taunts him the next with train oil, lard, and barbarism. A hollow, egotistical, slavish, and hypocritical community must expect only contempt and execration from the rest of mankind. Let the Yankees go ahead with their persecutions at home and their man worship abroad. Their humiliation, both at home and abroad, we trust, is not far distant.

THE CONFEDERATES AT KNOXVILLE

Official Dispatch

Mission Ridge, Tennessee, November 19, 1863

To General S. Cooper:—General Wheeler reports his attack upon and dispersion of the enemy's cavalry, pursuing them into the works at Knoxville, capturing three hundred prisoners. The infantry force is close up.

Braxton Bragg, General

GEORGIA LEGISLATURE

Milledgeville, Georgia, 19th—The House has unanimously concurred in the resolution of the Senate reenacting the resolution in reference to the secession of Georgia, pledging anew the resources of the state in vindication of the position then assumed, and declaring the determination not to tire of the war until independence is achieved. The House also unanimously concurred in the Senate resolutions endorsing the patriotism and wisdom of President Davis in the discharge of the arduous duties devolving upon him.

The Honorable Mr. Harrington, member of the House, from Terrell County, died today of pneumonia.

FROM CHARLESTON

Charleston, 20th—The enemy renewed his fire on the city this morning at eleven o'clock. At four o'clock this afternoon, the number of shells thrown was twelve. The shelling of Fort Sumter today has been more heavy than usual, with mortars. But few rifled shots were fired. No casualties either in the city or at the fort.

FROM THE SOUTHWEST

Abingdon, Virginia, 20th—Nothing definite. Encouraging indications westward.

CHARLESTON DAILY COURIER
November 19, 1863

[*The* Courier *states that the November 20 (Friday) issue would not be published and that publication would resume on November 21. No copies of the November 21 issue appear to have survived. The following articles are drawn from the Thursday issue.*]

FROM THE WEST
NEW BATTERY OPENED ON THE CHICKAMAUGA—SHELLING THE YANKEE CAMPS—ENEMY DRIVEN FROM HIS POSITION

Atlanta, 18th—Advices from the front are important.

A special dispatch to the *Atlanta Intelligencer* says, "A battery planted on an eminence near the mouth of the Chickamauga opened yesterday on the Yankee camps on the opposite side of the Tennessee River. A furious shelling was kept up for half an hour with great effect, dispersing the enemy in every direction. The Yankees attempted to reply with two guns, but were completely driven from their positions."

FROM WESTERN VIRGINIA
AFFAIRS IN EAST TENNESSEE

Abingdon, Virginia, 18th—The first number of Brownlow's *Whig and Rebel Ventilator* has been received. It contains nothing of interest, but is filled with abuse and vituperation. He says, "If the Union forces are compelled to leave the country, they will make it a howling wilderness. I glory in penning my lectures from my old fortifications, beginning with the hell-born and hell-bound rebellion, where the traitors forced me to leave off in my work of faith, labor, and love."

The Federal court, under Judge Bigg, was to convene shortly, and arbitrary arrests complained of by traitors will be tender mercies compared with the indictments to be brought before that court. In a lengthy article he says, "Slavery cannot any longer exist in Tennessee."

Charles McGhee, Columbus Powell, and Mr. Salter, of Kentucky, have been sent to that state upon the requisition of Governor Bramlette.

Heavy firing was reported in the direction of Bull's Gap, on Monday.

BOMBARDMENT OF FORT SUMTER

One Hundred Thirty-first Day of the Siege

The enemy's fire upon the fort during Tuesday night and Wednesday continued slow but steady. Our mortar batteries on Sullivans Island and Battery Simkins, in response, have also kept up a vigorous shelling of the Yankees at Gregg's and the Cummings Point mortar battery.

The number of rifled shots fired Monday night was 156, of which 55 missed; the number of mortar shells, 6, of which one missed.

On Tuesday, 14 rifled shots were fired, and 366 mortar shells. Five of the former and 117 of the latter missed the fort. No report from the fort was received Wednesday night.

The enemy fired a few shots up Cooper River Wednesday afternoon, believed to be at a passing steamer, but without effect. It is supposed to have been fired from the same gun that was used in firing toward the city.

None of the monitors were in action during the day. The *Ironsides* still remains quiet at her old anchorage.

NEWS FROM THE COAST

A correspondent on Johns Island, under date 17th instant, says: "Our men had a small skirmish with the Yankees last Sunday. It turned out to be altogether an artillery duel. Some of their shells exploded near us, but hurt no one. Our fire, it is believed, did some execution, as a number of dead and wounded were seen carried from the field. Our pickets say at least twenty were taken off.

"The impression here is that the Yankees wish to get possession of Seabrook Bay for the purpose of continuing their line of telegraph, which they are running from Fortress Monroe via Port Royal.

"Major Jenkins, with about forty men, went over Wednesday evening and returned on Friday night without accident. They caught in the creek, oystering, between Mr. Townsend's and Clark's Bay, two Yankee Negroes belonging to the 55th Massachusetts Regiment. One was a sergeant and the other a private. They said they were drafted and had to serve because they could not afford to pay three hundred dollars to the Lincoln government. Their company, they said, was on Clark's Bay, guarding an observatory which is in course of erection."

NORTH

BOSTON EVENING TRANSCRIPT
November 21, 1863

GENERAL SCHOFIELD AND SLAVERY IN MISSOURI

The order of General Schofield for the enlistment of colored men into the army is generally regarded in Missouri as the death blow to slavery in that state. The order is more stringent than that applied by the secretary of war to Maryland and Delaware. It dispenses with the owners' consent *from the first,* instead of requiring the consent of loyal owners during the first month and then dispensing with it, if necessary. *This was by General Schofield's request*. In conversing with a friend about these regulations for recruiting colored troops, General Schofield said: "Now the whole power of slavery in Missouri is destroyed." As showing the general's present position, it may be stated that it depended altogether upon him whether the recruitment of black men into the army should not be almost impossible in Missouri.

NEGRO REGIMENTS IN TENNESSEE

Major George L. Stearns has enlisted four regiments of colored men in Tennessee. Among these recruits are many Kentucky slaves, as it is very difficult to distinguish between contrabands from that state and Tennessee. Crowds of impoverished women and children are coming within our lines. Major Stearns proposes to put them on abandoned Rebel farms at Nashville.

NEW YORK TRIBUNE
November 21, 1863

PAST AND COMING EVENTS ON THE UPPER TENNESSEE

More than a week ago, advices from Chattanooga announced a movement by a portion of Bragg's army in the direction of east Tennessee. Of its progress toward Knoxville the intelligence of the appearance of a Rebel column before Loudon and the retreat of our forces from that place subsequently informed us. Still later, the news of the close approach of the enemy to Knoxville, contained in our special dispatches from that point printed yesterday morning, may have disturbed the public. We believe, however, that there is no occasion for any apprehension as to the safety of General Burnside's command.

To our certain knowledge, General Grant had positive information that the Rebel force advancing upon east Tennessee consisted of only three divisions of infantry. Allowing five thousand muskets for each of these—a very liberal estimate—we have an aggregate number little over one half the strength of the army we know to be at the disposal of General Burnside. A large portion of his troops, it is true, are mounted and hence will hardly be available in a pitched battle. Yet his infantry consists mostly of old and well-tried troops and must be more than numerically equal to the enemy's. If, then, General Burnside has his command well in hand, as accounts indicate, and has only to confront the force sent from near Chattanooga, we can see no ground for any fears as to the issue of the impending conflict. There might be cause for uneasiness if a second Rebel column were approaching Knoxville from southwestern Virginia simultaneously with that from Chattanooga. While it is possible that a force has been put in motion from the Virginia line, it seems certain that it has not neared Knoxville sufficiently to threaten General Burnside. A body of troops coming from that direction would have to march nearly a hundred fifty miles over extremely rough roads and could not come within many days' march of Knoxville without due notice of its advance to our army. No information to that effect is yet made public.

It is not probable that General Burnside will rely on fortified positions more than on the strength and prowess of his army to foil the plans of the enemy. In the former, the enemy would hardly attack him. Nor will his supplies and the necessity of keeping our communications with the North uninterruptedly open allow him to await an attack, if the enemy choose not to make it. His only safe mode of operation is evidently to trust to his numerical advantage and seek the chances of battle at once. Delay may bring the Rebel force from Virginia upon him; immediate action may enable him to meet both dangers successfully by defeating the Rebel bodies separately, one after the other.

While we believe that General Burnside has the means to defeat the enemy in front of him, we have also reason to think that the weakening of the Rebel army near Chattanooga, by the diversion of part of it into east Tennessee, will furnish General Grant the opportunity to relieve his command from the great perplexities and dangerous uncertainties that are still hanging over it.

Since our troops, by a finely conceived and executed coup, obtained control of the Tennessee River between Bridgeport and a point a short distance below Chattanooga, and two new wagon roads respectively on the south and north banks of the river, the impression has prevailed in the North that the difficulties experienced in supplying the Grand Army of the Tennessee had been entirely overcome. This is, unfortunately, not the case. But two steamboats of limited carrying capacity have been available so far for transportation by water, and this method of supply must depend upon the condition of the river. Wagon trains are a second means, but the wretched character of the roads and the exhaustion of the draft animals from long-continued insufficiency of food limit the supplies through this channel. The frequent destruction of the pontoon bridges over the Tennessee by Rebel rafts floated down from above Chattanooga has also proved a great obstacle to the rapid movement of provisions and forage. Up to the present time, indeed, our army has been subsisted from week to week, but that is all. General Grant's object, however, must be not only to feed it from day to day, but to reclothe it and equip it anew; replace the lost and broken-down horses and mules, numbering by thousands; accumulate supplies for the future—in short, to put it once more in condition for offensive movements.

The full means of communication with the North required for this end, and their undisturbed control during the winter, he can only secure by driving the enemy from his immediate front. And in addition to the question of supplies, there are strategic motives that will induce him to make an effort to relieve his army from the close pressure of the enemy. The Rebel guns from Lookout Mountain, as well as from other points of the Rebel front, cover our position. Their spasmodic use has hitherto occasioned but little annoyance to our troops, but there can be no doubt that they might be made to render them exceedingly uncomfortable. Again, Lookout Mountain, by its abutment on the very bank of the river, forms a kind of huge disconnecting wall between that part of the army at Chattanooga and that ranged along the slope of the Raccoon Mountains, under General Hooker. As long as this formidable barrier remains in the hands of the enemy, communication can only be had between the two divisions of the army by crossing the Tennessee River twice, so that ready mutual support cannot be given and the destruction of either of the connecting bridges isolates each from the other.

It cannot be questioned, in view of the division of Bragg's army for the flank operation in east Tennessee, that if General Grant means to strike a blow this winter, now is his time and opportunity. Since General Sherman has effected a junction with him, the strength of his army is as great as it will ever be until the old regiments are filled up. We cannot print the figures, but know that the Army of the Cumberland alone is believed, in Chattanooga, to be equal in point of numbers to the Rebel force still in front of the place. And there is a weakness in the Rebel position which has been long apparent to our generals and renders the chances of success even of a direct attack upon it by no means desperate. Lookout Mountain intervenes between the Rebel right and left just as it does between our two wings. Longstreet's corps, though now reported in front of Burnside, has been, and, we incline to believe, still is, confronting Hooker on the western slope. Succor can only reach him from the Rebel left by an extremely difficult road over the mountain itself. Any movement on our part that would give us possession of the eastern avenues to the mountain would ensure his capture or destruction.

General Grant, ever since he took command, has been anxious to solve the problem of the security of our possession of Chattanooga definitely and decisively in our favor. We are convinced that he will not let the winter pass without working the solution, whether he seizes upon his present opportunity or not. This much is certain: Chattanooga, so far, has been to us a barren conquest—a mere possession of a piece of Rebel territory. Another battle will be necessary to secure us not only a permanent title to what we now have, but also the real value of the tenure—that is, the access to and control of the roads leading east and south from the place, all of which the enemy at present firmly holds. Without them, Chattanooga is not a gateway, but a gate, locked by Rebel hands, from behind which we cannot move in any direction.

DECEMBER 19, 1863

SOUTH

RICHMOND DAILY DISPATCH
December 19, 1863

A YANKEE REVIEW OF WHAT THE ABOLITIONISTS HAVE ACCOMPLISHED

Last week the abolitionists held jubilees in New York and Philadelphia. The *Tribune* claims for them that they elected Lincoln in 1860 and that "posterity will do them justice." That paper, however, is entirely too modest. The abolitionists have done a good deal more than elect the Gorilla, and in the matter of doing them justice we will anticipate posterity a little and copy the following from the *New York Herald* of Saturday last:

> In 1860, the American abolitionists, pure and simple, numbered about 100,000 persons. In 1840, when they ran Mr. Birney for president, the abolitionists polled 7,000 votes. In 1844, with the same candidate, they polled 62,000 votes. In 1848, they intermingled with the Free-Soilers and gave Van Buren 300,000 votes.[34] From that time forth the pure abolition vote is so mixed up with the Free-Soil vote and the Republican vote that we cannot get at it with much accuracy. Still, we believe that 100,000 is a fair estimate of the number of true, radical abolitionists who have followed the flag of Garrison and Phillips, and who are entitled to share in the credit of the abolition work and in the glory which now crowns the labor.[35] In this number we include all such old women as Greeley and such young women as Tilton.[36]

What these one hundred thousand abolitionists have accomplished may be stated in a very few words. They have accomplished the present war. They have worked for it thirty years, and here it is. They have wrecked a powerful, peaceful, and happy country. They have arrayed brother against brother, father against son, children against parents. They have filled the land with widows and orphans. They have transformed the country into a vast graveyard. They have shed an ocean of blood and squandered mountains of money. They have made the air heavy with the shrieks of the wounded, the groans of the dying, and the lamentations of the mourners. They have devastated the fields and plantations of the South and destroyed the commerce of the North. They have given a check to the progress of civilization and democratic institutions, from which it will take years to recover. All this they have accomplished in thirty years. One hundred thousand fiends let loose from the lowest hell and inspired by the most infernal malice could not have accomplished more mischief in the same space of time. If this be any-

34. Free-Soilers: members of the Free-Soil party (1848–54), the politics of which were defined by its opposition to the extension of slavery into the western territories.

35. William Lloyd Garrison, founder of the abolitionist journal *Liberator* and the American Anti-Slavery Society.

36. Theodore Tilton, journalist and reformer, was the editor in chief of the *Independent* and the founder of the weekly *Golden Age*.

thing to rejoice over, let the abolitionists rejoice. If they desire to raise a monument to perpetuate the remembrance of their triumphs, our battlefields will furnish them with enough human skulls for a pyramid, and Wendell Phillips or Beecher would be only too happy to deliver the address at the laying of the corner skull.

During this abolition war, at least 100,000 men have been killed, 400,000 have been disabled for life. Thus, half a million have been subjected to death, wounds, and to sickness worse than wounds, in the armies of both sides. What amount of human misery has occurred beyond and behind the armies we shall not now inquire. The amount of property destroyed during the war may be roughly estimated at $500 million. The injury inflicted upon our commerce and carrying trade may be stated at $100 million. This is rather under than above the mark; for the Rebel Maffit asserts that he alone has destroyed $11 million worth of ships and cargoes, and Semmes has certainly destroyed much more. The war debt of the North and South amounts to about $5 billion. If the war ends by the abolition of slavery, we shall have to keep a standing army of a hundred thousand men and support two or three million indigent Negroes for several years. But we will leave that probability out of the account and will also refrain from estimating the millions and billions of dollars which the now impeded industry of this country would have produced had not the abolitionists caused this war. We wish to confine ourselves to facts and figures of indisputable authenticity. And what do these facts and figures show? Estimating the white population of the United States in 1860 at 26 million—and this is within a few hundred of the official figures—we find that the abolitionists have been instrumental in causing the death of one man out of every 260 people, and the crippling or otherwise disabling of one man out of every 52 people. Also, that the abolitionists have caused the destruction of property valued at $600 million and a war expenditure of about $5 billion. If these are things to be proud of, let the abolitionists hold a perpetual jubilee.

Taking the above statistics as a basis, a very simple process of arithmetic will demonstrate that each one of our one hundred thousand abolitionists has caused the death of one man and the lifelong disability of four men and has already cost the country fifty-six thousand dollars. What are the cruelties and the expenses of slavery when compared to this? It is very evident, however, that the loss of life and limb and money during the war should not be so equally divided among our one hundred thousand fanatics. Individual abolitionists have been more or less guilty according to their opportunities and their influence. Garrison, for example, should have more than one dead man, four wounded and crippled men, and fifty-six thousand dollars' worth of destroyed property set down to his account. Wendell Phillips is in the same case. Greeley has probably caused the death of at least a thousand men, and the remainder of the injury which he has inflicted upon the nation and upon humanity must be increased in proportion. The same remark will apply to Beecher, Cheever, Tilton, and such prominent abolitionists. Sumner, Wilson, Chandler, and other abolition politicians have even a larger share for which to answer. This sad account will certainly have to be settled someday—not in this world, perhaps, but certainly in the next. Then, if the abolitionists can find any food for gladness in these facts, it will be when they enter Hades and discover that the worst fiends receive them with respect and that Satan, Mephistopheles, Beelzebub, Moloch, and the other devils vacate their thrones to offer the newcomers all the insignia of preeminence in evil. The jubilee in Philadelphia will be nothing in comparison to this grand satanic reception.

CHARLESTON DAILY COURIER
December 19, 1863

FROM THE WEST
GENERAL JOSEPH E. JOHNSTON APPOINTED TO COMMAND THE ARMY OF TENNESSEE—ENEMY FALLING BACK FROM KNOXVILLE

Dalton, Georgia, 18th—General Joseph E. Johnston has been appointed to the command of the Army of Tennessee and is expected here in the early part of next week.

Major General Hindman has arrived and resumed command of his old corps.

Persons desiring permission to enter these lines with clothing for the soldiers should address their communications to the commanders of the regiments to which their friends belong in order that their statements may secure the necessary vouchers and guides for the action of the commanding general.

Information has been received that Sherman's corps has fallen back from Knoxville. It passed through Cleveland the day before yesterday on the way to Chattanooga.

FROM RICHMOND
THE STONEWALL JACKSON STATUE

Richmond, 18th—At a late meeting of the Executive Committee of the Stonewall Jackson Statue Association, President Davis, General Lee, the governor of Virginia, and other prominent officers were present. The report of the treasurer stated that Volick, the artist, had reached the continent and entered upon his work. Fifteen bales of cotton have been shipped to Liverpool to meet the sum of five thousand dollars agreed to be advanced to Volick.

The statue will cost $250,000 in foreign exchange.

FROM ORANGE COURTHOUSE
AFFAIRS IN THE ARMY OF NORTHERN VIRGINIA—A DESERTER SHOT

Orange Courthouse, Virginia, 18th—There is no change in the military situation on either side.

Dennis Driscoll, of the Johnson's battery of Richmond, was shot for desertion at noon today.

The weather is clear and cool, but the roads heavy.

SIEGE OF CHARLESTON

One Hundred Sixty-second Day

The enemy, between ten and eleven o'clock, Friday morning, opened an ineffectual fire upon the city from one gun mounted upon the mortar battery on Cummings Point. Five shells were thrown, all of which fell short.

Batteries Bee, Marion, Rutledge, Simkins, and Cheves responded and kept up a brisk fire on the Yankee gunners for about two hours.

About half past three in the afternoon, the enemy again opened on the city from one gun at Battery Cummings and fired five more shells, doing little or no damage. Batteries Bee, Rutledge, and Simkins replied.

The enemy fired a few shots in return from Battery Gregg at our batteries on James Island.

Some firing was heard throughout the day in Stono.

The Yankees are still engaged in revetting and building obstructions to the approaches of their batteries on Morris Island, interrupted and annoyed by our fire. The number of shots fired by the enemy on Friday is reported at sixteen, ten on the city and six on James Island.

The fleet remains inactive. A sloop of war and two gunboats were observed to leave the fleet inside the bar on Friday afternoon and sail south. The number of vessels reported inside the bar on Friday evening was twenty-nine, including the *Ironsides,* four monitors, the flagship, one gunboat, two mortar hulks, one propeller transport, three tugs, three barks, ten schooners, and three brigs; in Stono sixteen, Folly River nine, Lighthouse Inlet twenty-three, consisting of four river steamers, three tugs, hospital boat, derrick boat, two brigs, and eleven schooners.

GENERAL BEAUREGARD AND CHARLESTON

From the *Richmond Dispatch*

General Beauregard has entitled himself to the gratitude and admiration of the country by his magnificent defense of Charleston. Under his auspices it has withstood triumphantly such a combination of naval and military engineering as was never before brought to bear upon any fortified place. The defense of Charleston stands without a parallel. The boasted skill of the best engineer in the United States army, the terrific armaments with which his fortifications were supplied, and the naval monsters which cooperated with the land forces have for more than four months expended all their power upon the Palmetto City, and still its flag floats in proud defiance, and the *New York Times* now virtually admits that Charleston cannot be taken! What a lame and impotent conclusion of all the gigantic efforts and prodigious vaporings of the vindictive foe! What? Charleston cannot be taken! The hotbed of the rebellion! The nest of treason! The accursed city! For nearly three years the object over whose attainment Yankee malice has gloated, and over which it has rained fire and iron upon day and night, in an incessant storm, for four months! Where is your Swamp Angel?[37] Where is your Greek fire? Where are your monitors? Where is your Gillmore? And, after all, to find out that Charleston cannot be taken—that even Fort Sumter cannot be taken! That all the enormous mass of iron hurled upon it has only made it stronger and more impregnable! We can almost hear the Yankees gnashing their teeth and yelling in impotent rage as Charleston looks serenely down upon the baffled malice of these fiends in the shape of men.

Good reasons have these wretches to hate the name of Beauregard! He has been their evil genius from first to last. The Swamp Angel has

37. The "Swamp Angel" was an 8-inch 200-pounder Parrott gun, Parrott being a class of rifled cannon created by inventor Robert Parrott to handle increased gas pressure. Built specifically for the bombardment of Charleston, South Carolina, it was capable of delivering an incendiary projectile at a range of 7,900 yards. It was operational for two days, August 22–23, 1863, and fired thirty-six shots, the last of which disabled the gun. The Swamp Angel is, now, part of a public monument in Trenton, New Jersey.

had to succumb to the Guardian Angel of Charleston and looks up at his master as Lucifer may be supposed to have looked up as the purer and more powerful spirit who hurled him headlong from the battlements of Heaven to his proper place. From the time the first gun was fired at Fort Sumter to the present hour, Beauregard has inflicted such mortal blows upon Yankee pride and vanity that they can never forgive him till the crack of doom. Fort Sumter, which with a few feeble guns he snatched from the Yankees in two days, they have not been able to regain with the most powerful armaments in the world in four months. At Manassas he punctured the grandest military gasbag of the age and sounded the keynote of the grand march of Southern victories. All honor to the glorious soldier. In the grand galaxy of Southern heroes, his star will shine forever in unsurpassed brightness and majesty.

Let Charleston rejoice, but let her never relax her vigilance. The Yankee serpent is scotched, not killed. The price of her security is eternal watchfulness. Providence has signally rescued her from the malice of the invader; let her prove herself worthy of that interposition by continuing to work out her own salvation with redoubled energy and eyes that never sleep.

NORTH

BOSTON EVENING TRANSCRIPT
December 19, 1863

FROM TENNESSEE AND GEORGIA

Chattanooga, Tennessee, 18th—The Rebel general John Morgan escaped across the Tennessee at Gillispies Landing, sixty miles above here, on Sunday afternoon. Captain William Cummings and Robert Cummings, who escaped with him, were captured together with fourteen of his escort of thirty. Reaching the neighborhood of the river, they pressed every citizen to prevent alarm's being given, and hurriedly constructed a raft at the mouth of Miles Creek, on which an attempt to cross was made. A citizen who eluded their pickets gave the alarm, and the attempt was nearly frustrated. Morgan escaped on a valuable racehorse, which was presented to him in Kentucky, going in the direction of Athens. General Howard, who commands at Athens, has cavalry scouting the country, and possibly Morgan may be taken.

Wheeler has rejoined Hardee and is reorganizing his cavalry force near Dalton.

Refugees and deserters say that the Rebel cavalry will be actively employed during the winter.

On Wednesday, Ferguson, the guerrilla, with a small force, captured a part of the train of the 1st Cavalry Division on the march from McMinnville to Sparta. Peter Ebee, a sutler of the 9th Pennsylvania Cavalry, and three others were murdered.

Hardee's headquarters are at Dalton, and pickets as far as the Tunnel. His army, including the Georgia militia, is eighty-five thousand strong and is represented as utterly demoralized.

Generals Grant and Sherman left for Bridgeport today.

Steamboats make trips from Bridgeport to Loudon, whence stores are transported by rail twenty-two miles to Knoxville.

There is no news from General Granger, who, with General Burnside, is probably fighting Longstreet near Rogersville.

FROM MEMPHIS

Cairo, Illinois, 18th—Memphis dates of the 16th are received. The force sent out against the Rebels, who had been firing into a steamer at Waterproof, found them, killed sixteen, wounded several, and took some prisoner.

The steamer *Mars* had arrived at Memphis from New Orleans with nearly two hundred bales of cotton; also the steamer *Des Moines* from Friars Point with three thousand bales; also the *Silver Lake* from the White River with three hundred bales.

The cotton market was dull, with little business doing in consequence of the confusion arising from soldiers' arresting parties who have not complied with the late military orders. There were sales of 223 bales of middling at 62@65 cents; good ditto 67@68 cents.

The steamer *Silver Moon,* from Memphis, with a barge loaded with cotton, has arrived. She is bound for Cincinnati. She takes 150 bales from here, being a part of a lot of 917 bales seized here on the steamer *Crescent City,* on account of a charge against the owners for violating the regulations of the Treasury Department.

The steamer *Albert Pierce,* from New Orleans, has arrived with 150 bulkheads of sugar for St. Louis. Her news is anticipated. The gunboat convoying the *Albert Pierce* was fired into from batteries near Rodney. The marine fleet nearby moved down and commenced a vigorous shelling of the place.

The steamer *Effie Dean* collided this morning with a gunboat in sight of Cairo and sank. Her lower deck was tight, and she can be raised.

NEW YORK TRIBUNE
December 19, 1863

THE REBEL WORKS IN FRONT OF KNOXVILLE— HOW THEY BURIED THEIR DEAD—NUMBER OF THEIR WOUNDED FOUND IN HOUSES—LONGSTREET OBLIGED TO DESTROY AMMUNITION AND STORES

From Our Special Correspondent

Knoxville, Tennessee, December 5, 1863

An inspection of the Rebel lines just abandoned by them reveals a very extensive system, but not a very perfect description, of rifle pits, forts, and redoubts. In some prominent positions they had double lines. In their principal fort there were embrasures for eight guns. It is evident that they feared an attack from us. Their chief idea was to carry Fort Sanders, as the approach here afforded a cover of woods and other protection until within a hundred yards of the work. The enemy's dead are scattered all through the woods, very poorly buried. The leg or arm of at least one dead soldier protruded from the ground. Those in front of Fort Sanders are not sufficiently covered and will, if not attended to by our men, be rooted out by the hogs. A house or mill about three miles out on the Clinton Road has over two hundred wounded in it. They will be cared for by our medical officers.

Nearly a hundred prisoners have come in or have been captured today, and squads are everywhere wandering in the woods.

I learn from some of the Alabama and Georgia troops who were at Loudon that three locomotives and a large number of cars were dumped into the river of that place by the Rebels when General Sherman advanced upon them. They also destroyed a considerable quantity of Rebel clothing.

The country outside of the town is full of people inspecting the Rebel lines and gathering relics, muskets, etc., from the field.

E. S.

FROM THE MISSISSIPPI ATTACK ON A STEAMBOAT BY GUERRILLAS— ORDER CONCERNING COTTON BY GENERAL HURLBUT—MEMPHIS COTTON MARKET

Cairo, Illinois, December 18, 1863

The steamer *Julia,* which just arrived from New Orleans, reports that the *Brazil* was fired into below Rodney on the 11th. Three women and one man were killed and several wounded. The *Julia* reports that the steamer *Tecumseh* was burned on the 16th of November. The *Julia* brought 250 passengers and 212 barrels of sugar for St. Louis.

Five hundred fifty stragglers, deserters, and recruits were sent to Memphis and Louisville today.

The steamer *St. Patrick,* from Memphis 14th, has arrived.

General Hurlbut has issued a special order to the effect that guards be established on three designated roads leading into the city.

Cotton will be admitted on the roads, but none other than officers in charge of pickets will make memorandum of the name of the owner, consignor, and consignee; mark the number of bales; and report the same daily to the local Treasury agent. The time of day is also specified when cotton and produce may be brought in and, otherwise than in compliance with this order, will be seized. The commanders at La Grange, Corinth, and Columbus will be authorized to make similar regulations at the posts named when, in their judgment, the state of their commands and the adjacent country will permit.

Guerrillas are reported at various points along the river between here and Memphis.

The Memphis cotton market was dull; sales of two days, 95 bales at 66@70 cents. Receipts from below, 940 bales.

NEWS OF THE DAY: THE WAR

On Thursday night a force of Rebel cavalry, of Mosby's command, said to be eight hundred to one thousand strong, fell upon Company I, 155th New York, at Sangster's Station, three miles west of Fairfax, wounded one man, captured four, burned the tents of the company, robbed two women of their jewelry, and tried to burn the railroad bridge. Our boys fought them bravely from behind their encampment and succeeded in driving them off. The Rebels had wagons with them and took off all but one of their killed and wounded. Cavalry was sent in pursuit on Friday morning.

The steamship *Arago,* Captain Gadsden, arrived on Friday morning from Port Royal, with dates to 3:00 P.M. Tuesday from Charleston bar. Among her passengers is Brigadier General R. S. Foster and a portion of his staff. The *Arago* brings further details of the loss of the *Weehawken,* from which it appears that thirty-one persons lost their lives. A prize, the sloop *Josephine,* has been taken. The bombardment goes slowly on. The late high tides and storms have washed away eight feet of the beach of Morris and Folly islands.

A dispatch from Cumberland Gap, of the 16th instant, says that a portion of Longstreet's army, on the 14th, attacked the Union advance at Bean's Station and captured twenty-two loads of quartermaster's stores; also, that General Wilcox had fallen back to Tazewell and was fortifying. A later dispatch, of the same day, says that the Union citizens are leaving Knoxville and going in the direction of Big Creek Gap. Fighting was in progress at Blair's Crossroads.

There has been a severe snowstorm on the western Plains. Many persons are believed to have perished from cold, and cattle by thousands have died from lack of food. A large number of trains are out, and great anxiety is felt for them. At Leavenworth, on the 18th, snow was fourteen inches deep, and so drifted that the roads were blockaded.

During the march of our troops from Chattanooga against Longstreet at Knoxville, Granger's corps got in advance of Longstreet's ammunition train, while Howard's corps was in the rear. There being no escape for the train, forty loads of ammunition and two locomotives were run into the river at Loudon.

On the 11th instant, the steamboat *Brazil,* while passing below Rodney, Mississippi, was fired upon by Rebels on shore. Three women and one man were killed. The firing of shot and shell into a boatload of women and children is, of course, a high act of chivalry.

The Congressional Committee of Elections have now before them five contested cases from Wisconsin, two from Pennsylvania, one from Massachusetts, one from Kentucky, one from Maryland, one from Iowa, and one from Virginia.

The *City of Washington,* from Liverpool December 2nd, and the *Australasian,* from Liverpool December 5th, via Queenstown December 6th, arrived here yesterday. Their news has been anticipated, but they bring, seven days later, foreign files.

Dispatches of the 17th from Chattanooga say that the army will soon go into winter quarters. All is quiet, the situation unchanged.

Five deserters were executed on Friday in the Army of the Potomac.

1864

TIMELINE

January 31: In dire need of recruits, the Confederates draft those who obtained exemptions by paying for substitutes. In February, the draft age is raised to fifty.

February 1–2: The Confederates fail to recapture New Bern, North Carolina.

February 7–20: After capturing Jacksonville, Florida, Union troops move inland and are defeated in a minor action at Olustee depot.

February 14: Union General Sherman occupies Meridian, Mississippi. Federals spend five days destroying the facilities in Meridian and then return to their Vicksburg base.

February 17: CSS *Hunley,* at Charleston, becomes the first submarine in history to sink a warship, USS *Housatonic*. The *Hunley* herself is sunk, most likely as a result of an accident.

March 2: Colonel Ulric Dahlgren is killed during an abortive raid into Richmond to release Union prisoners. It is alleged that his real mission was to assassinate Jefferson Davis.

March 9: Grant is appointed to command all Federal armies. Halleck is to serve as chief of staff; Sherman is to oversee the forces in the West; and Meade is to continue serving as commander of the Army of the Potomac, but under Grant's supervision.

March 10: The Federals launch the combined army-navy Red River campaign, Louisiana, with the aim of taking a portion of Texas. The ill-advised campaign is aborted some two months later.

April 12: Confederate General Nathan Forrest captures Fort Pillow in the most controversial action of the war. He will be accused of murdering African-American Federal troops after they had "surrendered and were begging for mercy." After the war, Forrest will serve as the first Grand Wizard of the Ku Klux Klan.

May 4–7: The Army of the Potomac moves across the Rapidan River and clashes with Lee's forces. The Battle of the Wilderness ensues and, though bloody, ends inconclusively. Casualties: North, 17,666; South, 7,750.

May 5–16: Union General Benjamin Butler lands troops at City Point, Virginia, and begins an indecisive move toward Petersburg. Confederate General Beauregard stops Butler and seals him in behind the Union works at Bermuda Hundred, a neck of land at the confluence of the James and Appomattox rivers.

May 7: Sherman launches the Georgia campaign with a series of flanking movements around Johnston's strongly entrenched Confederates.

May 8–12: The Battle of Spotsylvania, Virginia, ends as a draw. On the final day, Grant and Lee clash at "Bloody Angle," the combined casualties numbering almost twelve thousand.

May 9–24: Union General Philip Sheridan undertakes a sixteen-day cavalry swing around Lee. On May 11, Sheridan's forces defeat J.E.B. Stuart's Confederates at Yellow Tavern, Virginia; during the action, Stuart is mortally wounded and dies the next day.

May 15: The Confederates win the Battle of New Market, Virginia. Engaged: Union, 5,150; Rebels, 5,000, including 247 cadets from the Virginia Military Institute. Casualties: North, 831; South, 577.

May 31: Radical Republicans splinter from the party and, on this date, nominate General John Frémont for president, in Cleveland, Ohio. Frémont withdraws on September 17, citing his concern that his candidacy would divide Union votes and could result in a Democratic victory.

June 1–3: Battle of Cold Harbor, Virginia. On June 3, in a one-hour frontal assault, the Union loses 7,000 in killed and wounded. Cold Harbor is Lee's "last great battle in the field."

June 7: The Republicans nominates Lincoln for a second term. In August, the Democrats nominate McClellan for president.

June 10: Forrest, with 3,500 men, is confronted by 7,800 Federals at Guntown, Mississippi, and, in a stunning victory, captures artillery, the entire train of supply wagons, and 1,623 prisoners.

June 15–18: The Army of the Potomac makes a quick move across the

James River, but fails to take Petersburg. However, the city is put under siege, and Lee is pinned down.

June 19: CSS *Alabama* is sunk off Cherbourg, France, by USS *Kearsarge*.

July 5: Confederate General Jubal Early makes a run on Washington, D.C. As the Union forces defending the city are composed of new recruits and troops on leave, Lee hopes Grant will be forced to pull reinforcements from the Petersburg trenches. Grant sends two divisions, not enough to divert the pressure on Lee, but enough to force Early to retreat to Virginia on July 12.

July 17: Sherman presses Atlanta. Confederate General Johnston is replaced by John Hood.

July 22: Hood attempts an unsuccessful offensive to halt the Union advance on Atlanta. The city is put under siege by Sherman.

July 30: Battle of the Crater, Virginia. Eight thousand pounds of explosives are detonated in a tunnel under the Confederate lines at Petersburg, producing a crater 170 feet long, 80 feet wide, and 30 feet deep. Poor preparation dooms the coordinated Federal attack, however. Casualties: North, 3,798; South, 1,500, including some 300 from the explosion itself.

General Early demands an assessment of $100,000 in gold or $500,000 in greenbacks from Chambersburg, Pennsylvania. When the money is not forthcoming, the town is burned. Grant dispatches Sheridan to handle Early.

August 5: Admiral David Farragut wins the battle for Mobile Bay, Alabama, shutting down one of the last Confederate ports. Some shore defenses surrender, but the city remains in Confederate hands.

August 18–21: The Federals capture and dismantle the Weldon Railroad, cutting off vital Confederate communications with Petersburg. Confederate efforts to dislodge the Federals fail.

September 2: Sherman takes Atlanta. Five days later, civilians are ordered to leave the city.

October 19: Sheridan drives Early from the Shenandoah Valley, depriving the Confederates of one of their last supply sources.

November 8: Lincoln receives 55 percent of the popular vote and 212 electoral votes, to McClellan's 21.

November 11: Sherman orders the destruction of the rail center at Rome, Georgia, and of nonresidential buildings, except for churches, in Atlanta. General Hood snipes at supply lines and tries to draw the Federals into Tennessee.

November 30: Battle of Franklin, Tennessee. Hood mounts an assault, but cannot penetrate the Federal positions at Franklin. Federals withdraw under cover of darkness. Casualties: North, 2,326; South, 6,252.

December 10: Sherman reaches Savannah.

December 10–21: Federal cavalry destroys the Confederate saltworks and lead mines in southwestern Virginia.

December 15–16: Outnumbered, Hood's forces are defeated at the Battle of Nashville, the last major battle for his Army of Tennessee.

December 18–27: General Butler, removed from command in Virginia and sent home, wangles the command of an expedition headed for Fort Fisher, which guards the last open Confederate seaport at Wilmington, North Carolina. Butler's offensive is stymied by strong Rebel defenses, bad weather, and mismanagement.

December 22: Concluding his planned "March to the Sea," Sherman announces to Lincoln, "I beg to present you, as a Christmas gift, the city of Savannah."

JANUARY 16, 1864

SOUTH

RICHMOND DAILY DISPATCH
January 16, 1864

WHIPPED

Dandridge, slave of T. Oliver, was ordered twenty lashes for stealing chickens in the Second Market. The fowls were recovered and delivered up to the owner.

A like number of stripes was inflicted on Alsey, the property of Dr. Walke, of Chesterfield, for entering the house of Mary Lazzarioni and taking, without permission to do so, one plaid worsted dress.

Martha, a Negro woman belonging to Dr. John Dawson, was ordered a whipping for stealing several articles of wearing apparel from Mr. David Brown.

THE SITUATION OF THE CONFEDERACY

We feel perfectly confident in the belief that the despondency which to a certain extent has lately spread over the country is due, in a great degree, to the murmurings of those who have been subjected to the operation of the conscription by the repeal of the substitute laws. Those gentlemen who in the prime of life—with all their limbs sound and intact, with their bodily condition in a state of perfect health, strong and active—thought themselves secured from accident by shot and shell under cover of their substitutes have found themselves mistaken; and there is no end to their lamentations. Of course the country must be gone to the dogs, since *they* are called upon to fight for it. What more terrible calamity can befall it than that they should be disturbed in their patriotic occupations of fleecing the public and hoarding up money, to bear arms, like common people, in defense of their lives, their homes, their families, and their firesides? As long as the question was left to be decided by others, everything was going on well enough. No reverse could daunt their courage, since it did not fall on them; no defeat could abate their hopes, since it did not endanger their moneybags. Now, however, the scene is completely reversed. These patriots see ruin in everything—even in our very successes. The idea of having to shoulder their muskets and face the enemy in person tinges all their contemplations and causes them to see everything through a veil as murky as the very pit of perdition. They live in an atmosphere rendered gloomy by their own personal apprehensions, and they fancy that it is the *only* atmosphere in the world. Because everything looks black and gloomy to them, they believe that everything *is* black and gloomy, in very truth. "Pat," said a gentleman, sleeping at an inn, to his Irish servant, "Pat, open the door and see what sort of night it is." "Plase your honor," answered Pat, opening the door of a press and popping his nose upon a huge cheese, "plase your honor, it's dark and smells like cheese."

The discontent, the murmurs, the gloomy views of this class of malcontents have, we verily believe, done more to dispirit this people than all the disasters we have sustained from the beginning of the war to this moment. Instead of meeting their fortune like men—instead of being thankful that for nearly three years of unexampled trials, dangers, and hardships, they have enjoyed, by the mere payment of a sum of money, a total exemption from them all—instead of taking up their muskets like men and doing their duty as every man is called on to do in this day of trial, a large portion of these people are engaged in no other occupation than that of spreading gloom and discontent around them. And all for what? Because they are called on to serve their country, as well as the poor, ragged, hard-fighting veterans of Lee, Johnston, and Beauregard, to whom they owe it that they have not long ago been stripped of every dollar that they have in the world, and made the servants of their own Negroes and the mockery of the white scoundrels with whom they are associated. Let us not be understood as embracing in these remarks *all* or even the larger portion of the substitute hirers. Some of them, a large portion, accept their fate with cheerfulness; others, quite a large body, were compelled to procure substitutes by a necessity inferior only in its exactions to absolute duty. We speak of that class—and it is a very large one—which procured substitutes for the purpose of making money out of this war, and of that other class, a larger one still, which procured them merely to keep their own carcasses out of danger. These classes it is whose complaints and clamors have had so large a share in depressing the spirits of the people at large.

It must proceed from some such source as this, or how are we to account for it? The country, *certainly,* is in no worse condition now than it has been on more than one occasion heretofore. Compared with the situation in which it stood two years ago—when Donelson surrendered, and New Orleans and Memphis were taken; when McClellan had an army of 250,000 men behind the Potomac and Johnston had less than 40,000 to face him; when the volunteer system had failed to procure any more recruits and Congress was wasting its time, as it is now, in listening to bunkum speeches instead of passing a conscription law. Assuredly, it is not so bad now as it was when McClellan lay around this city with an army of 150,000 men; when every hour a disaster which might throw it open to his advance was expected; when the government was preparing to save itself by flight, and Congress, after hurrying through a conscription bill, just in time to save the country, did actually abandon their posts and fly like a rabble of militia before a charge of cavalry. We hear enormous boasting of their preparations from the enemy, and we give way to panic, just as if they had never boasted before, or as if we had not heretofore withstood them in spite of all their braggadocio. Why, when the war was about to open, they were confident of subduing us with seventy-five thousand men. Twenty-five thousand were to march from Cairo down the Mississippi, twenty-five thousand were to land and march on Charleston, and twenty-five thousand were to move upon Richmond. Not the least doubt was expressed of success, which was to be signalized by hanging Jeff Davis "over the *battlements* of Washington." Have the loud boasts and confident predictions that heralded the march of McClellan upon this city been forgotten? Is nothing remembered of that famous number of a Yankee periodical which contained a picture of his triumphant entry, in all the pomp, pride, and circumstance of glorious war, his gigantic troopers cutting down the poor diminutive "secesh" men, who were seen in crowds throwing themselves on their knees and lifting up their hands to their conquerors, as though imploring the mercy of beings belonging to another race and a higher sphere? Have we forgotten the pompous descriptions of the ironclad vessels and the continued glorifications of Yankeedom's invincible legions which crowded the columns of all their papers at that remarkable period? Have they not said every day in the year that from that day, in so many months, the rebellion was to be crushed? And are we weak-kneed enough now to succumb to what is nothing more than a repetition of their empty bravadoes? Will the people of this country permit their spirits to be cast down by the repinings of men who repine merely because they are compelled to fight for their homes instead of leaving others to do all the fighting for them?

That the Yankees are making desperate efforts to bring the war to a speedy termination cannot be doubted, and we, at least, are not at all disposed to deny it. But the very prices which they offer for the re-enlistment of their veterans proves that this effort will be their last. The very fact that they are enlisting our Negroes to do their fighting for them proves a scarcity of men who have any stomach for the war. Nevertheless, they will make this effort, and it will be gigantic. And how do we propose to meet it? Not, we presume, by a tame surrender; not by giving up our houses to be taken possession of by Negroes; not by turning over all our goods and chattels to be confiscated for the benefit of the Yankees; not by sitting with our arms folded, or wringing our hands and blubbering over our misfortunes. These are the inevitable consequences of submission, and we do not suppose even the most gloomy of the substitute purchasers contemplate such a surrender as that. If they do not, there is but one alternative. It is to obey the laws of Congress cheerfully and with alacrity—to fight the enemy, since better may not be done. While our congressmen are talking, they are preparing for their formidable onset. We must be prepared to meet them, and we can be prepared if the proper steps be taken. We *must* meet them, and we must beat them. What is more, we can meet them, and we can beat them. What is most of all, we will meet them, and we will beat them. Away, then, with all this childish despondency. There is no occasion for it, and if there were, this is not the time to indulge in it. The Confederacy has not yet put forth one half its strength. It has risen always with the occasion, and thus it will continue to rise, as fast as fresh occasions present themselves. For our own part, we never have doubted of the issue, even when McClellan was around this city; and that, we take it, was the darkest hour of the Confederacy.

CHARLESTON DAILY COURIER
January 16, 1864

DESPONDENCY

The tone of despondency manifested by some few journals, by no small number of persons, and by several members of Congress is by no means justified, either by the aspect our affairs exhibit at the present time, or by the prospect which presents itself to the view of the intelligent, manful, and brave.

It is true we are suffering grievously from a redundant and depreciated currency—that the evils flowing from that source have been greatly augmented by the selfishness and avarice of thousands of knavish speculators and extortioners—that our troops failed to win victory in one of the most important battles that have been fought during the course of this war, and that calamitous failure was owing to the influence of feelings that made their defeat a disaster and a disgrace. But even these things do not furnish reasonable cause for the gloom and despondency that have taken possession of so many minds.

We think that the great schemes the enemy is preparing to execute so soon as the incoming of spring, with its genial influences, makes marching and fighting feasible have no little to do with that depression and anxiety. And in truth, those plans he publishes with so imposing a show of boldness and confidence, when seen on paper, are calculated to disquiet even the resolute and hopeful. An army of 300,000 chosen men is to advance in columns of 100,000 on Richmond and Atlanta. Two columns are to assail the Confederate capital, one from the south side of the James, the other from the Rappahannock. These three columns together, composing an immense army, are to be under the command of Grant, and he is expected by the government and the people whom he serves to destroy the armies that oppose his progress; capture Richmond, Atlanta, Charleston, and Savannah; and put an end to the life of our nationality before the beginning of summer.

This is the program the redoubtable Grant has arranged and matured. It is magnificent, and if that lucky captain succeeds in carrying it out, even partially, he will deserve all the praise the Yankee press and people have lavished upon him, and will fairly win the place in the list of military conquerors to which his nation has already exalted him.

This is not the first time our enemies announced to the world that our armies would inevitably be crushed by the immense hosts arrayed against them. The anaconda simile is fresh in the minds of our readers, and we remember how signally that plan failed to crush the limbs and life of the infant Confederacy.[1] And when the great Grant moves his mighty host to assail Richmond, it will not be the first time that capital has been threatened from different quarters. Nor is it at all unlikely that his columns, numbering, according to authorized statements, 200,000 men by the time they are midway between Chattanooga and Richmond, will, together, equal the army at whose head McClellan reached the Chickahominy, whence he was driven in disorder with heavy loss by the very commander who now defends our capital with his army of seasoned and splendid soldiers. The column that is to assail Atlanta is confronted by a general than whom none stands higher, in the judgment of officers and men, for skill, talents, valor, and all the qualities that constitute a great captain. Under his leadership the Army of Tennessee will win new laurels.

And though the figures paraded by the enemy are somewhat formidable, we should consider that an invading army should be threefold stronger than an army of defense. So, far from the enemy being able to comply with that condition, we doubt not that if stragglers and skulkers are compelled to return to their commands, and all who have furnished substitutes are forced to do their own fighting, the armies under Lee, Johnston, and Longstreet will number quite as many as the hosts under the invincible Grant. But granting that our forces are outnumbered and that the Yankee general really brings to the accomplishment of his mighty undertaking the immense host with which we are threatened, who outside Yankeedom believes that he is able to manage an army of that size?—who of us so stupid as to regard him as the equal of any of the generals whose names we have mentioned? He had no reputation in the old army, and all the successes he has achieved have been gained through the aid of overwhelming numbers. And yet, forsooth, this is the man who is to annihilate the armies of the Confederacy, overthrow our government, and put an end to the war in the space of ninety days.

It behooves us to nerve ourselves against these dangers and to prepare to meet them with courage, energy, skill, and the earnest development of our resources. The enemy is full of boasting and presumptuously confident of executing his mighty schemes. But one disastrous defeat will dispirit him, and if we can rout those columns at a distance from their base of supplies and follow up the victory with energy and skill, bearing with manful fortitude meanwhile the sore evils we are suffering under, our heroic efforts may be crowned with success before the summer is gone.

1. General Winfield Scott's "Anaconda Plan."

TO THE CITIZENS OF CHARLESTON

By order of His Honor the Mayor, all persons owning and occupying buildings in the range of the enemy's shells are ordered immediately to have removed all papers, combustible material, etc., contained therein. This notice particularly pertains to the banks, insurance, printing, and law offices, as also the customhouse. Our citizens will see the necessity of this stringent order, and it is to be hoped that it will be cheerfully and promptly attended to, as it is in the interest of these concerned as well as the public authorities.

M. H. Nathan, Chief, Fire Department

NORTH

BOSTON EVENING TRANSCRIPT
January 16, 1864

A CONVENTION OF STATES

Mr. Garrett Davis, in his speech in the U.S. Senate on Wednesday, assumed "that if a convention of all the states were called together and should resolve to do away with the government, they had the right and power to do it." He put in as a salve, however, a remark that he was opposed to any such exercise of power as a practical thing. Again, Mr. Davis said, in answer to a question from a senator of Michigan whether he held that such a convention would have the right to abolish the present government and establish another—and from what source, the Constitution or any other power, it could derive the right—Mr. Davis answered that while he was opposed to such a course, as an abstract proposition the majority of the states had a right to meet together in convention and to do away with the best government on earth. The political partnership could be canceled by the consent of the partners.

Mr. Davis's recognition of an "abstract proposition" refers to his political belief in the Virginia and Kentucky Resolutions of 1798, the pestilent origin of most of the political heresies which have been uttered since the formation of the American Constitution.[2] Under these resolutions, the offspring of William B. Giles and other Jacobins of that day, a

2. In 1798, confronted by the possibility of a war with France, Congress passed the Alien and Sedition Acts, the intent of which was to strengthen the central government and suppress political opposition. At the end of that year, the Virginia and Kentucky legislatures adopted a set of resolutions—the Virginia and Kentucky Resolutions—declaring the Alien and Sedition Acts unconstitutional, in protest of the curtailment of civil liberties authorized by the Acts. Secessionists would later argue that the resolutions, in effect, affirmed the power of individual states to judge the constitutionality of federal legislation.

warfare was made upon the administration of John Adams, which was a Federative administration. Those superbly impractical nuisances in the body politic—the Virginia and Kentucky Resolutions—were the fathers of all the political treason and folly which have been uttered for more than sixty years by nullifiers, secessionists, rebels, and enemies to the Federal government in general.

John C. Calhoun, after he had had the advantage of occupying almost every station in the Federal government up to the second place in the nation, being disappointed at not attaining the first place, turned all his bitterness of soul against the continuation of the rightful government, of which he had hoped and expected to be the head; and then, in the manner in which his disciples have faithfully followed him, he uttered the oracular sentiment, "Nullification is the rightful remedy." All the claims made by the insurgent states resolve themselves into the single right to leave the Union if they please to do so, or to make war upon the Federal government whenever an opportunity for such a demonstration should arrive.

The people of the country have heard enough of conventions of the South. They are nullification conventions, one and all. All the pretended commercial conventions of the South, from their inception to their closing appearances, were disunion conventions. John C. Calhoun, with his followers and supporters, headed one of the first of them, and not one of them ever met which did not sow the seed of disunion.

GENERAL GANTT'S ADVICE TO COPPERHEADS

General Gantt of Arkansas addressed a large Union meeting at Harrisburg, Pennsylvania, Thursday night. In the course of his speech, he gave the following good counsel to grumblers and Copperheads:

> I hear men in the North denouncing secessionists with apparent bitterness, and they say exterminate them but save the Negro. They might as well say of a man bitten by a mad dog, kill the man, but for God's sake spare the dog! [*Laughter.*] We in Arkansas are going to kill the dog and try to save the man. Kentuckians say there are two parties, destructives and conservatives. They believed the destructives were the secessionists and their willing aiders; but these latter called themselves conservatives, forsooth! We in Arkansas are going to vote for whomever you nominate as an unconditional Union candidate for president. [*Cheers.*]
>
> I say to those conservatives that the only way you can stay this

desolation and bloodshed is to say to the South, yield to the government, then we will withdraw our armies. But no! The conservatives have not the time nor the men, they say. They see their true and gallant neighbors shedding their blood in defense of our rights, while you stay at home to watch the Constitution. If you can't fight, if you can't join either side, for heaven's sake keep quiet and say nothing; for when the rebellion is conquered and the soldiers come home, they can see for themselves whether the Constitution is desecrated or not, and punish the desecrators. [*Cheers.*]

By your present conduct in murmuring and muttering, you preach peace propositions and encourage the insurrectionists. I am a stranger. I expect nothing from you. I want nothing from the government.[3] But I tell you truly that the rebellion is looking anxiously upon the course of the so-called conservatives and would like to spur them on, for they expect it will bring delay and final victory to them. I want my suffering people relieved, but I want the old government to embrace the whole territory as of old. [*Cheers.*]

My friends in the South have denounced me because I am telling the truth about them, but I tell you I never met more consummate secessionists than these conservatives of the North. Would the South abuse me if I were not telling the truth about them? I have been among the Rebels, and I know that your conservatism is aiding the South. For once I appeal to you. Leave party and go for your country; nominate an unconditional Union man and elect him. This is what the Union men of the South want. The Rebels are waiting for the inauguration of a new president, and they want your conservatives to succeed. Then will be their time for success. The hardest blow ever struck the rebellion was the Emancipation Proclamation enforced by Union bayonets.

NEW YORK TRIBUNE
January 16, 1864

THE CUSTOMHOUSE

We recently called attention to the fact that the abuses and frauds in the New York Customhouse, which have become suddenly conspicuous,

3. Edward W. Gantt was originally a general in the Confederate army; he switched allegiances in November 1863.

have been for nearly a year investigated by the secretary of the Treasury. We stated also that in the opinion of the secretary, additional legislation was necessary to reach and completely uproot these abuses and frauds. We were obliged further to add that both the stealings from the government and the systematic extortions from merchants find their origin in the systems and customs of Democratic administrations. It appears that these statements, which are all true, do not give pleasure to the *World*—a circumstance which we regret, but which does not lessen the probability of their perfect correctness. We briefly point out its misrepresentations and perversions, disregarding the angry impertinence which seems to be meant as a screen for dishonesty.

The *World* speaks of Secretary Chase's investigation as "an admitted failure." It knows that the investigation is still in progress, that it has unearthed the very frauds which are the present capital of the *World* in its denunciation of Mr. Chase and of Republican corruption, and that it will not stop till not merely personal delinquencies but the system which fosters them is exposed and reformed.

The *World* represents us as specifying two points in which the present laws are at fault, and as being able to present no others; it disposes of those points to its own satisfaction and thereupon argues that there is no necessity of law reform.

We spoke of the prevalent system among merchants of paying customhouse clerks to perform official duties, and the *World* expects its readers to believe that we pointed out this pernicious custom as a provision of law which needs modification. This, too, although we expressly stated that the law and the custom are in direct contradiction. On such an assumption the *World* bases its argument and opinion. We can only say that between the *World,* which is opposed to having any more laws against fraud, and Mr. Chase, who thinks them necessary, we side with the latter. Mr. Chase must be supposed to understand what reform is needed in the customhouse, and we credit him with an honest intention to effect it.

Of course, the real secret of the *World*'s uneasiness is our demonstration that the customhouse troubles are not traceable to Republican corruption, but are the inheritance of Democratic mismanagement and of the organized rascality which Democrats practiced for a series of years. It thinks the revenue system a good one because Alexander Hamilton originated it. Precisely so. What we complain of is the extra machinery which has been tacked on to Hamilton's framework by Democratic administrations, in order to create patronage for the party. The *Tribune* does not "propose to throw aside the work of Hamilton," but only the work of the Democratic pilferers whom the *World* defends. If any corrupt Republicans have taken advantage of methods and customs established by their predecessors, let that corruption be exposed with the utmost fearlessness and punished with the utmost rigor.

The *World* wants to know who are the three clerks whom Solicitor Jourdan directed the district attorney to prosecute. If it sends a reporter to the office of the district attorney of New York, he may, perhaps, learn whether that officer has obeyed instructions to prosecute these persons and, if he has not, why he has neglected that duty. If there has been any dereliction in that quarter, the responsibility can hardly be said to rest with the secretary of the Treasury. He means—and, so far as we have any influence, we mean—that this whole matter of customhouse frauds shall be exposed and corrected, and the *World* shall not defeat that purpose by carping criticisms intended to make partisan capital at the expense of the public good.

FEBRUARY 20, 1864

SOUTH

RICHMOND DAILY DISPATCH
February 20, 1864

THE EXECUTION OF A YANKEE SPY

According to the terms of the sentence pronounced by a court-martial in his case, Captain Spencer Deaton of the 6th Tennessee (renegade) Regiment was hanged in the prison yard west of Castle Thunder yesterday at half past twelve P.M. Long before the hour of execution arrived, the neighboring housetops and fences were thronged with scores of people, anxious to gratify that curiosity which scenes of such a character seldom fail to excite in the minds of many people.

About a quarter past twelve o'clock, a detachment of the military marched into the enclosure and formed themselves in a hollow square around the gallows, soon after which the condemned man was escorted out of the prison between that venerable detective, Captain John Caphart; the Reverend Dr. Carpenter, chaplain of the Castle; and Mr. Wiley, assistant executioner, the rear being brought up by the mammoth black dog so well-known to the visitors of that institution. Arriving at the place of execution, the proceedings of the court-martial and order of execution were read by Captain Callahan in a clear and distinct voice, during the reading of which Deaton stood with his hat on and gazed anxiously around him, as if expecting some deliverance from his impending doom. As soon as the verdict of the court-martial was pronounced, the reverend chaplain gave the signal for prayer, when all heads were uncovered and he delivered a short but impressive invocation to God for mercy upon the unfortunate man's soul. Deaton then replaced upon his head the hat which he had, during the solemn ceremony of prayer, held in his hand, and ascended with a slow and tremulous step the platform from which he was soon to be launched into eternity. Detective Caphart followed and proceeded to adjust the rope over the beam of the gallows and about the neck, arms, and feet of the victim. During this ceremony Deaton looked about him in a half-unconscious state, and when the cap was drawn over his face, he seemed utterly overcome with emotion, exclaiming rapidly and in a feeble voice, "Oh, Lord, have mercy on my soul! I am innocent! Oh, Lord, save me! I am innocent!" The officers who ascended the platform with him had hardly reached the foot of the ladder before his knees gave way under him, and he crouched down as far as the rope would permit. From this sitting posture he was lifted to his feet three times, and had finally to be held up by Mr. Wiley till the support was knocked from under him and he was left dangling in the air.

After hanging about half an hour, he was taken down in the arms of two Negro men and deposited in a common flattop pine coffin, painted red, which had been placed beside the gallows to receive his remains. From the time the pins of the platform had been knocked away until he was taken down, there did not seem to be the slightest movement of his muscles or contortion of his limbs, and everyone thought his death was as sudden as that which usually ensues from the breaking of the neck. But upon examination by Dr. Upshur, the physician of the prison, assisted by the assistant surgeon, it was found that strangulation had caused his death and that his neck had not been broken. The expression of his countenance indicated an easy death, and there were no traces of agony depicted thereon.

In appearance Deaton seemed to be about thirty-five years of age, five feet ten or eleven inches tall, sallow complexion, dark eyes, prominent nose, a pretty, fair forehead, and wore a slight mustache and imperial. He was attired in light-brown pants, black frock coat, and a high-crowned black felt hat, all well worn, his *tout ensemble* exhibiting a common, ignorant man, from a social point of view.[4] He was captured at Knoxville, Tennessee, on the 27th of August. In the terms of the court-martial, he was charged with being a Yankee recruiting officer and spy in our lines, on both of which indictments he was found guilty. The trial took place in western Virginia and was conducted by the officers of General Sam Jones's command. Upon the headboard which is to designate his burial place, Deaton requested that the following memorandum should be made: "Captain Spencer Deaton, Company B, 6th East Tennessee Infantry." His father's address he gave as William Deaton, Strawberry Plains, Jefferson County, east Tennessee. He also claimed to have a brother who is colonel of a renegade Tennessee regiment.

Circumstances have rendered it expedient that we should witness a number of executions, but in no instance has the subject evinced such alarm and despair as was shown by the unfortunate victim who was hanged yesterday. Incidents which have occurred during the last two weeks of his life plainly indicate that he entertained a strong hope of being rescued from his impending doom by the Yankee forces. His execution was first set for yesterday week; but from a letter which he had written to President Davis, stating that he was not then prepared to die, his execution was put off for one week, and we are informed that during Thursday night, before the decision of the president had been made known to him, he would frequently inquire whether fighting was not going on in the streets and if it was not thought the Yankees would take Richmond before day. His attending physician expressed the belief that had it not been for stimulants which had been given him for a few weeks back, he would have died from mental, as well as physical, prostration, and is satisfied that he had fallen away at least forty pounds.

The execution was also witnessed by a large number of the prisoners confined in Castle Thunder, all of whom seemed to view it with the utmost interest. It is to be hoped that the fate of this man will have a tendency to make all who ever contemplated violating them respect the laws of the country in which they reside.

4. *tout ensemble:* French, "whole ensemble," meaning "outfit."

CHARLESTON DAILY COURIER
February 20, 1864

CONGRESSIONAL
SUSPENSION OF THE HABEAS CORPUS ACT

Richmond, 18th—The president has approved, and the injunction of secrecy removed from, the bill to suspend the Habeas Corpus Act. The preamble to the bill asserts that the power to suspend is vested solely in Congress and that Congress is the exclusive judge necessary to the exercising of that power. It declares, in the opinion of Congress, that the public safety requires it. Congress, therefore, suspends the writ until ninety days after the meeting of the next Congress. In cases of arrest by order of the president, secretary of war, or general commanding the Trans-Mississippi Department, to apply only in cases of treason; conspiracy; combinations to assist the enemy's attempts at servile insurrection; desertion; encouraging or harboring deserters, spies; unlawful intercourse or trading with the enemy; advising the enemy, or inciting others to abandon the Confederate cause; burning bridges, or destroying telegraph lines; destroying, or attempting to destroy, government foundries or workshops.

During the suspension of the writ, the president shall cause every arrest to be properly investigated, and if improperly arrested, the party or parties shall be discharged, unless the case can be speedily tried by due course of law.

The president has signed the bill to authorize the impressment of meat for the use of the army, and other provisions, heretofore reported.

FRÉMONT GOING TO FRANCE

Special to the *Marietta Rebel*

Dalton, Georgia, 17th—A Washington dispatch of the 4th says Frémont will succeed Dayton as minister to France. No difficulty with France is apprehended.

SIEGE OF CHARLESTON

Two Hundred Twenty-sixth Day

The enemy continues to shell the city with about the usual effect. One hundred seventeen shots were fired from half past five Thursday afternoon to half past five Friday evening.

It is reported that one of the Yankee blockading ships sank off the harbor during the heavy blow of Thursday.

The Yankees are still at work on their Cummings Point batteries.

NORTH

BOSTON EVENING TRANSCRIPT
February 20, 1864

LATER FROM NEW ORLEANS
NEWS FROM TEXAS—UNION TROOPS REENLISTING

New York, 20th—The steamer *George Washington,* from New Orleans 13th, has arrived.

Advices from Indianola, Texas, are to the 8th instant. Nearly all the troops are reenlisting. The expedition in search of Rebels and lumber found no Rebels, but brought in a lot of lumber.

General Benton comes North to testify in an important case at St. Louis. General Fitz-Henry Warren commands the division during his absence.

The *George Washington* passed the gunboat *Arizona* and bark *Anderson* going up the river, and on the 15th, a hundred miles west of Tortugas, the steamer *Merrimac* for New Orleans.

At New Orleans, gold was 162½@164. Cotton cull at 68½ for good ordinary to 76½ for strict middling. Sugar and molasses in good demand.

OCCUPATION OF JACKSONVILLE, FLORIDA—
CAPTURES OF PRISONERS AND ARTILLERY

Washington, 19th—The following has been received at headquarters:

Baldwin, Florida, February 9, 1864

To Major General H. W. Halleck, General in Chief:—I have the honor to report that a part of my command, under Brigadier General F. Seymour, convoyed by the gunboat *Norwich,* Captain Merriam, ascended the St. Johns River on the 7th instant and landed at Jacksonville on the afternoon of that day.

The advance, under Colonel Guy V. Henry, comprising the 40th Massachusetts Infantry, Independent Battalion of Massachusetts Cavalry, under Major Stevens, and Elders's Horse Battery of 1st Artillery, pushed forward into the interior. On the night of the 8th, passed by the enemy drawn up in line of battle at Camp Vinegar, seven miles from Jacksonville; surprised and captured a battery three miles in the rear of the camp, about midnight; and reached this place about sunrise this morning. At our approach the enemy absconded, sank the steamer *St. Mary's,* and burned 270 bales of cotton a few miles above Jacksonville. We have taken, without the loss of a man, about one hundred prisoners, eight pieces of artillery in serviceable condition and well supplied with ammunition, and other valuable property to a large amount.

Q. A. Gillmore, Major General Commanding

NEW YORK TRIBUNE
February 20, 1864

[UNTITLED]

The news from Georgia is significant. The Rebel governor has ordered all citizens to move with their property to the east side of the Chattahoochee. That river runs from northeast to southwest and cuts off a large triangular section from the northern half of the state, through which our armies are to advance from Chattanooga. The object of the order is to withdraw all supplies and leave the country barren of everything which could sustain our troops. It indicates that a line of defense is to be finally adopted north of Atlanta.

We question the reports that General Sherman's troops have destroyed the bridges on the Mobile and Ohio Railroad, severing the connection between Polk's forces, and that a battle has been fought at Enterprise. It is doubtful that any part of Sherman's column should be so far advanced, unless it was his cavalry. If any bridges have been burned on the Mobile Road south of Meridian, we shall hear next of a Rebel retreat.

[UNTITLED]

In the debate on the Enrollment Bill in the Senate yesterday, Mr. Wilson stated that Kentucky had been called on for eighteen thousand men and had enlisted *less than seven hundred*. As there remain over seven thousand to be furnished from either the white or the black population, it is possible Governor Bramlette may not find his opposition to the recruiting of colored troops especially popular among the whites, who, because of it, will become subject to draft. Mr. Powell said Kentucky did not desire to fill her quota with colored troops. He speaks for the slaveholders, disloyal like himself.

After a protracted debate, the report of the Conference Committee on the Enrollment Bill was adopted: yeas, 26; nays, 16.

THE REBEL DESTITUTION

On Wednesday last we gave, in an article embodying the general order of General Gillmore, the first positive information of the purpose of the expedition to Florida. Certain opposition journals—either from a habitual incapacity to comprehend the propriety of telling the simple truth, or else staggered by the statement that the Union was about to be reconstructed, so far as Florida is concerned, by a very simple method, at the same time that a side blow, and a heavy one, was to be struck at their friends, the Rebels—affected to believe that we were indulging in a vein of gentle irony. The news we publish this morning from the Department of the South will render it necessary for those puzzled journalists to meet the fact in some other way than by the supposition that we were making fun of it. General Gillmore has made a successful lodgment in Florida, has issued an invitation to the people to return to their homes, promises them the protection of the national government, and has thus taken the initiative step to restore the state to the Union. Have our opposition contemporaries any objection to this? Or do they prefer that Florida shall still continue out of the Union and all her resources left for the use of the Rebel armies and to sustain the rebellion?

That this expedition was a wise and timely one is proved in a remarkable way at the very outset. The disloyal portion of the people fled precipitately at the approach of the Union troops, leaving behind them, in some of their houses, a few copies of an important circular, which have fallen into the hands of the military authorities. We print this document in our news columns and hardly need commend it to a careful perusal. It has been for some time known to those whose business it is to learn such facts that the Rebel armies had no other recourse for their needed supply of beef cattle than Florida and that a weekly average of twenty-two hundred heads of beeves had been drawn from that state. To cut off this supply, as we intimated on Wednesday, was one of the purposes of General Gillmore's expedition, and he no sooner enters the state than he has the documentary evidence from the Rebels themselves of how serious a disaster he is about to inflict upon them. This circular was to be transferred only from hand to hand, and the greatest precautions were taken to guard against publicity, and no wonder. It discloses a state of impoverishment as terrible to them to feel as it is important to us to know.

"Bacon is exhausted, and beef our only hope," says the chief commissary of General Bragg's army. "The army must fall back. If the enemy break through our present lines, the wave of desolation may roll even to the shores of the Gulf and the Atlantic," unless "the imminent danger of our army suffering for the want of beef" is arrested. "The troops in Charleston," says the chief commissary of Georgia, "are in great extremity. We look alone to you for cattle; those in Georgia are exhausted."

"Our situation is full of danger. We are almost entirely dependent upon Florida," says the chief commissary of South Carolina. "Extraordinary efforts are required to prevent disaster. Starvation stares the army in the face! The handwriting is on the wall!" exclaims in despair Major Millen of Savannah. There is much more of this emphatic official testimony, and it is enforced in the strongest terms and with the most moving appeals by Commissary White. How hopeless, then, must be the condition of the armies and the people of those Rebel states, with their only source of supply for food completely cut off by General Gillmore? Even the knowledge of the fact of such destitution is worth a successful campaign, and it only needs to make a campaign successfully to see at least the beginning of the end of the rebellion. Forward the armies.

MARCH 19, 1864

SOUTH

RICHMOND DAILY DISPATCH
March 19, 1864

PENNSYLVANIA CAMPAIGN—SECOND DAY AT GETTYSBURG[5]

From Our Own Correspondent

Army of Northern Virginia, March 16, 1864

In two previous letters I have adverted to the parts which Ewell's corps and Heth and Pender of Hill's corps bore in the first day's fight at Gettysburg. Today I propose to speak of the second day's fight. Pickett's division of Longstreet's corps crossed the Potomac on the 25th, Hood's and McLaws's, of the same corps, on the 26th, and these three divisions reached Chambersburg on the 27th of June. Here the whole corps remained for two days. From this point Hood and McLaws moved to Greenwood. Pickett was left at Chambersburg to guard and bring up the rear. On the 1st of July, the corps received orders to move to Gettysburg. It was detained, however, several hours by Johnson's division and the train of wagons which came into the road from Shippensburg. McLaws's division, notwithstanding this delay, reached Marsh Creek, four miles from Gettysburg, soon after dark on the evening of the 1st of July.

5. The watershed Battle of Gettysburg, Pennsylvania, was fought on July 1–3, 1863, between General Lee's forces and General Meade's.

Hood's division got within nearly the same distance by the same time (except Law's brigade, which had been on picket at Guilford, on the road to Emmitsburg, and returned about noon on the 2nd); General Pickett had not yet gotten up.

About noon of the 2nd, Lieutenant General Longstreet began a movement which he had previously been ordered by General Lee to make, viz: to move around and gain the Emmitsburg Road on the enemy's left. The enemy, having been driven back by the corps of Lieutenant General Ewell and Hill on the first day, had taken up a strong position extending from Cemetery Hill along the Emmitsburg Road. On account of the difficulty of finding a route by which the movement could be made without being observed, McLaws did not get into position opposite the enemy's left until about four o'clock. Hood's division was moved farther to our right and was placed in position partially enveloping the enemy's left. Cabell's battalion of artillery, with McLaws's division, and Henry's battalion of artillery, with Hood's division, opened at once upon the enemy. Hood at the same moment moved forward, pressing the enemy upon his left, while McLaws attacked the enemy in front. The enemy was soon driven back upon a commanding hill, which was so steep and rough that ascent was most difficult. At the base of this hill were numerous stone fences, behind which the enemy sought shelter, and these they held with great pertinacity. The enemy were, however, driven from point to point until nearly night, when a very strong force of them met some brigades of Anderson's division of A. P. Hill's corps, driving back one of them and checking another. Barksdale's brigade of McLaws's division was also driven back at the same time.

A portion of Hood's division which had driven the enemy to the precipitous part of the mountain was repulsed about dark with considerable loss. After this, the troops were withdrawn to the position from which they had first driven the enemy. During the fight of this day, Lieutenant General Longstreet was with, and superintended the movements of, McLaws's division, leading the charge of Wofford's brigade in the attack on the enemy's first position on the Emmitsburg Road, and was exposed to a heavy fire of artillery and musketry during the action.

During the fight this evening, Longstreet's corps captured two pieces of artillery, several hundred prisoners, and two stands of colors, with heavy loss, however. Major General Hood was severely wounded, as was Brigadier General G. T. Anderson of Hood's division. Brigadier General Barksdale of McLaws's division was killed; and Brigadier General Semmes, of the same division, was mortally wounded, but has since died;

and fully one half of the field and line officers of these divisions were either killed or wounded in this evening's engagement.

The line of battle on this day was formed with Ewell on the extreme left and Longstreet on the extreme right, with A. P. Hill in the center. We have hurriedly and imperfectly alluded to the battle as fought on the right. Let us now look after the enemy on Ewell's front and see how he had disposed of them. All was ready on this end of the line to attack at eight o'clock in the morning, but word having been received that Longstreet would not be ready for some hours, the whole of the artillery that could be brought to bear was placed into position, the ground carefully reconnoitered, and every precaution taken to ensure success. Andrews's battalion of artillery, under Major Latimer, was placed in position on a hill, from which the batteries on Cemetery Hill, fronting the scene of the first day's fight, were taken in reverse, and two 25-pounder Parrott guns, belonging to the reserve artillery of the corps, were placed on the same ridge, 600 or 800 yards to their rear. Some of the other artillery of the corps was posted near the seminary, just to the right of the Middletown Road; but finding its position unsuitable for doing much against the enemy, they fired only occasionally, in order to draw the fire of the enemy.

About four o'clock in the evening, Longstreet's guns away to the right announced that the battle was opened, and from that time until night there was kept up one of the most magnificently grand and terribly loud cannonades ever heard, far more terrific than at Malvern Hill, though by no means so destructive to us.

Latimer's guns taking the enemy's in reverse, while those on Hill's front and on the right were engaged with them in front, completely silenced the enemy for nearly half an hour, but they soon put thirty or forty guns in position against him and, by far greater weight of metal and superiority of position, so damaged Latimer's guns as to compel his withdrawal from the field after a contest of one and a half hours, except one battery which he kept to repel any advance of the enemy's infantry. He himself remained with this battery and received the wound which resulted in his death, from one of the last shells which the enemy threw. His arm was much shattered, rendering necessary amputation above the elbow. He bore the operation with much cheerfulness of spirits and seemed to be rapidly recovering when secondary hemorrhage ensued. He had now been removed to Harrisonburg, Virginia, and at this point he died, after lingering some six or seven days. His immediate commander, in speaking of him, said, "No greater loss could have befallen the artillery of this corps." This was emphatically true. He was at the time of his death not more than twenty-one years of age, yet there was no better officer in the whole of this army or one more highly esteemed.

Just as Latimer ceased firing, Johnson's infantry was ordered forward to the attack. It was now not more than half an hour before sunset. In passing down the hill on which they had been posted, and while crossing the creek, they were much annoyed by the fire to which they were subjected from the enemy's artillery, which, from Cemetery Hill, poured nearly an enfilade fire upon them. The creek was wide and its banks steep, so that our men had to break ranks in order to cross it. Having passed the creek and getting close under the hill which the enemy occupied, General J. M. Jones, who was on the right, re-formed his line and advanced steadily up the hill to the attack. But before the brigade had proceeded very far, General Jones was wounded, and his senior colonel being also shot about the same time, the brigade was for a while without a commander, and was thrown into some confusion, and finally retired a short distance. The Louisiana brigade of General Nicholls, Colonel J. M. Williams commanding, conformed their movements to those of General Jones. On the extreme left General G. H. Steuart's brigade was more successful. Pushing around to the enemy's left, he enfiladed and drove the enemy from a breastwork they had built in order to defend their right flank, and which ran at right angles in the rest of their lines up the mountainside. The enemy, however, quickly moved forward a force in order to retake it, but were repulsed, our troops occupying their own breastworks in order to receive their attack. It was now dark, and General Steuart made no further effort to advance, the ground being new to him, and very rugged and precipitous.

General Early, upon hearing General Johnson's infantry engaged, sent forward Hays's Louisiana and Hoke's North Carolina brigades (under Colonel Avery). These troops, advancing as a storming party, quickly passed over a ridge and down a hill. In a valley below they met two lines of the Federals posted behind stone walls. These they charged. At the charge the Federals broke and fled up the hill, closely pursued by our men. (The enemy, after repulsing General Jones's brigade of Virginians, pushed a column down the valley, between them and General Early, with the view of turning Jones's right flank; but hearing Early's guns, they hastily returned.) It was now dark. But Hays and Avery, still pursuing, pushed the enemy up the hill and stormed the Cemetery Heights. Says a most intelligent spectator who witnessed this charge, "I have never seen or heard anything more intensely exciting and terrible than this contest. From the point where I stood, just outside of the town, lighted up by the flashes of the enemy's guns, thirty or forty pieces, perhaps more, were firing grape and canister with inconceivable rapidity at Early's column. It must have been that they imagined it to have been a general and simultaneous advance, for they opened on our men in three or four directions besides that which they were attacking. Fortunately, in the darkness they overshot, and our men did not suffer very severely. Hays's and Hoke's brigades pressed on and captured two or three lines of breastworks and three or four of their batteries of artillery. For a few moments every gun of the enemy on the heights was silenced, but by the time General Hays could get his command together, a dark line appeared in front of them and on either flank a few yards off. The true situation soon became clear. The Yankees were bringing up at least a division to retake the works. General Hays, being unsupported by the troops on his right (which were from Hill's corps), was compelled to fall back, bringing with him four stands of captured colors and some seventy-five prisoners." Colonel Avery, 6th North Carolina troops, commanding Hoke's brigade, was killed in this attack.

It is believed that if this attack had been supported by a simultaneous one on our right, different results would have followed. Major General Rodes commenced to advance simultaneously with General Early. He had, however, more than double the distance of Early to go, and being unsupported by the troops on his right, who made no advance, he consequently moved slower than he would have done had he been supported. Before reaching the enemy's works, Early had been repulsed, and so General Rodes halted, thinking it useless to attack, since he was unsupported, especially as the enemy had heavy reinforcements just coming up and over a hundred guns which could be brought to bear on the line of Rodes's advance.

When the second day closed, this was the position of Ewell's corps. Johnson's left had gained important ground, part of it being a very short distance from the top of the mountain, which, if once gained, would command the whole of the enemy's position, but his right had made no progress. Early's attack, *almost* a brilliant success, had produced no results, and he occupied nearly his former position. Rodes, having advanced nearly halfway to the enemy's works and finding there good cover for his troops, remained in the occupancy of his advanced position.

This was the condition of affairs on our extreme right and left. Hill, during this day, occupied the center, and only a part of his corps was actively engaged. Late in the afternoon of this day, while Lieutenant

General Longstreet's corps and a portion of Major General Anderson's division were assaulting the enemy's left, Major General Pender, having ridden to the extreme right of his command to put them in the fight, should the opportunity offer, received a severe wound in the leg from the fragment of a shell. The wound, at first pronounced not dangerous, subsequently proved fatal. Words from the writer in eulogy of this brave and accomplished officer are unnecessary. Speaking of him in his preliminary report of Gettysburg, General Lee says, "This lamented officer had borne a distinguished part in every engagement of this army and was wounded on several occasions while leading his command with conspicuous gallantry and ability. The confidence and admiration inspired by his courage and capacity as an officer were only equaled by the esteem and respect entertained by all with whom he was associated for the noble qualities of his modest and unassuming character."

Early in the morning of the 2nd of July, Wilcox's brigade began to take position, but finding that three regiments of Yankee sharpshooters had anticipated them and were occupying the position they had intended to take, Wilcox's men engaged the Yankees and, after a sharp fight, drove them off and occupied the ground from which the Yankees had just been driven. This brigade, with Perry and Wilcox, was formed on the right of Hill's corps, with the left of Longstreet's being joined onto Barksdale's brigade of McLaws's division. After the spurt of a fight in the morning, the troops of these brigades rested until about four o'clock, when the attack began on the right and gradually extended around to the left. After Barksdale's brigade of McLaws's division had been engaged for some time, Wilcox, Wright, and Perry were ordered forward, encountering a line of the enemy and soon putting them to rout. Still pressing forward, these three brigades met with another and stronger line of the enemy, backed by twelve pieces of artillery. No pause was made. The line moved rapidly forward and captured the artillery. The enemy, however, fought with greater obstinacy than usual, and their artillery mowed down our men at every discharge. On reaching, however, a ravine (some 300 or 400 yards beyond the captured artillery) of dense bushes, it was discovered that the enemy had another heavy line of battle immediately on the other side, with a large amount of artillery posted on the ridge behind them. Upon our reaching this ravine, the enemy attempted to drive us away by a charge, but was repulsed with heavy loss. Seeing the weakened condition of our men, another fresh line of battle was thrown forward by the enemy, but, after an obstinate fight, was repulsed. And now the condition of our troops became critical in the extreme. Wilcox, Perry, and Wright had charged most gallantly over a distance of more than three quarters of a mile, breaking two or three of the enemy's lines of battle and capturing two or three batteries of artillery. Of course our lines were greatly thinned and our troops much exhausted. By strange mismanagement, as yet unexplained, no reinforcements were sent to this column by the lieutenant general commanding! Perhaps when the official report of Lieutenant General Hill shall be given to the public, the whole matter will be made clear. Again the enemy made a third and most determined effort to force us back, and having succeeded in driving back Barksdale on the right of these brigades, they in turn were of necessity compelled to retreat.

It was now dark, and our troops were repulsed at all points save where Brigadier General Steuart held his ground. A second day of desperate fighting and correspondingly frightful carnage was ended. But our noble commanding general still believed himself and his brave army capable of taking these commanding heights and thus being able to dictate a peace on the soil of the free states. With what success this was attempted it will become us to inquire in our next installment, when we shall recount the events of the third day's fight at Gettysburg.

X

CHARLESTON DAILY COURIER
March 19, 1864

[UNTITLED]

Have any readers considered what would have been the indirect political results of an early completion of the project so urgently advocated thirty-five to forty years ago for a connection between the Atlantic and the Ohio River—Charleston and Cincinnati? The farsighted statesmen who desired that connection—among them Calhoun and Hayne, two of our brightest and best names—contemplated more than merely commercial results.

The dissolving tendencies of the old Union were aggravated and accelerated by the growth of the Northwest, exactly as that growth was connected with and derived through or from New England.

The first election of a distinctively western (northwestern) president was the signal for separation. Under such intercourse and connection as the South could and should have opened with the Northwest, the growth of that great region might have been corrected and trained into conservative channels. The best minds of that teeming region—excluding, of course, the raw immigrants, imbued with the destructive radicalism of the lowest European Red or Black Republicanism—are beginning to see that they have sacrificed much to the grasping and godless aspirations and policy of New England. They are now and have been fighting the battles of New England ideas and schemes against their own interests and in devotion to a noble and generous but mistaken sense of "loyalty."

The bravest and best soldiers and officers that the Yankees have shown of American birth have been chiefly from the Northwest. The villainous officers and commanders who have labored even to add new motives to Southern hatred of the Yankee are in some cases from New England, whence also come all of the obscene and grossly offensive letters, so far as we have seen letters taken from battlefields. In a large package, including more than twenty clearly legible letters, taken after the first battle of Manassas, all were from New England, and with two exceptions—both letters from one writer—all were such as no Southern woman would write to a friend, or sister, or husband.

The troubles which vexed Washington and his best generals through the Revolution were in large proportion from New England. The failures and violations of agreement which dissolved the old Confederation were mainly from New England. The factious opposition which embarrassed the government during 1812–14, a war undertaken for the rights of shipping, and mainly of New England, was all from New England.[6] Counterfeited novelties and inventions in so-called religion, morals, arts, literature, and science, and new discoveries generally in all resources, by which mean men seek to eke out a living without work and from the labors of others, are nearly all from New England.

The best men whom New England has reared—of men over middle age—have come from and out of New England. Old England keeps at home her best sons and colonizes the troublesome or lazy members of society. New England has for years sent off her best and worthiest representatives, and if specimens of the New England character, as lovingly depicted by old writers, are now wanted, they can be easiest found out of New England.

There must have been a gross mistake in political geography. New England was, perhaps, designed to keep house alone, or with Canada. Not a cause which ever threatened the American Union up to its dissolution but may be traced to New England.

6. War of 1812 (1812–14).

[UNTITLED]

The men of our army are not hirelings. They are mostly men who are voluntarily enduring untold hardships and encountering imminent peril for their country, to save it from subjugation and destruction. They are entitled to the utmost respect, and the officer who would put an indignity upon one of them wantonly is guilty of a cowardly crime. Efficient discipline, so far from being the result of severity, is not attained without that *esprit de corps* which results from mutual confidence and respect between officers and men.[7]

Is it not possible that many of the desertions from our army are caused by the character of some of our officers?[8] If the officer is complaining continually of his superiors, of the government, of the management of everything—if he is always expressing doubts of our success, uttering the most gloomy prognostications, and deploring the condition of the country—is he not encouraging and nursing discontent and sedition in the minds of his men? Can this be of any service to the cause? says the *Floridian*.

NORTH

BOSTON EVENING TRANSCRIPT
March 19, 1864

KENTUCKY UNIONISM

The *Louisville Journal*, commenting upon a communication from a Rebel young lady, justifies its adherence to the Union—how? By any broad and generous considerations of patriotic duty to the whole country? By the exhibition of any such spirit as moved the Northern and Eastern states to rush to the defense and preservation of the entire nation? Not at all. The *Journal*'s whole argument is that of intense and narrow local selfishness. Its object was to save Kentucky from being the battleground. It was the position of Kentucky between the belligerents, not unconditional loyalty, that induced the *Journal* to advocate and insist upon continuance in the Union. This is a frank avowal and accounts for the fact that not a little of Kentucky Unionism has been just so much Unionism as was necessary to save Kentucky from the sad experiences of Ten-

7. *esprit de corps:* French, "spirit of body," meaning "team spirit."

8. Desertions became an endemic problem in the Confederate army after the reverses of 1863. In October 1864, President Davis announced that "two thirds of the army are absent from the ranks." In the Union army the rate of desertion was 24 percent in the regular army and 6 percent in the volunteer army.

nessee. Anything beyond this was not to be granted. There was a time when the double-faced neutrality, loving the South and looking to the North for safety, had an influence. That time has gone by. The Federal cause does not need to consult Kentucky border policy, but Kentucky may discover that her politicians have succeeded in putting their proud state in a false and, for her, unfortunate position.

NEW HAMPSHIRE'S LAST QUOTA

By proclamation of Governor Gilmore, it is stated that the quota of New Hampshire, under the president's call for 200,000 men, is 2,626. The accredited excess of volunteers under the previous calls was 291, and the reenlistments of veterans number 1,676—leaving only 659 necessary to fill the new quota. The proclamation concludes as follows:

> On the first day of April, the munificent government bounties of four hundred dollars to veterans and three hundred dollars to fresh recruits will cease to be paid. Let us fill to the maximum, before that day, the ranks of our noble 1st New Hampshire Cavalry, which now numbers 457 men, and New Hampshire is again in excess of all demands upon her. But I would appeal to the patriotic citizens of our state to give to their government no stinted or niggardly support. Let each subdistrict see that its quota is full, beyond all question, by April 1. Let us unite in reiterating the statement that "there shall never be another draft in the Old Granite State."

ARKANSAS A LEGAL FREE STATE

Little Rock, Arkansas, 18th—Partial election returns from eleven counties give more votes than the whole number required by the president to replace Arkansas in the Union. The other counties will give full five thousand more. The new state constitution was almost unanimously ratified, there being only 137 votes against it. Arkansas is thus declared a free state in the Union, and the whole free-state ticket is elected. Guerrilla bands made violent threats; nevertheless, the citizens were enthusiastic in their determination to vote the state back into the Union, many going to the polls at the risk of their lives. The military used every exertion to protect the voters.

NEW YORK TRIBUNE
March 19, 1864

[UNTITLED]

The Senate debated yesterday the bill to promote enlistments of colored troops by freeing the wives and children of all enlisted soldiers. The second section provides for compensation, and Mr. Wilkinson moved to strike it out, declaring he did not want this government to become the purchaser of slaves and that we had already gone too far in acknowledging property in slaves. Undoubtedly, and it is quite time to begin to consider whether, if anybody is to have compensation, the slave should not have it a hundred times rather than the master. The master has had the lifelong unpaid toil of the slave. Why should he be paid for not continuing to steal it?

As to the bill, we cannot doubt that it will pass in some shape and, we earnestly hope, without the extension of this ruinous and demoralizing policy of compensation. No loyal or honorable senator can say that we ought to expect the enlistment of black soldiers to fight for a Union which keeps their families in bondage. We are swift to protect the rights of the master; let us at least acknowledge those of the Negro.

[UNTITLED]

New Jersey is discussing the right of soldiers to vote, and the New Jersey Copperheads, following the example of their New York brethren, are unanimous in opposing it. A majority of the Legislative Committee on Elections have reported against the bill which had been submitted—a bill against which they can find no argument in the Constitution, and no argument of any kind except the hatred which they bear to the defenders of the Union. The loyal minority of the committee presents a clear, brief statement of the question at issue, demonstrating that there is no constitutional restriction upon the place of voting and that the right of the soldiers to cast their ballots in camp is as perfect as the right to cast them at home. Indeed, the law is so plain that its opponents have no better suggestion to offer against it than that the exercise of the right of suffrage will be an infringement of the sovereignty of another state; to appreciate the force of which it is necessary to remember that the New Jersey soldiers are in Virginia and that the stay-at-home Copperheads disfranchise them to preserve intact the imaginary rights of the state which they are fighting to subdue. A still more ingenious proposal is that they should be sent home to vote at every election, no matter what may be the exigencies of battle or campaign. Such a plan would doubtless be approved by Mr. Jefferson Davis and was probably put forth as an assurance to him that his New Jersey allies are vigilant in his behalf.

The New Jersey legislature being strongly Peace Democratic, we presume the soldiers must make up their minds to be swindled out of their rights so long as they remain in the field.[9] But wait till they *can* vote, and see what side the state will take.

REBEL PLOTS

We have, within the last few months, published letters from a correspondent at Washington who escaped a few months ago from Richmond, where he had been constrained to occupy an official position in the Rebel War Office. If all that this gentleman relates be true—and we have no reason to doubt it—his statements are more interesting and important than any others that have been made public in relation to the rebellion and the character and plans of its leaders. Some weeks since, we published his bold impeachment of the genuineness of the letter of T. Butler King of Georgia, which the *News* of this city first made public as an evidence of the desire of leading Southerners for peace on some reasonable terms. Our correspondent denounced this letter as a forgery, got up in complicity with Northern Peace Democrats and promulgated for the express purpose of creating disunion at the North and aiding that party in the autumn elections. The exposure was so circumstantial as to carry with it a conviction of its truthfulness. If it were possible to meet a charge so serious, would it have been passed over in silence? With our Copperhead contemporaries the *Tribune* is a favorite paper. They sleep, as one of them has said, "with a file of it under their pillows." What the *Tribune* says, what they choose to assume it says, and what they would be very glad to have it say, however far it may be from our intention, form the staple of Copperhead editorials. *Tribune* here, *Tribune* there, *Tribune* everywhere—they have little else to talk about from day to day. Why have they not undertaken to crack this delectable nut of the alleged forgery of the T. Butler King letter? Manifestly because they were afraid of their own fingers. The *News,* which published the letter itself with a notable flourish of trumpets, has observed an absolute and ominous silence upon the exposure of our correspondent.

9. Peace Democrats, a faction of the Democratic party in the North, generally opposed the administration's war policies and called for a negotiated peace with the South. They were accused, with some justification, of prolonging the war by encouraging continued Southern resistance. Though of the same party, War Democrats, such as Andrew Johnson, supported the Union war effort.

We publish, this morning, another letter from the same source. Its revelations are interesting, and as with those heretofore received, we have no reason for doubting its statements, almost incredible as some of them seem. That the Rebel authorities should seriously propose to assassinate or kidnap Mr. Lincoln will startle many good people, but they are thoughtless as well if, after the experience of the last three years, they believe the Rebels would hesitate at any measure, however desperate, which promised to aid them in the desperate work of the rebellion. There is no doubt that the address which the Richmond papers assert was found upon Colonel Dahlgren, ordering the assassination of Mr. Davis, was a forgery. Is it not probable that their own plot to compass the death of President Lincoln suggested the imputation of such a plan to our forces, to be substantiated by the forged paper declared to have been found upon the person of the dead colonel? It is certainly probable.

At any rate, we publish the story of our correspondent as he sends it to us. That he states what he believes to be true we have not the slightest doubt. If anybody can prove it to be false, we shall accept the evidence.

APRIL 16, 1864

SOUTH

RICHMOND DAILY DISPATCH
April 16, 1864

FROM THE SOUTHWEST

Dalton, Georgia, 14th—Artillery firing was heard in the direction of Cleveland this evening, supposed to be the enemy practicing.

It is reported that McPherson's corps has arrived at Huntsville.

The weather is cloudy and threatening rain.

Meridian, Mississippi, 14th—Advices from beyond our lines confirm the report of the Confederate victory in the Trans-Mississippi Department. The wounded are arriving at Baton Rouge in large numbers.

Powers's cavalry had a fight recently at Plain's Store, near Woodville, whipping the enemy, taking a number of prisoners and one piece of artillery.

Colonel John Scott takes command of the cavalry of east Tennessee.

FROM TRANS-MISSISSIPPI

Mobile, Alabama, 15th—Western advices announce that Chalmers has captured Fort Pillow and two regiments of from 800 to 1,200 Negroes and eight guns and destroyed two transports.

Second Dispatch

Mobile, Alabama, 15th—Mississippi River advices from different points report great battles between Kirby Smith and Banks, near Shreveport, in which Banks was defeated with the loss of *fourteen thousand men* killed, wounded, and captured.

Baton Rouge and other hospitals are full of the Yankee wounded.

CHARLESTON DAILY COURIER
April 16, 1864

BRITISH AND FOREIGN OPINION—A WARM RECEPTION IN A COLD COUNTRY—THE FEELING IN NEW YORK—DIX AND DIXIE—NEW YORK POLITICIANS—THE CARNIVAL OF GREENBACKS—THE SNOBBERY OF SHODDY—BROADWAY AS IT WAS AND IS, ETC.

Special Correspondence of the *Courier*

Montreal, Canada East, March 25, 1864

After following the calls of business in the West Indies and Europe, I am at length enabled to catch a breathing spell here in Canada, to give you the results of my observations upon matters and things abroad. This remark I can make, and I think it will be gratifying to all your readers—wherever I have wandered upon God's footstool, I have, as a *Southerner,* found myself in the midst of friends. There can be no mistake about the world's sympathy. Ministers and diplomatists may wrap themselves in the frigid reserve of *expediency,* and fractions of the masses may run after the theories of pseudo-philanthropists, but the people are with us everywhere. If hospitality is a test, in London, in Paris, in Havana, in Montreal, no stranger is more eagerly sought after and more warmly cherished than he who represents the land of Stonewall Jackson. And I firmly believe that this heavy burden in our favor will bear fruit in the shape of active intervention, should we ever be pushed to the wall.

Canada is in intimate commercial relations with the Northern states, but those interests cannot smother that innate and characteristic sentiment of the British heart: sympathy for the little fellow who pluckily contests his rights against the overgrown bully. For these reasons, a Rebel can have a good time of it here. The British possessions are crowded with refugees from the South, most of them the victims of expatriation from Kentucky, Tennessee, and the banks of the Mississippi River. There are a few families from the Atlantic coast. I have met two from Charleston. Donegana's Hotel is the Confederate headquarters. The alliance between England and the Confederacy was cemented in formal style a few weeks ago. Lord Abinger, who is an officer of the Guards, one of the "crack" British regiments now in garrison here, was married to Miss Magruder, the beautiful and accomplished niece of the Confederate commander in Texas. All that was lovely and chivalrous of the two empires, sojourning in Montreal, appeared at the nuptials.

Winter reigns with a cruel sway over the Canadas. As far as the eye can sweep, the landscape lies covered with its mantle of snow. The St. Lawrence is frozen solid. Heavily laden teams make it the common thoroughfare. The river is icebound as far down as Quebec. Until the last of April, Canada is closed to traffic with the world, save by the lines of railway which have their termini in the Yankee ports. The Canadian Company's steamers to Liverpool sail during the winter months from Portland. This will explain why I ran the risk of my neck by trying to get to Canada through the Federal states. About six weeks ago I took passage from Liverpool to New York on one of the Cunard steamers. A little disguise and an assumed name permitted me to stop in New York about ten days, in tolerable security, interrupted occasionally, I must admit, by qualms of nervousness and visions of Lafayette. However, I discovered myself to old friends whom I could trust, and during the brief stay I made, I was enabled to gather items and information which may perhaps be of some interest to the readers of the *Courier*.

Just now I alluded to the sympathy felt for our cause in Europe and Canada. But nowhere is that sentiment stronger than in the city of New York. I was astonished at its extent and depth. A little explanation is necessary to account for the anomaly of a community opposed to the war and yet represented in the army by thirty thousand soldiers. While the mass of the people are for peace and, if necessary, recognition, the city is governed by the party in power in Washington. General Dix reigns supreme, backed by the whole military strength of the government. As long as the Federal army is successful in the field, that moral influence is strong enough to keep the people quiet. But let disaster loom up, and the popular discontent manifests itself—witness the draft riots in July last, when the mob turned its wrath upon the Negro as one of the causes of the war and would have proceeded to the hanging of the abolitionists had not the Democratic idol of the time, Governor Seymour, interfered, with treacherous promises of state protection against the government. Time was thus procured to import fifty thousand foreign soldiers, and the people found themselves bound hand and foot. I have heard it stated that not one in five of the soldiers recruited in New York are citizens. The ranks are filled up from the continual stream of European immigration. When the war broke out, the Democratic masses in the city were opposed to Lincoln's plan of coercion. But the furor from the country reached New York. The abolition newspapers took courage and launched out in the most insane ravings. A mob of Black Republicans, really contemptible in number, visited the offices of the peace newspapers with threats of destruction. Bennett, who is in his dotage, was frightened, and the *Herald* went over in a day and devoured all its previously expressed opinions. The Democratic leaders in New York finally gave way to the outside pressure, and the flag excitement then carried everything before it. The fanatics raised flags on the church steeples (I saw one still flying from Grace Church the other day). An illustration of the want of backbone in the Democratic politicians was related to me. I do not think it has ever appeared in print. After the "firing upon Sumter" (the era from which everything is reckoned in the North), and while the excitement was beginning to rage, a meeting of prominent Democrats was held at the New York Hotel. Resolutions of the strongest character against coercion were passed, and among those who delivered speeches, in which they made use of the stereotyped threat that Federal armies must pass over their Democratic dead bodies on their way to subjugate the South, were Daniel E. Sickles and Thomas Francis Meagher. Their knees gave way a week afterward, and they sought commissions in the army. Other Democratic politicians, like Daniel S. Dickinson and "Beast" Butler, who formerly considered it a privilege to "lick the Southern boots," followed suit. But the conservative masses, I am satisfied now, were always opposed to the war. A reign of terror existed for above a year. People were dragged from their beds at night and thrown into prison. Newspapers were suppressed, and the administration indulged in every enormity with impunity, until the election of Seymour as governor of New York broke the chains. Since then, the partisans of peace have unloosed their tongues. Vallandigham, an avowed peace man, received the largest vote ever thrown for a Democrat in Ohio—184,000. He was beaten by the soldiers' vote and a series of outrageous frauds. In November last, Gunther, an open and decided peace man, swept the city of New York for mayor. The *New York Day Book,* a furious opponent of the war, has nearly a hundred thousand circulation. The *New York News,* Ben Wood's paper, is avowedly for peace. A prominent Democrat whom I met, and who had just returned from stumping New Hampshire, asserted to me that eight out of every ten Democrats in that state were opposed to the war, and the stronger he talked peace, the more he delighted his hearers. It is well-known that the administration carries the state elections by permitting those soldiers, and only those, who agree to vote the abolition ticket, to go home on furlough at election time.

I have dwelt upon these evidences of an antiwar element at the North because I regard its existence as of the utmost importance in determining the length of the contest. I shall allude more at length to the subject in its bearing upon the presidential election in a future letter. But let me remark here that there cannot be in our own country more bitter *haters*—that's the word—of Lincoln and the party in power than those I met with in the North. I verily believe that if the floodgates of antiabolition wrath could be opened today in New York, not an abolitionist, from Beecher down to Greeley, would escape instant immolation. They would be torn to pieces, burned alive, or blown from the cannon's mouth—so furious is the feeling against them.

This, however, is under the surface. It will seethe and boil until the day of the great reaction. At present, New York holds high carnival. The enormously inflated currency gives an apparent gilding to everything. Every man has more money (greenbacks) in his pockets than ever he had before. It comes so easily—therefore, he spends it lavishly. Retail trade is stimulated to an extravagant degree. Never before was there such a glitter and show, and bustle, and pleasure-seeking in New York. Mansions outvying the magnificence of European palaces are going up on Fifth Avenue. Five thousand showy equipages stream through the broad pathways of Central Park every afternoon. The great thoroughfare, Broadway, is a jam of omnibuses, carriages, and wagons; the sidewalks are a confused crush of pedestrians; the shop windows dazzle with their splendor. A dozen theaters, a score of lesser shows, and a host of underground "concert and pretty waiter girl" saloons are crammed to suffocation. Grand balls follow each other nightly, where, as well as at the Italian Opera House, the ladies blaze with diamonds and precious stones and are gorgeous in silks, and tulle, and lace, and moiré antique. Delmonico's three restaurants and a new palatial eating house, with gilded windows and doors, on Fourteenth Street, called the "Maison Doree," are filled with people at all hours, gorging themselves with rich food and getting merry over expensive wines. John Morrissey has a huge gambling den on the most public part of Broadway, where greenbacks are shoveled around by the bushel. The countrypeople swarm into town to get rid of their money and join in the frenzied dance around the altar of pleasure. The hotels turn away hundreds daily. Sometimes travelers ride from hotel to hotel for hours in a despairing search for accommodation. Houses are almost impossible to procure, and rents are enormous. The Stock Exchange is the scene of the wildest excitement. Six sessions of the Stock Board are held daily, and as those are not enough to satisfy the passion for gambling, two more have been commenced, for evenings, at the Fifth Avenue Hotel. Fifty million dollars' worth of stocks are sold daily and nightly. Half of these stocks are acknowledged bubbles. Fortunes are made in an hour. I have been told of a clerk who ventured into the exchange with $160 and cleared the week with $100,000, every cent of which, however, he lost in one week more. Vanderbilt and George Law, the stock kings, are wealthier than the Astors. It has become unfashionable to cavil at a charge. Ask any price, and it will be given. A lady pays two thousand dollars for a piece of brocade to make a dress; a man gives ten thousand dollars for a span of carriage horses and thinks nothing of it; another spends five thousand dollars on a dinner party; another pays fifty dollars for a choice seat at the opera; another pays ten thousand dollars a year rent for a three-story house on Fifth Avenue. (I know these figures will hardly look *large* to the eyes of the Confederate readers, but it must be remembered that gold is at a premium of only 64 percent in New York City at present.) And thus everybody is taking a part in the saturnalia. Even the soldiers receive from four hundred to one thousand dollars' bounty for reenlisting and contribute to the general jollification. This picture is not overdrawn. I doubt if the world's history ever knew of a similar era of popular delirium. Some of the newspapers are alarmed and cry out loudly against the outrageous extravagance of the hour. The abolition organ, the *New York Times,* entreats the people to go back to entrenched expenses and private economy, or make up their minds for financial ruin. The fact is, almost everyone regards the Federal currency as eventually worthless, but "we have got into the scrap, and it's too late to help it now." "The country is bound to go to the devil anyhow," and "we might as well have a good time while the fun lasts."

New York is not alone the abode of madmen. Boston, Philadelphia,

Chicago, Cincinnati, and Washington display the same features, though to a more moderate extent. But the disease is a national one, and it will be discovered prevailing among the land speculators in the interior of Michigan as well as among the merchants and stock gamblers of the "Empire City." Foremost of those who have thrived by the war are the government contractors. Thousands have risen from comparative poverty to great affluence through their dealings with the Washington authorities. So many of this class, vulgar and illiterate but shrewd and unscrupulous men, with their wives and families, have prospered that a new order has been created in society—the "Shoddy Aristocracy," so called. They spend money with unbounded extravagance and may readily be recognized by their impudent assumptions of "ton" and a ridiculous display of jewelry. I met one of these people in Montreal a few days ago, who assured me that he had made half a million dollars since the war commenced, and added he with a chuckle, "Everything I sell to the government I make a hundred percent on."

It would not require the wisdom of a prophet to foresee where this will lead the Yankees. It is one of the most hopeful signs of our ultimate triumph that our enemies are wasting their strength and substance in riotous living.

With the depreciated currency, prices have gone up; taking into consideration the difference in the value of exchange and gold, every article of prime necessity is higher at the North than in the Confederate states. And the advance is felt to be more burdensome by the Yankees than by our own people, because they have not, like us, been inured to privation, nor accustomed to feel in every fiber of their being that any personal sacrifice is better than a failure of the cause.

It was the custom of our people, before they became a separate confederation, to spend their summers at the North, and I presume that to nine out of ten of your readers, Broadway has been almost as familiar as any street in Charleston or Richmond. Perhaps it will interest them to know whether it has changed in its appearance these last three years. Many new and magnificent stores have arisen. Stewart has a marble palace at the corner of Tenth Street. It is finer than any store I have seen in London or Paris. Wallack's Theater is in a new building on the block next to Fourteenth Street. There is a splendid hotel, with a marble front, on the corner of Twenty-sixth Street, called the St. James, and another of equal magnificence lower down called the Albemarle. Nearly all of Broadway below Broome Street is occupied with wholesale stores. The fashionable part of the street now extends as high up as Thirty-fourth

Street. A horse railway runs through the upper part of Broadway. Madison Square is becoming the center of the city. It is faced by several fashionable hotels. A new theater is projected there, and the local authorities talk of building a new city hall in the park. The lower part of Broadway preserves its olden features. There is the same apparently inextricable jam of omnibuses opposite Barnum's Museum, and the Battery clings to its latter-day characteristics of dirt and unsavoriness. The City Hall Park is covered with unsightly wooden barracks for soldiers. You remember the story of the countryman who got up on the steps of the Astor House to wait "until the procession passed by." There is the same eternal procession passing up and down the sidewalks. A fair proportion are soldiers, but the uniform appears much less frequent than in our cities. To a Southern eye there is something very odd-looking in the crowds of smartly dressed men, in broadcloth coats and "stovepipe" hats, who pass by. Uptown, the ladies trip along, arrayed in all the hues of the rainbow and rejoicing in carefully displayed Balmoral skirts and coal-scuttle bonnets, trimmed profusely with artificial flowers. On the street corners, newsboys yell in your ears the latest editions of the daily papers, with appetizing morsels of war news. During the first two years of the war, these industrious gamins had a fresh Yankee victory for every hour of the day, but they have got over that sort of thing now. Even the most verdant pedestrian cannot now be taken in with a vociferous announcement of the "Capture of Richmond," or the "Fall of Fort Sumter." When night falls upon the city, Broadway above the St. Nicholas is illuminated far and wide with the gaslight from the shop windows. The principal theaters and minstrel halls announce their presence in letters of fire. Crowds throng about these places of amusement, waiting for the doors to open. The gilded and brilliantly lighted rumshops and oyster saloons and ice-cream gardens bustle with eager customers and breathless waiters. And the gay multitude, scarcely thinned from its daytime proportions, continues to crowd the pavements. Later in the evening, after the theaters have dismissed their patrons and sent them homeward bound, the street is given up to the orgies of sin. Drunken soldiers, spreeing on their bounty, reel along, with vocal accompaniment; female frailty displays its painted cheek and bedizened charms; and the underground concert halls, which line every step of the sidewalk, sound with revelry and music, and oftentimes with the tumult of personal conflict. Broadway, in all its phases, is a fair daguerreotype of that curious and versatile species of the "genus homo," the universal Yankee nation.

A prominent feature of New York has always been its newspaper press. Before the war, our people used to be familiar with the peculiarities of all the leading journals. They preserve still the same characteristics. The *Herald* is quite as ridiculous and bombastic as of old. A while ago it was urging Lincoln for president. Suddenly it dropped Abraham and took up General Grant. Now the only man to save the Yankees from ruin is this same Grant, while "Old Abe" is nothing but a "smutty joker," to use the *Herald*'s refrain. Bennett goes in for whipping England and France offhand, but is willing to pardon the "Rebels" if they will embrace the amnesty, and would not object to the escape of "Jeff Davis," provided he crawls off quietly through Texas into Mexico. The *Tribune* has distinguished itself lately by coming out as an advocate of amalgamation. That reminds me that Reverend Dr. Tyng has declared lately in the pulpit that the Negro is the *superior* of the white man. Greeley belongs to the anti-Lincoln faction of the Republican party and inclines toward Chase or Frémont. The *Times* is the official Lincoln organ. It is violent, vindictive, and mendacious in its abolitionism. The *World* belongs to the piebald Democracy; that is, a small clique of weak-headed and weak-kneed politicians who believe "slavery is dead" and the war ought to be prosecuted, though it is all wrong. It is the vehicle of considerable high-sounding rhetoric. The *News* and *Day Book* are peace papers, even to the extent of recognizing the independence of the South. The *Journal of Commerce* gives the war a weak support and would advocate peace if it had the courage. The *Post* is a malignant enemy of the South. It is rabid on the war question. The *Express* has a mixed creed. It supports the war and goes for peace, and praises Jeff Davis and wants to see him hanged, and denounces slavery and opposes abolitionism, and is in a muddle generally. The old *Commercial Advertiser* is now conducted by Hurlbut, formerly of Charleston, and still later of the Richmond prisons. When our authorities arrested him, he was indignant that his devotion to the South should be questioned, but he goes for a "vigorous prosecution of the war" now. The *Courier and Enquirer* is dead. Its proprietor, Colonel James Watson Webb, who wanted to head the 7th Regiment and drive the Rebels into the Gulf of Mexico, has gone off to Brazil as Old Abe's ambassador.

But I will break off at once, for I must remember the *Courier* is not back to a "peace establishment" and its old blanket dimensions yet and its correspondents may not ramble on unchecked.[10] In a future letter, however, I will endeavor to jot down some observations upon the pres-

10. blanket: a full-size newspaper sheet.

ent political situation in the United States and venture a "guess" at the probable length of the war.

Palmetto

NORTH

BOSTON EVENING TRANSCRIPT
April 16, 1864

REBELS RETREATING FROM EAST KENTUCKY

Louisville, Kentucky, 15th—Headquarters are advised of a dispatch from Colonel Gallup, received at Lexington, that the Rebels are in full retreat from east Kentucky. The force that made the attack on Paintsville was about a thousand strong. Colonel True is pushing forward from Mount Sterling in the direction of Pound Gap to intercept them. No fears are entertained of the result of this incursion.

A small band of Bennett's men is reported to have gone from Harlansville to Hartford and there robbed the People's Bank and several stores.

Rumors also prevail that about twenty-five guerrillas are within five miles of Shelbyville.

THE FORT PILLOW ATROCITIES CONFIRMED—DISPATCHES FROM GENERAL SHERMAN—THE REBELS TO SUFFER IN RETALIATION—THE REBEL ATTACK ON PADUCAH INEFFECTUAL

Washington, 16th—Yesterday afternoon dispatches were received from General Sherman, confirming the surrender of Fort Pillow and the brutal conduct of the Rebels immediately afterward, which bids fair to be amply retaliated in that quarter in due time.

The *Star* says according to General Sherman, our loss was 53 whites killed and 100 wounded and 300 blacks murdered in cold blood after the surrender.

Fort Pillow is of no value whatever to the defenses of Columbus, and the Rebels have no doubt left that vicinity, having been disappointed with considerable loss in the object of their raid, which was the capture of Columbus, whence they were promptly repulsed with no loss on our side. The commander of the fort occupied it against direct orders.

The Rebels, according to official dispatches received here last night, effected nothing at Paducah, losing a soldier killed or wounded for every horse stolen and doing us no other damage than by a few thefts.

It is not believed that Forrest will next appear in the vicinity of Memphis, where they can effect no more than at Columbus and stand a very fair chance of being surrounded by overwhelming forces.

NEW YORK TRIBUNE
April 16, 1864

SHOCKING FROM THE MISSISSIPPI
ATTACK ON FORT PILLOW—A SURRENDER DEMANDED—THE SUMMONS REFUSED—A DESPERATE AND PROLONGED FIGHT—OUR FORCES OVERPOWERED—INDISCRIMINATE SLAUGHTER OF THE PRISONERS—THE DEAD AND WOUNDED BAYONETED—400 SOLDIERS BUTCHERED—ONLY 200 OUT OF 600 SURVIVE—MEN SHOT WHILE IN THE HOSPITAL—THE HOSPITAL BURNED—NEGROES BURIED ALIVE BUT ESCAPE—SHOCKING SCENES OF SAVAGERY—SIX GUNS CAPTURED BY THE ENEMY—MEMPHIS TO BE NEXT ATTACKED

Cairo, Illinois, 14th—On Tuesday morning, the Rebel general Forrest attacked Fort Pillow. Soon after the attack, Forrest sent a flag of truce, demanding the surrender of the fort and garrison, meanwhile disposing his force so as to gain the advantage. Our forces were under command of Major Booth of the 13th Tennessee (U.S.) Heavy Artillery, formerly of the 1st Alabama Cavalry.

The flag of truce was refused, and fighting resumed. Afterward a second flag came in, which was also refused.

Both flags gave the Rebels the advantage of gaining new positions.

The battle was kept up until 3:00 P.M., when Major Booth was killed and Major Bradford took command.

The Rebels now came in swarms over our troops, compelling them to surrender.

Immediately upon the surrender ensued a scene which utterly baffles description. Up to that time comparatively few of our men had been killed; but insatiate as fiends, bloodthirsty as devils incarnate, the Confederates commenced an indiscriminate butchery of whites and blacks, including those of both colors who had been previously wounded.

The black soldiers, becoming demoralized, rushed to the rear, the white officers having thrown down their arms.

Both white and black were bayoneted, shot, or sabered. Even dead bodies were horribly mutilated and children of seven or eight years and several Negro women killed in cold blood. Soldiers unable to speak from wounds were shot dead and their bodies rolled down the banks into the river. The dead and wounded Negroes were piled in heaps and burned, and several citizens who had joined our forces for protection were killed or wounded.

Out of the garrison of six hundred, but two hundred remained alive.

Among our dead officers are Captain Bradford, Lieutenants Barr, Ackersbrom, Wilson, Revel, and Major Booth, all of the 13th Tennessee Cavalry.

Captain Poston and Lieutenant Lyon, 13th Tennessee Cavalry, and Captain Young, 24th Missouri, acting provost marshal, were taken prisoner.

Major Bradford was also captured, but is said to have escaped; it is feared, however, that he has been killed.

The steamer *Platte Valley* came up at about three-thirty and was hailed by the Rebels under a flag of truce. Men were sent ashore to bury the dead and take aboard such of the wounded as the enemy had allowed to live. Fifty-seven were taken aboard, including seven or eight colored. Eight died on the way up. The steamer arrived here this evening and was immediately sent to the Mound City Hospital to discharge her suffering cargo.

Among our wounded officers of colored troops are Captain Porter, Lieutenant Libberts, and Adjutant Lemming.

Six guns were captured by the Rebels and carried off, including two 10-pound Parrotts and two 12-pound howitzers. A large amount of stores was destroyed or carried away.

The intention of the Rebels seemed to be to evacuate the place and move on toward Memphis.

Cairo, Illinois, 15th—Two Negro soldiers, wounded at Fort Pillow, were buried by the Rebels, but afterward worked themselves out of their graves. They were among those brought up in the *Platte Valley* and are now in hospital at Mound City.

The officers of the *Platte Valley* receive great credit from the military authorities for landing at Fort Pillow at imminent risk and taking our wounded on board and for their kind attentions on the way up.

No boats have been allowed to leave here for points below Columbus since the first news of the Fort Pillow affair.

The attack on Paducah yesterday proved to be a mere raid for plunder made by a couple of hundred men, who were shelled out by the fort and gunboats after occupying a portion of the city in squads.

About noon they left, taking away a number of horses and considerable plunder and leaving behind about six of their wounded. No one hurt on our side.

Several of the guns captured by Forrest at Fort Pillow were spiked before falling into his hands.

Others were turned upon gunboat *Number 7,* which, having fired some three hundred rounds and exhausted her ammunition, was compelled to withdraw. Although a tinclad, she received but slight injury.

General Lee arrived and assumed the command at the beginning of the battle. Previous to which, General Chalmers directed the movements. Forrest, with the main force, retired, taking with him the captured funds.

While the steamer *Platte Valley* lay under flag of truce taking aboard our wounded, some of the Rebel officers, and among them General Chalmers, went aboard, and some of our officers showed them great deference, drinking with them and showing them other marks of courtesy.

St. Louis, 15th—The correspondent of the *Union,* who was aboard the steamer *Platte Valley* at Fort Pillow, gives even a more appalling description of the fiendishness of the Rebels than our Cairo dispatches:

Many of our wounded were shot in the hospital. The remainder were driven out, and the hospital was burned.

On the morning after the battle, the Rebels went over the field and shot the Negroes who had not died from their wounds.

Many of those who had escaped from the works and hospitals, who desired to be treated as prisoners of war, as the Rebels said, were ordered to fall into line and, when they had formed, were inhumanly shot down.

Of 350 colored troops not more than 56 escaped the massacre, and not one officer that commanded them survives. Only fourteen officers of the 13th Tennessee escaped death.

The loss of the 13th Tennessee is three hundred killed; the remainder were wounded and captured.

General Chalmers told this correspondent that although it was against the policy of his government to spare Negro soldiers or their officers, he had done all in his power to stop the carnage. At the same time, he believed it was right.

Another officer said our white troops would have been protected had they not been found on duty with Negroes.

While the Rebels endeavored to conceal their loss, it was evident that they suffered severely. Colonel Reed, commanding a Tennessee regiment, was mortally wounded. There were two or three well-filled hospitals at a short distance in the country.

MAY 21, 1864

SOUTH

RICHMOND DAILY DISPATCH
May 21, 1864

THE YANKEES GIVING AWAY THE LANDS OF THE SOUTH

Late Northern papers bring accounts of the passage, in the House of Representatives of the Federal Congress, of a bill to give as homesteads to soldiers and sailors, *without regard to color,* "the confiscated lands in insurrectionary districts." It passed by a vote of seventy-five to sixty-four—a majority of eleven. The chief defender of the bill was one Julian of Illinois. In the course of the debate on it, Mr. Pendleton of Ohio contended that under the present law the forfeiture of lands was not to extend beyond the lifetime of the owners and, besides, that at the present time they had not required lands to be divided into homesteads. Julian replied that large districts were coming into their (Yankee) possession, which were to be sold for taxes, and there was no law (Yankee) on the statute book which stood in the way of acquiring the fee of estates. Of course! Mr. Julian is right. There never is anything either in Constitution or law which stands in the way of the appropriation of the property of the Southern people to their own uses, by the Yankees. Yet the meager majority of *eleven* on the passage of the bill in the House was a small, fanatical majority to boast of, and much too small for the passage of a measure such as the bill on which it was obtained, proposing, as it does, to eject a people from their homes and lands and cutting them up among soldiers and sailors of all colors as rewards for their services in the war of invasion.

It is quite in keeping with the Yankee character and cunning that such a bill as this should pass the Yankee Congress at this time. It is not that they possess lands that they may, with impunity, cut up and give as rewards to the myrmidons they are now sending to spread devastation wherever they can in the South. It is merely to hold up to them the charming seductions to the service in the war of invasion—to stimulate them to the prosecution of that war in the most ferocious and brutal manner. A "home in Dixie" has been the blissful anticipation of the mercenary invader from the beginning of the war—the rich reward of his hardships in camp and his trials and perils in the terrible encounter with the Southern soldiers, whose prowess and courage they so well appreciate that nothing short of a promised reward like that of this Yankee bill could tempt a vast number of them to come in the way of. The war has been waged from the beginning on this principle of dividing the spoils of invasion among the invaders. At first there was some little caution, some kind of deference for the opinion of the world. The laws took not the responsibility of the spoliation; the work was left to military commandants of posts and to those brutal bands which plundered undefended districts. At first even Lincoln admitted that there was no authority in the Constitution to disturb the institution of slavery in the South. But gradually all respect for the Constitution, all respect for public opinion, yielded to the dishonest and brutal designs which the government had harbored in the beginning, and now they have arrived at the point which they designed at first to reach—of claiming the entire property of the people of the South as belonging to the Yankees and their government!

It may be asked, How is it that the satanic Federal Congress can presume to divide our lands among the mercenary soldiers and Negroes of their armies at the time when the Southern troops are repelling them in every field, and when the heaviest disasters that have fallen upon Federal arms since the war began have followed in quick succession the present year? Very plainly because this is the very time that they need troops, and the bribe of the rich lands of the South, with their comfortable homes, is held up to stimulate enlistments among foreigners and Negroes, the riffraff of all nations, so that their armies may be replenished and they may yet continue a little longer the bloodshed and the rapine of their barbarous war of invasion of the South. It is the very time for such a bill. Had they met with no reverses—had they conquered everywhere and been sure of the subjugation of the South without further extra exertion—they never would have offered the lands of the South to soldiers of all colors. They would have set them apart to pay the war debt, and the soldier would have been left to his bounty and pay as quite sufficient for his services. But there is more work to be done. More men are wanted, and they are willing to pledge lands that they have not yet conquered—to give valuables never yet in their possession—to those who will peril their lives in acquiring it! It is a safe bargain—one of that description especially agreeable to the Puritans. If they succeed by it and don't like it, they can repeal it. It is a handsome specimen of Yankee craftiness, subtlety, and dishonesty.

CHARLESTON DAILY COURIER
May 21, 1864

LATEST FROM VIRGINIA
DANVILLE RAILROAD BRIDGE REPAIRED—
NEWS FROM GENERAL BEAUREGARD'S DEPARTMENT—
YANKEE GENERAL AMES KILLED—YANKEE
ACKNOWLEDGMENT OF FAILURE, ETC.

Richmond, 20th—The bridge over the Staunton River, on the Danville Railroad, has been repaired. The continuation of the Richmond and Danville Railroad connecting Danville with Greensboro, North Carolina, is completed. The trains will commence to run through tomorrow.

The *Petersburg Express* of yesterday says General Ames (Yankee) was killed in the fight on Monday, at Chesterfield, and General "Baldy" Smith lost a foot.[11]

Butler remained aboard the *Greyhound*, with steam up to the top of the gauge.

The Washington correspondent of the 18th says, "The simple truth is, we have yet failed to get a victory and have suffered a terrible loss in killed and wounded."

FROM GENERAL JOHNSTON'S ARMY
HEAVY SKIRMISHING AT CASS STATION—FIGHTING
JOE HOOKER REPORTED KILLED—BATTLE ORDER
OF GENERAL JOHNSTON, ETC.

Atlanta, 20th—A press reporter who left Cass Station last night brings intelligence of heavy skirmishing near that place, which continued till night. Our loss was comparatively small. General Cleburne's division held the enemy in check. Report says "Fighting" Joe Hooker was killed and that his body fell in our hands.

General Johnston issued his battle order yesterday, telling the troops that our communication with the rear was now safe, and asked them to

11. The report of General Ames's death was incorrect, as was the report of General Hooker's death in the subsequent article.

imitate their brothers in Virginia and the Trans-Mississippi. This was received with the wildest enthusiasm. Our forces are in the line of battle just beyond the Etowah River, with the left resting on the stream.

Augusta, Georgia, 20th—Our exchanges this evening contain the following:

Marietta, Georgia, 19th—There was heavy skirmishing on the 15th between the enemy and General Maney's brigade. Wheeler has been resisting the advance of the enemy all day, but was driven on by our infantry, when Maney's brigade took up the fight.

Atlanta, 19th—Thursday morning our army was in line between Cass Station and Kingston. The enemy was within two miles and advancing. There had been no fighting for twenty-four hours.

The reported capture of twenty-two hundred prisoners by Cleburne is a canard.

Our position is now secure against any flank movement. General Johnston's headquarters are at Cassville. Another battle is imminent. The utmost confidence is felt throughout the army.

Atlanta, 20th—The train which arrived this evening brought no additional news nor reports of fighting.

NORTH

BOSTON EVENING TRANSCRIPT
May 21, 1864

THE DUTY AT HOME

Nobody who knew anything about the matter ever imagined that General Grant was to have a holiday march to Richmond.[12] It was clear that he was to win victory by severe fighting, heavy losses, and trying hardships. The enemy had been gathering up his strength for the final struggle, so far as he is concerned, and such an enemy, desperate and powerful in his very madness, was not to be easily conquered. To ensure his defeat, he must be met by a power superior to his own, and the means put in operation must be equal to the heavy work to be accomplished. The campaign thus far, taking into view all its combinations, is in no degree discouraging. The favorable result, it must however be remembered, cannot probably in the nature of things be reached in a day or many days. It is not worthwhile, therefore, to be wasting time in criti-

12. Refers to the Battle of the Wilderness, Virginia, May 5–7, 1864, and the Battle of Spotsylvania, Virginia, May 8–12, 1864.

cism if that criticism leads to a neglect of the paramount obligation to leave no act undone and no sentiment unexpressed which will sustain and cheer the Federal armies on to victory.

All who believe that the conflict is for ideas and principles, and for the saving of a nationality consecrated to a true democracy and a republican civilization, must let this belief hold in their minds its transcendent importance and make their daily speech and daily deeds correspond with their convictions. Taking this view, the community should put itself bravely and cheerfully into the struggle and be ready to sacrifice everything to secure the triumph of the right. The spirit wanted at home is one that will show itself in a calm, steady determination not to be baffled by any difficulties. That spirit ought to appear in the readiness of property to acknowledge that it owes its security to the men fighting the rebellion on the fields of battle, and in the willingness of property to give itself to any extent demanded to put down insurgent despotism and ward off chaotic anarchy. It ought to be manifested in fresh efforts to increase our forces to the degree that may be required to replenish their losses and make them invincible in numbers in their onward march. It ought, in a word, to be evident in all directions in an earnest and practical patriotism, willing to spend and suffer for the great cause in whose defense our soldiers are giving their lives so heroically.

The grave mistake is in the delusion that all the work of the hour is to be done by the army. The army is not fighting for itself. It is fighting for us. It is fighting for our country. It is fighting for the peace and unity of the nation—for the people, for humanity. Consequently, every citizen should be fighting with it. This is no moment for selfish considerations of business, or heartless considerations of personal enjoyment, to rule. This is no moment for party bickerings, or for anxieties caring only for one's own insulated comfort or welfare. This is no moment for asking how little can be done in the way of furnishing men and matériel. Rather is this the moment for everybody to be courageous, active, and generous—to identify himself with the public—to inquire what and how much he can do for his country so as most speedily to end the strife, and end it by the utter discomfiture of the country's only deadly foe. More is required than weeping over the killed and wounded. Their graves and their sufferings have a summons in them. As they died or suffered, so should all strive now to live. The call upon all is to rise out of the narrowness of individual lives and act upon the truth that each man is greatest and noblest when he identifies himself with his race, shares the common lot, and consecrates himself to the service of the highest principles. In a very few years, the youngest among us will be where the consciousness of having been true to the country will be worth infinitely more than any memory of a life given merely to the getting of gain or to catering for low and frivolous and unmanly self-indulgence. These are the views to be cherished and acted upon now. The signs are that the military despotism of the slave power is staggering to its fall. It becomes all to seek to have a share in the final blows that are to overthrow this gigantic tyranny and deliver half a continent from its oppressions.

NEW YORK TRIBUNE
May 21, 1864

NEWS FROM RICHMOND
WHAT THE REBELS THOUGHT OF GENERAL GRANT'S PLANS—MEASURES FOR THE DEFENSE OF RICHMOND—THE WASHINGTON MONUMENT—OUTRAGES ON THE MEMORY OF WASHINGTON—THE CITIZEN MILITIA OF RICHMOND—HOW THE REBEL RANKS ARE RECRUITED—NEGROES EMPLOYED FOR THE DEFENSE OF RICHMOND—JEFFERSON DAVIS WITH LEE'S ARMY

Correspondence of the *New York Tribune*

Washington, May 19, 1864

In a previous letter I mentioned that when I escaped from Rebeldom, I left behind me several friends, Union men, who were determined to come North at the first opportunity. One of these gentlemen, Mr. George H. Harris, arrived here yesterday, having left the Rebel capital on the 12th instant, and the intelligence he brings is so interesting and important that I hasten to communicate it.

Mr. Harris is an Englishman, who for upward of two years has been employed in the publishing house of West and Johnson, 145 Main Street, Richmond. Soon after the beginning of the war, he presented to General Winder, and a few days later to the secretary of war, the proper evidence that he was an alien, and requested permission to leave the country. But those functionaries, thinking probably that if not allowed to leave, he would be obliged to enlist in the army to avoid starving, refused him a passport. Fortunately, however, he obtained a clerkship with the above firm, at a salary which enabled him to subsist without aiding the Negro-driver's abhorrent cause.

Four weeks ago the Rebel authorities became satisfied for the first that it was really General Grant's purpose to attempt the capture of

Richmond. Before this, they believed that the demonstrations in that direction were a mere feint to conceal his real intentions. They flattered themselves that "On to Richmond" had been tried so often without success that it would not be ventured on very soon again, and that Grant was endeavoring to accomplish by strategy some grand result not attainable by the valor and strength of the Union armies if his designs were anticipated. As soon as Davis and company became satisfied that a grand movement was to be directed against their capital, they commenced anew extensive preparation to resist it. Not only were reinforcements collected from every quarter for Lee, but the erection of new defensive works previously suggested by Beauregard, but believed by Jefferson Davis to be superfluous, was proceeded with.

Additional measures were also adopted to render the "citizen militia" more patriotic and effective. The members have been for several weeks assembled every afternoon in Capitol Square for company and battalion drill, after which they are gathered around the equestrian monument of Washington and around the steps of the Capitol and exhorted and implored by eloquent speakers—each of whom imagines himself a Patrick Henry—to welcome the Federals, with bloody hands, to hospitable graves.

The Washington Monument, as the reader who has seen it knows, is an elegant structure, both in design and artistic finish. It stands in the center of a circular base about twenty-five feet in diameter and consists of a column about fifteen feet in height, mounted on a polygonal pedestal, or star. On the top of the column is a statue of the Father of His Country on horseback. On each projecting angle of the star, a few feet from the column, stands on a small pedestal one of the lesser lights of the Revolution. On the circle of the main base, opposite the points of the star, are placed large eagles, standing on blocks of stone.

On the breast of each of the Revolutionary heroes surrounding Washington is a placard quoting some of his distinguished sayings in the days that tried men's souls. As a sample, on the breast of Dr. Franklin, quoted from his remarks in the first American Congress, is written, "Independence will cut the Gordian knot at once and give us freedom." What would that great man say now, if he could speak, at being thus made the advocate of the slaveholders' rebellion!

From the beaks of the eagles are suspended placards with flaming mottoes in Latin. It must have been noticed that the Rebels' leaders are prone to interlarding their speeches and inscribing their banners with mottoes from the dead and foreign languages, but the reason of their doing so no Yankee, perhaps, has ever yet guessed. It is because to their ignorant and deluded followers, there is something awfully imposing in a dead-language saying or inscription. Should they see or hear the same sentiment in English, they would scarcely notice it. But having seen it in Latin, they will not rest until they find someone who can interpret it, and then they will mentally repeat the translation until it becomes as familiar to them as, and more sacred in their estimation than, any of the Ten Commandments. To give all the inscriptions on these cards would be tedious, but one or two of them may prove interesting. On the eagle nearest the Capitol steps hung the ancient saying *"Dulce et decorum est pro patria mori,"* or "It is sweet and glorious to die for one's country." On another hung *"Pro aris et focis,"* or "For our altars and our firesides."

There can be no doubt that the Rebel leaders have succeeded by artifice and chicanery such as this in convincing many an unsophisticated youth that it is sweet and glorious to die for the Confederacy and that they are fighting for their altars and their firesides; and many thousands more must be led to the slaughter before the terrible delusion is dispelled from the Southern mind.

Had their desecration of the monument ended here, they might, perhaps, be forgiven, but not a tithe of their sacrilege has yet been told. They most outrageously insulted the memory of the immortal Washington. They tied in his hand, or rather in the hand of his statue, a long staff, from the top of which floated, insulting alike the Father of His Country and the pure air of Heaven, a dirty Rebel rag. The principal instrument of this outrage, thank God, speedily received a merited reward. He had barely secured the flagstaff when his foot slipped and he fell headlong to the stone base below, fracturing his skull and dying in a few moments.

An impulsive Irishman, who had been forced into the militia then drawn up in the square, seeing the man fall, thoughtlessly shouted, "Bejabbers, Washington gave him the shillelagh—he will have nothing but the Stars and Stripes." The words had scarcely passed the lips of the unfortunate man when he was sabered by his captain; and as he fell, and after he had fallen, he was kicked by the chivalry around him—his companions-in-arms—and afterward dragged by the legs to the rear in a dying condition. It is almost a wonder that at this time there was not a resurrection at Mount Vernon. The great spirit of the hero entombed there must have felt like resigning its high post in Heaven and taking up the flesh again, to resent the insult offered its earthly image by making it a standard-bearer for the infernal rebellion.

Demonstrations such as I have described have been common throughout the South ever since the war began, and trifling as they may appear to the Northern reader, they are not without their effect. They are designed to delude the weak and ignorant, and catch the rabble, by reminding them that Washington was a Southern man and a Rebel. Speakers are always at hand to expatiate to the gaping crowd on the emblems before them and to stuff them with sophistry that they should be proud to be called Rebels because Washington was a Rebel, that all Rebels must be right because Washington was right, and that the position of the Rebel states toward the Federal government is analogous to that occupied by this country toward Great Britain in '76. To the Southern people such comparisons are not odious.

They never reason or reflect. They take the law and the gospel from their superiors in education and craft and have done so for so long that today they are as planets, lesser stars, and meteors, who either revolve around their great luminary, Jefferson Davis, or occupy the post in the firmament he assigns to them. There are, to be sure, many exceptions—Union men. To keep up the simile, I might call them fixed and shooting stars; for some of them are content to remain quietly in their places, though their luster is for the present obscured by the brilliancy of the great Rebel bodies around them, while others occasionally shoot off, explode, and disappear forever, like the poor Irishman mentioned a moment or two ago. The Southern people are generally very ignorant and the veriest slaves of their official masters of any people on earth.

But I am digressing. The "citizen militia" of which I was speaking includes every man and boy in and around the city capable of bearing arms or rendering any kind of military service. Aliens, citizens of other states who happen to be at the capital, as well as the denizens of the place have been gobbled up in the streets and forced into the ranks, and nothing that they can say or do will get them released. Such as complain too emphatically of their treatment are hurried off to Castle Thunder. A whole company, composed mainly of Irishmen, revolted and were at once thrown into the Castle. Not less than three hundred had been incarcerated for refusing to do militia duty before Mr. Harris left.

Some of the companies, composed of lawyers, merchants, clergymen and others, of unquestionable loyalty to Jefferson Davis, are permitted, after drilling in the square for a time each day, to return to their homes and businesses, to be assembled suddenly, if necessary, at the signal ringing of the bells. But all who are suspected of a disposition to shirk duty are kept together.

The Rebel soldiers confined in Castle Thunder awaiting trial for desertion, absence without leave, and other offenses, as well as those convicted and undergoing punishment in the chain gang, have all been pardoned and returned to their regiments. The jails and penitentiary have been ransacked for recruits, all receiving pardon who will enlist. The Confederate authorities do not consider that they are letting felons loose on Southern society. Governor Smith declared to several persons, in the hearing of Mr. Harris, that should these convicts desert, it would be to the enemy's lines and that they would soon commence plying their avocations of theft, robbery, and murder among the Yankees, so that even if they deserted, the Confederacy would receive some satisfaction from having released them and at the same time get rid of feeding them. Even the murderer, R. S. Ford, convicted recently of manslaughter for the premeditated and deliberate killing of Mr. Dixon of Georgia, clerk of the House of Representatives, a little more than a year ago, has been reprieved and placed in command of a company of pardoned felons.

The Rebel War Department has also determined to employ Negro soldiers for the defense of the Rebel capital. These soldiers are to be bondmen and are not to be enrolled or mustered into the service like white soldiers, but are to be hired by the government, of their masters. In case they are killed or lost, or rendered worthless, their owners will receive their value in money, as they do for horses, mules, and other property impressed or hired by the government and lost in its service. These Negroes are recruited upon these terms with the consent of their owners. There are hundreds of farmers, large slaveholders, in the counties of Goochland, Hanover, New Kent, and Henrico, who, in view of the advance of General Grant, have no inclination to seed their lands; and being, therefore, glad to be relieved for a time of their Negroes, they heartily second the arrangement of the War Department.

But while the Rebel authorities will regard these soldiers merely as armed property, they will claim, if any of them are taken prisoner, that they are soldiers and should be exchanged as such. None but the best men with families will be employed, and they are assured by their masters that if they desert, or are taken prisoner and refuse to be exchanged, their wives will be flogged to death or sold south on the rice plantations. They are too familiar with the cruelty and brutality of their Rebel masters to disregard this fiendish threat, and their affection for their wives, if they can be so called, would prompt most of them to endure anything, even bondage, to keep them from destruction.

Several companies of this character have already been organized and are under instruction. It is supposed that they will be employed principally within the fortifications, as they are being taught mainly to load, fire, and handle the heavy guns. In short, no effort is being spared to hold General Grant at bay. Thousands of reinforcements are being sent every day from the south and southwest to General Lee. Nearly all the troops have been taken from Charleston and Mobile, and so many have been withdrawn from Johnston that if pressed by our forces, he can only escape destruction by another masterly retreat.

The Rebels are bound to stake everything on their capital. If they lose it, they know their cause is irreparably lost. The Army of Virginia could not, in such case, be kept together for a day. A great battle between Grant and Lee must soon be fought, compared with which the battles of last week and the week before will appear like skirmishes. Jefferson Davis is to take the field in person—not to command the army, but by his presence to endeavor to inspire the despairing soldiers with enthusiasm. Since the battles with Grant, Davis has reviewed a portion of Lee's army and is reported to have said in an address to them that the time had arrived when by putting forth all their energies they could crush the enemy in almost a single blow and put an end to the war and that it was his intention to be with them and share their dangers in the next great conflict.

THE DRAFT IN KENTUCKY

Paducah, Kentucky, 20th—The draft for McCracken County, Kentucky, was made yesterday.

Five hundred forty-two names were drawn, and among them are many merchants and businessmen of this city.

There was considerable excitement, but no disturbances occurred. The lines are closed to prevent the persons who were drawn from leaving.

The draft in Graves County will take place today, and in Lexington County on Monday.

JUNE 18, 1864

SOUTH

RICHMOND DAILY DISPATCH
June 18, 1864

FROM LYNCHBURG

A gentleman who left New London, ten miles above Lynchburg, at six o'clock on Thursday evening says a sharp engagement was going on between the enemy and Imboden's, McCausland's, and Jones's cavalry, and it was reported yesterday morning that our men fell back after the engagement to secure the advantages of a more favorable position. The same gentleman says that the enemy burned the depot and public stores at Liberty. The following letters give additional details of the situation about Lynchburg:

From Our Own Correspondent
Lynchburg, Virginia, June 16, 1864

Very little is known which is proper for publication. The enemy in heavy force passed through Liberty, Bedford County, yesterday morning, and have been moving cautiously in this direction. It is thought by some that they will attempt to go on to Danville instead of attacking this place, which may now be considered safe. Should they attempt to get to Danville, I think they will be foiled. All of the enemy are reported to have left the Amherst side of the James. The raiding party that burned Concord made a circuit around Lynchburg, being closely pursued by Imboden's men, and a greater portion of them joined the main body near Liberty night before last. They took off very few Negroes, who manifested no desire to go away but got out of their way. They had no time to injure or take off property of any other description while making the circuit. Nothing was injured at Campbell Courthouse, where they passed themselves off for Confederates and were entertained by the citizens in a handsome manner. The publication of newspapers here is discontinued for the present, and the editors and employees of those papers are in the trenches. The enemy was reported near Forest Depot this morning at sunrise.

B.

Lynchburg, Virginia, June 17, 1864

For reasons some of which are given below, it is almost impossible to obtain reliable and well-authenticated intelligence of movements in this quarter, hence the inaccuracy of many of the statements which obtain circulation. Citizens of entire reliability on other subjects have brought in most erroneous statements in regard to the movement of the enemy and their numbers since active operations commenced hereabouts. Having been unaccustomed to the presence of the enemy, they honestly believe what they report, having been deceived in some cases by others, but in most instances have deceived themselves; and in nine cases out of ten, intelligence through such channels proves incorrect.

From headquarters we get no official information, as the present military head has thought proper to withhold all intelligence from the press. With this explanation I will proceed to make some corrections of previous incorrect statements and then give your readers a correct statement of what is *known* to be correct. Campbell Courthouse was not burned by the enemy, nor was any property destroyed by the raiders who passed that place while making the circuit around Lynchburg. The enemy seem to have concentrated their forces for the attack on this place in a southwestern direction from the city, on the Forest Depot Road and the Abingdon or Southwestern Turnpike. Their entire force is under Hunter, which is estimated—from authentic information received—to be from 15,000 to 20,000 strong. Crook and Averell have not more than four thousand cavalry, which composes the entire cavalry force now operating in this quarter. They camped on Fancy Farm, seven miles from Liberty, on Wednesday evening, and yesterday evening were reported to be within eight miles of this city and were skirmishing with our men; which report I have the best reasons for believing correct. It is also reported, on what is deemed reliable authority, that yesterday morning they burned three considerable bridges on the Virginia and Tennessee Railroad over the following creeks: Little Otter, Big Otter, and Elk.

It was apprehended yesterday by some that they would not attack our position at this place at all, but would attempt by a flank movement to reach Danville. The developments of today, however, will decide this question.

A number of flagrant outrages were committed in Amherst—some on the persons of females—the particulars of which are of too beastly a character to be recorded. The burning of the Military Institute and other property at Lexington is fully confirmed. The residence of ex-Governor Letcher was also fired by the vandals, who would not even let his wife save her clothes. The residence of General F. H. Smith was saved by his daughter, who was in a state of health that would not justify her removal from her bed.

The very latest we have is a report that the enemy have advanced on the Charlemont Road from Liberty, and it is reported that they were crossing the James at an early hour last night at Waughs Ferry, which is nineteen miles above this city. We have another report that still another column of the enemy is advancing from above by the Mountain Road, which is next to the James, but from other information received, the correctness of such report is of a doubtful nature.

The citizens of Lynchburg have responded to the call in the present emergency in the most energetic manner and have exhibited their patriotism by turning out, and every man and boy who can shoulder a musket is now in the ranks, prepared to defend to the last extremity that sacred spot called home. Even the cripples volunteer their services, and in many instances fill positions which relieve men capable of bearing arms, thus adding another to the number of guns to be leveled at the invading foe.

B.

FROM DANVILLE

All was quiet in Danville yesterday. The report that the Yankees had appeared at Pittsylvania Courthouse was erroneous, and the whole statement regarding an advance upon Danville was premature.

CHARLESTON DAILY COURIER
June 18, 1864

LATEST FROM PETERSBURG
ENEMY'S ASSAULTS HANDSOMELY REPULSED—CAPTURE OF 450 PRISONERS—YANKEE GENERAL BARTON MORTALLY WOUNDED

Petersburg, Virginia, 17th—An assault made on Battery 16 last evening was handsomely repulsed by General Bushrod Johnson's division. About four hundred fifty prisoners were captured belonging to Hancock's corps. They state that General Barton was mortally wounded.

Our forces met a slight reverse at the same point this morning. Another assault made at the same place this afternoon was repulsed. It is believed that the enemy's forces are heavily massed in front of Petersburg. Colonel Page of Wise's brigade was killed this morning. Captain Fred Carter of the Richmond Blues, wounded Wednesday night, died today. Colonel Randolph Thomson, severely wounded in the same fight, is doing well. Lieutenant Colonel Wise, who was seriously wounded, is improving.

FROM RICHMOND
ACCOUNTS FROM PETERSBURG—THE ENEMY IN CHESTERFIELD COUNTY—FIGHT NEAR CHESTER—GENERAL LEE IN COMMAND OF ALL OUR FORCES

Richmond, 16th—We have received nothing definite today from Petersburg. The Yankees have advanced their lines in Chesterfield. Some fighting took place near Chester today. By last advices, Sheridan was moving through Spotsylvania and is reported crossing the Rapidan.

General Lee has been placed in command of all the forces of Virginia and North Carolina.

FROM GENERAL JOHNSTON'S ARMY
ASSAULTS ON OUR LEFT—ENEMY DRIVEN BACK

Three miles west of Marietta, Georgia, 17th—The enemy made several attacks today in six lines of battle on our extreme left, near Lost Mountain, and were received with terrific volleys of artillery and musketry. They were driven back, and our forces hold the ground from which they have been driven. The fight occurred at two o'clock this afternoon.

Full accounts of the battle have not yet been received.

The enemy continues to cannonade our works on the center of our lines furiously. Both lines remain substantially the same as yesterday. The enemy continues fortifying. They also attempted to shell our Signal Corps on Denver's Mountain, but could not reach the top.

FROM THE SOUTHWEST
COLONEL SCOTT'S ATTACK ON THE YANKEE GUNBOATS—MARMADUKE MARCHING ON LITTLE ROCK

Clinton, Louisiana, 17th—On Wednesday morning last, at daylight, Colonel Scott's batteries attacked and drove off the Yankee gunboat 53 and the *General Bragg* at Como Landing and Ratcliffe Ferry. The engagement lasted four hours, when the ironclad gunboat *Lafayette* came and Scott withdrew. Last night the engagement was renewed, and the *Bragg* was towed off with thirty shots through her.

There is great stir and much moving of Yankee transports from here and down the river between Port Hudson and New Orleans.

Meridian, Mississippi, 17th—The latest reports from the Mississippi River state that Marmaduke has gone toward Little Rock. The Yankee troops under A. J. Smith were landed below Marmaduke, and an attempt was made to flank him. Marmaduke withdrew, taking all his booty and stores with him. He destroyed a great many of the enemy's vessels on the river.

The smallpox is raging in the Yankee camps at Vicksburg and is also spreading among the citizens.

Gold is quoted at 207.

OFFICIAL DISPATCH FROM GENERAL FORREST
HIS VICTORY CONFIRMED

Guntown, Mississippi, June 14, 1864,
via Mobile, Alabama, June 14, 1864

To the Honorable Isham G. Harris:—I met the enemy under Generals Stewart and Grierson, 10,000 strong—7,500 infantry and 2,500 cavalry, and 20 pieces of artillery—on the 10th instant, with 4,000 cavalry and 18 pieces of artillery. After a hand-to-hand fight for six hours, I completely routed him. Their battle cry was, "Remember Fort Pillow."

My loss was 150 killed and 450 wounded. Among the killed were many valuable officers.

The enemy's losses were 1,000 killed, 2,000 prisoners, 250 wagons and ambulances, and all their artillery and ordnance stores. We are still following and killing many in the woods. Their loss cannot be less than five thousand.

Buford, Bell, and Lyon distinguished themselves, as all the officers and men did on this occasion.

N. Bedford Forrest, Major General

NORTH

BOSTON EVENING TRANSCRIPT
June 18, 1864

PETERSBURG

We infer, from the great strength of the works defending this place, the estimate which the Rebels placed upon its strategic importance. Its fortifications are described in the official dispatch of Secretary Stanton, which we published in the *Transcript* yesterday afternoon, as being even more formidable than those of Missionary Ridge, where Federal valor found truly heroic illustration. The meaning of such formidable defenses is that the Rebels purposed to hold possession of the Petersburg and Richmond Railroad, as the most important line of communication radiating from Richmond to the southward. Losing this, they are confined to one road of comparatively recent construction, passing through a different section of the Confederacy—and hold even this line only upon the supposition that they can withstand the efforts of Grant, which will be, or have already been, directed toward its destruction.

Intelligence of the occupancy of Petersburg by General Grant's forces has not yet been received, but we have been officially informed that the main line of the enemy's works there has been stormed by General Smith and that his guns command the city. Prisoners of Beauregard's corps have been captured, who report they had crossed the James River, above Drewry's Bluff, and marched to Petersburg—a distance of from sixteen to eighteen miles. From this fact we can see how the enemy were outgeneraled and outmarched by General Grant. The Richmond papers show that Lee was expecting an attack at Malvern Hill, while Grant was quietly crossing his troops over the James River. General Smith is dispatched to Bermuda Hundred, moves on Petersburg, and, perhaps, begins the assault before the Rebels fairly apprehend the designs of the lieutenant general. They then unsuccessfully attempted to throw a sufficient number of troops into the place to defend it from the first attack. Had it not been for the celerity of movement on the part of the Federal troops, it may be that Rebel reinforcements, sufficiently numerous, would have so delayed the reduction of Petersburg as to have seriously interfered with other operations against Richmond.

THE DEFEAT OF THE ANTISLAVERY AMENDMENT

All the Democrats in the House, with the exception of four, voted against the passage of the amendment to the Constitution abolishing slavery. The effect of this action is to prevent, at present, the people from voting on a question of such vital importance. It would seem that nothing but a preference for slavery itself could have prompted the opposition to adopt such a course. There could be no constitutional objection to the amendment, as the Constitution especially provides for the proposed action of Congress and the people of the states; and the power is admitted by Mr. Calhoun himself, in the following passage of a speech defending nullification:

> As high as this right of interposition on the part of a state may be regarded in relation to the general government, the constitutional compact provides a remedy against its abuse. There is a higher power—placed above by the consent of all the creating and preserving power of the system, to be exercised by three fourths of the states—which, under the character of the amending power, can modify the whole system at pleasure—and to the acts of which none can object. Admit, then, the power in question (nullification) to belong to the states—and admit its liability to abuse—and what are the utmost consequences, but to create a presumption against the constitutionality of the power exercised by the general government, which, if it be well-founded, must compel them to abandon it; or, if not, to remove the difficulty by obtaining the contested power in the form of an amendment to the Constitution. If, on an appeal for this purpose, the decision be favorable to the general government, a disputed power will be converted into an expressly granted power. But, on the contrary,

if it be adverse, the refusal to grant will be tantamount to an inhibition of its exercise; and thus, in either case, the controversy will be determined.

[UNTITLED]

Governor Johnson of Tennessee is just the man, in his antecedents, whom the Copperheads, if they had a particle of sincerity, ought to commend. He was a Democrat—a genuine, honest Democrat. He was not an abolitionist. He had no part or lot in the election of President Lincoln. He refused to have anything to do with secession and maintained his allegiance to the Union when his old political associates rebelled against the Federal government. He insists now that a state cannot secede. He has accepted the logic of events and adopts now, as a patriot, the only principles and views that can be effective in overthrowing the traitorous Southern Confederacy—whose despotic character and purposes he thoroughly understands. Such is the man whom the Copperheads are swift to abuse, with every term at the command of upstart, arrogant aristocracy, because, in their kid-glove estimation, he is not a gentleman and rhetorician. But then, these Copperheads, so anxious for dignity and refinement in high places, do not sympathize with Rebels and are not admirers of Jefferson Davis! They are Simon-Pure Democrats.

NEW YORK TRIBUNE
June 18, 1864

THE CAMPAIGN

The new movement proceeds with long strides. While the country waits to hear that the Army of the Potomac is well across the James, comes the news that Petersburg has been attacked and taken. Whether the town itself has been occupied or not, as a late and somewhat unauthentic dispatch affirms, is of little moment, the decisive fact being that the works which command it were gallantly assaulted and carried by General Smith on Wednesday evening at twenty minutes past seven o'clock. Those works, it is officially stated, were stronger than Missionary Ridge at Chattanooga. However that may be, they were evidently enough of great strength, and their storming is one other evidence, where no evidence is needed, of the heroic courage of the Negro troops who took them. General Smith was impelled to offer them his thanks for their gallant work and to declare that they cannot be exceeded as soldiers. It ought to be at least a week before the Copperhead papers renew their sneers at the courage and capacity of Negro troops.

Petersburg lies south of the Appomattox. It is a little remarkable—it is certainly unexpected—that the first movement of the campaign south of the James should have been made south of the Appomattox also. The operations against Petersburg have been hitherto from Bermuda Hundred as a base, and the Appomattox was crossed by a pontoon within the line that enclosed that peninsula. But General Grant, with the originality and boldness which have marked his conceptions from the beginning of this campaign, chose not only to throw his army across far down the James, but to move instantly upon the first point which presented itself as an objective, regardless of the base existing at Bermuda Hundred. His army crossed the James at Windmill Point. Thence to Petersburg is eighteen miles. The abandonment of the Cold Harbor line, north of the Chickahominy, began on Sunday night, and his shortest route to the James was twenty-five miles. Yet on Tuesday his enormous army crosses the river; on Wednesday its advance corps, which had gone around by transports, has taken Petersburg; and eight hours later the V Corps, which marched all the way, comes up to the support of the leading column and forms its line of battle in front of Petersburg. We know not where in military history to look for a more extraordinary example of rapidity in moving by the flank large bodies of troops in the face of the enemy, or of that swift steadiness which advances over all obstacles to the accomplishment of its purpose.

None of Lee's army, it is said, had reached Petersburg when Smith assailed its defenses, but there were indications that a force had arrived after the entrenchments were carried and that the left bank of the Appomattox was to be held. What truth there is in this, time will show.

THE EAST TENNESSEE ORPHANS

Mr. C. C. Tracy, the western agent of the Children's Aid Society, has just returned from his journey to provide homes for the east Tennessee orphans. We condense some facts from his most interesting report.

These orphans were the children of the poor and loyal farmers of the Tennessee mountains, and, as Mr. Tracy describes them, the most poor, wretched, half-starved company he ever saw gathered, even from the miserable dens of city poverty. They were so weak from want of food that many had to be lifted into the omnibus! Several of the parents had died of exhaustion and starvation. One little group of three children attracted much sympathy. Their father had been conscripted into the

Rebel army and had then escaped to Nashville to join the Union ranks. The Rebel neighbors, hearing of it, came and burned the man's house and destroyed all he had, and turned the sick mother and her three little ones out of doors. Weak and exhausted as she was, and half starved, she managed to walk some one hundred fifty miles to Nashville and just reached her husband to die in his arms! The father consigned the three children to the Christian Commission and Children's Aid Society and rejoined his regiment, saying, "Now I can fight with free hands."

Two other bright, merry little creatures were in a house on Chickamauga Creek during the great battle and took refuge in the cellar. They had been told that the Yankees would murder them, but they found themselves very kindly treated, of course. Their mother had probably died of want of food, and the father fell in the Union ranks. One woman, with two children, had been "raised" in South Carolina, but her husband was conscripted in Tennessee and then had run away to our forces and had been killed. Mr. Tracy describes them all as remarkably good looking, with blond features, but thin and weak from want and suffering. As they journeyed on in Ohio to their places of destination, they were delighted beyond measure at the thriving look of the country. One said, "Why, in my country there isn't so much as a chicken or fence left—everything swept clean off—but here, the farther north we go the better it is." The most unbounded sympathy was shown them everywhere. In one town where the party stopped, all the ladies gathered together, fed and washed and clothed the poor orphans, and took them to their own homes.

They were speedily provided with the very best places in families, more as children adopted than servants. Nothing was spared to make them comfortable, and there, in that free and intelligent western community, far from the miseries of war, they will grow up happy and useful. Out of the whole company of thirty, only one or two could read, though some of the girls were fourteen or fifteen years old. There would have been over a hundred but for a report spread by the secessionists that "they were to be sold as slaves in Ohio."

It is not unlikely that others will desire to be removed by the Children's Aid Society when they hear of the success of these.

The suggestion of this most charitable and practical movement to cure some of the sad ills of war in our country is due to that excellent organization, the Christian Commission.

JULY 16, 1864

SOUTH

RICHMOND DAILY DISPATCH
July 16, 1864

THE WAR NEWS

The city was excited yesterday by a rumor of vast proportions. It was said to have emanated from official sources and was in effect as follows: The people of Baltimore had "risen" upon the Federal forces in that city, overcome them, and invited the Confederates to enter and take possession, which they accordingly did. Upon application at the War Department, we could get no confirmation of this report; if Baltimore was in our possession, the authorities here knew nothing of it. Thus, the rumor had no foundation in fact, though as it progressed, it gathered proportions and by nightfall had spread through every portion of the city. It was stated that it had its origin in this way: That a gentleman connected with the press was informed by a member of Congress that a staff officer had told him that the government authorities had a Washington paper of the 13th which furnished the important news. It is almost needless to add that the news in the paper of the 13th (given in another column) contains no such intelligence.

Last evening it was reported that a Yankee deserter, who yesterday came into our lines at Chester, stated that Washington was in the hands of the Confederates. If it be true that such a statement was made, it is entitled to no credit, for deserters are not usually to be relied upon. The latest news we have is from the *Washington Chronicle* of the 13th instant, which will be found in this morning's paper. We learn, in addition, that General Lew Wallace, who was defeated by the Confederates at Monocacy Bridge and fled from the field in confusion, has been relieved of his command and superseded by General Ord.

A gentleman from the Northern Neck of Virginia reports that forts Lincoln and Stephens, which constitute a portion of the defenses of Washington, were carried by the Confederates on the 13th. We are not prepared to vouch for the accuracy of this statement, though we see no reason for doubting it.

We have it from the best authority that Grant has moved two corps and a large quantity of artillery from the front of Petersburg and sent them to aid in the defense of Washington.

A gentleman who arrived in Lynchburg on Wednesday night from Fairfax County, which place he left on Monday last, states that the excitement in Washington was intense and that the Lincolnites were in great fear and trepidation consequent upon the advance of the Confederates into Maryland. The Yankees were removing all stores from Alexandria and Washington and all public archives and property of every description. Confusion worse confounded prevailed in the Federal capital. This gentleman derived his information from parties just from Washington, and it may be relied upon.

Private advices from Maryland affirm that by order of the general commanding, private property was strictly respected by our army in Maryland and Pennsylvania. This disagrees totally with the Yankee accounts, and we hope, so far as it applies to the miscegenators, that it is untrue. They should be made to feel some of the evils of the war which they are so relentlessly waging upon the South.

THE CONFEDERATES IN MARYLAND— HUNTER GONE TO PENNSYLVANIA

We had a conversation with an intelligent gentleman from our army in Maryland, who arrived here last night, having been within three miles of Washington City with the Confederate cavalry Monday at one o'clock. He gives some interesting particulars about the "raiders" in that state, some of which we can make public.

The cavalry on Monday was in three miles of Washington City and met on the roads leading from the city many citizens who had come out from the place, not desiring to be there when it was "carried by assault," as they supposed it would be. Several of them claimed to be good "secesh" and said they hoped our troops would go in, that now was the time. The soldiers there, they said, were nearly all heavy-artillerymen and most of them new hundred days' men from the North. All the old soldiers and fighting troops had been sent a week before to Sigel and are now with him on top of Maryland Heights. They were sent under the impression that the Confederate raiders were a small force and would not think of going around the rear of the Heights and leaving Sigel in their rear. With Sigel, they are now cut off from Washington. These citizens said there were not two full regiments of real soldiers in Washington City. There were a good many long faces among the Union people living along the roads in the vicinity of Washington, and they got a good deal longer Monday when a farmhouse about three miles distant from the city was burned by the Confederates. Our informant did not know the name of the owner of the house. A gentleman living near the city handed over about a hundred fat cattle to our cavalry, to be driven into Dixie. He refused to take pay for them.

At Baltimore our cavalry was hovering around the town in sight of its fortifications, which are about two miles distant from the city. The Yankees are all inside of the works and have no pickets out, our cavalry having run into town the few they did have out. Governor Bradford's house, which was burned, was within a stone's throw of one of the works—so close that a Yankee holloed out, "Never mind, d——n you, we'll pay you for that." To this a ragged Rebel replied, begging him not to mind that little bill, that the Confederates intended to burn Baltimore next day and he could settle it all at once.

Citizens who came out of Baltimore said the place could easily be taken by the cavalry then around it, as the soldiers of the garrison were out aiding General Lew Wallace in search for a large body of Rebel infantry, which were reported to be near Monocacy Bridge.

The fight at Monocacy Bridge, our informant says, was just no fight at all. It was a big run, and if the Yankees lost one thousand men, most of them must have broken their necks running. There wasn't a soldier with Wallace who fired more than once. They found the Rebels getting around them in all directions and, using discretion, took to their heels. The hundred days' men are described as "splendid." They all had on nice, new blue uniforms, shiny brass buttons, and muskets as bright as if they had just come out of the store. They also had brand-new shoes, many pairs of which some of the Rebels in delicate health, who had gotten their feet wet, were forced to borrow. These warriors didn't seem disposed to hurt anybody. Some of them didn't know which end of a cartridge went in first, and the general impression among them was that the regulation mode of getting the ramrod out of a gun was to blow it out.

Some Pennsylvania men who were in Maryland and had not been able to make their escape back home were quite talkative to our troops. They themselves were Democrats (of course), and didn't favor the war, and didn't intend to come out at anybody's requisition. They disclosed, however, a state of feeling on the part of the Republicans which is rather interesting. They say that their Republican neighbors won't come out to defend their homes, though Curtin's call had been out a week. These miscegenators say they cannot join the patriots for a hundred days any more than a hundred years, as one day among the Rebels might damage them beyond the chance of repair at any price. They say there are no regular troops about there now who can be sent out to drum them up, as was done during the invasion last year, and they intend to stay at home and smoke their pipes in peace.

General Hunter had reached Martinsburg and had gone into Pennsylvania by the Greencastle and Chambersburg Road. Our scouts saw his force as it moved along the Greencastle Road, and he did not have over six thousand infantry with him. He is going to Gettysburg, to put himself between the Confederate raiders and Philadelphia.

The stock gathered by the raiders in Maryland is said to be immense. Droves of fat cattle, hogs, sheep, etc., throng the roads. The gentleman from whom we get these facts says that in coming back from near Baltimore, on the route by way of Shepherdstown, he "didn't see as much as a chicken left."

A report was circulated at the North about three weeks ago that the Confederates were about to make an effort to release the prisoners at Point Lookout, whereupon, according to the statements of persons who came out from Baltimore, the government impressed every steamer "from Maine to Baltimore" and, sending them to the Point, removed the prisoners farther north.

The Maryland troops with the raiders were having the finest sort of time in the way of eating and drinking and warm welcomes from parents and friends.

The roads in Maryland were in splendid condition and the marching easy and rapid.

LOCALITIES AROUND WASHINGTON

The tollgate on the Seventh Street Road, where a portion of our forces were on the evening of the 11th instant, is only three miles from Washington. A clergyman informs us that within a quarter of a mile of this tollgate formerly stood the only Methodist church in the district connected with the Baltimore Conference, which seceded and joined the Southern wing of the church. It was demolished by the Yankees when constructing batteries for the protection of Washington. Tenleytown (or Tenallytown, as the dispatches have it) is to the west of this point, on the Rockville Road, about two miles from the suburbs of Georgetown. In this locality another column of our forces, according to the Northern accounts, appeared on the evening of the 11th.

LATEST FROM MARYLAND

At a late hour last night, we received by telegraph a summary of news from Northern papers of the 13th. It will be seen that no allusion is made to the "capture" of Baltimore or Washington, which formed the staple of such magnificent rumors yesterday.

FROM PETERSBURG

The situation of affairs on the Southside has almost ceased, pending the exciting events now transpiring in Maryland, to attract public attention. Grant is still displaying his strategy in the way of "masterly inactivity" and gradually detaching portions of his army for the defense of Washington. We hear that there was some heavy artillery firing on the lines yesterday morning, the cause or consequences of which we have not been able to ascertain. The sharpshooters have an occasional skirmish, but beyond this and the persistent shelling of the city by the Yankees, military operations have lately been very limited. Most of the families have removed beyond reach of the enemy's missiles, while those whose means enabled them to do so have secured a refuge outside of the city limits. The inhabitants are animated by a spirit of firm resolution and have the most unbounded confidence in our military leaders and the gallant troops whom they command.

BELOW RICHMOND

Everything continues quiet. Our artillery indulge in an occasional shot at the Yankee transports and are reported to have done them some damage. The enemy's gunboats reply and continue to shell every locality on the north bank which is supposed to shelter a "Rebel."

Alexander Duvall, Jr., of the 2nd Company Richmond Howitzers was wounded and taken prisoner on Wednesday. He had volunteered to go on a reconnaissance with some cavalry and, after he received his wound, was taken off in a boat by some Yankee sailors.

FROM NORTH CAROLINA

Recent intelligence from New Bern states that the raid into Onslow County resulted badly for the Yankees. It appears that they got separated and came together unexpectedly, when, each taking the other for an enemy, they fired into each other, killing an orderly-sergeant and two or three privates and wounding many others.

It is universally acknowledged by the Yankees at New Bern that a failure of Grant to whip Lee must put an end to the war, and none believe that he will succeed. The force at New Bern is now very small, composed of only enough men to garrison the forts, with a small number of cavalry to send out occasionally and keep up a show of strength.

FROM MISSISSIPPI

The following official dispatch was received at General Bragg's headquarters yesterday:

> Okolona, Mississippi, July 14, 1864
>
> To General Braxton Bragg:—We attacked a column of the enemy, under Smith, yesterday, on the march from Pontotoc to Tupelo, causing him to burn many wagons. We attacked him in his position at Tupelo this morning, but could not force his position. The battle was a drawn one and lasted three hours.
>
> S. D. Lee, Lieutenant General

CHARLESTON DAILY COURIER
July 16, 1864

[UNTITLED]

One hundred of the Yankee deserters held at the Castle in Richmond were lately transferred to the Libby, and their status changed from deserters to that of prisoners of war. It is, at last, the deliberate conviction of the Confederate government that deserters can never become of any service to us, either in the army or the workshop, and that it is better to get man for man by an exchange of them under the cartel.

THE PUBLIC FEELING

At no period since this war began its course of blood, devastation, and anguish has the mind of the combatants been more deeply excited than at the present time. Both parties realize the tremendous importance of success and are putting forth all their power to achieve it, and never have the soldiers under the two flags exhibited greater valor, more persistent energy, firmer resolution. Those qualities have been exhibited in an unwonted degree by the men under Lee and Johnston, Grant and Sherman. The last named has received some compensation for the severe repulses inflicted upon him at various points, thereby maintaining the spirit of his soldiers and persuading the people of the North that he was on the high road to complete and glorious triumph. But the former of those Yankee captains has met with a series of disastrous defeats, has been obliged to adopt another line of approach to Richmond after publishing to the world his determination to reach that city by pursuing the road from Fredericksburg, has utterly failed in the attempt to carry

Petersburg by a coup; and yet he was enabled to hurl his heavy columns day after day against our solid lines and, after sustaining frightful losses, to preserve unimpaired the discipline, order, and spirit of his immense army. The sublime heroism and unsurpassed skill of the generals at the head of our two great armies and the men under their command have been applauded with enthusiastic ardor by the whole of Christendom, and even our enemies have given copious and cordial expression to their admiration of the brilliant strategy and indomitable valor displayed by these great masters of the art of war and by the men who are proud to fight and endure under such leaders in such a cause. The courage and obstinacy with which our enemies have fought has redounded to the glory of our troops; every assault they have made has shown the superiority of Southern generals and soldiers in martial gifts and qualities. In this emphatic manner do the men composing the hostile armies show and declare that they are fully sensible of the value of the stake they contend for. And while the soldiery of both countries have been fighting, marching, and suffering, in order to gratify the hopes and desires of their government and people, the whole continent has been watching the progress of the campaign with an interest so intense and long sustained that at times it has been painful. All eyes have been fixed on the two great theaters of the conflict. The scenes of blood enacted there have absorbed universal attention. Operations in other quarters have been regarded as important only in proportion as they affected the results of those mighty campaigns. The ear has been eagerly open for the latest news from Virginia and Georgia, and readers of daily journals begrudged the space devoted to every other subject.

But while the mind of the South has been refreshed by pleasing intelligence and altogether hopeful since the inauguration of those campaigns, that of the North has been actuated by a variety of conflicting emotions. Today the dwellers in the United States have rejoiced over some dispatch whose falseness the morrow has discovered, and the truth has turned their joy into sorrow. They have been greatly elated by high-sounding promises and predictions and then troubled and cast down by the extinguishment of their sanguine hopes. When we could not delight ourselves over the narration of splendid successes, we have been able to keep our spirits against the assaults of gloom and despondency, and throughout the course of the campaigns in progress, we have maintained a firm, calm, trustful, dignified attitude. It has not been so with our enemies. Their joy has been intemperate, their expectations extravagant, their feelings mixed and various, the excitement they have been so long under painful and exhausting. The diverse nature of the events that have moved our and their minds has produced these different effects, and today we are better able to bear defeat, though it take the proportions and color of disaster, than our enemies, with their vastly greater resources.

The deplorable condition of their finances has a great deal to do with the feverishness of the public mind of the people, over whom Lincoln holds despotic sway, and it is because aware they are that they are fast approaching the abyss of anarchy and ruin that they are so restless under the misfortunes that have befallen their arms. They are conscious that they have undertaken a work too formidable even for their magnificent resources, and, stricken with terror and dismay, they contemplate dissensions, starvation, bankruptcy, and a troop of horrors, whose presence is already felt. Although no military success, no matter how important and decisive, could prevent the coming of those woes and save them from certain destruction, still they long for such a victory with eager hope.

The movement under Breckinridge has raised that excitement to the highest point, and it is easy to conceive the perplexity, dismay, and anguish that have taken hold of the spirit of our foes at the announcement of the approach of that able and adventurous leader. That movement, whether it be a raid or an invasion, has sorely disquieted the blatant foe, for he is conscious that if justice is meted out to him, his enormities will be visited with a heavy hand.

While the mind of our enemies has been more and more disturbed as the campaign progresses, and is now the prey of all manner of direful apprehensions, that of the South has been steadily growing more firm and hopeful. Expectant of success, we are not unprepared for reverses. Our spirit has been chastened into humility and moderation, and while we shall receive victory with glowing thanks to Almighty God, we shall submit with resigned hearts to any misfortune He sees proper to let befall us.

NORTH

BOSTON EVENING TRANSCRIPT
July 16, 1864

FROM PETERSBURG RETURN OF THE 13TH MASSACHUSETTS REGIMENT—THE SIEGE IN GOOD PROGRESS— SUCCESSFUL RAID UP THE JAMES RIVER—REBELS DEFEATED AND PROPERTY DESTROYED

New York, 13th—The *Herald*'s army dispatch states that the 13th Massachusetts Regiment left for home on the 13th instant, their term of service having expired.

There was nothing new respecting the siege on the 14th. Operations are steadily in progress for the reduction of Petersburg.

A raid was made up the James River by Lieutenant Chambers and 130 men of the 31st Pennsylvania Artillery and 10th Connecticut Volunteers. Our force made an assault on a Rebel station, where three hundred Rebels were stationed, capturing fourteen.

The Rebels were then burned out of their quarters, by setting them on fire, and were compelled to give fight on open ground, where they were punished severely in killed and wounded, and driven off. Our loss was one man.

Lieutenant Chambers captured a torpedo which the Rebels were about to sink in the river, and destroyed a large quantity of grain, also a grist and saw mill.

Lieutenant Chambers is to be promoted.

THE RETREAT OF THE REBELS ACROSS THE POTOMAC— OUR ARTILLERY SHELLING THEIR REAR—THOUSANDS OF LIVESTOCK SECURED BY THE RAIDERS—1,500 REBELS KILLED AND WOUNDED IN FRONT OF WASHINGTON— PHILADELPHIA AND BALTIMORE RAILROAD

New York, 16th—The *Herald*'s Washington dispatch says no fort in front of Washington was captured by the Rebels.

It is reported today that trains were heard on the Orange and Alexandria Railroad, and it is supposed that reinforcements were coming to the Rebels, or to carry off their plunder. The prevailing opinion is that they are hurrying away.

The last of their rear guard passed Rockville at noon Wednesday.

The *World*'s dispatch says advices from the upper Potomac confirm the retreat of the Rebels into Virginia. Our artillery shelled the Rebel rear last evening, and some stragglers were taken, but it was impossible to intercept the main body. They had, when at Wilson's Farm, 576 prisoners, taken at Monocacy.

The *Tribune*'s dispatch says it is estimated that the Rebels secured eleven thousand head of cattle and horses, besides droves of sheep and hogs, which they got across the Potomac while threatening Washington.

Brief as was the combat before Washington, it was bloody. The Rebel killed and wounded must have reached 1,500.

The *Herald*'s correspondent says Admiral Lee, of the James River Squadron, has gone to the North Carolina sounds on an inspecting tour.

General Meade had an hour's interview with General Butler on the 13th.

Washington, 15th—It is certain that small portions of Rebels have reentered Virginia and are traveling with their plunder through Loudoun County toward Snicker's and Ashby's gaps. A large force of our troops is in pursuit.

It is reported that Breckinridge and staff were in Leesburg Wednesday morning, superintending the movements of the enemy. A number of stragglers have been picked up by our troops.

Baltimore, 15th—The Philadelphia Railroad Company has made arrangements for running their trains over their road tomorrow. Gunpowder Bridge has not yet been repaired, but a footbridge is constructed around the burned portion.

The reports today of Rebel cavalry being around the city are believed to be unfounded. Our cavalry made a thorough examination of the country in the vicinity, but could not find an armed enemy anywhere.

NEW YORK TRIBUNE
July 16, 1864

"MY MARYLAND"

Maryland is probably some millions of dollars poorer this day for the late Rebel raid, most of which she would have saved by seasonably organizing and drilling her militia. She ought to have been able to put fifty thousand militia into the field for the defense of her own buildings, crops, and cattle within forty-eight hours after hearing that an enemy was on her border. Five thousand militia cavalry, mounted on their own horses, armed only with revolvers for close fighting and carbines for use when dismounted, might have saved at least half of what they have lost. Such cavalry could not be expected to use swords effectively, nor yet to resist artillery; but hovering on the flanks and front of the enemy, driving in or capturing his vedettes, making dashes at his wagons, and picking up his stragglers, it could do him great injury with little loss or risk.[13]

Now that the raid is over, the pro-Rebel organs in the loyal states will endeavor to magnify its fruits to the utmost. Thus the *Daily News* says of the raiders on their retreat, "They are strong enough to repel any assault that may be made. They obtained several thousand recruits and a vast amount of supplies."

Maryland gave Breckinridge 42,482 votes in 1860, while Howard, the Democratic "Peace" candidate for governor, had but 26,086 in 1861; and the party has done no better ever since, owing to its heavy depletion to swell the ranks of the Rebel armies. If "several thousand" more of them have just gone, their prospect for carrying the state for president this fall must range considerably below zero.

ONLY A NIGGER

Lieutenant Hunt of Utica (U.S. regular artillery) recently fell overboard from a tug in the James River and was drowned. His body not being recovered by the tug, some relatives went down and dragged the river for it in vain, being afforded every facility by our naval officers. Finally they inquired along the riverbank, and found two Negroes who told them of another Negro who had buried the body of a Federal officer which he found on the riverbank. Proceeding to that Negro's hut, they met his wife, who showed them the clothing, spurs, etc., of the buried officer, which they readily recognized as Lieutenant Hunt's. She also produced and gave them fifty-seven dollars in cash with his wallet, which her husband had taken before burying the body, decently shrouded in coarse cloth, in the best coffin he was able to make. In a little while, the husband returned and, before aiding them to exhume the remains, produced three hundred dollars more, with certain important papers, which he had also taken from the body, but which he had carefully concealed even from his wife, because (he said) the guerrillas often came there and they might frighten her into giving up to them documents and money which they ought not to have. All these were brought away with the body. Of course the Negro only proved shrewd, thoughtful, and strictly honest, but there have been instances of white men doing considerably worse.

13. vedettes: mounted sentinels positioned in front of the pickets.

AUGUST 20, 1864

SOUTH

RICHMOND DAILY DISPATCH
August 20, 1864

A YANKEE REVIEW OF GRANT'S CAMPAIGN[14]

The *National Intelligencer* contains a review of Grant's campaign, written with considerable candor and evidently by a person who was present with the army and probably held a prominent position. It professes not to give the losses on both sides, yet it does give those on the Yankee side, as they were stated by their newspapers; that is to say, it admits sometimes half, and sometimes about one third of the truth. Yet, as things are, having probably no better resource for information than Stanton's telegrams, and considering that it comes from a Yankee, the story is told, as we have said, with tolerable fairness. It begins with the day on which Grant broke up his camp to cross the Rapidan, that is, on the 3rd of May. It admits a loss on the 6th of May of 15,000 men, from which we may fairly infer that the actual loss was fully 25,000. Here the misstatement of the Yankee press is repeated when it is said that at daylight on the 7th, General Lee was *retreating* in good order to Spotsylvania Courthouse. General Lee was *not* retreating. He was following the movement of Grant, who, having lost, according to the statement of the Yankee newspapers—admitted by this author to be correct, but believed by us to be an underestimate of at least one third—35,000 men, drew off his whole left wing and the greater part of his center and was endeavoring to anticipate Lee by taking possession of Spotsylvania Courthouse. Lee *followed* him, which would not have been the case had he himself been executing a movement in retreat, not quick enough to prevent him from taking possession of the ground, but soon enough to drive him from it before he had succeeded in fortifying it to any great extent. Lee would never have left the Wilderness had Grant remained before it; and the latter left it because he found himself utterly unable to drive Lee from his position. Thus, early in the campaign, he had failed in his grand object, which was to turn Lee's right, attack him on that flank, and force him to fight with his back to the mountains. There can be no doubt, from all the information we have been able to obtain, that Grant lost in the battles of the 4th, 5th, 6th, and 7th of May at least

14. Refers to the Battle of the Wilderness, May 5–7, and the Battle of Spotsylvania, May 8–12. In the principal actions, the Union lost 29,000 in killed and wounded.

50,000 men. The Yankee papers, as we have seen, admitted a loss of 35,000 thousand, and this writer, as we have also seen, endorses the admission.

On the 10th of May, the writer admits a loss of 10,000 men. We may therefore conclude that the real loss was at least 15,000. We have never seen a Confederate officer who estimated it at less than 20,000. The same may be said of the 12th of May, on which day the Yankees and this writer admit a loss of 10,000 men, while no Confederate officer rates their loss at less than 20,000 and many place it as high as 30,000. It was, we suspect, about 25,000. Contrary alike to the strong logic of *facts* and to the inferences of common sense, the reviewer claims a substantial victory this day, because Hancock's corps, in the morning, surprised the division of General Edward Johnson and captured several thousand men. Yet he himself acknowledges that they were afterward repulsed and that all attempts to regain possession were foiled with the most tremendous slaughter ever experienced in this war. On the 18th, the battle was renewed along the whole line, and the Yankees were everywhere repulsed. On this occasion they lost, the reviewer says, 1,200 men; we may say about 3,000. He does not tell the reason why the attack was comparatively so feeble and the Yankee loss comparatively so small. We must do it for him. It was because the Yankee soldiers could not be brought up to the scratch any longer. The tremendous lessons of the 6th, 10th, and 12th had not been lost upon them. They had lost all heart and were no longer the men they were in the beginning of the campaign.

Grant failed *here,* as he had failed at the Wilderness, to drive Lee from his position; and having done so, he took *himself* off, in strict pursuance of Dogberry's advice. Here, according to this writer, commenced his grand flanking operations, which consisted in retreating from before a position he had been unable to carry and attempting to place his army between Lee and Richmond. In this, of course, he failed again. On the North Anna River, he found Lee still in his front—still interposing between him and Richmond, still ready to fight, and still determined to force *him* to fight, if he would obtain the prize he sought, at every disadvantage. He had already lost, according to the statement of the Yankee papers, 75,000 men; *in point of fact,* his losses had reached 100,000, and these were the very flower of his army. He had been reinforced, while in Spotsylvania, by 25,000 good troops, the larger portion of which had already been expended. He had been reinforced by Butler with 20,000. He had received 40,000 from Ohio and other states, but they were mere hundred days' men. We may, therefore, safely say that now, having crossed the Pamunkey, opened McClellan's old line of communication with West Point, and set himself down at Cold Harbor, he was not more than one half as strong as he was before he crossed the Rapidan. With this diminished force he was still facing Lee behind his breastworks, with troops reinforced and in the highest spirits; and he was compelled to get him out of his way or abandon all thought of entering Richmond by that line, on which, however, he had promised "to fight it out, if it took him all summer." But three days of summer were gone, when, on the 3rd of June, he made his last attack on the north side upon Lee and was repulsed with greater slaughter than he had ever yet met with. The two armies remained opposite to each other for several days, when Grant flanked himself over James River, General Lee not attempting to interrupt him. "On the 11th of May," says the reviewer, "after six days of heavy fighting on the overland route, General Grant had written to the secretary of war, 'I propose to fight it out on this line, if it takes all summer.' On the 14th of June, just a month afterward, and when the summer was only two weeks old, he had turned his back on this line; and the Army of the Potomac, at least what remained of its original number on the day when it took up the bloody march across the country from Fredericksburg, was set down by its commander on the banks of that river, from which it was removed by General Halleck in 1862, and where it might have been replaced by General Grant long before the 14th of June in the present summer, and that, too, without the loss of a man, if he had chosen to convey it there in transports instead of marching overland, where every foot of its progress was marked with precious blood—the blood of trained and brave and skillful veterans."

After announcing this singular circumstance, the reviewer pauses to inquire into the causes which led to the choice of the overland route. He mentions three, which have been conjectured by various persons: First—complaisance to the president, whose favorite route this was well-known to be. This is rejected as at variance with the well-established character of Grant for independence, etc. Second—General Grant expected to overpower and beat General Lee so badly that his troops would be much too demoralized to defend Richmond. This, we suspect, was the *true* reason for choosing the overland route. It shows that he had underestimated his enemy, which is not characteristic of an able general. Third—by this route it was supposed Washington would always remain covered. The force of that reason is entirely destroyed by Grant's exodus across the river, which leaves no force at all between Washington and Lee's army.

We have room for very little more. The writer says that the offensive movements against Petersburg were suspended because Grant was entirely exhausted, but doubts whether he will be allowed to rest.

The writer admits that the campaign has been a stupendous failure.

CHARLESTON DAILY COURIER
August 20, 1864

A FAITHFUL SERVANT

It will be a pleasure to all who shall undertake the record of this war from a Southern view to preserve and report the well-attested instances of the constancy and endurance and fidelity of servants. Many such cases have occurred and have been reported in the newspapers, and we earnestly invite reports of all such from witnesses and observers.

A soldier who has lately reached this city, after enforced acceptance of Yankee hospitalities as a prisoner, reports a case which came to his knowledge, although the Yankees, of course, generally endeavor to conceal such cases. On one of the islands of our coast, now infested by Yankees, is a Negro servant who has been forced off from his master's premises. Great efforts have been made to enlist him as a soldier, as, from his character and qualifications, the Yankees have great hopes for him. Promises of the most alluring kind, persuasions, and entreaties having failed, the opposite course was tried, and he was exposed to trials and punishments of all kinds that could be devised to overcome his foolish obstinacy, as the Yankees supposed. He has now been for some months subjected to close confinement and short diet, with a heavy ball and chain, not only to prevent escape but to punish him severely. He told our informant that his mind was fixed and fully prepared to endure everything and anything, even the death of confinement and starvation, before he would take a gun against his master or his master's friends.

Do not such cases and the claims of all good servants who have been by force placed in the ranks of power of the enemy deserve consideration? We have urged, and we now repeat the suggestion, that the governors of the states, under consultation and cooperation with the War Department, through the generals in command, could and should give public and general notice of amnesty and safety, so far as military laws and state laws are concerned, to all servants returning within our lines who can show clearly that they have not willfully or deliberately committed offenses or desertion but have been dragged into Yankee service by force.

SIEGE OF CHARLESTON

Four Hundred Eighth Day

The firing on Fort Sumter has fallen off rapidly in the past two or three days. During Thursday night, Gregg fired 23 and the "Swamp Angel" 8 shots; on Friday, Gregg fired 45 and the "Swamp Angel" 15 shots; giving a total of 91 shots since last report, a falling off of between 30 and 40 shots from the firing of the previous day.

Several Yankee vessels passed the bar, going south, yesterday, and two from the south sailing north.

A tug which was observed cruising eastward all Thursday night returned inside the bar Friday morning.

There was no news from the coast.

TO THE CITIZENS OF THE CONFEDERATE STATES

Savannah, Georgia, August 15, 1864

Upon the commencement of hostilities between the Confederate States and the United States, when the call was made for volunteers, my services were accepted, and I enlisted in the 17th Regiment Georgia Volunteers, commanded by Colonel Benning. Having faithfully served and been stricken down by disease, an honorable discharge was given me.

Since my return to Savannah from a visit to the counties of eastern Georgia, the intelligence has reached me that my son, Nathaniel G. Sutton, a private in Company I, 31st Regiment Georgia Volunteers, is wounded and in the hands of the enemy. The villains having drawn the blood of one of my family, revenge is mine, and I shall proceed forthwith to Virginia and occupy the place in ranks made vacant by the accident which has happened to my child.

I call on all who are able to load and shoot any description of gun or firearm to follow me and my gray hairs, drive the vandals from our soil, and dictate to them our terms of peace. A glorious future is opening brightly to us all. Let them all rally to the banner of the Holy Cross, and all will be well with us.

Francis Sutton

NORTH

BOSTON EVENING TRANSCRIPT
August 20, 1864

THE RECORD OF MASSACHUSETTS

No son of the Old Bay State need blush for its course during the present war. When the national capital has been in peril, her native-born citizens have rushed to its defense. The safety of Washington and Fortress Monroe are due to the patriotic promptness of Massachusetts volunteers. It was her militia who baffled in its inception a plot to seize Fortress Monroe, and who were the first to reach Washington, marching *through* New York, Philadelphia, and Baltimore. Since that time, the state has been equally prompt to answer the call of duty. Five thousand hundred-days' men have recently been raised in twenty-five days and sent from the commonwealth, while Pennsylvania, with her border constantly threatened, has recruited only eight thousand such troops and New York, with her thronging population, has probably contributed a lesser number. Pennsylvania soldiers are needed to guard their own state, while Massachusetts men are available for service in distant portions of the Union. The 60th Regiment is reported to be at Indianapolis.

This commonwealth has an excess of females over males of one hundred thousand. It pays 12 percent of the internal revenue of the country and manufactures a larger proportion of the articles necessary to the prosecution of the war than any other state. With a population more than two thirds of whom are American born, no state besides has been so fully represented in the ranks of the Union army by its best citizens. From many communities, quotas have been composed of what is called the "refuse" of society, while Massachusetts was sending men whose absence created a real void in the places they had left. With such facts the commonwealth can challenge the closest scrutiny as to the thoroughness and effectiveness of the support it has rendered the government.

A SINGULAR DESIRE FROM A STRANGE QUARTER

The "opposition" appears to be very much exercised that no ratification or mass meetings, torchlight processions, and other electioneering demonstrations have appeared in support of the nominations of the Baltimore Convention.[15] This anxiety is exceedingly disinterested and mag-

15. The 1864 Republican convention, held in Baltimore, nominated Lincoln for a second term. With the war seemingly at a standstill, Lincoln's popularity was at a nadir; Andrew Johnson, a Southern War Democrat, was chosen as vice president to prop up the ticket.

nanimous! The "opposition" would doubtless enjoy an excited political campaign, distracting the attention of the Northern communities from the war and giving an opportunity for arousing and working upon the passions and prejudices by whose help it hopes to accomplish its ends. But this amiable desire will not, perhaps, be gratified.

The people understand the Baltimore platform and see that it is made of straight planks. They know the Baltimore nominee, and why, at this crisis, he is the nominee. They believe he will be reelected, because that reelection is a part of the process by which the rebellion is to be put down—the one supreme object they have at heart. It may be necessary for those who are struggling for an opportunity to negotiate with Jefferson Davis, ready to concede the honor of the republic and abandon its democratic institutions to the arch-unbeliever in the rights of majorities, for the sake of a peace politically profitable to them—it may be necessary for such parties to indulge in scenic displays to cajole the novelty-loving populace.

The great body of the people, however, have more serious work to do. Their object is to crush Richmond and its military despotism and not to strengthen the hands of secession by a Northern tender of aid and comfort. If President Lincoln prosecutes the war with steadiness and fair success, he will not be called upon to quit the White House because the usual but now unseasonable appliances were not employed to secure his reelection. He will be chosen by the serious and earnest patriotism of the country.

NEW YORK TRIBUNE
August 20, 1864

FROM SHERMAN'S ARMY
SWINGING TO THE RIGHT—ANOTHER FORWARD MOVEMENT

From Our Special Correspondent
Right Wing Southwest of Atlanta, Georgia
August 10, 1864

Our extreme right has gained another and still stronger position upon the southwest side of Atlanta. Following up the advantages obtained by the operations of the past three or four days, having discovered and driven back the enemy's left, the 2nd and 3rd divisions of the XXIII Corps yesterday succeeded in advancing their lines for another mile.

On the afternoon of the 8th, as I stated in a previous letter, we came to an open field, across which the enemy's works and a portion of the infantry and cavalry force could be distinctly seen. This field is about two miles long from west to east, with an average breadth of 600 to 800 yards, having a creek running through it from east to west. It is crossed by hedgerows and divided by farm fences. A road crosses it toward the west end. At the east it is bounded by a ridge running transversely, with farmhouses along its base embowered in clusters of shade trees. Beyond this ridge is the line of the Macon Road; the sound of the cars as they go in and out, by day and night, is distinctly heard. Across the west side or end of this field, earthworks for infantry, with embrasures for artillery, have been constructed within plain view of the enemy, whose vedettes are seen moving about; and the troops are lolling around or engaged in camp routine at the edge of the woods. This is doubtless the enemy's last line toward the railroad, and here and nearby are massed all the troops which can be spared from the defenses of the city.

Permit me, in the outset of this letter, to do away with any impression that may have gained currency at home that the Rebels are likely to abandon their position here some dark night and leave us to walk quietly into the town. The signs are all against it, and I no more expect that we shall occupy Atlanta without a severe struggle—perhaps a prolonged and bloody one—than that Richmond will be evacuated by Lee. No country ever furnished such natural opportunities for defense, and not even Georgia has anywhere in its northern section land so rough and difficult in which to prosecute offensive warfare. It would extend too far the limits assigned to this letter (my time also is brief) to fully describe the situation. A daily account of operations is the most that I have the time to give.

There never have been more than one or two points at most from which we could reach the city with our artillery, and since the XXIII Corps has been withdrawn from the left and that position abandoned, I doubt if many shots or shells have been thrown into the place.

But to return to the advance of yesterday. General Hascall took General Cooper's and Colonel Hobson's brigades and, with a section of the 6th Michigan Battery, marched around to the right of this open field I have described. A heavy line of skirmishers was deployed, which, swinging upon their left as upon a pivot, overlapped the left flank of the enemy, which was chiefly composed of cavalry with a battery. The skirmishers, after advancing for half a mile, went forward with a cheer upon the double-quick, and the Rebels gave way, retiring to the next hill and belt of woods. From there they shelled General Hascall's line quite vigorously for some time, and were replied to by our guns. The troops, closely following the skirmish line, steadily advanced, coming out upon an open field, forming an indentation into the edge of the woods. This was the ridge sought after for our position, and here was a good position to locate works. A semicircular line of entrenchments was built, which guarded against attack from any quarter, and the main line was so refused as to be protected against attack or surprise on the flank. It was on this ridge where the Rebels made a spirited stand, and from which our troops, having no time to construct defenses, were attacked after night, on the 8th, and were obliged to give way. Here Lieutenant Colonel Elstner lost his life while engaged in deploying his skirmish line about nightfall. Afterward the Rebels burned a barn on the end of the knoll toward the field.

Captain Kerstetter, General Hascall's able adjutant general, came back to the battery position about 3:30 P.M. and reported to General Schofield that the division had gained the important position they were sent to occupy. From the open field they could see plainly, a mile and a half to the northeast, obliquely across the field, a large Rebel force engaged in building a large fort or earthwork.

While the 2nd Division was getting the place secure, they were constantly cheered, and the enemy's sharpshooters, occupying the skirmish pits in and along the meadow at the left, kept up an annoying fire.

The 3rd Brigade of the 3rd Division, Colonel Byrd, with a section of battery, meantime moved in on the left, also under cover of the woods, driving back the Rebel skirmishers and gaining a new position on the northeast side of the field. These operations occupied the best part of the afternoon. Toward evening the 19th Ohio Battery posted in front opened upon the Rebel skirmish pits within range to drive them out, but failed to dislodge them from the meadow. They were too securely burrowed in their holes to be reached. Everything was made secure for the night, the troops bivouacked on the field, and General Hascall, according to his usual custom, moved his headquarters close to the front, so as to be near his line during the night. We distinctly heard the Rebel tattoo at dark and could see their campfires beyond the field. The night passed without any unusual demonstration, the customary skirmish firing being kept up from both sides.

E. S.

SEPTEMBER 17, 1864

SOUTH

RICHMOND DAILY DISPATCH
September 17, 1864

THE WAR NEWS

The enemy, within the past day or two, has crossed a force to the north side of the James River, at Curles Neck, and has shown some signs of hostilities. The object of the movement is yet undeveloped, though Grant has always resorted to a feint of this description when he had any important enterprise afoot. Many well-informed persons believe that he contemplates some bold movement at an early day on the south side, and if so, this explains the crossing of the troops. We shall probably soon hear of stirring events on and about the Weldon Railroad.

From official information received last evening, we learn that the enemy yesterday morning drove in our pickets at New Market, but in the afternoon our forces advanced, drove them back, and reestablished our original picket line.

A MOVEMENT OF THE ENEMY CHECKED

We heard, on Thursday evening, a vague report of a movement of the enemy in the direction of the Southside Railroad, but it came in such indefinite shape that we forbore any notice of it yesterday. The affair, as it turned out, possessed no great importance, though if any reliance can be placed on the assertions of prisoners, the enemy intended a bold push for the Southside Road. It appears that early Thursday morning Warren's V Corps of the Yankee army left their works in the vicinity of the Weldon Railroad and broke through General Butler's lines below Poplar Springs Church. This is a point in Dinwiddie County, between the Vaughan and Boydton plank roads, about two miles west of the Weldon Road, and between three and four miles south of Petersburg. The Yankees attempted to advance, but were soon met by Colonel D. D. Ferebee, commanding General Dearing's brigade, who fought them four hours with varying success and finally repulsed them with considerable loss. Our loss in the affair was small. The enemy succeeded in reaching Poplar Springs Church and threw up breastworks at that point, but were compelled to abandon them. A number of the enemy were killed and wounded and several captured. The prisoners reported that this movement was an attempt to advance their lines in the direction of the Southside Railroad, though in military circles it is believed to have been only a reconnaissance to feel the strength and position of our forces.

After their repulse by Colonel Ferebee, Warren's troops retired to their old position, and our original picket line was reestablished.

LATEST FROM PETERSBURG

Passengers by last evening's train report that the enemy yesterday made an attempt to advance his lines on the Weldon Railroad but was met by Wilcox's command and driven back. We captured eighty-nine prisoners, who were brought over by the train. There were among them one or two commissioned officers. Doubtless this was a repetition of the movement of the previous day, and it is now apparent that the Yankees are determined, if possible, to extend their lines in the direction of the Southside Railroad. Indeed, it has been all along known to be a part of Grant's plan to establish himself upon that line of communication, as he has upon the direct southern route, but he has made a bad beginning and, it is hoped, will be held in check permanently.

THE ARMY OF TENNESSEE

Official information has been received that the Army of Tennessee is in splendid condition and spirits.

In a dispatch to General Bragg, dated September 15, 1864, General Hood says he is very much gratified at the feeling now existing among the officers and men of his army and that they are in better condition for battle than at any time since they crossed the Chattahoochee.

Official information has also been received that the extra-duty list (consisting of detailed men) is being materially decreased.

DESERTERS AND DELINQUENTS

We call attention to the proclamation of the governor concerning deserters and other delinquents owing military service to the Confederate government. The law of the state makes it obligatory upon magistrates, sheriffs, sergeants, and constables to take steps for the arrest of all such persons as may be found within their respective counties, cities, and towns, and imposes penalties for a failure to do so. In addition to this, the governor promises, in the event that the present apathy in this respect continues, to revoke the military exemptions of many justices of the peace and other county officers, and we feel assured he will keep his word. The government now needs the services of every able-bodied man who can be spared from civil employment, and if all deserters and skulkers were placed in the ranks, our armies would be largely reinforced. The proclamation is timely, and we trust that those who are most interested will heed its warnings. A law more plain in its provisions was never passed by the General Assembly, and we can only account for the neglect of state officers to comply with it by supposing them ignorant of its existence. They can have no such excuse now.

CHARLESTON DAILY COURIER
September 17, 1864

OAK ASHES WANTED

Persons having oak ashes which they are willing to dispose of will do us a great favor by sending them to this office, for which a fair price will be paid. Anyone in the country having any on hand which they will sell, or anyone who is willing to undertake to collect some for us, will please make the fact known by letter. We use it, instead of potash, for making lye to wash the ink off the type.

[UNTITLED]

"Peace on the base of the Union" is the McClellan motto. If disposed at all to accept this peaceful tender, we would ask, what Union or what stage or standard of the Union shall we accept? The Union as formed by thirteen states, of whom twelve actually held slaves and all recognized slavery—or the Union of which one large section organized and aided and encouraged the John Brown raid against the other section and the home of Washington?

[UNTITLED]

Even according to the bloodiest codes of recognized war, it is not allowed, we believe, to fire into a city that is not simply and merely a military post, until it has been invested and attacked and effectually surrounded by a force apparently sufficient for occupation when surrendered.

Charleston is not besieged in any sense approaching this condition—its land approaches, two rivers, and three railroads are open and in free use, and the only token of a siege, or summons, or pretext for treating it as a city liable to shells is a few batteries only near enough to annoy and alarm and disturb noncombatants, invalids, and others, and not to weaken in any way the military defenses.

The shelling is not—even after General Foster's emphatic assertion—directed to or at any works, shops, or arsenals, or other military posts—or if so, the Yankees are bad artillerists.

Judged by its effects and mode in reference to the rules of war, the shelling of Charleston can only be pronounced by impartial witnesses an experimental school of practice in developing new results in artillery.

Are we ready to continue champagne courtesies and frequent flags of truce with persons ordering and approving such shelling, and branding us falsely for cruelties to prisoners whom they will not relieve by exchange?

THE CRISIS

The duties devolving upon us at the present crisis are numerous, weighty, and imperative. After suffering a long series of disastrous defeats, the enemy has at last achieved a success.[16] That success has filled his corrupt heart with rejoicing and inspirited and emboldened him to such a degree that he has come up to the wicked work he has enterprised with renewed determination and boundless confidence.

Feeling himself strong enough to carry out that offensive measure, Lincoln has ordered his enrolling officers to proceed forthwith with the enforcement of the draft. McClellan's construction of the Chicago platform and the declaration of his purposes and intentions oblige us to see that the hope of receiving help from the party opposed to the administration is altogether delusive.[17] Hood's successful retreat from Atlanta has so wrought upon the minds of our unstable and conceited enemies that the voices that were recently lifted up for peace are now silent, while they who cried out loudly for the continuance of the war are urging their government and generals with greater clamor and augmented fierceness to move their armies forward with rapid step and to smite with relentless fury. Throwing off the doubts and anxieties that beclouded and disturbed their spirits, and encouraged to believe that glorious success stands ready to crown their efforts, the people and the soldiers of the United States, burning with strong desire after the fruit

16. Refers to the fall of Atlanta, September 2, 1864.

17. The 1864 Democratic convention, held in Chicago, nominated General George McClellan for president. Intended to appeal to the peace faction, the platform condemned "arbitrary military arrests" and "suppression of freedom of speech and the press" and pledged to preserve the right to hold slaves—in its elliptical language, to leave "the rights of the states unimpaired." It decried the "four years of failure to restore the Union by the experiment of war" and demanded "that immediate efforts be made for a cessation of hostilities . . . so that, at the earliest practicable moment, peace may be restored on the basis of the Federal Union."

of their labors and sufferings, are confident that in a very short time their dominion over the states that have chosen a government of their own will be completely reestablished.

These are the purposes and intentions, the hopes and expectations, that now move and impel the heart of our enemies. Moreover, the administration is aware that the renewal and prolongation of its power can be secured only by important military success. A great victory will replace Lincoln in the presidential throne and redound to the solid advantage of that great company of rogues who are increasing their substance by speculation and contracts. The number directly interested in the reelection of Lincoln is reckoned by hundreds of thousands. The hopes of that vast number and of the great host of army officials and clerks are bottomed upon the success of their president, and that depends upon the success of Grant and Sherman.

We should expect those generals to make some daring and determined efforts in the course of the next thirty or forty days, and we may also count upon demonstrations in other quarters. It is not unlikely that the redoubtable Farragut will pay Charleston a hostile visit.

With these dangers staring us in the face, it behooves us to exercise watchfulness, diligence, courage, and energy. This crisis must be met in a manner worthy of our righteous cause, in harmony with the precious interests at stake, and with the lofty reputation we have earned for splendid gallantry, invincible courage, and heroic fortitude.

The armies confronting the foe in Virginia and Maryland must not be allowed to suffer defeat. And in order that they may do the work assigned them, arrest the course of the invading hordes, discomfit and scatter them, those armies should be reinforced. Those blessed with sound bodies and strong arms who, under various pretexts and subterfuges and pleas, have been enabled to remain at home and pursue gainful avocations; that large army of clerks who have only heard of battles by the hearing of the ear; all able-bodied sons of the South who rightfully belong to our generals, should be removed from the rear to the post of honor in the front and compelled to share the miseries and perils of a soldier's life with the noble men to whom we look for victory, deliverance, and success. Those gallant spirits whose fortitude and valor are beyond praise should not be suffered to contend against large odds while there are so many legally liable to the duties they are discharging, enjoying their ease and amassing wealth. The noble ends we aim at accomplishing, the sacrifices cheerfully made by the men in service, the long list of the martyred dead, the increased boldness and confidence of the enemy, the mighty efforts he is now putting forth for our subjugation or extermination, urge and admonish those in power to augment our fighting force and to use all the material at their command, to ensure successful resistance and glorious victories.

NORTH

BOSTON EVENING TRANSCRIPT
September 17, 1864

"PERSUADED"

An opposition paper, whenever any thoroughly patriotic order is issued, or decidedly loyal opinion is expressed, by Lieutenant General Grant, has a quiet way of affirming that this officer has been "persuaded" by the president or the War Department to say so-and-so. It has recently included General Sherman in its intimations that the leaders of our armies are in slavish subservience to the authorities in Washington. That dodge will not work. The people cannot be "persuaded" that such men as Grant and Sherman are "persuaded" by anybody to utter anything but their honest views, however unpalatable they may be to Copperheads.

FROM THE IX ARMY CORPS

The following family letter from a staff officer in the Army of the Potomac furnishes new proof of the hopeful and patriotic spirit which pervades the troops in the field. Under date of "Near Petersburg, September 11," the writer says:

> Not many days will elapse before the telegraphic wires will carry news to the people that "something has happened." Everybody is confident here—there is no discontent, no demoralization. It is most gratifying to see the cheerful unanimity that pervades our troops. They are all inspired by one grand purpose, that, despite the lack of interest at home, or, rather, the lack of sympathy on the part of too many who should be our warm supporters there, they will, under the leadership of our noble Grant, and a merciful Providence permitting, bring this war to its proper and desired issue—to wit, an *honorable and permanent peace*. Hence it is that they so cheerfully respond to every call and readily undertake every duty, however arduous. Hence it is that our Burnside assured the people of New Hampshire that he had "heard more grumbling during his three days with them than dur-

ing the whole summer campaign in the army." I assure you, the heart of the army is all right. I wish I could say as much of the whole people.

Democratic politicians are counting upon a large McClellan vote in the army, but when the time comes to act in the matter, they will find where the army stands. The soldiers are not blind; they know who are their friends and who are not. McClellan was once their favorite. They remember that the same party which has used most strenuous measures to take away their right to citizenship—their privilege to vote—now tries to court their favor by inserting an ambiguous clause as the last plank in a rotten platform. They know, too, that the party which would elect McClellan is *pledged to render futile all their past efforts to restore the Union.* As they remember their labors for the past three years—as they think of the treasure that has been spent, and bring to view their comrades whose lives have been sacrificed in the struggle—they are disposed to say to these disloyal apologists for treason: "Stand out of our way—Grant, lead us on—*Our labors shall not be unavailing.*" Be assured, the army knows which way the wind blows—they will vote while they fight—and they will vote for Lincoln while they fight for the Union.

Is there not great reason to be hopeful? Never since the war began have I felt so really confident as now that the end is approaching. The recent glorious victories at the South and West—the failure of the raids to cut Sherman's communications—the fizzle of Early in his attempt to scare Grant—the persistent bulldog grip which he has here, and which he tightens every day—these and other things are cheering signs that our work is hastening to its close. All we want here is men, and I am happy that they are coming in goodly numbers. "Now, by Saint Paul, the work goes bravely on," and we are content to await the issue in firm trust—"as we go marching on."

Frank

NEW YORK TRIBUNE
September 17, 1864

THE CANVASS

The McClellanites are working desperately, but the tide is against them. They make much noise, especially with their powder, but they make no headway. There were more men willing to vote their ticket the day after it was nominated than there are now—and more now than there will be on the day of election. Their equivocation respecting their platform hurts them badly. The people demand of a party that it shall at least have faith in its own principles and not be ashamed to own them. When the convention puts forth one creed, its candidate another plainly irreconcilable with the former, and not even an effort is made to efface or explain their discrepancy, be sure the fates are against them. Discussion must render their position more and more awkward, less and less tenable. Their motley garb cannot abide the rough handling of an earnest, stirring, vigorous campaign.

If the vote of the loyal states were polled tomorrow, it would present aggregates of just about two million for Lincoln and Johnson against fifteen hundred thousand for McClellan and Pendleton. But we must and shall do better in November. An important Union victory in Virginia would double the Lincoln majority in several states and increase it everywhere. On the other hand, a staggering Union defeat would diminish the Lincoln vote and majority, but it would take two or three stunning blows in quick succession to remand us to the gloom and paralysis of August. We even doubt if the rout and dispersion of Grant's army could do it.

Of the contested states, our hardest work is to be done in Indiana and Illinois, because the soldiers absent from their homes in those states cannot vote. After all has been done that can be in the way of furloughs, we must bear up against a net loss of at least ten thousand in the popular vote of each of these states for want of a Soldiers' Voting Act. We can stand this since Atlanta, but only last month these two states would have gone for McClellan.

We had supposed New Jersey morally sure to go against us, but her Unionists say no—they can and will carry it. Their works honor their faith. From end to end the masses come forth to hear Unionist speakers and respond to their appeals. We reckon that 100 Lincoln meetings were held in this state last week and that the number is rapidly rising to 500 per week. It may be 1,000 before November. In spite of a heavy loss by the absence of soldiers, New Jersey will poll more votes for Lincoln this year than she did in 1860.

By the way, is there not some McClellanite so hardy as to attempt to answer this question: If the soldiers are mainly on your side (as you say), *why has no single legislature of your party ever passed an act enabling them to vote?* It surely is not that party's custom to disfranchise men who were ready and eager to vote for it.

Let there be no blind trust that all will come out right. We shall triumph because we shall deserve to triumph. We shall sow the land broadcast with Union newspapers and documents and shall reap therefrom a harvest of loyal votes. And when the result shall have shown that the Unionists stand firm as a rock, meaning to have a peace that will endure, that peace will be close at hand.

RIDING TWO HORSES

The *Daily News,* two days ago, declared, upon the authority of a delegate from Indiana to the Chicago Convention, that the peace platform, adopted by that convention, was presented two months ago to General McClellan "and was by him approved both in its letter and in its spirit." Nobody pretends now, however, that his letter does not repudiate that platform. The *World* thanks God for it, and such of the Peace Democrats as assume to have any principles are preparing to repudiate him and to nominate another candidate.

It matters little whether General McClellan was persuaded by his friends thus to break faith with the peace men, or whether the news of the capture of Atlanta convinced him that he had no chance before the people as a peace candidate. The fact remains that he held that "circumstances altered cases," and that he violated his pledge to one party, so that he might please the other. Whether the fall of Atlanta had any influence upon his mind, it certainly had upon the minds of such Democrats as believed that the defeat of the party was a foregone conclusion if they went to the country with a proposition to lay down our arms at the very moment when it was clear that a vigorous prosecution of the war for a little while longer was sure to secure the suppression of the rebellion. Such men naturally accept General McClellan's letter as a timely deliverance from a political blunder of their own making. They were in a dilemma from which they could not be extricated without some loss. To adhere to the platform was evidently to lose everything, though they might still poll a respectable minority of votes. To abandon it, however much they might trust to the cohesion of party—not trusted to in vain in the case of such men as Fernando Wood, who announces that he shall support McClellan—is to lose the votes of the honest peace men. The question was to be solved only by the doctrine of chances, and the chances seemed to be that McClellan on a war letter stood better than McClellan with a white feather in his soldier's cap.

We assume that there are among the Democrats many men who do not believe in an ignominious peace with Rebels, who have filled the land with mourning and have laid our best and bravest in bloody graves.

But General McClellan, if, as the *News* asserts, he ever agreed to accept the Chicago platform, is not one of these. His position is one of expediency, simply, not of principle or patriotism; his appeal is for votes, not for the honor of the nation. He has cheated one party; he may cheat the other. Expediency has made him a war man; expediency may make him a peace man. In the calculation of chances some possible elements of the situation seem to have been left out in the ciphering of these wily politicians. We are a people given, unfortunately, to despondency. The hope of carrying the election for the Chicago nominees was based, a month ago, upon the despairing temper of the people. Who knows how it will be a month hence? War has diverse aspects; the enthusiasm for victories won today may be checked tomorrow by temporary reverses; the hope of a speedy end cherished by today's success may sink into disappointment next month at the slow progress of events. Before November, General McClellan's haste to deliver his friends from one dilemma may turn out only to have plunged them into another. They may wish that his letter had never been written, and the honest Democrats who believe in him now may find themselves cheated, in their turn, by assurances held out to the fainthearted, the weary, and the desponding that he means, after all, to stand on the Chicago platform and that, once in power, his first duty will be to listen to and grant any terms of peace that the Rebels may choose to demand. This riding two horses is ticklish business; and those who get up behind the general on his war steed may find themselves kicked off in his awkward attempts to shift to the other animal. As he mounted the Democratic gelding when that seemed likely to be the winner, and only *because* it seemed so, he may try to mount the mare when she, in her turn, promises better speed. A man, governed by no higher motive than to commend himself to the wavering temper of a party hungry for power, should never be trusted by the honorable and thoughtful men of that party, who, however dear they may hold their allegiance to it, are bound by ties a thousand times stronger to their country. Nor is all this mere speculation. We *know* there are Democrats in this city, high aforetime in the party's confidence, and who have never been tainted by that peace delusion, which only means disunion; who are not taken in, and do not mean to be, by the McClellan war letter. They will support for president the man who, unmoved by the despondency that creeps periodically over a portion of the popular mind, but strong in the determination and zeal that animates the great majority of the people, they know will bring the war to an honorable conclusion and secure for us a permanent peace.

OCTOBER 15, 1864

SOUTH

RICHMOND DAILY DISPATCH
October 15, 1864

SHERMAN'S REPORT OF THE ATLANTA CAMPAIGN

The *Times* contains the following telegraphic dispatch from Washington:

> General Sherman's official report of the Atlanta campaign is published in the official *Army and Navy Gazette* of this week. It is dated September 15 and fills twenty columns of that paper. He estimates the enemy's strength to have been between 45,000 and 50,000 infantry and artillery and 10,000 cavalry. General Sherman says that he maintained about the same strength during the campaign, the number of men joining from furlough and hospitals about compensating for loss in battle and from sickness.
>
> The report is composed in General Sherman's terse and trenchant style and forms a most interesting history of perhaps the most brilliant and complete campaign of the war. He terminates his recital with the following deserved tribute to his subordinate commands:
>
>> My three armies in the field were commanded by able officers, my equals in rank and experience—Major Generals George H. Thomas, J. M. Schofield, O. O. Howard. With such commanders I had only to indicate the object desired, and they accomplished it. I cannot overestimate their services to the country and must express my deep and heartfelt thanks that, coming together from different fields, with different interests, they have cooperated with a harmony that has been productive of the greatest amount of success and good feeling. A more harmonious army does not exist.

THE SHELLING OF CHARLESTON—A NIGHT OF HORROR

A correspondent of the *Macon Confederacy,* writing from Charleston on the 30th, gives an account of the cruel shelling of that place, in the corporate limits of which there are not probably a dozen Confederate soldiers.

Wednesday night will long be remembered by the residents of this city as a night of horror. The shelling of the place had been almost continuous and rapid on Monday and Tuesday, but the bombardment of the last forty-eight hours has exceeded it all. On Tuesday evening I counted four shots within eight minutes and thought it remarkably rapid firing, but the cannonading Wednesday night beat even that. It commenced a little after six o'clock and lasted until ten—the shells averaging forty and forty-five to the hour. The firing is said to have been from four guns, but I think more must have been used, as anyone at all acquainted with heavy artillery practice knows that it takes considerable time in the loading and firing of heavy ordnance.

That the enemy have mounted additional and heavier pieces is evidenced from the fact that the shells were thrown in a part of the city hitherto considered safe and beyond the reach of these devilish missiles. Where that neighborhood is I shall not be so indiscreet as to mention for the information of the enemy.

Much damage was done to buildings and considerable injury to persons—the family of one of our oldest and most respectable merchants, consisting of a lady and four children, were all wounded by the explosion of a percussion shell in the room in which they were seated at tea. The lady had her collarbone broken; the children were less seriously hurt. During the day, one man had an arm taken off, and another lost a leg from the shells. Up to this writing, I have heard of no loss of life from the bombardment of the last forty-eight hours.

Had it not been a matter of life and death, some of the scenes witnessed, by the flight of the darkies from the shelled district, would have been ludicrous and mirth-provoking.

Many old wenches passed the window at which I was seated, loaded down with every conceivable useful and useless article of household plunder, with their young ones screaming and tugging at their skirts. Others, with more maternal feelings, abandoned all their kitchen goods and bore off their sooty pickaninnies alone. I noticed one of the latter loaded down with no less than three—two in her arms and one riding on her back. One old African, in hobbling past, cordially but irreverently wished that the Yankee who invented those big guns "was in hellfire, and the d——d rascals dat was firing dem, too."

It is a singular idea, but no less true, that the Negroes hereabouts seem to think themselves a doomed race, so far at least as shells are concerned. But they bade defiance to fate on this occasion by leaving at the first fire. I have heard of but few whites leaving the neighborhood.

Had a fellow been ironclad or bombproof, top and bottom, the sight would have been a grand and imposing one, but when my attention was even at its height, the thought that the flight of these fiery monsters might be turned in my direction caused a cold chill to run through my veins.

The firing ceased at ten o'clock, and was not renewed until eight the next morning, and was kept up steadily but slowly all day, the shots not exceeding eight to the hour.

The Yankees war not only with women and children, but even with the dead. Several shells fell on Tuesday night in the graveyard of Trinity (Methodist Episcopal) Church, tearing up the graves and demolishing the tombstones of the sacred dead. They may have been chance shots. I think otherwise, and that they were but following the hyenalike instincts of their projectors.

The yellow fever, I am sorry to say, is on the increase. It is now among our German population, with whom it is generally very fatal, as all previous yellow fever seasons have abundantly proved. Prayer for its abatement was offered up in several of the churches last Sunday.

The *Charleston Courier* adds to the above this paragraph:

The enemy renewed their fire upon the city rather feebly Thursday morning. Some thirty-three shots were fired up to six o'clock Thursday evening. No further casualties were reported, but several very narrow escapes were made. In one house the family, but a moment previous to the entering of a shell, had retired to the dining room, when the sitting room was struck, making a complete wreck of the room and contents. A prayer book on a side table appeared to be the only article that escaped destruction. It was opened at the Forty-ninth Psalm, commencing with "Deliver me from mine enemies, O my God; defend me from them that rise up against me. Deliver me from the workers of iniquity and save me from bloody men."

[UNTITLED]

The desire of Secretary Floyd to engage the country in a great foreign war was a very natural desire on the part of a man who believed that a foreign war alone could prevent the dissolution of the Union. Yet we think it fortunate for the South, at least, that he did not succeed. It could only have postponed the separation, without rendering it impossible. The day was destined to arrive, and sooner or later it would have brought in its train all the evils and inconveniences that belong to it. Postponement, we are disposed to think, would only have added to our difficulties.

We should have been victorious in any war which we should have waged with any European power. The enormous armies which the two sections have brought into the field, and the unparalleled obstinacy with which they have fought, leave no doubt whatever of that fact. No European power could have stood before the combined strength of the whole country once known as the United States. The navy was, it is true, confined to a few ships, but in the course of a two years' war it would probably have reached the number of a thousand. It would have swept that of either France or England from the ocean. It is probable that in the beginning of the war, France or England might have landed an army upon our shores. But events have clearly shown that it could not have sustained itself here a week, let its size have been what it might. The navy having become irresistible, a million men, if necessary, could have been thrown on the shores of either France or Great Britain, and neither France nor Great Britain, let them vapor as they may, could have withstood the onset of such an army. Of course, Canada would have gone overboard at the very first rush, for Great Britain, so far from defending her, is anxious, even now, to give her away to the Yankee. That we are not drawing upon our imagination, we think, the gigantic proportions of the present war sufficiently indicate. What might not the whole country united have done?

The United States would have come out of such a war with a high reputation, a mighty army, and an invincible navy. As was the case in the Mexican War, the South would have done all the fighting, and the Yankees would have taken all the profit and claimed all the glory. They would have taken all the navy and as much of the army as they could have induced to join them. Their resources would have been multiplied beyond measure, and their arrogance would have grown far beyond even their actual acquisition of wealth and power. They would not have failed to assert, more offensively than ever, their mission to settle the affairs of the whole earth and, more especially, those of the Southern states. The Black Republican party would still have been predominant—would still have insisted upon their mission—would still have persevered in their determination to ignore the rights of the states and to make them all bend to their will. Separation and war would still have been inevitable. We should still have been compelled to meet the Yankee hosts in the fields, and that, too, under far greater disadvantages than we actually encountered when the war began. Suppose they had had in the beginning such an army and such a fleet as they now have. There is hardly a possibility that we could have resisted them, utterly unprepared as we then were for war. Such an army and such a fleet they would have had, had there been a war with Great Britain in 1858, as there was very near being. We regard it as providential that it did not take place.

CHARLESTON DAILY COURIER
October 15, 1864

OUR OBLIGATIONS

The nature of the cause we are engaged in is one of the grounds on which we bottom the hope of final success. We are not disturbed at the thought of the greater number, power, and advantages of the enemy, because we believe that the work we are doing is approved of Heaven. If we institute a comparison between ourselves and our enemy in regard to morals, we are painfully conscious of the fact that we are very little, if at all, better than they. At any rate, we are forced to admit that our transgressions are so numerous and atrocious that they would justify the Most High in afflicting us far more grievously than we have been chastised. There is none self-righteous to such a degree as to dare claim the potent help of Heaven on the score of national or individual purity, fidelity, and consistency. But we have hope that God has taken part with us, because the cause for whose success we are fighting and suffering is just and righteous.

It is that precious fact that sustains our spirits under heaviest disasters, emboldens us in the face of imminent perils, braces our resolution, nerves our arms, and inspires our bosoms with invincible courage and dauntless valor. It is that assurance which causes our noble soldiers to fight with such furious earnestness; which makes them so patient under manifold privations and miseries; which imparts so fervent and importunate a spirit to the supplications of those who have power to prevail with God in prayer.

While the holy nature of our cause assures the hope of eventual triumph, we should consider that its high character imposes imperative and weighty obligations, which if we fail to meet with sincerity, heartiness, and faithfulness, we expose ourselves to the wrathful displeasure of the Most High.

The motives, purposes, and objects of the enemy we are contending with are altogether wicked, and his conduct toward us is in perfect keeping with the vile ends he aims at accomplishing. There is harmony between his designs and the means he makes use of to secure their completion. The destruction of mills, barns, corncribs, livestock, agricultural implements, the murder of women and children, pillage, robbery, and devastation—all those shocking crimes which he avails himself of are fit instruments for the execution of his base and bloody purposes. The means become the cause. No matter how infamous and cruel in his dealings with us—no matter how black and huge his iniquities—they are no whit more wicked than his motives and objects.

As sins of the vilest sort are in keeping with the ends our enemy is endeavoring to secure, so iniquity of every class and color, of every hue and form, is utterly out of harmony with the objects we desire to compass. Our conduct and character should be in keeping with the noble, grand, and glorious ends we purpose accomplishing. As our cause is holy, so we should be holy. As our cause is righteous, so likewise should we be righteous. As our cause has received the approval of God, so we should by repentance and faith obtain the pardon of our transgressions and the gracious favor of the Most High.

It is in that way we should honor the name of the Most High. Of what worth is the gratitude we pretend to feel if we regard our victories as pleasing proofs of the skill of our generals and the prowess of our soldiers, thereby taking all the praise to ourselves and increasing the pride and vanity of our hearts? Or, if we really refer our successes to the interposition of God in our behalf, is the thanks grateful to Him if it is poured from corrupt minds? That honor which comes from the lips only is an offense and abomination. If we would honor and glorify God, we must do it with holy lives. We must have our sins washed away, our hearts justified and renewed, and we must live in all good conscience before God and man.

The purification of our moral nature would produce a beautiful harmony between ourselves and the cause we are engaged in. It would exalt, embolden, and inspire our hearts and arm us with a power that would make unavailing all the mighty resources upon which the foe grounds his expectation of success. God would then indeed be our God.

His all-powerful help would be freely vouchsafed us; and, prepared and qualified for the enjoyment of the inestimable blessings for which we are battling, we would be speedily placed in possession of them.

LINCOLN'S CHANCE

The power of the government—the power, not the influence—is now actively employed, without any check or fear of punishment, to secure its existence. In the army, military regulations secure the vote of Lincoln. Officers have already been cashiered, by orders over the signature of the secretary of war, for distributing McClellan's tickets to their soldiers. Throughout the land the vast militia called the Loyal League is armed and drilled to preserve peace at all the polls—in other words, to arrest or kill those who come forward to vote against a truly despotic government. The ordinary public meetings in favor of McClellan are almost everywhere broken up by volleys of stones from soldiers posted for the purpose. If this machinery is not found efficacious, there remains much more of it, always employed in countries where republicanism is transforming itself into despotism. In a word, says the *Examiner,* Lincoln has the upper hand in the matter because he has the *armed hand*. Perhaps the Ruler of events, intending to create and save the Southern Confederacy, so wills. If McClellan were elected, there are doubtless many, very many, persons in the South who would believe the restoration of the Union to be possible. But while Lincoln is president, there is no one man who will, or who can, submit. Lincoln and his gallows, Lincoln and the confiscation of property, the depopulation of cities, the desolation of vast countries, the death of millions, the long train of exiles—these are things that place the safety of the Confederacy beyond the reach of hazard. They leave no choice to anyone. Any man will fight rather than be kicked out of his own house, or be hanged, or starved in the wastes and wilds of Central America. And these are Lincoln's alternatives.

DESERTING HIS COLORS

Benjamin Smith, a deserter from the 18th South Carolina Regiment, was committed to the Castle on Sunday, in Richmond, having been taken in a Yankee regiment, with arms in his hands, fighting against the Confederate flag.

NORTH

BOSTON EVENING TRANSCRIPT
October 15, 1864

WORK

It may be considered settled that of the two candidates for the presidency, Abraham Lincoln is to be elected by a very large majority of the electoral vote. In ordinary times this would be enough. But more than this is wanted now. In one sense, the men in this political contest are of little account. Their respective merits or demerits have entered into the canvass, merely as one side or the other has endeavored to win votes by showing its fitness or unfitness to stand as the head of the administration of a great republic. The real issue is an issue of principles, and in view of this fact, an overwhelming expression of public sentiment on the right side is to be labored for with unremitted diligence and unwearied earnestness.

Grant that the Chicago party means to insist upon a Union of some sort as a condition of peace; grant that it means to stand upon its own solemnly resolved platform, or upon whatever of definite purpose can be inferred from the adroit and ambiguous letter of McClellan; grant this, and it is still easy to see what policy must come of giving the whole power in the management of public affairs, or even of any considerable influence as a strong minority, to the political plotters who have disguised their antirepublican designs by assuming to represent the democracy. That policy, to make the best of it, means to try negotiations first with the leaders of the rebellion, not with the people of the South, and in these negotiations the Chicago party would stand ready to concede to those leaders their old relations to the Federal government.

This is what they intend by making "Union" the only condition of peace. They do not start with the fact that Jefferson Davis and his fellow conspirators are traitors and guilty of armed treason—the authors, by the admission of Alexander H. Stephens, of a civil war with all its horrors, for which they had, at the time of its assaults upon the national flag, no justification.[18] They do not start with this fact. They have an entirely different theory as to the past doings and the present attitude of the Richmond leaders. At most, they are misguided political adversaries, who are to be conciliated, and won back to the allegiance they have spurned, by compromise. This is the policy: Armistice, conference,

18. Alexander H. Stephens served as Davis's vice president (1861–65) and, after the war, as congressman and governor of Georgia.

concession, and such a Union as the secessionists may be pleased to agree to. If this encouragement fails, then, say a portion of the Chicago party, we will fight on for a Union. But amid the contradictions in that party, the fighting, even in the last resort, will be a very mild kind of skirmishing.

On the other side, the ground taken is that the nation is engaged in overcoming rebellion, in compelling treason to submit unconditionally, and in restoring the authority of the Federal government all over the land, so that it shall not be again periled by sectional treason and an ambitious aristocracy that holds free institutions and popular rights in supreme contempt.

Here is the issue of principles and of policy presented to the voters of the North on the 8th of November. The result of the election is not to be merely the expression of a choice as between the two nominees, but a pronunciamento by the people as to the view they take of the war and the sort of nation they mean to be. This being the case, how clear is the duty of working in season and out of season to secure an overwhelming expression of the popular will in favor of Union and free institutions—a democratic nationality.

THE ARMY VOTE

The Democrats, before the late elections, had a great deal to say about McClellan's popularity with the army. To be sure, they were shrewd enough to go generally against allowing soldiers to vote, but they were anxious to show that their opposition to the measure was not prompted by any fear that the soldiers would vote against their candidate.

Well, the soldiers have voted, and voted overwhelmingly against all covert and all open Copperheadism—against the Chicago platform and its nomination—against the principles and against the persons of the Democratic party. In the camp, Pennsylvania and Ohio vote one way, and the result might have been expected. Soldiers are always skittish about their communications; they dislike, in advancing upon an enemy that openly smites, to leave behind them an enemy which secretly stabs; and the meaning of the army vote is simply this, that the Federal troops have a deep-rooted distrust of a nomination which is received with cheers in the Confederate camps.

NEW YORK TRIBUNE
October 15, 1864

NEWS OF THE DAY: THE WAR

Richmond papers of Sunday show that the battle on Friday week created the most intense excitement and uneasiness in the Rebel capital. All business was suspended, and every person capable of bearing arms, working on fortifications, or otherwise aiding in repelling Grant's raiders was hurried to the front. The *Enquirer* contains advertisements from schools, stating that they have been suspended on account of the teachers' being compelled to lay down the pen for the sword. Trains of railroad companies were suspended. Theaters and other places of amusement were all closed. Express companies could make no deliveries, the clerks being out with the local forces. All persons employed in printing offices, between the ages of sixteen and fifty-five, were ordered to enroll themselves, and an officer, appointed to see that this order was complied with. All the Union prisoners confined in the city were rapidly hurried farther south. The *Examiner* says, "The papers, by a mistaken piece of policy, claim that the Confederates won a victory on Friday." Referring to the need of more troops, the *Enquirer* says, "Let the call be enforced, not merely in Richmond, but on every farm, in every house, and in every cabin of Virginia, and of all other states, for the loss of Richmond is the immediate loss of Virginia."

Among the passengers from City Point, Virginia, by the mail boat on Tuesday afternoon, was Mr. John Libby, the owner and former occupant of the large storehouse in Richmond which, since the war, has been notorious as a prison for Union soldiers. Mr. Libby, with several other gentlemen, had long been suspected by the Rebel authorities as disloyal to the cause of the Confederacy, but had managed to escape the wholesale conscription until the last order—the revocation of all details—was issued, in the face of which he received one evening an order to prepare for military service the next day. With the assistance of several Union citizens in Richmond, he formed a plan to escape, which he carried into effect the next day, having managed to secure a pass to leave the city on a pretense of visiting some friends in the country.

On the morning of the 5th instant, a party of seventeen men from the Rebel ram *Albemarle* came down in a launch, with the intention of capturing a dispatch boat plying between the Union fleet in Albemarle Sound and Roanoke Island, and also intending to blow up a powder schooner lying close by, but our forces, hearing of the plan, frustrated them; they, however, succeeded in destroying the Croatan Lighthouse, situated eight miles north of Roanoke Island, in Croatan Sound, and taking the lightkeeper and his wife prisoners.

A gang of Mosby's guerrillas, in strong force, on Thursday, made an attack on the outer picket of the 2nd District of Columbia Regiment, stationed at White Plains, on the Manassas Railroad. The guard of eight men was captured, and the officer in command was shot in several places and abandoned to his fate.

A party of guerrillas captured the westward-bound train on the Baltimore and Ohio Railroad on Thursday night, robbed the passengers, and burned the cars.

Two privates of the 6th Pennsylvania Heavy Artillery were killed by guerrillas on Thursday, between Accotink and Burkes Station.

GENERAL SHERMAN'S POSITION

The report which was circulated yesterday on Rebel authority—that Rome had been captured by Hood—seems to have caused a little commotion among the gold gamblers in Wall Street, but is most unlikely to be true. That town is fortified and strongly garrisoned and, not being on Sherman's direct line of communications, would not have been attacked for the purpose of interrupting them, nor would its loss be important. The story rested upon a reported advance of the main body of Hood's army northward and, if it had any foundation, would in fact be taken to indicate that such a movement was in progress. But we do not deem that probable.

The Rebel Department, which includes Georgia and Alabama, has been put under Beauregard. Just when Hood was superseded we do not know, but it is not likely that the new commander has found time to undertake a new campaign on a large scale. If not, then all the Rebel operations in northern Georgia and Alabama relate to the efforts of Wheeler and Forrest to break up the Chattanooga and Nashville Railroad and the cooperating attempts on the Chattanooga and Atlanta Road. Both these efforts have been made and repulsed. Forrest has been driven back across the Tennessee, and the very serious attempt on Allatoona, on the 6th instant, by a large force under French, resulted in the total defeat of the Rebels. Both those expeditions were undertaken at the moment most favorable for their success, while General Sherman was concentrated at Atlanta, and before he had detached any considerable force for the protection of these railway lines. When Forrest crossed the Tennessee, few troops could be got together at first to oppose his advance, yet it was less than a fortnight before he was sent "whirling" back again. So of the attack on Allatoona. It was arranged for just in time.

General Sherman subsequently telegraphed, "I had anticipated this attack and had ordered from Rome General Corse with reinforcements." He himself reached Kennesaw Mountain so as to witness the repulses—the enemy losing two hundred dead and a thousand wounded and prisoners. So thorough was the defeat that this Rebel force has not since been heard from in any quarter. And, in fact, Forrest was driven beyond the Tennessee River on the same day, October 6, that this Allatoona defeat occurred, so that the two main columns of the Rebel advance came simultaneously to grief. Forrest has been reported again this side of the Tennessee, and we now have the story about Rome. But against all rumors of mischief is to be set the sure fact that Sherman has had abundant time to meet all such marauders; to get his posts in order; to dispose his forces; and though it is impossible to guard every single rail on a line of three hundred miles, yet to defend effectually the points of importance that were exposed. He himself assured us in a dispatch of the 9th that "Hood, observing our approach, has moved rapidly back to Dallas and Van Wert, and *I am watching him in case he tries to reach Kingston or Rome*. Atlanta is perfectly secure to us, and this army is better off than in camp."

We do not suppose Hood can, at that time nor since, have moved his main army so far north as Dallas, which is forty miles northwest of Atlanta and ten or twelve west of the railroad. It seems pretty certain that the Rebel leader, though retreating first on Jonesboro, drew gradually off toward the West Point Road and scattered his divisions on that line in order to feed them. His wagons are said to have been in good part lost at Atlanta, and he would therefore lack the means for a movement to the north. It was further reported that the iron of the West Point Road was being removed for the construction of a new road from Griffin, on the Macon line, to West Point, which might facilitate a move through Alabama, but not to northwestern Georgia. And it is an evidence of how little General Sherman feared an attack on Rome that he summoned from that place the division which marched to the relief of Allatoona.

It is only necessary to remark further that some sort of continuous operations in Sherman's rear are to be expected as matters of course. Hood or Beauregard, whichever commands in the field, cannot afford to lie still and see their armies melt away by desertion while Sherman is preparing for a new campaign. They must try something. They have tried and lost what was their best chance of mischief, but it need not be supposed they will give up. An attack upon Sherman's front is the one thing they are not crazy enough to attempt, but every other means of harassing him, however desperate, may be looked for. Sherman looks for it and has laid his plans accordingly. At Allatoona and Atlanta it was his first business to collect magazines of provisions, and he is supposed to be supplied for a month without another carload from the North.

He has all central Georgia to forage in. He has a numerous and victorious army, and he has a better head for war than Hood and Beauregard, and Bragg and Davis, all together. These childish apprehensions of disaster, which have no better excuse than a Rebel lie, and which are fomented by gamblers and traitors in Wall Street, deserve nothing but rebuke and contempt.

NOVEMBER 19, 1864

SOUTH

RICHMOND DAILY DISPATCH
November 19, 1864

SUICIDE OF A NEGRO

A Negro man, named Royall, slave of Benjamin Garrett, of Halifax County, Virginia, who had escaped from the batteries a few days since but was subsequently arrested and committed to the Engineer Hospital building, on the corner of Nineteenth and Cary streets, jumped into the dock, near the Libby Prison, on Thursday night, about half past ten o'clock, and was drowned. He had attempted his escape from the hospital in company with another Negro, when the guard on duty fired at but missed him. Royall continued his flight, but was pursued so closely that he ran for the dock, pitched in, and was drowned. His body was soon afterward recovered and Dr. Little, the coroner, called to view it, but on learning the circumstances of his death, he declined to hold an inquest.

YANKEE DESERTERS

A large number of Federal deserters, desiring to avail themselves of the advantages afforded under the provisions of "Order No. 65," came into our lines yesterday and were consigned to Castle Thunder to await their turn to be forwarded home.[19]

19. Issued on August 15, 1864, the order was intended to encourage desertion among Union soldiers. It promised that Union deserters "coming within the lines of the Confederate armies shall be received, protected, and supplied with means of subsistence, until such of them as desired it can be forwarded to the most convenient points on the border, where all facilities will be afforded them to return to their homes."

One-hundred-odd deserters were sent off yesterday under Confederate escort, in conformity with said order.

[UNTITLED]

The market was better supplied yesterday, and a favorable reduction was observable in the prices asked by some vendors. Good beef sold at from $3.50 to $4 per pound—a reduction of one dollar since Thursday. It is to be hoped that the citizens who are in the habit of attending market will refuse to submit to sudden and unreasonable advances in prices whenever they take place.

[UNTITLED]

We should be inclined to believe that Sherman's movement from Atlanta to the south was designed to draw Beauregard from Tennessee, where his presence must be a serious inconvenience, at least to the Yankees, were it not that such a theory does not correspond with the tearing up of the track from Chattanooga to Atlanta. The better opinion seems to be that he designs to obtain possession of a base upon the Atlantic or the Gulf, from whence, with renewed resources and increased strength, he may prosecute a winter and early spring campaign. In the former view, he will make for Augusta and Savannah; in the latter, we may hear of his moving in the direction of Selma and Mobile. In either case, his journey is a long one, and we do not see that his success will decide any great question. By withdrawing from Atlanta and tearing up the railroad, he gives us all the country between the two places. By going either to Mobile or Savannah, he likewise abandons all the intermediate country; for it cannot be expected that his force is large enough to spare garrisons, all along the route, sufficiently large to keep the country, and such garrisons must inevitably be captured, wherever they may be left.

This movement, it is very possible, may be regarded as formidable only because it is novel. In such a light we are disposed to regard it, for we cannot see any great object it would accomplish without losing something equally valuable in the attempt to secure it. The similar movement made by Sherman last spring ended in nothing except the injury inflicted on the population as he passed along. If the people of the country are only true to themselves, it may be the means of securing us a great triumph. In this connection, we are glad to see that gallant soldier and true patriot, General Howell Cobb, is in the field and at the head, we should judge, of quite a considerable force. Gustavus Smith, too, is in the service of the state of Georgia, and we hope the means will be afforded him to show himself that great officer which he has everywhere heretofore had the credit of being. With such men at the head of such a force as we are informed Georgia can still furnish, it will be a very difficult job to march to Savannah, we should think. It cannot, at least, be done with shouldered arms the whole march.

We know not whether this march of Sherman's was designedly so timed. But we think nothing is more certain than that Grant designs to make a grand attack, all along our lines, at a very early day, both naval and military. That he will be repulsed on both elements whenever he may try it we confidently believe, for we place the most implicit confidence in our brave troops and their officers and the great general by whom they are commanded.

CLEARING OUT A NEST OF DESERTERS

The deserters who form themselves into bands in Mississippi to rob the country do not seem to have a very quiet time of it. A letter in the *Mobile Advertiser,* from Gainesville, Mississippi, gives an account of Seals's band in Jones and Perry counties. It says:

> Seals soon came across two soldiers, Daniel McCall and John Knight, who had been captured at Port Hudson and paroled, and lately exchanged, and told them that they should join him or leave the country. They left, but soon returned and captured four of his men, two of whom they hanged, and shot another. This encouraged the citizens, who soon organized and went in pursuit of the outlaws. In their first day's scouting they captured five—two Smiths, one Leonard, and one Holleman—with stolen horses, cattle, bedclothes, and bedding in their possession. They were tried and sentenced to be shot. These men made confessions, implicating some forty-two others. The next day they captured two and killed two. One of these, named Stewart, was a native of Hancock County, who has been buying stolen horses and cattle from the deserters and shipping them to New Orleans. Another, named Moody, of respectable connections, was taken with thirty head of beeves in his possession. I believe this was his first offense, but the sentence was inexorably executed. In all, there have been ten shot and three hanged; and four are still in the hands of the citizens, who are still after them; and I hope, before this reaches you, the list will be at least doubled.

CHARLESTON DAILY COURIER
November 19, 1864

THE CRISIS—OUR DUTY

We have need of self-denial, generosity, patience, courage, firmness, forbearance, wisdom. Our minds are harassed and perplexed by questions of great difficulty and delicacy; our spirits are grievously tried by evils under which we are groaning, or which are hanging black and heavy over the future. Those grave questions must be considered, and our course in relation to them determined upon, with calmness, fairness, earnestness, and candor; those evils must be endured with equanimity, and met with firmness, or turned aside with boldness, promptitude, and energy. This is no time for wrangling and bickering, for avarice and ambition, for sluggishness and cowardice. We must see to it that there is no disagreement between our personal interest and the public behoof. If the calling we are pursuing is harmful in the smallest degree to our cause, patriotism and the instinct of self-preservation make its abandonment a sacred and imperative duty. And we should not only refrain from doing damage to the righteous cause in whose success is involved the welfare and happiness not only of the present generation but of those who shall live after us for ages to come, but we should give it our cordial and energetic support.

In times such as these, our country's interest should be paramount. Indeed, if we occupy the right position and are under the influence of proper feelings, there can be no conflict between our individual good and the good of our country. They must be harmonious, identical. If they clash, we must sacrifice our personal interest to the public good, no matter how great the cost. All cannot do service with sword or musket. Disease, age, or physical disability of some sort gives exemption from the army to a large number, while many are more useful in the pursuit of their callings and trades than they would be as soldiers. But after deducting those honorably and rightly exempt, there still remains an exceedingly great number whose bounden duty it is to join our brave sons who have gone forth to do what they can toward vindicating and establishing our right to self-government. By remaining at home, they incur eternal infamy, inflict detriment upon our cause, and expose it to the hazard of failure. Never was there a time when we needed brave, strong, earnest, resolute men so greatly as we do at the present crisis. The enemy is moving forward with increased confidence and more furious earnestness. He is firmly resolved to conquer, subdue, and subjugate us;

and unless we put forth our utmost power, unless every man capable of bearing arms will take his place in the ranks, unless every man comes up to the help of our cause resolved to discharge the duties patriotism, manhood, the love he cherishes for wife, child, and mother, make incumbent, the foe will certainly visit direful woes upon us, if he does not despoil us of our substance and reduce us to a degrading and remorseless thralldom.

The call the present emergency makes upon us comes with all the force and emphasis given it by every fine and noble sentiment of our nature. Honor, national existence, the purity of our homes, the blood of those heroes who have fallen on so many gory battlefields, unite to swell the solemn call that urges us to do our duty in this terrible crisis. Away with all false, unworthy, insufficient excuses. Let us desist from the pursuit of gainful, ambitious, selfish ends. Our country demands and requires our strong arms, our stout hearts, our firm wills, our clear heads. Let us render her service, let us obey the call with hearty readiness, with eager haste, with unconquerable spirit. Let us show what sort of stuff Southern men are made of, and oblige the world to admit that we are worthy of the blessings we are contending for, worthy of the high dignity we aspire after.

There is ground for apprehension, but not for despondency. The evils that threaten are just near enough, and their occurrence to that degree probable, to animate the heart of the true Southerner with a more heroic valor, to stimulate to greater effort, to call into active exercise all the high qualities of manhood. Let us contemplate the perils with clear vision, obtain a thorough acquaintance with them in all their completeness and magnitude, and, perfectly aware of their nature, let us confront them and prepare to turn them aside with all the skill, strength, resolution, and valor God has given us. And if we meet the crisis in a spirit worthy of our glorious cause and the precious interests imperiled, worthy of the noble men who have sealed their devotion with their hearts' blood, and of those equally noble who are now confronting the presumptuous foe, humbly depending on Almighty God for success and victory, we shall come forth out of this dreadful contest gloriously triumphant.

NORTH

BOSTON EVENING TRANSCRIPT
November 19, 1864

[UNTITLED]

The gold speculators in New York and Boston are now mercilessly preying upon one another after having for a long time subsisted at the expense of the body politic. It is one of the pleasantest of phlebotomizing operations for a spectator to witness a gold buyer at 218, when ten minutes after the purchase the price is quoted at 210. But it is unsatisfactory to reflect that the seller is not obliged to produce any gold, but only pockets the difference—especially as speculators in other articles do not reduce their rates to correspond with even the reported decline of the precious metal—which, at its real value, should now stand between 170 and 180.

FROM NEW ORLEANS
FREE TRADE ESTABLISHED—FRENCH EVACUATION OF MATAMOROS

New York, 19th—By the steamer *Morning Star* from New Orleans, 12th, we learn that the French troops have evacuated Matamoros, leaving the inhabitants to take care of themselves.

At Brownsville, Texas, there is a small Rebel force, who apprehend an attack from the Union troops, now that their imperial friends have withdrawn from the neighborhood. There is nothing to prevent our forces' capturing Brownsville.

The recent Treasury order declaring New Orleans in an insurrectionary district and prohibiting trade to that market has been countermanded, and commerce is again permitted.

It is stated that General Canby's wound is of such a nature as to prevent him from taking the saddle for six months.

The reported capture of a large number of cattle by Colonel Farrar, which the Rebels were trying to get across the Mississippi from Texas to supply Hood's army, is confirmed.

PEACE RUMORS INCREASING—FRENCH OFFER OF MEDIATION—PRESIDENT LINCOLN'S PROPOSED ACTION

New York, 19th—The *World*'s Washington correspondent says the French minister had an interview with Secretary Seward, in which he reviewed the offer to place the services of his government at the disposal of the president to facilitate negotiations with the South. Secretary Seward told him he would consult the president and invited him to another interview in the matter.

To Independent Newsroom

New York, 15th—The *Herald*'s Washington dispatch says the proposed appointment of peace commissioners to the Rebels grows more in favor the more it is discussed. High officers here say there is no question that propositions alike honorable to both parties will soon be made by Mr. Lincoln, which will afford an opportunity for the Confederates to lay down their arms and resume their places in a stronger and more powerful Union than has ever existed.

THE DESTRUCTION AT ROME, GEORGIA—POSITION OF HOOD'S ARMY

New York, 19th—General Corse, the Union commander at Rome, Georgia, on the 10th destroyed such buildings there as would be of use to the Rebels, and abandoned the place for the purpose of withdrawing to some important point.

The latest Rebel accounts from Hood say he is in a position to march into middle or west Tennessee. They admit the report of the capture of Decatur by them to be a hoax, stating that the attack in that place was a ruse to get Hood's army trains well past it.

NEW YORK TRIBUNE
November 19, 1864

ACQUIESCENCE IN THE POPULAR VERDICT

Nearly sixty-four years have passed since Thomas Jefferson, in his first inaugural, pronounced "acquiescence in the decision of a majority, the vital principle of republics, from which there can be no appeal but to force, the vital principle and immediate parent of despotism." Mr. Jefferson may have seen (though *we* do not) how to reconcile this axiom with the spirit and purport of his Kentucky "resolutions of '98." But there can be no doubt that his "sober second thought" was right, whatever may be said of his first. And the heartiness, the unanimity, with which the people's verdict, pronounced in their late presidential election, has been accepted as conclusive throughout the loyal states and loyal portions of disloyal states afford fresh proof of the tenacious vitality of our republican institutions and the new force and emphasis which their cardinal principle has acquired from the sad but wholesome experiences of the last four years.

A few days ago we were involved in the fierce and angry strife of a presidential contest. The waves of party spirit rolled mountain-high; crimination begot recrimination. Anticipations of military despotism at the polls and threats of resistance unto blood in case the election were thus vitiated resounded throughout the land. A newly landed foreigner, glancing at our long processions, our mass meetings, and listening to the violent language which was therein received with thundering acclamations, might well have supposed that we were on the brink of a fresh and formidable convulsion. But the day of election passed—passed in general quiet, with scarcely a trace of violence or riot—and the early hours of the next morning saw the result flashed from Maine to Kansas without evoking one defiant or menacing utterance—without unmasking one traitor who had not been known as a traitor already. The supporters of the opposition ticket had made a most determined canvass —they had commenced it with resolution and prosecuted it with enthusiasm—they had polled a very large popular vote, though not enough to win—and they frankly and promptly accepted the result, as they would have expected us to accept it had we, instead of they, been outnumbered. They did not surrender their preference, but they readily admitted that it had been overborne, and recognized the successful candidates as the elect of the people, the chosen administrators of the government for the ensuing four years. Journals that had been most vehement in their opposition to Mr. Lincoln were among the foremost in recognizing and deferring to his reelection as a fact, and in all the loyal portion of our Union, there was not one single voice raised in favor of resistance or demur to the popular verdict. Thus, the republic stands stronger in the hearts of the masses and is based on surer foundations in this fourth year of a vast and terrible civil war than ever before. And even were it longer possible for the rebellion to succeed in dividing our country, it could not hereafter disorganize and gradually disintegrate that portion which it failed at the outset to tear away with it. The immense majorities in Indiana and Illinois are fit responses to the dark and traitorous conspiracies whereby those states have specially been distracted, while the unanimity and emphasis with which the Pacific states have spoken afford a fresh and strong attestation of the vitality and perpetuity of the American Union.

The disappointment and chagrin which this majestic exhibition of loyalty and concord have excited in the breasts of the Rebels are but clumsily disguised in the bitter comments and feigned gratulation of their journals. In the substantial unanimity and hearty accord of the loyal states they read the doom of secession. And what they tremblingly foresee they will ere long realize.

COTTON—GOLD—WAR

The *New York Times,* discussing and discouraging the suggestion that the government may and will so act as speedily and largely to reduce the premium on gold, says:

> Let it be understood that whenever the agents of the government here have a million of gold more than it requires for its own use, that million will be sold in open market and the government will have done all it can do directly toward controlling its price.
>
> There are other ways legitimate and proper for the government to use, by which its influence can be exerted to the same end. Whatever it can do to increase the amount of exchange tends to reduce the price of gold. Every bale of cotton which it brings forward from the South has the same effect. A law was passed at the last session of Congress for the express purpose of procuring cotton from the Rebel states, but nothing practical has yet been done toward carrying it into effect. It has been reported that regulations have been devised, and agents appointed, for that purpose, but they do not seem to have accomplished anything; and unless we are misinformed as to their character, they never will. It is well-known that there are very large quantities of cotton in the Rebel states, perfectly accessible to private traders, if they were allowed by our government to get it, but thus far no facilities have been afforded for doing so.
>
> If the government will take up this matter practically, it can throw into market half a million bales of cotton within six months, and that will do more to bring down the price of gold, and to keep it down, than all the edicts it can issue against speculation, or all the efforts it may make to control speculation by direct interference of any kind.

We trust the government will think twice—yes, three times—before adopting and acting on the above suggestions. For, assuming it to be true that there is a large amount of cotton within the Rebel lines that might be bought and brought away "if private traders were allowed by our government to get it," we see not how this operation could be effected without giving instant and important aid and comfort to the rebellion. Let us suppose, at a venture, that this cotton could be bought for a hundred dollars in greenbacks per bale of four hundred pounds. Here would be not less than $50 million paid over to Rebels for property now lying dead on their hands and rendering next to no support to their belligerent operations, because it is too bulky, too cumbrous to be sent away and converted without incurring great risk of capture and confiscation. With the $50 million the case would be bravely altered. Confederate agents, with carpetbags stuffed with hundred-dollar greenbacks, would permeate our whole country unwatched and unsuspected, finding everywhere persons ready enough to take their greenbacks and give their full value in niter, bacon, percussion caps, revolvers, blankets, gray cloths, or whatever else may be most needed by the Confederate armies. Or if any should fear to operate here, they have only to stop by the way at Nassau or Bermuda, where they can exchange their greenbacks for whatever may be most essential to the efficiency of the graybacks—the same to be delivered within the Confederate lines, if required. This $50 million of greenbacks in the hands of Rebel purchasing agents would be equal to a fresh conscription of one hundred thousand recruits to the Rebel armies.

There may be another side to this matter, but this is the view that it presents to our mind, and it impels us to entreat the government to deal very gingerly with this cotton business. We can readily see how "private traders" might make a good thing—a *very* good thing—of buying half a million bales of cotton in Dixie at twenty-five cents per pound and selling it in New York for a dollar. We can realize that the first effect of this transaction would be to depress the premium on gold by supplying a considerable amount of exchange on London. But if the rebellion should (as we fear) be thereby set on its legs again for six months or so, the ultimate effect of the operation would not be salutary. There is a Scotch proverb importing that he needs a long spoon who takes his soup with the Evil One, which we have no doubt Secretary Fessenden will thoughtfully consider before he lets loose the horseleech crowd of "private traders" who are so fierce for making their several piles by buying Rebel cotton.

THE ROMAN CATHOLIC CLERGY ON HUMAN LIBERTY

The *Tablet* dissents from some portion of our recent strictures on the attitude and teachings of the Roman Catholic clergy in our country touching the slaveholders' rebellion and its causes—dissents more especially to our remark that the influence of said clergy coincides with that of the grogshops in keeping our Irish-born population in an attitude of sympathy and virtual cooperation with the slave power now struggling desperately to destroy our Union. We do not understand the *Tablet* to deny the substantial truth of our assertion, but rather to dissent from our grouping as disrespectful and irreverent. But the truth is always to be spoken when anything is, and it seems to us that this substantial accord between the clergy of one of our most numerous bodies of Christians and the keepers, almost without exception, of the haunts of low dissipation and moral ruin properly challenges investigation and reflection. Why *should* the great body of the clergy of *any* Christian denomination be of one mind in politics with the keepers and frequenters of the haunts of vice and infamy? What is the "mystic tie that binds" these seemingly incongruous classes in political fellowship? Here is a grave fact—the priests of a great and venerable Church and the keepers of the dance houses of Water Street and the rum-holes of Corlears' Hook, Mackerelville, and the Five Points ardently supporting, with scarcely an individual exception, the same candidates in our recent election. What purpose, what impulse, what sympathy, have they in common? Who will give us the true reason of their accord?

Do you say that they are alike opposed to intermeddling with what is none of their (or our) business? Then let us shift the scene, and see how your explanation adapts itself to the resulting parallax:

The city of New Orleans, now nearly a century and a half old, was originally settled by Roman Catholics, who have always been its most numerous and wealthy denomination. It is the residence of an archbishop, with a numerous and influential clergy. That city was very early, if not at its foundation, cursed with slavery, for on its transfer by France to Spain in 1763, of its 3,190 inhabitants no less than 1,225 were slaves. In 1860, its population had increased to 168,823, whereof barely 13,380 were slaves. But New Orleans had now become the greatest slave mart on earth, Havana and Dahomey not excepted, and the focus of the harshest and most exacting system of slave working ever known in a Christian, while far crueler than was ever tolerated in a Muhammadan, country. In that city of New Orleans, under the shadow of a Roman Catholic cathedral, crimes against humanity and decency were constantly and publicly perpetrated by wholesale at barracoons and slave auctions, in the way of handling, stripping, and selling women and female children, who often commanded enormous prices, notoriously for the gratification of the most brutal lust. At these auctions, husbands were sold away from wives, mothers from their young children, not occasionally but by wholesale and almost daily, for scores of years. Many of the victims as well as many of the perpetrators were Roman Catholics; yet, notwithstanding that the Catholic Church propounds and maintains the most rigorous and salutary doctrines with regard to the sanctity and indissolubility of marriage, we have never heard of a protest by any archbishop of New Orleans against these slave auctions, which were the scandal of Christendom. That Catholic women and girls were sold by hundreds to libertines for the most infamous purposes has never, within our knowledge, evoked even a spirited remonstrance from the archiepiscopal champions, at New Orleans, of the Immaculate Conception.

Nay, more: Today Louisiana has rival governors and governments—one of them located in New Orleans and based on the right of all men and women to freedom; the other somewhere in the northwestern quarter of the state, and fighting to destroy the Union in the interest, and for the perpetuation, of Negro slavery. And today the archbishop of New Orleans and all (or nearly all) his clergy are the ardent, active, bitter, obstinate partisans and champions of the Rebel, disunion, proslavery government of Louisiana and the relentless foes of its free rival. In other words, they are doing their utmost to restore at New Orleans the crimes, infamies, and abominations of the system of divorce at the dictate of a master's caprice, lust, or avarice, and of rape, enforced concubinage, and bestiality, which has been banished from that city by the triumph of the Union arms.

Now, if there were anything in the ordinances, the inculcations, or the traditions of the Catholic Church Universal that required this, we could understand, though we could not approve or justify it. But the fact seems to be emphatically otherwise than this. The antipathy of races, so often cited to justify Irish persecution of "naygurs," is utterly unknown at Rome, where a Negro black as midnight is received in society, ordained to the priesthood, and consecrated a bishop, precisely as if he were a white man, and whence the most memorable papal bull issued in our time—that of Pope Gregory, 1839—condemns and denounces slavery as inhuman and unchristian. So Bishop Dupanloup and other eminent Catholics of our day are ardent contemners of slavery, while Augustin Cochin was recently knighted by the pope for his admirable, convincing treatise showing the beneficent results of West India emancipation. We cannot recall the name of a single eminent Catholic in Europe who is an upholder or advocate of slavery. Will anyone explain to us the proslavery attitude and course of the Catholic clergy in this country?

RICHMOND ON SHERMAN

The latest Richmond paper which has reached us, the *Enquirer,* of the 16th, occupies itself with speculations upon Sherman's movement. Sherman is the subject of its leading article, as he has been of the leading articles of most of the Rebel papers since his contemptuous neglect of Hood and his return to Atlanta were first reported. The *Enquirer* has "no doubt but that Grant planned a movement from Atlanta toward Mobile, for we learn that a fleet of transports laden with supplies had arrived in Pensacola." Yet we get small light from this piece of information, for in the next sentence we learn that "General Hood defeated the plan; and the movement so far from being southward from Atlanta, has been turned northward, and *Sherman is at Bridgeport;* and Atlanta, if not already evacuated, is an actual impediment to its captor." Considering the date of this declaration, we can infer one of two things: that the War Department has prevented all intelligence of Sherman from reaching the Richmond editors, or, which is the real fact, that they are persistently misleading their readers. For when the above-quoted sentence was written, Sherman had been gone seven days from Atlanta.

A subsequent section of this article shows still more strongly that the Richmond press is really in possession of news about Sherman, but dissembles for a purpose.

> The arrival of a supply fleet at Pensacola, of which the government received advices several days ago, must be regarded as conclusive that an advance from Atlanta was seriously entertained by the enemy at one time. Whether Sherman, after following Hood to the Tennessee River, is in a condition to return to Atlanta, surrender Tennessee to a Confederate army, and, at the opening of winter, undertake a march to the Gulf Coast may very well be doubted. But it is not so improbable that attention should not be given to it. *Whether there is or is not a force to meet him he will ascertain when he makes the attempt.* He might reach the Gulf, overpower all opposing force, and fix his new base upon the waters of the Gulf. *But what then? The march would be all; the damage repaired, he would have accomplished nothing to impair our means of defense and would find himself opposed in the spring by another army.* But what would become of Tennessee and Kentucky

> when Sherman is on the Gulf! Relieved of Federal bayonets, and certain of four years more of despotism, the people of those states would rally to the Confederate flag in such numbers that Beauregard could send a force to watch Sherman on the coast, and march his army to Cincinnati.

The sentences we italicize show clearly enough that the *Enquirer* is indulging, as its habit is, in a game of bluff. Why threaten us with an army to meet Sherman on an expedition which a moment before has been pronounced impracticable? Why talk of a force which we know does not exist, since in the Confederacy there are but two armies—the armies of Hood and of Lee—the first of which cannot be sent at all to oppose Sherman, and the second of which cannot be without abandoning Richmond? Similarly absurd is the threat that Beauregard can raise one force in Tennessee to pursue Sherman and another to march to the Ohio. It is the effort of the *Enquirer* at once to fortify the public mind of the South against the immediately expected news of Sherman's advance through Georgia and to hold out vague hopes of penalties he will have to pay for his daring. That Thomas has an army ample for the defense of Tennessee is a fact which in Richmond is not thought worthwhile to state.

On the whole, it strikes us that the talk about "detailing" editors for the Richmond journals might be omitted. Those journals do now, as during all the war they have done, register the rule and opinion of the military authorities on military subjects, and on other matters it is of small consequence what they say. Their protests against censorship are for stage effect, full of sound and fury, signifying nothing.

DECEMBER 17, 1864

SOUTH

RICHMOND DAILY DISPATCH
December 17, 1864

THE WAR NEWS

All was quiet yesterday on the lines below the city.

There has been a good deal of cannonading on the lines about Petersburg during the past few days. Wednesday and Thursday the enemy's batteries on the left shelled our works on the Chesterfield side of the Appomattox for an hour or so and threw a good many bombs from their mortars, but accomplished nothing.

It was reported here yesterday that a fight had taken place at Petersburg on the previous night, during which we had captured a thousand prisoners. The story was without foundation.

One hundred nine prisoners, including a captain and two lieutenants, belonging to Warren's column and captured by General Hampton near Bellfield, were brought to this city last evening.

THE RAID INTO SOUTHWESTERN VIRGINIA—THE SALTWORKS CONSIDERED SAFE

The raiding columns which on Wednesday burst into southwestern Virginia are still in motion, having met with no check. They are believed to consist of five thousand mounted men, under Stoneman. It will be recollected we stated yesterday that on Thursday morning, at nine o'clock, they had reached Glade Spring, taking the people there by surprise and capturing all of the railroad employees, with one exception, and that, at last accounts, a portion of them were advancing up the railroad in the direction of Marion. Information was received here yesterday that the main body had left the railroad at Glade Spring and started toward the saltworks, six miles distant, and that the smaller party, previously mentioned, had passed Marion and were advancing on Wytheville, which is fifty-five miles this side of Abingdon. The object of this party is doubtless to break up the railroad and thereby prevent reinforcements from being sent from the east to our troops at the saltworks. They will, of course, destroy as much property as possible along their route.

The main body, who moved on the saltworks, have by this time, we think, discovered that that position is safe from their attack, for we are glad to be able to state that it is held by a first-rate general and an abundance of troops to hold it against any force the Yankees can muster. Stoneman, if he be indeed, as we think, commander of the raiders, has also discovered that his sudden irruption into southwestern Virginia was not entirely unexpected by our military authorities, although he did catch the citizens and railroad people asleep. We hope he will find this out to his cost before he gets through with his raid. It has only been a few months since a previous raid of his, begun under quite as auspicious circumstances as this, was brought to a disgraceful conclusion by himself and most of his men being made prisoners. A similar fate may again be in store for him.

FROM SAVANNAH

We have no news from Sherman which was not published yesterday. He has captured Fort McAllister and invested Savannah on the south and west. No fighting has yet occurred.

THE LATEST FROM SHERMAN

The latest Yankee advices from Sherman are by the *Arago,* from Port Royal, South Carolina. They say:

> The latest advices from Sherman at the time the *Arago* left—on the 8th instant—were that his advance troops, comprising mostly cavalry and light artillery, had reached a point only forty miles from Savannah and were steadily feeling their way toward that city, with every prospect of capturing it with very little loss to his army. He had succeeded in severing the railway communication leading to and from Savannah and had cut off the most important routes of supplies for the troops that were hastily assembling in the defense of the city.

CHARLESTON DAILY COURIER
December 17, 1864

YANKEE NEWS

Richmond, 15th—Northern papers of the 13th instant have been received.

A Nashville telegram of the 12th only gives details of the fight near Murfreesboro between Bates's division and Milroy.

A Louisville telegram of the same date says General Lyon crossed the Cumberland River on Saturday, with twenty-five hundred men, moving toward Hopkinsville.

A Cairo telegram says Lyon captured a transport twenty miles above Fort Donelson and used her for crossing the river. The boat was loaded with forage and was burned after the Rebels crossed. This telegram says Lyon's force is estimated at four thousand.

Breckinridge is reported at Sparta, Tennessee, with ten thousand men.

The steamer *Donegal,* from Port Royal on the 7th, arrived at Philadelphia with the news of the destruction of the Pocotaligo Bridge by the

Yankee forces on the 6th. Foster's scouts had communicated with Sherman's forces, which were marching on Savannah.

Farragut has arrived at New York.

Rosecrans will command a force designed to operate in the rear of Hood.

In the Yankee Senate, Davis submitted lengthy joint resolutions for the restoration of peace and union, which were laid on the table and ordered to be printed. The resolutions propose a convention of all the states, to which shall be referred eleven amendments to the Constitution, one forming the New England states into one and another providing for the alternate election of president from the free and slave states.

Gold in New York 233⅝.

SIEGE OF CHARLESTON

Five Hundred Twenty-seventh Day

The steamer *Celt* took down the harbor Friday forenoon the balance of the Yankee prisoners due on the present exchange. The number of Yankee prisoners delivered thus far, since the commencement, in Savannah and Charleston harbors is as follows: Privates, 10,685; officers, 225, making a total of 10,910. The truce expires at ten o'clock this morning, at which time the usual firing between the batteries and the shelling of the city may be expected to be resumed.

AN APPEAL

Summerville, South Carolina, December 10, 1864

Now that the blessed season is approaching in which our "Lord Jesus Christ came to visit us in great humility," and in which we were wont to hail His advent with our sweetest songs and prepare both hearts and homes to greet Him. Now that this return of the high festival of Christmas, when so many of us are too sad to deck our homes with garlands, seeing there is scarcely one from which some cherished member will not be absent, either in camps or on the battlefield, languishing in hospitals or sleeping in a clay-cold bed at home or in foreign soil. When, for these causes, our hearts are desolate and the Christmas fires burn dim upon our hearthstones, let us see what our sad hearts can suggest, and our hands prepare, to honor the Prince of Peace and serve Him through His friends, remembering His blessed words: "Inasmuch as ye have done it unto the least of these my brethren, ye have done it unto me." Let us think of our brave soldiers, those afar off and those near at hand, and do everything in our power to supply their wants.

I call upon you, in the name of God and of humanity—in the name of freedom for which we are fighting, and which we intend (Heaven helping us) handing down to our children—to help these devoted men.

But especially at this time I plead for those in the Summerville hospitals, for, although under exemplary surgeons and efficient officers, yet are they in want of many comforts, which, perhaps, it is only necessary should be brought to the mind of the public to have supplied.

Five hundred men are now in these hospitals, and four hundred more daily expected.

The articles most needed are stimulants—brandy, whiskey, etc.; mutton suet and bandages, used for wounds; pickles and Irish potatoes, excellent in scurvy; vinegar and dried fruits of any kind; bandages, whether white or colored, provided the colors do not run; cotton and feathers, for making soft beds and pillows; butter, eggs, chickens, and milk, particularly wanted; woolen and cotton yarns, for socks; books, pamphlets, and newspapers, to beguile the tedious hours and turn the poor fellows' thoughts from their far-off happy homes.

These are some of the things required; your kind hearts will suggest the rest. Blockade runners could send oranges, lemons, and the like peculiar and acceptable articles not so easily procured by others.

All donations are allowed to come free of charge on the railroad and can be directed to the Ladies' Summerville Hospital Association, care of H. T. Peake, Esq., Summerville, South Carolina.

Communications can be addressed to Mrs. S. Miles, Summerville, and local donations sent to her or any of the Board of Visitors: Mrs. Ann Toomer, Mrs. Sarah Stone, Mrs. Miller, Mrs. Carrington. All boxes, jugs, demijohns, and bags will be returned, if directed and directions for so doing sent with them.

May the blessings of this holy season rest upon the heads of all who respond to this appeal, and the next year bring them peace, and peace to all the land, ere again the angel's song heralds the Virgin-Born.

NORTH

BOSTON EVENING TRANSCRIPT
December 17, 1864

[UNTITLED]

The news of the present week has been of the most encouraging nature. We have received definite tidings of General Warren's great raid upon the Weldon Railroad, in which many miles of its track were rendered unserviceable and quantities of food accumulated for the Rebel army destroyed. The enemy is now deprived of the use of a larger portion of this important road than at any time since Grant established his lines around Petersburg. This must materially increase the difficulty experienced in securing adequate supplies for the army defending the Confederate capital.

A grand expedition has sailed from Fortress Monroe southward. It embraces, besides a very powerful fleet, quite a large number of troops, which, taken from different corps of the Potomac Army, have been consolidated into one corps, called the XXIV. General Graham accompanied the expedition and will lead the land force, although General Butler is reported to be its supreme commander—a fact, if it be such, that almost proves the destination of the expeditionary column to be within the department over which General Butler has been placed. His department, it will be remembered, includes the state of North Carolina. If the sagacious Massachusetts general really commands the expedition, he could not help contrasting the formidable collection of armored vessels, and the heavily armed wooden gunboats comprising it, with the fleet, consisting of the fifty-gun frigates *Minnesota, Wabash,* and *Cumberland,* with four other, smaller vessels and the force of eight hundred men, with which he and Commodore Stringham entered Hatteras Inlet on the 28th of August, 1861, and captured forts Hatteras and Clark—715 prisoners, 25 cannons, and 1,000 stands of arms falling into Federal hands by the achievement.

There is a report that the fleet and the troops above mentioned are destined for Wilmington. The announcement of the capture of Kinston, by a force sent from New Bern, indicates that an attempt is to be made to seize Goldsboro, about sixty miles from New Bern. Kinston is halfway between New Bern and Goldsboro. If the Federal soldiers can establish themselves at the last-named place, no reinforcements can be sent by rail to Wilmington from the northern sections of North Carolina or Virginia. The only assistance the city could receive, when attacked, must come from regions farther south, in which the Rebels are now busily employed in warding off the blows of General Sherman.

But the most memorable intelligence of the week, at the time of writing these paragraphs, is the safe arrival of General Sherman upon the Atlantic Coast. His splendid army marched triumphantly through Georgia, bearing down all opposition and creating confusion and terror in the Rebel ranks everywhere. Emerging from the cloud of Rebel misrepresentation, but not of Rebel soldiery, as the Confederates were too weak to oppose its progress by such substantial obstacles, it has fixed a base upon Ossabaw Sound, some ten miles south of Savannah. The Federal force, under General Foster, operating north of Savannah, is also in communication with the victorious troops of General Sherman. That city is practically invested on all sides, and its defenders are enclosed within lines which they cannot break. The Richmond papers do not express very great confidence in the ability of the city to hold out a long time when once seriously attacked by Sherman's army.

In the Gulf Department a raiding party under General Davidson is devastating the country over which it passes, and causing the traitors in Mobile to tremble from fear of a visitation by these ministers of justice. An expedition consisting largely of colored troops, sent out from Vicksburg, has rendered immense service to the Union cause by cutting Hood's army off from the supplies accumulated at Jackson for its support. In western Virginia, Federal cavalry are destroying Rebel subsistence and crippling the railroad by which alone Breckinridge could reinforce Lee with sufficient dispatch to be of service in pending operations throughout North Carolina, South Carolina, and Georgia.

Before Nashville, a series of battles, begun between General Hood and General Thomas, have resulted, so far as is known, successfully for the Federal arms.

The fruits of the last day's contest are not yet definitely ascertained. If present indications are not fallacious, Hood's army has been dealt a staggering blow by the brave soldiers under General Thomas. Hood seems to have almost as ill luck in contending with Thomas as when he fought Sherman.

Thus, the Federal columns are moving victoriously wherever the enemy confronts them, and the close of the week is bright with promise of future Union successes.

Since the foregoing was written, General Thomas's official dispatch brings the gratifying information that a complete victory was gained over Hood yesterday—one that must entirely destroy the efficiency of the Rebel army threatening Nashville a few days since. The importance of the success can hardly be overestimated. It virtually puts out of the way one of the most numerous bodies of veterans the Rebels have in the field, and will release the West from all fears, hereafter, of Southern invasion.

NEW YORK TRIBUNE
December 17, 1864

THUNDER

CAPTURE OF SAVANNAH—11,000 PRISONERS CAPTURED—FORT McALLISTER TAKEN BY SHERMAN—GLORIOUS VICTORY AT NASHVILLE—A FIERCE FIGHT WITH THE REBEL ARMY—UNION RAID IN MISSISSIPPI—DESTRUCTION OF BIG BLACK BRIDGE—HOOD'S COMMUNICATIONS CUT—SUCCESSES IN EAST TENNESSEE—THE RAILROAD THERE BROKEN UP—OUR FORCES INVADE VIRGINIA

Baltimore, Maryland, December 16, 1864

The *American* has just received a dispatch from Annapolis, stating that the steamer *Varuna* had just arrived from Charleston with the news that General Sherman had captured Savannah, with eleven hundred prisoners, after eight hours' fighting.

Second Dispatch

The correspondent of the *American* at Annapolis telegraphs as follows: "The steamship *Varuna* left Charleston Barren on the 14th instant, at eight o'clock in the morning. The report had reached there by the Rebel flag-of-truce boat that Sherman was in possession of Savannah after an eight hours' fight, capturing *eleven thousand prisoners.*"

FROM THE WAR DEPARTMENT

Washington, December 16, 1864, 8:15 P.M.

To Major General Dix, New York:—Official dispatches from General Canby have been received today, showing the complete success of an expedition sent out by him from Vicksburg to cooperate with General Sherman's operations and cut Hood's communications with Mobile.

General Canby also reports the probable success of another expedition from Baton Rouge, under command of General Davidson, the details and object of which it is not proper now to disclose. When last heard from, Davidson was reported as having caused quite a panic in Mobile, and to be devastating the country generally. Lieutenant Colonel Earl, commanding a special party, was severely wounded and fell into the hands of the enemy at Fayette, Mississippi.

The Richmond papers of today confirm the reported capture of Bristol by an expedition supposed to be under the command of Stoneman and Burbridge; and, also, the surprise and capture of Glade Spring depot, on the railroad thirteen miles south of Abingdon, Virginia.

They also contain General Hood's official report of the battle of Franklin, in which he acknowledges the loss of many gallant officers and brave men, among whom he enumerates Major General Cleburne, Brigadier Generals John Williams, Adams, Gist, Strahl, and Granbury, killed; Major General John Brown and Brigadier Generals S. Carter, Manigault, Quarles, Cockrell, and Scott, wounded; and Brigadier General Gordon, taken prisoner.

They also state that on Wednesday General Sherman carried Fort McAllister commanding the entrance to the Ogeechee River, by storm, and that the capture of this position puts Sherman in communication with the Yankee fleet and necessitates the reinforcement of Savannah.

The dispatches of General Canby, so far as is proper for publication, and the extracts from the Richmond papers giving Hood's official report of the battle and our success in southwestern Virginia and in Georgia are subjoined.

Up to this hour (8:30 P.M.), nothing has been heard from Nashville since last night and nothing from General Sherman later than the Richmond newspapers report of the capture of Fort McAllister on Wednesday.

New Orleans, Louisiana, December 9, 1864

On the 25th ultimo, I reported that movements cooperative with General Sherman's operations would be made from Vicksburg and Baton Rouge for the purpose of cutting Hood's communications with Mobile. The expedition sent from Vicksburg, consisting of about two thousand cavalry and eight pieces of artillery, under the command of E. D. Ostrand of the 3rd Colored Cavalry, returned on the 4th instant, having met with a complete success. After an admirably executed flank movement on Jackson on the 14th ultimo, the expedition started for the Big Black Bridge on the Mississippi Central Railroad, which was reached on the 27th, and, after a stubborn resistance, captured and destroyed it.

This cuts Hood's army off from the large quantities of supplies and stores accumulated at Jackson, Mississippi, and makes that railroad, which was his main reliance, unavailable to him for months to come.

Besides this important bridge and trestlework, the following property was completely destroyed: thirty miles of track, including culverts; the wagon bridge over the Big Black; Vaughn, Pickett, and Goodman stations, with all the railroad depots and buildings; 2,600 bales of cotton, 2 locomotives, 4 cars, 4 stagecoaches, 20 barrels of salt, and $166,000 worth of stores at Vaughn Station.

The expedition was considerably harassed on its return by large bodies of the enemy's forces, but suffered no material losses, and brought back more recruits than its entire loss in effective men. Major J. B. Cook, commanding the 3rd Colored Cavalry, distinguished himself and his regiment greatly by the gallantry with which the force guarding the Big Black Bridge were driven behind their strong stockades on the opposite side of the river. Our men had to charge across the bridge dismounted, with nothing but railroad ties for a path, and in the face of a sharp fire. I have announced Major Cook in general orders as promoted to the vacant lieutenant colonelcy of the regiment, subject to the approval of the president.

E. R. Canby, Major General

City Point, Virginia, December 16, 1864

The *Richmond Dispatch* of today, after fully confirming the previous reports of the capture of Bristol, states that the enemy then advanced up the railroad toward Abingdon, which we presume fell into their hands, though we have no information of the fact. The next we hear of them, they had at nine o'clock yesterday morning pounced on Glade Spring, a depot on the railroad thirteen miles this side of Abingdon, taking everyone there by surprise and capturing all of the railroad employees except one, who managed to escape to tell the tale. At last accounts, the enemy were pushing up the railroad in the direction of Marion, which is twenty-seven miles on this side of Abingdon. This is a raid in Breckinridge's rear. The raiders, leaving his forces somewhere in the neighborhood of Knoxville, came up the north side of the Holston River and crossed over to Bristol. It is probable the raiders separated, one party proceeding to Bristol and the other to Abingdon. If unchecked, it is likely they will come up the railroad even as far as Salem and thence escape to the Kanawha by the route followed by Hunter last summer. It is unknown who is in command of this expedition, but it looks very much like some of Stoneman's galloping work. None of the dispatches received say anything about Saltville. If it is unprotected, it has doubtless been visited by the enemy. If, however, there were any troops there, the Yankees were apt to fight shy of it and confine their operations to the railroad.

THE BATTLE OF FRANKLIN

General Hood's official report of the battle of Franklin has at last been received. It will be seen that our reported extraordinary loss of general officers is but too true. The following is General Hood's dispatch:

> Headquarters, Army of Tennessee
> Six Miles from Nashville, December 8, 1864,
> via Mobile, December 9, 1864
>
> To the Honorable J. A. Seddon:—About 4:00 P.M., November 30, we attacked the enemy at Franklin and drove them from their center line of temporary works into their inner lines, which they evacuated during the night, leaving their dead and wounded in our possession, and retired to Nashville, closely followed by our cavalry. We captured several stands of colors and about a thousand prisoners. Our troops fought with great gallantry. We have to lament the loss of many gallant officers and men. Major General Cleburne and Brigadier Generals John Williams, Adams, Gist, Strahl, and Granbury were killed. Major General John Brown and Brigadier Generals S. Carter, Manigault, Quarles, Cockrell, and Scott were wounded. Brigadier General Gordon was captured.
>
> J. B. Hood, General

A subsequent telegram from General Hood says that our loss of officers was excessively large in proportion to the loss of men.

FORT McALLISTER TAKEN BY SHERMAN

Official intelligence was received yesterday that the enemy on Wednesday carried Fort McAllister by storm. The garrison of the fort consisted of a hundred fifty men. Fort McAllister is on the Ogeechee River, fifteen miles southwest of Savannah, at the point where the river is crossed by the Savannah, Albany, and Gulf Railroad, and about six miles from the Ossabaw Sound. The capture of this position put Sherman in communication with the Yankee fleet.

Without attempting any military criticism, we cannot withhold the opinion that the exposing of one hundred men to the assault of Sherman's whole army was a piece of extravagance that our present military resources do not seem to warrant.

The *Examiner* has the following:

> Fort McAllister commands the entrance of the Ogeechee River and has prevented the enemy heretofore from ascending the river; we believe there are other works farther up the stream which would render the navigation of the stream by the enemy extremely uncomfortable. The fall of Fort McAllister does not by any means involve the loss of Savannah, but will necessitate the reinforcement of the troops defending that city.
>
> **FROM SOUTHWEST VIRGINIA**
>
> At Glade Spring the enemy captured an engine and fourteen flats with some railroad hands. On these cars a party of men were mounted and sent up the road toward Marion, and a dispatch from the operator at that place on yesterday tells us that they were at two o'clock within a mile of that place. Their object is easily divined: It is to burn the bridge over the Holston River and break the road to prevent troops from being sent down the line by steam to reinforce Saltville. To Saltville the main body will undoubtedly go, and in all human probability has already gone. There are some fortifications at Saltville, and some reserves, whose members we do not know. If these can check them by any sacrifice, reinforcements will soon put the place out of danger. At present it is certainly in great danger.

Edwin M. Stanton, Secretary of War

1865

TIMELINE

January 13–15: The Federals launch another assault on Fort Fisher, North Carolina. A frontal offensive by the naval landing party is repulsed, but the army troops attack from the rear and prevail. Confederate blockade runners are decoyed into capture.

January 31: The Union House of Representatives follows the Senate action and passes the Thirteenth Amendment, abolishing slavery.

February 3: At Hampton Roads, Virginia, Lincoln and Secretary of State Seward meet with a delegation of "Peace Commissioners" from Richmond, but the discussions stall. Lincoln rejects the Southern position that the Confederate states constitute an autonomous nation, and insists that the Confederates cease all hostilities and unconditionally recognize Federal authority.

February 6: Lee is made commander in chief of all Confederate armies.

February 7: Grant extends his line around Petersburg, forcing Lee to defend a 37-mile perimeter with 46,000 men.

February 17: After 567 days of blockade and bombardment, Confederate troops evacuate Charleston. On the same day, Sherman accepts the surrender of Columbia, South Carolina. Wind-driven embers from cotton bales torched by the retreating Confederates soon set the city ablaze.

February 22: The Confederates evacuate Wilmington, North Carolina.

February 27: Union General Sheridan, with ten thousand cavalry, returns to the Shenandoah Valley, where he faces feeble opposition from Confederate General Early. A few days later, after overwhelming Early's forces and capturing two hundred wagons and one thousand prisoners, Sheridan moves to rejoin Grant in Petersburg.

March 3: Congress establishes the Freedman's Bureau to assist former slaves.

March 4: Inauguration day in Washington, D.C.

March 12: Sherman occupies Fayetteville, North Carolina.

March 13: In desperation, the Confederate Congress passes a bill authorizing the enlistment of African Americans, promising freedom to those slaves who serve.

March 18–21: Battle of Bentonville, North Carolina. Sherman engages Johnston in the last major action in the state. Casualties: North, 1,646; South, 2,606. Johnston withdraws upon hearing that Goldsboro, North Carolina, has fallen to the Union. He later repositions his troops in an attempt to block any Federal movement toward the north.

March 25: The Confederates break through the lines around Petersburg and capture Fort Stedman. But in a matter of hours, the attack falters, and the Confederates are beaten back behind the lines. Casualties: North, 1,044; South, 3,500.

March 26: Sheridan joins up with Grant at Petersburg. Lee begins to look west, hoping to join with Johnston.

April 1: Sheridan routs the Confederates at Five Forks, Virginia.

April 2: Lee orders the evacuation of all troops from Petersburg. President Davis and the Cabinet leave Richmond.

April 3: Early in the morning, Richmond is evacuated, and ammunition and other supplies are destroyed and buildings set afire. By the time the Federal troops accept the Confederate surrender, at 8:15 A.M., wind has spread the flames throughout the city center.

The first Federal soldiers to occupy Richmond are members of the 1st Division of Colored Troops, whose presence is resented by the white citizens of Richmond as well as by Federal units that enter soon after. Also, the first Federal forces to march into Petersburg are the 7th and 8th Colored Troops. Efforts will be made to purge these facts from the historical record.

April 4: Lee retreats toward Amelia Courthouse, with Sheridan in pursuit.

April 7: Grant sends a note to Lee, suggesting that further resistance is futile, and requesting the surrender of the Army of Northern Virginia.

April 9: Surrounded and without supplies or support, Lee surrenders to Grant in the McLean house at Appomattox Courthouse, Virginia.

April 12: With all defenses finally taken by the Federals, the Confederates surrender Mobile, Alabama.

April 14: Major General Anderson raises the same flag he lowered in surrendering Fort Sumter four years ago to the day.

While watching a play at Ford's Theater, Washington, D.C., President Lincoln is shot by the actor John Wilkes Booth. Secretary of State Seward and his son, at home, are also wounded as part of an obvious conspiracy.

April 15: Lincoln dies, and Vice President Andrew Johnson becomes president.

JANUARY 21, 1865

SOUTH

RICHMOND DAILY DISPATCH
January 21, 1865

STATISTICS OF SLAVERY

According to the United States census for 1850, the number of slaves then in the United States was 3,204,013, distributed as follows: Alabama, 342,844; Arkansas, 47,100; District of Columbia, 3,687; Delaware, 2,290; Florida, 39,310; Georgia, 381,682; Kentucky, 210,981; Louisiana, 244,809; Maryland, 90,368; Mississippi, 309,878; Missouri, 87,482; New Jersey, 236; North Carolina, 288,548; South Carolina, 384,984; Tennessee, 239,459; Texas, 58,161; Virginia, 472,528; Territories, 26. In 1776, the slaves were as follows: Massachusetts, 3,500; Rhode Island, 4,373; Connecticut, 6,000; New Hampshire, 629; New York, 15,000; New Jersey, 7,600; Pennsylvania, 10,000; Delaware, 9,000; Maryland, 80,000; Virginia, 165,000; North Carolina, 75,000; South Carolina, 110,000; and Georgia, 16,000. Total in 1776: 502,132.

The first introduction of African slaves was in 1620, by a Dutch vessel which brought twenty from Africa to Virginia. In his work upon the slave trade, Mr. Carey of Pennsylvania says, "The trade in Negro slaves to the American colonies was too small before 1750 to attract attention." The same writer says that the slaves numbered 55,850 in 1714, of which 30,000 were brought from Africa. The importations between 1715 and 1750 are estimated by Mr. Carey at 90,000; between 1751 and 1760, 35,000; between 1761 and 1770, 74,000; between 1771 and 1790, 34,000; between 1790 and 1808, 70,000—total: 333,000. The number in the last-mentioned decade is considered by the census to be evidently too small: Charleston alone, in the first four years of that decade, imported 30,075, which were consigned to 91 British subjects, 88 citizens of Rhode Island, 10 French subjects, and 13 natives of Charleston. Foreigners and New Englanders always conducted the traffic.

Making a correction for Mr. Carey's underestimate, the whole number of Africans at all times imported into the United States will not exceed 400,000. Thus, the number of Africans and their descendants in this country is nearly eight or ten to one of those that were imported, while in the British West Indies there are not two persons remaining for every five of the imported and their descendants. This is shown by Mr. Carey as follows: Imported into Jamaica previously to 1817, 700,000 Negroes, of whom and their descendants but 311,000 remained after 178 years, to be emancipated in 1833. In the whole British West Indies, imported, 1,700,000, of whom and their descendants 660,000 remained for emancipation, the rest having been previously emancipated by death, the result of the hard treatment they received from the philanthropical nation that is so very much concerned about American slavery.

Conventions of delegates of Virginia and North Carolina anticipated the Continental Congress of 1774 in resolving to discontinue the slave trade. On the 1st of March, 1807, Congress passed an act against importations of Africans into the United States after January 1, 1808. An act in Great Britain in 1807 also made the slave trade unlawful. Denmark made a similar prohibition as to her colonies, to take effect after 1804. The Congress of Vienna, in 1815, pronounced for the abolition of the trade. France abolished it in 1807. Spain, to take effect after 1820. Portugal abolished it in 1818. The slave trade continued in spite of the abolition. The average number of slaves exported from the coast of Africa averaged 85,000 per annum from 1798 to 1805, and from 1835 to 1840, there was a total of 135,810; in 1846 and 1847, it was 84,000 per annum. Between 1840 and 1847, 249,800 were taken to Brazil and 52,027 into the Spanish colonies.

Slavery was abolished in Pennsylvania in 1780. In New Jersey it was provisionally abolished in 1784, all children born of a slave after 1804 to be made free in 1820. In Massachusetts it was declared after the Revolution that slavery was virtually abolished by their constitution (1780).

In 1784 and 1797, Connecticut provided for a gradual extinction of slavery. In Rhode Island, after 1784, no person could be born a slave. The Ordinance of 1787 forbade slavery in the territory northwest of the Ohio. The constitutions of Vermont and New Hampshire abolished slavery. In New York it was provisionally abolished in 1799, twenty-eight years' ownership being allowed a slave born after that date, and in 1817, it was enacted that slavery was not to exist after ten years, or 1827.

There were 1,602,535 male and 1,601,778 female slaves in this country in 1850.

[UNTITLED]

We devoutly wish there was some other subject to write about except Yankees and Lincoln. We are as sick and tired of the disgusting monotony as anyone can well be. Even roast beef and plum pudding would lose their charms if one were compelled to dine on them every day in the week, and every week in the year, for four years, much more pork and beans, and codfish and potatoes. We are nauseated with the whole subject of Federals and flank movements, ditching and entrenching, bombshells, ironclads, and torpedoes. We are disgusted with the name of every prominent man in the United States, not simply because they are grand rascals, but because they have become tedious. To have to indict the same thieves at the Old Bailey every day in the week, to see the same ugly, vicious faces peering over the dock every day of the year, is equal to being mayor of the city of Richmond. Nothing is so offensive as a stale rogue. The interest that villainy at first arouses wears off by repetition. Even the inventive genius of the Yankees fails to keep up our curiosity. The novelty of both their crimes and absurdities has disappeared, and they can no longer produce a sensation. They have made arson, robbery, and murder so common that the newspapers, in order to keep up with these performances, have become little better than Newgate calendars. We wish, just by way of variety, they would become decent and civilized and relieve us from a bore which has become more intolerable than the bores of their cannons. We wish they would all go home, if only to give the newspapers something else to write about. Only to think of four long years, in which every article, every day of the year, is about war and Yankees.

We appeal to them as fellow beings on two legs, and having the same external aspect of humanity as other men, will they not begone and let the newspapers alone? How would they like to be invaded in this way and have nothing to write about but drums, trumpets, and gunboats?

We say nothing of bloodshed, burning, hanging, confiscation, and the like. It is a fearful thing to have only one subject to write and talk about for four years.

CHARLESTON DAILY COURIER
January 21, 1865

[UNTITLED]

The *Augusta Register* and other exchanges have referred to some remarks of the *Courier* concerning Sherman's triumphant progress through Georgia, as designed or at least calculated to impeach the valor and good faith of Georgia. We regret that some of our editorial friends in Georgia and North Carolina are so thin-skinned and susceptible and deem it necessary to smell out and denounce assaults on Georgia or North Carolina where none were designed or intended. If the character or good fame of either of our adjoining states has suffered at all from the press, it has not been from any editorial utterances in and through the *Courier*. If Georgia papers have brought Georgia into doubt and North Carolina papers have been quoted as authority for gross disaffection in North Carolina, it is not according to our wishes or desires, or the result of any efforts on our part. Some editors, however, of these states —we mean not to imply that other states have not editors equally prone to superfluous zeal in repelling supposed assaults—cannot see in any South Carolina journal a fact recorded concerning any Georgian or North Carolinian without inferring some attack on the state.

Whatever inferences may be extorted from any remarks that have appeared in these columns, we hope all editors who have suspected or smelled attacks will accept our assurance that nothing of the sort was designed. So far as the number, proportion, and conduct of field representatives are concerned, we shall not stop to decide by fractional calculations whether Georgia or North Carolina has done better.

We freely and thankfully admit that both have done well; and should we hear now and then of a deserter, or a skulker, or of white-livered mammonites taking the oath in either state, or of gangs or squads in either state going about committing disorders or outrages, we should not consider these exceptions and rare cases as characteristic of Georgia or North Carolina, any more than we could or would admit like instances as presenting the character and claims of our own state.

We must say in candor, however, that in all states—and in North

Carolina, South Carolina, and Georgia, three states placed in situation and resources so as necessarily to meet the brunt of the war—there have been exhibitions of shortcomings. All have suffered in territory, and in particular cities, because too much reliance was placed on the brave men who had gone forth, or too much was expected of brave men in some cases, sacrificed for want of officers and military management, and too little was done in evoking, improving, and organizing the resources of the state beyond the conscription.

We believe that more could have been done, and some of our disasters have been avoided, if governors of states, including Governors Vance and Brown, had done more in earnest and actual efforts and less in proclamations and appeals aimed, perhaps, against Richmond or Washington. We believe that iron, copper, and other metals of some value in war can be found in North Carolina and Georgia, and many other elements or resources that could and would have been more improved than they have if the work had been attempted in good time and in the full, earnest assertion and appreciation of states as to rights, duties, and privileges. We believe one tenth of the zeal and capital and efforts and official patronage directed to blockade running, if applied and directed to the cultivation, development, and improvement of our own resources, would have done more for ending the war successfully, for keeping up the better spirit and purposes with which our better class of citizenship entered the war, and for convincing and assuring all concerned—our foe and our very complacently neutral spectators—that we were in earnest and were fully resolved and fully able to be free and independent.

After all, this, and not any mere military result or achievement, is the problem before us. We believe there were men enough in Georgia nominally enrolled or strictly liable to local and special and limited duty and service, if not for the conscription proper, to have defeated Sherman before he reached Millen.

He gave fair and full notice of his intention, and it was known to everyone competent to have any opinion that Millen was in his line if he started toward the Atlantic at all.

We make no imputation, or impeachment, or insinuation against Georgia as a state, or against her organized government, or her noble army of sons in the field, when we say that blame must rest somewhere for Sherman's march through Georgia; and it is difficult to believe that some persons then in and of Georgia are not justly included in this censure.

We simply state obvious facts, and no exchange need reply, or ask a merely captious discussion, by retorting as to states or by calling on South Carolina. These columns will show that we have steadily endeavored to stir up all within our state to duty. No state, however, can be exposed to the same ordeal and challenge offered to Georgia by Sherman—for his success in that state has largely increased his resources.

If, however, after this warning, any citizen of South Carolina neglects his duty either in going out for the field, or in giving information, or in removing servants, horses, and provisions before Sherman, or in furnishing supplies to them who will fight for him, or in any other particular, we request and beg all exchanges of other states to give the full facts, and we shall not accuse them of assailing or impeaching South Carolina.

[UNTITLED]

Headquarters District, Augusta, Georgia
January 19, 1865

Honorable R. H. May, mayor of Augusta:—Lieutenant General Hardee directs me to have the cotton burned in the city on the approach of the Yankees. This order I am bound to execute even at the peril of the city. It is to be hoped that your patriotic citizens will at once remove this temptation to Yankee invasion, either to distant parts or to the commons, where the torch can be applied when the emergency shall occur.

The military will render you all the assistance in its power for the removal.

With great respect,
D. H. Hill, Major General

NORTH

BOSTON EVENING TRANSCRIPT
January 21, 1865

FROM SAVANNAH
20 SHIPLOADS OF COTTON—EXAGGERATION OF SUFFERINGS—SHERMAN'S MOVEMENTS

New York, 21st—Letters from collector Draper at Savannah state that a number of vessels are being loaded with cotton for this city and would soon sail.

No account has been taken of the amount of cotton, but it is estimated that it will require twenty vessels to convey it. The collector advises traders to hold off for the present. The stories of suffering in Savannah have been greatly exaggerated by Julian Allen and others.

Recent movements of our army were made with nearly all Sherman's troops, whose numbers are much greater than generally supposed. The army fairly adore their general, and though the time of some of them has expired, as the saying is, they "will stay late with him."

PROMOTION OF A COLORED OFFICER FOR GALLANTRY

Sergeant Stephen A. Swails, 54th Regiment Massachusetts Volunteers (colored), was commissioned second lieutenant in that regiment, on the recommendation of Colonel Hallowell, for his conspicuous gallantry in action and his merit as a man of character and intelligence, 11th of March, 1864.

The usual application for his discharge for promotion was made by the governor, June 1, 1864, which discharge was not granted by reason of the "African descent" of the sergeant. The case has been a subject of examination and correspondence between the War Department, the general commanding the Department of the South, and the governor until the present time.

The fitness of Sergeant Swails was not denied by anyone, unless his inheritance of some "African blood" could be a disqualification. Major General Foster seems to have been fully impressed by his character and claims to promotion, and evinced no objection whatever to his taking rank as an officer; but he understood the order of the War Department to preclude it.

Today the governor has received the copy of an order from the secretary of war expressly authorizing the discharge of the sergeant and his muster-in as a second lieutenant. Thus, by degrees, does "the world move."

NEW YORK TRIBUNE
January 21, 1865

[UNTITLED]

The glorious victories of Sherman and Thomas are producing much good in England. The most skeptical critics of the military situation begin to see and to admit that the cause of the South is fast becoming hopeless. The Confederate loan during one week declined 10 percent, although the news of the capture of Savannah had not then been received.

On the continent of Europe, the papal bull may lead to serious complications. The French government, in a circular to the bishops, has declared that the bull and the "Appendix," containing the catalogue of errors, are contrary to the laws of the empire and that, therefore, they cannot be published by the bishops. A large meeting of the French clergy is soon to be held to express the general dissatisfaction with the contents of the bull. This forebodes a violent commotion within the Church, which may more or less affect all the Catholic countries of Europe.

[UNTITLED]

Bennet G. Burley, the Lake Erie raider, whose trial has been going on at Toronto before Justice Duggan, has been committed, so we learn by special dispatch, as subject to extradition under the treaty. His counsel immediately applied for a writ of habeas corpus. The decision of Justice Duggan had a depressing effect upon the Southerners present, whose little plans of robbery and arson will be sadly interfered with if this is the way in which they are to be dealt with.

PEACE EFFORTS

The *New York Times* has certainly swallowed wrong end foremost its story about "terms of peace and adjustment" suggested by us last summer, and brings it up so transformed as to bear but slight resemblance to its proper self. We made some suggestions for the consideration of the president of the United States, and for no one else unless and until approved and adopted by him, with such modifications as he should see fit to make; and so far from being precluded from submitting them, or having them submitted, by the president's "withholding his needed assent," we have since learned with surprise that the president expected that we *would* submit them informally to certain Rebel agents in Canada, and was disappointed that we did not. *We* had no thought of doing anything of the kind.

The *Times* evinces "anxiety and alarm" in view of our inference from the fact of Mr. Blair's repeated journeys Richmond-ward "that the president does not insist on unconditional surrender" by the Rebels, and says:

> If it be true that our government is prepared to accept a *conditional* surrender at the hands of the Rebel authorities, the coun-

> try would like to know what conditions it is prepared to grant, and we applied to the quarter most likely to be well-informed upon that point.

No, sir! That "quarter" is the government itself, which (we presume) is quite able to keep its own counsel. We do not see how it could make a public proclamation of "what conditions it is prepared to grant," pending their consideration and possible modification. *We* neither know nor seek to know them, but rest in the confident trust that the Executive is equal to the high trust reposed in him by the people.

"PUBLIC SPIRIT" IN RICHMOND

The red-hot rebellious newspapers in Richmond are letting numerous cats out of the bag in a way which is far from prudent. It is natural to suppose that there are a great many persons in the Confederacy who are quite sick of insurrection and uncommonly sorry that it was ever undertaken. These wise apostates from a foolish faith are, to a considerable extent, defended from wrath and violence by the fact that to hang them, flog them, or tar and feather them would be creative of a most damaging scandal. But the ferocity of desperate editors is not always to be restrained, and even in the wise House of Representatives we perceive that it has been thought necessary to resolve that the Confederate states will stick by each other and mean to fight either to the death or the Day of Judgment. When solemn declarations like these are judged to be fit and proper, it does not require a great deal of logic to prove that the disaffected are neither meager in numbers nor poor in character. It does not, therefore, surprise us to find the *Richmond Examiner* of the 12th instant in a depressed frame of mind over what it is pleased to call "the decay of public spirit." The *Examiner,* if we may credit its trumpet-toned defiance, fears neither our old armies nor our new drafts, our guns nor our generals, our ships nor our steamboats; and it goes into an elaborate calculation intended to prove that we are at the present moment not only used up, but upon our marrowbones, bawling lustily for quarter. Under such rejuvenating and stimulating circumstances, it really does strike us as greatly and inexplicably queer that "public spirit," like other "spirits," should be growing scarce in the Rebel stronghold. Yet the *Examiner* admits the "decay" and avows that it is "greatly to be feared." Why this "decay"? It isn't to be attributed either to the loss of battles or to sieges or to blockades, to diminishing provender or painfully diluted potations; but rather, as we are confidently informed, to "the continual spectacle of executive folly and legislative subserviency." One reason may, perhaps, be as good as another in an emergency. But if we were that mongrel thing, a "citizen" of the Confederacy, we think that it would give us exceedingly unpleasant interior feelings to be told that in the first period of our brand-new commonwealth, our pretty new Congress, the pick of an enfranchised people, the quintessence of slaveholding wisdom and virtue and patriotism, was proving subservient to one who is no better than a "fool." Yet there it is in black and white! Executive folly! Legislative subserviency! Nay, the *Examiner* goes further than this. The army, it declares, is demoralized by a lack of "manliness" in Mr. Davis and of "common sense" in his Congress. All this indicates a most portentous depression, both civil and military!

While the lawmakers and the law executors are thus giving out, we are proud to say that the secession editors are more blatantly bold than ever. The number of long poles with which Mr. Davis and his senators are being continually stirred up surpasses computation. The valor of the newspapers, we are bound to confess, shows not the smallest sign of abatement. The ready writers of the Confederacy are still most murderously metaphorical and brilliantly belligerent. Were not our cause excellent, we should surely succumb before the broadside of bad names which is every morning discharged at us. We should have supposed that the natural effect of these lurid leading articles would be a revival of "public spirit." Fine writing sometimes does wonders. A lucky song once gave fresh impulse to the French Revolution when it threatened to stop revolving—but the Richmond editors appear to manufacture both hot and heavy articles in vain. They have nearly exhausted the resources of their classical dictionaries. Their pens must be worn down to the stumps. Their ink pots must be almost dry. But Public Spirit wants its breakfast. And its dinner. And its supper. Public Spirit evaporates with beef at five dollars per pound and brandy at five hundred dollars per gallon. Public Spirit requires coats and shirts and breeches.

On the other hand, if Public Spirit is a little down in Richmond, the other kind, i.e., Private Spirit, would appear to be upon the rise. Nobody can tell exactly how many people in the Rebel states are sick of the Davis government, but if the number be not increasing, why these continual rousers in the newspapers? One thing is evident: Wherever our victorious soldiers march, they are civilly saluted as deliverers. There is no desperate defense—no fighting in the streets—no firing from the windows—no disputing inch by inch our advance. So when we capture Richmond, as capture it in time we must, Mr. Davis will undoubtedly run away, but he will have but a slim following. There will be meetings in New York and Boston to raise funds for the famishing people of Richmond, and when we send them food, be sure they will not quarrel with it.

FEBRUARY 18, 1865

SOUTH

RICHMOND DAILY DISPATCH
February 18, 1865

THE FALL OF COLUMBIA

Columbia has fallen. Sherman marched into, and took possession of, the city yesterday morning. This intelligence was communicated yesterday by General Beauregard in an official dispatch.

Columbia is situated on the north bank of the Congaree River, just below the confluence of the Saluda and Broad rivers. From General Beauregard's dispatch it appears that on Thursday evening the enemy approached the south bank of the Congaree and threw a number of shells into the city. During the night they moved up the river and, yesterday morning, forded the Saluda and Broad. While they were crossing these rivers, our troops, under General Beauregard, evacuated Columbia. The enemy soon after took possession.

Through private sources we learn that two days ago, when it was decided not to attempt the defense of Columbia, a large quantity of medical stores, which it was thought impossible to remove, was destroyed. The female employees of the Treasury Department had been previously sent off to Charlotte, North Carolina, a hundred miles north of Columbia. We presume the Treasury lithographic establishment was also removed, though as to this we have no positive information.

The fall of Columbia necessitates, we presume, the evacuation of Charleston, which, we think likely, is already in process of execution. It is impossible to say whither Sherman will next direct his columns. The general opinion is that he will go to Charleston and establish a base, but we confess we do not see what need he has of a base. It is to be presumed he is subsisting on the country, and he has had no battle to exhaust his ammunition. Before leaving Savannah, he declared his intention to march to Columbia, thence to Augusta, and thence to Charleston. This was uttered as a boast, and to hide his designs. We are disposed to believe that he will next strike at Charlotte, North Carolina, which is a hundred miles north of Columbia, on the Charlotte and Columbia Railroad; or at Florence, South Carolina, the junction of the Columbia and Wilmington and the Charleston and Wilmington railroads, some ninety miles east of Columbia.

There was a report yesterday that Augusta had also been taken by the enemy. This we do not believe. We have reason to feel assured that nearly the whole of Sherman's army is together at Columbia and that the report that Schofield was advancing on Augusta was untrue.

FIRING BELOW RICHMOND

Several heavy guns were heard in the direction of Dutch Gap yesterday evening. The cause of the firing has not been explained. Probably some wet guns were being fired off.

FROM PETERSBURG

On Wednesday and Thursday some movement was going on in Grant's camp opposite Petersburg. Deserters state that Grant has sent eight thousand men to City Point since Saturday, and say it is the impression in the Yankee army that this force is to be sent to New Bern or to reinforce Sherman. Sherman does not want reinforcements; Terry, at Wilmington, may require more.

GENERAL JOHNSTON'S REPORT

General Johnston's report of his campaign from Dalton to Atlanta was yesterday made public by the Confederate Senate and ordered to be printed. The publication of this report will give a fresh impetus to the great Bragg–Johnston–Hood controversy which, for six months, has engrossed so much of the attention of the press and the country.[1]

1. Bragg–Johnston–Hood controversy: Following the humiliating defeat at Missionary Ridge, Tennessee, on November 25, 1863, General Braxton Bragg resigned as head of the Confederate Army of Tennessee. President Davis replaced him with General Joseph Johnston, whom Davis disliked. Bragg was then made Davis's own "military adviser." In a later action in Georgia, with Union General William Tecumseh Sherman pressing Atlanta and a cautious Johnston faltering, Bragg urged Davis to appoint the aggressive but, to some observers, reckless John Hood to replace Johnston. The removal of Johnston on July 17, 1864, was supported by the government but criticized by the army. After Hood suffered a series of disastrous defeats, Commanding General Robert E. Lee restored Johnston to the command on February 23, 1865. Bragg was appointed to command a division in Johnston's army for the last month of the war.

CHARLESTON DAILY COURIER
February 17, 1865

[*No copies of the February 18 issue appear to have survived. The following articles are drawn from the Friday issue.*]

[UNTITLED]

If we lose our independence, we lose all our property of every kind, in the country—our debt, our slaves, and our lands. But we lose more. The people of the United States have a greater debt than we, and we shall not escape without being obliged to pay our proportion of their debt. In what condition will that leave us, with our property, our lands, bonds, houses, and slaves all gone and the mighty debt incurred by the enemy in his war for our subjugation still to be borne in part by us and our children? Then our subjugation, with all its personal evils, the utter degradation it involves, must be considered. Subjugation—submission—presents no hope; but in continuing the war it is otherwise. We can see clearly the end and the evils of submission. It involves our utter degradation and the turning loose among us on a footing of equality, to the destruction of our society and civilization, millions of Negroes. The final result of prosecuting the war is not now discernible, but it certainly holds out to us hope.

[UNTITLED]

General Lee has been announced as commander in chief of the Confederate armies. The following is the order of Adjutant General Cooper:

"General Robert E. Lee, having been duly appointed general in chief of the army of the Confederate States, will assume the duties thereof and will be obeyed and respected accordingly."

[UNTITLED]

Let Confederate officers, by every means and appliance possible, stimulate the pride and fire the zeal of the men who are absentees without the purpose of desertion, so that they may return to their command and give our glorious old leader, General Lee, such an army as will enable him to chastise the invader and drive him from our soil. Public meetings should be called in every city and town in the Confederacy and our most eloquent and patriotic men be engaged to address them. There should be concert of action among the people, and a determination expressed by them in primary assemblies, to sustain the government and the army and to make every sacrifice that may be required to sustain the cause of freedom and independence.

[UNTITLED]

The army is all right. Only let the people at home do their whole duty. Let them exert every energy to provide for the comfort of the soldiers and their families. Let them return to the ranks the men who have deserted their colors and are lounging about the country without any sufficient excuse. Let them create a public opinion that will not tolerate such unpatriotic conduct and that will make every neighborhood in every state too hot for the skulkers who have abandoned their faithful companions-in-arms.

[UNTITLED]

Let the horrors of the war teach us what the horrors of subjugation will be. The *Philadelphia Inquirer,* in a late issue, contained in one column the exaggerated accounts of certain newspaper correspondents who had been imprisoned at Salisbury. Their sufferings were magnified with the art which is peculiarly the Yankee's own—the art of lying. But another column of the same paper contained the depositions of a number of poor women who had been employed to make clothing for the Yankee government. Their average week's pay, after six days of continuous labor, from early dawn until nearly midnight, was four dollars. Four dollars for one hundred hours' hard labor. One woman declared that she could make but two and a half dollars a week. Other women avowed that it was with great difficulty they could get paid at all, however small their weekly pittance might be. Remember, these women were working for the Yankee government—making clothes for the soldiers at the Philadelphia arsenal. If Yankees act thus to their own women, what will be their tender mercy toward the women of the South when they have them in their power? God forbid that day shall ever come!

[UNTITLED]

Perhaps our military chiefs may know something more than they are willing to give to the outside world, although, to tell the truth, says the *Wilmington Journal,* we cannot see the object of any particular reticence in regard to the enemy's movements, if we have been able to fathom them. If there was a plausible reason for this while the enemy, cut off from his base, was wending his way through Georgia, we cannot see that there is any such reason now, while he is operating in South Carolina, in full connection with his base and in full communication with his government.

NORTH

BOSTON EVENING TRANSCRIPT
February 18, 1865

GENERAL SHERMAN'S ARMY AND THEIR ANTAGONISTS

The *New York Daily News* (Ben Wood's organ), which labors hard to make it appear that General Sherman is in a desperate condition in South Carolina, cannot, with all its efforts, increase the force opposing him beyond fifty thousand. To produce even this amount, Hood's broken army, Hardee's discomfited troops, and the South Carolina militia are aggregated into one mass, no account being taken of the wide area comprising the theater of battle in the Palmetto State. There is no evidence yet that these different bodies are not hopelessly separated, at Branchville, Augusta, and Columbia. If brought together for an attack, the concentration would not probably be as rapid as that of Sherman's army, which is abundantly able to defeat any fifty thousand Rebel soldiers the Confederacy can furnish. The men who were so unmercifully beaten from Dalton to beyond Atlanta and subsequently whipped in every encounter in Tennessee will have very little relish for meeting Sherman's veterans, with whom "success is a duty" always thoroughly performed.

SHERMAN STILL ADVANCING—THE REBELS CONTINUING THEIR RETREAT—REPORTS ABOUT THE EVACUATION OF RICHMOND

Special Dispatch to the *Transcript*
Washington, February 18, 1865

The report, published yesterday, that General Sherman's heretofore invincible troops had been checked in their march through South Carolina is entirely without foundation.

Richmond papers of yesterday, just received here, state that the Union forces were still marching on, overcoming all opposition. As a military and physical necessity, the Rebels fall back as Sherman advances. Thus far, he has brushed aside the enemy with only a partial demonstration of his power.

Well-authenticated reports are said to have reached General Grant that the Confederates have begun the evacuation of Richmond. If these stories are confirmed, we may soon expect another movement of the Potomac Army. General Lee cannot afford to have General Sherman scour South Carolina, destroying all the means of transportation whereby Lee obtains his supplies from South Carolina, and then march into North Carolina with the powerful army intact, which has accomplished the destruction of Rebel food. It may therefore be anticipated that Lee will change his base, unless Sherman meets with a reverse.

President Lincoln will send in the name of the new secretary of the Treasury to the Senate next week.

Kappa

NEW YORK TRIBUNE
February 18, 1865

NEWS OF THE DAY: THE WAR

Rebel cavalry are hovering around Nashville, making little raids here and there, but they are not strong enough to do serious damage.

The case of the Rebel raiders at Montreal has gone over until Monday. The defense professes to have more witnesses to examine.

Advices from Knoxville to the 15th represent everything quiet in east Tennessee.

THE NATION'S AGONY

The last sands of the rebellion appear to be nearly run. It may be, as is urged by those who would gladly depress the national credit, that Lee will insist on fighting one more great battle in the hope of surprising and overwhelming Grant or arresting the majestic progress of Sherman, but we do not believe it. Unless our more ferocious philanthropists—of the female persuasion especially—shall succeed in persuading the Southern people that our triumph involves their annihilation, we have high hopes that what remains of the Rebel forces will crumble and melt away before the majestic advance of the Union armies like snow before the breezes of spring. All our advices concur in representing the Southern masses as thoroughly sick of the rebellion and anxious for a peace that shall reconcile them to their country, not trample them under the bloody feet of her legions. In fact, the ravings of the Richmond press concerning "despondency," "croakers," etc., and their publication of assurances that the army does not despair—that General Lee considers their case by no means hopeless, etc.—what would evince desperation if all these do not! Unless prevented by some extraordinary and most improbable disaster, we confidently look for a complete and auspicious pacification of our country at a very early day.

But that will be by no means the end of our trials, though it ought to mark the utmost limit of our public burdens. When the war ends, our public debt should have reached its maximum, and its reduction should, within a few weeks thereafter, have begun. We are now paying into the national Treasury about $400 million per annum—more than $1 million per day—and we would reduce no tax till after the reduction of the principal of our debt shall have fairly begun. Give us peace, industry, and frugality, and we may very soon be paying off the principal of that debt at the rate of at least $100 million per annum.

The indispensable condition of our financial solvency is national economy, and that is yet to be secured. Our Congress, but especially the House of Representatives, seems incapable of even comprehending our financial condition—in fact, how could it be expected to do so when its leader imagines that irredeemable paper may be made equal in value to gold by the easy process of enacting that it shall be and remain so? Do we not hear from various respectable quarters suggestions that our currency shall be suffered to remain irredeemable for an indefinite period after peace? Are we not told that the country will not be ready for resumption for years? And how does this differ from the assumption that slavery must be indefinitely continued because the blacks are unfit for freedom? Or that counterfeit money must be allowed to circulate because the volume of genuine currency is insufficient?

We hold it the interest of everyone who lives by honest industry, or by the honest employment of capital, that we shall return to a currency at par with specie at the earliest possible moment and that this moment will arrive within sixty or at most ninety days after the government shall be able to desist from further borrowing. But to render such presumption practicable, it is essential that we have peace and national frugality.

The peace cannot be far distant—but where is the frugality? What single expenditure does Congress propose to retrench? In what department is the tendency to increased outlay successfully resisted? Only think of the proposition to pay the builders of ironclads 20 percent extra being seriously entertained by Congress at such a crisis as this! Think of the patent-extension jobs, involving the abstraction of millions on millions from the sweat and toil of the many to swell the riches of the few that are now being piloted through the House! Think of voting twenty-five thousand dollars at such a time to a painter of very moderate pretensions—at least, of very moderate achievement—for a picture to ornament the Capitol! Think of the millions lavished on that Capitol throughout the years when the national existence was at stake, and when the soldiers who stood between the republic and her ruin were vainly asking for the money they had so nobly earned, and for which their wives and children were famishing! Truly, the patience of the masses is explicable only by their profound unacquaintance with what is most vital in the conduct of their public affairs.

The new internal tax bill now before Congress proposes to exempt members of either House from the payment of income tax on their three thousand dollars per annum and mileage from the Treasury. We trust the advocates of common decency in the House will take care that we have the yeas and nays on this when the bill comes out of committee. We would rather give a hundred dollars than not have them. Do let us see who vote that a clerk who earns $1,600 per annum shall pay $100 of it into the Treasury, but that he who lays the taxes shall not pay a cent on his $3,000. There is an audacity in that sort of voting that we rather admire, provided it does not seek to dodge the yeas and nays. Gentlemen in Congress, let us know who will vote to frank your own salaries as well as your letters!

MARCH 18, 1865

SOUTH

RICHMOND DAILY DISPATCH
March 18, 1865

COLORED TROOPS
AN APPEAL TO THE PEOPLE OF VIRGINIA

It will be seen by the order of the secretary of war, published above, that the undersigned have been authorized to proceed at once with the organization of companies composed of persons of color, free and slave, who are willing to volunteer under the recent acts of Congress and the legislature of Virginia. It is well-known to the country that General Lee has evinced the deepest interest on this subject and that he regards prompt action in this matter as vitally important to the country. In a letter addressed by him to Lieutenant General Ewell, dated March 10, he says, "I hope it will be found practicable to raise a considerable force in Richmond. . . . I attach great importance to the result of the first experiment, and nothing should be left undone to make it successful. The sooner this can be accomplished, the better."

The undersigned have established a rendezvous on the 21st, between Main and Cary streets, at the building known as Smith's Factory; and every arrangement has been made to secure the comfort of the new recruits and to prepare them for service. It is recommended that each recruit be furnished, when practicable, with a gray jacket and pants, cap and blanket, and a good serviceable pair of shoes, but no delay should take place in forwarding the recruits in order to obtain these articles.

The governments, Confederate and state, having settled the policy of employing this element of strength, and this class of our population having given repeated evidence of their willingness to take up arms in the defense of their homes, it is believed that it is only necessary to put the matter before them in a proper light to cause them to rally with enthusiasm for the preservation of the homes in which they have been born and raised, and in which they have found contentment and happiness; and to save themselves and their race from the barbarous cruelty invariably practiced upon them by a perfidious enemy claiming to be their friends.

Will not the people of Virginia, in this hour of peril and danger, promptly respond to the call of our loved general in chief and the demands of the Confederate and state governments? Will those who have freely given their sons and brothers, their money and their property, to the achievement of the liberties of their country now hold back from the cause their servants, who can well be spared, and who will gladly aid in bringing this fearful war to a speedy and glorious termination?

Let every man in the state consider himself a recruiting officer and enter at once upon the duty of aiding in the organization of this force by sending forward recruits to this rendezvous.

Every consideration of patriotism, the independence of our country, the safety of our homes, the happiness of our families, and the sanctity of our firesides—all prompt to immediate and energetic action for the defense of the country. Let the people but be true to themselves and to the claims of duty, and our independence will be speedily secured and peace be restored within our borders.

J. W. Pegram, Major P.A.C.S.
Thomas P. Turner, Major P.A.C.S.

[UNTITLED]

The altered tone of both the English and Yankee newspapers, when they speak of each other's respective country, is the most remarkable incident connected with journalism in these latter days. Before this war had revealed the strength of the United States—while they were still entire—the language held by the *London Times* with regard to them was always slight, often sneering, and, on some occasions, absolutely insulting. On one occasion, it spoke of the ease with which Britain had throttled "the Northern giant," Russia, and intimated that it could, at the same time, with all the ease imaginable, administer castigation to Jonathan. Even after the war had actually commenced on this side of the Atlantic, while the parties were marshaling their forces and preparing for the mighty conflict that was so shortly to ensue, the *Times* indulged its satirical vein, without stint, at the expense of the combatants. After the battle of Manassas, it told the Yankees that they had mistaken their calling; that they never could be a great military nation, how great soever might be their aspirations after military fame; that "war was not in their line of business"; and that to excel, they must take to something else. When Messrs. Mason and Slidell were piratically seized on a British vessel upon the high seas, by a ship belonging to the United States, the tone of the *Times* was, beyond measure, bold, insolent, and defiant.

At the same time, the Yankee press was as obsequious and cringing as the British press was arrogant and domineering. Both are wonderfully altered since that time. The Yankee is now as loud and insulting as he was formerly meek and submissive. The change has not taken by surprise any person who has been accustomed to study the policy of the British. That government has always been famous for dealing out what it calls exemplary justice upon culprits whom it believes unable to help themselves. Let not such hope to escape the lash of British vengeance. Greece, or Brazil, or any of the little states on the continent—such as Denmark, for instance—cannot hope to escape upon any conceivable pretext whenever it may be so unfortunate as to incur the wrath of the British lion. It is only strength that secures impunity from that magnanimous animal. Even now the *New York Herald* is calling upon the British queen to revoke her proclamation of neutrality—that is, we suppose, to take part with the Yankees in their war upon this country. We do not see why this should not be done. It would be perfectly consistent with the whole conduct of Great Britain throughout the war. Should Ambassador Adams choose to demand it, a good-natured, easy soul like Russell could hardly refuse so small a favor to his amiable ally after having already granted him so many others. He has already placed Canada at his disposal; he has but to stretch out his hand to grasp it. Why refuse anything, when so much has already been given? we ask again.

We sometimes feel disposed to be a little astonished at the facility with which Great Britain has been brought to play second fiddle in this concert of the nations. Who that lived a century or even a half century ago would have believed it possible that such a thing could ever happen? But we suppose it is with governments as with individuals: The greatest bullies are always the first to succumb when real danger presents itself.

CHARLESTON DAILY COURIER
March 18, 1865

[*On the first page of the February 21 issue, Lieutenant Colonel Stewart L. Woodford announced, by command of Major General Q. A. Gillmore, "The* Charleston Courier *establishment is hereby taken possession of by the Military Authority of the United States. All the materials and property of said newspaper of every kind will be immediately turned over to Messrs. George Whittemore and George W. Johnson, who are hereby authorized to issue a loyal Union newspaper."*]

THE ENEMY BECOMING DESPERATE

The news which we published yesterday of the reported evacuation of Richmond by the Rebel forces and the refusal of the Virginia troops to fight outside the limits of their own state is deserving of close attention. Whether or not the reports are well-founded, it has been evident to prominent officers in Grant's army that preparations for the evacuation of that city have been in progress for some weeks. The Union combinations have been consummated with such masterly skill that the Rebel leaders see no way of saving themselves and their army but in the immediate abandonment of Richmond. And even then they must grope in the dark. The very fact of their leaving Richmond, after all that has been said and written against such a course by the Rebel military authorities and the editors of the Southern press, is an evidence of the desperate strait in which the leaders find themselves. The question is asked, where will Lee go to after evacuating Richmond and Virginia? The most sanguine of the Rebel sympathizers predict he will make a new battlefield in Tennessee, while others who have watched the waning fate of the rebellion for many months do not hesitate to declare that in the evacuation of Richmond the whole fabric of the rebellion becomes dissolved.

It is by no means probable that Grant, with his splendid army and well-trained veterans, will quietly smoke his cigar while Lee is attempting to form a new base. On the contrary, we are inclined to the belief that Lee will discover he has "jumped from the kettle into the fire." Wherever he may turn, there he will find Grant clutching at his throat with a firm grasp. Sherman, too, is another source of difficulties to the Rebels. They cannot comprehend why Joe Johnston has not been able to impede Sherman's march in North Carolina. The very thought of Sherman joining his forces with those of Grant in front of Petersburg is sufficient to excite the wildest alarm. Grant and Sherman together! What is left for the enemy to do? Nothing but to surrender, or take to flight. In either case the result will be nearly the same. The moral effect of the evacuation of Richmond will be heavily felt throughout the Southern dominions, and the act will be considered as an acknowledgment on the part of Jefferson Davis that he has lost all faith in his own scheme. In Europe the effect will be most damaging for the Rebel cause. Their bonds will decline in value to such a point as to be nearly worthless even with John Bull to endorse them.

Then again, another ominous element which protrudes itself from the mass of Rebel military perplexities is the dissatisfaction prominent among the Virginia troops. While Lee keeps his forces in Virginia, the state troops are willing to remain by him, but the moment he expresses a determination to abandon her soil, a mutiny in the army is at once created. The soldiers believe with the Richmond editors that the "game is up" when the capital is suffered to fall into the hands of the Union forces. That it will fall into their hands, if it has not already done so, is one of the certainties of the war.

Are the people of the South prepared to see the Union reestablished? We take the ground that the majority of the people are so prepared and would be greatly disappointed, after experiencing four years of distressing ruin, should the prospect which they now have held out to them, to live a peaceful and happy life under the protection of the "Stars and Stripes," be withdrawn from their gate. In North Carolina the popular feeling in favor of the Union seems to increase every day. The members of the House of Commons have gone so far as to agitate the question of returning to the Union in open session. On that point Mr. Hanes recently said that North Carolina had a perfect right to dissolve her allegiance with the Rebel government and enter into a separate negotiation with the United States for peace.[2] Secession, he said, was a failure, and that Sherman, in marching forward through South and North Carolina to co-operate with Grant, would greatly imperil the safety of Lee's army and perhaps effect its capture. The following are his own words:

> Can we prevent the success of our enemy? Can we recover back the majority of the Confederate states which have been taken from us by the armies of the United States? Can we hold our remaining territory? Can we even prevent the fall of Richmond and the capture or destruction of our only remaining army, recruited to the full extent of our white population? Sir, these questions have already been answered by the government itself in the negative by its leading organs, the *Richmond Sentinel* and *Richmond Enquirer,* who have declared the contest to be too unequal to be longer maintained unless we arm our slaves.

He was opposed to arming the slaves. On this subject he said:

> We have ten male slaves at home to one white man. Excite them to frenzy by passing a law to conscript them, and we would have an immediate insurrection, which, to put down, would require the withdrawing of our armies, thus leaving the field to our enemies. If no insurrection took place, they would either go over to the enemy in a body or turn their guns upon us, with bold conscripts for leaders.

On the subject of a reconciliation he said:

> There are those who think, after so much strife and bloodshed, that reconciliation is impossible. This is a mistake. All history refutes the idea. The case of England and Scotland, which was in some respects similar to ours, divided, as they were, into kingdoms and at war for centuries, effected a reconciliation, and Scotland started on a new career of prosperity and glory. Her people, from being one of the most turbulent, have become one of the most quiet and refined, as well as one of the most contented and happy in the world. This is because nature never intended that the island of Great Britain should comprise more than one nation. Such will prove to be our own case.

2. Lewis Hanes, a Whig, was a member of the North Carolina House of Commons (1860, 1864–65).

On the subject of a divided country he said:

> When we take a view of the country which composes the United States, it is difficult to resist the conviction that nature intended it to contain but one great nation. Nature never intended the mighty Mississippi to water or drain but one nation. Close this river to the Northwest by transferring its mouth to another nation, and they become the most completely landlocked country in the world. Were they to consent to this, they would sign their own death warrant. This country can never be divided so as to separate the northwestern states from the Gulf states, without reversing an inexorable law of nature. The only hope I have ever seen in this struggle was that the northwestern states might be induced to join our Confederacy. The manner in which these states voted in the late presidential election has dispelled that hope forever and, in my judgment, has sealed the fate of the Confederacy.

The speech of Mr. Hanes, of which the above are only a few extracts, we set down as the most bold and defiant Union effort in behalf of peace that has come from the South at any time during the war. On hearing that Mr. Hanes had expressed the sentiments as above quoted, Jefferson Davis ordered his arrest, but was prevented from carrying out his design by the action of the North Carolina legislature, which extended over Mr. Hanes the protecting shield of the state. North Carolina is not the only state that is beginning to discuss the question of re-union. We see favorable symptoms in Georgia, which we believe will soon spread to that extent that the demand of the people to place that state back into the old Union will be irresistible. The Rebel press in Virginia observes all these movements and has, until quite lately, written a series of articles to discourage them, but they cannot prevent their progress any more than they can impede the revolutions of the sun.

THE SCARCITY OF WOOD

Editors, *Charleston Courier:*—In your issue of yesterday you speak of the scarcity of wood in the city and say that "at a few miles in the country the wood is cut and piled up in cords, ready to be transported to any given point. It seems to us the owners of this property might do a profitable business by having it brought to the city." Perhaps, Messrs. Editors, you are not aware that the owners of the wood of which you speak have no teams with which to haul it to the city, they having recently undergone the double process of stripping or cleaning out of livestock, etc. First, the retreating or evacuating army took what they wanted, and, second, the occupying army took what was remaining.

You very justly say that owners of wood in the vicinity of Charleston "would find a ready sale for their wood if they would bring it to the city, where it is greatly needed, both by the army and citizens." You can rest assured that if they had the teams or the means wherewith to purchase teams, they would willingly bring in a supply of the much needed article and return with a load of groceries and provisions to their families, as you suggest.

While upon this subject, allow me to make a suggestion or two to our worthy commanding officer, Brigadier General John P. Hatch, who is proverbial for his kindness and is held in high estimation by all who have had occasion to seek his advice, not only on account of his courteous manner, but because in him they find a gentleman who sympathizes with them in their misfortunes, and one who always affords relief if within his power, to wit: If he (General Hatch) could find it convenient, or compatible with his duty, to restore to the farmers in the vicinity of Charleston such animals and wagons as were necessarily taken by the Union forces upon their occupation of the city, he would thus afford great relief to the citizens, generally, by ensuring them a better supply of wood than they now have, as I feel satisfied that upon the restoration of their teams the farmers would gladly haul wood to the city in connection with their other agricultural pursuits. Such a course would not only afford relief upon the perplexing question of a supply of wood, but it would also afford many anxious minds relief upon the still more perplexing question as to a supply of vegetables and provisions for the coming summer and winter. Possibly many of the animals taken have been removed from the city and cannot be readily found; if so, perhaps the department has spare animals which could be loaned to those from whom they have taken. The commanding general can rest assured that there are many farmers in the vicinity of Charleston who really stand in need of such relief as is mentioned above, and who would ever appreciate him who will step forward in their day of distress and assist them to make an honest livelihood for themselves and their families.

A Farmer

NORTH

BOSTON EVENING TRANSCRIPT
March 18, 1865

[UNTITLED]

Sheridan's ravages on the Virginia Central Railroad will effectually prevent the accomplishment of one of the plans of campaign which have been invented for Lee in case he evacuates Richmond. It was supposed he might make a dash northward and attempt to carry the war into Pennsylvania. The destruction of the Charlottesville Railroad and the Virginia Central relieves the North from any fear of an invasion. Sheridan has done his work so thoroughly that Grant could have a force in Lee's front before the latter could traverse half the distance between Richmond and Washington.

The Virginia Central Railroad is a line of communication not new to Sheridan. In the campaign which opened last May, he went over the same route and penetrated to the outer defenses of Richmond. His present raid, including, as it does, the destruction of the James River Canal, the Lynchburg and Charlottesville Road, as well as the Virginia Central, has so far been one of the most devastating, even of his sweeping and desolating incursions. The destruction of property, we are told, was enormous, but the destruction of communications is a greater calamity to Lee than the destruction of property and cannot but have an important influence in the decision of the approaching campaign.

A SPEECH BY PRESIDENT LINCOLN

Washington, 18th—A Rebel flag captured by the 14th Indiana at Fort Anderson was presented to Governor Morton today. During the ceremony, President Lincoln, who was present, spoke as follows:

> Fellow citizens, it will be but a very few words that I shall undertake to say. I was born in Kentucky, raised in Indiana, and lived in Illinois—[*laughter*]—and now I am here, where it is my business to care equally for the good people of all the states. I am glad to see an Indiana regiment on this day able to present the captured flag to the governor of Indiana. [*Applause.*] I am disposed in saying this to make no distinction between the states, for all have done equally well. [*Applause.*]
>
> There are but few views or aspects of this great war upon which I have not said or written something whereby my opinions

might be known. But there is one—the recent attempt of our erring brethren, as they are sometimes called—[*laughter*]—to employ the Negroes to fight for them. I have neither written nor made a speech on that subject, because that was their business, not mine; and if I had mine and I had a wish upon the subject, I had not the power to introduce it or make it effective.

The great question with them was whether the Negro being put into the army will fight for them. I do not know and therefore cannot decide. [*Laughter.*] They ought to know better than we. I have in my lifetime heard many arguments why the Negroes ought to be slaves, but if they fight for those who would keep them in slavery, it will be a better argument than any I have yet heard. [*Laughter and applause.*] He who will fight for that ought to be a slave. [*Applause.*] They have concluded at last to take one out of four of the slaves and put them in the army, and that one out of the four, who will fight to keep the others in slavery, ought to be a slave himself, unless he is killed in a fight. [*Applause.*]

While I have often said that all men ought to be free, yet would I allow these colored persons to be slaves who want to be and, next to them, those white people who argue in favor of making other people slaves. [*Applause.*] I am in favor of giving an appointment to such white men to try it on for themselves. [*Applause.*]

I will say one thing in regard to the Negroes being employed to fight for them. I do know he cannot fight and stay at home and make bread too—[*laughter and applause*]—and as one is about as important as the other to them, I don't care which they do. [*Renewed applause.*] I am rather in favor of having them try the slaves as soldiers. [*Applause.*] They lack one vote of doing that, and I wish I could send my vote over the river so that I might cast it in favor of allowing the Negro to fight—[*applause*]—but they cannot fight and work both.

We must now see the bottom of the enemy's resources. They will stand out as long as they can, and if the Negro will fight for them, they must allow him to fight. They have drawn upon their last branch of resources—[*applause*]—and we can now see the bottom. [*Applause.*] I am glad to see the end so near at hand. [*Applause.*]

I have said now more than I intended, and will therefore bid you good-bye. [*Applause.*]

NEW YORK TRIBUNE
March 18, 1865

LATER FROM SHERIDAN
HIS OPERATIONS TO THE 15TH INSTANT—THE JAMES RIVER CANAL DESTROYED TO GOOCHLAND—15 MILES OF THE VIRGINIA CENTRAL ANNIHILATED—ENORMOUS AMOUNT OF PROPERTY "CONFISCATED"—A SLIGHT BRUSH WITH THE ENEMY

War Department, Washington, March 17, 1865, 3 P.M.

Major General Sheridan reports on the 15th instant, from the bridge of the Richmond and Fredericksburg Railroad across the South Anna River, that, having destroyed the James River Canal as far to the east as Goochland, he marched up to the Virginia Central Railroad at Tollsville and destroyed it down to Beaver Dam Station, totally destroying fifteen miles of the road. General Custer was then sent to Ashland and General Devin to the South Anna bridges, all of which have been destroyed. General Sheridan says the amount of property destroyed in his march is enormous. The enemy attempted to prevent the burning of the Central Railroad bridge over the South Anna, but the 5th United States Cavalry charged up to the bridge, and about thirty men dashed across on foot, driving off the enemy and capturing three pieces of artillery—20-pounder Parrotts.

C. A. Dana, Assistant Secretary of War

FROM CHARLESTON
OPENING OF THE SCHOOLS

From Our Special Correspondent

Charleston, South Carolina, March 4, 1865

The great event of today—the inauguration of two workingmen, a farm laborer and a tailor, as the future rulers of a mighty people—was fitly celebrated by Charleston, the conquered stronghold of the feudal spirit in America, by the reopening of the public schools of the city for all the children thereof, without distinction of rank or race, of color or creed. The Morris Street School was selected as being the best preserved and the largest for the first assemblage of the children, and it was not thought that there would be any immediate necessity for opening the others. But by nine o'clock the first and third stories were so crowded with colored children that it was impossible to classify them, and in the second story, which was exclusively appropriated for the whites, there were over two hundred. Between 300 and 400 white children have reported their names, but some have been kept away today by the report, industriously circulated by the enemies of free schools and by the old Rebel teachers, that colored women would be put over them as their instructors. There were 1,000 colored children by an actual but incomplete count, and at least 1,500 have promised to attend before the close of another week. As this outpouring of children was so much larger than was expected, it became necessary to announce that another school building would be opened on Monday, when the classification will be completed and the system of instruction commenced.

Addresses were made to the children in the different wards by the Reverend Mr. Newcombe, Freedmen's Aid Society; Chaplain Lynch, 50th Massachusetts; and Mr. Kane O'Donnell of Philadelphia.[3] They were taught some school hymns, and sang various songs, and the exercises were closed by a short prayer, which all the freed children slowly and distinctly repeated after the superintendent: "God bless—Abraham Lincoln—our president—and liberator."

Many hearts were touched by the sight of more than five hundred of these little children, all so lately slaves, with clasped hands and closed eyes, asking God to bless the instrument of their freedom on the day of his reinstallment in authority, and in the city which was the first to rebel against it. And in all the wide land, there were no more sincere prayers offered up for our president.

So the thing is done. The loyal white people—the Irish and German population—have shown that they are quite willing to let their children attend the same school building with the loyal blacks, although it is true, also, that no attempt to unite them in the same rooms or classes would have been tolerated at this time. But in the playground, white and black boys joined in the same sports—as they do in the public streets—and there can be no doubt that, now that this great step has been made, all the prejudice against equal educational advantages will speedily vanish. And, indeed, it is the veriest hypocrisy in the city where every old family has aided in obliterating all complexional distinctions by mingling their blood with that of their slaves. In the rooms in which the colored children assembled, there were many pupils with clear blue eyes, pure white skins, long, silky hair without a single kink—and

3. Concerned citizens established Freedmen's Aid Societies in major cities—Boston, New York, Philadelphia, and Cincinnati, among others—to assist emancipated slaves. These nongovernmental organizations were not connected with the Freedman's Bureau, which was established in March 1865 by the U.S. government for the same purpose.

yet they were classed with the Negro population by the former rules of this city.

The white children were told that no insult to the colored pupils would be permitted, and they expressed themselves not only willing but glad that everyone had now a chance to be taught.

The Freedmen's Aid Societies will furnish teachers.

The old teachers and directors (who did much to incite and keep alive the rebellion here by causing the children to sing insurrectionary airs) are doing their utmost to have the instruction of the colored children brought to an end. But their representations have no influence at post headquarters, and only General Gillmore has the necessary authority to grant their dastardly and arrogant desires. I will not do that officer the wrong to suppose for one moment that he would be instrumental in turning out the truly loyal children of the city in order to conciliate men whose hands are red with the blood of our brothers. But the Rip Van Winkles here do not know the times we live in, and act and talk exactly as if the Fugitive Slave Law were in full force and they could browbeat the truth still, as in the bad old times. They will wake up and find their mistake by and by, and scenes like these will help them to know that this is the nineteenth century.

The colored people are arranging to have a grand procession in honor of the arrival of their liberators. No public demonstration of satisfaction has been made by the white loyalists yet, and an attempt to organize a brigade of them has been abandoned as impracticable. The officer who attempted to raise it declared that he found that "the best of the loyalists of Charleston would be the worst kind of Copperheads up North," although he did not blame them as he did their erring Northern brethren, because they had no opportunity to know any better.

The Christian Commission has furnished through its agent, Reverend Mr. Spencer, all the schoolbooks that are needed.

Berwick

APRIL 15, 1865

SOUTH

RICHMOND DAILY DISPATCH
April 1, 1865

[*Publication of the* Dispatch *was suspended on April 3. The day before, the news of the fall of Petersburg had reached Richmond, and in anticipation of Federal occupation, the Confederate government had ordered all public property in the city to be set afire, triggering a conflagration that reduced much of Richmond to ashes. The following articles are drawn from the April 1 issue, the only Saturday issue published that month.*]

THE RICHMOND AND PETERSBURG LINES

All continues, and seems likely to continue, quiet on the north side of the James River. The enemy are expending their activity on our right.

Immediately at Petersburg, in front of General Gordon's lines, there has been no stir since the *feu d'enfer* of Wednesday night.[4] The performances of that night are quite sufficient to last a considerable length of time. The heroes of that dark and sulphurous but bloodless field can afford to rest on their laurels for the present. General Lee, in his official report of this affair, which we received late Thursday night and published yesterday, says: "General Gordon reports that the enemy, at 11:00 P.M. yesterday, advanced against a part of his line, defended by Brigadier General Lewis, but was repulsed."

We have quoted this dispatch to call attention to the fact that, whereas it says the enemy advanced at eleven o'clock Wednesday night, the cannonade, as everyone in Petersburg and Richmond who is not stone-deaf knows, began before ten o'clock and was at its fiercest before eleven. The report to the contrary notwithstanding, we cannot help adhering to our opinion, expressed yesterday, that there was no attack at all. Of course, we do not think our officers willfully misrepresented the case, but that in the shadow of that darkest of nights they were mistaken. We look with interest to the Yankee account of the affair, which we will receive tomorrow. We should not be surprised if they have a flaming account of a repulse of the Rebels, with the usual "horrible slaughter."

4. *feu d'enfer:* French, "hellfire."

AFFAIRS ON THE RIGHT

The enemy have pushed a heavy column beyond our right, southwest of Petersburg, but we have heard nothing from that quarter that we can rely upon as authentic since General Lee's report of Thursday, published yesterday, in which he says "there was skirmishing near Dinwiddie Courthouse yesterday [Wednesday] without decisive result."

The *Petersburg Express* of yesterday says Grant's long-contemplated movement to extend his left toward the Southside Railroad has begun and that he has forty thousand men on the field.

We make a summary of the *Express*'s account of the recent operations on our right:

On Tuesday night the enemy advanced up the Military Road to within one mile of the Boydton Plank Road, threw up entrenchments on either side, built a large fort at the Lewis House, and pushed forward a body of troops to within a few hundred yards of the plank road.

On Wednesday this column was attacked by our troops and driven back, our vanguard entering and for a time holding the fort at the Lewis House. Not receiving immediate or sufficient support, the fort was yielded. After driving the enemy thus far with beautiful success, our troops fell back a short distance and offered battle, but the Yankees declined to accept it and failed even to make any pursuit.

The fighting in the vicinity of Hatcher's Run on Wednesday afternoon was quite severe for a while, and the Yankees suffered heavily.

Yesterday morning the enemy's cavalry were ascertained to be approaching the Five Forks, on the White Oak Road, leading from the plank road, near Burgess's Mill, across to the Southside Railroad. This point is about midway between these two points. This cavalry column had passed around our works and was confidently making for the railroad. But a lion was found in their path in the person of General Fitz Lee and his brave troopers. Heavy firing was heard near the Five Forks subsequently, and from the direction it took at a late hour, it is believed that battle was joined and the enemy driven.

Just beyond Burgess's Mill, and to the southeast, skirmishing commenced early in the day. Here, Grant had his infantry massed and his flanks supported by cavalry, and here the heaviest fighting occurred. The discharges of artillery and the volleys of musketry could be distinctly heard in the city—the former, at times, very heavy and the latter, with occasional intervals, almost incessant. While we have the gratifying intelligence that all was well with us, we are yet unable to give any official account of the fighting. We held our own, and the enemy gained no advantage. Between 2:00 and 4:00 P.M., the heaviest fighting occurred, and at sunset the firing still continued, but was changed both in direction and severity. It was evident from the direction of the firing late in the afternoon and that of an earlier hour that the enemy had either been driven back or had changed the point of attack—most probably the latter.

It is stated that some 500 or 600 prisoners were captured. Their condition was pitiable. They were covered with mud from head to heels.

Generals Grant, Meade, and Sheridan were on the field, or in its vicinity, during the day. All the prisoners and several deserters who came over to us assert this fact.

Both prisoners and deserters state that the enemy's intention is to strike the Southside Railroad—probably at the junction. These statements are so uniform as to cause some credence to be placed in them. The prisoners state their loss to be very heavy.

It is supposed that the battle will be renewed today unless the enemy entrenches and assumes the defensive.

ANOTHER ACCOUNT

Yesterday evening's *Whig* contains the following telegram:

> *Petersburg, Virginia, 30th—10:00 P.M.*—A heavy fight has been progressing all day in Dinwiddie, near Hatcher's Run, eight miles from Petersburg.
>
> Nothing official has been received here, but reports, up to five o'clock, deemed reliable, state that three furious assaults were repulsed.
>
> At half past two o'clock the enemy came up in overwhelming numbers and drove Bushrod Johnson's division one mile and a half.
>
> The Confederates were then reinforced, which turned the tide of battle. We then drove the enemy, with great slaughter, to and beyond their original position of the morning.
>
> The ground is strewn with their dead and dying, and seven hundred prisoners are reported sent to the rear.
>
> The affair of last night, for roar of cannon and musketry, which lasted two hours, exceeded anything ever heard in this section.
>
> It turns out today that both belligerents conceived the idea that they were being charged behind their works, when, in fact,

neither had left their entrenchments; hence the prodigal expenditure of ammunition.

It was one of the most novel events of this remarkable war.

The loss was small on our side and is now not supposed to be large with the enemy.

All quiet on that front today.

FROM EAST TENNESSEE

The latest advices from east Tennessee are that the advance guard of Thomas's army were threatening Bristol on Wednesday and it was thought likely they might have occupied the place yesterday. Some skirmishing with the enemy's cavalry has occurred west of Bristol.

Yankee raiders are reported to be advancing toward Marion, in Smyth County, Virginia, and toward Salisbury, North Carolina.

FROM NORTH CAROLINA

The Raleigh papers report all quiet in that vicinity on Wednesday. There was not even a rumor from the front.

CHARLESTON DAILY COURIER
April 15, 1865

FORT SUMTER

The historic old flag was yesterday replanted in Fort Sumter. The day, the occasion, and the event mark a new era for South Carolina and hereafter will be among the most memorable in her annals.

At an early hour in the morning our streets were made lively by crowds of citizens wending their way along the principal streets to the wharves. National flags were to be seen waving from numerous private as well as the public buildings. Vehicles of every description were in great demand. Crowds of army and navy officers as well as citizens were at the hotel waiting for carriages to convey them to the different steamers upon which they had been invited to take passage to the fort. A band of music in front of the hotel discoursed most charming music and made that rendezvous doubly attractive.

About six o'clock the arrival of the steamer *Diamond,* General Gillmore's flagship, with that officer and his staff, together with a number of distinguished visitors on board, was announced by a salute. Long before ten o'clock the wharves and streets leading to them, along which it was supposed the visitors would pass, were thronged by the crowd, anxious to see the distinguished strangers. All the vessels in the harbor were decorated with colors, and made a gay appearance.

The following order of Major General Gillmore for the carrying out of the president's intentions was issued:

Headquarters, Department of the South
Hilton Head, South Carolina, April 10, 1865
General Order, Number 41

Friday next, the 14th instant, will be the fourth anniversary of the capture of Fort Sumter by the Rebels. A befitting celebration on that day, in honor of its reoccupation by the national forces, has been ordered by the president, in pursuance of which Brevet Major General Robert Anderson, United States Army, will restore to its original place on the fort the identical flag which, after an honorable and gallant defense, he was compelled to lower to the insurgents in South Carolina in April 1861.

The ceremonies for the occasion will commence with prayer at thirty minutes past eleven A.M.

At noon precisely the flag will be raised and saluted with one hundred guns from Fort Sumter, and with a national salute from Fort Moultrie and Battery Bee on Sullivans Island, Fort Putnam on Morris Island, and Fort Johnson on James Island, it being eminently appropriate that the places which were so conspicuous in the inauguration of the rebellion should take a part not less prominent in this national rejoicing over the restoration of the national authority.

After the salutes, the Reverend Henry Ward Beecher will deliver an address.

The ceremonies will close with prayer and a benediction.

Colonel Steward L. Woodford, chief of staff, under such verbal instructions as he may receive, is hereby charged with the details of the celebration, comprising all the arrangements that it may be necessary to make for the accommodation of the orator of the day and the comfort and safety of the invited guests from the army and navy and from civil life.

By command of Major General Q. A. Gillmore.
W.L.M. Burger, Assistant Adjutant General

Admiral Dahlgren issued the following order:

Flagship *Philadelphia*
Charleston Harbor, South Carolina, April 13, 1865
General Order, Number 36, Third Yearly Series

The public prints announce the surrender of the Rebel army, under General Lee, to the commanding general of the United States army.

As the ceremony ordered for the formal restoration of the Union flag to Sumter will occupy the greater part of tomorrow, it only remains to give the rest of the day to some appropriate recognition of an event which seems to leave no further power of effective resistance to the rebellion.

The vessels of the squadron will, therefore, dress ship, in full colors, tomorrow at 8:00 A.M., and at the same time every vessel will fire a national salute of twenty-one guns.

Twenty-one guns will also be fired at sunset, when the flags are hauled down.

John A. Dahlgren,
Rear Admiral Commanding,
South Atlantic Blockading Squadron

NORTH

BOSTON EVENING TRANSCRIPT
April 15, 1865

THE MURDER OF THE PRESIDENT

It was with a strange thrill of mingled surprise, grief, horror, and exasperation that the American people heard this morning that assassination had become a political power and had struck at the most honored life in the land. The crime was so new to our politics, and was so abhorrent to all our ideas and feelings, that its commission came upon the public mind like a thunderbolt from a clear sky. The horror of the deed was all the more deepened by the fact that its victim was the kindliest and most magnanimous of great magistrates and seemed to fall a martyr to his own goodness of heart.

There can be no doubt that this crime had its motive in political fanaticism and that it will terribly react on the faction in whose service it was performed. It was as stupid as it was wicked; for it will deprive treason of the little remnant of sympathy which it retained abroad, and will associate the government of Davis with the pistol of Booth. No assassination of the head of a government ever benefited the cause it was intended to avenge or advance; and the assassination of two such men as the president and secretary of state, both well-known as the calmest and most moderate of statesmen, and least disposed to suffer passion to interpose the least obstacle to peace, seals the death warrant of the Confederacy and forbids all compromise with its leaders. The cause that animates the hand of the assassin must abide by the stern decrees of justice and law. Clemency lies murdered in the Capitol.

The immediate plotters of this scheme of assassination doubtless had no direct official connection with the Confederate government, for the members of that government could not be so fooled by fanaticism as not to know that the assassination of Mr. Lincoln and Mr. Seward would be even a greater blunder than crime. But what associates the act with them is the brutality and hatred against the North with which they have filled the hearts of the Southern people. The satanic sentiments they have inculcated have their legitimate outcome in the deed at which the nation now stands aghast. The cool malignity of thoughtful treason appears all the more diabolical, now that it has touched springs of influence which have resulted in the mad act of blind and brutal assassination.

THE MOURNING IN WASHINGTON— THE PRESIDENT'S BODY REMOVED TO THE WHITE HOUSE—SECRETARY SEWARD AND SON BOTH IN A CRITICAL CONDITION—GUILT OF JOHN WILKES BOOTH AND HIS ACCOMPLICES

Special Dispatch to the *Boston Transcript*

Washington, 15th—All business has been suspended, and the city is draped in mourning. The excitement is intense. Travel has been suspended between Washington and Baltimore. Only the United States mails are allowed to come into the city. Every point is guarded by military, and large corps of police are on the alert.

President Lincoln's body has just been removed to the White House.

Both Secretary Seward and his son Frederick are still in a very critical condition. It is very doubtful whether either recovers. The skull of Frederick Seward is ascertained to be broken in two places.

It has been definitely ascertained that the perpetrator of the horrible deed was John Wilkes Booth. It appears that he had a number of accomplices.

From correspondence found in Booth's room, and other strong circumstantial evidence, the assassinations were to have taken place before the 4th of March, but from some cause or other their courage failed them at that time.

From the direction in which Booth's horse was discovered, it is pretty certain that he has made his escape into Virginia, having crossed the Potomac from some point in Maryland.

Kappa

NEW YORK TRIBUNE
April 15, 1865

THE PRESIDENT SHOT—
SECRETARY SEWARD ATTACKED

First Dispatch

To the Associated Press

Washington, 14th—The president was shot in a theater tonight and perhaps mortally wounded.

Second Dispatch

To Editors:—Our Washington agent orders the dispatch about the president "stopped." Nothing is said about the truth or falsity of the dispatch.

Third Dispatch

Special Dispatch to the *New York Tribune*

The president was just shot at Ford's Theater. The ball entered his neck. It is not known whether the wound is mortal. Intense excitement.

Fourth Dispatch

Special Dispatch to the *New York Tribune*

The president expired at a quarter to twelve.

Fifth Dispatch

To the Associated Press

Washington, 15th, 12:30 A.M.—The president was shot in a theater tonight and is, perhaps, mortally wounded.

The president is not expected to live through the night. He was shot at a theater.

Secretary Seward was also assassinated.

No arteries were cut.

Particulars soon.

Sixth Dispatch

Special Dispatch to the *New York Tribune*

Washington, 14th—Like a clap of thunder out of clear sky spread the announcement that President Lincoln was shot while sitting in his box at Ford's Theater. The city is wild with excitement. A gentleman who was present thus describes the event: At about ten-thirty, in the midst of one of the acts, a pistol shot was heard, and at the same instant a man leaped upon the stage from the same box occupied by the president, brandished a long knife, and shouted, *"Sic semper tyrannis!"*—then rushed to the rear of the scenes and out of the back door of the theater. So sudden was the whole thing that most persons in the theater supposed it a part of the play, and it was some minutes before the fearful tragedy was comprehended. The man was pursued, however, by someone connected with the theater to the outer door and seen to mount a horse and ride rapidly away. A regiment of cavalry have started in all directions with orders to arrest every man found on horseback. Scarce had the news of this horror been detailed when couriers came from Secretary Seward's, announcing that he also had been assassinated. The following are the authentic particulars.

Seventh Dispatch

Special Dispatch to the *New York Tribune*

Washington, 14th—The president attended Ford's Theater tonight, and about ten o'clock an assassin entered his private box and shot him in the back of the head. The ball lodged in his head, and he is now lying insensible in a house opposite the theater. No hopes are entertained of his recovery. Laura Keene claims to have recognized the assassin as the actor John Wilkes Booth. A feeling of gloom like a pall has settled on the city.

About the same hour a horseman rode up to Secretary Seward's and, dismounting, announced that he had a prescription to deliver to the secretary in person. Major Seward and Miss Seward were with their father at the time. Being admitted, the assassin delivered the pretended prescription to the secretary in bed and immediately cut his throat from ear to ear. Fortunately the jugular vein was not severed, and it is possible Mr. Seward may survive. Secretary Stanton was undisturbed at his residence. Thus far, no other murderous demonstrations are reported. It is deemed providential that General Grant left tonight for New Jersey. He was publicly announced to be present at the theater with the president. Ten thousand rumors are afloat, and the most intense and painful excitement pervades the city.

Eighth Dispatch

Special Dispatch to the *New York Tribune*

Washington, 14th—The assassin is said to have gained entrance to the president's box by sending in his card requesting an interview. The box was occupied by Mrs. Lincoln and Colonel Parker of General Grant's staff. The villain drew his pistol across Mrs. Lincoln's shoulder and fired. Colonel Parker sprang up and seized the assassin, but he wrested himself from his grip and sprang down upon the stage as described. His spur caught in the American flag as he descended, and threw him at length. He unloosed the spur and dashed to the rear, brandishing his knife and revolver.

Ninth Dispatch

To the Associated Press

Washington, 14th—President Lincoln and wife, with other friends, this evening visited Ford's Theater for the purpose of witnessing the performance of *Our American Cousin*.

It was announced in the papers that General Grant would also be present, but he took the late train of cars for New Jersey.

The theater was densely crowded, and everybody seemed delighted with the scene before them. During the third act, and while there was a temporary pause for one of the actors to enter, a sharp report of a pistol was heard, which merely attracted attention but suggested nothing serious, until a man rushed to the front of the president's box, waving a long dagger in his right hand and exclaiming, *"Sic semper tyrannis,"* and immediately leaped from the box, which was on the second tier, to the stage beneath and ran across to the opposite side, making his escape amid the bewilderment of the audience, from the rear of the theater, and, mounting a horse, fled.

The screams of Mrs. Lincoln first disclosed the fact to the audience that the president had been shot, when all present rose to their feet, rushing toward the stage, many exclaiming, "Hang him, hang him!"

The excitement was of the wildest possible description, and of course there was an abrupt termination to the theatrical performance.

There was a rush toward the president's box, when cries were heard: "Stand back and give him air." "Has anyone stimulants?" On a hasty examination, it was found that the president had been shot through the head, above and back of the temporal bone, and that some of the brains were oozing out.

He was removed to a private house opposite to the theater and the surgeon general of the army and other surgeons sent for to attend to his condition.

On an examination of the private box, blood was discovered on the back of the cushioned rocking chair on which the president had been sitting, also on the partition and on the floor. A common single-barreled pocket pistol was found on the carpet.

A military guard was placed in front of the private residence to which the president had been conveyed. An immense crowd was in front of it, all deeply anxious to learn the condition of the president. It had been previously announced that the wound was mortal, but all hoped otherwise. The shock to the community was terrible.

At midnight the Cabinet, together with Messrs. Sumner, Colfax, and Farnsworth, Judge Curtis, Governor Oglesby, General Meigs, Colonel Hay, and a few personal friends, with Surgeon General Barnes and his immediate assistants, were around his bedside.

The president was in a state of syncope, totally insensible and breathing slowly. The blood oozed from the wound at the back of his head. The surgeons exhausted every possible effort of medicinal skill, but all hope was gone.

The president and Mrs. Lincoln did not start for the theater until eight-thirty. Speaker Colfax was at the White House at the time, and the president stated to him that he was going.

Although Mrs. Lincoln had not been well, because the papers had announced that General Grant and they were to be present, and as General Grant had gone north, he did not wish the audience to be dispirited.

He went with apparent reluctance and urged Mr. Colfax to go with him, but that gentleman had made other engagements and, with Mr. Ashman of Massachusetts, bade him good night.

Tenth Dispatch

Special Dispatch to the *New York Tribune*

Washington, 15th, 1:00 A.M.—One of our reporters is just in from the presidential mansion, who says an orderly reports the president still breathing, but beyond all probable recovery. The circumstances of Secretary Seward's assassination are thus narrated by a member of his household: A man on horseback rode to the secretary's house, rang the bell, and told the servant attending upon the door that he had a prescription from Dr. Verdi, Mr. Seward's attending physician, for the suffering secretary, which he must deliver in person. The servant took him upstairs and ushered him into Mr. Frederick Seward's room, where he delivered the same message but was assured by young Mr. Seward that he could not see his father. He then started to retire, when he turned with an inaudible mutter and leveled a blow at Frederick with a slung-shot. A scuffle then ensued, in which the assassin used his knife and very seriously wounded the assistant secretary; then, rushing by him, he passed through the door into the father's room.[5] He found the secretary in the charge of his male nurse, and with an instantaneous rush he drew his knife and cut the secretary's throat from ear to ear; then, plunging his knife into the nurse, he darted out, when he encountered young Major Seward, who seized him and endeavored to detain him, without knowing the horrid tragedy he had enacted.[6] He again used his knife and billy, but was most eager to escape, and, as soon as he had cut himself loose, fled to the outer door, mounting his horse, and was off before the inmates could give anything of an alarm. In fact, the wonderful suddenness with which both acts of brutality were enacted is perhaps the most surprising feature of this dire national calamity.

Eleventh Dispatch

Special Dispatch to the *New York Tribune*

Washington, 14th, 1:15 A.M.—The president is slowly dying. The brain is slowly oozing through the ball hole in his forehead. He is, of course, insensible. There is an occasional lifting of his hand and heavy stertorous breathing; that's all.

Mrs. Lincoln and her two sons are in a room of the house opposite to Ford's Theater, where the president was taken, and adjoining that where he is lying. Mr. Sumner is seated at the head of the bed. Secretaries Stanton, Welles, Dennison, Usher, and McCulloch and Mr. Speed are in the room. A large number of surgeons, generals, and personal family friends of Mr. Lincoln fill the house. All are in tears. Andy Johnson is here. He was in bed in his room at the Kirkwood when the assassination was committed. He was immediately apprised of the event, and got up. The precaution was taken to provide a guard of soldiers for him, and these were at his door before the news was well through the avenue. Captain Rathbone of Albany was in the box with the president. He was slightly wounded.

We give the above dispatches in the order in which they reached us, the first having been received a little before midnight, for we know that

5. Frederick Seward served as assistant secretary of state.
6. Augustus Seward was a major in the Union army.

every line, every letter will be read with the intensest interest. In the sudden shock of a calamity so appalling, we can do little else than give such details of the murder of the president as have reached us. Sudden death is always overwhelming. Assassination of the humblest of men is always frightfully startling; when the head of thirty million people is hurried into eternity by the hand of a murderer—that head a man so good, so wise, so noble, as Abraham Lincoln, the chief magistrate of a nation in the condition of ours at this moment—the sorrow and the shock are too great for many words. There are none in all this broad land today who love their country, who wish well to their race, that will not bow down in profound grief at the event it has brought upon us. For once all party rancor will be forgotten, and no right-thinking man can hear of Mr. Lincoln's death without accepting it as a national calamity. We can give in these, its first moments, no thought of the future. God, in his inscrutable providence, has thus visited the nation; the future we must leave by Him.

Later.—The accounts are confused and contradictory. One dispatch announces that the president died at 12:30 P.M. Another, an hour later, states that he is still living but dying slowly. We go to press without knowing the exact truth, but presume there is not the slightest ground for hope. Mr. Seward and his son are both seriously wounded, but were not killed. But there can be little hope that the secretary can rally with this additional and frightful wound.

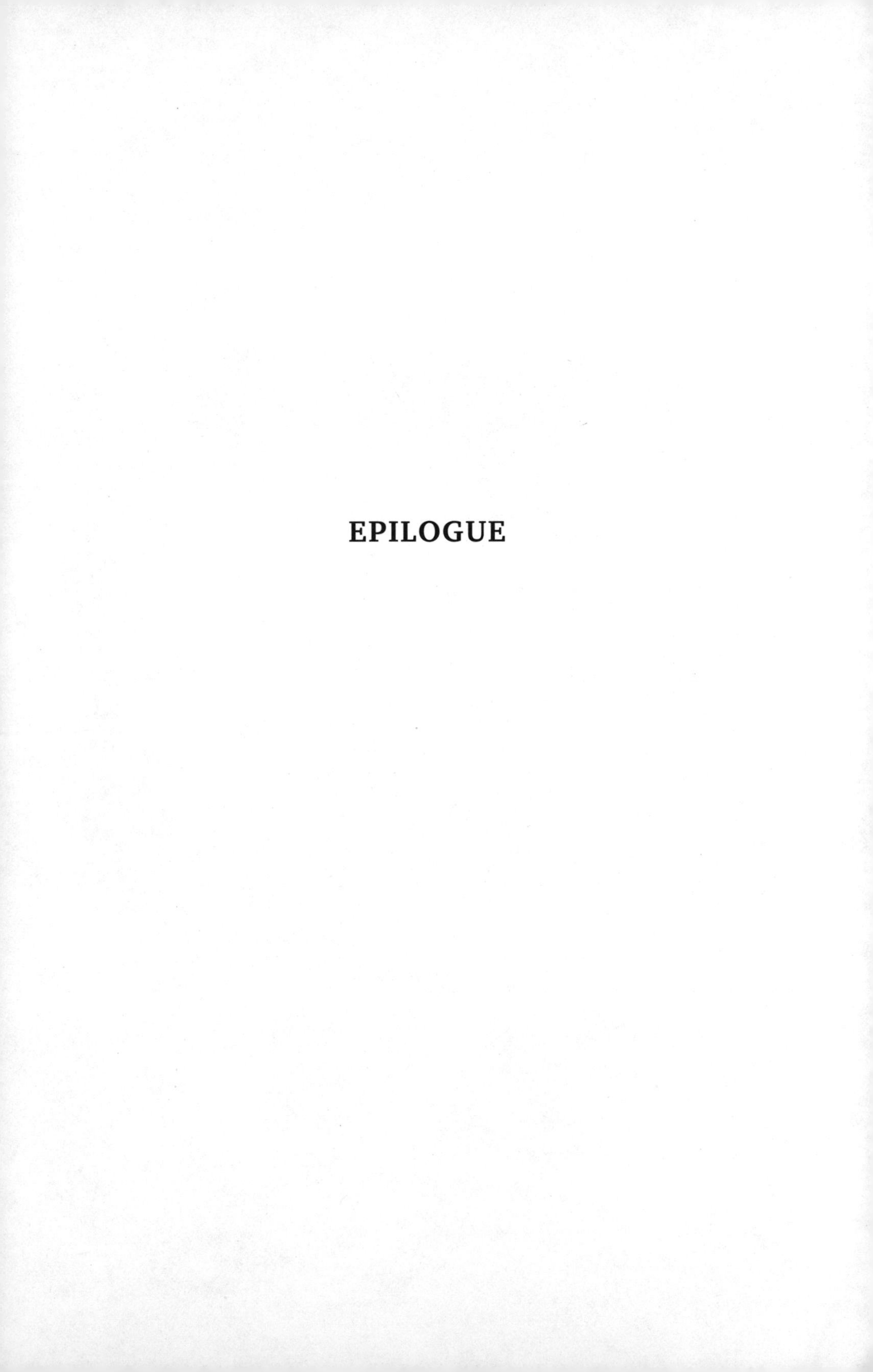

EPILOGUE

TIMELINE

April 26: Lincoln's assassin, John Wilkes Booth, is cornered and killed in a barn near Bowling Green, Virginia.

May 10: Jefferson Davis is captured near Irwinsville, Georgia. Because he seems to have grabbed his wife's raincoat by mistake in dim light, rumors fly that he attempted escape disguised as a woman, in full petticoats.

May 23–24: The Army of the Potomac conducts a two-day grand review for the residents of the nation's capital.

May 29: President Andrew Johnson grants a general amnesty and pardon to most persons who participated, directly or indirectly, in the rebellion, except high-ranking military and government officials and the wealthy, who must apply individually. All property, except slaves, will be restored, upon approval.

May–June: Various Confederate army forces give up arms. The last significant group, a regiment of Native Americans in Oklahoma Territory, surrenders on June 23.

June 31: The conspirators in the Lincoln assassination are convicted in military court. Four are hanged on July 7.

November 6: The Confederate raider *Shenandoah* surrenders to British officials at Liverpool, England. It is the last Confederate military force to surrender.

December 18: Approved by twenty-seven states, the Thirteenth Amendment to the Constitution is ratified, abolishing slavery and involuntary servitude.

December 24: Six Confederate veterans meet in Pulaski, Tennessee, and form the Ku Klux Klan.

1866: Edward Pollard, the former editor of the *Richmond Examiner,* writes in his book *The Lost Cause,* "The Confederates have gone out of this war with the proud, secret, deathless, dangerous consciousness that they are the better men. . . . The war did not decide Negro equality; it did not decide Negro suffrage; it did not decide states' rights." Pollard exhorts his readers to join him in pursuing the "true cause" of the rebellion—white supremacy—which is to be achieved by keeping the freed slave "in a condition where his political influence is as indifferent as when he was a slave."

MAY 20, 1865

SOUTH

[*The fire of April 2–3, 1865, in Richmond consumed the offices of the* Dispatch, *and publication was suspended during the period covered in the Epilogue. Articles of the* Dispatch, *drawn from the December issues, are presented at the end of this section.*]

CHARLESTON DAILY COURIER
May 20, 1865

FOREIGN RELATIONS

Now that the great struggle for the life of the nation is over and our armies are about being disbanded, many restless, eager spirits are anxiously inquiring what they shall do in the future. The excitement of a camp life has dissatisfied them with the quiet avocations of a business life, and already we see many making preparations to join the Liberal party of Mexico, while others are hoping for a war with England. At the first glance, both might seem reasonable and just, to relieve the oppression of one and punish the perfidy of the other.

But the sober-thinking man can readily see that a war with a foreign power would at this period be unfortunate. We have to recover and recuperate our energies and resources after the long and desperate struggle we have undergone. Internal trade and commerce have to be reestablished; a reconstruction of state governments in the South, a settlement of many social and political points, and a careful blending of conflicting elements so as to produce harmony have to be made. This alone will be enough to occupy our attention for some years, while those who desire a more restless, exciting life will find their element in the territories of the far West, in the gold regions, or establishment of settlements along the contemplated line of the great Pacific Railroad; while a filibustering expedition to Mexico would compromise us and involve us in difficulty with foreign powers.

The death of the Mexican empire is but a question of time. Daily are the Liberals gaining strength and power, and soon will, unaided, drive the invaders from the soil. With our power and prestige and the well-known defense of the Monroe Doctrine by President Johnson, France will not dare to support the empire—the cost would be too great.

That a war with England would be a popular war at this time no one will doubt, but would the great principle of liberty be advanced by such a war? England and America being the two exponents of free speech, free press, and free governments, it would seem that a tacit moral alliance would be more to the advancement of republican ideas and principles, as must be plain to all thinking men.

The United States have established themselves as the first military power of the world, both on land and at sea. Let it rather be our province to act as peacemaker and gradually pave the way for more liberal forms of government. We shall always be respected and feared and, in a congress of nations, could act as arbitrator of all questions. This is a more enviable and desirable position than that of the conqueror of nations. All can easily find employment in developing the resources of our own land that have been brought to light in the last few years. Cities are to be rebuilt and railroads to be opened and the ravages of an internal war to be removed.

So far, the government has been able, without compromising our dignity, to preserve friendly relations with all foreign powers. Let not the acts of party and unthinking men disturb those amicable relations at this important period. Now that the bayonet has finished its task, statesmanship and diplomacy must complete the work. The old and oft-quoted phrase, "Time sets all things right," is a living truth. Let us have patience, and ere this generation shall pass away, we shall see a flourishing sister republic on either side of us—a Mexican republic and a Canadian republic. It may be sooner, it may be later, but it will surely come to pass.

REMOVAL OF THE RESTRICTIONS ON TRADE

As will be seen by the communication from the general agent of the Treasury Department, which we publish this morning, only cotton is allowed to be purchased by agents on account of the United States. All other products of the states included in the president's proclamation of April 20, 1865, may be shipped to the loyal states on payment by the shippers of the internal revenue tax. Persons having taken the oath of allegiance are at liberty to receive goods, not contraband of war, without restrictions as to quantity. All local special agents of the Treasury are to be dismissed, there being no duties for them to transact. This settles the questions as to trade pursuits which heretofore have not been fully understood by the business community. Under this new incentive we shall doubtless see in a very short time a heavy amount of goods of various kinds coming into this port.

NORTH

BOSTON EVENING TRANSCRIPT
May 20, 1865

GENERAL SHERIDAN'S NEW COMMAND—RECALL OF GENERAL BANKS—ARRIVAL OF JEFFERSON DAVIS AT FORTRESS MONROE—NEW EVIDENCE AGAINST DAVIS IN THE CONSPIRACY

Washington, 20th—The appointment of General Sheridan to a Trans-Mississippi Department necessitated the recall of General Banks and materially limits the department of General Pope. Orders for the same will be issued today.

A dispatch just received announces the arrival of Jefferson Davis at Fortress Monroe. The government has not yet decided what disposition will be made of him.

Governor Vance of North Carolina was brought here today.

Government has just received additional information implicating Jefferson Davis in the assassination conspiracy.

Secretary Seward is expected to testify today.

Kappa

A SOUTHERN PATRIOT—UNION MEN STILL IN DANGER

Raleigh, North Carolina, 15th—James C. Johnson, one of the wealthiest men of the South, aged 80 years, died near Edenton on the 12th instant.

He disinherited all his relatives because they deserted him (a Union man) and espoused the Rebel cause. At the outbreak of the rebellion he told his slaves—numbering near one thousand—the war would free them and they could go or remain. It was he who discharged Henry Clay's indebtedness of thirty thousand dollars, unknown to the latter.

Many of Johnston's paroled men are under the impression, by a report that France has recognized the Confederacy, that they can prevent Union men holding meetings. A Northern man will not be safe in the South after the withdrawal of the Union troops, unless Negroes are used for garrison duty.

SHOT BY A NEGRO SOLDIER—MORE REBELS SURRENDERED

Louisville, Kentucky, 19th—Mr. McGrath was shot and killed in Shelbyville this morning by a Negro soldier of Captain Kirt's company. McGrath and two or three others violently objected to Negro troops' occupying the United States rendezvous, and in this altercation the shooting took place.

The *Nashville Union* says the Rebel general B. Hill has turned over all his men—some seven hundred—with their arms and horses, to the United States. The men were paroled.

NEW YORK TRIBUNE
May 20, 1865

EMPLOYMENT FOR THE SOLDIERS

It will not be many days before the soldiers of the armies of the Union will be coming home. Next week is the great review in Washington, speedily after which, it is understood, the armies of the Potomac, of the Tennessee, of Georgia, and the rest will be mustered out of service—their long toil honorably over, their new life at home to begin. What shall that life be?

We press that question upon the public. What shall the future of our soldiers be? They come back to us after three or four years of military life, their old occupations long since forsaken, their prospects sacrificed to the patriotic zeal that called them into the field. The question for us is whether we will allow the men who have saved the country to suffer because they saved it. It is a practical question and appeals to practical men for its answer. To a considerable extent, it is a question not of intent or of goodwill—for we should all say instantly that the soldiers *ought* to be cared for—but of method, of means, of good sense, and of organization. It is a question how we will endeavor to recognize the claim of the soldiers on the country—how we shall receive them on their return, how we shall take them back into civil and peaceful society, what employment we shall provide them, and what effort we shall make to reinstate them into positions not less advantageous than those they occupied before the war.

The Sanitary Commission is trying to answer these questions. It has established a Bureau of Employment for Disabled and Honorably Discharged Soldiers. The purpose of this bureau is to bring employers and those seeking employment together, and without charge to either. Its office, at 35 Chambers Street in this city, is meant to be a rendezvous for returning soldiers, who may there register their names with a memorandum of the kind of employment they desire and with such other information as employers will naturally expect. Those wishing workmen of any kind are invited to register their applications, stating wages, locality, prospect of permanent employment, and especially whether their work can be done by disabled men and what sort of physical disability does not disqualify a soldier for the specified occupation. Those who are interested will find more precise information at the bureau itself and from the circulars which it distributes.

We heartily commend this and all kindred efforts as likely to be useful and as indispensable, but we by no means stop there. While urging due attention to these facilities—these means of help which make it easy for those desiring to help the soldier to direct their efforts in some safe channel—we are far from thinking that all our duty is done in calling attention to them. We urge still more strenuously that each individual ought to feel himself bound to contribute his personal efforts toward the same end which the bureau contemplates and works for. We want every man and woman to feel that they *owe* something to the armies that have saved the country. Asking for nothing on the ground of charity, we ask for everything on the ground of duty and of obligation. Let no one appeal for charity to the returning soldiers. No man who has shouldered a musket in this war ought to be insulted with the proffer of alms. If he needs money or anything else, let him have it—but not as charity. Let him have it as a right, as something due to him and from us, but never as a charity. And so with the furnishing of employment. It ought to be given to the soldier by those who want work done—given with generous pay, and given to the soldier in preference to any other, and as his right. It will be found also that the armies contain great numbers of men who left excellent positions to enter it, and who are no worse but better qualified by their long service in the field for the duties of civil life. They have the first claim both on private employers and on the government.

One other point. This Bureau of Employment which the Sanitary Commission has opened in Chambers Street is a sample of those which are to be or have been established all over the country. As they make no charge for services to either of the parties whom they benefit, their existence involves an expense, and we beg those who cannot in any other way help the soldiers to send a few dollars to these bureaus. It is not possible at this moment to invest money to better advantage.

JUNE 17, 1865

SOUTH

CHARLESTON DAILY COURIER
June 17, 1865

SECTIONALISM

Mr. Editor:—I have read with much interest the remarks of your correspondent "J. P." upon sectionalism and approve of them most heartily, for I have always been strongly opposed to this Southern exclusiveness —politically, commercially, and socially—on the broad ground that it stultifies, cripples, cramps, and kills all our energies, thereby putting an insurmountable barrier in the way of every effort or attempt at advancement, hemming us in on every side with an adamantine wall of self-superiority; and I have no hesitation in saying that to this feeling of exclusiveness, we are indebted more than any other single fact for our present deplorable condition, and I very much fear that there is at this moment a very strong effort being made by certain parties in our midst to keep alive and retain that ancient relic of fossilism. This is not as it should be, for all the blessings of free institutions will be lost to our heretofore benighted country if this sectional wall, now only cracked and fractured, is allowed to be repaired and rebuilt with Southern materials and workmen only. Let us therefore look well that this ancient partition wall be not only not rebuilt, but that every brick and stone of it be pulled down and every vestige of it, even to its very foundation, be utterly and forever obliterated, so that its place shall know it no more. We read in the Scriptures that at the death of our Savior the veil of the temple was rent in twain and that the hidden mysteries of the sanctuary which the Jews had claimed as their own were thus thrown open for the good of universal man. Has not the death of slavery rent in twain this adamantine wall of sectionalism and opened up a vast extent of rich and fertile country which has for centuries been held by the exclusive few, thereby giving to all alike, whether they come from the North or from the South, from the East or from the West, the greatest of all blessings—universal freedom, both corporeally and intellectually?

A Federalist

PUSH FORWARD THE GOOD WORK

By all means let us push forward the good work of rebuilding the city of Charleston. We cannot afford to lose a single day, or a single hour, which can be profitably employed in the advancement of a movement of such vast importance to the people. To be sure, we are in the midst of summer, but that is no reason why we should falter in the execution of our plans and enterprises. We desire to see the ruins which now mark the burned district cleared away and fine, substantial buildings erected in their place. This must be done sooner or later, and it is important for the prosperity of the city that the work should be commenced immediately. There is no use of waiting for the approach of cooler weather before anything is attempted in this direction.

It will be four months before we get cool weather, and in the meantime, hundreds of buildings might be erected and placed in readiness to receive occupants. Thousands of sojourners in the country, towns, and cities of the state are making preparations to come to the city to reside in the fall, and then there will be an unprecedented demand for houses. Anyone possessed of even moderate discernment will not fail to recognize the fact that in three or four months hence we shall see a great change in the streets of Charleston. Trade will spring up in every quarter of the city and will go on increasing and extending till the times gone by are not only equaled, but excelled, in point of industry and activity.

We would like to hear something further concerning that line of steamers which, it was stated a short time since, was to be run between this port and Florida. Where, too, is the proposed Wilmington line of steamers? The time is coming shortly when it will be indispensable that we should have water communication with Florida and North Carolina. It will be a paying investment for some enterprising men to establish these routes of steamers. Here again is the Savannah Railroad completely forsaken in its damaged condition. That road must be rebuilt sometime, and why not take hold of the work at once? Don't let us neglect doing all we can to contribute to the prosperity of Charleston.

NORTH

BOSTON EVENING TRANSCRIPT
June 17, 1865

THE SALE OF WOOD

It has long been suspected that the Honorable Ben Wood of the *New York Daily News* had sympathetic relations with the leading Rebels, but it was not supposed that money considerations had any influence in inducing him to seek this elevating communion with congenial souls. It appears, however, from the evidence elicited yesterday in the trial of the conspirators that there were financial reasons for his complicity with treason and that he did not discredit the name of Wood by indulging in disinterested disloyalty.

Jacob Thompson, the Judas who had charge of the Rebel purse, and who varied the business of buying up incendiaries, assassins, and poisoners, with speculations in members of the Federal Congress, sent to the Honorable Ben Wood last August a check for twenty thousand dollars, drawn by the Bank of Montreal on the City Bank of New York, in favor of D. S. Eastward, who endorsed it over to the proprietor of the *News*. Mr. Thompson, who seems to have had a still larger experience in the purchase of men after the rebellion than before it, and who appears to have pursued his vocation regardless of expense, paid, in the case of Wood, a very heavy price for a very poor article. The Negroes may be not the best judges of the commercial value of flesh and blood, but if Thompson had paraded Ben Wood before the blacks of his plantation as "a twenty-thousand-dollar nigger," no respect for so distinguished a "massa" could have prevented an outburst of ironical jeers at the palpable badness of the bargain.

It is announced today by telegraph that the government has ordered the arrest of Wood, and there is thus a probability that the proprietor may join the editor of the *Daily News* in Fortress Monroe. Our readers will not fail to note in this a twofold violation of the liberty of the press and the liberty of the citizen—of the liberty of the press in arresting the proprietor of a journal guilty of nothing but giving aid and comfort to the enemies of the country, and of the liberty of the citizen in objecting to a purely commercial transaction between a resident of Montreal and an inhabitant of New York for the sale of a Copperhead.

NEW YORK TRIBUNE
June 17, 1865

THE COMING FOURTH

We hope this nation will celebrate its next birthday in a somewhat more becoming and significant way than has always been attempted heretofore. We refer not so much to the method as to the spirit of the celebration. It is no matter that Fourth of July orations have become proverbial for patriotic exaggeration, or for rivaling in matter of rhetoric the pyrotechnic displays by which they are followed in the evening. It is no matter that Europe used to laugh—let her laugh now with what grace she can, since she has learned that vainglorious America can burn powder to other purposes than empty noise, sound and fury, signifying nothing. We do not care so much to urge a reform in those outward observances as in the motive of them, and we appeal now to the Yankee common sense of the people to remember what it is that ought to be celebrated on the fourth day of July in each year.

This republic never before this year had full right to make the anniversary of the Declaration a national festival. It might have chosen other days—Washington's birthday, or the adoption of the Constitution, or the discovery of America, or anything else—but the one day it had little right to appropriate was the day on which Congress adopted the theoretical affirmation of Thomas Jefferson that "all men are created equal." In every day of those years, the nation has practically cast contempt on Jefferson and his immortal doctrine. Ruled by a despotic faction that hated democracy, the republic has lived a lie and, when it appealed to Heaven to bear witness to its respect for the great founder of American institutions, oscillated in idle indifference between atheism and perjury. Today, for the first time, it has a partial claim to lift its right hand in such an asseveration. Today it is at least settled that wherever the flag of the Union floats, no fetter shall hold a slave and that so much of "equality" as consists in the freedom to move from place to place is the law of the United States.

We would have that for one text of the thick-coming ovations that begin to murmur in our ears. Be there no stint to the rejoicings over what four years of strife have brought us, for it is just and patriotic to make the most of our victory. But in order to make the most of it, we must remember what it has failed to secure and how far short of the goal we are still halting. And that will be another text for another class of speakers, for the enthusiast and reformer whose eye fixes steadfastly on the future, and whose faith does not stop short of the perhaps distant day when the inspiration of Jefferson shall be the moral and political law of the state. How far are we from yet admitting that governments derive their just powers from the consent of the governed? Whether Negroes are citizens or not may be a question—whether they are part of the people presidential proclamations seem to leave uncertain. But that they are among "the governed" the most "conservative" politician will not venture to deny—until he is reminded that only from the consent of the governed can any government derive its right to authority—and then his speculative casuistry may seek to find a term for the political designation of the emancipated slave which may put him outside the pale of even the exhaustive statement of the Declaration. Let him task his ingenuity well—still will he fail. The irresistible progress of events presses upon the country the alternative of denying the fundamental dogma of the Declaration of Independence, or of conceding suffrage to the Negro and opening to him those conventions which are to resettle the fundamental law of the returning states.

In view of the exigency pressing upon us, we incline to believe that the pivotal statement of the Declaration is not the equality of all men, but to seek for it in the more precise, necessary, and practical assertion above quoted—that governments are instituted among men to secure the inalienable rights of life, liberty, and the pursuit of happiness and that their just powers are *wholly* derived from the consent of the governed and rightfully exist only so long as they are directed to these ends. And it is with reference to this affirmation that we would interpret the guarantee in the Constitution of a republican form of government to every state. The phrase means something, and one of our present duties is to give a legal and beneficial effect to its meaning. Nor do we admit for a moment that it can be construed historically or politically so as to exclude the loyal, free men of the South—be their complexion what it may—from a share in the reconstruction of their local or state form of government.

These, then, are the two themes for the coming Fourth—the splendor of the triumph already won and the greater splendor of that which it remains to win. The din of arms grows still, but the conflict of ideas is irrepressible until the republic becomes homogeneous—until the schoolhouse goes down to the Gulf—until the slaveholder is educated up to the Declaration, and until the ballot is in every Negro's hand.

JULY 15, 1865

SOUTH

CHARLESTON DAILY COURIER
July 15, 1865

PAYMENT OF CAPTURED COTTON

The pall which for the last four years has covered the land with its gloomy folds has been removed. The country has emerged from the darkness by which it was surrounded. The sunshine of a restored unity, not only of authority but of interest and hope, has begun to cast its rays from between the passing clouds and to light up with bright anticipations of the future the mountaintops and valleys of our vast expanse. It is not to be expected that we shall at once be blessed with the full splendor of its radiance or reap the rich and copious prosperity which will gradually flow from its influence. But it may well be hoped that every encouragement will be offered, and every aid rendered, to relieve the calamities of the past and the stern desolation of the present.

The cessation of hostilities finds this section of the South in an exhausted condition, without a currency, with its wealth in slaves, both in capital and interest, gone. In fact, with scarcely any other resource than that which is afforded by the land itself, and that subject to a system of experimental labor, or such products as the ravages of war may have left, the people are bereft of their opulence. They have again, in the homes of their fathers, to commence, as if in a new world, and struggle for maintenance and support. They have not lost, however, either their heart or hope. They realize and accept the existing condition of things and, like men, are seeking to devote their energies to the revival of agriculture, commerce, and manufactures and to the restoration of those channels of trade and business on which the welfare and prosperity of a country depend. A common destiny binds them to the Union. A common interest requires that not only no obstacle should be placed in their progress, but that they should receive every assistance in this laudable endeavor. Cotton has heretofore constituted the chief export of the state and its chief source of wealth. It was the basis of, and therefore may be considered as the representative of, coin. The larger portion has been destroyed by either army. And now what of this staple has been preserved amid the devastation and wrecks forms the reliance of our people for the recommencement of life and the establishment of the foundation on which business operations are to be based. There is not a great deal in the state. But to make available that amount, whether it be large or small, was essential to furnish the capital for a beginning, and therefore of vital importance. It formed the essence of our business life. That part which was saved in the country cannot but partially be turned into profit, on account of the destruction of the lines of communication and the therefore inadequacy of price. That which remained in and adjacent to the city was taken possession of by the government.

Prior to the evacuation of this city, the merchants and other citizens of the community had purchased cotton, on account of the depreciated condition of the then currency, and with a view to furnishing the means of defraying their liabilities, of support of their families, and of resuming again their business operations. There was scarcely a house where some of it was not stored, or an individual who had not measurably provided himself with it as a basis of capital and credit. It is a mistake to suppose that this belonged to, or was in any wise connected with, the affairs at Richmond. It was in truth and in fact the property of individuals by lawful purchase and held for lawful purposes. When, therefore, the government, through its authorities, required that all cotton should be reported and delivered to its control, the principal source of recuperation was taken from the hands of the citizen, and he was deprived of the means either of discharging his indebtedness or of again renewing his customary vocation. His business required some capital, and that which had been provided for that purpose had been taken away.

The Northern creditor is interested in this question, because upon its restoration depends the ability to pay his demands. The Southern merchant is deeply concerned, because it constituted his chief dependence in the hour of ruin and need. The government appears to have been impressed with this view of the case and the necessity for some remedy. The cotton had been shipped to New York and other ports. It could not well be restored in kind. It was therefore directed that claims for all cottons which had been seized by the authorities should be presented to the proper department, with full proof of ownership and a statement of the marks and weights, by which it might be traced and identified and a proper value ascertained. These claims were duly presented. No action that we are advised of has yet been taken in regard to them. It is of importance to our own people and to all who are or have been connected in business relations with them that these claims should be proved and payment made at the earliest possible day.

This duty cannot too urgently be pressed upon the consideration of the government. Our merchants have acted with great fidelity. They are desirous to commence again with integrity and honor. They desire to deal fairly and justly with their Northern creditors. The cotton and stores which they had acquired by their labor for this purpose have passed into the power of the government. What they now require is that compensation therefor should be promptly provided. We cannot but believe that all that is really needed is to call the attention of the government to this duty and necessity. It will be a measure of great relief. It will be an act of justice. It will afford succor to our people and promote the interest and prosperity of all.

POLITICS

We see that the wire-pullers at the North are already deeply engaged in concocting schemes wherewith they hope to install themselves and friends in good, fat offices. Many of these gentlemen doubtless have an eye to appointments at the South, but we judge from what we can learn of affairs in Washington that a large majority of office seekers will be disappointed in their Southern anticipations. While the political warfare is being waged at the North, we sincerely trust a scene of words, and speeches, and violent contentions will not be entered upon here. We want quiet. Our people desire to peaceably engage in their accustomed pursuits without being compelled to take part in an excited and angry political discussion. It is time for us to think of politics when civil law and order shall have been fully and thoroughly restored throughout the state. Of course, we will eventually be called upon to decide many weighty questions, but now is not the time to drag those questions before the people.

NORTH

BOSTON EVENING TRANSCRIPT
July 15, 1865

[UNTITLED]

The president, the Cabinet, and Congress, together with the loyal people of the country, may take a vacation from all charge of public affairs.

Reconstruction or restoration is none of their concern. They are relieved from the responsibility of even trying to pacify the nation and cement the Union anew. All this is to be done by the Southern patriots, recently in arms against the republic, conducting such nice institutions as the Andersonville Pen and the Libby Prison, legislating at Richmond in a spirit so democratic and with such sacred regard to the rights of humanity and of political freedom.[1] Overcome by force, unable to carry out their fine plans by cannons and muskets, thefts and barbarities, they are now prepared to dictate the terms on which they will again live in legal amity with the North. They claim to be the best interpreters of the Constitution and strenuously insist that it will be for the good of the free states to listen to the policy of conciliation they are graciously willing to grant.

Certain journals at the North, eminent for the zeal with which they have supported the Federal government and the persistency with which they have cold-shouldered Jefferson Davis and his associates, are joining with these Southern patriots, acknowledging the singular propriety of their movements, the sound wisdom of their counsels, and urging the administration and the people to allow themselves to be instructed by these "natural leaders," these statesmen so remarkable for their unselfish consistency, the clearness and liberality of their political theories, and their fidelity in their unwavering allegiance to republican institutions! Under the circumstances President Johnson has nothing to do but retire to the Soldiers' Rest for the summer, keep quiet, and wait until "the brave Anglo-Saxons" (as Mr. H. W. Hilliard calls them)—revolutionists in the most righteous of causes—have decided what is the best for the United States and on what condescending conditions they are prepared to give the United States the benefit of their forgiveness and the return of their guardian care.[2] Indeed, if these Southern gentlemen have their own way and are left to their own devices, our readers must not be surprised if they wake up some fine morning and find that all the schemes of reconstruction have resulted in annexing the United States to what Mr. Hilliard calls "his country."

1. Established in February 1864, Andersonville Prison (Georgia) housed only enlisted men. The inmates lived in squalor and received little to eat and no medical attention. More than twelve thousand are believed to have died there.

2. Henry W. Hilliard, Confederate general and Alabama politician.

NEW YORK TRIBUNE
July 15, 1865

FROM NORTH CAROLINA
THE MUSTERING OUT OF TROOPS—THE NECESSITY OF MILITARY AUTHORITY—THREATS OF THE SLAVEHOLDERS—NO WAGES PAID TO THE NEGROES—AN INGENIOUS SWINDLE—MEDICAL ATTENDANCE WANTED—DOMESTIC MATTERS—OUTRAGES OF UNION SOLDIERS ON THE NEGROES

From Our Special Correspondent
Raleigh, North Carolina, July 10, 1865

Under the last order for mustering out troops now garrisoning different portions of North Carolina, the forces will be reduced to seven infantry regiments of the XXIII Army Corps and six of the X Army Corps, with all the colored troops now in the state and one regiment of cavalry—the 5th Ohio and the 2nd Massachusetts Heavy Artillery. The infantry regiments destined at present to remain are the 120th, 123rd, 124th, 128th, 129th, and 130th Indiana and 28th Michigan (XXIII Corps), and the 3rd, 47th, and 48th New York, 4th New Hampshire, 97th Pennsylvania, and 13th Indiana (X Corps). These, with those mentioned above, will constitute the entire force in the state, and number not to exceed thirteen thousand men. They will all be paid after reaching their respective state rendezvous.

There are widely different opinions expressed and feelings entertained among different classes of citizens, touching the propriety and safety of removing the military forces from the state. One party has been clamoring for it almost from the time of Johnston's surrender and are daily manifesting more and more impatience at the presence of the bluecoats in the streets. They feel so entirely confident of their ability to go alone now, without the steadying hand of Uncle Sam, that they are earnest to have all the troops withdrawn. Not being a native here, and therefore incapable of judging as accurately as one to the manner born, touching the motives of this class, I fall back upon the editor of the *Progress*. In a recent article on this subject, he refers to this impatience to be rid of military restraint, and states that he hears constant threats from the ex-slaveholders and aristocrats as to what they intend to do with the "niggers" as soon as the bluecoats get out of the way, and warns them that so long as they keep up these threats, the troops will be kept in the state. He charges that those who are most violent against the continued occupation of the state by the troops are the still-unsubdued and -rampant class of Rebels and aristocrats in nearly all cases.

Having stated Mr. Pennington's views on this subject, I will now affirm that they accord fully with my own observations, which are daily confirmed by unmistakable evidence from all parts of the state by a multitude of witnesses. Even now the small garrisons at different points are insufficient to hold in check a class of the old slaveholders; I think they are exceptions to the general rule, who seem determined to retain their old grip upon the laborers. They either intend to "use their service without wages and give them naught for their work," absolutely, or give them such paltry compensation therefor that with the loss of all the old franchises, such as free rent, clothes (such as they were), and medical attendance, it makes their condition vastly worse than the state of actual slavery.

If I take the condition of affairs in this city—the center of the state, where the treatment of the blacks is a matter of publicity, and where, being mostly house servants, they would be likely to receive much better treatment than plantation hands—some idea may be formed of the program which the late owners of the slaves have marked out for themselves.

As to wages, I venture to say not one in ten has been paid a cent of wages since we occupied the place. An old, religious, and faithful servant near me has spent his life in drudgery for the people who claimed him, his wife, and children as slaves and now insist upon allowing him only five dollars per month and board without clothes, at the same time charging him five dollars per month rent for the quarters he and his family occupy on the "lot."

They can now get *no medical attendance*. The better and more sensible farmers have made fair and, in some few cases, liberal arrangements with their hands. Mr. J. P. Kennedy, near Kinston, and Colonel Smith, of Johnston County, have agreed to give their hands one half of the crops raised, furnishing seed and animals to do the plowing, and furnishing the subsistence while the crops mature. Such men do not trump up old charges against their hands, just as the corn is getting ripe, to drive them away and save the trouble and expense of paying them for their work. This has been done in some cases. I shall mention the names of good planters who deal justly with their hands.

The worthy pastor of the African Methodist Episcopal Church, Mr. Croom, informs me that a great deal of sickness prevails in his parish, that the old physicians are sent for but they won't come. In many instances the case is made worse by promises to come, when they wholly fail to appear or, calling once, never come again. Thus, the patient lingers in expectation of medical relief, until his case becomes unmanageable and he dies for the want of the simplest attention at the proper time. I appeal to Dr. Barnes, medical director of the X Army Corps, for the truth of my statements, and to Colonel Whittlesey and his assistant superintendents of freedmen here. Dr. Barnes has regularly provided medical attendance and medicines for a large number of the colored people, who, but for his timely and humane attentions, would have perished. The masters, in some cases, turn away the servant when he or she becomes disabled by sickness. A grievous case of this kind came to my notice on the 4th, where the young woman was turned, sick and unpaid, into the streets by a family in this place.

And these are the people who propose, or have undertaken, to import *Irish girls* from the North to do the work in their kitchens!

I continually hear of great mortality among the freed people on the plantations in different parts of the state. The masters lament the unhappy condition of the poor free Negroes, but take no pains to get them a physician or procure medicine for them. They think themselves wholly absolved from any of these humane obligations now—the Negro is no longer property! If I mistake not, Colonel Whittlesey has informed General Howard of the great needs of the freed people of this vicinity for medical attendance and medicines.

One or two good physicians who would come to Raleigh, bringing a stock of drugs and medicines with them, and devote themselves wholly to the care of the colored people would do a living business now and ultimately establish themselves in a handsome business. These people are now able to pay moderately for medical attendance and will soon be as well, or better, able to maintain good physicians as the white folks. But they should have the best physicians in every respect.

MARRYING AND GIVING IN MARRIAGE

I do not wish to alarm the young ladies at home, but I ought to mention that a considerable number of young men whose regiments are about being mustered out—such as the 47th and 48th New York and 97th Pennsylvania Zouaves—have made up their minds to stay in the country. There are too many eligible openings to be resisted. They are fast marrying the disconsolate young ladies and widows and settling down for life upon the vacant farms which on every hand invite their labor and enterprise.

CHANGE OF PROVOST MARSHALS

By the mustering out of the 9th Maine we have obtained a change in the officers commanding this post. Major Dyer has been relieved as provost marshal, and Captain J. A. Barrett, commanding the 48th New York Veteran Volunteers, succeeds him. The change will be welcomed by the colored population, who have had little occasion to be thankful for any leniency or consideration shown them during Major Dyer's administration. It has been no uncommon thing to see Negroes tied up by the thumbs in the Capitol grounds for petty offenses, or walking under guard with their heads protruding through a flour barrel in the most public streets, wearing a large sign with the word "thief" displayed in large letters thereon, to the great delight of Rebels. In this case the culprit was guilty of the heinous offense of picking two or three plums out of a basket in Market Street, and charged with saying something impudent to a soldier. The colored people have been knocked down, robbed, and regularly assaulted by scamps wearing the Union uniform in our public places, apparently without any attempt to punish the assailants. The last case of this kind occurred on the 5th instant, when two quiet and inoffensive colored men were set upon near a certain stable while peaceably passing along the street, and outrageously pummeled with the intention of robbing them. They complained to the provost marshal, who took the lying statement of the soldiers that the black men called them hard names, tied up the colored men by the thumbs, and let the guilty white men go free.

There are other abuses which have been committed here, which, for the present, I abstain from mentioning. No one will complain at even-handed justice when it is meted out to white as well as black, but hitherto it has been too much like Balcom's comb—all on one side. I shall predict nothing as to Captain Barrett's administration, only that he is an energetic and temperate man. Colonel Coan of the 48th New York, now commanding the 2nd Brigade, X Army Corps, will command all the troops in the vicinity of Raleigh.

E. S.

RICHMOND DAILY DISPATCH

[*Publication of the* Dispatch *resumed on December 9. The following articles are drawn from the first three Saturday issues of that month.*]

RICHMOND DAILY DISPATCH
December 9, 1865

THE PAST AND THE PRESENT

The *Richmond Dispatch,* which met a temporary suspension of its existence in the expiring flames of the recent Confederacy, is this morning restored to life. It is again endowed with the Promethean fire and speaks to its readers as though it never lost its breath or its voice. Welcome it, "dear reader," with the same kind and genial sensibilities which warm its own heart, and let there be established once more between it and thee the same confidential and affectionate relations which formerly existed, and which blessed and rewarded all its toil, all its struggles, through the thorny and flinty way of journalism.

These Southern states have passed through an ordeal of trial and suffering seldom the lot of a generation of people. They entered upon a struggle in which they failed, and in which these trials and sufferings were incurred. Unlike most rebellions, as they are called, especially when they have failed, those who undertook it were not merely a set of malcontents, recklessly resisting the clearly defined political organisms of the country. They were fortified by a sense of rights under the Constitution and a conscientious conviction of the justice of their position, which had at least the semblance of support in the debates of our ancestors who framed the Constitution itself, under which the republic was formed. Those truly great men left the question of the relations between the states and the general government an open one. There were strong parties in the very convention which framed the compact of union upon the questions at issue touching those relations. The very able and patriotic men who figured in that body, after much debate, gave the question the go-by, and while they failed to settle it themselves, they appointed no umpire to which it could be referred. They thus left us as a legacy a bitter and disastrous war—a war which was fought, and fought bravely, to its final conclusion. The South entered upon it with more unanimity and determination than have been known to characterize the resisting party in any civil war that we read of. It fought through it under its sense of constitutional right, with a courage and constancy which has challenged the admiration of other nations.

But the question thus submitted to the arbitrament of war was decided against them, and they submitted, as brave men ever submit, to the Fates, which all their fortitude and power cannot control. They were overwhelmed by superior numbers and resources and succumbed after a resistance which vindicated the honesty and sincerity of their intentions. Their heroism has lately received a tribute that is alike honorable to the head and heart of the magnanimous commander in chief of the powerful armies they encountered in the field. Such a tribute is the most fitting rebuke—the most scathing denunciation—of those wretched attempts to dishonor the gallant dead who fell in hecatombs on the field in proof of the truth and sincerity of their devotion to the cause they sustained. Regarding the result as the settlement of the question, those who so nobly periled their lives in support of the principles they espoused readily acquiesced and submitted to the authority of the Federal government; and order and quiet were instantly restored in a country where the devastations of war and the exhausting exertions of defense against overwhelming odds had reduced the people nearly to famine. The subsequent history we need not recount. The steady efforts of all to restore order, and the patient and cheerful manner in which a people reduced from the happiest independence to utter poverty have undertaken to provide for immediate want and rebuild their fallen fortunes, constitute one of the noblest examples in the history of mankind.

In this struggle the *Dispatch* took its part. It was honest and earnest and does not mean to retreat, or, in the everyday parlance, to crawfish from its position. It sympathized with the Confederacy, did all it could to cheer the hearts of the people in the struggle, and continued with it, and, we may say, fell with it in the calamitous fire of the 3rd of April. Its voice was heard up to that hour. While the carrier conveyed its communications to the public in one part of the city, its types and presses were melting in the fires of another.

But like the noble people in the midst of whom it was published, and whom it now addresses, it, too, accepts the situation and the clear decision of the trial of arms—of blood. It means to abide by the oath which its conductors have taken, and sustain the government under which we now live. It feels, today, as though it had never been suspended—in fact, its seat at the round table of the fraternity has only been temporarily vacant—and it speaks as though only twenty-four hours had passed since its last appearance. It is true there is no war, but that was over, in fact, when it last appeared. It resumes its mission, then, before the war—which was to encourage and stimulate the improvement of

Richmond and assist in the development of the resources of our dear old mother, Virginia. To these purposes it will bring all the energies of its improved and enlarged means and power, and hopes in its day to do some real service in this noble cause.

Renewing our expressions of gratification at once more holding communication with our dear friends of Richmond and Virginia, the *Dispatch* promises at once to direct all its influence to the promotion of their good. Nothing on this earth would make its conductors so happy as to see our people safely and prosperously through that trying transition state in which they are now struggling; and it shall be our most enthusiastic occupation to try to facilitate their passage, dry-shod, through this Red Sea of their difficulties. That our own townsmen and the good people of Virginia—God bless and preserve her!—may pass through their trials successfully and become, as they deserve to be, prosperous and happy is the devout prayer of the *Dispatch*.

REBUILDING THE CITY

There is a great mistake prevailing with many people that all the money employed in rebuilding this city comes from the North, and very doleful prophecies are indulged upon this hypothesis concerning the future. We are sold! We are both bought and sold—and must wind up with general bankruptcy and poverty! Now, there is no use in this—no reason for all this anticipation of evil. There is a better and a truer view of the subject. The money employed in the active enterprise of rebuilding this city is not all from the North. Nearly all the very best buildings in progress of construction in this city are built up with the money of our own enterprising citizens. For, thank God, notwithstanding the desolation which swept over the South, and especially over this devoted city, some of the wisest and most farseeing of our people saved a part of their means, and this they are now using in the most enterprising and public-spirited manner. So we are not entirely dependent on Northern capital—very far from it. But what should we fear from the Northern capitalists? We know that, commercially speaking, under the influence of steam transportation, by water and rail and telegraphs, there is an inevitable concentration of commerce in the great cities and settling points of the continent and that all other localities must be subsidiary and tributary to them. So, do what we will, we cannot escape that subordinate relation. Now, since that is the case, what objection can we have to the drawing of capital from the commercial center to build up and adorn our recently desolated and forlorn city? Money put in the bricks, in the stores and dwellings and public edifices of Richmond, cannot be easily taken away. At most, the proprietorship of the buildings can only be changed. The money remains in the buildings, and they are permanent —permanent places of business, permanent tenements to live comfortably in, permanent ornaments of the city. Not only, therefore, are we fortunate in having this borrowed capital to revive the city, but our good fortune will be increased precisely to the extent of the amount that may be so contributed from abroad to this important object.

There need be no fears on the subject. The more capital that is drawn thither, the greater the interest that will be felt by capitalists abroad in the general prosperity of this city. They would be unwilling to see their investments wholly unproductive, and their influence and means would, if necessary, be surely given for the promotion of that general commercial thrift which would contribute to their individual benefit.

So let us look ahead and be hopeful, assured that every dollar brought here and placed in the houses of Richmond is a permanent investment and a guarantee of the confidence felt in the future of the place, as well as an earnest of the disposition to aid in the promotion of its growth and welfare.

RICHMOND DAILY DISPATCH
December 16, 1865

FEARFUL DESTITUTION!

The "destitute ration," which has been the solitary dependence of so many of our people for their daily bread, ceased yesterday, and it is ascertained that there are now in this city three thousand forty-six women and children entirely destitute, with the rigors of winter upon them and nothing between them and death but charity.

The fact is appalling. It carries its own appeal with it. Words cannot convey its inexpressible horror. Many of these persons, threatened with an awful fate, have never, in former days, known want. Not a few of them are delicate, refined, gently bred, possessed of every household virtue and adorned by every social grace. Something must be done, and done quickly. The whole head and heart of the community must be devoted to instant, practical, thorough measures for their relief. We had never expected to see such a state of things in America—least of all in Virginia. Every man who can spare aught, however little, must now deny himself all but the bare necessities of life to save his perishing brethren. Will not the benevolent everywhere assist us in these efforts of common humanity? America, which has dispensed her bounty to the famishing of foreign climes, will not look coldly on and see Christian people—flesh of their flesh and bone of their bone—dying of starvation at their own doors.

RICHMOND DAILY DISPATCH
December 23, 1865

THE SOUTHERN STATES ADMITTED TO BE STILL IN THE UNION BY THADDEUS STEVENS HIMSELF

Monday, the 17th, and Tuesday, the 18th, of December, were remarkable days in the history of this country. On the former of these days, Thaddeus Stevens, on the question of referring the president's message, delivered himself of all the venom which has been accumulating since the memorable day on which his iron mills were burned. It is to be hoped he felt better after the operation, and the probability is that he did, for on the very next day he made a tacit confession that the view he had taken of the situation the day before had been wrong and that the states of the South were not territories but bona fide states, acting in their capacity as such and entitled to have such acts recorded as the acts of so many states. On the latter day Mr. Secretary Seward sent in the vote of the states upon the amendment of the Constitution which abolishes slavery. It was found that twenty-seven states had voted, making the constitutional two thirds. Among those that had voted and that were counted in order to make up the constitutional number were the names of Virginia, North Carolina, South Carolina, Georgia, and Alabama. Without them there would not have been the required number. The inclusion of these states among the number of those which had voted for abolition affords a proof that Mr. Seward, as well as Mr. Johnson, regards them still as states, acting, as states always do in their transactions with the general government, through their legislatures. The formal declaration of Congress that these states were states could not have settled their status more decidedly than the action—or rather the failure to act on that occasion—by Congress did. Mr. Stevens had not a word to throw to a dog. His Radical comrades were perfectly mum. The action of the five Southern states, deciding the question, was received as fair and legal. If the Radicals now insist that these five states are out of the Union, they entirely upset the great constitutional amendment. It will thus be seen that the president has gained a complete victory.

In spite of this triumph, however, the Radicals will still continue to keep the Southern members out of their places. We are not sure that it is not the best thing they can do for the South. If left alone, it is evident enough that they will destroy their party utterly before the existence of the present Congress shall have terminated. Give them rope, and they will inevitably hang themselves. Their proceedings have already disgusted many of their party, and the disgust must become universal as they advance. They are of that description of men who know not what to do with power when they have it. They will, in less than twelve months, if left entirely to themselves, make the very name of Republican hateful for centuries to come. Parties of that description always do. In the meantime they cannot do us much harm. They may pass the Negro suffrage amendment, but it will be voted down in the states.

As for their right to keep Southern members-elect from their seats, it is clear to us that they have none. The Constitution defines the qualification of a representative. He must be twenty-five years old and have been a citizen of the United States seven years. These are all the qualifications required; and when the privilege is conceded to each House of judging and deciding the qualifications of its own members, nothing more is meant than that it shall decide whether such members have or have not the qualifications required by the Constitution. To give to a House of Representatives the power to establish an arbitrary standard of qualification is what the law never intended. It would be to give one branch of the legislature the power to alter the Constitution. No new qualification can be fixed but by amending the Constitution. Both Houses are plainly violating the Constitution in enforcing their own will in this respect; but it is all the better. The people will give them only the more signal overthrow when they come to act upon their cases.

NEGRO SUFFRAGE IN WASHINGTON

The vote given in Washington, on Thursday, on the question of Negro suffrage was as nearly unanimous in the negative as almost any vote upon any imaginable question submitted to popular decision could be. It stood: *for* the right of suffrage to the Negro, 35; *against* it, 6,603! The vote was the largest ever polled—exceeding in the aggregate by 928 that cast for mayor in 1864 and by 3,583 the vote polled at the general election in June.

It is said that old citizens who had not voted for years went to the polls to cast their votes on this occasion and that prominent Republicans cast their votes *openly*—notwithstanding that the ballot is the legal mode of voting—in order to express their emphatic censure of the indignity proposed by a party in Congress to be inflicted upon their community.

INDEX

ABOUT THE EDITOR

Brayton Harris, a retired U.S. Navy captain, has worked as a printer, publisher, editor, freelance writer, and aerospace public relations executive. With a lifelong interest in Civil War journalism, he is the author of the 1988 special edition of *Civil War* magazine on "The Press and the Civil War" and, in 1999, provided a more comprehensive treatment of the subject in his book *Blue and Gray in Black and White: Newspapers in the Civil War.* He has published several hundred magazine articles and seven books, including *The Navy Times Book of Submarines: A Political, Social, and Military History* and *Johann Gutenberg and the Invention of Printing*.